Visual FoxPro 5.0 for Windows

Developing an Application Framework

Nelson King

M&T Books
A Division of MIS:Press, Inc.
A Subsidiary of Henry Holt and Company, Inc.
115 West 18th Street
New York, New York 10011
http://www.mispress.com

Printed in the United States of America

First Edition—1997

ISBN 1-55851-560-7

MIS:Press and M&T Books are available at special discounts for bulk purchases for sales promotions, premiums, and fundraising. Special editions or book excerpts can also be created to specification.

For details contact: Special Sales Director
MIS:Press and M&T Books
Subsidiaries of Henry Holt and Company, Inc.
115 West 18th Street
New York, New York 10011

10 9 8 7 6 5 4 3 2 1

Associate Publisher: Paul Farrell
Development Editor Laura Lewin
Technical Editor: Shar Feldheim
Production Editor: Stephanie Doyle
Managing Editor: Shari Chappell
Copy Chief: Karen Tongish
Copy Editor: Betsy Hardinger

CONTENTS

CHAPTER 5: USING DATABASE ELEMENTS 127

CHAPTER 6: SQL AND THE QUERY AND VIEW DESIGNERS 175

CHAPTER 10: PROCEDURAL PROGRAMMING 355

SECTION 4: OBJECT-ORIENTED PROGRAMMING 405

CHAPTER 11: UNDERSTANDING OOP, PART II: CLASSES 409

CHAPTER 12: EVENTS AND METHODS........441

CHAPTER 13: DEBUGGING........................465

SECTION 5: PLANNING AN APPLICATION 493

CHAPTER 14: APPLICATION ANALYSIS......497

CHAPTER 15: DESIGNING AN APPLICATION....................................519

SECTION 6: BUILDING AN APPLICATION FRAMEWORK 569

CHAPTER 16: WORKING ON THE FRAMEWORK..571

CHAPTER 19: MASTERING THE DATABASE....707

CHAPTER 20: ADVANCED SQL AND VIEWS 751

SECTION 7: COMPLETING AN APPLICATION FRAMEWORK 795

CHAPTER 21: TESTING AND DOCUMENTATION 799

CHAPTER 22: STANDARD COMPONENTS AND MODULES 827

Preface

Sometimes I get really angry with Microsoft. I've reviewed all of the major client/server and C++ development systems for national publications (testing scripts and benchmarks included), and Visual FoxPro stands with the best of 'em. Visual FoxPro is a very good product and deserves a much better fate than to languish in the shadow (PR-wise) of Visual Basic. At the same time, Microsoft is driving toward a goal of homogenizing the user interface for all its application development products, leaving (in theory) the underlying programming language at the back end. Whether or not this means the end of FoxPro as we've known it for about a decade, it seems certain to lose some of its distinctiveness. I hope it retains the edge in data management—a world-class database engine and great flexibility in the future some three to five years. In the here the language. If not, there's little point in using it. All of this, however, is in and now, Visual FoxPro 5.0 is one of the best database application development systems you can buy. This version has added some wonderful touches for the developer. I hope you enjoy using it as much as I have. I can't get too angry with Microsoft. The company has earned some credit for enabling the FoxPro team to get this far.

—Nelson King

Acknowledgments

No author finishes a book like this without people to egg him on, or simply to throw eggs. I'd like to thank Jan Smith and Shar Feldheim (the technical editors) for their unerring aim, and Laura Lewin (Development Editor at MIS:Press) for enduring my constant game of chicken with deadlines.

INTRODUCTION

It's tempting to start this introduction on a grand note by quoting a famous person who died long before computers were invented. But it's more appropriate to stick with describing the reality you are about to face. The process of building applications, especially the bigger ones, is a unique challenge. As you may have heard, application development isn't always successful. In fact, the figures say that about 60 percent of all corporate applications fail. I'm not sure what is meant by "fail," but there are plenty of well-documented disasters.

There's an even bigger problem, and it's called backlog. For a long time we haven't been able to build applications fast enough and well enough to keep up with the demand. This is obviously related to the failure problem, but even if projects didn't fail, we'd still be up to our keisters in deadlines and nearly impossible specifications. That's why for at least a decade there have been many attempts to solve the problems. So far, one approach seems to work best: object-oriented programming.

In a nutshell, object-oriented programming provides a way of designing and constructing an application so that it's made of many reusable parts—objects. Each object is relatively independent and can be tested to make sure it does what it's supposed to do. Then you piece together many objects to create not just one but (potentially) a whole series of applications, each built with only relatively minor changes. In this way it's possible to create robust applications quickly.

Unfortunately, when confronted by complexity and scale (big applications with complicated requirements), the object-oriented approach itself becomes complicated and difficult to manage. That's why, in the past five years or so, there have been many attempts to organize object-oriented programming so that it can handle numerous and large-scale applications without overwhelming our ability to understand the work. The most successful of these approaches has been the application development framework, such as Microsoft's Application Framework for C++ and Borland's OWL. In a sense, these frameworks are like blueprints for the development of an application combined with the raw materials needed for construction. It's an effective combination.

Assuming that you want to build an application (hopefully many of them) and you're not sure how to do it with Visual FoxPro, this book uses an application development framework to describe how it's done. Visual FoxPro doesn't have an application framework of its own, and maybe Microsoft should have provided one, but that's not a great loss. In the long run, it's better for you to build and assemble your own framework. You'll understand it better, know how to manipulate it more easily, and know how to fix it.

As you might suspect, there are many ways to build, buy, or borrow an application framework. Does this book have its own approach and demand that you learn it? No. There is a disk full of programming stuck to the back cover that contains a class hierarchy and application modules that can be used as the basis of an application framework, but that's not the point. If this book has a thesis, it's that in the process of building your own framework you need to learn how to stitch together ideas and code from many sources. As you will see, this is not easy with a class hierarchy, so planning and intimate knowledge of your framework is a must. I maintain that the only way you can get that intimacy is to do it yourself, which means hours of study, sweat, experiment, and occasional anger. It can also be fun—a lot of fun.

Of course, building the framework has its own pitfalls and challenges. In that regard, this book can help. It's a guide that attempts to show you the road ahead but lets you go at your own speed and in your own way. I know that's a cliché, but it's also true. You don't master a program like Visual FoxPro in a couple of evenings, and ultimately you have to learn it your way. The same is true for building an application framework.

Who Can Benefit from This Book?

Who can benefit from this book? This seems to be an obligatory question for an introduction, as if you should exclude someone. The temptation is to say that *everyone* can use this book! But that's not accurate. If you're not interested in programming or, more specifically, in building applications, then this book is not for you. But I suppose you wouldn't be reading this if that were true. The real issue is whether a Visual FoxPro application development framework is relevant to you. Here are some quick criteria concerning applications you may be considering:

- Should they be object-oriented?
- Are they database-centric—that is, do they use a lot of data?
- Do you plan to develop more than one?
- Will they be used by more than one person?

Yes answers to these questions make you a candidate for an application framework tailored to Visual FoxPro.

This book does not assume that you know how to program, much less that you know the specifics of the FoxPro language or object-oriented programming. Instead, learning the language and the object-oriented tools is woven into the description of how to build applications and an application development framework. Even if you already know this territory, it won't hurt to review the basics so that it's clear how they fit into the framework. For example, did you know there are 42 potential components of a full-scale application, many of which are considered standard? They include obvious things such as reports and data entry forms but also less familiar elements such as business rules and error trapping. That's one of the things about applications: They can cover a lot of territory. The problem is, until you build an application or two, it's very difficult to fit all this in your head. This book tries to be a map of this brave new world, giving you an overview you can use while you fill in the details with your own experience.

Previous versions of this book attempted to be a reference work and guide to application development. No more. Visual FoxPro has grown too big and too complex for me to shoehorn both a description of application development and a reference to the details of programming into one book. Now the task is to clarify the *why* and *when* of things and, above all, to explain the entire scope of building an object-oriented application and an application framework. In a similar sense, this is not a "code book"—no particular style of coding is promoted—nor is the focus exclusively on programming.

As you can see by the following section descriptions, the material covered has a wide range—from fundamentals to grand architectures.

Section 1, "Starting an Application Framework," dives right in with some hands-on basics, such as getting a (very) mini program running and illustrating the fundamental concepts and jargon behind object-oriented programming.

Section 2, "Data Management for Applications covers the basics of the FoxPro database management system and other concepts you'll need for integrating data with your applications.

Section 3, "Good Old-Fashioned Programming," demonstrates the standard procedural programming concepts and techniques, with emphasis on the FoxPro database management commands.

Section 4, "Object-Oriented Programming," expands on the main concepts of the FoxPro object-oriented approach and explains some of the most important techniques.

Section 5, "Planning an Application," builds on the necessary concepts and techniques from the first three sections to explain how full-scale applications are analyzed and designed with an application development framework in mind.

Section 6, "Building an Application Framework," goes into the details of developing the components of an application framework using the Visual FoxPro tools and object-oriented techniques.

Section 7, "Completing the Application," covers what it takes to deliver an application with framework components, including testing, documentation, and utility programs.

The New FoxPro for FoxPro Vets

It's true that Visual FoxPro is a long way from FoxBASE+, or from FoxPro for Windows 2.6 for that matter. Different as it is, for those of you who have programming experience from the older versions of FoxPro, there's no reason to fret over lost knowledge. Almost everything you know about programming will find a place in the new FoxPro—except the development context, which is almost totally different. Object-oriented programming is a different way of thinking, especially when it comes to making all the components (classes and objects) fit. Be warned: Spending hours attempting to link your previous experience to perceived similarities in Visual FoxPro is risky. It's too easy to think you've understood an object-oriented concept when all you've done is to transpose some concept from your previous experience. For example, making generic functions for a procedure file is not like making generic classes in a class hierarchy.

Whether you're a vet or a beginner, there's a lot of effort involved in mastering Visual FoxPro. The details of object-oriented programming and FoxPro's use of the Structured Query Language (SQL) run very deep. But almost everyone who has made the effort comes away not only with appreciation but also with stars in their eyes. If you've programmed before, especially with other versions of

FoxPro, you'll discover that there are visions possible in this universe that we've never had before. It's enough to make a grizzled FoxPro veteran smile broadly.

TYPOGRAPHIC CONVENTIONS

Every book that deals with computer software must explain why certain things are printed the way they are—the so-called typographic conventions. This is not very stimulating information, but a quick glance at what follows might save you some confusion.

TYPOGRAPHIC CONVENTIONS

CONVENTION	DESCRIPTION AND EXAMPLES
General language syntax	FoxPro commands and functions are presented in a special typeface—**BROWSE, TRIM( )**, and particularly when they are used to illustrate syntax, the formal description of the language.
Language examples	Whenever the commands and functions are used as an example that would be typed, they are presented like this: `SET FILTER TO STATE = "CA"`.
Menu and control options	All options of the FoxPro system menu and controls are bolded and have the first letter capitalized: **File, Save As...**. They are often presented in a sequence of selections separated by commas.
Option prompts in windows and dialog boxes	Similar to menu options, buttons, prompts and other special markings of FoxPro windows are bolded: **File Select List**.
Object-oriented programming elements	Classes and events are presented in mixed case and bolded: **Grid**, **FormSet**, **Init**. All syntax and methods in the body of the text use the same typeface as other FoxPro syntax and functions: **SHOW()**, **ADDOBJECT()**. Properties and objects are in normal text but use mixed case: AutoActivate, Form, Grid, Movable.
Names of folders, files, tables, fields and variables	So that the numerous references to fields, tables, and variables don't get lost in the text, they are capitalized: ACTIVITY (table), GUESTID (field).

The most unusual of the typographic conventions are the ones used to highlight the syntax of commands and functions. Where system menu approaches exist, they are also listed. It's important to note that no attempt is made to duplicate the full syntax of the Visual FoxPro *Language Reference*. You can, and should, make frequent use of that book or, better, the on-line reference. What's provided in this book are forms of the commands and functions that are actually used most of the time. This follows a reverse of the 80/20 rule: 20 percent of the programming language is used to do 80 percent of the programming.

The following syntax conventions are used for commands:

System menu: File, New, Table/DBF

Command syntax: **CREATE cFileName**

Arguments: **cFileName** The name of the file to create.

Examples:

```
CREATE GUEST
CREATE \DEMO\DATA\GUEST
```

Both the system menu and command options are presented together, along with some typical examples for programming. The command syntax is the formal presentation of a command, its clauses, and the various items that go with it, followed by the arguments, the clauses and variable values that can be used.

The following syntax conventions are used for functions:

Command syntax:

STUFF(cExpression, nStartReplacement, nCharactersReplaced, cReplacement)

Arguments:

cExpression The character expression to be stuffed (the stuffee).

nStartReplacement The starting position for the substring to be stuffed.

nCharactersReplaced The ending position for the substring to be stuffed.

cReplacement The character expression to stuff (the stuffer).

Example:

```
? STUFF("  My dog, Spots, has fleas   ",1,2,"Gosh! ")
```

Returns: `"Gosh! My dog, Spots, has fleas   "`

Functions start with the formal syntax, followed by an explanation of the arguments (the information being sent to the function for processing) and then one or more examples of the use of the function. Finally, the word **Returns:** explains the information the function returns when it's finished.

SECTION 1

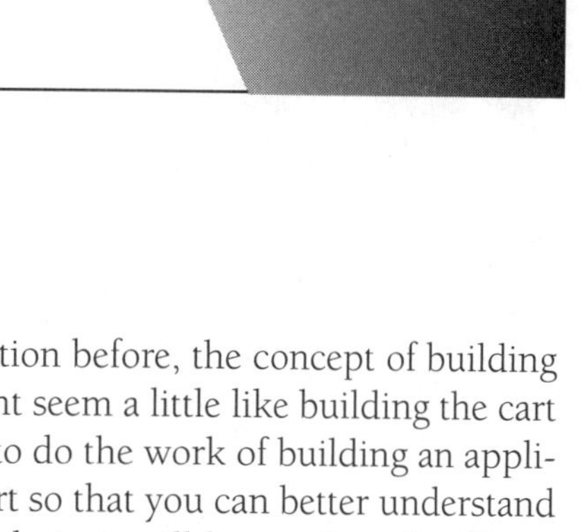

STARTING AN APPLICATION FRAMEWORK

If you've never developed a software application before, the concept of building an application development framework might seem a little like building the cart before buying the horse. But if you're going to do the work of building an application in any case, why not harness that effort so that you can better understand the process? In that way, the next time you do it, it will be much easier. There are only two chapters in this section, but they're crucial for introducing you to the predominant concepts and terminology of the book.

- Chapter 1, "Organizing and Application and Its Framework"
- Chapter 2, "Understanding OOP, Part I"

Chapter 1 is devoted to giving you a sense of the whole: what application building is about and how to organize it with an application development framework. You probably won't comprehend everything in this first encounter, but it will be helpful to see where you're going.

Chapter 2 introduces the basics of object-oriented programming. There are a couple of reasons for introducing it in two parts (here and in Chapter 11), the most compelling being that until some of the concepts and jargon are explained, much of the interaction among database management, object-oriented programming, and application building will be impossible to describe.

CHAPTER 1

ORGANIZING AN APPLICATION AND ITS FRAMEWORK

Right from the top: building applications is one thing; building them with a particular language or development tool is another. All applications, loosely defined, are computer programs that perform, or help the user perform, certain related tasks such as accounting or word processing. In modern graphical environments, all applications have menus, windows, buttons, and other screen devices. They use data to one degree or another. They have a beginning, a middle, and an end. No, an application isn't like a story, although the development of a large application can require at least as much creativity and skill as writing a novel.

Applications contain similar elements and have similar structures. This makes it possible to learn about applications in a generic sense without reference to a programming language or development system. To a certain extent, that's what this first chapter is about. However, as soon as you implement an application using a specific approach, such as Visual FoxPro's, you'll see the development tool that dictates the structure of an application. For example, if you are familiar with developing applications but new to object-oriented programming, you'll discover that using a class hierarchy is a very different way to construct applications.

Because you are building applications with Visual FoxPro, it's assumed that data will play a big role. FoxPro started as a data management program, and that remains its greatest strength. However, with the power comes a certain amount of complexity. As a result, when you learn about building applications in Visual FoxPro, there are three big areas to cover:

- Application structure and design
- Data management
- Object-oriented programming

Needless to say, this is a lot, and it gives an indication of why an application development framework can be valuable: a framework is both a conceptual structure and a practical guide you can use to organize everything that goes into an application.

What Is an Application Framework?

It will take the entire book to flesh out an explanation of an application development framework, but with really big subjects it's often helpful to start with an overview—even if you don't understand it fully—so that you can fix in your mind a rough outline of the whole.

Figure 1.1 shows the main components of an application framework.

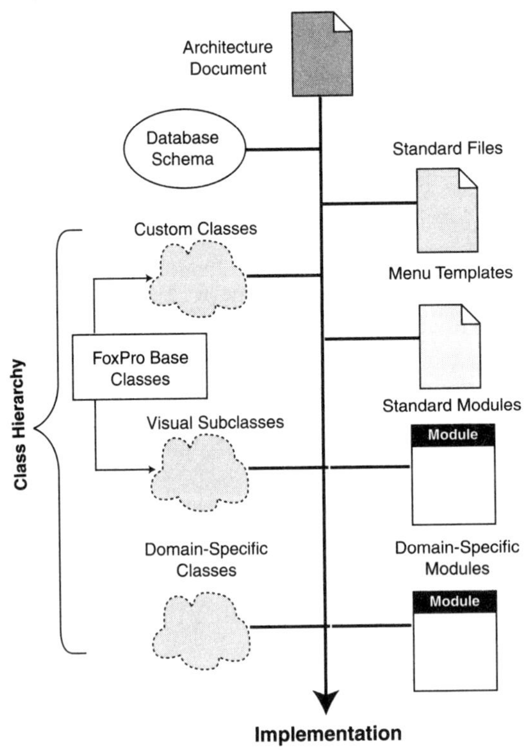

Figure 1.1 An application development framework.

The diagram presents the primary elements of an application from the perspective of the developer—these are the biggest pieces you put together, and they constitute the design and structure of an application. The diagram includes some generic elements, such as designing databases and building object-oriented program classes, but it moves from top to bottom toward elements that are specific to a particular application, sometimes called the *domain* of an application.

At the bottom is *implementation*, where you take all the designs and program elements from above and combine them into a working application. At the top you'll notice something called the *architecture document*. This is a fancy label for something basic: documenting what you do.

We won't stop here to explain the items in the framework diagram. Even a short description would take a full chapter and wouldn't make much sense without first covering basic concepts and jargon. From here to Chapter 13, we'll proceed down the left side of this framework, primarily covering those concepts and basic techniques. From Chapter 14 to the end of the book, we'll cover the less abstract components and the analysis and design process that leads to programming an application.

NOTE

I want to make it clear that this diagram, or any other scheme for an application framework, is not waiting somewhere, ready for you to effortlessly snap together the pieces. In a way, the diagram in Figure 1.1 is an idealization—a goal—something you need to create and thoroughly understand for yourself. Murphy and his law are forever present in applications development, and when something goes wrong, the only way to fix it is to know where (and how) to look. Even if you could acquire a completed framework, without intense study of how it's constructed you would find it more trouble than it's worth.

Whether you try to construct a formal application development framework, something that can be used to produce many applications more quickly and reliably, or you just want to understand how *an* application is created, the framework can be a guide for what you must do. Keep in mind that you don't need to create a pharaoh's pyramid. The scale of applications is almost infinitely varied, and so is the scale of an application development framework. We'll hit on this theme often, because the scale of an application is an important factor in many of the decisions you will make about how to develop it.

The working assumption of this book is that you plan to program more than one application, in which case the value of an application framework is easily demonstrated. It's usually characterized as "programming without reinventing the wheel." Using a framework, especially in conjunction with object-oriented programming techniques, is one of the best ways yet discovered to reuse your programming. An application development framework may not be the only solution to the current industry wide software development bottleneck, but it does seem to be part of the solution.

GETTING STARTED

Almost the first topic you'll find in the Visual FoxPro *User's Guide* is how to use the Project Manager. From the developer's point of view, this priority is exactly right. You are going to live in the Project Manager from start to finish. If the application framework is the conceptual collection point for an application, the Project Manager is where the real work of an application is collected in the form of files.

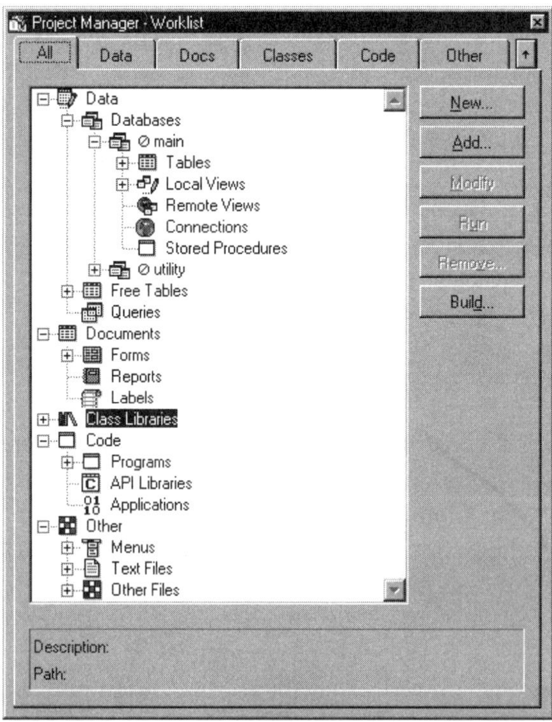

FIGURE 1.2 THE PROJECT MANAGER, THE CENTER OF ACTIVITY.

As you can see in Figure 1.2, there are many file categories in the Project Manager. **Data** lists all the databases, tables, queries, and views. **Documents** contains the screen forms, reports, and labels. **Classes** lists the class libraries, which are the heart of object-oriented programming. **Code** lists the files that contain programs, applications, or programming provided externally to FoxPro (API libraries). Finally, the **Other** tab houses the menu files and other miscellaneous files such as bitmaps for icons and various text files. All this reinforces the idea that even a middle-size application might have a hundred or more files.

Although this is not a tutorial book, in the spirit of showing you that implementing an application isn't forbiddingly complex and mysterious, let's step through a small example. We'll start very simply by making a new Project Manager and three files that will give you the beginning, middle, and end of an application.

Assuming you know how to start Visual FoxPro, you'll soon be at the main FoxPro window, which is nothing more than a system menu at the top, followed by a toolbar row, a status bar at the bottom, and the Command window in between. Follow these steps:

1. Open a new project. The mechanics are simple, but the real question is, where are you going to put the project file? Almost everything you do in FoxPro creates a file, and files have to go somewhere. The most obvious route is to create a new subdirectory (*folder*, in Winspeak). The topic of configuring your hard disk (or a network's drive) for your project is important (you'll encounter the details in Chapter 8), but for now create a new directory. To continue with the project file, select **File** from the menu, followed by **New**. When you see the New File dialog box, make sure **Project** is selected (it should already be selected unless you've recently created some other kind of file). Click the **New File** button, and you'll be presented with the Create dialog box (the operation of which should be familiar from similar Windows programs). In the folder you created, save the project file with an appropriate name.

2. Once you have a new Project Manager window, select the **Code** tab and then the **Programs** line. Click the **New** button on the side of the Project Manager window; this will open a new program file.

   As you stare at this blank window, knowing it's some kind of program file, you'll probably realize this "little" example is going to breeze by a lot of territory, including how to program in Visual

FoxPro, in order to give you some very basic entry and exit points for an application.

3. Type the following in the program window:

```
*MAIN.PRG
SET TALK OFF
PUSH MENU _MSYSMENU
DO MAIN.MPR

READ EVENTS
POP MENU _MSYSMENU
SET TALK ON
```

This MAIN program will be the one that starts the application. It doesn't do much. Like all programs, each line is a command or instruction that will be executed in order by FoxPro. **SET TALK OFF** stops FoxPro feedback messages from showing up on the screen. **PUSH MENU _MSYSMENU** stores the main FoxPro menu in a memory-holding area (a *stack*) so that you can display your own menu with **DO MAIN.MPR**. This MAIN.MPR file is a menu program that controls the flow of the program.

The **READ EVENTS** command is crucial, because it sets the internal status of FoxPro to continuously wait for events such as keystrokes, menu choices, and mouse clicks. Technically, this is called an *event loop*; it's what keeps a FoxPro program running. Every FoxPro program must have this command, and, as you will see, they all end by canceling it.

When **READ EVENTS** is terminated, the program resumes in the MAIN file. Notice that two commands are reversed: **POP MENU _MSYSMENU** restores the FoxPro system menu, and **SET TALK ON** allows information from FoxPro to display on the screen again. After that, FoxPro automatically ends the program and returns you to the main FoxPro window.

When you're finished typing, click the **Save** icon in the toolbar or use the menu (**File**, **Save**) and use the Save As dialog box to save the file in your project folder with the name MAIN.PRG. Close the Program window. Many people prefer to use the **Ctrl-W** keyboard combination, which closes the window and saves the file at the same time. Notice that the **Programs** line in the Project Manager now has a + in front of it. Click it, and the line will expand to reveal the MAIN program. Highlight the program and notice the buttons on the right that become active (*enabled*). From this point, you can select the **MAIN** entry and use the **Modify** button to edit the file or the **Run** button to run the program. That's how your program gets started. Before you do that, however, there are a couple more steps.

4. Select the **Other** tab in the Project Manager and highlight **Menus**. Click the **New** button and you'll have a small dialog box (Figure 1.3) that lets you choose between a standard menu and a shortcut menu (the right mouse menu, new in this version of FoxPro).

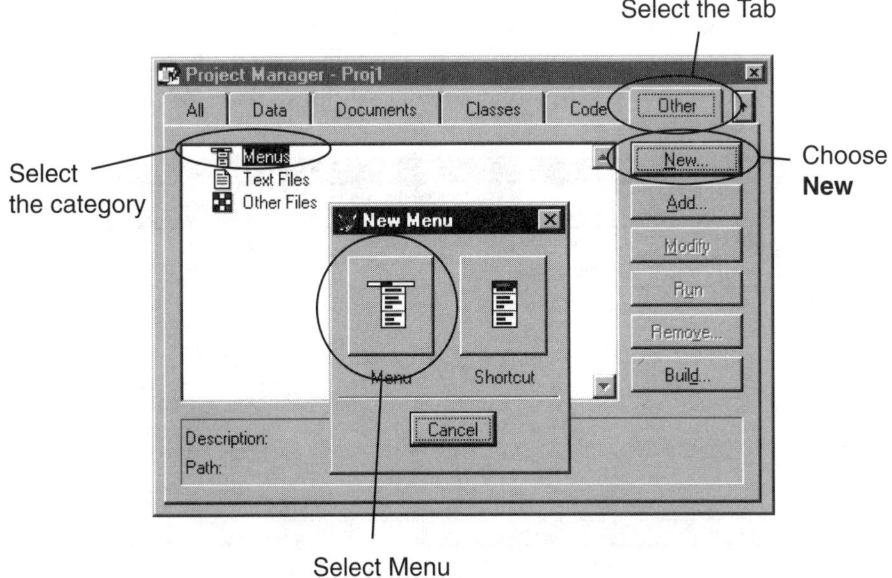

FIGURE 1.3 STARTING A NEW MENU.

Choose the **Menu** button, which opens the Menu Designer window. We won't go into the details here, but this is where you create all the menus for an application (see Figure 1.4). Start by typing **\<Show** in the prompt column of the designer. You enter and edit these options as you would any other text field. Use the \< characters, because they create the *hot key* access (**Alt-S**) to the menu option. Next, move over to the Result column and use the drop-down box to change from Submenu to **Command**. In the blank box to the right, type **DO FORM main**. Now, when you click the **Show** option of the menu, it will start the screen form called MAIN (which you'll create shortly).

One more addition to the menu is necessary. In the prompt box beneath Show, type **\<Quit**. Change the Result box from Submenu to **Procedure** and click the **Create** button in the next column. This action puts you into a Program window, one that is specifically attached to the menu. In this window, enter:

```
_SCREEN.ActiveForm.Release()
CLEAR EVENTS
```

The first line closes the form window, and the second line is the command that terminates the **READ EVENTS** that keeps the program running. The completed menu should look like Figure 1.4. Save the menu to your project folder with the name MAIN.

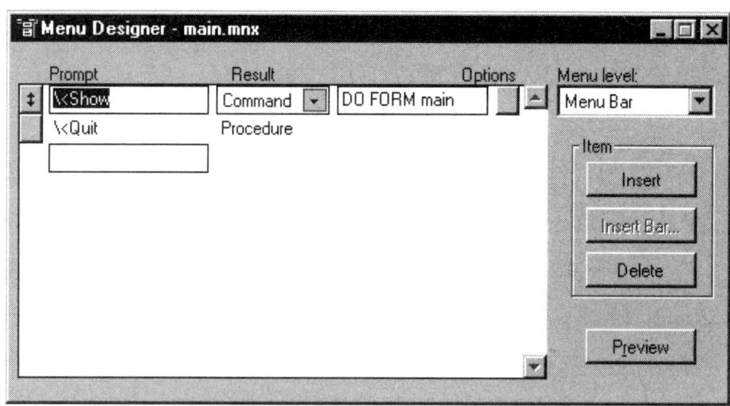

Figure 1.4 Menu Designer with completed revisions.

5. The final step is to create the screen form referenced in the menu. A form, which is nothing more than a standard window, is the basis for most of the user interfaces you will create in your applications. A form is also the most complex programming *object* in the realm of object-oriented programming, but more on that later. For now, we'll create a simple form so that you can see how forms are integrated into an application.

Select the **Documents** tab in the Project Manager and highlight **Forms**. Click the **New** button and choose **New Form** from the New Form dialog box. The Form Designer window will appear, as in Figure 1.5, although your configuration may be somewhat different.

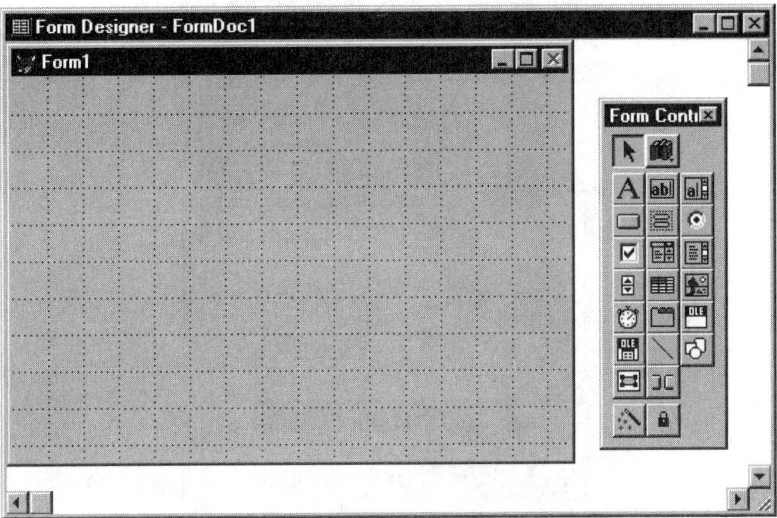

FIGURE 1.5 A NEW FORM IN THE FORM DESIGNER.

For the most part, we'll ignore the toolbars and Properties window that also appear. We'll make only a couple of cosmetic changes to give you the flavor of working in the Form Designer. In the Properties window (see Figure 1.6), find the word **BackColor** in the gray-shaded left column. This is the *property* of the form that determines the background color.

Double-click this row, and the FoxPro Color dialog box appears. Select a color of your choice, click **OK**, and the background color of the form will be instantly transformed. That's why this is called *visual programming* and why you are working with *Visual* FoxPro.

We'll finish by adding some text to the form. Find the Form Controls toolbar and the button with a large letter *A* in it. This is the **Text** icon. Click it so that the normal arrow cursor changes to a cross-hair cursor (+). On the form itself, click and hold the cursor at some point to the left of the middle and drag the dotted drawing box (called a *marquee*) down and right to mark off an area. In the box you've created, type **THIS IS A PROGRAM FORM** and press **Enter**. You've actually typed into the entry box of the Properties window, and the text shows up immediately in the form.

FIGURE 1.6 THE PROPERTIES WINDOW WITH BACKCOLOR HIGHLIGHTED.

NOTE

I know, big deal. You've probably seen this sort of visual programming before, and we're certainly baby stepping. But, you have 96 more properties of the form to understand, not to mention 30 methods and 22 types of controls that fit into a form. You'll get to the serious stuff soon enough.

As with everything else you've done so far, you need to save this form as a file. Give it the name MAIN.SCX and put it in your project folder. It, too, will be registered in the Project Manager, where you can access it again with the **Modify** button.

All that's left to do is start the fireworks. Go back to the **Code** tab of the Project Manager and highlight the **Main** program. Click the **Run** button.

6. In all likelihood you will get a Program Error message: `File 'main.mpr' does not exist`. This error is a bug. You wouldn't want this example to be unrealistic, would you? However, we're going to cheat, because you don't need to figure out this bug for yourself. What's missing is that the Menu Designer does not automatically generate code for the menu program. This is one of several ways in which menus are different from most programming in FoxPro.

   First things first: get out of the error message by clicking the **Cancel** button. You'll probably notice that the program window reappears and highlights the line of code that caused the error. This would be very convenient, especially if it worked like that all the time, but it doesn't. Besides, the error isn't in the code; rather, we get it because the file doesn't exist. That's typical of the misdirection you'll find whenever you debug software. Close the program window and go back to the Project Manager.

   To fix the bug, select the **Other** tab and highlight the **Main** menu entry. Click the **Modify** button, and the Menu Designer reappears, along with the **Menu** option in the system menu. Choose the **Generate** option under **Menu**, and in the Generate Menu dialog box make sure the output file goes to your project folder with the name MAIN.MPR. Then press **Generate**. FoxPro will flash a few messages while it generates the code. When it's finished, close the Menu Designer window (there's nothing to save) and try to run the main program again. This time, hopefully, it will run.

NOTE

If you go through these steps, it will appear that you've created four files (one each for the project, program, menu, and form). Actually, FoxPro creates nine files, each with a specific file extension: two for the project (PJX, PJT); one for the program (PRG); four for the menu (MNX, MNT, MPR, MPX); and two for the form (SCX, SCT). That's how your application's files proliferate like rabbits and why the Project Manager is needed to keep track of them.

IT'S THAT SIMPLE?

Take another look at the application development framework diagram in Figure 1.1. What parts of it were involved in the example? None, actually, because nothing you created is ready for reuse in multiple applications. The closest would be MAIN.PRG, the main program file, which, with a great deal of augmentation, could be used as a template. But the example illustrates some key elements of all applications. Maintaining the analogy we started earlier, the MAIN program is the beginning and end of an application, the MAIN menu provides the bridge from beginning to middle and from middle to end, and the MAIN form is the middle. The "middle" is where the user spends most of the time, working with an application's user interface. When all is said and done, this is also where you, as the developer, will spend most of your time.

NOTE

You might want to hang on to what you did with the example. It works and can be used as a *test bed*—a quick way to run tests on forms, menus, and other program elements. Eventually, it could form the basis of a sophisticated application. Someday, when you've created a huge class hierarchy, hundreds of forms, dozens of menus, and many standard application modules, you can remember this humble kernel of an application.

THE APPLICATION DEVELOPMENT CYCLE

Time is an important factor in application development. Unless they're trivial, most applications take many days to develop, and some can require years. Even if you're not under the gun of a deadline, the ability to complete an application in a reasonable amount of time is the search for the Holy Grail of software. The need to save time was one of the motivations behind the creation of object-oriented technology, visual programming, and application development frameworks.

Here's a truism to consider: The time it takes to create an application is much greater than the sum of the time it takes to create each of the component parts.

This truism has a couple of wrinkles. One is that through object-oriented programming and modularization you try to reduce the amount of time spent developing the component parts. As mentioned, the goal is to reuse them. Of course, it takes time to build the reusable parts in the first place.

The other wrinkle is that you don't merely build parts when you create an application. Programming isn't the only thing an application developer typically does. Unless you are working in a large company where specialists are involved, most applications require analysis, design, integration, setup, and a host of other things, such as client management, that have little direct relationship to programming. All these peripheral activities take time.

In any application of size (however that's defined), you go through many steps or phases. It's a process, and a lengthy and complicated one at that. The process has a name—the *application development cycle*—and it's illustrated in Figure 1.7.

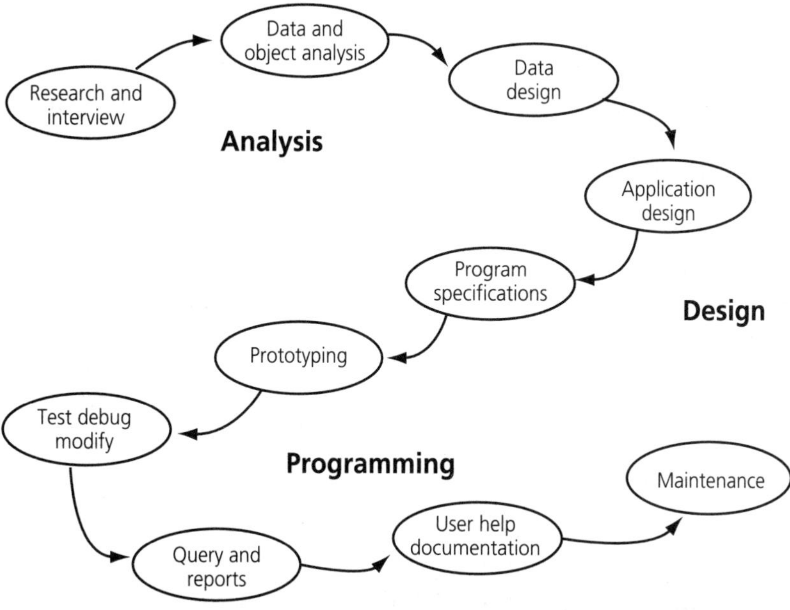

FIGURE 1.7 THE APPLICATION DEVELOPMENT CYCLE.

There are scores of ways to describe the application development cycle. Some are academic, others are proprietary (part of a product), and still others are based on experience. All of them reflect a repetitive life cycle of building an application or of developing revisions to existing software. Planning for the phases and steps of the cycle is a strategic consideration for large applications and can be applied even to small ones. Of course, some developers ignore any definition of the development cycle and prefer the "Just do it" approach. Just doing it works, to a point, but in developing full-scale applications, especially object-oriented ones, the "point" may come well before the completion of the project.

In this book, we'll use an approach to the application development cycle based largely on experience and adapted for database applications in the object-oriented programming environment. Boiled down to the essentials, there are just four phases:

1. **Analysis:** Find out what the application is supposed to do, what data is involved, and who's supposed to use it.
2. **Design:** From knowledge gained by analysis, you design the necessary components of the application: databases, class hierarchies, processing routines, user interface.
3. **Programming:** Design in hand, you do the programming, which as described later is a cycle of its own: program, compile, debug.
4. **Maintenance:** Once the application is completed, it must be maintained. Often it will be revised, bringing you back to analysis and design. That's why it is called a cycle.

The actual development of software is not as sequential as it appears in the diagram; phases overlap, are dropped, cycle among themselves, and generally move forward in a much messier fashion. But the cycle exists, and understanding it will help you to think about your application from the point of view of how much time and effort should be spent along the way. The development cycle is another framework that can help you organize yourself, the application, and the users. Following is a brief description of the phases of the cycle (with details to follow in later chapters).

Research and Interview

For one project, the manager down the hall comes in and says, "Hey, we need a program to register the daily mail. Can you whip something up?" Another project, a half-million dollar customer information application, is expected to take more than a year to develop and will involve most of the people in the company. The scale of the research, interview, and analysis phases of these two projects is quite different, but the objective is the same. You need to find out who's involved and what's needed.

In both cases, you sit down with the principals and find out what they want. You locate and study documents and other information that will help you decide what data is involved. You also try to understand who will use the application—users' job environment, business rules and processes, perhaps even their work habits.

Understanding what the user wants is often difficult. For most users, developing software (or even using a computer) is not part of their job. How could they suddenly become articulate about what they want in a program? But it's only a half truth that users don't know what they want until they see it. They have a notion of what they want, and it's the developer's job to reach an understanding of their notions.

Collecting information about data requirements is usually much easier than understanding user requirements. Existing computer programs, reports, data sheets, even loose notes can be gathered and analyzed. The usual practice is to cast a wide net in the beginning and catch as much information as possible about data. Later, you can throw out items as you begin to decide what information is relevant.

Many applications can be understood only if you learn about the user's business. What is the line of work? How like (or unlike) is it to other applications? What is the working environment, including all computer technology? What business rules apply in the area of the application? Much of this can be learned only by observation, interview, and even participation.

The focus of most efforts in the research and interview phase is to get a clear picture of the functions involved in the application—often called *functional analysis*—the processing, updating, reporting, and other operations the application must perform. At the end of the phase, your aim is to create a list of requirements and observations that add up to an outline of the application's functionality.

The previous paragraphs don't begin to do justice to the importance or subtleties of analysis and research. To learn more, it's highly recommended that you read specialized literature, perhaps take a course in school, and if possible talk to people who do this kind of analysis. Keep in mind that application analysis is a profession in its own right, and that speaks volumes about how complex and special it can be.

DATA AND OBJECT ANALYSIS

It's assumed that you've chosen FoxPro because the application you're developing has a prominent data management requirement. With Visual FoxPro, you also need to include the object-oriented approach to application development. The blend of data and object analysis will be crucial to almost every application.

If you're familiar with data analysis but not object-oriented analysis, there is good news: the two approaches are quite similar. Even though FoxPro is a relational and not an object-oriented database system, the work you do to create a database design is based on a very similar kind of analysis used for object-oriented designs. It's essentially function-oriented, with groups of people, forms, work flows, and so forth providing data elements in one system and objects (classes) in the other.

At this stage of analysis, you spread out the collected documents and notes about project data and start to identify individual items of information (often called data *items*, or data *elements*). While making this identification, you can also begin to categorize the data by type and other properties, a process that leads more or less naturally to thinking about the classes involved in the application, many of which will be closely related to the data.

FoxPro applications are often user-centric, and the focus of analysis is on the interaction between the user interface and the data. When you're analyzing these applications, the user's point of view about the information is the most important, and the object-oriented model for applications is most useful. However, some elements of applications (or even whole applications) have little or no user participation. In these cases, approaches such as transaction analysis or data flow diagramming may be more appropriate. Object-oriented approaches should never be considered the only way to do analysis.

As an example, here's a line from an analyst's notebook: "Sally in PR generates the work order, but Bill in production needs to read and approve it before it's sent to the layout staff." In such notes, you read that a work document—which in a FoxPro application means a screen form—is filled out by Sally. When she's finished, a database is updated (perhaps with additional calculations), and a notification is sent to Bill. You will need a form to present the order for review and a way to capture an approval. Finally, the order is transferred to the appropriate person in the art room, who acknowledges the receipt (needing an entry screen) and continues working with the order.

This one short note indicates the need for at least three review and entry forms (data and objects) as well as data transfer and updating—including user notification (transaction processing)—and a running documentation of the procedure (data flow). You would also make explicit note that the system runs on a network and needs some minimal security for sign-off. At least half of this sce-

nario doesn't involve a user interface. That doesn't mean the application will leave the object-oriented framework but only that other kinds of analysis may also be appropriate.

DATABASE DESIGN

The database design phase is characteristic of applications built around data management. In this phase, you are moving from generic data items to fields in specific FoxPro databases and tables. You may have made a list of items; now you decide data types, length, and field names. At the same time that you are identifying fields, the table design should be taking shape. It's part of this process to develop the *relational schema*, usually a diagram that outlines the structure of a database with tables and the relations between them. You are also identifying indexes, filters, and other aspects of the data system, such as partitioning for business rules and other client/server considerations.

If you ask experts in object-oriented design (OOD), they will tell you that OOD should come before the database design. This is a cart before the horse problem, compounded by not being sure which end of the horse goes first. Much depends on the scale of the application, the amount of data processing vs. user interface, and the general complexity of the application. Not all applications need a formal database design—or a class/object design, for that matter. This is one of those points where the scale of the project and the developer's resources come together to force a decision about how the application will be developed.

APPLICATION DESIGN

If you don't do the object-oriented design during or before the database design phase, in Visual FoxPro you would usually do it during application design. During this phase, you define an application's modules, forms, menus, and other major structural elements. These elements mostly fall into the realm of FoxPro's visual classes (menus are an awkward exception), so OOD is virtually required. However, many developers have difficulty finding the connection between the data and functional abstractions and the visual classes used in a FoxPro implementation. As you will see, this design task requires a mixture of what FoxPro calls custom classes (nonvisual classes) and the forms-oriented visual classes.

In this phase you will also make decisions about what elements of a complete application are needed. As an application grows in scale, you may need to include elements such as: application security, installation procedures, system codes management, report management, a help system, and more. Many of these elements arise from of the requirements of any application and not from any specific functions of the application.

APPLICATION SPECIFICATIONS

Application specifications, the *specs*, are typical of applications built on contract. Most applications benefit from spelling out the details—including the number of screen forms, reports, and other program elements—to which are often attached time, materials, and cost estimates. You may also specify hardware, networking, communications, and other "application environment" requirements.

In general, an application specification is a method of communication, a way of telling the users what to expect in the application. It may also be the basis of a contract or part of an elaborate project management scheme. Much depends on the scale of the application and the kind of working environment.

PROTOTYPING

It's becoming chapter and verse in modern programming that applications begin as prototypes. The prototypes, usually of modules from the application, are subjected to review with the user or client, and then go through refinement and modification. Its trendy name implies—rapid application development (RAD)—that prototyping is slick and fast.

As a technique for speedy development, RAD is largely an illusion. Yes, the prototype may appear quickly, but with most projects there is almost constant tweaking of screen layout and other elements to suit the needs (and frequently the whims) of the users. That's what prototyping is really about—getting the developer and the user to understand the application before the programming is completed.

For full-scale applications, so much analysis and design time has been (or should have been) expended that prototyping is more or less confined to refining the user interface rather than testing major functional assumptions. Although it is true that object-oriented programming emphasizes reusable components and

quick modification of stock elements, a strong design framework is necessary to hold together an application of any size.

TEST, DEBUG, MODIFY

As the prototypes of modules are completed, they go into the testing, debug, and modification phase. This step may be, in effect, a series of prototypes that may or may not involve the users in further review and testing. Given names such as *alpha* or *beta testing*, these more or less formal procedures involve seemingly endless rounds of revision and debugging. Depending on the size of the application and how many modules it has, this period may involve a team of programmers. This means that this phase is usually the most difficult one to manage.

QUERY AND REPORTING

Often, but not always, queries and reports begin development somewhat after initial module prototyping. This arrangement allows time for the data definitions to be accepted and stabilized, and that helps to avoid changing reports every time a change occurs in the database design. This aspect of data retrieval and output shouldn't be confused with FoxPro's SQL views, which are an integral part of the data environment for an application's forms.

This aspect of an application is usually segregated as a separate phase because of the volume and detailed requirements involved. Creating reports, especially with tools such as FoxPro's Report Designer, is one part repetitive mechanics and one part art. Programming the complete reporting environment usually involves user input to determine which reports to run and what filtering is required. It can be astonishingly complex, and when you consider that even a small application may have 50–100 reports, it is no small piece of the application pie.

HELP SYSTEMS AND DOCUMENTATION

For the user there is on-line help, which is part of the application. In Visual FoxPro 5.0, you must use the native Windows help system and its related development tools. For some applications (especially the large ones), user documentation includes printed material in the form of manuals or procedure books. A third kind of documentation is written for the programmer. Maintenance and modifications to the program depend on having appropriate information about how the system was designed, specified, and coded.

Although it's essential, this phase of developing an application has little glamour. If documentation of any sort becomes an afterthought, it's usually unavailable or worthless. Some projects get by with nonexistent or bad on-line help and documentation; most don't.

MAINTENANCE

As a rule, you don't throw your finished application over the wall and run. Delivered software has an afterlife, and it's called maintenance. Whether this means revisions, bug fixes, or simple housekeeping, all software needs maintenance. Database applications, in particular, need maintenance, because no matter how well they are designed or how robust their machinery, data tables become corrupted and accumulate bogus data. Some of this maintenance can be built into your application, and at other times this task will require the direct attention of someone else. Whatever the case, it's important to plan for the maintenance part of the cycle.

Being a cycle, the application development process could very well start over—with a new version perhaps. If the previous sections have been a Grand Tour (if this is Monday, we must be in prototyping), then we've merely been gawking at the highlights of what can become the dominant factor in all your waking hours. Buried in the cycle are major decisions about your approach, scheduling, and resource requirements (time and money). If you take up application building professionally, these decisions are the basis for profit or loss. If you didn't know it before, building applications is a challenge.

CHAPTER WRAP-UP

If there are bigger topics in software than the application development cycle and application development frameworks, we're in trouble. One covers the process of initiating, preparing, programming, and installing applications. The other covers the software elements that produce the applications and how you go about organizing them. No doubt the introductions in this chapter have raised many questions and have provided few answers, but it was important to get started. Unfortunately, an unwanted by-product may be a sense of apprehension. You may be asking, are applications really this complicated? We haven't even started the object-oriented programming. What have I gotten into?

Relax. As the Japanese are fond of saying, "One can appreciate the mountain before climbing it." Once you start climbing the learning curve you'll see that, as in so many other things, taking one step at a time makes an awesome task require nothing more than attention and patience.

Applications can be big, complex, and difficult. Most of them are not. It helps to maintain perspective. There is no requirement for an application development framework. Visual FoxPro doesn't provide one, and most of the people who ask you to build applications won't even know what it is. Similarly, there's often no one around to insist that you do analysis and design before building an application or that you spend time documenting what you do. There are even applications, albeit small ones, that *shouldn't* labor under the machinery of the two frameworks. Keep things simple if you can.

That does not mean, however, that the elements of the cycle or the framework don't apply to smaller projects. They do—but not all of them in every instance. An application development framework will provide you with a way to reuse your programming efforts, and, if you're organized about it, even smaller projects will go more quickly. Similarly, the development cycle can be abbreviated, but you're still going through most of the phases if only informally. It helps to understand where you are in the process and, better still, to have made conscious decisions about what you will and won't do.

NOTE

This chapter has a lot of philosophizing and finger-wagging. That's in keeping with the scale and impact of the topics. However, you'll need experience to discover whether what I've written is true or even makes sense. So go forth and experience, which in this case means get started with an application. If you're unlucky, you may have to create a real application immediately. In my experience, first applications (in FoxPro or any other system) are like the first pancake: usually far from perfect. It would be better if you started an application that is useful but not required. In any case, start looking around at other software and think about something that you might want for an application. In the next chapter, we'll get started with some object-oriented programming fundamentals, and the real work begins.

CHAPTER 2

UNDERSTANDING OOP, PART I

And now we come to the main event, object-oriented programming (OOP), about which you may be in fear and trembling—or chomping at the bit. Unless you are experienced with other object-oriented programming languages, the Visual FoxPro implementation of the so-called object model will probably be a challenge, although the difficulties are often exaggerated. It's true that you don't learn OOP overnight. That's not because of the difficulty but because it's so different, at least different from other kinds of programming. If you've never done any programming, that may be a point in your favor. You'll have no habits and preconceptions to unlearn.

In Visual FoxPro, most people learn OOP by doing it and seeing it, usually while creating screen forms. It's not that forms are all there is to the FoxPro OOP (hardly), but they make up the bulk of an application's user interface, and they embody almost every aspect of the object-oriented approach to programming. So this chapter will use a form and the Form Designer as the main point of illustration. Because the focus is on OOP concepts, you won't learn the fine points of working in the Form Designer (that will come in later chapters), but you will cover the basics.

Although hands-on is probably the best way to learn OOP, it is good to be aware of the ancient Chinese proverb: "One who learns doing without thinking will soon be undone." For many people, it is just as necessary to develop an intellectual framework for understanding new concepts such as OOP as it is to just do it. Ideally, practical experience and an understanding of how things work should go together. Along with using the Form Designer, this first OOP chapter will indulge in a good deal of theory and explanation.

Tucked into the end of this chapter is a short glossary of OOP. If it suits your style of learning, you can jump back and forth from the glossary to confirm some of your suspicions about the meaning of jargon.

NOTE

In this exposition of object-oriented programming, you will see concepts explained, defined, and characterized more than once. There's no one way to perceive a complex subject like this. It's hoped that by looking at the same thing from different angles, sooner or later, you'll have an *aha!* experience.

OOP and the Application Framework

It would be hard to overemphasize the importance of object-oriented programming to an application development framework, or to programming FoxPro in general. If you look at the diagram in Figure 1.1 (Chapter 1), you might get the impression that the object-oriented part is large but not overwhelming. In fact, it is almost everything, including roughly 90 percent of the real work involved in creating an application. Moreover, the principles behind OOP drive much of the application's design and make it possible to realize the goal of an application framework: reusable code.

The Object-Oriented Approach

First, we'll jump in with a description of object-oriented programming—well before you probably can understand it—to lay the concepts and buzzwords on the table. Then we'll go to the Form Designer and illustrate the concepts and jargon as you will encounter them in FoxPro. At the end of the chapter we'll put all the pieces together and look at object-oriented programming from several perspectives.

One aspect of objects tends to confuse almost everybody: what is an object? The Microsoft *Developer's Guide* uses the example of a telephone as an object. This seems clear enough, because we sometimes refer to telephones and other things as objects. The telephone can also stand as a metaphor for objects in a program, because we know what it does, but we don't need to know how it does it. However, saying that a telephone has characteristics like a program object is really looking at things backward. In most cases, you want to say that a program object has characteristics like something in the real world. This applies to telephones, cars, and many other physical things. In object-oriented programming, you can have a telephone object, and what it would do is to *model* the real telephone—capture its attributes and behavior. This is what the telephone dialer programs do.

The correlation between physical objects and programming objects is usually easy to understand, but object-oriented programming is not limited to objects that represent physical objects. A programming object can also model (among other things) a process, a concept, or a relationship. In daily life we don't usually call "lunch" an object, but a restaurant management program might certainly have a program object called **Lunch**.

Programming objects are *abstractions*: condensed and selective representations of many observable (or at least perceivable) aspects of either the real world or the world of a software program. The latter is where the FoxPro *visual objects* come in; they are abstractions of computer processes and entities: data entry screens, reports, and so forth. In object-oriented programming you will encounter both kinds of objects: those that represent or model something in the real world, and those that do the same thing for elements of software. It will probably take a while to understand the similarities and differences between the two types of objects; but you must remember that it usually takes both kinds of objects to make an application.

Object-oriented programs are constructed with objects derived from classes. Within a running program, objects provide information and services to other objects through their *properties* and *methods*. As illustrated in Figure 2.1, objects store their own information and have specific characteristics or attributes (properties). They can respond to things that occur (events) using programming procedures that are event-specific methods. They can also execute procedures (methods) without external events.

If objects are the building blocks of a program, then *classes* are the blueprint for the blocks. Classes define how objects are to be initially constructed. The phrase "initially constructed" is important because in FoxPro you can add things to objects that are not originally defined in their class. Although we spend most of our active programming time working with objects, it is really the classes that are fundamental to what the objects can do. That's why design and implementation of classes and their relationships (the *class structure*) is considered important in object-oriented programming.

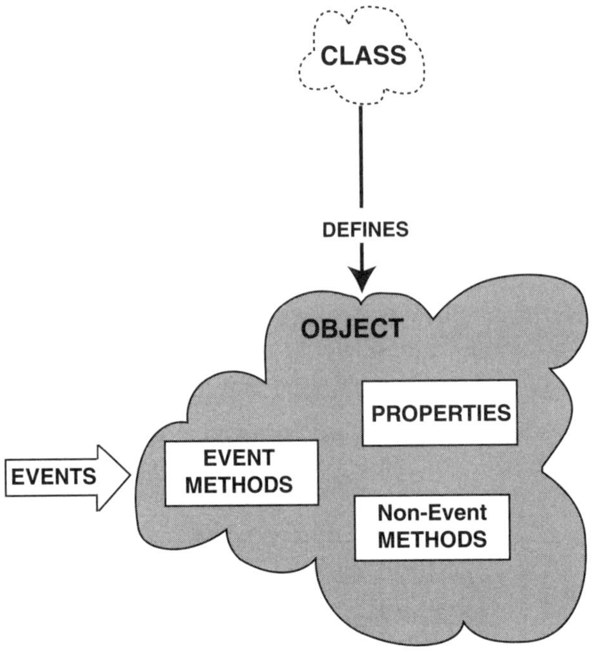

FIGURE 2.1 OVERVIEW OF AN OBJECT.

Associated with objects and classes are a number of fundamental concepts, which for better or worse have an intimidating jargon: instantiation, encapsulation, inheritance, polymorphism, and class hierarchy. Figure 2.2 illustrates most of these (and other) conceptual associations.

Starting at the top, as one can do with a hierarchy, are the *base classes*. (Don't ask why the top of a hierarchy is called a base.) Base classes are either defined by the language, are built-in, or constitute the most fundamental user-defined classes. In Visual FoxPro, there are only the built-in base classes; all others are derived from them (*subclassed*).

Let's take, for example, the base class **Grid**. This class is the rough equivalent of the old FoxPro Browse, the spreadsheet-like display of data. Because **Grid** is a base class, you cannot modify the definition of a grid object (the object that the **Grid** base class creates). However, you can create your own class based on the **Grid**:

```
DEFINE CLASS myGrid AS Grid
```

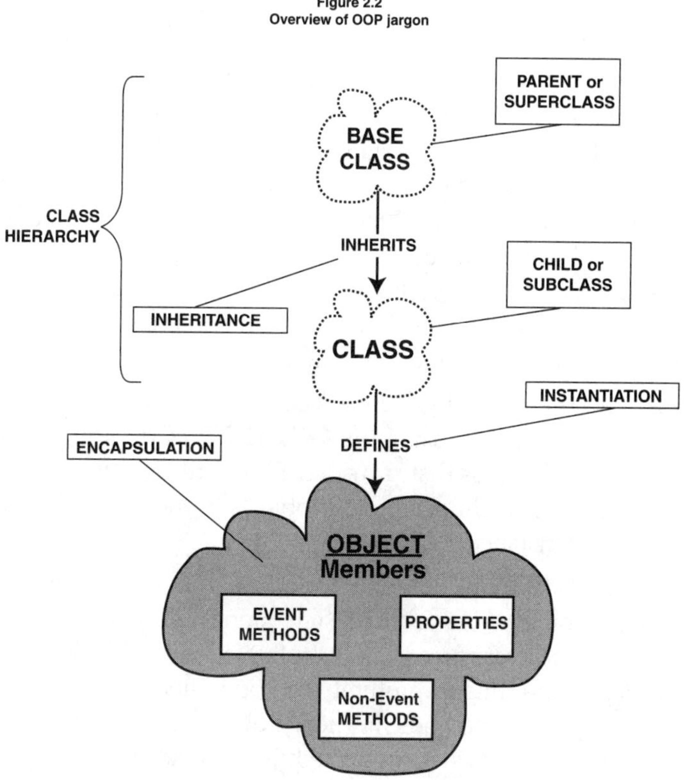

FIGURE 2.2 OVERVIEW OF OOP JARGON.

In this *subclass*, you can define additional properties and add new methods or other objects. In addition, the subclass *inherits* all the properties and methods from its *parent* class (sometimes called the *superclass*). This means, for instance, that if the base class has a white background for the grid, your subclass will also have a white background, at least until you change it. Suppose you change the background color to blue and add a new method, **BlueColumn()**, that puts a decorative blue column with stars in the grid. Now suppose you define another class based on your subclass:

```
DEFINE CLASS myNewGrid AS myGrid
```

It would inherit the blue background and the blue column. This chain of *inheritance* is called a *class hierarchy*. The top of the hierarchy (the base class) is the most generic, and each succeeding level adds (or modifies) properties and methods for its own purposes.

Another important aspect of inheritance and the class hierarchy is that you can create a method in a parent class, such as the **BlueColumn()** mentioned earlier that adds a blue column with stars in it to a grid; then in the subclass you can create another **BlueColumn()** but change the stars to dollar signs in the column. This ability to use the same name in different classes for a method that is somewhat changed from the parent class is called *polymorphism*. If you couldn't do this, inheritance would hardly be worth the bother. It's the ability to selectively modify (also sometimes called *overload*) inherited class *members* (properties and methods) that makes object-oriented programming powerful.

At each level of the hierarchy, the class can be used to create—the technical word is *instantiate*—an object, using the **CREATEOBJECT()** function. An object is the active *instance* of a class that provides information through its properties, and services through its methods, to other objects in the program. (An application may have many instances of a class.)

However, it is usually not desirable for all the members of an object to be accessible to other objects. As with the telephone example, knowing what a member does is not necessary to using it. In fact, it's often better that some elements are explicitly off-limits to prohibit the possibility of inadvertent changes to important properties or methods. In theory, objects are fully self-contained—*encapsulated*—having their own data, procedures, and structure. In practice, it is necessary to expose some members of the object to other objects (sometimes called the *public parts* or *interface*) and hide other members (sometimes called *private parts*). Sorry, but this jargon is for real.

FoxPro and OOP

There is no such thing as *the* object-oriented programming language. More than a score of OOP implementations are currently in use, and the number is growing. If you picked a set of 20 concepts and techniques to represent a basic OOP capability, no one product would have more than 15, and products would overlap almost at random. Visual FoxPro is not unique in this respect. It supports a healthy variety of OOP features but by no means all of them.

Fortunately, it's unnecessary to worry about which OOP features FoxPro does or does not have (leave that for the debates on the FoxForum). Instead, concentrate on what you have to work with, which is rich and deep enough to keep you learning for years. However, it is useful to note that in a purely object-oriented programming language, everything is an object. This is not strictly true for FoxPro, which has three feet in and one foot out of object-orientation. Certain elements of the FoxPro system—namely menus, databases, reports, and program files—are not fully object-oriented. This lack of complete integration produces some rough edges, as you will see. It's also the reason that an application development framework isn't just the class hierarchy and its by-products.

Visual FoxPro gives you several tools that are either specifically designed for managing classes and objects or use object-oriented elements:

- Form Designer
- Report Designer and Label Designer (partially object-oriented)
- Class Designer
- Class Browser (Professional Edition)
- Control Builders (in the Form Designer)
- Data Environment (in the Form Designer and the Report Designer)

Considering that the Form Designer can also create classes, its importance in the list is almost overwhelming. Like many development environments (Visual Basic, Delphi, PowerBuilder), Visual FoxPro is *form-centric*; the form is not only the center of the user interface but also the center of most of the procedural programming. If you're going to learn OOP, the Form Designer is a good place to start.

THE FORM DESIGNER: A FIRST LOOK AT OOP

Now it's time for hands-on work. Rub your knuckles, stroke the mouse, and open a new form in Visual FoxPro. The examples here work as if you were creating the form for the example in Chapter 1 and a table found on the accompanying disk. You might instead use a form of your own, specifically one that needs at least one table. It should be a very simple form, because the focus is on the object-oriented programming and not the form itself.

Figure 2.3 was created by first selecting **Forms** and then **New** in the **Documents** tab of the UTILITY project manager (bypassing the Form wizards).

Once the form is open, either right-click in the form to get the shortcut menu and select **Data Environment** or use the system menu under **View**.

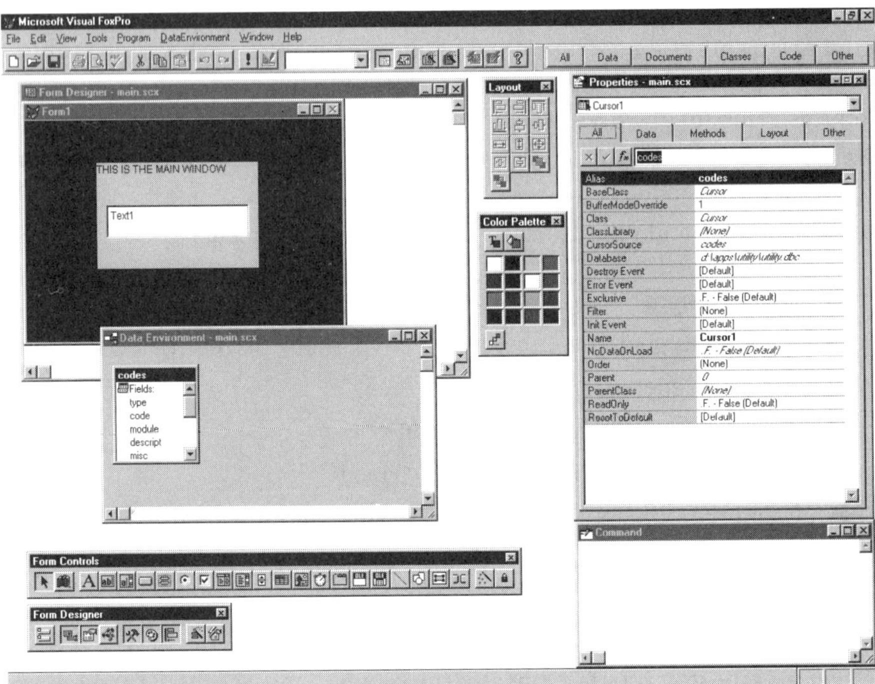

FIGURE 2.3 THE FORM DESIGNER AND DATA ENVIRONMENT.

You might also want to open the other forms-related toolbars: Layout, Color Palette, and Form Designer. (Use **View**, **Toolbars** from the menu or right-click on any open toolbar.)

The first order of business, usually, is to attach data sources (tables or views) to the form. That's the purpose of the Data Environment window. Right-click in the window to open the shortcut window and select **Add**. In the current example, with the UTILITY database already open, we'll select the CODES table. This action puts the CODES table box into the Data Environment window.

The Data Environment is itself one of the base objects (not a base class because it can't be subclassed), and as an object it has its own properties and methods. You can see them by opening the Data Environment property window (Figure 2.4) using the shortcut menu.

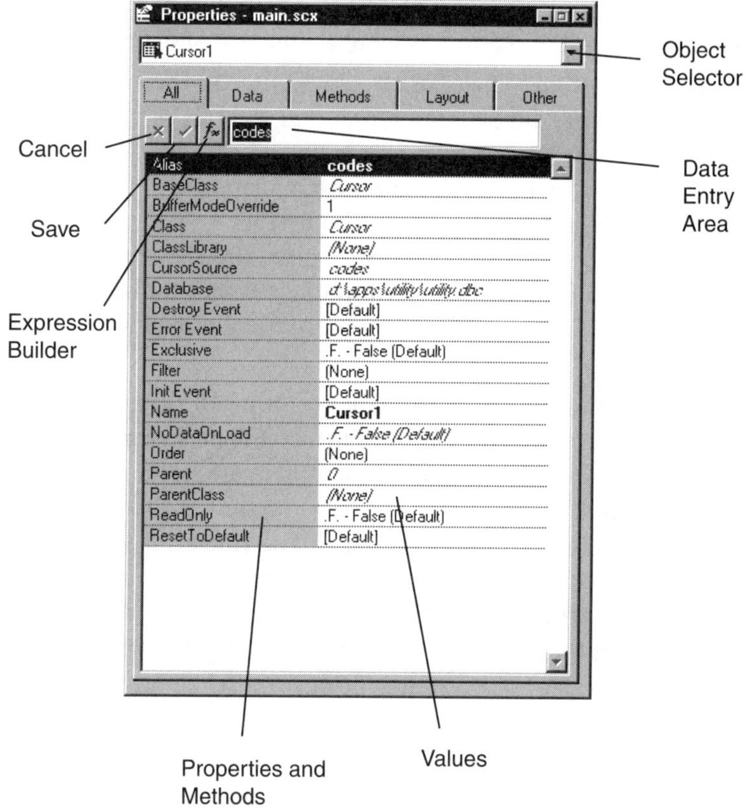

FIGURE 2.4 DATA ENVIRONMENT PROPERTY WINDOW.

All property windows have the same format: tabs for **All**, **Data**, **Methods**, **Layout**, and **Other**, the currently selected object in the object selector box, and, most prominently, the list of properties or methods. Actually, "property window" is a bit of a misnomer, because it displays more than just properties of the object.

If you have just added a table to the data environment, it will be listed in the object selector box as **cursor1**. In Visual FoxPro, cursors are treated as objects, and that is the main link between the database system and object-oriented programming. Incidentally, you know that something is an object when it comes with a property window. Cursors have one, and menus do not.

If you haven't already done so, try all the tabs and pay close attention to the changing list displayed. Although it takes a while, you will become accustomed to reading these lists like the daily newspaper—with instant recognition. As you tab along, move up and down the list with the mouse or arrow keys.

You'll notice that some lines put an active entry in the editing box, others put a shaded entry (not editable) in the box, and still others do nothing. In general, Visual FoxPro has done a tremendous job of simplifying and supporting your work in this somewhat bewildering array of properties and choices. For instance, you can't edit things that are read/only. A constant help line at the bottom of the window identifies every property or method. Right-click on any line and you can **Reset to Default**, or use **Help** to get details of the options. The **Fx** button on the left of the edit box will bring up the Expression Builder window when appropriate.

Of particular interest for the **cursor1** object is its **Methods** tab. You'll notice that it has only four entries: **Init Event**, **Destroy Event**, **Error Event** and **Reset to Default** This is a minimum set of events; there are 41 more. No one object has all of them (thank goodness). All of these events are program-triggered (as opposed to being triggered by user activity). The **Init** event is activated when, in this case, the table is opened. Similarly, the **Destroy** event occurs when the table is closed. The **Error** event is triggered whenever an error occurs during the operations involving the object, such as, in this case, an error opening a file or a multiuser conflict.

Double-click on any one of these methods, and the Code window will open (Figure 2.5). During most of the development cycle, you will live in this window because it's where you create and maintain most of the programming for your application.

The window is simple: it displays the object list box to select which object to work on, and the procedure list box to select the method to add or edit.

NOTE

If you're coming from previous, non–object-oriented versions of FoxPro, forget snippets, forget Startup and Cleanup code, and, for the most part, forget program files (PRGs). They're not relevant to the OOP in Visual FoxPro, and any retro thinking will only confuse you. The new word for code is *method*, and methods are written as part of objects and the events they respond to.

Close the Code window for now and switch to the **Data Environment** object (in the object list box) to look at its options. Note especially the **Other** tab, which contains information about the object and its classes. You'll see that **DataEnvironment** is listed as a base class (although, as mentioned, it is really an object). The Data Environment window you see on your screen is an object. It is created by the definition stored in its class, which in this case is built into FoxPro as a base class. Understanding and modifying the FoxPro base classes (and their objects) is one of the fundamental requirements for FoxPro object-oriented programming.

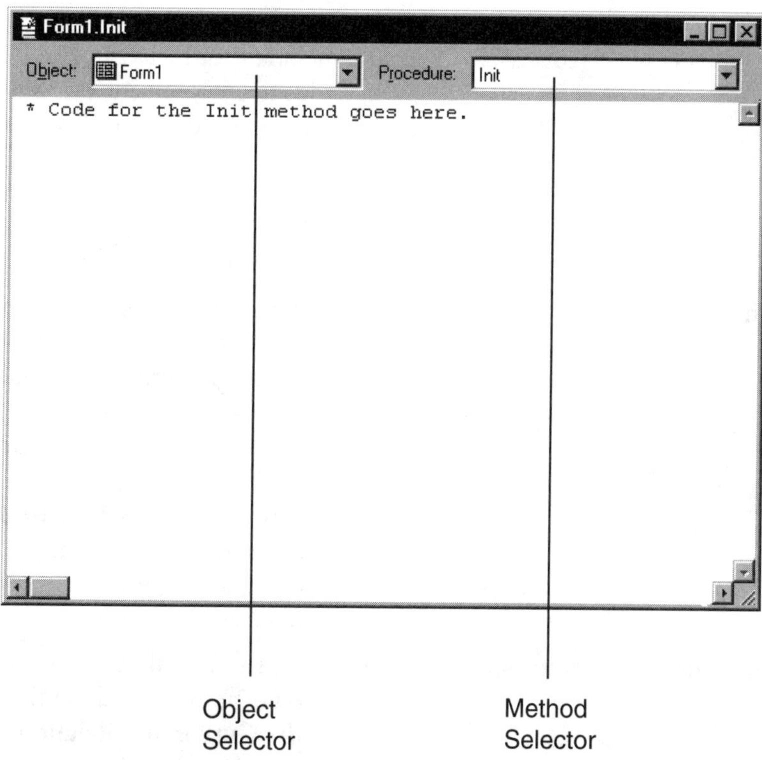

FIGURE 2.5 CODE WINDOW.

BASE CLASSES AND OBJECTS

When you buy an object-oriented programming system such as Visual FoxPro, it's customary to receive a set of base classes. They are sometimes called *primitives*, although this term is misleading because many of them are sophisticated screen objects. Table 2.1 lists all the Visual FoxPro base classes and objects by type. Sooner or later you will need to recognize them all from memory.

TABLE 2.1 VISUAL FOXPRO BASE CLASSES AND OBJECTS

CLASS	TYPE	DESCRIPTION
Cursor Object	Non-visual Object	Tables and views placed into a data environment are automatically **Cursor** objects. **Queries** and **Views** also produce **Cursor** objects outside the data environment. In most respects, a **Cursor** is another name for a table.
Custom Class	Nonvisual Class	A **Custom** class is, essentially, a class template with a very limited set of properties, methods, and events, an arrangement that allows you ample freedom to define its capabilities. User-defined classes **AS CUSTOM** are essentially nonvisual and are extremely useful for application management routines.
DataEnvironment Object	Nonvisual Object	This is actually a container object (and not a base class) that holds the **Cursor** and **Relation** objects for **Forms**, **FormSets**, and reports. You can set its properties only at design time.
Relation Object	Nonvisual Object	Relations established between tables and views (cursor to cursor) in a data environment are automatically **Relation** objects. Their properties cannot be set at run time.

CLASS	TYPE	DESCRIPTION
FormSet	Nonvisual Container	**FormSets** are a way of grouping two or more **Forms** (and possibly **ToolBars**). They are very similar to the Screen Sets of FoxPro 2.6.
OLE Container Control	Nonvisual Container	Contains OLE controls (OCXs if you have Visual FoxPro Professional) and other OLE objects from external applications such as Word and Excel.
PageFrame	Nonvisual Container	A **PageFrame** contains and lends properties to **Pages**, but it's important to note that it isn't visible unless it's inside a **Form**.
Timer	Nonvisual Control	A **Timer** is a good example of a **Custom** class, because it performs tasks and is not visible. It is used in any situation in which time control is required.
Column	Visual Container	**Columns** are where the action is in a **Grid**. They contain a **Header** and any object except **Form**, **FormSet**, **Cursor**, another **Column**, or **ToolBar**. Because a **Column** is integral to a **Grid**, it can't be subclassed.
Command ButtonGroup	Visual Container	Used to create two or more **Command** buttons (the old push buttons) as a group. This is a favorite object for creating what are called *push button menus*, or PBMs.

(Continued...)

CLASS	TYPE	DESCRIPTION
Container Object	Visual Container	This might be best described as the utility container, because it can house any controls in any combination. It is particularly useful for grouping related controls in a form. Objects in a **Container** are fully accessible at both design time and run time.
Control Object	Visual Control	Although similar to a **Container** object, **Control** objects are not accessible during either design time or run time—the ultimate in protected controls.
Form	Visual Container	For most applications this is the keystone class, the one that contains page frames, any controls, containers, custom classes, and almost anything that's important for the user interface. Mastering the **Form** class (in the Forms Designer) is a requirement for developing in Visual FoxPro.
Grid	Visual Container	Although superficially like the old FoxPro Browse, the **Grid** is a sophisticated container for all base-class–derived objects except **Form** and **FormSet**. Along with the **Form** class, this is the most important user interface tool in Visual FoxPro.
OptionGroup	Visual Container	This is the container for two or more **Option** buttons, which present the user with a "pick one" selection. Don't forget to use the Option Group Builder.

CLASS	TYPE	DESCRIPTION
Page	Visual Container	A **Page** is integral to a **Page-Frame** and can't be subclassed. It may contain any controls, containers, or custom class.
ToolBar	Visual Container	The icon toolbar has become a standard for Windows programs, and this class makes it relatively easy to create one. As a container class, it may hold any controls, page frame, or other container class, although in practice it usually contains only command buttons.
CheckBox	Visual Control	A **CheckBox** control is used for "yes or no"–type options. It displays an **X** in the box when selected.
ComboBox	Visual Control	One of the most important data entry controls, the **ComboBox** allows either text entry in its upper portion or selection from a drop-down list. Because of its many options, it's a good idea to use the ComboBox Builder.
CommandButton	Visual Control	Creates a single command button.
EditBox	Visual Control	The standard control for entering character data (text) into variables, memo fields, and arrays. It automatically features all the usual FoxPro editor capabilities. Remember to use the Edit Box Builder.

(Continued…)

CLASS	TYPE	DESCRIPTION
Header	Visual Control	The **Header** class provides text headers for grid columns. This is a very limited class; it's integral to a grid and can't be subclassed.
Image	Visual Control	In a way, the **Image** class is really a container for image objects (in the form of BMP files). In addition to framing a bitmap image, it has all the usual control properties, events, and methods, giving it a great deal of flexibility.
Label	Visual Control	This control is used to place text into a **Form**. As a prompt for other controls, a **Label** may have an access key (defined by \< before a letter) that puts focus on the next control in the tab order.
Line	Visual Control	A **Line** control is simply a vertical or horizontal line, usually in a **Form**.
ListBox	Visual Control	Displays a list of items for the user to choose. The List Box Builder simplifies the many options.
OLE Bound Control	Visual Control	Allows you to place an OLE object into a **Form** or report. This class does not have its own set of events and can be used only in connection with a GENERAL field.
Option Button	Visual Control	Option buttons are integral to an **OptionGroup** and can't be subclassed. Moreover, you can use this class only to add a single option button to an Option Button Group container.

CLASS	TYPE	DESCRIPTION
Separator	Visual Control	This is a special little object to put spaces between controls in a grid. It is integral to the **Grid** class and cannot be subclassed.
Shape	Visual Control	This class can create squares, rectangles, and circles in many variations.
Spinner	Visual Control	Allows entry (or selection) of numeric values with the mouse.
TextBox	Visual Control	The standard control for entering data into fields (or variables, memo fields, and arrays). It automatically features all the usual FoxPro editor capabilities. Remember to use the Text Box Builder to set properties. This is what's happened to the old FoxPro @GET/SAY.

Table 2.1 is organized into five categories: nonvisual base objects, nonvisual container classes, nonvisual control classes, visual container classes, and visual control classes. *Non-visual* means that the class has no representation on the screen. The visual classes, which are in the majority, are those that put something on the screen, and they come in two subcategories: containers and controls.

The table annotates which of the classes can be modified while the program is running (at *run time*) or can be changed only while you are working in a Designer window, at *design time*. This seemingly subtle distinction can become important. For example, you might want to change the way something works in response to the user, but you can't because it's modifiable only at design time.

NOTE

Because all the FoxPro visual base classes can be modified by subclassing and are vital to the user interface of an application, they get most of the attention. However, there are several important base classes that cannot be subclassed: **Page**, **Option**, **Column**, **Separator**, and **Header**. There are several *base objects* that cannot be subclassed: **Cursor**, **DataEnvironment**, and **Relation**. Base objects are, in most respects, like base classes that cannot be modified.

Container Classes

As the name implies, container classes are designed to create objects that contain something, usually control objects. As a group, container classes are the most important classes in FoxPro because of their role in creating the large (composite) objects in the user interface. The "big three" of this group, if you count the pairs as one, are **Form**s and **FormSet**s to create data entry screens or all-purpose dialog windows, **PageFrame**s and **Page**s to create familiar tabbed dialog boxes or wizard-style dialog boxes, and **Grid**s and **Column**s to create the Browse-like grid screens. It will be a rare application that doesn't use the objects from all three of these pairings.

To return to the CODES example, one of the container classes is already open as an object: a form. Before we put anything into it, check out the property window. It's the same property window for every object in the form; you just click on the item, or change the object selector box. You'll notice that because a form is a visual object, it has a large number of layout properties attached to it. In general, FoxPro gives you fine-grained control over the appearance, shape, and presentation of objects on the screen.

The form also has a large number of events that may potentially be associated with a method, but you'll notice that, by default, none of them contains any code at the time the object is instantiated. That will change. Much of the code for an application can be found in the methods of a form. For a container class, forms and grids are the two most active in terms of programming.

Control Classes

Because a blank form isn't very interesting, let's put a control into it. Most forms in FoxPro applications will contain fields. Placing a field into a form is easy: just drag a field name from a table box in the Data Environment window onto the form. This action automatically instantiates a **TextBox** class into a text box object.

If you open the properties window for a text box, you'll notice that it has a large number of properties and methods—88, to be exact. That's why FoxPro provides you with a TextBox Builder to help guide you through the many options. Click on the **Builder** icon, and you'll see the screen shown in Figure 2.6.

With this builder to provide organization and support, it's much easier to decide which of the many properties you can change to suit this particular field.

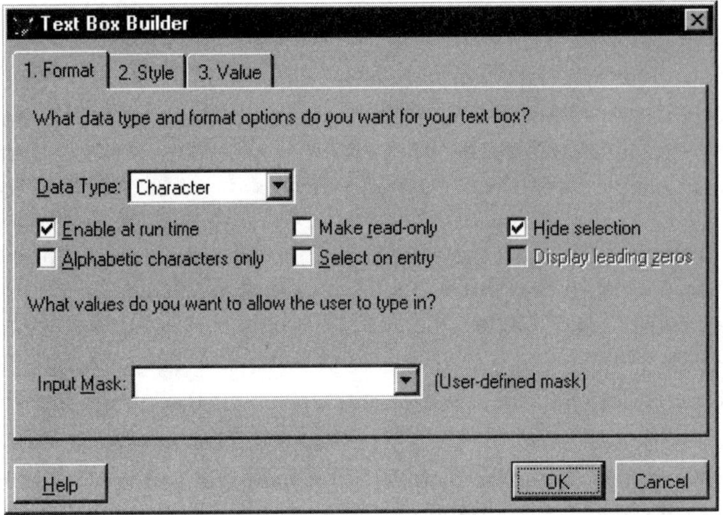

FIGURE 2.6 TEXT BOX BUILDER.

PROPERTIES

Properties are usually one of the more understandable aspects of object-oriented programming. After all, we use the equivalent words—*attribute*, *characteristic*—in everyday speech: "Being a gas guzzler was characteristic of the car." Similarly, in OOP when we say a form has a BackGroundColor property set to blue, it describes one of the characteristics of a particular form object—it has a blue background.

A property, however, is more than a characteristic. As it is defined in the Microsoft *Developer's Guide*, a property is "An attribute of a control, field, or database object that you set to define one of the object's characteristics or an aspect of its behavior." The behavior element of this definition is important, because a large number of properties are associated with how an object *behaves* (what its methods do). For example, the Stretch property controls how an image is shaped to fit a particular area and has several options that determine the behavior of the stretching.

Making these distinctions between types of properties wouldn't be so important if there weren't so many properties. There are 232 built-in FoxPro properties, and, as with functions, it's of little use to list them all at once. They need to be grouped and explained in context. Categorizations, such as the ones that follow, may help you recognize different kinds of properties, or as is often the case, different capabilities for the same property under different circumstances.

- **Properties that provide information only** (read only), for example, Object.Class, which returns the name of the class that defined the object. You'd have to change the class, and not this property, to change the value.
- **Properties that specify a characteristic of the object**, for example, Object.FontSize, which sets the size of an object's font.
- **Properties that control behavior**, usually by turning something on or off (enabling or disabling), for example, Object.Movable. When set to true (.t.), it allows a form to be moved on the screen, and, when false (.f.), it freezes the form in its current location.
- **Properties that specify behavior**, for example, Object.BufferMode, which takes values 0,1, and 2 to specify which mode of record updating is to be used (none, pessimistic, or optimistic).

NOTE

Note that the syntax of properties (also methods and events) is *always* referenced to objects. If the object is of a specific type, it will be used: DataEnvironment.Cursor.CursorSource. Otherwise the generic object is used: Object.ShowTips.

Most of the properties you manipulate will be of the built-in variety. You can also create your own properties when you define a class.

Going back to the text box property window (from the previous topic), click on the **Layout** tab (Figure 2.7). This is where most of the properties of control objects are located. Scan through this list and see whether you can identify the types of properties.

Because the properties window lists properties (or methods) only in alphabetical order, you need to learn how certain properties are associated. For example, in this illustration, the font properties are easy to spot because they all begin with Font and sort together. However, the Height property and the Width property (which obviously belong together) are not usually both visible in the list.

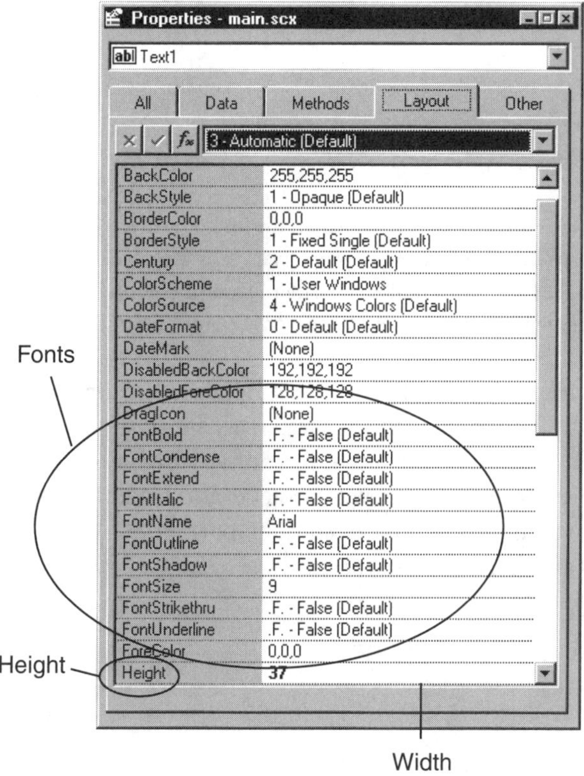

FIGURE 2.7 TEXT BOX CONTROL LAYOUT PROPERTIES.

DESIGN TIME VS. RUN TIME

Design time refers to the time you are working in the Form Designer or Report Designer, and *run time* refers to the time the program is running. In the Form Designer, you can change the values of any (non–read-only) property simply by entering the new value in the Properties window. This is equivalent to writing the following code:

```
Thisform.caption = "Sample Registration"
Thisform.caption = "Sample Login"
```

When the program is running, however, the values can be changed only by using a conditional expression or a user-defined function:

```
Thisform.caption = IIF(lLogtype,"Sample Login","Sample;
  Registration")
```

or

```
Thisform.caption = TitleChange(1)
```

WARNING

When you work in the Form Designer, the form is *active*, much as if it were running. This means that if you change a property such as Movable to false, you won't be able to move the form while designing, either. It pays to set up the more critical behavior properties with the appropriate conditions *before* you activate them.

When you're confronted with this kind of properties list for a text box, keep in mind that normally only a handful of properties are changed (or are even relevant) for a specific control. At this point in your learning curve, it's hard to know which properties are important for what objects and under what circumstances. As we go along, you'll continually encounter properties. We'll highlight those that are routine (and crucial), as well as those that are less often used but are really cool.

EVENTS

Most programs don't run from top to bottom without stopping (with the exception of short, procedural programs to do things such as database maintenance). As soon as a program pauses in its execution, it needs a way to start again. It needs an *event*, such as a selection from a menu or a specific keystroke.

That's the significance of the one command that rules the execution of your applications: **READ EVENTS**. As you saw from the example in Chapter 1, near the beginning of every application you will issue this command to, in effect, allow the program to stop execution while it waits for an event.

Events, whether generated by the program itself or coming from the activity of a user, are what direct the flow of execution in most programs (and all applications). In fact, any program with a user interface will have many kinds of events. It should be stressed that events are not unique to object-oriented programming; FoxPro had events long before it called them that or had any systematic way of dealing with them.

It's one of the great strengths of the object-oriented model that it can help to organize and control the complexity of events associated with a modern application. Figure 2.8 illustrates the main types of events recognized by FoxPro. Some of them, such as various kinds of mouse actions and keystrokes, are obvious; others are more specific to objects and object management. There are also the three minimum events—**Init**, **Destroy**, and **Error**—which are recognized by all objects.

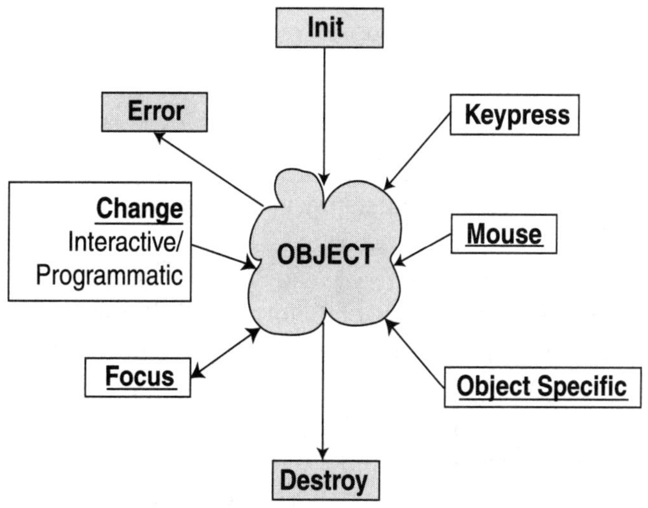

FIGURE 2.8 FOXPRO EVENT TYPES.

The main point is that whatever their type, events are not scattered throughout an application in inaccessible corners of your code. Instead, events are organized *by object*.

Visual FoxPro 5.0 has 43 events, a list that cannot be modified. You can tell something about the events from looking at the list in Table 2.2.

TABLE 2.2 FOXPRO EVENTS

Activate	DropDown	QueryUnload
AfterCloseTables	Error	RangeHigh
AfterDock	ErrorMessage	RangeLow
AfterRowColChange	GotFocus	Resize

(Continued...)

BeforeDock	Init	RightClick
BeforeOpenTables	InteractiveChange	Scrolled
BeforeRowColChange	KeyPress	Timer
Click	Load	UIEnable
DblClick	LostFocus	UnDock
Deactivate	MouseDown	Unload
Deleted	MouseMove	UpClick
Destroy	MouseUp	Valid
DownClick	Moved	When
DragDrop	Paint	
DragOver	ProgrammaticChange	

Not every object can respond to every event. Some events are highly object-specific, such as **UnDock** for toolbars or **BeforeRowColChange** in a grid. Most objects, such as the text box control, have a fairly long list of supported events, as you can see in Figure 2.9.

The key point is that each one of these events is a *potential* method. You simply double-click on an event's line, and a code window will open for you to program a method. In this scheme, an event is a straightforward concept: it's an action relative to an object, either from a user doing something, such as clicking the mouse, or from the program doing something, such as initializing an object.

What can become complicated is the pattern of events, for example in a complex form that has many objects and each has many methods responding to events.

Methods

Methods are the part of an object that *do* something—they are said to exhibit *behavior*. That's because they're program routines, code that performs operations, retrieves information, and a zillion other things that programming can do. In terms of programming, methods are very much like user-defined functions or procedures. In fact, when you define a class and create its methods, they *are* functions and procedures.

In the FoxPro brand of object-oriented programming, there are two kinds of methods: those that respond to specific events, and those that don't (sometimes called *event* methods and *free* methods). The event methods are those attached to specific objects and specific events, as shown in Figure 2.9. The event methods are open-ended in what they can contain. They must be programmed in one of the designers and are permanently associated with an event and object combination. They also take on the same name as the event, that is, the **Init** event has an **INIT()** method.

Free methods, on the other hand, are given their own names and are not necessarily associated with a specific event or object, although many methods are designed to work with specific types of objects. This is true of most of the built-in FoxPro methods, which are listed in Table 2.3.

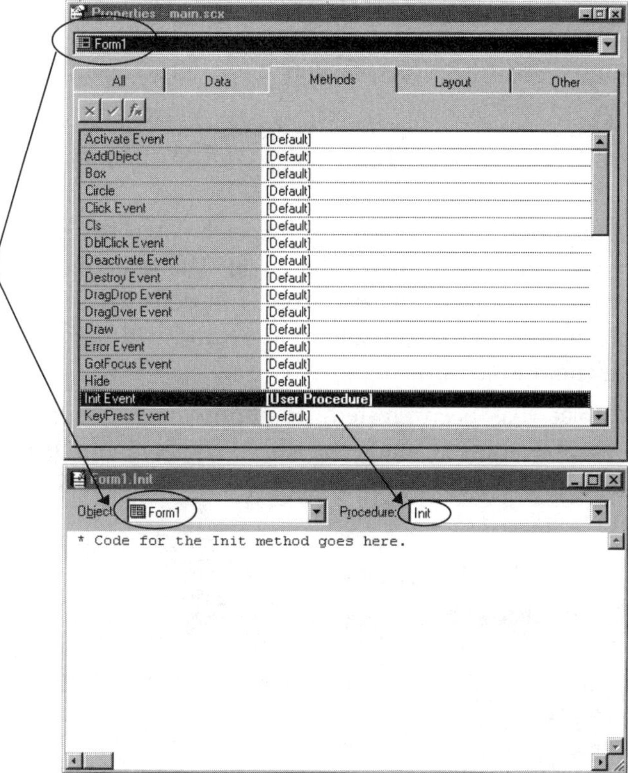

FIGURE 2.9 PROPERTY WINDOW, METHOD TAB, AND CODE WINDOW.

TABLE 2.3 FOXPRO METHODS

ActivateCell	DoVerb	Release
AddColumn	Drag	RemoveItem
AddItem	Draw	RemoveListItem
AddListItem	Hide	RemoveObject
AddObject	IndexToItemId	Requery
Box	ItemIDToIndex	Reset
Circle	Line	SaveAs
Clear	Move	SaveAsClass
CloneObject	Point	SetAll
CloseTables	Print	SetFocus
Cls	Pset	Show
DeleteColumn	ReadExpression	TextHeight
Dock	ReadMethod	TextWidth
DoScroll	Refresh	WriteExpression

Most of these methods are valid only with specific objects (in this case, objects derived from base classes and their subclasses). The same method shows up in a number of different objects, but in each case it does what it's supposed to do because of polymorphism, which allows a method with the same name to be adapted for different objects.

Once an object has been created, its nonprotected methods are available throughout an application in much the same way as functions and procedures in a procedure file. Using a method is simply a matter of *calling* it with the following syntax:

Parent.Object.Method

Examples:

```
myForm1.Button1.Show()
myForm2.GetTopValue()
myForm3.DoShift(3,5)
```

In the usual OOP manner, the active element is qualified by references to objects. There will be much more about referencing (and methods in general) later.

PERSPECTIVES ON OBJECT-ORIENTED PROGRAMMING

You've been introduced to the major elements of object-oriented programming: classes, objects, properties, events, and methods—and the major concepts—inheritance, encapsulation, polymorphism, and the class hierarchy. Now it's time to put all these pieces together to develop a composite view of OOP—or rather several views. There is no one way to understand object-oriented programming, so I'll offer several perspectives that may be helpful.

PERSPECTIVE: A DIAGRAMMATIC VIEW

For those who like to *see* the relationships between OOP elements, Figure 2.10 presents the whole picture (if not complete in every detail).

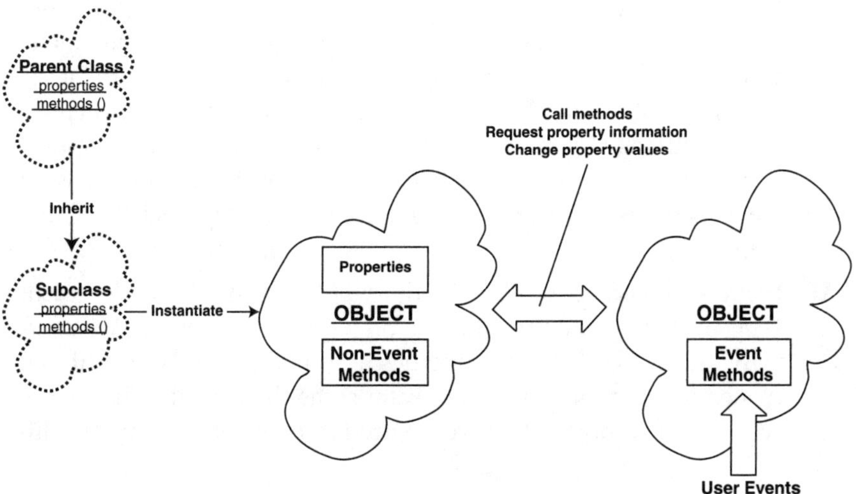

FIGURE 2.10 BASIC OOP ELEMENTS AND CONCEPTS.

PERSPECTIVE: OOP INTERACTIONS

Another useful perspective is to think of OOP in terms of the interactions (or dynamics) between key elements or concepts:

- **Class to subclass.** The ability to create a class based on another class is crucial to object-oriented programming. However, it takes careful planning to create a hierarchy of classes that cleanly separates the more generic characteristics and operations from the specific ones. There is always the danger of creating so many classes that they confuse not only you but also the FoxPro compiler, resulting in programs crashing from misplaced variables or program routines.
- **Classes and objects**. Classes define objects. If it isn't in the class definition, as a property or method, then it won't be in the object created by the class. However, once an object has been created (instantiated), it is an independent entity and can be modified by programming. The best example is the use of forms in which you create a form object from the FoxPro base class **Form** and then use **ADDOBJECT()** to put other objects into the form, even while the program is running.
- **Events, objects, and methods.** Events happen to objects, whether caused by users or generated by the program. There are many events, but objects respond only to a specific subset of them. Of the events that affect an object, you select the ones you need to create event methods. These methods contain programming code appropriate for the event (although there are few limitations on what event methods can do). For example, you might select the **Click** event.
- **Properties and methods.** On the whole, these are two different OOP elements with little in common, especially when you're working with built-in FoxPro properties and methods. However, if you create your own properties and want some that actually change the behavior of an object, then you'll need to couple the property with a method.
- **Encapsulation and inheritance.** With encapsulation, you try to hide properties and methods from other objects; with inheritance,

you expose some of the properties and methods to modification. There is always a design tension between these two elements.

- **Object to object**. Most of the program execution in object-oriented programming is from object to object: one object requests information from or modifies the properties of another object, or it calls (invokes) the methods of another object. In the latter way, program execution is passed from object to object, subject to the internal logic of the program and especially the events triggered by the user.

PERSPECTIVE: THE FOXPRO 2.X PROGRAMMER

If you are already a FoxPro user or developer, then you are a candidate for a temporary feeling of dislocation. For example, the Form Designer looks a lot like the old Screen Builder, but below the surface the two tools don't work alike at all. There is much new jargon, but just when you think you understand something, you'll discover that you've just transposed one of your familiar procedural concepts onto an OOP concept, usually with misleading conclusions.

The attempt to find equivalencies between procedural techniques and object-oriented techniques will have limited success; the only clear connection is using commands and structures from FoxPro 2.6 in the class and object methods. This connection is very useful at the micro level. At the macro level, however, where you must understand the interactions among the major OOP elements, things are very different. This is not your father's FoxPro, to borrow a phrase.

PERSPECTIVE: THE BIG LEAP

Most people find that creating forms, using controls, and working with the other visual aspects of OOP (at least as implemented by FoxPro) are relatively easy with hands-on experience. There will be some moments of confusion, particularly if you're familiar with the old FoxPro, but the instant feedback of seeing your work run (or not run) helps to settle the ideas in place.

Not so with the development of a whole application's worth of databases, forms, dialog boxes, and classes. With OOP, the problems lie mostly at the points of integration where the many objects of a program interact. The deeper you go, the more you will discover the necessity of creating program management routines that can be used to keep track of what's going on between the objects and, if necessary, control them. That's where the application development framework comes into play. Its forte is in providing standard ways of connecting the elements of an application.

WHY USE OOP?

Perhaps by this point you've begun to see that OOP is both a challenge and a blessing. For most people it will be a steep learning curve (perhaps even a cliffhanger), but there are payoffs. Still, it is not an empty question to ask, why use OOP?

Many expositions of the principles of object-oriented programming sound like justifications for using it. That's because OOP is still a relatively new approach, and it has its detractors. However, OOP has been a major force in application development for about a decade, and the products that implement it have skyrocketed in both number and importance—not the least of which are Microsoft's C++, Visual Basic, Access, and Visual FoxPro.

Here are some of the major advantages of object-oriented programming:

- **It provides a way to reuse code.** In most people's books (including this one), this benefit is the big one. Although reusable modules or functions are nothing new to programming, the OOP model lays down a comprehensive approach and provides a mechanism—inheritance—that is more efficient in making code reusable than any other known scheme.
- **It lends itself to building complex user interfaces.** From the start, OOP grew up with the need to build complicated graphical user interfaces. Its embrace of events and the encapsulation of major GUI elements such as forms give it the appropriate tools to manage sophisticated user interfaces.
- **It provides a way to organize and handle events.** The potential chaos of event driven programming, with users and the program vying with the programmer for control of program execution, has been avoided by placing events and the response to them within objects, This arrangement provides a location for the programmer to cleanly deal with events.

- **It helps to provide organization for a program.** Ultimately, the structure of a program (or application) depends on the design of the class structure. The OOP principles of inheritance and encapsulation provide the guidelines for the organization. Although OOP not the only way, it's an organizing approach that works.
- **It helps to modularize the design of a program.** In OOP, modules can be complete programs (or *applets*) or simply a collection of related objects and their defining classes. The principles of encapsulation make it possible to plug modules into a larger application without much danger of conflict between the elements. This point brings us back to OOP's first benefit—it enables reuse of code.

A Short Glossary of OOP

Because jargon is one of the primary barriers to understanding object-oriented programming, here's a short list of the most important terms. I've defined them with as little jargon as possible, although inevitably it becomes necessary to define one piece of jargon with other pieces of jargon. Most of these words are fleshed out with context elsewhere in the chapter.

abstraction Because the real world is complex, human beings long ago learned how to manage it by creating abstractions (concepts) that stand in for the real thing. The classic example is a chair. We know that chairs come in many shapes and sizes (a chair has many properties), but we all understand when somebody says, "I sat in the chair." In object-oriented programming, an object is an abstraction that more or less crisply defines something in the content (domain) of the program. Abstraction is also the process of focusing on the essential characteristics of an object.

base class A base class is the most generalized class in a class structure, or, put another way, it's at the top of the hierarchy. In FoxPro, this concept is easily understood because Visual FoxPro base classes cannot be modified and all other classes are derived from them (subclassed).

class In Visual FoxPro and most other OOP languages, a class is a blueprint (definition) for an object, and it is composed of variable definitions (properties), procedures (methods), and other instructions on how to create the object. When you run a program, classes are instantiated into objects.

class category A class category is a grouping of related classes, such as a "utility" class category composed of classes that perform application utility functions. In Visual FoxPro, this can be represented by a class library that is stored in a VCX file.

container class This is a class that is designed to contain objects. Visual FoxPro has nine container classes: **Form**s, **FormSet**s, **Grid**s, **Grid Column**s, **PageFrame**s, **Page**s, **Control Group**s, **Option Button Group**s, and **ToolBar**s.

custom class Visual FoxPro has two types of base classes: visual and custom. In practice, the main difference is that a custom class is not a container and can't define any other visual type of class. Custom classes are important for creating more abstract, processing-oriented objects. For example, you might create a **Customer** class to contain information (properties) and procedures (methods) about customers. This class doesn't necessarily have a visual aspect—no form, grid, or control—although you might involve visual objects in some of the methods.

domain In program analysis we refer to "the domain of the application," meaning the area of functionality covered by the application. For example, the domain of an inventory program includes all the things pertaining to inventory: counts, storage, picking, restock, and so on. *Domain* is a technocratic word, but the alternatives are even more awkward.

encapsulation
As one of the hallmark concepts of OOP, encapsulation simply means that a class or object is largely self-contained. It has the information and procedures necessary to perform its function. In practice, it's important to emphasize the term *largely*. Classes are designed to create objects having two segments: one segment, hidden from everything except itself and its subclasses, contains the methods and properties it needs to do the job; the other segment is public and provides the interface to the services offered by the object or accepts needed information and services from other objects.

event
An event is an occurrence in a running program that can be detected by the system and for which you can write programming that responds to it. This is a fancy way of saying that a mouse click is an event, and you can write a routine to tell FoxPro how to respond to the click. Events are always relative to specific objects. For example, a mouse click event is available for a command button but not for a form set.

framework
Creating an application requires a large number of components. A framework provides a way of organizing those components, usually in terms of classes and objects but in FoxPro including non–object-oriented items such as menus. An essential element of a framework is its architecture document, which spells out what components are available and how they can be used.

generic class
Any class that can serve as a template for other classes is a generic class. This class relationship is different from a purely inheritance relationship, because you cannot use a generic class without providing values for its generic parameters.

hierarchy
A hierarchy is used as a ranking among classes in two senses in object-oriented programming. One definition concerns the abstractions of the domain, in which one abstraction inherits the structure and behavior of the more generic abstraction. The classic example is the classification system of biology (order, species and so on). The other sense refers to the hierarchy of classes used in programming, in which a subclass inherits the properties, events, and methods of the class above it in the hierarchy.

inheritance
Inheritance is a relationship between classes in which one class inherits the structure and behavior (properties, events, and methods) of one or more classes. Inheritance is always associated with the class hierarchy, where a subclass inherits from its superclass. In FoxPro most inheritance is *single*—one superclass only—but container classes may define objects that contain any number of other objects, which is a form of *multiple* inheritance.

instantiation
Creating an object from a class is called instantiation; you're creating an instance of the class.

interface
Among its many meanings in computing, the interface of a class and its objects is the part that provides services (methods or data) to other objects.

method
In Visual FoxPro, methods are procedures or functions defined within a class (as part of the class definition). There are 44 built-in methods provided by FoxPro, and you can create any number of methods for your own classes. Methods are programming routines executed by an object when called upon for its services. Many methods are triggered by events such as a mouse click.

object Grady Booch has a nifty definition for an object: "something you can do things to." Technically, objects are instances of their classes, meaning that classes provide the definition of what objects can do and what information they contain.

OOA Object-oriented analysis studies the domain of an application for all the operative abstractions that can be represented as classes and objects. Or, put less formally, OOA tries to analyze the structure and operations of an application in terms of objects and classes.

OOD Object-oriented design takes the abstractions discovered in OOA and turns them into a design for a particular application developed in a particular language.

OOP Object-oriented programming is a way to build programs using the collaborative interaction of a collection of objects. The objects are defined by classes, which are organized in a hierarchy in which each successive class (and the objects it creates) inherits the structure and behavior of the class above it.

polymorphism Within a class hierarchy, polymorphism is the ability of one class member (usually methods) to have the same name as other members in the hierarchy and inherit basic structure and behavior, but be able also to have individualized (customized) behavior. This is one of the key object-oriented programming concepts, because it allows developers to customize inherited characteristics without losing the benefits of the class hierarchy.

property Objects have properties and, as a result, usually have associated information or states. For example, an object may have a color property or may return a value for a property.

protected In Visual FoxPro, this is a declaration in the class definition that separates methods and properties into two kinds: those that are hidden (visible only to the class's own objects and subclasses) and those that are public.

subclass A class that inherits from one or more classes above it in the hierarchy.

superclass The class from which another class (the subclass) inherits.

visual class In Visual FoxPro, visual classes are base classes associated with a visual object—something that is visible on the screen, such as buttons, windows, forms, and so forth.

Chapter Wrap-Up

Object-oriented programming, at its most fundamental, has two facets: one provides a blueprint for the construction of the building blocks of a program, and the other provides configurations of the building blocks that make it possible to handle complex user interfaces (and all the other elements of a full-scale application). Classes and the class hierarchy are the blueprint, which in turn creates the objects of an operational program. The objects, given the ability to respond to events (internal and external) and containing all the information and functionality they need, communicate among themselves to create the running program.

That, in a nutshell, is what OOP does. This chapter was like jumping between mountain tops, covering the main points of a subject that is vast and deep. It will become more comfortable in later chapters, as we fill the gaps in detail.

SECTION 2

DATA MANAGEMENT FOR APPLICATIONS

This section covers the data management capability of Visual FoxPro and explains how it relates to the construction of an application framework. Working with data is a reasonable place to start, not only because in some ways it's easier but also because data management is fundamental to FoxPro. Most applications are built on a foundation of data. There are few programs that don't manage data in one way or another, and when it comes to software for business, data is usually the reason for the program. You probably wouldn't be working with Visual FoxPro if you didn't have database management as one of the primary requirements of your applications.

Before you launch into developing a database application, especially a large one, it's important that you understand and feel comfortable using the data management capability of FoxPro. The chapters in this section are graduated, beginning with data fundamentals and ending with reporting.

- Chapter 3, "Data Management Fundamentals," introduces you to the basic concepts behind FoxPro's data management system, including data types, FoxPro expressions, and a selection of data-oriented functions.

- Chapter 4, "Creating Database Elements," covers the role of SQL in FoxPro and begins the cycle of data management, by showing you how to create your own database, including the tables, indexes, and relations.
- Chapter 5, "Using Database Elements," picks up after the database has been created and continues the cycle of data management including data editing, searching, and a host of maintenance tasks.
- Chapter 6, "SQL and the Query and View Designers," explains the use of SQL to extract information from a database and focuses on the powerful capabilities of FoxPro's new SQL views.
- Chapter 7, "Output and the Report Designer," completes the data management cycle by explaining FoxPro's report creating capabilities in the Report Designer. This chapter introduces some of the more useful wizards that work with the Report Designer.

NOTE

These chapters cover a lot of technical ground. I've tried to be inclusive, but of necessity things are introduced quickly and without much elaboration. For a more gradual approach, a companion book is available. *Teach Yourself...Visual FoxPro 5* (MIS:Press, 1996) focuses on the FoxPro database management tools.

CHAPTER 3

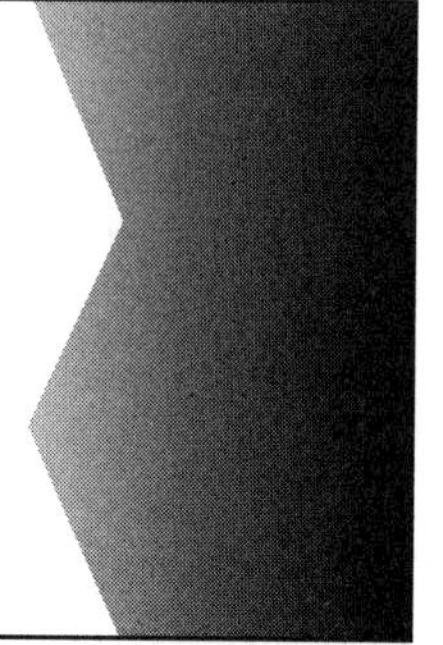

DATA MANAGEMENT FUNDAMENTALS

Most business applications are a user interface for data, and, more often than not, the data was the reason for developing the application. That makes data a good place to start the road to an application framework. This chapter reviews data management concepts and jargon from the perspective of a Visual FoxPro application developer.

NOTE

How important is data to an application? In the years before client/server computing, object-oriented programming, and the Internet, there was another major buzzword in FoxPro programming: *data-driven applications*. Essentially, a data-driven application reflected a goal: to let information stored in tables provide the operating parameters for an application. For example, instead of hard coding the specifications of a window, you put the parameters, such as height, width, and color, into a table, which fed the specs to the program when the window was created. Why would you do this? Because it's much easier to change values in a table than in a compiled program. At heart, data-driven applications were all about giving the programmer and user more control over a program's details, without resorting to programming.

Certain elements of FoxPro still reflect the data-driven approach. For example, there are commands to store variables, screens, and other program elements in tables. These days, "data-driven" isn't mentioned much, but the concept is still useful—for example, in tables that store user preferences. It's something to think about as you design your applications, and I'll continue to mention it. Incidentally, note that FoxPro uses data tables to store all the code of an application. Son of a data-driven program.

DATA BASICS

The biggest difference between database information and most ordinary information is that database information is highly structured—categorized, typed, labeled, sized, and formatted. This structuring has a dual purpose: to take advantage of what a computer can do and to provide people with a way to organize the information. For example, computers are good at searching text, but they do it faster if the search isn't random. By structuring text so that it exists in a specific file, is categorized (for example, by CITY and STATE), and then is indexed by category, you let the computer search for a particular item (such as a city) much more rapidly.

Structuring data usually goes hand-in-hand with the design and development of an application. As illustrated in Figure 3.1, for most applications the database sits between the information of the real world and the software user interface.

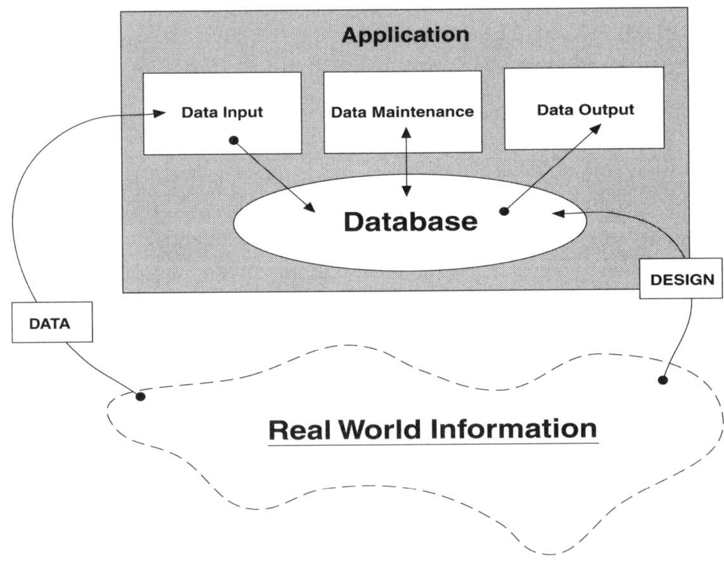

FIGURE 3.1 THE RELATIONSHIP OF DATA TO AN APPLICATION.

The data and database are structured to reflect, or model, the way information is used in the real world so that the information can be appropriately captured and stored for retrieval. Then the user interface is built to provide the most relevant and easiest use of the data. Because you're working with FoxPro—a database management system—it's crucial to understand how it organizes data before you build the application elements that collect and display the information.

UNDERSTANDING DATABASES

Generally speaking, a *database* is a collection of one or more files that store related information; the content of a flowers database doesn't contain information about fish. Although it's loose, this semantic definition works. Many applications are developed around a single database. A key component of the definition is that whatever the data, it is stored in files on disk. It's the ability of programs such as FoxPro to perform file operations quickly that gives them special power for data management.

As of version 3.0, Visual FoxPro supports a database system, called a *database container*, that's composed of three database files with file extensions DBC, DBT, and DCX. These files contain information about the files that actually contain the data, which have the extension DBF or FPT. "DBF" stands for database file, the old dBase concept, which you may find confusing now. Here's another potential source of confusion: you won't read more than a few pages in the FoxPro manuals before you'll see data files referred to as *tables*. This is the jargon of Structured Query Language (SQL) which you've probably heard about. In SQL, everything is stored in a table, which is usually a file on disk.

This is one of those overlaps of terminology that in practice aren't really a problem. For most people, when the reference is to something stored on a disk, the word is *file*. This is the realm of the operating system, and there's no good reason to impose database jargon on it. You open a file, delete a file, copy a file, and save a file, because these are more or less direct references to operating system actions. However, when you talk about the structure, content, and relationships of a data file, it's a *table*. In this context, you create a table, index a table, and append to a table, because these actions affect the content or structure of the information in a data file.

FOXPRO TABLES, RECORDS, AND FIELDS

Although FoxPro's database container defines the large-scale collection of information, on a day-to-day basis in applications development you will mostly talk about tables. The structure of FoxPro tables in large part defines how you organize an application's data. That structure takes the form of a table similar to the one in Table 3.1 or a grid format from a spreadsheet program.

TABLE 3.1 THE LOGICAL STRUCTURE OF A FOXPRO TABLE.

	FIELD / COLUMN 1	FIELD / COLUMN 2	FIELD / COLUMN 3
Record / Row 1	data value	data value	data value
Record / Row 2	data value	data value	data value

The most fundamental element of a table is the *field* (or *column*, in SQL jargon). A field is a categorization of information; if you create a field as a category of prices, it should contain only price values. All fields must have names (a *field name* or *column name*), which should reflect the categorization of the field. For example, a PRICE field would contain prices, or COMPANY field would contain names of companies. The combination of a row of data values from each field is called a *record* in FoxPro (*row* in SQL) and is technically called a *tuple*. (There is an old pun about tables being tupleware containers.)

Tables, fields, and records form a crucial three-way relationship in data management. The fields define the specific data to be stored, and a collection of fields defines a table. The choice of which fields go into a table is not arbitrary. If you have a PRODUCT table, it should have fields that contain information about products. It might be helpful to note that in other database systems, fields are called *attributes* of a table. If the table contains products, the attributes might be the name of product, the manufacturer, price, and color. This relationship between fields and tables is confirmed by each record, because a record is an *instance* of what is being defined by the collection of fields that make up a table. That's a long way of saying that in a PRODUCT table, each record contains information about one product. At this point, a visualization might help (see Table 3.2).

TABLE 3.2 A PRODUCT TABLE WITH DATA.

	PRODUCT	MANUFACTURER	MODEL	PRICE
1	Widgetizer II	WidgetWare Inc.	LC1231	399.95
2	Veggymiser	VeggyLand Corp.	101A	49.99

In the way most FoxPro developers look at it, Table 3.2 is a representation of a table and data. At the top are the field names, which might also be considered column headers. On the left side is a column for record numbers. It's important to note that FoxPro stores record numbers for all records, but the numbers don't constitute a field. The junctions of a record (number) and each field (name) contains the data for that record. Most of FoxPro's data operations (such as deleting, appending, and updating) take place at the record level—you delete a record, append a record, and so forth. Most of the references to data occur at the field level—you search for a value in a field or edit a field.

Fields and records represent the *logical* structure of a FoxPro table; the representation of the *physical* structure of a FoxPro file (Figure 3.2) is somewhat different.

The illustration doesn't actually show how FoxPro data is stored on disk; it's a conceptual diagram that is helpful to keep in mind for later discussions.

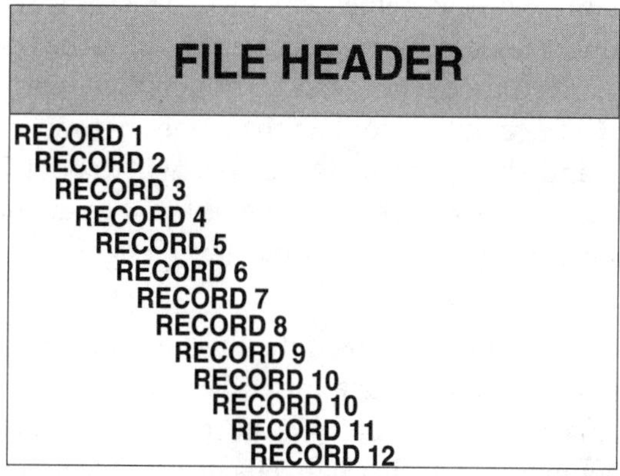

FIGURE 3.2 THE PHYSICAL STRUCTURE OF A FOXPRO DBF FILE.

The part of the file structure to note is the *header*, which contains the information FoxPro needs about the table (for example, field names and the number of records in the table). The header plays an important role in a multiuser environment, because FoxPro must lock the header—make it unavailable to all but one user—for certain operations. Following the header is the body of the file, which contains the data (and associated record numbers).

DEFINING FIELDS

Fields are the cornerstone of FoxPro databases—or perhaps to be more accurate metaphorically, the base of the pyramid. Above the fields are records, and then tables, and finally databases. The field is the element of a database that most directly corresponds to items (and properties of items) in the real world. For example, if you have a database of cars, you will probably have fields such as MAKE, MODEL, and COLOR to contain information about each car.

A field is defined in FoxPro by five properties: field name, field type, width, decimal, and null. The first three properties are required. All five will be covered as practical issues in Chapter 4; but we're working at the conceptual level here, so the focus is on field names and field types.

Field Names

Think about fields as columns of data, and recall that all the values in the column must contain the same kind of information. If the field is called CITY, it's supposed to contain only the names of cities. This is a *semantic* definition, because it can be understood only in the context of how the contents of the field are described. Semantic descriptions can be difficult to interpret. For example, if a field is named CITY, should it contain the names of towns and villages? New York City is a city and should be included, but what about Zap (a very small town in North Dakota)? This is not a problem if you've defined the field CITY to contain the names of communities officially recognized by the postal service—but is that what you really want?

A semantic definition may also be difficult to enforce. What's to stop someone from entering the name of a state into a field defined as CITY? It could be stopped by checking every CITY entry against a list of states, but this would require a lot of machinery. And what happens if someone enters a person's name in the CITY field? Among other things, you'll get a bogus mailing label.

Fortunately, the majority of fields are understandable by normally literate people, who quickly grasp the idea that if a field says CITY (and is seen in conjunction with STATE and ZIP), a city name in the postal sense is wanted. Unfortunately, the semantic description of a field is vital—it's the only clue to a correspondence with items in the real world—but there are plenty of items in the real world which are difficult to characterize with field names. That's why data analysis is important when you're building applications.

All of this emphasizes how important the design of fields (names and definitions) can be to a database. In some cases, you can get by with conventional field names (CITY, STATE, ZIP), but in other cases you may need much more precise names and definitions (for example, POSTALCITY, COMMUNITY, STATE, ZIPCODE). We'll come back to this and related topics many times.

DATA AND FIELD TYPES

In addition to defining fields, tables, and databases, there is another fundamental data concept: *type*. Most people beyond infancy can distinguish between a cat, a rose, a chair, and a rock. A little later in life, people learn to distinguish between the words *cat*, *rose*, *chair*, and *rock* as symbols (abstractions) of the real thing. We remember the properties of these things in the real world (such as smell or shape) that help us to distinguish each word as representing a *type* of something. In this way, the word *cat* can be applied to a large number of furry animals that we recognize as a type of cat. All data in FoxPro is distinguished by type, such as numeric, character, or date. Data types are also abstractions, of course, and are applied to data so that like items can be stored the same way.

NOTE

The ability to use the process of abstraction (finding a computer representation for things in the real world) is a crucial skill. Just as data types are abstractions that fit how a computer works, you will encounter many similar approaches in object-oriented programming.

Data types are based on information people want to store, adjusted for the behavior of computers, which can sometimes be mystifying. For example, it may be hard at first to understand why 5 + 6 = 11 but "5" + "6" = "56." The trick is to see that 5 and "5" are different. The former is a number (a numeric data type), and with numbers you can do math. Because it is in quotes, the latter number is a character (a character data type), just like the letter "b." You can't do math with characters; the + sign used in "5" + "6" indicates *concatenation*—joining characters together.

In FoxPro, data types apply to all data, including the contents of programming elements such as variables and arrays. Database tables share these data types as well as seven more field types. Table 3.3 lists the FoxPro data types and field types and highlights some of their quirks.

TABLE 3.3 BASIC FOXPRO DATA AND FIELD TYPES.

FIELD TYPE	DESCRIPTION AND SPECIFICATIONS
Character	This basic text field includes ASCII characters 32–126. This means that character data includes all the keyboard symbols, such as #, @, and $, as well as letters and numbers. Because there are far more

(Continued...)

FIELD TYPE	DESCRIPTION AND SPECIFICATIONS
Character *(cont.)*	ways to manipulate character data than any other type, the rule of thumb is to create most fields as character fields unless there is a good reason for them not to be. For example, numbers such as phone and Social Security numbers are always stored as character fields because they require no math calculations. In most applications, character fields will contain the bulk of your data. The maximum size of a character field (often called the *width*) is 254 characters—about four or five sentences. If more text must be stored, then Memo fields are used instead. References to character fields are abbreviated as *C*. Maximum field size in bytes: 254.
Numeric	This is the basic number data and field type. With numeric and float fields, you can have as many as 20 numbers total (for example, 99,999,999, 999,999,999,999). This is a fairly large number. If you need something larger (or much smaller), FoxPro supports scientific notation written in the format E+#. For example, the range of permitted numeric values in FoxPro is expressed as .9999999999E+20–.999999999E+19. Numeric precision: 1–16 places. References to this type are abbreviated as *N*. Largest field size: 20 numbers (or bytes) total, including decimal point.
Integer	The integer field may contain only whole numbers (no decimal values) up to 2 billion. Use it to store counts, sequence numbers, and other whole number values where no possibility of fractional entry is desired. The integer type is more compact in storage size (half that of even a currency field), although the other binary numeric types (currency, double) are slightly quicker for calculations. The range of accepted values is from–2147483647 to 2147483646. References to this field type are abbreviated as *I*. Size in bytes: 4.

FIELD TYPE	DESCRIPTION AND SPECIFICATIONS
Double	A double (numeric precision) field provides more accuracy and control over numeric values than a numeric field, which can accommodate only 20 digits. Double type can also provide better floating-point flexibility, because the position of the decimal is entered with the value into the field. The range of values is from–4.94065658541247–324 to 1.79769313486232E+308. Like the currency type, doubles are stored in binary format. Fields type references are abbreviated as *B*. Size in bytes: 8.
Float	This is the same as a numeric field (which means it is redundant—use numeric fields instead). Numeric precision: 1–16 places. Largest field size: 20 numbers (or bytes).
Currency	This type is not just for currency. It can store most numeric values in less space than a standard numeric type does: 8 bits for most practical uses. Whereas a numeric field stores the actual numeric characters (as ASCII characters) and must be converted to do binary arithmetic, the currency type is already in binary format and is somewhat faster for calculations. Of course, you can also use this type to store monetary values (not necessarily dollars). It will maintain as many as four places after the decimal. The display of this field will follow the FoxPro currency settings (**SET CURRENCY**). This type is referenced by the abbreviation *Y*. Field size in bytes: 8.
Date	All dates are stored in the character format yyyymmdd but are usually displayed in the character format ddmmyy (for example, 01/01/94). However, for calculations the date is handled as a number. Internally, the format conversions are handled automatically. However, as input values, you will need to frequently deal with date conversions, using a battery of functions including **CTOD( )**, **DTOC( )**, **DTOS( )**, and the quasioperators **{ }**

(Continued...)

FIELD TYPE	**DESCRIPTION AND SPECIFICATIONS**
Date (cont.)	(more on all this later). The details of the date format respond to the **SET DATE**, **SET MARK**, and **SET CENTURY** settings. This type is abbreviated as *D*. Size of field in bytes: 8.
DateTime	This type combines date and time in the format ddmmyyhhmmss, (for example, 2/09/97 14:57 PM). You can use it to store only date or time or both. Because there is no Time field type, this type is particularly useful for storing times. If you store only one element, FoxPro will set the other element to its default. The default for time is 00:00:00 (midnight). The default for dates is 12/30/1899 (go figure). By default, Time values are displayed in AM or PM format: 12:30:45 PM. The details of the date format respond to the **SET DATE**, **SET MARK**, and **SET CENTURY** settings; the time format, to **SET HOURS** and **SET SECONDS**. The DateTime type is stored in a binary format and is somewhat more compact and quicker to calculate than the standard Date type. The type abbreviation is *T*. Size of field in bytes: 8.
Logical	A true or false type and field (Boolean logical true or false), represented by .T. for true and .F. for false. This type is used extensively for flags ("Is record active?"—.T. or .F.) and for storing values for the FoxPro CheckBox control. Reference to this type is abbreviated as *L*. Size of field in bytes: 1.
Memo	Originally, this field was used to store only text. Now, however, it can be used to store a variety of information, including memory variables, window definitions, and other programming data. Still, its primary use is to store notes and other extended text entries. The data is not stored in the DBF file but rather in another file of the same name but with the extension FPT (for example, CUSTOMER.DBF and CUSTOMER.FPT). For database files (DBC), the memo field file has the extension DBT. Fields of

FIELD TYPE	DESCRIPTION AND SPECIFICATIONS
Memo *(cont.)*	this type are abbreviated as *M*. Size in the DBF or DBC file in bytes: 4. Size of the FPT or DBT file: limited only by disk space.
General	The general field is a close cousin of the memo field and is housed in the same FPT file. This field, however, is specialized to contain visual images, sounds, and other information coming from programs other than FoxPro through Microsoft OLE (object linking and embedding) connections. Fields of this type are abbreviated as *G*. Size in the DBF file, in bytes: 4. Size of the FPT file: limited only by disk space.
Character (Binary)	Essentially, this is the same as the regular character field type except that its values will not be changed if a code page (national character definition) is changed. This is of obvious value for applications that must be used across language (national) boundaries. Maximum field size in bytes: 254.
Memo (Binary)	Like the Character (Binary) field type, the Memo (Binary) field is a memo field that will not change values if the code page is changed. Size in the DBF file in bytes: 4. Size of the FPT file: limited only by disk space.

Even a quick glance at the list of data and field types indicates that many of them are for special purposes. For most applications, Character, Date, DateTime, Logical, Memo, and General are used routinely. Among the numeric types, people switch between Numeric (when the format of the number is paramount), Integer (to keep it simple), and Double (for maximum capacity and calculation speed). Character data predominates, in part because most information is in the form of characters and because character data is the most flexible. For example, Visual FoxPro gives you more than 20 functions to manipulate Character data.

NULLS

A *null* is sometimes listed with the data types, but a null is an absence of type. In fact, it represents an absence of data. "From nothing will come something."

In database management, that something can be trouble. For example, when a new record is added to a table and one of the fields is of the currency type, what is its value? Should it be a zero? Zero is hardly nothing—ask an accountant whether or not a zero balance means something. So perhaps a new currency field should contain nothing. What, then, is "nothing"? In FoxPro, as in most other mature database systems, it's a null. A null is a value that has no value. This is an accurate statement, even though it sounds contradictory. In fact, a null is also data-type–neutral; it has no data type of its own, and it doesn't affect the data type of anything that contains it.

Nulls are primarily a marker (a *token*) to signify that the current item (field, variable, and so forth) contains nothing. Among other things, a null is used to distinguish the absence of value in fields that may contain something easily mistaken for "nothing," such as 0 for numerics and spaces for character fields. You can enter a null into a field (or other data container) by assigning the **.NULL.** token to it or using **Ctrl+0** from the keyboard. Choosing when to use nulls can be important to an application, and we'll revisit this topic several more times.

FoxPro Expressions

Just as data and field types span FoxPro programming and data management, FoxPro *expressions* are ubiquitous. There are expressions in data selection criteria, in the database commands, and in the programming language, and there are even mathematical expressions. As a concept, expressions encompass many fundamentals of data management and programming, but their overlapping use in so many contexts can lead to confusion. Hopefully, the explanation presented here will help keep things straight. As a general approach, we'll proceed from the simplest of expressions (constants, variables) to the most complex (compound logical expressions) in a building-block fashion—each simple expression being used as part of more-complicated expressions.

Commands and Expressions

In FoxPro, *commands* tell the program what to do. They are part of the programming language, and most of them are related to database management. For example, here are four of the most fundamental commands: **LOCATE**, **EDIT**, **REPLACE**, and **DELETE**. **LOCATE** searches a table to find a match for a value in

a specific field. **EDIT** provides the means to edit a record. **REPLACE** can change the value in specific fields for the whole table. **DELETE** marks specific (or all) records for deletion.

These commands, like most FoxPro commands, have a number of associated *command clauses* that qualify or control the command's behavior. Here, for example, are the clauses associated with the **REPLACE** command:

REPLACE FieldName1 **WITH** *eExpression1* **[ADDITIVE]**
[, FieldName2 **WITH** *eExpression2* **[ADDITIVE]]** ...
[Scope] [FOR lExpression1**] [WHILE** *lExpression2*]
[**IN** nWorkArea | cTableAlias]
[NOOPTIMIZE]

This is the full *syntax*—the elements and format for using the command. The words **WITH**, **FOR**, and **WHILE** are the principal command clauses. Notice that in each case the clause is associated with an expression (*eExpression1* and so on). This is typical. Although commands provide the machinery for doing something, the clauses and their expressions define what, precisely, should be done.

USING THE COMMAND WINDOW

As various kinds of expressions are introduced, you are encouraged to experiment with them in the Command window (see Figure 3.3).

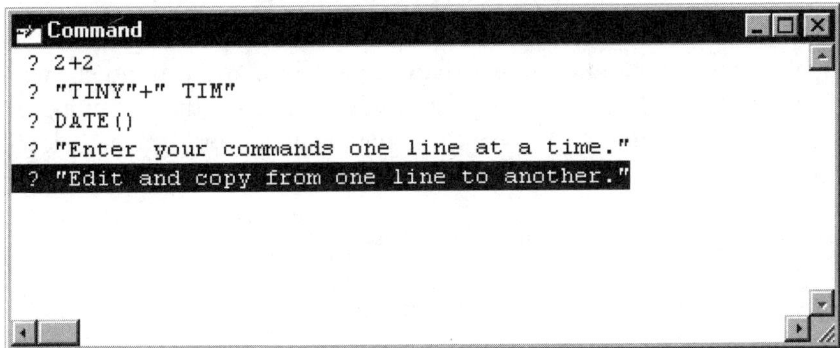

FIGURE 3.3 COMMAND WINDOW.

There are two main advantages of entering commands and expressions here: it's very direct, and you can use commands not available in the menus. Because FoxPro is an *interpreted* language (it can execute commands in a line-by-line fashion), you type the command you want and FoxPro executes it immediately. Although there are some limitations, using the Command window gives people a sense of control over data, and experienced programmers use it frequently to do data maintenance and prototype FoxPro expressions.

Using the Command window is like working with a slightly eccentric version of the standard FoxPro program editor. You type commands as text, and you can use **Cut**, **Copy**, **Paste**, and **Find** from the **Edit** menu as you would expect. However, in contrast to the program editor, you type one command at a time. When you press the **Enter** key, FoxPro executes the command.

As you might have gathered, FoxPro expressions are not complete *command statements*; by themselves, expressions (of any kind) can't be run by the computer. They need to be used in conjunction with a FoxPro command. For example, to evaluate (execute) many kinds of expressions in the Command window, you will need to use the **?** command, which works like asking "What is—?" Here are some examples:

```
? 1+3
? DATE()
? 1 = 2
```

In each case, FoxPro performs the operations indicated by the expression and displays the result on the screen. As you work, the Command window retains everything you type. As the window fills with commands, you can scroll up and down, not only to see where you've been but also to cut and paste any of the previous commands or modify them to make a new command.

You should size the window to have plenty of room for longer commands, although you can type lines longer than the window. You can either have the window scroll (which is a nuisance, because you can't see the beginning of the line) or use a semicolon (**;**) to continue the command on the line below. For example:

```
REPLACE ALL contact WITH customer.fullname ;
  FOR NOT EMPTY(customer.fullname) ;
  AND customer.enterdate > {"11/01/92"}
```

Even using continuation markers (the semicolon), you can't enter more than one command at a time. This means that extended programming structures (such as loops) can't be used in the Command window.

CONSTANTS

The first building block of FoxPro expressions are *constants*, which are simple values such as these:

```
3.1416
"Visual FoxPro version 5.0"
12/31/99
```

They're called constants because, as a simple expression of value, they don't change while a program is running. They're also identified by data type: numeric constants, character constants, and so forth. You'll see many references to constants throughout the FoxPro manuals, in most cases indicating that you should supply a value to a function, screen prompt, or other data input. Most FoxPro applications also define constants to use in programming through what are called *preprocessor directives*, such as this:

```
#DEFINE PI 3.1416
#DEFINE APPVERSION 1.01
```

After using one of these directives, instead of writing 3.1416 throughout a program, you just type **PI**. (More on this in later chapters.)

VARIABLES AND FIELDS

Variables are easily contrasted with constants, simply because the values of variables can change while the program runs. You already know about one kind of variable: fields. A field is like a container whose content conforms to a certain definition (data type, width, and so on), but the specific content can change from record to record. Regular variables are also containers for data, but they exist only in RAM and are sometimes called *memory* variables.

A variation on memory variables are *field* variables, which are variables in memory that contain data from fields. Field variables are distinctively expressed by prefixing the field name with `m.` like this: `m.city, m.state`. There are also *arrays*, which are a type of variable that may have multiple elements sharing the same variable name but differentiated by an indexing number: `aState[1], aState[2]`. (Arrays are important, and there's a whole section on them a few chapters ahead.)

NOTE

In FoxPro, fields, memory variables, field variables, and arrays are classified as containers—a concept you will see often in object-oriented programming.

The simplest way to create a variable in FoxPro is by *assignment*—that is, by assigning a value (as a constant expression) to the variable's name:

```
cartype = "MINIVAN"
```

The equal sign isn't like a math equation; in this case, it's more like saying, "Store the value MINIVAN to the variable named CARTYPE." In fact, there is an older FoxPro command that looks like this:

```
STORE "MINIVAN" TO cartype
```

This statement expresses variable assignment better than the equal sign but requires more keystrokes to enter, so programmers (being natural keyboard efficiency experts) don't use the **STORE** command very much.

Variable names may be as many as 254 characters long, but unless you're addicted to typing (and therefore not a keyboard efficiency expert and therefore not a programmer), they should be only as long as necessary to convey what they contain. By convention (meaning that you'll see it done a certain way all the time, but no one says you have to do it), FoxPro variables are written in mixed case, using capitals to separate portions of the name: `LastName`, `AutoModel`. If the name needs to be longer than two such segments, it's separated by an underscore (again by convention): `Name_By_Birth`.

You should practice creating some variables in the Command window. Enter the command **SET TALK ON** before you start so that you can see the values as they are being assigned. You can also see the results of an assignment by using the **?** command with a variable like this: `? cartype`. Table 3.4 shows more examples of variable assignments.

TABLE 3.4 EXAMPLES OF VARIABLE ASSIGNMENTS

VARIABLE ASSIGNMENT	DESCRIPTION
`cLastName = LASTNAME`	Character data from a field
`dToday = DATE()`	Today's date from the **DATE( )** function.
`cNada = .NULL.`	Assigning a null to a variable.
`lOk = .f.`	A variable taking a logical value of false.
`x = 3`	A numeric variable.

Variables take on different data types. Unlike most other programming languages, FoxPro is very flexible about the data types of variables. For one thing, you don't need to declare a variable (that is, name it) before using it. You also need not define its data type, because this happens automatically when you assign a value. You can change the content, and hence the data type, at any time. For example, it's legitimate to use the following two assignment statements back to back:

```
first = 14
first = "Mary"
```

This sort of flexibility makes programming language experts scream. Changing the data type of a variable can lead to unpleasant difficulties—bugs—when a program encounters a data type it didn't expect. That's why naming conventions for variables have evolved over the past few years. They are not required by FoxPro but have become standard practice. As illustrated in Table 3.5, the simplest of these conventions involves prefixing each variable name with a lowercase letter of its data type followed by capitalizing the first letter of the variable name.

This naming convention doesn't guarantee that a variable will contain data of the specified type, but it does help to spot one that doesn't.

Variables, like constants, are a type of expression. They are most commonly used to convey values into other (often more complex) expressions. For example:

```
x = 3
y = x + 4
```

TABLE 3.5 DATA TYPING VARIABLE NAMES

DATA TYPE	PREFIX	EXAMPLE VARIABLE
Array	a	aMonths
Character	c	cLastName
Currency	y	yCurrentValue
Date	d	dBirthDay
Datetime	t	tLastModified
Double	b	bRemainder
General	g	gGeneral
Integer	i	iCount
Logical	l	lFlag
Memo	m	mComments
Numeric	n	nCounter

This use of a variable is just like that of a mathematical expression, where x takes on the value of 3 and, when 4 is added to it, passes the value of 7 into the variable y. A less familiar example might look like this:

```
m.LastName  = LASTNAME
cLastName   = UPPER(m.LastName)
```

In this case, the field variable m.LastName is loaded with the value stored in the field LASTNAME. Depending on which record is active, the name will change. Then the value stored in m.LastName is passed to the function **UPPER( )**, which converts all the letters to uppercase (all caps), and the result is stored in the variable cLastName.

FUNCTIONS

Functions are also expressions and another building block for complex expressions. FoxPro has nearly 380 built-in functions, and that's an indication of how important they are. Essentially, a *function* is a type of program that does one of three things: provide information, process data, or test for something.

As you saw in the previous section, the **UPPER( )** function converts character data to uppercase letters; that function is a processing function. The **DATE( )** function returns the current system date, and is the type of function that provides information. **EMPTY( )** tests whether it is true or false that a field or variable contains a value. All functions are said to *return* a value (appropriate to their type), which can then be stored in a variable or used as part of another expression:

```
dToday = DATE()
? dToday
Displays:  3/22/97
```

The property of functions to work *in-line* with other expressions and commands makes them uniquely valuable. For example, here is the **DATE( )** function working with an important database command, **REPLACE**:

```
REPLACE ALL LASTDATE WITH DATE()
```

This command (also called a *command statement*) replaces the value in all LASTDATE fields with the current date.

Next is an example of one function *nested* inside another function:

```
REPLACE ALL MONTH WITH MONTH(DATE())
```

The **DATE( )** function returns the current date to the **MONTH( )** function, which returns the current month as a number, which in turn is used to replace the value in the MONTH field. In this example, the **DATE( )** function is used as the expression for the **MONTH( )** function's *argument*—the jargon for part of a function's syntax. The full syntax looks like this:

MONTH(*dExpression* | *tExpression*)

dExpression a valid Date expression

tExpression a valid DateTime expression

The argument **dExpression** specifies what kind of data may be passed to the function, in this case a date expression. This same approach lies behind all the FoxPro expression types (see Table 3.6) used for functions.

TABLE 3.5 FOXPRO EXPRESSION TYPES

cExpression	Valid Character Expressions: `"Spot runs"`—text constants (character strings). `Clastname`—variables or fields containing text. `UPPER("spot")`—functions or other expressions that return character data.
nExpression	Valid Numeric Expressions: `3.1416`—numeric constants. `NCount`—variables containing numbers (numeric, integer, or double). `SALECOUNT`—fields containing numbers. `RECNO()`—functions or other expressions that return numeric data.
dExpression	Valid Date Expressions: `{12/12/94}`—date constants. `DStartDate`—variables containing dates. `ENDDATE`—fields containing dates. `DATE()`—functions or other expressions that return dates.
tExpression	Valid DateTime Expressions: `{12/12/94 10:30:45 PM}`—DateTime constants. `TStartDateTime`—variables containing dates and times. `ENDDATETIME`—fields containing DateTime values. `DATETIME()`—functions or other expressions that return dates.
lExpression	Valid Logical Expressions: `.T./.F.`—logical symbols. `Ldone`—variables and fields containing a logical value. `FOUND()`—functions or other expressions that return true or false.

Unlike command verbs, in which the order of the clauses is generally not important, functions are very fussy about the order and data type of their arguments. Most of the time, if you use an expression with the wrong data type—or forget a required expression—you'll get an error message.

NOTE

This is a good spot to introduce what I call a programmer's trained sensitivities: things for which there are no hard-and-fast rules but that you need to sense and avoid—or sense and do. This one involves mixing data types. You can't do it, except where it's specifically part of the syntax. In most expressions and in either term of a logical expression, you can't mix types—for example, date and character values. Typically, you must convert one of the values to match the other. Most of the time, FoxPro will complain if you make this mistake, but not always. To avoid problems, you need to develop a sense of where types are involved and especially when they're going to need conversion.

FUNCTIONS: A STARTER SET

Visual FoxPro has so many functions (and later you'll meet their object-oriented twin, methods) that it's hard to know where to begin learning them. Here's a recommended starter set that you can use almost immediately in both programming and data management. Use the on-line help to get precise definitions and practice using them in the Command window.

GENERAL USE FUNCTIONS:

EMPTY(*eExpression*)

Tests an expression to see whether it contains any data. Very useful, but don't confuse empty with a null value. Returns true or false.

ISNULL(*eExpression*)

Tests an expression to see whether it contains a null. Returns true or false.

BETWEEN(*eTestValue, eHighValue, eLowValue*)

Tests whether a value can be found between two other values. Normally used for numbers but can also be used with characters. Returns true or false.

IIF(*lExpression, eExpression1, eExpression2*)

Called the condition IF, this is the most important function in the language. Tests whether a logical expression is true or false and returns the corresponding result. Learn how to use this one in your sleep.

DATE AND TIME FUNCTIONS:

DATE( )

Returns the current system date.

DAY(*dExpression* or *tExpression*)

Returns the current day of the week based on the date expression argument.

YEAR(*dExpression* or *tExpression*)

Returns the year, as in "1996," based on the date expression argument.

DATETIME( )

Returns the current date and time from the system clock.

TIME( )

Returns the current time as a character string: 12:03:45.

CTOD(*cExpression*)

Converts a character date (such as 12/21/97) to a FoxPro date.

DTOC(*dExpression* or *tExpression* [,1])

Converts a FoxPro date into a character string.

{ }

Converts a character string into a date and is quicker than **CTOD( )**.

DTOT(*dExpression*)

Returns the time portion of a date time.

CTOT(***cExpression*** **)**

Returns the date time value as a character.

NUMERIC FUNCTIONS:

INT(***nExpression*** **)**

Returns the integer (whole number) value of a number.

ROUND(***nExpression , nDecimalPlaces*** **)**

Returns the rounded value of a number to a specified number of decimal places.

VAL(***cExpression*** **)**

Converts a character string into a number.

STR(***cExpression*** **)**

Converts a number into a character string.

DATA MANAGEMENT FUNCTIONS:

RECNO(**[*cTableAlias* | *nWorkArea*]** **)**

Returns record number of the current record in a table.

DELETED(**[*cTableAlias* | *nWorkArea*]** **)**

Returns whether or not the current record in a table has been deleted.

RECCOUNT(**[*cTableAlias* | *nWorkArea*]** **)**

Returns the number of records in a table.

OPERATORS

Constants, variables, fields, and functions are the primary expressions, but to put them to use in more-complex expressions requires an *operator*—the plus sign (+) and greater than sign (>) are typical. There are always two *terms* (expressions "to the left of" and "to the right of") surrounding an operator, and the operator either performs an action (such as adding) or a comparison (such as greater than) with the two terms. For example:

```
DATE( ) + 31
```

This is equivalent to saying, "Add 31 (days) to the current date." Most of this is familiar from basic math. But, as you can see in the list of operators in Table 3.7, some operators are obvious, others are unfamiliar but useful, and still others are truly arcane.

TABLE 3.7 FOXPRO OPERATORS

OPERATOR	DATA TYPES	DESCRIPTION	EXAMPLE
+	N,I,B,F,Y,D	Addition	`3.56 + 3`
+	C	Concatenation	`"Ab" + "by"`
+	D,N,I	Adding days to dates	`DATE()+ 3`
-	N,I,B,F,Y	Subtraction	`356 - 3`
-	C	Trimmed concatenation; `blanks are added to end`	`"Tom & " - "Jerry "`
-	D,N,I,T	Subtract days from dates	`DATE()- 3`

=	C,F,N,I,B, D,T,Y	Equal to	`"Ab" = "Ab"`
			`2 = 2`
			`DATE()=CTOD ("12/1/93")`

= =	C	Equal to and equal in length (exact match)	`"Tom" == "Tom"`
<>	C,N,F,B,I,Y,T,D	Not equal to:	`"Ab" <> "Tom"`
#		<> math style	`4 # 3`
!=		!= C language style # dBase style	`nType != cType`
>	C,N,F,I,B,D,T,Y	Greater than `"Jerry" > "Tom"`	`1000 > 999`

OPERATOR	DATA TYPES	DESCRIPTION	EXAMPLE
>=	C,N,F,I,B,D,T,Y	Greater than or equal to	999 >= 999
<	C,N,F,I,B,D,T,Y	Less than	999 < 1000
			"Tom" < "Jerry"
<=	C,N,F,I,B,D,T,Y	Less than or equal to	999 <= 999
^, **	N,F,B,I,Y	Exponentiation	x^2, x**2
*	N,F,B,I,Y	Multiplication	2*4
/	N,F,I,B,Y	Division	x/3
%	N,F,B	Modulus (remainder)	2%3
$	C,M	Substring comparison (string contained in)	"Ab" $ "Abby"
AND, .AND.	L	Logical AND. Without dots is modern usage.	AND ("Ab"$"Abby")
OR, .OR.	L	Logical inclusive OR. Without dots is preferred.	OR ("Ab"$"Abby")
NOT, .NOT., !	L	Logical NOT. Without dots is preferred. Don't use the ! symbol.	NOT ("Ab"$"Abby)

EVALUATION AND ORDER OF PRECEDENCE

With the addition of operators, you can build expressions of many kinds. In many respects, each expression is a self-contained unit, and everything in it relates to the data type of the expression and what it is supposed to accomplish. For a simple example, SALES + RETURNS is a numeric expression (presuming both fields are numeric fields). A more complex expression, SALES + RETURNS = 10,000, is a logical expression, because it *evaluates* to true or false depending on the values contained in SALES and RETURNS.

Functions, along with character, logical, and mathematical expressions and their operators, are said to evaluate to something. When an expression is evaluated, it produces a result. A character expression evaluates to characters, a numeric expression to a number, a date expression to a date, and a logical expression to true or false. Table 3.8 lists some examples.

TABLE 3.8 EXPRESSIONS BY TYPE

TYPE	EXPRESSION	EVALUATION
Character	`TRIM(LASTNAME)`	`"Johnson"`
Numeric	`SALES + 10,000`	`25,000`
Date	`DATE()- 30`	`11/01/92`
Logical	`"Ab" $ "Tintern Abbey"`	`.t.`

The evaluation of an expression is performed by FoxPro when you execute a menu option containing an expression, enter an expression in the Command window, or run a program containing expressions. Evaluation usually moves from left to right in an expression, but there is an *order of precedence* (especially in numeric and logical expressions) that determines the order in which parts of an expression are evaluated. It is easy to make mistakes in logic that are really mistakes in the order of precedence. For example:

```
dDAYS_OVERDUE + DATE() / 30
```

This statement will create a "Data type mismatch" error, because FoxPro will follow its default order of precedence and carry out the division before the addition. Put another way, the expression looks like this to FoxPro:

```
                DATE()
dDAYS_OVERDUE + ------
                  30
```

but FoxPro can't divide a date by a number. Problems like this can be avoided, not by memorizing the table of precedence (Table 3.9), but by using three rules of thumb:

1. Evaluation flows from left to right.
2. Parentheses always control the order of evaluation.
3. If need be, you can refer to a table of precedence.

Using parentheses to control the order of evaluation is your best tool. For example, the preceding problem expression is easily fixed:

```
(DAYS_OVERDUE + DATE()) / 30
```

This statement tells FoxPro to evaluate the addition expression before doing the division. When you look at one of your expressions and you're not sure how it will evaluate, don't hesitate to use parentheses to make it evaluate the way you want.

TABLE 3.9 FOXPRO ORDER OF PRECEDENCE

1	Expressions enclosed within parentheses
2	Functions
3	Exponentiation
4	Multiplication and division
5	Modulus calculation
6	Addition and subtraction
7	Character string operations
8	Relational operators
9	NOT
10	AND
11	OR

NOTE

I can't stress enough how important it is to become fluent in constructing expressions, complex or otherwise. Start by working with these data-oriented expressions and practice all you can in the Command window. Make mistakes and learn from them. Soon we'll be adding object-oriented expressions to the mix. That's no time to be wondering how functions work.

LOGICAL EXPRESSIONS

Now it's time to turn our attention to *logical expressions*. As has been mentioned, logical expressions always evaluate to either true (.t.) or false (.f.). They are also sometimes called *conditional* expressions, because they're used to do something based on satisfying a logical condition. This is what makes logical expressions important. Among other things, they are used to qualify SQL statements (in the **WHERE** clause). Nearly every major data management command can use a logical expression attached to either a **FOR** or a **WHILE** clause.

BUILDING LOGICAL EXPRESSIONS

The form of a logical expression is like that of an algebraic relation. There's a left side (left term), a right side (right term), and, in the middle, one of the *relational operators* (=, <, <=, >, >=, <>, or $). For this type of expression, "relation" means that the left side relates in some way to the right side, and this relation evaluates to either true or false. The examples in Table 3.10 will help to make this clear.

TABLE 3.10 THE FORM AND EXAMPLES OF LOGICAL EXPRESSIONS

LEFT TERM	OPERATOR	RIGHT TERM
Constant, field, variable, function, or a combination	=, <, <=, >, >=, <>, $	Constant, field, variable, function, or a combination
13	>	4
"CA"	<>	STATE
cSTATE	=	"CA"
SALES	>	10,000
DATE() + 31	<=	DUE_DATE

The variations in logical expressions are infinite. Most of the time, you'll use them to test for some condition in a field (or fields), and, depending on whether the result is true or false, an action will occur. The nature of the action will help you determine how to build the expression. For example, if you want to delete some old records from a table, you might use a date of entry field to test whether the record is older than 90 days and, if it is, delete it. Your command and conditional expression might look like this:

```
DELETE ALL FOR ENTERDATE + 90 < DATE()
```

Similarly, in FoxPro's SQL statements you'll use logical expressions such as this:

```
SELECT ALL CUSTOMER_NAME, CITY, STATE;
  FROM CUSTOMER ;
  WHERE STATE = "CA"
```

The **WHERE** clause, a selection criterion in SQL, causes the **SELECT** command to return only those records that match the logical expression.

THE EXPRESSION BUILDER

Creating logical expressions is important enough to FoxPro that a specialized dialog box, the Expression Builder, has been provided (see Figure 3.4).

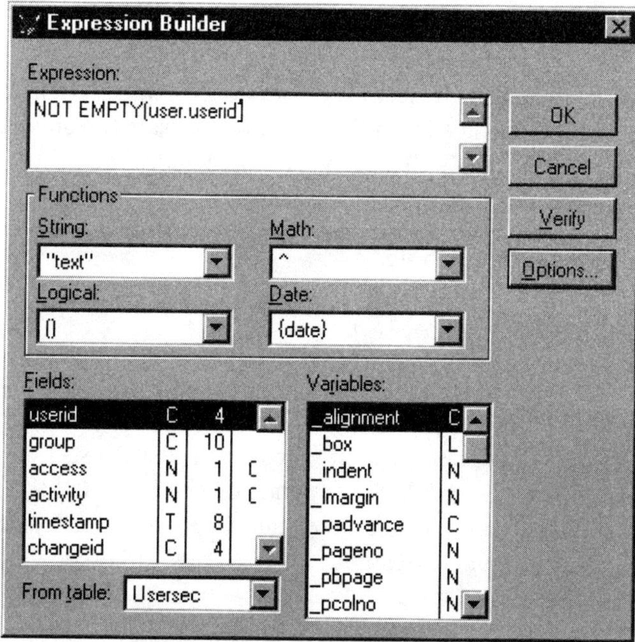

FIGURE 3.4 EXPRESSION BUILDER DIALOG BOX.

The Expression Builder is found in the FoxPro user interface as an option attached to the **For** or **While** clause of commands such as **Locate**, **Index**, and **Replace**. It can also be used in your applications with the **GETEXPR** command. It's important to understand that the Expression Builder is intended to support building expressions and is in no way a tutorial or one of Microsoft's wizards. It's usually reserved for programmers.

Compound Expressions

It's guaranteed that at some point you will need to construct logical expressions that contain more than one expression. These so-called *compound* expressions are constructed of multiple logical expressions glued together with the Boolean operators **AND, OR,** and **NOT,** usually clarified by the liberal use of parentheses. For example, consider this compound expression:

```
"JOHN" $ LASTNAME AND ;
STATE="CA" AND ;
(SALES >= 10,000 OR GROSSMARGIN > 5)
```

In English this could mean, "Select all records of salespeople where "JOHN" is part of the last name, who live in California, and have sales greater than $10,000 or else a gross margin higher than 5 percent." Breaking down the compound expression, it has these simple logical expressions:

```
Character:    "JOHN" $ LASTNAME
Character:    STATE = "CA"
Numeric:      SALES >= 10,000
Numeric:      GROSSMARGIN > 5
```

The overall flow of logic makes five tests. The first two (designated by the first **AND**) are character tests. Then there are the two numeric tests (signified by the **OR**). The fifth test (the second **AND**) depends on the results of the two numeric tests. The parentheses are not required, but they make this expression easier to understand, and in some cases may make a huge difference in the way an expression is evaluated.

There are two simple rules that might help to guide your use of **AND** and **OR**. In an expression that uses **AND**, both logical expressions must be true for the **AND** to return true; for example, "You can go to the movies only if you've done the dishes AND you have the money." Using **OR** in an expression such as "condition x OR condition y," only one of the conditions needs to be true: "You can eat dessert if you've broken your diet OR it's not fattening."

The **NOT** is, of course, a negation, and it is most often used to exclude something from a search or a database process. It can be used to test for the negative of a conditional expression, as in this example:

```
LOCATE FOR NOT STATE = "CA"
```

Also quite commonly, it is teamed with two preliminary tests of the **AND** or **OR** variety:

```
LOCATE FOR NOT (STATE = "CA" OR STATE="OR")
```

There are many formal ways to approach Boolean logic, and if you go on to study database administration you will encounter the more precise and mathematical definitions. However, in the less academic atmosphere of day-to-day database management, you can usually get by using common sense and the standard English meanings.

CHAPTER WRAP UP

Going through the basic terminology of data management may seem like a long way from application development, but it's like learning a language—everyone needs to start with the same vocabulary. If you're new to database management, some of the concepts, especially table definitions and complex expressions, may be difficult. Like many concepts, these will become much more understandable once you've had experience with them.

For emphasis, here are the terms and concepts that are most crucial for programming and database management:

- Data types
- Files (tables), records, fields, and databases
- Field types
- Constants
- Variables
- Functions
- Operators
- Logical expressions

CHAPTER 4

CREATING DATA MANAGEMENT ELEMENTS

This chapter and the next one describe FoxPro's primary data management commands, the ones you'll use to create and maintain databases. In this regard there are three major roles for data management in application development: Interactive data management, data management within an application, and the data management that users do with your application.

Interactive data management is what you, as developer, do interactively with FoxPro. Throughout the life of an application, it's necessary to get at the database and tables to manipulate them directly. Test tables need to be created and loaded with data. Field values are checked and cleaned. Problems in processing data are discovered and corrected. Much of this data management is separate from the application programming, and you'll do most of it interactively by issuing commands from the Command window. The FoxPro tools come from its roots as a data management system, and they're some of the best in the industry. Mastery of these tools—mainly the Database Designer and Table Designer as well as the command language—will not only speed your application development but will also prepare you for programming.

Most applications also need some programming routines that do nothing but data management. These routines may be used for transferring data from one place to another, updating information, or a thousand other purely data-oriented operations. The programming involved uses sequences of data management commands and is commonly called *procedural* programming to distinguish it from object-oriented programming.

Also typical of most applications is a need to put the user into the data management loop. This kind of data management runs all the way from the user making simple operational choices, such as which report to print, to direct involvement with data maintenance. Many parts of an application, such as a data entry screen, operate as front ends to hide complications but still give the user control. In this area of application development, you'll often mix FoxPro's data management commands with object-oriented programming.

In most FoxPro applications you're never far from the data. Even in the heart of object-oriented user-interface programming, most of the time you'll be manipulating data in the background to provide something for the user interface.

FoxPro and SQL

The first version of Visual FoxPro was a watershed product in FoxPro's commitment to Structured Query Language (SQL). In previous versions, SQL was an important but peripheral capability, one mainly associated with queries. In this version, SQL has moved front and center to take its place with the original FoxPro commands that do the work of data management. This arrangement presents an interesting set of options (or dilemmas, depending on how you look at it) for someone planning data management for an application. How much SQL should you use? This is not a question to be answered quickly.

SQL, variously pronounced "sequel" or S-Q-L, has evolved from an academic relational database theory into the common language of the database management industry. Put another way, SQL is everywhere. It has become standardized through official committees and shoehorned into almost every database product. It's almost the only way to manipulate databases across hardware and software boundaries.

It's this latter capability that makes SQL important for products (such as FoxPro) that feature connectivity to many different database systems. In many cases, the only way to manipulate data in other products' tables is through SQL, so FoxPro added SQL commands to its repertoire, as you can see in Table 4.1.

There is considerable overlap between the SQL and FoxPro commands, and that naturally causes confusion. Which command do you use? If you lean in the direction of conceptual purity, SQL is clearly the direction FoxPro (and the industry) is moving, and it will pay to use it fluently. If you want the best command for the job, the honest answer is, "It's a mixed bag." Commands such as **SQL-SELECT** and **CREATE SQL VIEW** are unique to SQL. The **DELETE-SQL** command is not only slower than its FoxPro counterpart (it doesn't check to see whether the record is already deleted), but it also can be dangerous, because its default is to delete *all* records. And so it goes. We'll consider the pros and cons of the two alternatives as we go through the chapters.

TABLE 4.1 SQL BASICS (* COMMANDS SUPPORTED BY FOXPRO)

SQL COMMAND	DEFINITION	OLD FOXPRO COMMAND
***ALTER TABLE**	Change (modify) tables.	**MODIFY TABLE**
***CREATE TABLE**	Create a new table.	**CREATE TABLE**
***CREATE DATABASE**	Create databases.	
***CREATE PRIMARY**	Create primary (also secondary) indexes.	**INDEX ON**
***CREATE VIEW**	Create SQL views.	
***DELETE**	Delete records in a table.	**DELETE**
***DROP...**	Delete tables, indexes, views, databases.	**DELETE...**
GRANT/REVOKE	Grant or revoke user access privileges.	
***INSERT**	Insert records into a table.	**APPEND**
***SELECT**	Retrieve a set of records.	**SET FILTER TO**
SHOW...	Display a list of all databases, data items, and so on.	**DISPLAY DATABASE**
***UPDATE**	Update a group of records.	**REPLACE**

THE PROGRESSION OF DATA MANAGEMENT

An application built on a database will almost inevitably reflect what is called the *progression of data management*:

1. The database and tables are designed and created.
2. New data is entered into the tables.
3. Data is retrieved, edited, and maintained.
4. The stored data is retrieved for output and presentation.

When you develop an application, you will include elements (summarized in Table 4.2) from each phase.

Table 4.2 The Progression of Data Management in an Application

The Developer's Work	In the Application
1. Create the Database	
Design and create the necessary tables and indexes, store them in a database, add referential integrity, triggers, and stored procedures	Deliver the application's database(s) and tables, ready for use (or at least ready for loading data).
2. Enter Data	
Pre-load tables with codes and other default data.	Default data (code tables etc.)
Build a data import capability, if needed.	Data import capability.
Build data entry forms for all tables.	Forms for manually entering new data.
3. Edit and Maintain Data	
Build search mechanisms for data to be retrieved and edited,	Ability to locate and scan data.
Create views and forms for data editing.	Forms for data editing.
Program data processing elements.	Utilities for data maintenance.
Program data integrity and maintenance routines as needed.	
4. Retrieve Data for Output	
Create views and queries.	Queries for viewing data on screen.
Create reports, labels, mail-merge, graphs, and other output options.	Reports, mail-merge, and labels for printing.
Build data export capability, if needed.	Graphs and other visual presentations Data export capability.

At this point the table is sketchy, and some of the items may not be familiar to you. You will eventually learn that the work briefly outlined here covers about 80 to 90 percent of most applications. This data management sequence is often well masked by the user interface, but you might be surprised how many applications consist of little more than database tables, data entry and edit screens, and reports.

CREATING DATABASES AND TABLES

Building an application doesn't begin with creating database and tables. It begins with an analysis and design phase that determines, among other things, which data should be included in the tables. However, this chapter is about hands-on data management, so for the time being we'll forgo the formal analysis and design and use an example that is both common and simple: a database and one table that contains information about the people who use an application.

NOTE

Data for this example is part of the Application Utilities database on the accompanying disk. The database file name is UTILITY.DBC.

DEFINING DATABASES AND TABLES

The first step is to create a database file. This file is called a *database container*, one of many containers in FoxPro. What it contains is not the tables, which have their own files, but rather information about the tables. This "data about data" is sometimes called *metadata*. So much for the jargon. As you will see, it's easy to create or modify FoxPro databases and tables. The mechanics are relatively simple, and FoxPro is usually very quick about it.

CREATING A SIMPLE DESIGN

Even with a simple database, it's helpful to do your homework for the design of the tables. The choice of tables and fields is important, and decisions about field names, type, and width have many implications in an application. The example we'll use is typical for a fairly large application that needs to track who is using the program, along with the user's basic information (name, phone, and so on), work assignments, and security clearances. To create the design in this case, I grabbed some personnel lists and network administrator documentation, studied them for a while, and then listed potential data items and field definitions as in Table 4.3.

Table 4.3 Rough Draft of a User Table

Data Item	Field Name	Type	Width
User's Unique ID	USERID	C	4
Network ID	NETWORKID	C	8
Last Name	LASTNAME	C	25
First Name	FIRSTNAME	C	15
Middle Name	MIDNAME	C	15
Division	DIVISION	C	15
Department	DEPARTMENT	C	15
Building	BUILDING	C	20
Room Number	ROOM	C	8
Job Title	TITLE	C	35
Birthdate	BIRTHDATE	D	8
Security Clearance Level	SECURLEVEL	C	1
Employee Status	EMPLOYSTAT	C	1
Date Record Last Changed	RECUPDATE	D	8

The next step is to use the Database Designer.

Using the Database Designer

A FoxPro database is a file that contains information about your data—not the actual data itself—and is therefore sometimes called a *data dictionary*. It would be natural for you to wonder what this means for an application. Broadly speaking, the FoxPro database now helps to document an application, standardize data values, validate data entry, enforce business rules, and protect data integrity, and it stores two of the most important tools in the FoxPro kit: connections and views. We'll come back many times to the items in this list, and their value will become clearer. You can create tables without using a database, but for now, let's just say you'd need a very good reason to do it that way.

The FoxPro Database Designer was created to make the task of defining databases, tables, and table relations not only easier but visually more interesting. Using the Database Designer guarantees that you are defining tables within an open database and that you will have full access to all the extended capabilities.

As with all files, the best place to start a new database is from the Project Manager (see Figure 4.1). Select the **Data** tab and then the **Databases** line. Select the **New** button. In the Open File dialog box, give the database a name and locate it in an appropriate folder. (For the current example, the file and folder were named UTILITY.) When you're finished, the Database Designer window will open and the new database will be registered with the Project Manager.

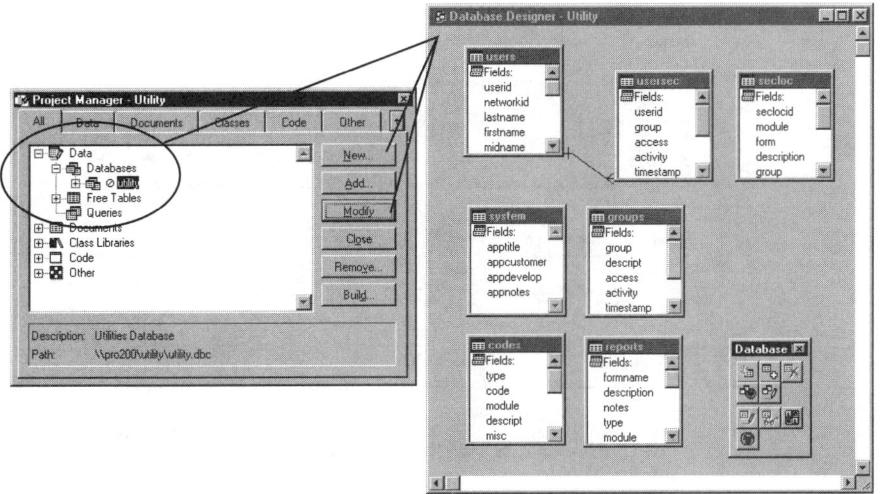

FIGURE 4.1 THE DATABASE DESIGNER.

NOTE

If you keep the Project Manager open while you are working in the Database Designer, all the tables you create (and other objects as well) will be automatically registered. You can also start new tables from the Project Manager, and they will be associated with the open database. As is usually the case, FoxPro provides multiple ways to do the same thing.

Because most of the capabilities of a database don't come into play until you have one or more tables in it, we'll move along to that operation.

To create a new table, click the **New Table** icon in the Designer toolbar and select the **New Table** icon in the next dialog box. You'll be asked to give the table a file name and a folder (directory) location. The folder should be one associated with the project, and the file name should reflect the contents of the table—in this case, USERS. When these steps are completed, FoxPro opens the Table Designer window (Figure 4.2), where the table specifications (and much more) are entered.

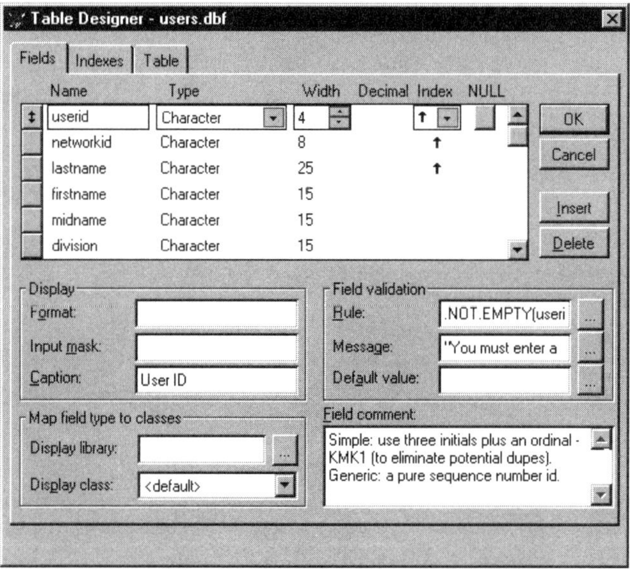

FIGURE 4.2 THE TABLE DESIGNER.

NOTE

You may have noticed that I skipped over the Table wizard. It might be a good idea to try it. This wizard attempts to give you templates (sets of field definitions) to jump start a table. If the shoe fits perfectly, it might be okay. Usually, it doesn't fit.

USING THE TABLE DESIGNER

There are four steps to complete the table definition:

1. Enter the basic definition of fields (name, type, width, decimal, null).

2. Create indexes (primary, candidate, regular).
3. Set relationships between tables (persistent relations, referential integrity rules).
4. Enter processing and validation logic (field validation, triggers, default values).

The first three steps are usually done in order. The fourth, defining the business rules, can be done separately. We'll cover that step once you've had more exposure to FoxPro programming.

DEFINING FIELDS

As you can see in Figure 4.2, defining fields has six elements (or *properties*, to use the object-oriented terminology): field name, type, width, decimal, index, and null. The first three are required, and FoxPro won't let you start another field without finishing them. You can enter all of a table's fields at once, insert or delete fields as needed, and move them up or down by dragging the buttons on the left. Most people like to enter the primary index field first, and other important fields near the top so that they are quickly visible in dialog boxes.

The first property, field name, is often the only clue to the contents of a field, so it helps to make the name descriptive. Visual FoxPro may have field names as long as 254 characters, but don't get carried away with long field names. A good name tells you about the contents of a field in as few characters as possible. There is also a **Field Comment** space where you can fill in the details. Use this box, and not the field name, for description.

Field names in FoxPro have some restrictions. The first character of the field name must be a letter. (Numbers and other symbols are not allowed in that position.) Spaces are not allowed, nor are the following characters:

` ~ ! @ # $ % ^ & * ( ) + = \ | / > < , ? ; : " -

It's good practice to establish field name conventions, at least within a database if not all your projects. Here are some examples:

- Make the fields names mnemonic; they should remind you of what's in the field.

- You can use the underscore (_) in a field name, typically to link words (because no spaces are allowed).
- Use identical field names in different tables when they mean the same thing. If you need a last name field in two different tables, call the field LASTNAME in both tables. The benefits of this convention include easier transfer of data between similar files and easier creation of relations between files. Most important, it makes it clear that the contents of the fields are the same.

NOTE

If you ever have to remove a table from a database, all the field names longer than 10 characters will be chopped or changed by FoxPro. Many programmers still try to stick with field names within the 10 characters just in case.

Field Types, Widths, and Table Sizes

Every field must have a type and a width. Width, or field length, is the amount of space allocated for a field in each record. Some widths are automatic by data type: Memo (4), General (4), Logical (1), Date (8), and DateTime (8). For Character, Numeric, Integer, Currency, and Float fields, you must assign the width. With Numeric, Currency, and Float you may also need to indicate the number of decimal places. Be sure to add decimal places and the decimal point to the total width of the field.

It used to be conventional wisdom that you should always size fields at the minimum to save disk space. The calculation is simple:

1. Add up the widths of all the fields; the result equals the record size in bytes.
2. Multiply by the expected number of records. For example:

   Record Size 300 bytes x Total Records 1,000 = 300,000 bytes (300K)

Having enough disk space is not the problem it once was. The standard disk size is approaching two Gigabytes. That isn't a license to throw away space, but there's no need to scrape for every kilobyte. In particular, make character fields (such as a company name) long enough to cover most cases; otherwise, users are inclined to abbreviate in unpredictable ways. However, if you're going to have millions of records in a table, "a few bytes here and there" can really add up.

NULL-VALUED FIELDS

The final piece of field definition is the **NULL** check box at the end of each field, which tells FoxPro to accept null values in the field. A full explanation of a null value is complicated (it's covered fairly well in the FoxPro *Developer's Guide*), but, in short, a null value is used to distinguish between fields that contain no value of their own data type and those that contain so-called empty values of their data type. An example serves as the best explanation. Currency fields that contain a zero (0) might be considered "empty," but ask any accountant whether a zero balance is significant. To distinguish between a zero value and no value, FoxPro allows nulls. With a null value, a field will contain a **NULL**, which is a marker (or token). You can enter these into fields by using **Ctrl+0** or by replacing a field with a null marker: `REPLACE BALANCE WITH NULL`.

In most general database work, you will not need to use nulls very often (if at all). Because of the complications they can cause, they are usually avoided. But in applications that have sensitive data (such as money fields) and when the entry of nulls can be automated through programming, they can be extremely important.

CREATING TABLES USING A COMMAND

Table creation is usually done through the Project Manager, Database Designer, and Table Designer connection—but not always. There are times when you may need to create a table, especially tables for temporary storage, in the programming. The SQL **CREATE TABLE** command does the job. The full command can also specify indexes, validation rules, and table relations. For that reason, **CREATE TABLE** is one of the monster commands, with more than 20 clauses and options. The following is a bare bones syntax typically used for creating temporary tables. (If you wish, check the *Language Reference* for the gory details.)

Command syntax:

```
CREATE TABLE TableName1 [FREE]
  (FieldName1 FieldType [(nFieldWidth [,nPrecision])]
    [NULL|NOT NULL]
  [, FieldName2 ...])
```

Arguments:

TableName1 The name of the table. In most cases this should be an eight-character DOS file name complete with path, if appropriate.

FREE Create a free table not attached to a database file. This is often the case for temporary files.

FieldName1 FieldType [(nFieldWidth [,nPrecision])] [NULL|NOT NULL]

This is the format for specifying a field and its properties. See the following example.

Example:

```
CREATE TABLE tempuser FREE ( userid C(4),networkid C(8),;
    lastname C(35), firstname C(20), salary C(6,2)NULL )
```

NOTE

Creating a table with this command raises a couple of points:

The table is opened exclusively, meaning that it is not available to other users unless you reopen it to be shared. If you don't use the **FREE** clause, the table will be attached to the open database (if there is one).

INDEXING TABLES

Once you've entered the fields of a table, you should be ready to consider the type of index associated with them.

THE IMPORTANCE OF INDEXES

One of the cornerstones of database technology is the ability to rapidly search for data. Suppose you want to find the city of Seattle in a table containing addresses. You could use a Browse window and scroll through the table looking for the word *Seattle*, but if there are more than a few hundred records, this method is impractical. So you want the program to find Seattle for you. It does this in two ways: first, Seattle is a city, and tables that contain addresses always have a CITY field—so this is the relevant field to search. Second, you can index the CITY field. This technique creates a list of the values in the CITY field, and this list is stored (usually) in a compound index file (CDX). When you tell FoxPro to find the word *Seattle* in the CITY field using the CITY index, FoxPro employs an extremely sophisticated search algorithm that will produce a match

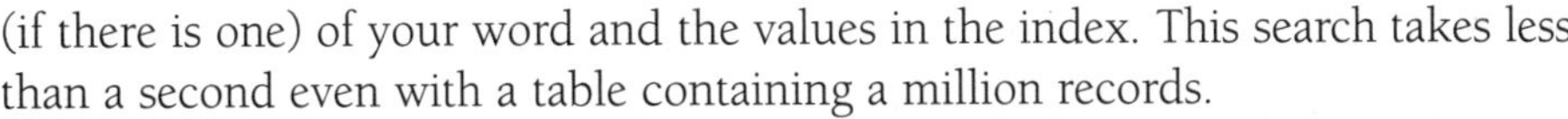

(if there is one) of your word and the values in the index. This search takes less than a second even with a table containing a million records.

This match (or not) between a search value and the index values is the principle behind the mechanisms of FoxPro's relational technology. When you "link" two tables in a relation, it's based on the values in one table being appropriate for a search in an index of the other table.

Indexes and index types play a variety of roles in FoxPro:

- **Primary keys:** In a relational system, every table must have one (and only one) *primary key* (index). By definition, the primary key does not permit duplicate values. There are times, however, when it's necessary to create a table whose primary key (in the logical sense) permits duplicates, for example in a PURCHASE table that has repeating customer IDs as the primary key. You can't use FoxPro's Primary Key type for this table, because it enforces the no-duplicates rule.
- **Foreign keys:** In a relational system, some fields may be used to reference indexes of other tables. This kind of field is called a *foreign key*. Most applications use a number of foreign key links into what are called *lookup tables*—for example, from a product code in one table to a table that contains the definition (name, price, and so on) of the code.
- **Search and query:** In addition to serving as linking fields for relations, most indexes are also used for searches. In either a lookup (using commands such as **SEEK** and **LOCATE**) or a SQL query, indexed fields are essential for high performance.
- **Sort order:** If your field isn't indexed for one of the preceding reasons, it may be useful to index the field so that it will be displayed or printed in sorted order. You can choose between ascending (A–Z) and descending (Z–A) orders.

WARNING

As important as indexes are, don't get carried away with them. They exact a performance penalty when you're adding new records and performing other operations. In some cases, especially for reports, it may be more efficient to create temporary indexes or to use SQL queries, which have a built-in sorting capability.

Creating Indexes

There are two ways to create indexes in the Table Designer. The first is very quick. Take a look at the **Fields** tab in Figure 4.2, and you'll see the **Index** column. Clicking in this column produces an arrow that indicates that the field is indexed and whether it's in ascending (A–Z) or descending (Z–A) order. For fields in which the index key is the same as the field, this is the way to go.

For more-complicated indexes with compound keys, and for general index maintenance, the **Index** tab of the Table Designer window is the place to be (Figure 4.3).

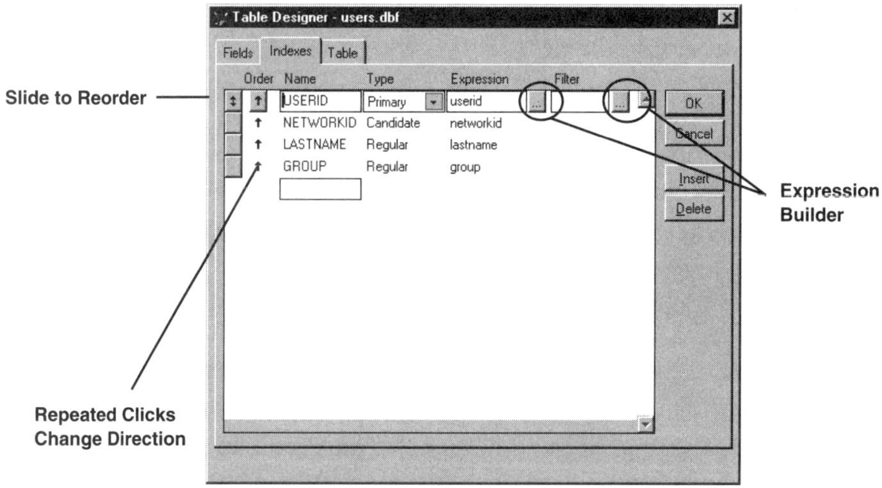

FIGURE 4.3 THE INDEX WINDOW.

As you can see in the figure, each line for index definition has five parts: **Order**, **Name**, **Type**, **Expression**, and **Filter**. The **Order** column works just like the **Index** column in the **Fields** tab; you click to set the direction of the order. The name, also called a *tag*, is the way to identify the index. (In a compound index file, you may have a number of indexes.) Tags are usually the same name as the field, although for complex indexes people use a variety of naming conventions. Unlike field names, here you are limited to 10 characters, so you sometimes need to be inventive to create a useful name for complicated indexes (for example, LASTFIRSTMI for a LASTNAME+FIRSTNAME+MIDINIT key).

TYPES OF INDEXES

Each index line has a combo box that gives you four choices for type of index, as described in Table 4.4.

TABLE 4.4 FOXPRO INDEX TYPES

INDEX TYPE	DESCRIPTION
Primary	A primary index does not permit duplicate values, following the rules of a relational database system. FoxPro will allow only one primary index per table.
Candidate	Any index you create as a Candidate type is a "candidate" to become a primary index. This index type has exactly the same properties as the primary index, except that you can have as many candidate indexes as you need. In practice, this type is not used frequently, because the requirement for uniqueness in field values is relatively rare except for primary keys.
Regular	This index doesn't do anything special; it simply orders the values in the index expression. Most of the indexes are of this type.
Unique	Indexes of this type contain only unique field values. This is not the same as the uniqueness enforced by primary or candidate indexes. A field with a unique key may still contain duplicates, but the duplicate values won't be in the index; it will contain only the first occurrence of the duplicated value. As you might suspect, this index type is not used very often.

INDEX EXPRESSIONS

An *index expression* is your instruction to FoxPro about which values are to be stored in the index for searching. Around 60 to 70 percent of all indexes use a single field as the index expression. If you index the CITY field, then CITY is the index expression and the values in that field become part of the index. If you use CITY+STATE as the index expression, then the contents of both fields will be stored in the index, presumably because you want to do lookups based on the combination of city and state. This is called a *compound index*, and it constitutes about 15 to 20 percent of all indexes.

You can also create *complex indexes*, which may contain a combination of fields and other FoxPro expressions, including functions. For example, perhaps you have a mailing routine that needs only the first three digits of the ZIP code. You can use an expression such as `SUBSTR(zip,1,3)`, and the function will extract the first three digits of the ZIP for the index. These more complex indexes may be used only 10 to 15 percent of the time, but they tend to be important.

Creating Indexes Using a Filter

The final option for FoxPro indexes, the **Filter** box, uses a logical expression to select which records are included in the index. For example, if you have a large table with more than 100,000 records and a STATUS field with two conditions ("A"=Active and "I"=Inactive), you might create two filtered indexes with this type of expression: `STATUS = "A"`. Switching index tags means that only those records that match the expression are in the index. This technique is somewhat faster than using SQL or any FoxPro commands, which must actually search an index or the table.

In your applications, you'll need to balance the gain in convenience or display speed against the general performance hit you'll take by having filtered indexes. (For one thing, they're slower to update.) In practice, filtered indexes aren't used much, except for very large and rather static tables. Most developers prefer using ad hoc filters, as in SQL.

Compound Indexes with Mixed Field Types

Most of the time you will create indexes using character fields, but there are times when other field types may be involved. (Remember that you can't index Memo or General fields.) As long as you are using single field indexes, this is no problem. Compound indexes with mixed field types, however, require special attention.

The most common of these are date and character indexes—for example, an index on a person's last name and date of birth. You can't create an index expression such as LASTNAME +BIRTHDATE, so one field type must be converted. Universally, conversions are to the character type, so in this example the date could be converted using the date-to-character function: `lastname+DTOC(birthdate)`.

When you complete the definition of indexes in the Index window, click the **OK** button. FoxPro will ask you whether you want to compare the rules against existing data and make structure changes permanent. This is a bit misleading, because creating an index in no way affects the data in the table. What you need to know, however, is that FoxPro is serious about checking existing values. If you specify a field as a Primary or Candidate key and if FoxPro finds duplicate values in it, you won't be allowed to create the index.

FoxPro is extremely flexible in its ability to create indexes, more so than almost any other database system. Although most applications use standard single field indexes, you should always consider some of the other index approaches. This is clearly one of those many instances in which you usually do standard things, but you need to know enough about other options so that you think of them when you need them.

CREATING INDEXES USING A COMMAND

Creating indexes in the Command window, especially for on-the-fly data manipulation, is common. If you can type at all quickly, entering the rather simple command is much easier than wending your way to the **Index** tab of the Table Designer. Traditionally, and in the current manuals, the FoxPro command is used to create indexes on any open table:

Command syntax:

INDEX ON eExpression TAG TagName [FOR lExpression] [ASC | DESC] [UNIQUE]

Arguments:

eExpression Index expression (single field, compound field, complex)

TagName Name of the index (tag)

FOR lExpression The "filter" clause

ASCENDING|DESCENDING Index order

UNIQUE Index containing unique values, not the same as a primary or candidate index

Examples:

(With a table open and selected.)

```
INDEX ON userid TAG userid DESCENDING
INDEX ON status TAG status_a FOR status = "A"
INDEX ON DTOS(indate)+status TAG datestat
```

Using SQL commands, you have two options: create indexes at the time the table is defined with **CREATE TABLE**, or add them later with **ALTER TABLE**. Both options have a complex syntax, which you should check out with the on-line help. Because they are cumbersome, they're often relegated to use in programming where the ability to define the index types is fully available. The commands look like this:

Command syntax:

CREATE TABLE TableName1 (FieldName1 FieldType <(nFieldWidth [, nPrecision])]

[PRIMARY KEY eExpression2 TAG TagName2 FOREIGN KEY eExpression4 TAG

TagName4

Arguments:

FieldName1 FieldType [(nFieldWidth [,nPrecision])] This is the format for specifying a field and its properties; see the following example.

PRIMARY KEY eExpression2 TAG TagName2 This argument applies to the whole table, where you supply the key expression and tag name.

FOREIGN KEY eExpression4 TAG TagName4 Creates a regular index for the table, where you provide the expression and tag name.

Example:

```
CREATE TABLE tempuser ( userid C(4),networkid C(8),;
   lastname C(35), firstname C(20), salary C(6,2)NULL ) ;
   PRIMARY KEY userid TAG userid;
   FOREIGN KEY networkid TAG networkid
```

If the table has already been created and is part of a database, you can use the **ALTER TABLE** command, which also happens to be one of the most versatile and important of the SQL additions to Visual FoxPro. Again, the syntax has been abbreviated to highlight the indexing options.

Command syntax:

ALTER TABLE TableName1

[ADD PRIMARY KEY eExpression3 TAG TagName2]

[ADD UNIQUE eExpression4 [TAG TagName3]]

[ADD FOREIGN KEY [eExpression5] TAG TagName4]

Arguments:

[ADD PRIMARY KEY eExpression3 TAG TagName2] Use this clause to create the primary key of a table, where you supply the index expression and the tag name.

[ADD UNIQUE eExpression4 [TAG TagName3]] As before, this clause creates a unique index with your index expression and tag name.

[ADD FOREIGN KEY [eExpression5] TAG TagName4] Similar to the preceding arguments, this creates a regular index with your index expression and tag name. It's also the one you're most likely to use for creating indexing on-the-fly in an application.

Examples:

```
ALTER TABLE users ADD PRIMARY KEY userid TAG userid
ALTER TABLE users ADD FOREIGN KEY networkid TAG networkid
```

When you're programming for applications, each approach has its uses. **CREATE TABLE** is used when a complete table definition (including indexes) is required. **ALTER TABLE** is ultimately the most flexible (as long as the table is attached to a database), and because it is a SQL command it represents—more or less—the trend for the future of FoxPro. **INDEX ON** is easier to remember and quicker to type. Guess which command gets used most often.

CREATING PERSISTENT RELATIONS

Once the data fields have been created and the indexes defined, the tables of a database are ready for relations. A relational database uses links between tables to allow distribution of information into many files. These links are created between one table (the source or parent table) and the index key of another table (the target or child table).

Once a relation has been established between tables, and provided there are matching values, you can draw on information from any field in the current record of a linked table. This is how you provide data to most of the forms, grids, reports, and other data processing in your applications.

Continuing the ongoing example, the USER table could be extended by assigning security clearances to each user. However, because a user might have from 1 to 20 (or more) clearances, it's fairly obvious that a second table, USER-SEC (shown in Table 4.5), would be a better place to store the repeated values.

TABLE 4.5 USER SECURITY TABLE

DATA ITEM	FIELD NAME	TYPE	WIDTH	KEY
User's Unique ID	USERID	C	4	Foreign
Dept. or Workgroup	GROUP	C	10	Regular
Access Security Level	ACCESS	N	1	
Activity Security Level	ACTIVITY	N	1	
Date Record Changed	RECDATE	D	8	
ID of Person Making Change	CHANGEID	C	4	

In this way, an unlimited number of clearances (by department or workgroup) could be assigned to a user. Each clearance would be accessible either through the user's unique ID, which is a foreign key of the new table, or through a combination of the user's ID and the workgroup, which is the primary key of the table. When the USERS table is linked to the USERSEC table via a relation between the USERIDs, all f the security clearances are available for display using a grid.

TEMPORARY VERSUS PERSISTENT RELATIONS

Visual FoxPro makes an awkward distinction between *temporary* and *persistent* relations. The distinction is important and needs to be fully explained.

In the FoxPro user interface (Command window and system menu) and especially in programming, when you open tables, set index orders, and establish relations between tables, you are making active connections. Specifically, as you move through records in the parent table, the relational link does a lookup in the child table and, if it finds a match, moves the record pointer in the child table to the matching record. The command, which will be covered extensively in Chapter 5, is as follows:

SET RELATION TO [field expression] INTO [table name/alias]

This statement creates what FoxPro calls a *temporary relation*.

A persistent relation also sets a link between tables, but it uses an index in the parent table connecting to an index in the child table, and link information is stored in the FoxPro database file (.DBC).

The most important difference between the two types of relations is the context in which the relationships become active. The persistent relations activate automatically when you're using the following: Query Designer, View Designer, Database Designer, Forms Data Environment, and Report Data Environment. Elsewhere—in the Command window and some programming—temporary relations must be used.

The two relation types do not overlap. If you are in the Database Designer and set a relation, it has no effect on the actual condition of the tables (whether or not they're open). Similarly, if you open tables and set relations in the Command window and then go to a report that has a defined Data Environment, FoxPro will ignore the currently open tables and their relations.

NOTE

If the two types of relations seem confusing, it's because they reflect rough edges between the FoxPro command language and the FoxPro SQL orientation. Here's a rule of thumb to help keep the two kinds of relations straight: if you're working in any kind of Designer (or something produced by a Designer), it's a persistent relation and will be used automatically. If you're working with the system menu, the Command window, and programming, it's a temporary relation and you must set the relations yourself. In practice, persistent relations are most helpful for interactive data management, because they show up automatically when you open tables and perform browses. However, from time to time in programming they can be a nuisance, because relations are set *sotto voce* and you may not realize what's happened. This subtlety can lead to some errors in data that are difficult to track.

SETTING PERSISTENT RELATIONS

Persistent relations are usually created visually in the Database Designer. To set a relation between tables, start by making sure that you can see the indexes for both tables (they're usually buried at the bottom of the field list). Then highlight the desired index in the parent table and drag it to the desired index in the target table. Figure 4.4 illustrates this operation. This procedure is somewhat different from the one you use to set relations in the Data Environment window, because it is from index to index rather than from a field to an index. If FoxPro accepts the link, you'll see the Edit Relationship dialog box (Figure 4.5).

FoxPro has already inserted the index expressions from each table, but there's a chance you might need to edit them. When you're finished with the Edit Relationship window, FoxPro will draw a line between the parent and the child table.

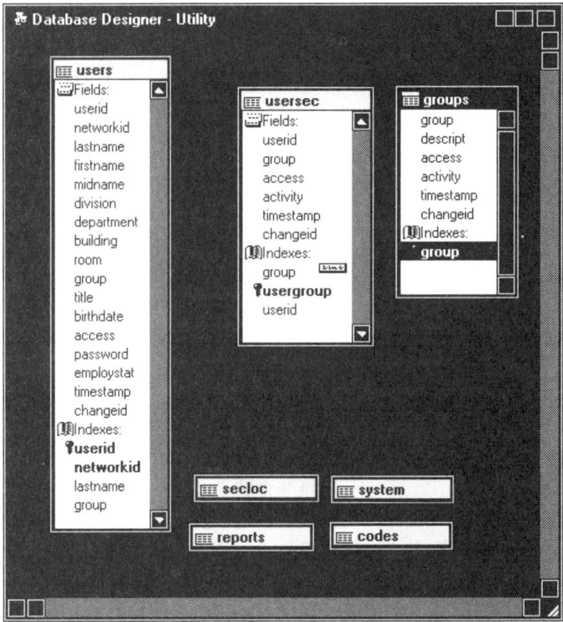

FIGURE 4.4 RELATIONS IN THE DATABASE DESIGNER.

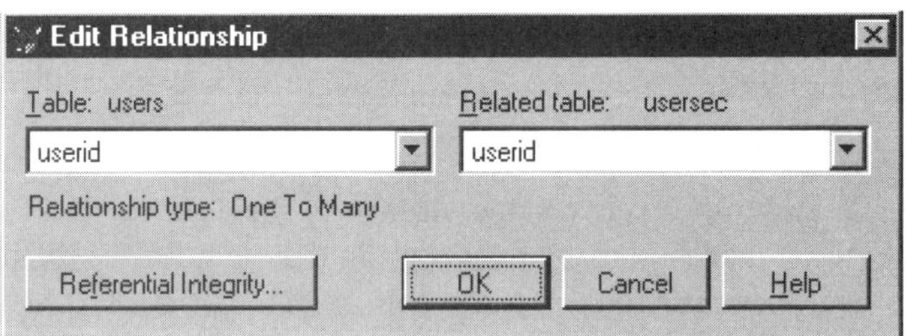

FIGURE 4.5 EDIT RELATIONSHIP DIALOG BOX.

NOTE

If the relationship is one-to-one (one record in the parent table to one record in the child table), the line will end in a single line. If the relationship is one-to-many, the line terminates at the child table with "crow's feet" (three lines). Incidentally, Visual FoxPro can be capricious about what it accepts for persistent links. Don't be surprised if some obvious relations fail or have to be done "backward," from child to parent and then changed in the Edit Relationship dialog box.

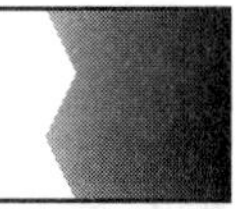

If you need to change the relations, simply double-click on the relationship line and the Edit Relationship window will open.

This visual presentation of a database schema (design) is not only easier to understand but also self-documenting. Anyone can tell at a glance which tables are involved in the database, which fields and indexes are available, and what the persistent relations are between the tables.

CREATING PERSISTENT RELATIONS USING A COMMAND

Persistent relations can be set through the **CREATE TABLE** command when a table is defined, or with the **ALTER TABLE** command. Because these relations are stored in the database file, a database must be open for the commands to work. Compared with the visual method, this technique is so clumsy that it's done only in programming—and then only rarely.

Example:

```
OPEN DATABASE utility
CREATE TABLE usersec (userid C(4),networkid C(8);
  FOREIGN KEY networkid TAG networkid ;
  REFERENCES bindery TAG networkid
```

Example:

```
OPEN DATABASE utility
ALTER TABLE usersec ;
  ADD FOREIGN KEY userid TAG userid ;
  REFERENCES users TAG userid
```

CHAPTER WRAP-UP

The first pieces of almost every application are the database and tables. The Database Designer and Table Designer are the two FoxPro tools you'll use most of the time to create and maintain databases and tables, although occasionally there will be places in programming where you'll use commands to create tables. (Databases aren't created on-the-fly, although with FoxPro it's possible.) Creating indexes is a normal part of establishing an application's database, but you'll find that indexes come and go during the development process. You'll create many indexes by using commands, both in the Command window and in programming. Relations are even more ad hoc, although now that Visual FoxPro supports persistent relations by storing them in the database, you can set some typical relational links ahead of time.

CHAPTER 5

USING DATABASE ELEMENTS

Chapter 4 breezed through the creation of databases, tables, indexes, and persistent relations, keeping in mind that the real work for this phase of data management is analysis and design (which will be covered in Chapters 14 and 15). This chapter focuses on the immediate data management concerns of a developer at work.

In a sense, the database and tables are just shells—containers—that have little meaning until you fill them with data and start the process of data manipulation and retrieval, steps two and three of the data management progression:

1. The database and tables are designed and created.
2. New data is entered into the tables.
3. Data is retrieved, edited, and maintained.
4. Data is retrieved for output and presentation.

FoxPro has a cornucopia of tools, especially commands, for this part of data management. Although some of the commands are suitable only for the programming environment, most of them are also valuable in the Command window, where you will do much of your routine data maintenance.

Database and Table Setup

Here's the picture: You've finished creating a database and some tables. However, because there's no data, it doesn't do much good to connect tables to forms or make reports; in fact, FoxPro will often behave strangely when tables are empty. So the next thing to do is to *populate* your tables, that is, enter some data. Typically you'll want enough data to see data in the forms and to test any data management routines, and that means entering from 10 to 100 records. Later, when you begin to stress test your application, you may need far more data than that.

To begin a session, you start Visual FoxPro as usual and then stare at the Command window. Now what? Open the appropriate databases and tables. In general, the sequence goes like this:

1. Set the working environment.
2. Open a database or table, usually setting indexes at the same time.
3. Open more tables as needed.
4. Set relations, if any.

As is typical for FoxPro, there are several ways to go about this sequence: through options in the system menu, by typing in the Command window, or by using the Data Sessions window. All three approaches will be covered, so you can try them and decide what works best for you. If you're learning the FoxPro language, using the Command window is most helpful, at least in the beginning.

Using the Command Window

In previous chapters you've seen a few examples that involved the Command window. Visual FoxPro is one of the few application development environments that still give you unfettered access to interactive, command-driven data management. You type in the commands, and FoxPro executes them immediately. Keep in mind that this process is not the same as programming, because you can't use loops or conditional structures, but it's a great way to test expressions and prototype data management routines.

Using the Command window is a lot like working in a standard text editor. **Cut**, **Paste**, **Find**, and other editing features are available. However, you can't clear the Command window, because every time you press **Enter** to execute a command, the window is redrawn and saves your previous command. This arrangement provides a useful history. Not only can you see where you've been, but you can also cut and paste to create a new command.

Make the Command window big enough, about 60 characters wide, so that you can enter typical commands without losing them. The window will scroll to the right if your commands exceed the window size, but you'll find it a nuisance not to see the beginning of a command. Many programmers use a continuation marker—a semicolon (;)—to continue a command on the ensuing line:

```
REPLACE ALL contact WITH customer.fullname ;
  FOR NOT EMPTY(customer.fullname) ;
  AND customer.enterdate > DTOC("11/01/92")
```

This technique has a couple of benefits: It keeps the entire command visible in the Command window, and it teaches you how to break up long commands (especially the SQL commands) so that they are more readable in your programming.

NOTE

If you don't like the Command window's default font or size, use the font picker in the menu (**Format**, **Font**) to select something else. In most cases, a *monospaced* font (all letters are the same size), such as Courier New or FoxFont, works best. Similarly, the colors used for text in the Command window (shared with the Program Editor) can be altered to suit your taste (or color blindness). The settings for text color are found in the menu under **Tools**, **Options** in the **Syntax Coloring** tab. It might be a good idea to become familiar with the FoxPro language before you fiddle very much with the colors.

THE SETUP SEQUENCE

From time to time during application development, you'll close the programming elements, such as the Form Designer, and start a data management session. Although there are many ways to do this, there is an informal sequence: Set the environment, open tables, and set relations.

SET THE WORKING ENVIRONMENT

Before you open any files, it's customary to set up a working environment or, more accurately, to check a few things so that you know your environment is appropriate for database work. Some of this setup is automatic; for example, if you're using the Project Manager (as you should be), the environment may already be open. Minimally, you should also inform FoxPro where the working files (in this case data related files), are located and, if your computer is on a network, you should be set to share files. We'll cover this topic, called *configuration*, in much more detail in Chapter 8, but the following items are needed from the beginning:

- Even though the Project Manager will track your files, for interactive sessions in the Command window you need to make sure that the data files are on the FoxPro path. This can be done a number of ways. Here's one that uses the menu: In the **Tools**, **Options**, **File Locations** tab, enter the **Default Directory** and **Search Path** or use the three-dot buttons to have FoxPro provide a directory picker dialog box.
- If you are on a network, use the **Tools**, **Options**, **Data** tab to uncheck (turn off) the **Open Exclusive** option. This makes all your files open in shared mode so that other people can access them. Normally, you should also turn on **Automatic File Locking**, **Buffering**, and **Multiple Record Locks** to enable FoxPro's multiuser locking capabilities.
- Also in the **Options**, **Data** tab, deselect **Ignore Deleted Records**, (you normally want to see all records) and **SET EXACT on** (so that searches with trailing spaces will still find a match).

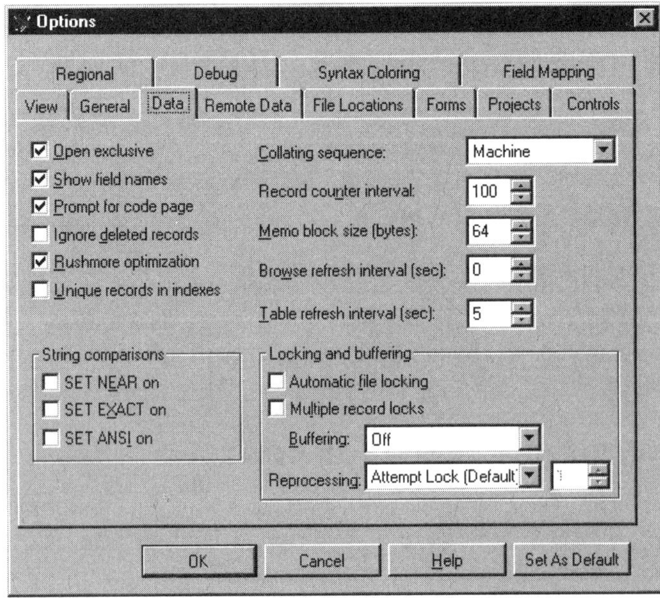

FIGURE 5.1 OPTIONS DIALOG BOX, DATA TAB.

OPENING DATABASES

When you open a data file that belongs to a database, FoxPro automatically opens the database file. Consequently, you'll rarely need to open a database explicitly. When you do, the best approach is through the Project Manager—double-click the desired file—and into the Database Designer. On a few occasions in programming you may need to open a database on command—for example with the SQL **ALTER TABLE** command, which requires that the database be opened exclusively. Here's the basic syntax for opening and closing a database file:

OPEN DATABASE [FileName| ?] [EXCLUSIVE]

CLOSE DATABASE [FileName] [ALL]

Arguments:

FileName| ? The name of the database file (DBC), or ? to open a file locate dialog box.

EXCLUSIVE Network only: Open a database so that no other user may access it. Typically done only for maintenance purposes.

Examples:

```
OPEN DATABASE ?
OPEN DATABASE utility
OPEN DATABASE utility EXCLUSIVE
CLOSE DATABASE utility
CLOSE DATABASE ALL
```

There are also times in programming when you may want to make a specific database active. This is technique similar to using **SELECT** for tables:

Standard toolbar: In the databases drop-down list, select the database.

Command syntax:

SET DATABASE TO [DatabaseName]

Example:

```
SET DATABASE TO utility
```

Opening Tables

When a table is opened, FoxPro establishes a space in memory to contain information about field names, indexes, and pointer status. This space is called a *work area*, which FoxPro numbers 1 through 32,754. (That's right—theoretically, you can open that many tables.) When you're opening several tables, each one must be assigned its own work area; otherwise, you'll wind up closing tables as you open new ones. This assignment is handled automatically in the Project Manager and the Data Session window, but with commands you must assign work areas explicitly.

Each work area has its own environment, including data buffering, index order, field lists, and data filters. These properties are all accessible in the Work Area Properties dialog box (Figure 5.2), which is reached from the menu (once a table is opened and you're in a Browse window) via **Table**, **Properties**. We'll refer to this window several times in this chapter.

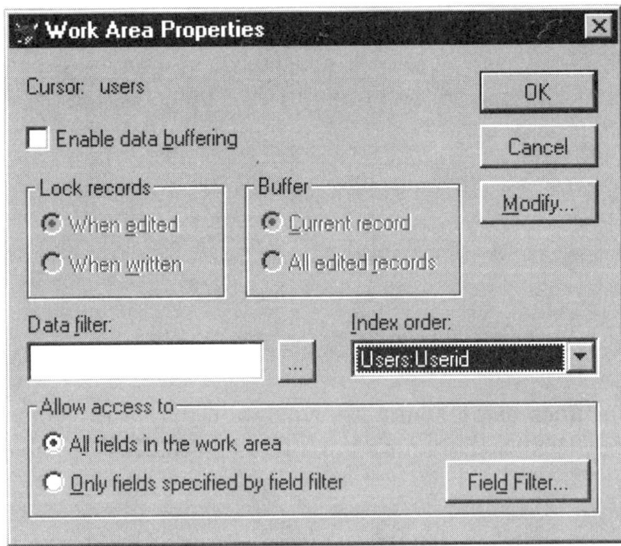

Figure 5.2 Work Area Properties dialog box.

Now we come to the main event: opening tables. For interactive work, there are three ways to open tables from the menu, but many people find the basic FoxPro command, **USE**, to be quick and direct. Here are the various approaches:

- System Menu: Select **File**, **Open**, and be sure to select **Tables (DBF)** in the File Open dialog box.
- Project Manager: From the **All** or **Data** tab, expand the **Tables** line and then double-click a table or use the **Browse** button. If you don't want a Browse window, this is not a good way to open a sequence of tables.
- Data Session window: In the menu, select **Window**, **Data Session window**. When the window is open, use the **Open** button to display the Open Table dialog box, where you can select the table.

Command syntax (selected):

USE [cTableName] [IN nWorkArea] [EXCLUSIVE]

USE cTableName

Arguments:

cTableName The name of the table to open. Keep in mind that you may need to include the entire path to the table or the name of the database (if one isn't already open). In general, FoxPro will open a file name faster than one with a lengthy path, provided that the file is on the path FoxPro searches.

IN nWorkArea The number of the work area to use, normally 0, or else the name or alias of the file.

EXCLUSIVE Network only: Open a table so that no other user may access it. A number of commands require this argument. Most of the time, files are opened in shared mode and then, when required, reopened in the **EXCLUSIVE** mode.

Examples:

```
USE users
*
USE users IN 0
* To close a table
SELECT user
USE
* On a network
SET EXCLUSIVE OFF
```

```
USE usersec IN 0 EXCLUSIVE
* Including the database, notice the ! separator.
USE utility!users IN 0
* Closing a table
SELECT user
USE
```

Several command options for the **USE** command should be highlighted: First and foremost, **USE** with no clauses (see the preceding example) will close any open table in the currently selected work area. This is the primary way to close tables. **IN 0** is used routinely to let FoxPro assign the next available work area to a table; **AGAIN** is a potent option that lets you open multiple copies of the same table—for example, one to browse and another one to do a search. Because there are many commands that reference a table name or alias, **ALIAS** is sometimes used to reduce the size of long table names. Aliases are required for tables that are opened with the **AGAIN** clause (if you don't use one, FoxPro will make one for you). Here are some examples:

```
USE customer IN 0
USE customer IN 0 AGAIN ALIAS cust
```

With **USE**, it's important to pay attention to whether or not the table's work area has been selected. For example, `USE customer IN 0` opens a CUSTOMER table in the next highest work area, but it does not select the table. What does this mean? For example, let's say you already had the PRODUCTS table open in work area 1 and then executed the **USE** command to open the CUSTOMER table. If you don't also switch the work areas, any other command you invoke will be executed on the PRODUCTS table and not the CUSTOMER table. This arrangement can lead to major, and sometimes insidious, errors. The solution is to use the **SELECT** command, which switches FoxPro from one work area to another.

Command syntax:

SELECT nWorkArea | cTableAlias

Arguments:

nWorkArea The number of a table's work area, or 0 to use the next lowest area.

cTableAlias The name of the table or its alternative name (alias).

Examples:

```
SELECT 0
USE customer
*
USE customer IN 0
SELECT customer
```

Because **SELECT** also helps to document which work area is in use, many programmers insert **SELECT** commands even when it's not strictly necessary.

SETTING AN INDEX ORDER

You can set the index order of a table at the time you open it or any time thereafter. It's a common practice in programming to change the index on-the-fly, and that makes it important to keep track of which index is currently active. Setting indexes from the menu is clumsy, so many people do it only from the Command window.

Command syntax:

USE cTableName ORDER nIndexNumber

Arguments:

ORDER nIndexNumber The tag name of the index or the number of the index (in the order you see them in the Index window).

Examples:

```
USE users   IN 0 ORDER userid
USE usersec IN 0 ORDER 1 ALIAS sec
```

Once a table is open, you can change the index order from the menu (two ways) or by using the **SET ORDER TO** command:

- System menu: Once the table is open and you are in a Browse or Edit window, select **Table**, **Properties**, **Index Order** and then the name of the index (tag).

- Data Session window: With the table open and selected in the Data Session window, use the **Properties** button and then **Index Order** to select the name of the index tag.

Command syntax:

SET ORDER TO TagName [IN cTableAlias]

Arguments:

TagName the index number or (more commonly) the tag name to be set.

IN cTableAlias specify a work area or alias for the index order to set.

Examples:

```
SELECT users
SET ORDER TO userid
```

or

```
SET ORDER TO userid IN users
SET ORDER TO birthdate IN users DESCENDING
```

A work area may have only one index order at a time, but each instance of a table opened multiple times with the **AGAIN** clause (each in its own work area) may have a different index order. The **IN** clause, which you will see with many commands, means that you can change the index order in a different work area without **SELECT**ing it. This approach can be convenient, and it saves a few CPU cycles by omitting commands. As a rule, the table alias—which is usually the same as the table's file name—is used instead of work area numbers, which are much harder to track.

You can use the **ASCENDING** and **DESCENDING** clauses of both the **USE** and the **SET ORDER** commands to change the direction of the index sort. Ascending goes from A to Z and descending from Z to A. For example: `USE customer IN 0 ORDER custid DESCENDING` or `SET ORDER TO custid ASCENDING`.

NOTE

Because FoxPro goes back several generations (versions), it carries a certain amount of baggage, including two types of index files. Unless you are dealing with older FoxPro or FoxBASE systems, the indexes you need to know are in the CDX (compound index) files. By default, FoxPro creates and maintains CDX indexes automatically, and there is no need to reference the index file (which has the same name as the table). The *Language Reference* and the *Developer's Guide* cover the other index types (IDX, compact) in detail.

SETTING TEMPORARY RELATIONS

The final step in this process of setting up a data management session is usually to establish the relations between tables. There are two places where you work interactively with relations: the Command window and the Data Session window.

Select **Window**, **Data Session**. In the Data Session window, follow these steps:

1. Open all the files in your database, each in its own work area, usually with the parent table in the first work area.
2. To set relations, select a parent table. Click the **Relations** button to start a link. Click on the table to be linked (the child table). This action displays a Set Index Order dialog box. Select the appropriate index in the child table and click **OK**.
3. The next dialog box you see is the Expression Builder. If the field to be used isn't already showing in the window, enter the linking field and click **OK**.
4. Repeat this process for each of the relations you need.

The result will look something like Figure 5.3.

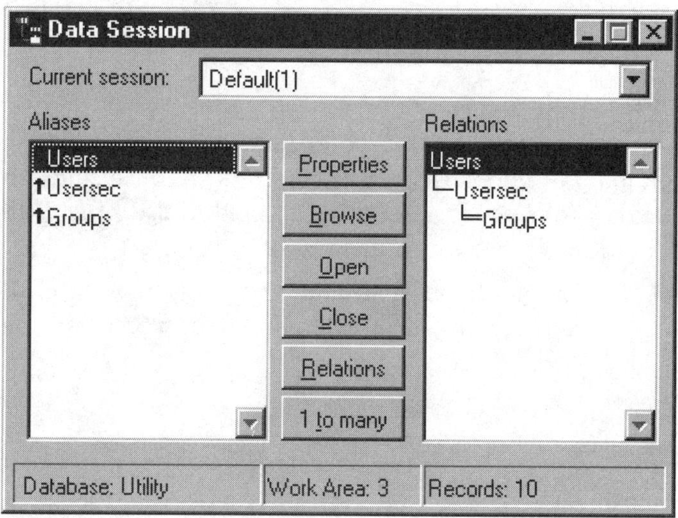

FIGURE 5.3 DATA SESSION WINDOW WITH RELATIONS SET.

To see exactly what a relation does, use the **Browse** button in the Data Session window to open a Browse window for both a parent and a child table. Then move the cursor in the parent Browse window and watch the records automatically change in the child table.

NOTE

From the Data Session window you can save the entire table configuration to a VUE file using **File**, **Save As** from the menu or **CREATE VIEW <path + file>** in the Command window: `CREATE VIEW C:\APPSDEMO\DBF\UTILITY.VUE`. At any time thereafter, you can open view files to re-create the configuration by using **File**, **Open** or **SET VIEW TO <path + file>** in the Command window. Because many steps are involved in opening files, indexes, and relations, view files can be great time-savers for interactive work. Incidentally, don't confuse view files with SQL views. They're not the same.

Setting Temporary Relations Using a Command

As you might recall from Chapter 4, FoxPro makes a distinction between persistent relations (stored in the database file) and temporary relations created with commands. In programming, the way to set temporary relations is with the **SET RELATION** command. Before this command can be used, both tables must be open, and the child table must be indexed on the key used in the relation.

Command syntax:

SET RELATION TO <index key expression> INTO cTableAlias [ADDITIVE]

SET RELATION OFF INTO cTableAlias

Arguments:

index key expression INTO cTableAlias The parent table's relational expression into the work area or table name (alias) of the child table. This is an index key (often a single field name), and **cTableAlias** is the name (or alias) of the table into which the relation is being set.

ADDITIVE If a table already has a relation, you must use this clause to set another one. Otherwise, any other relations will be closed.

Examples:

```
USE usersec IN 0 ORDER userid
USE users IN 0
SET RELATION TO userid INTO usersec
*
SET RELATION TO networkid INTO netdirs ADDITIVE
```

TYPES OF RELATIONS

Relations come in many varieties, but three are most important: one-to-many, many-to-many, and one-to-one. As illustrated in Figure 5.4, relation types are determined by examining both directions of the relation: table A to table B, and table B to table A. For example, the classic one-to-many relation is between a customer table and an invoice table. In the direction from customer to invoice, each customer may have none to many invoices. In the direction from invoice to customer, one invoice will have one (and only one) customer.

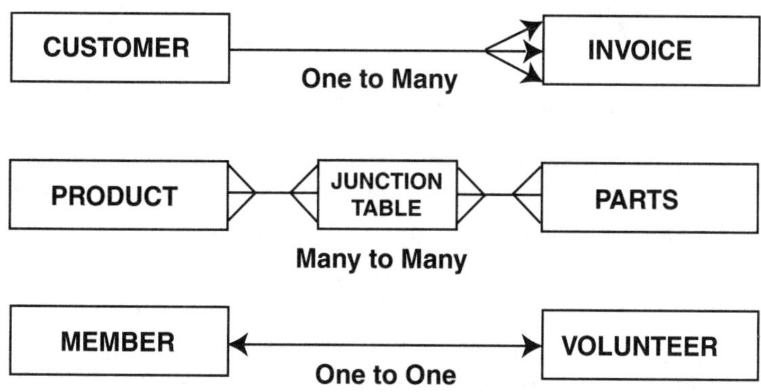

FIGURE 5.4 TYPES OF RELATIONS.

The one-to-many relation is by far the most common in data management. If you recall one of the rules for a relational database—repeating values belong in another table—you can understand why. However, one-to-many is not the default for temporary relationships in FoxPro. When you set a temporary relation, it is from one record in the parent table to the first match (one record, if any) in the child table. If you need a one-to-many relation, you create it with the **SET SKIP** command or in the Data Session window.

In the Data Session window create a relation between two tables, highlight the parent table, and click the **1-To-Many** button. In the 1-To-Many window, select the child table for the relation (you can select more than one).

Command syntax:
SET SKIP TO TableAlias1

Arguments:

TableAlias1 The names (or aliases) of child tables for the one-to-many relation.

Example:

```
USE users IN 0
USE usersec IN 0
SELECT users
SET RELATION TO userid INTO usersec
SET SKIP TO usersec
```

JUNCTION TABLES AND MANY-TO-MANY RELATIONS

Many-to-many relations are somewhat special. Examples based on real data are rare, but this type of relation is standard for junction tables. This needs some explanation. Consider two tables: PRODUCT and PARTS. Most products are made of many parts. Parts are often found in many products. If you link these two tables, what might happen to the uniqueness of each product or each part? For example, a product might contain two or three of the same part. How would you know which part (or product) is the "real" one? The solution is a third table, a *junction table* (see Figure 5.4). It contains an identifier (usually an ID field) for each part related to a product and for each product related to a part. In fact, it might be a two-field table. Keep this approach in mind for your own database designs.

ONE-TO-ONE RELATIONS

It may be hard to find an example of a one-to-one relation: one record in table A may match none or one record in table B, and one record in table B may match none or one record in table A. Here's one example: In a table of club members and a table of club members who are volunteers, a particular member can appear in each table only once. This sort of situation might not even require two tables. If all you need is to know whether a member is, or is not, a volunteer, then a single field in the MEMBER table would be enough. However, if a lot of specific data is collected about volunteering, you probably wouldn't clutter the member file with it and would create a VOLUNTEER table.

DATA ENTRY AND EDITING

When the relations have been set, you have completed the setup for a working session. Each open table that is linked by relations can now provide data from all its fields for your commands, including entering and editing data. This is not the sexiest part of data management, but it's important. Fortunately, data entry doesn't necessarily mean you sit at the keyboard typing for hours. In fact, typing is the last resort. It's obvious that most applications must provide for manual data entry—typically with forms—but many programs must also have ways to import data from other sources (usually through files) or may need to generate data with programming.

As a developer, you'll almost certainly need to load tables with data prior to the use of the application. I've mentioned test data, which all applications need. But as the delivery time nears, you may also become involved with conversion of existing data and the creation of system-related information (codes, descriptions). Both of these tasks may be problematic: Developing system data is often a minefield of policy issues, and as for data conversions—well, let's say every developer will have a story about a data conversion from hell. More on this later.

NOTE

It's a good idea to keep in mind two primary data management platitudes:

- If you haven't got it, you can't use it.
- Garbage in, garbage out.

If you don't have the fields, you probably can't enter or retrieve the information. Without data entry, however, empty fields are of no value. This leads to the second platitude, which indicates that throwing data willy-nilly into a database isn't necessarily a good thing. There is also a corollary: It's much easier to catch bad data before it goes in than to clean it later.

APPENDING NEW DATA

Entering new data starts with the ancient dBase command **APPEND**. This command is, or should be, strictly an interactive command. It can be executed through the menu. First you must have a table open and be in Browse mode:

View, **Browse** (or **Edit**). Then, in the Table menu, select **Append New Record**. Using the keyboard shortcut, **Ctrl-Y**, does the same thing.

Appending puts you into an Edit window and lets you add one record at a time to a table. Here's the command syntax:

Command syntax:

APPEND [BLANK]

Arguments:

BLANK Create a blank record.

Examples:

```
SELECT usersec
APPEND
*
APPEND BLANK
```

APPEND BLANK used to be the primary command for adding new records to a table with programming. However, this command has an important side effect: It locks the header of a table to update the count of records. During that time, the file is unavailable to all others. The amount of time lost is minuscule, but if you are adding hundreds of records sequentially, the impact would be noticeable.

One reason to use **APPEND BLANK** is in conjunction with the **SET CARRY** command. When this command is on, data will be copied from the fields of the previous record into a new record, and that can be a major time-saver if most of the data needs to be repeated. The command syntax is quite simple: **SET CARRY ON** and **SET CARRY OFF**. In the menu, you can use **Tools**, **Options**, **General** (tab), and click on or off the **Fill New Records with Current Values** button.

INSERT-SQL

For adding single records in programming, **INSERT-SQL** is preferred, not only because it's a SQL command but also because it executes faster than **APPEND**. Its drawback is the lengthy syntax if you specify many fields.

Command syntax:

INSERT INTO dbf_name [(fname1 [, fname2, ...])]
VALUES (eExpression1 [, eExpression2, ...])

INSERT INTO dbf_name FROM ARRAY ArrayName

INSERT INTO dbf_name FROM MEMVAR

Arguments:

dbf_name Specifies the table to insert into.

(fname1 [, fname2,]) Specifies the fields that will contain values. They must match the field names in the table, although the order does not matter.

VALUES (eExpression1 [, eExpression2, ...]) Specifies the values to be inserted into the fields. The eExpression1 entries indicate you can use any kind of valid FoxPro expression to provide the field values. The values must correctly match the field types.

FROM ARRAY ArrayName As a shortcut, you can use an array that contains values.

FROM MEMVAR Similar to the array clause but uses the field variables.

Examples:

```
cGroup    = "ACCTG"
cStaffid = "OPS"
INSERT INTO usersec ;
   (userid,group,access,activity,recdate,changeid);
   VALUES ("HRJ1", cGroup, 5, 3, DATE(), cStaffid)
*
SELECT user
SCATTER MEMVAR
m.userid = "HRJ1"
m.group  = cGroup
m.access = 5
INSERT INTO user FROM MEMVAR
```

The **INSERT..FROM MEMVAR** form is particularly useful for controlling the data entry. "Memvars" are a legacy from older versions of FoxPro and would be obsolete if it weren't for **INSERT..FROM MEMVAR**. They are memory variables created from fields and are preceded by **m.**—for example, **m.city**, **m.state**. It's helpful that the field name identifies what's in the variable. If you use the **SCATTER MEMVAR** command, FoxPro will create **m.** variables for an entire record and fill them with the values in the current record. This is exactly like using **SET CARRY**. On the other hand, if you use **SCATTER MEMVAR BLANK**, it's like the **APPEND BLANK** command, and you must assign values to the memory variables before issuing **INSERT..FROM MEMVAR**. The preceding example shows how this is done.

APPEND FROM

Whenever possible, most people prefer to import data from some other source instead of typing thousands of records by hand. This data might come from a mainframe computer or a simple data transfer from one DBF file to another. If the file format involved is DBF or one of the ASCII text files, then **APPEND FROM** may be the command of choice. It is available in the menu, but you must have a Browse window open and then use **Table**, **Append Records**.

Command syntax:

APPEND FROM FileName [FIELDS FieldList] [FOR lExpression] [TYPE] [DELIMITED]

Arguments:

FileName The name of the file to append from, if necessary with a complete path.

FIELDS FieldList Specifies a list of fields to be included in the transfer (for DBF files).

FOR lExpression Uses a logical expression for a selection criterion of which records to transfer (DBF files).

TYPE Specifies the type of file format (if not DBF).

[DELIMITED [WITH Delimiter|WITH BLANK|WITH TAB] These are the various options for handling ASCII text files. The **DELIMITED WITH Delimiter** clause allows you to use any delimiter.

Examples:

```
SELECT users
APPEND FROM newuser
*
```

```
APPEND FROM userlist.txt DELIMITED WITH ","
APPEND FROM userfee.xls TYPE XL5
*
APPEND FROM newuser FIELDS userid, lastname ;
  FOR newuser.state = "CA"
```

APPEND FROM assumes that you have selected the work area of a table that's ready to receive records. It also assumes that you know something about the structure of the file you are going to append from. You may recall from Chapter the recommendation to give identical fields in different files the same field name, data type, and width. **APPEND FROM** is one place where this practice will pay off. In transferring from DBF to DBF, if the field names, data type, and width are the same, the data will move without a hitch. If the fields don't match completely, some fields may not transfer at all, especially if they're the wrong data type, or they may be truncated because of different field widths. Such situations call for data conversion and programming, a topic that will be covered later.

Table 5.1 lists the types of file formats supported by FoxPro.

TABLE 5.1 SUPPORTED FILE FORMATS FOR ALL COMMANDS

FILE TYPE	COMMAND	SOURCE OF FILE
ASCII	A,C	Text file, fields separated by a comma
ASCII	A,C	Text file, fields separated by a tab
ASCII	A,C	Text file, fields separated by a space
DBF	A,C,E,I	Xbase Database File (FoxPro, dBase, Clipper)
DIF	A,C,E	Data Interchange Format (old spreadsheet programs)
FOX2X	C	FoxPro versions 2.0, 2.5, 2.6
FOXPLUS	C	Original FoxBASE+ format
FW2	A,I	Borland Framework II
MOD	A,C,E,I	Microsoft Multiplan v.4.01
PDOX	A,I	Borland Paradox v.3.5 and 4.0 (DB files)
RPD	A,I	Borland RapidFile v.1.2

(Continued...)

FILE TYPE	COMMAND	SOURCE OF FILE
SDF	A,C	Text file, in Standard Data File (row/column) format
SYLK	A,C,E,I	Symbolic Link format, used by old spreadsheet programs
WK1	A,C,E,I	Lotus 1-2-3 v.2x, spreadsheet files
WK3	A,I	Lotus 1-2-3 v.3x, spreadsheet files
WKS	A,C,E,I	Lotus 1-2-3 v. 1A, spreadsheet files
WR1	A,C,E,I	Lotus Symphony 1.2, spreadsheet files
WRK	A,C,E,I	Lotus Symphony 1.0, spreadsheet files
XL5	A,C,E,I	Microsoft Excel v. 5.0
XLS	A,C,E,I	Microsoft Excel

(I=Import, E=Export, A=Append From, C=Copy To)

Most of these file types are associated with a specific product and often have specialized file formats and content. The version number is also significant in most cases.

IMPORT

To make **APPEND FROM** work properly, you need to know the type, alignment, and order of data. This isn't always possible, especially with file formats of other programs. That's where the **IMPORT** command is most useful. It converts files by creating a new DBF based on the field information in the source file, provided it's one of the supported formats (see Table 5.1). You can perform this operation from the menu, where you can call up a File Import Wizard (helpful for ASCII imports). Use **File**, **Import** and pick your method.

Command syntax:

IMPORT FROM FileName [TYPE <type>]

Arguments:

FileName The name of the file to be imported. The DBF created will be the same name.

TYPE The file format of the imported file (see Table 5.1 for a description of options).

Example:

```
IMPORT FROM sales TYPE WK1
```

IMPORT does not provide you with amenities such as the ability to choose fields or a **FOR** clause to select data on a conditional basis. It merely converts data from one file format into the DBF format. You'll often need to do further manipulation on the file **IMPORT** creates and then use **APPEND FROM** (or its sibling **COPY TO**) to get the data into a final table.

FINDING AND EDITING DATA

At this point, we shift from entering new data to editing existing data. There is one guiding principle: You must find it before you can edit it. In other words, editing begins with locating one or more records. There are many ways to do this, the simplest being to open a table and Browse through it until you find what you want. But with tables containing more than 1,000 records, this kind of searching can become tedious and unreliable. That's when you switch to one of FoxPro's search and edit modes.

Essentially, there are two flavors (a la mode) for finding data to edit: *one record at a time* or a *set* of records. **GO**, **SEEK**, and **LOCATE** search one record at a time; **SET FILTER**, **BROWSE FOR**, and **SQL-VIEW** work with sets (groups) of records. All these commands may be used in an application, although **SQL-VIEW** will see the most duty because of its connection to Data Environments.

GETTING LOCATED IN A TABLE

Before going on to discuss finding data, let's review a little geography concerning positions within a table. FoxPro maintains a *record pointer* for every open table; it stores the record number of the currently active record. The record pointer has five basic positions that you need to recognize:

1. **Beginning of File (BOF)**
2. First Record of the Table

3. Other Records of the Table
4. Last Record of the Table
5. **End of File (EOF)**

The relationship between an index, a search, and the position of a record in a table is illustrated in Figure 5.5.

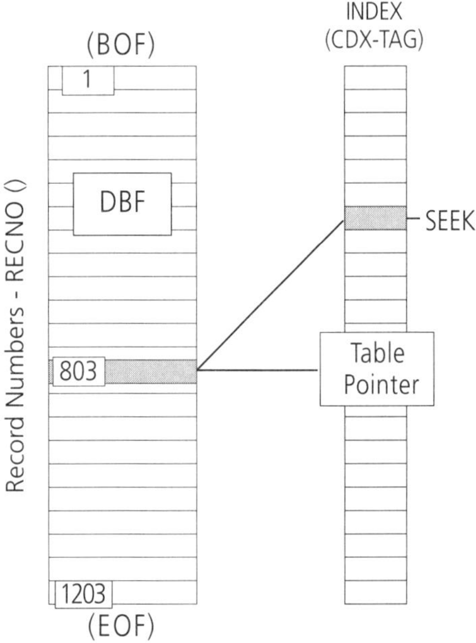

FIGURE 5.5 TABLES AND POINTERS.

There are two pointer positions that do not correspond to a record: Beginning of File and End of File. These positions are actually *beyond* the records of the table. Why? When you search for something in a table and it's found, the pointer is on the located record. What happens if nothing is found? The pointer can't be on a record. The solution uses **EOF**, the End of File position, which has the characteristics of an empty record. Although much less used, the **BOF** (Beginning of File) position exists for the same purpose. If you try to go beyond these positions with a command, you'll get an error message.

Most of the FoxPro table operations and search commands have specific behavior associated with the table pointer; Table 5.2 lists most of them.

TABLE 5.2 POINTER POSITIONS AT THE COMPLETION OF A COMMAND

COMMAND	POINTER POSITION AT COMPLETION
SEEK	Found: **RECNO**
	Not found: **EOF**
LOCATE	Found: **RECNO**
	Not found: **EOF**
INDEX, **REINDEX**	First Record
REPLACE ALL	**EOF**
DELETE / RECALL ALL	**EOF**
SUM, **AVERAGE** etc.	**EOF**
TOTAL	**EOF**
COPY TO	**EOF**

In many data processing routines, it's important to know how the record pointer behaves after a command so that the next command performs properly. It's too easy not to realize that with the pointer already set at EOF, another command may cause an error.

Go

The epitome of record-at-a-time searching is **GO**, which literally goes to a specific record number. (There is also an alternative, redundant command: **GOTO**.) Of course, you need know an appropriate record number, a significant assumption. **GO** is available in the menu: With a table open and in a Browse window, select **Table**, **Go to Record**, and then **Top**, **Bottom**, or **Record #**.

Command syntax:

GO nRecordNumber [IN cTableAlias]

GO TOP | BOTTOM

Arguments:

IN cTableAlias Specifies a work area or a table name to go to.

TOP|BOTTOM Goes to the first record or last record of a table. These options are frequently used in programming.

Examples:

```
SELECT users
GO 123
GO BOTTOM
GO TOP IN usersec
```

For the most part, **GO** is used only in programming with temporary record pointers. You might start at one record, do something, and then wish to return to the original record. It might look like this:

```
*Save the current record number to a pointer variable.
nPrevRecord = RECNO()
*Do something in the table, such as a search and edit, which *will
change the record number.
LOCATE FOR city = "Seattle"
EDIT
*When finished, go back to the original record.
GO nPrevRecord
```

Always keep in mind that record numbers are not permanent in FoxPro. Whenever records are added or deleted, the numbers are adjusted. This arrangement makes them unreliable for anything except short-term reference.

A closely related command to **GO** is **SKIP**, which moves one or more records forward or backward in a table.

Command syntax:

SKIP [nRecords] [IN cTableAlias]

Arguments:

nRecords The number of records to skip (forward, toward the bottom of the table). Using negative numbers moves the pointer backward (toward the top of the table).

Examples:

```
SKIP
SKIP -1
SKIP 100 IN users
```

NOTE

The minute record adjustments provided by **GO** and **SKIP** are characteristic of FoxPro's record-oriented data management. They're not available to purely SQL systems. I can't tell you how many times they're used in data manipulation routines, but they give you controls over record positioning, especially in loops, that are invaluable.

A Familiar Trio: For, While, Scope

Another aspect of positioning within a table is associated with three command clauses that appear with great regularity: **FOR**, **WHILE**, and **SCOPE**. The **FOR** clause has already been mentioned in connection with logical expressions. Its function is to provide the primary selection criteria for a command, indicating which records will be processed. When you specify a **FOR**, as in `LOCATE FOR city="Seattle"`, FoxPro begins at the first record in the table and searches forward until it finds a match or winds up at EOF.

WHILE has a similar purpose and uses similar logical expressions, but it begins at the current record and will continue to process only *while* the logical expression is still true. In practice, **WHILE** is typically used after a search.

SCOPE in FoxPro is another way of referring to the range of records to be processed by a command. It helps select which records a command will affect. Wherever it appears in the user interface, you can choose from several clauses, which are summarized in Table 5.3.

Table 5.3 SCOPE Clauses

Clause	Meaning
ALL	All records in the table.
NEXT <expN>	The next <number> records.
RECORD <expN>	A specific record.
REST	All records from the current record to the end of the table.

In general, scope clauses are not used very often, with the exception of **ALL**. The basic data management commands have a default scope of one record. That is a good thing, because many of these commands can do a lot of damage if unleashed prematurely on the entire table. It's common to practice with some of these commands by having them act on a harmless record in the current table or on a dummy table. When everything seems to be working, you turn on the **ALL** clause and let the command fly.

As for the other scope clauses, knowing exactly how many records to include with **NEXT** is often difficult. Working on an exact **RECORD** is a special case. **REST** is used occasionally with indexed searches when it is known that the rest of the table contains candidate records.

LOCATE

LOCATE is the generalist in the FoxPro record-by-record data searching business. With this command you can find a single record, with or without indexes and with any field type (except Memo and General).

Command syntax:

LOCATE FOR lExpression1 [Scope] [WHILE]

Optionally followed by: **CONTINUE**

Arguments:

lExpression1 The logical expression for selection of records to be searched.

Scope The specification of the scope of the search.

WHILE Used if the search begins from an already selected record.

CONTINUE This is a separate command used in conjunction with **LOCATE** to continue searching until the next match of the **FOR** criteria.

Examples:

```
SELECT users
LOCATE FOR birthdate < {12/31/50}
LOCATE FOR lastname = "Johnson"
*
LOCATE FOR UPPER(lastname) = "JOHNSON"
CONTINUE
```

LOCATE is available in the menu: With a table open and in a Browse window, select **Table**, **Go to Record**, **Locate**. The Locate Record dialog box (Figure 5.6) is very simple.

FIGURE 5.6 LOCATE RECORD DIALOG BOX.

It has only **Scope**, **For**, and **While**. The **For** clause is the workhorse where you specify a logical expression; it must contain one or more fields. FoxPro will check whether anything in the search expression can be linked to an existing index. If it can be, then all or part of the expression will be sent to the Rushmore processor. Otherwise, FoxPro will proceed to traverse the entire table from top to bottom, checking each record as it goes. This latter process, called a *sequential search*, is relatively slow. If your table is very large, it can take a lot of time (even hours).

SEEK

SEEK, and its function clone, **SEEK( )**, is one of the key commands in the arsenal of FoxPro data management. To master it, you need only the skills for building expressions and the knowledge that this is one of the most heavily used and fastest of all search commands in or out of programming. Note that it is not available from the system menu.

Command syntax:

SEEK eExpression [ORDER TagName] [IN cTableAlias]

SEEK(eExpression, cTableAlias), [TagName]

Arguments:

eExpression A valid FoxPro expression that produces a searchable value (and matches the field type of the current index key).

ORDER TagName Used to set the order of a table for this command.

IN cTableAlias Specifies the work area or table to be searched.

Examples:

```
SELECT users
SET ORDER TO city
SEEK "Seattle"
SET ORDER TO
*
SEEK 4 ORDER activity IN usersec
* As a function
IF SEEK("Seattle","USERS"), "CITY"
   ...
ENDIF
```

Unlike **LOCATE**, **SEEK** must be used with an indexed field. This means you must form an expression that will correctly fit the key of the index (tag) currently ordering the table, or the index you specify in the command. For example, if the index tag key is **LASTNAME**, then you need to form a character expression that can reasonably be matched in this key, e.g. "JOHNSON". **SEEK** can work with any legitimate key expression—numeric, character, date, logical, and compound keys.

A **SEEK** is always very fast, taking less than a second or two even in extremely large tables. That's the nature of an indexed search and explains why so much of FoxPro relies on it. If a **SEEK** finds a match for your expression, it is often the first record of a series, in which case you may want to open a Browse window to examine all the records. If the **SEEK** fails to find a match, the current record will be at EOF.

The function form, **SEEK( )**, is found mostly in programming, as in the preceding example, where you can use it to verify whether something was located. Both function and command are often used to do quick lookups in secondary tables, a task that is far less demanding of resources than maintaining a relation is.

EDITING

To edit data, the most common pattern is to open a table, execute a **LOCATE** or **SEEK** to get to a specific record, and then use one of the basic tools for interactive editing: **BROWSE** and **EDIT**. These commands can be used in applications, but from the programming and user interface point of view, it would be a giant step backward from grids and forms.

BROWSE

By now you've seen references to a Browse window at least a score of times. It seems that any kind of interactive data management automatically involves a browse. In fact, it usually does. If you're new to the Xbase tradition, *browse* may remind you of cows and horses. Well, it is a form of data grazing, and it's worth your time to become familiar with all the capabilities.

The Browse window is readily available (see Figure 5.7). From the Project Manager, select a table in the **Data** or **All** tab, and use the **Browse** button. (With the **Projects** option **Run Selected File** set on, double-click on a table in the **Data** or **All** tab.) In the Database Designer, double-click a table box or use the right-mouse shortcut menu to select **Browse**. Finally, with a table open and selected, you can use **View**, **Browse** in the menu.

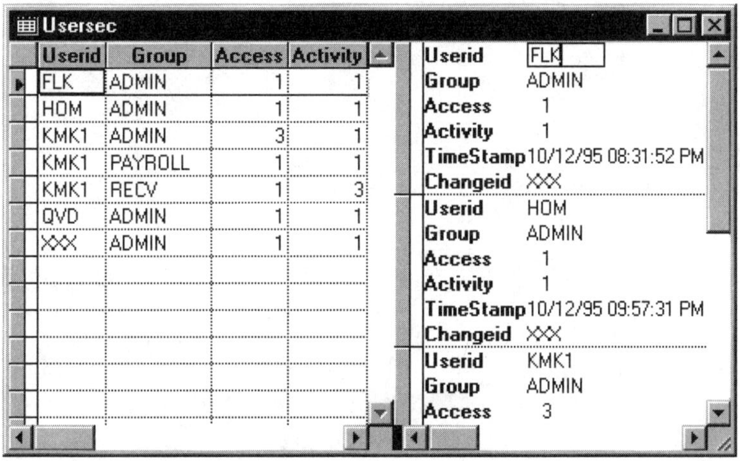

FIGURE 5.7 BROWSE WINDOW.

As illustrated in Figure 5.7, you can split (partition) windows and move and size fields to see the data in a way that's useful. You'll find yourself dropping out of a running program—or even while it's still running—to see what's happening to data. Either in the Command window or embedded within other programming, you can use one of the **BROWSE** forms to look for problems. Here's the command syntax most often used for interactive browsing:

Command syntax (selected):

BROWSE [LAST]

BROWSE [FOR lExpression1]

BROWSE [FIELDS FieldList] [FOR lExpression1]

BROWSE [FREEZE FieldName]

Arguments:

FIELDS FieldList A list of fields (separated by commas) to be displayed in the Browse window. Without a fields list, all fields will be displayed. The order of the fields in the list determines their order in the display.

FOR lExpression1 The standard **FOR** with logical expression to determine which records will be included in the Browse display.

FREEZE FieldName Locks the editing cursor in one field.

LAST Causes FoxPro to re-create the previous (last) configuration of the Browse window. This is the default for the system menu and Project Manager. To remove a previous configuration, start Browse without the **LAST** clause.

Examples:

```
BROWSE LAST
BROWSE FIELDS userid,lastname,firstname,midname ;
  FOR division = "LEGAL"
BROWSE FOR city = "New York" FREEZE zip
```

You may have noticed that the View menu contains an **Edit** option, which acts as a toggle with the **Browse** option. They're two faces of the same coin. **Browse** is the horizontal, multiple-record presentation, and **Edit** is the record-at-a-time, vertical format. You can also put the two formats into a window side by side.

WARNING

Because it is an open window on a table, a Browse lends itself to accidental data damage. As soon as you move from one field into another, data can be written to the table, and that makes it easy to introduce random errors. Your best defense is to be alert. If you make an entry error and don't know the original value, use the **Esc** key to cancel the browse without updating the table.

BROWSE can be configured to include fields from multiple tables. You can use either of two ways: Use the **FIELDS** clause to specify fields, or use the command

SET FIELDS TO, which specifies the available fields for *all* commands. The latter command, which can also be found in the menu (with all tables and a Browse window open, select **Table**, **Properties**, **Field Filter**), is not used very much. That's because it takes a while to set up, and it applies to all commands, thereby forcing you to turn it on and off.

By far the most important clause is **FOR**, which makes it possible to filter the visible records. As soon as your tables reach 1,000 or more records, you'll find that using conditional expressions with **FOR** is essential.

NOTE

The full syntax for the **BROWSE** command has 43 clauses and options! (If you think that's impressive, the grid has 93 such options—*properties*, *events*, and *methods* in the object-oriented programming jargon.) Although the Browse window is great for interactive data management, it's not an object-oriented tool and doesn't fit well in that environment.

TABLE AND DATABASE MAINTENANCE

It follows from the maxim, "Data, if left to itself, tends to degrade," that all databases need maintenance. Information needs to be updated, errors fixed, data deleted, and tables, indexes, and databases occasionally changed or even removed. All this is database maintenance or, more precisely, table maintenance. You will do some of the work interactively, as a developer. Most applications must provide some ability for the users to do maintenance.

The essence of good table maintenance is to let FoxPro do most of the work. Whereas editing is often done on a record-by-record basis, table maintenance attempts to make the computer do as much as possible with large numbers of records. Most of the commands involved, such as **REPLACE** and **DELETE**, are capable of working with an entire table.

NOTE

Table maintenance commands are used in program routines that are almost always *procedural*, meaning that commands are executed one after another until the processing is completed. There is usually little or no user intervention in these routines, and only a modest amount user interface is required. Data maintenance belongs to a facet of FoxPro applications—data processing—that is almost untouched by object-oriented programming, and for which you will need traditional programming skills.

WORKING WITH SETS OF DATA

The ability to edit a specific set of data is the specialty of the SQL view (Chapter 6), but you should also know that you can work with a set of data using a native FoxPro command. Whereas the SQL view must first execute a query and create a temporary table, the FoxPro command works directly on a table. When you need to process data under program control—for example, if you're updating a complex inventory scheme—this direct table access will execute much faster than the SQL approach.

SETTING A FILTER

You've already seen how you can use the **FOR** clause to select which records a particular command will affect. The **SET FILTER** command does the same thing except that it is a global command. All subsequent operations—whether **BROWSE**, **REPLACE**, or any other table-oriented command—will work only with records that have come through the filter. To create a filter in the menu, with all tables and a Browse window open, select **Table**, **Properties**, **Data Filter**. You can type a filter (logical) expression in the edit box, but it will probably be easier to use the three-dot button (...) to open the Expression Builder dialog box. This is another case in which typing the command language may be quicker.

Command syntax:

SET FILTER TO lExpression

Argument:

lExpression The logical expression that specifies the criteria for selection.

Examples:

```
USE users IN 0
SET FILTER TO state = "CA"
GO TOP
SET FILTER TO
```

You can set a separate filter for each open table. When you're using the command for processing, it's important to realize that the condition specified by **SET FILTER** isn't evaluated until the record pointer is moved in the table, and that is often accomplished by issuing the **GO TOP** command after setting a filter. A filter is cleared by the command **SET FILTER TO**.

MASS UPDATES

Nowhere is the power of a database manager more evident than when you're using commands for mass update. Instead of typing a price change in each record of 10,000 products in a PRODUCTS table, you instead type this command in FoxPro's Command window:

```
REPLACE ALL PRICE WITH PRICE*1.1
```

A few seconds later, the job is finished. The more experienced you become at maintaining data this way, the more you'll be on the lookout for ways to expedite the task with these time saving techniques. Never do manually what you can figure out how to do with FoxPro.

REPLACE

REPLACE is the most heavily used tool in data maintenance. Essentially, it does for table fields what **=** or **STORE** does for variables: load values. Here are some typical examples of its use:

- Updating fields, such as replacing a date field with the current date.
- Repairing or changing character fields, such as replacing a state field with all uppercase letters.
- Replacing one field with another, such as replacing a total field with the contents of that field plus the entry in a sales field.
- Replacing one field with the contents of a field in another table. This is based on a relation being set between the tables.

Here are the most common elements of syntax:

Command syntax:

REPLACE FieldName1 WITH eExpression1 [, FieldName2 WITH eExpression2
[Scope] [FOR lExpression1] [WHILE lExpression2]

Arguments:

FieldName1 The name of the field to be replaced (all fields must be in the same table).

eExpression1 Any valid FoxPro expression to supply the value to replace the value in the field. It must match the field type.

FieldName2 WITH eExpression2 A sequence of field replacements is allowed (see the following example). In fact, this is much preferred to issuing a series of **REPLACE** commands.

Scope Sets the scope to **ALL**, **RECORD n**, **NEXT n**, or **REST**.

lExpression1 The standard logical expression for the **FOR** clause.

lExpression2 A logical expression for the **WHILE** clause.

Examples:

```
REPLACE ALL indate WITH DATE()
*
USE users IN 0
REPLACE userid    WITH "00001",;
        networkid WITH "WILLY",;
        lastname  WITH "Williamson",;
        firstname WITH "Micheal"
*
REPLACE ALL lastname WITH UPPER(lastname);
  FOR NOT EMPTY(lastname)
*
dDate = DATE()
SELECT users
SET ORDER TO city
SEEK "San Francisco"
REPLACE REST city WITH "SAN FRANCISCO" ;
  WHILE city = "San Francisco"
```

You can also use **REPLACE** in the menu: With a table open and in a Browse window, select **Table**, **Replace Field**. As shown in Figure 5.8, start with the field list at top left and select a field to be replaced **WITH** something. Selecting the **With** button (three dots) brings up the Expression Builder, where you specify what should replace the field. You can also type something directly into the entry field. The three entry areas in the lower half of the window are the familiar **Scope**, **For**, and **While** options, which limit the records affected by **REPLACE**.

Getting the most from **REPLACE** is a matter of thinking creatively about how it can be brought to bear on a wide range of data manipulation tasks. Its effectiveness is limited only by your understanding of how to use expressions in the **WITH** and **FOR** clauses.

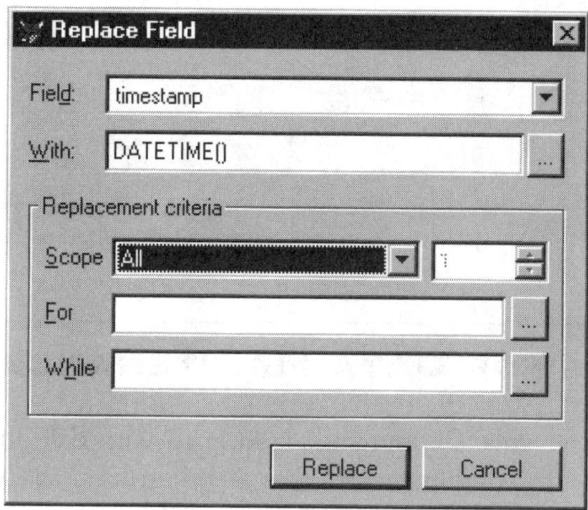

FIGURE 5.8 REPLACE FIELD DIALOG BOX.

UPDATE SQL

The **REPLACE** and **UPDATE-SQL** commands are largely redundant, at least for now. It has been hinted that **UPDATE-SQL** will be able to work with multiple tables in the future, but in the here and now, **REPLACE** is more versatile (having both **FOR** and **WHILE** clauses) and runs faster. Here's the basic syntax for the SQL version:

Command syntax:

UPDATE TableName SET Column1 = eExpression1 [, Column2 = eExpression2 ...]

WHERE FilterCondition1 [AND | OR FilterCondition2 ...]]

Arguments:

TableName Specifies the table to update and, optionally, the database.

Column1 = eExpression1 Specifies the list of columns (fields) and the expression that will be used to replace the field's value.

Column2 = eExpression2 A column list, separated by commas.

FilterCondition1 [AND|OR FilterCondition2 This has the same function as the **FOR** command: to set criteria for record selection in the update.

Examples:

```
UPDATE users SET userid = "0001",;
        lastname = "Williamson",;
        firstname = "John"
UPDATE utility!usersec SET activity = 1 ;
  WHERE activity = 0
```

Functions for Data Maintenance

Most of this chapter covers commands associated with data management, but you should also learn some functions that are often used in the same context. Most of these functions are informational; they tell you the status of something or give you information about the databases, tables, indexes, and relations. This list includes the more commonly used functions; others will be introduced when we cover network data management.

Database-Related Functions

DBC( )

Use this to see which database is currently selected. Returns the path and name.

DBUSED(cDatabaseName)

Given the name of a database, it returns .T. if it is open; otherwise it returns .F.

INDBC(cDatabaseObject, cType)

Returns .T. if the name of a database object, such as a table name, and the type of object (CONNECTION, FIELD, INDEX, TABLE, or VIEW) are in the current database.

Table-Related Functions

ALIAS( )

Returns the name (or alias) of the currently selected table.

DBF( )

Returns, the path and name of the currently selected table.

SELECT([0] [1] [cTableName])

Returns with the 0 argument, the number of the current work area; with 1, the highest available work area; with a table name, the work area of that table, if any.

USED(cTableName)

Given the name of a table or its alias, this returns true if it is currently open.

Index-Related Functions

KEY([nIndexOrder] [cTableAlias])

Used to get the index key expression from a given open table or index order number.

ORDER([cTableAlias])

Returns the active index tag name for the current workspace or a given table.

PRIMARY([nIndexOrder])

Used to find out whether an index is a primary type.

TAG(nTagNumber)

Returns the name of the tag for a given index order number.

(See also the following in on-line help: **CANDIDATE()**, **CDX()**, **DESCENDING()**, **FOR()**, **KEYMATCH()**, **TAGCOUNT()**, **TAGNO()**, and **UNIQUE()**.)

RELATIONAL FUNCTIONS

RELATION(nRelationNumber)

Used to get the relational expression for a relation. The argument requires a number based on the open relations, such as 1-4.

TARGET(nRelationNumber)

This function returns the table alias for the target of a relation. In combination with **RELATION()**, you have both pieces of information from the **SET RELATION <exp> TO <table>** command.

REMOVING RECORDS

Every database system must have a method for removing unwanted data. In Xbase systems, you delete records (one or more at a time), a process that marks them as deleted but does not physically remove them from a table. The deletion is completed only when you issue the **PACK** command, which runs through an entire table and removes deleted records forever. Until the time a **PACK** has been run, you can still retrieve deleted records by using the **RECALL** command.

DELETE AND RECALL

DELETE and **RECALL** could be called polar twins, because they are almost look-alikes in syntax but opposite in effect. **DELETE** marks records for deletion, and **RECALL** removes the marks. Both commands are available from the menu: With a table open, select **Table**, **Delete Records** or **Table**, **Recall Records**. To do the same things with commands, here's the syntax:

Command syntax:

DELETE [Scope] [FOR lExpression1] [WHILE lExpression2]

RECALL [Scope] [FOR lExpression1] [WHILE lExpression2]

Arguments:

Scope Sets the scope to **ALL**, **RECORD n**, **NEXT n**, or **REST**.

lExpression1 The logical expression to select records in the **FOR** clause.

lExpression2 The logical expression to select records for in the **WHILE** clause.

Examples:

```
SELECT users
DELETE ALL FOR indate > {12/31/89}
*oops
RECALL ALL FOR indate > {12/31/89}
```

NOTE

You can also efficiently delete and recall individual records in a Browse window by using the **Ctrl+T** key combination.

DELETE - SQL

DELETE - SQL is redundant with the FoxPro **DELETE** command, but, as in other cases, you may choose to standardize on the SQL approach.

Command syntax:

DELETE FROM TableName [WHERE FilterCondition1...]

Arguments:

TableName Specifies the table (and optionally the database) in which to delete.

FilterCondition1 Uses a logical expression in the same way you would with a **FOR** clause. You may add expressions using a Boolean **AND** or **OR**.

Examples:

```
DELETE FROM utility!users WHERE lastname = "JOHNSON"
```

PACK (TABLES AND DATABASES)

When you've decided that it's time to clean house and remove deleted records in a table or database, use one of the **PACK** commands. Scheduling of a **PACK** is an important part of maintaining active databases, because all files must be opened exclusively (only one user allowed), and, in the case of a database, all attached tables and views must also be closed. To execute a **PACK** from the menu, with a table selected, use **Table**, **Remove Deleted Records**. From the Database Designer, select a table and then use **Database**, **Remove Deleted Records** from the menu. For a database, while in the Database Designer, use **Database**, **Clean Up Database**. The command language is as simple as it gets:

Command syntax:

PACK and **PACK DATABASE**

Examples:

```
*For tables
USE usersec IN 0 EXCLUSIVE
PACK
*For databases
SET DATABASE TO utility
PACK DATABASE
```

ZAP

ZAP is a vicious little command (no syntax other than **ZAP**) that removes all the records in a table in about one second. The command requires exclusive use of a file. If you have **SET SAFETY ON** (FoxPro's protection against inadvertently deleting or zapping tables), you will be asked whether you really want to zap all records. The command is used when you want to reuse a table starting from scratch. This is a common occurrence during software testing and occasionally in data processing, where you may have scratch files for holding data that need to be quickly wiped clean of records.

VALIDATING A DATABASE

Because database files play an active role in FoxPro data management, their contents change frequently and so, too, do many of the objects about which the DBC file contains information. Not surprisingly, this information can get out of sync, for example when attached tables are moved to different folders but the location is not updated in the database. Visual FoxPro has provided an interactive tool, **VALIDATE DATABASE**, to check through all the components of a database and report out, and attempt to recover, any problems encountered. If you run **Clean Up Database** from the menu, it will also do a **VALIDATE DATABASE** as part of the routine.

Command syntax:

VALIDATE DATABASE [RECOVER] [TO PRINTER [PROMPT] | TO FILE FileName]

Arguments:

RECOVER Validation will use dialog boxes to let you correct table and index locations.

TO PRINTER [PROMPT]|TO FILE FileName Sends validation messages to the printer or to a file name (as a text file).

Examples:

```
OPEN DATABASE utility EXCLUSIVE
SET DATABASE TO utility
VALIDATE DATABASE
```

RESTRUCTURING DATABASES, TABLES, AND INDEXES

One of the most important benefits of the relational database design, and of FoxPro's approach to data management, is how easily you can modify tables and indexes. Most operations are simple and don't take very long, although working with very large tables (100,000 or more records) can still require considerable processing time.

MODIFYING, REBUILDING, AND REMOVING INDEXES

Although FoxPro has an extremely robust file system, from time to time power outages and other computer (or network) crashes may damage tables or indexes. Recovery from such a crash often requires nothing more than restoring files from a routine backup (which, of course, everyone has done). For a variety of reasons, however, it may be more expedient to rebuild or re-create indexes.

Keeping in mind that on a network all forms of rebuilding indexes require exclusive use of a table (and kicking everyone out of it), there are two ways to rebuild FoxPro indexes: **REINDEX**, or delete the index tag and execute an **INDEX ON** (or **ALTER TABLE**). The **REINDEX** approach is an all-or-nothing proposition, because it will rebuild every index in a compound index file (CDX). In small tables, this rebuilding is no problem, but with very large tables it could take many minutes or even hours. **INDEX ON** and **ALTER TABLE** work with one index at a time, giving you more options. These commands also are more thorough than **REINDEX**, which doesn't remove unused space from the CDX file.

You can access the **REINDEX** capability from a couple of places in FoxPro: With a table and Browse window open, use **Table**, **Rebuild Indexes** from the menu, or in the Database Designer, select the table and then **Database**, **Rebuild Table Indexes** in the menu. The command, with the appropriate table open, is simply **REINDEX**.

The alternative approach, re-creating the index, goes like this:

```
USE usersec IN 0 EXCLUSIVE
DELETE TAG fullnameINDEX ON lastname TAG lastname
```

The other available option uses **ALTER TABLE**:

Command syntax (selected):

ALTER TABLE TableName1 [DROP PRIMARY KEY] [DROP UNIQUE TAG TagName4]
[DROP FOREIGN KEY TAG TagName6]

Clauses and arguments:

DROP PRIMARY KEY Removes the table's primary index key.

DROP UNIQUE TAG TagName4 Removes the unique index named **TagName4**.

DROP FOREIGN KEY TAG TagName6] Deletes the foreign (regular) index.

Examples:

```
ALTER TABLE user DROP PRIMARY KEY ;
  DROP FOREIGN KEY TAG networkid
*You can execute both a drop index and add index in the same *ALTER
TABLE command:
ALTER TABLE newuser DROP FOREIGN KEY TAG fullname ;
   ADD FOREIGN KEY lastname TAG lastname
```

MODIFY DATABASE AND MODIFY STRUCTURE

Changes to a database or a table are most easily accomplished in their respective designers (for a database, *only* in the Database Designer). Typically, you would start in the Project Manager: Highlight a database name and click **Modify**. There is also a command, **MODIFY DATABASE [DatabaseName]**, that is very seldom used. Its one argument, **DatabaseName**, specifies the name of the database to be modified.

Don't count on the design of your tables being perfect. Even if they were, information requirements change over time, forcing changes in your tables. In any event, tables need to be restructured—dropping, adding, and redefining fields. Most of the time you'll do these modifications in the Table Designer. As usual, the table needs to be opened exclusively. Then go through the Project Manager, highlight the table, and click **Modify**. Alternatively, use the Database Designer. Select the table box and, from the right mouse shortcut menu, select **Modify**. **MODIFY STRUCTURE** is available as a command, and it's relatively quick to type:

```
USE usersec IN 0 EXCLUSIVE
MODIFY STRUCTURE
```

Some people will prefer the Command window approach. Within a program, however, the preferred approach is to use **SQL-ALTER TABLE**. This command has a lengthy syntax, which you can check out in the *Language Reference*. Here are a few examples:

```
ALTER TABLE usersec DROP COLUMN entrydate
ALTER TABLE user DROP PRIMARY KEY;
  DROP FOREIGN KEY TAG networkid
ALTER TABLE RENAME COLUMN chgdate TO datechg
```

REMOVING AND DELETING TABLES AND DATABASES

On occasion, you may need to remove tables from databases to make them free tables. This is the way you should handle moving a table from one database to another. From the Project Manager, select the table and then use the **Remove** button. From the Database Designer, select the table box and then **Database**, **Remove** from the menu. You can also use the **REMOVE TABLE** command.

Command syntax:

REMOVE TABLE TableName [DELETE]

Arguments:

TableName Name of the table to be removed.

DELETE Not only removes the table but also deletes it from the disk.

Examples:

```
REMOVE TABLE usersec
REMOVE TABLE newuser DELETE
```

As you can see in the preceding example, **REMOVE TABLE** can be used to delete a table attached to a database. Free tables are deleted with the **DELETE FILE** command.

Command syntax:

DELETE FILE [FileName | ?]

Argument:

FileName Specifies the name of the file to be deleted, complete with extension.

Example:

```
DELETE FILE newuser.dbf
```

WARNING

Deleting database tables from their folder with a standard Windows utility can be very bad for the database file (it goes out of sync). **REMOVE** the table from the database before deleting it, and, if possible, run **VALIDATE DATABASE**.

Command syntax:

DELETE DATABASE DatabaseName | ? [DELETETABLES]

Arguments:

DatabaseName Provides the name of the database to be deleted.

DELETETABLES This clause will cause FoxPro to delete all the tables associated with a database—use with caution!

Example:

```
DELETE DATABASE utility
```

THE MORGUE

As long as we're on the subject of deleting and removing, here are some data management commands that are still available in Visual FoxPro but are either obsolete, dangerous, or on their way out. Don't waste your time with any of them: **ACCEPT**, **INPUT**, **INSERT** (not the SQL command), **JOIN** (not related to SQL in any way), **SET DO HISTORY ON**, **UPDATE**, **CHANGE**, and **FIND**.

CLOSING DOWN

Last but not least, you need to gracefully exit your work session. Here are the standard commands. Take your pick:

CLOSE TABLES ALL Closes tables but not databases.

CLOSE DATABASES Closes all databases and their open tables, but not free tables.

CLEAR ALL Closes all databases and tables, and releases all variables.

QUIT Closes everything, including FoxPro.

PUTTING IT ALL TOGETHER

This chapter runs the gamut of FoxPro's database management capabilities. Just to prove that it all belongs together, here's a simulated (but not too far-fetched) database session that you could do in the Command window or in a short program.

The asterisks (*) are not for looks. They're comment markers that tell FoxPro that the text on that line isn't programming.

```
*We're on a network. Let other people use the files.
SET EXCLUSIVE OFF
*Home folder (directory) for this session.
SET PATH TO c:\demo\data
* Open a database
OPEN DATABASE utility

*----[Open a set of tables with indexes and relations
* Users table
USE users   IN 0 ORDER userid
* User's security clearances table
USE usersec IN 0 ORDER userid
* Set up a relation between two tables: users -> usersec
SELECT users
SET RELATION TO userid INTO usersec
* one-to-many
SET SKIP TO usersec
* Open for a separate browse in users.
USE users IN 0 ORDER userid AGAIN ALIAS user2
SELECT user2
BROWSE FIELDS lastname, firstname, userid, division

*----[Add some users from a paper list
APPEND IN users

*----[Add some new users from a table
```

```
* Their names are in a scratch table
SELECT users
APPEND FROM newuser FIELDS lastname, firstname, midname,;
  division, department, birthdate
* Check the appends for ok transfer, new employees only.
BROWSE LAST FOR EMPTY(employstat)

*——-[ Update new users with USERIDs
* Get the last userid assigned.
SELECT user2
SET ORDER TO userid
GO BOTTOM
* Assign the value to a variable
cUserID = user2.userid
* Return to users and start assigning new userids.
SELECT users
LOCATE ALL FOR EMPTY(employstat)
* Create a new ID (functions involved described later).
cUserID = ALLTRIM(STR(VAL(cUserID)+1))
REPLACE userid WITH cUserID
CONTINUE
* In Command window, scroll back and reuse commands for
* each new user.

*——-[ Finished, clean up
CLOSE DATABASES
```

Chapter Wrap-Up

There are enough commands in this chapter that you could make a career of using them. It's worth your time to experiment and look up some of the details of the syntax in the on-line help (or *Language Reference*). You've walked through almost the entire data management cycle—data entry, editing, maintenance, and retrieval—but the emphasis has been on maintenance. These commands and functions are the tools you'll need to create test data, build routines for data maintenance into applications, and manipulate data within programming. Whether you're diving out of a program that's hit a bug or you're crafting a data conversion program, you'll need to know how to conduct a complete data management session, including configuring your environment, opening tables and databases, setting index orders, and establishing relations. It's all here, but only practice and experience will make the procedures comfortable.

NOTE

This is a "big picture" sort of book, but having worked with FoxPro's data management capabilities for more than a decade, I know that some of the nuances make a big difference. I've tried to include subtleties, but there's no opportunity to give you the complete flavor of a real working session or to cover the quirks and gotchas. In addition to gaining your own experience, I highly recommend spending some time in the FoxPro Forum on CompuServe, reading the messages about bugs and other issues. As a reference book, Granor and Roche's *Hacker's Guide to Visual FoxPro* (Addison Wesley, 1996) has no peer for depth of details. If you want to cover the data basics in a more leisurely fashion—here comes a plug—I have written *Teach Yourself..Visual FoxPro 5.0* (MIS:Press, 1996).

CHAPTER 6

SQL AND THE QUERY AND VIEW DESIGNERS

Chapters 3 through 5 covered the part of FoxPro data management concerned with getting data into a database and maintaining it. Storing data is necessary, but the point of the exercise is to be able to look at the data: extract it, analyze it, and make reports from it. Now we come to the payoff—retrieving the data.

When you're considering this aspect of data management, think of it as a two-step process: the retrieval of data, which may or may not be visible to the user, and the display (output) of the data. For example, you might include in the programming of the application a SQL query that retrieves information from a number of tables and delivers it to a cursor. Then you use a report, created in the Report Designer, to display that information on paper.

FoxPro has so many ways to retrieve and present data, each with its own advantages, that it takes a while to learn which technique to use when:

- Query Designer
- View Designer
- Report Designer
- Label Designer
- Browse window
- OLE links
- Summarizing commands such as **CALCULATE** and **TOTAL**
- File Output commands such as **COPY TO**
- Simple listings with commands such as **DISPLAY**

Collectively, these methods will provide the data underpinning of many elements of the application framework. We'll cover most of them in the next two chapters, beginning with the SQL tools: the Query and View Designers and the associated command, **SELECT-SQL**.

The FoxPro Database Engine

Before having a look at the crown jewels of FoxPro database management—**SELECT-SQL** and SQL views—it's helpful to put the FoxPro approach into perspective with the world of database application development, namely client/server applications.

Client/server application development separates the *back end* (the database server) from the *front end* (the client application program). In general, these terms define separate classes of products. Yet Visual FoxPro, reflecting its PC heritage, combines one of the better database engines with some back end database capabilities and the capability of developing state-of-the-art client applications. It may seem that FoxPro sits somewhat uncomfortably between the industrial-strength database servers, such as Oracle, Sybase, or even Microsoft's own SQL Server, and client development software such as Sybase's PowerBuilder and Microsoft's Visual Basic.

There has been a trend for the past year or two for nearly all client application development programs to incorporate data management capability. There are two compelling reasons for this: Even when you're connecting to database servers, there is often a need for local (at the user's computer) manipulation of data; and second, not all applications require the power (or complexity) of a database server. To handle both situations, PowerBuilder, for example, incorporated the Watcom SQL database manager, and Visual Basic 3.0 added numerous database management commands with the Jet database engine from Microsoft Access. In the context of this trend, FoxPro's powerful database engine and the rich assortment of data management capabilities distinguish it, very favorably, from most other application development programs.

The Rushmore Technology

The program code for the FoxPro database engine has come from many sources. Much of the technology discussed in this chapter that deals with updating a SQL view was first developed for Microsoft Access. Similarly, another important part is the so-called Rushmore technology. (The name came from the Hitchcock movie *North by Northwest*, which was filmed at Mt. Rushmore—no pun originally intended.) This technology came from Fox Software before it was acquired by Microsoft.

The Rushmore technology is a battery of file management techniques—indexing, data compression, bitmap storage, query optimization, I/O management, and memory management—under one roof. The secret Microsoft consistently exploits is to avoid data management on the disk drives and to work instead in memory.

Computing in memory (RAM) is much faster than using disk drives, but RAM is not unlimited. You can't put massive databases (or even relatively small ones) entirely in RAM. Indexes are a different story. They're already more compact than the data file, and when a compression algorithm shrinks indexes to one-sixth of their original size (or smaller), many indexes can fit in memory space. That's where much of the speed comes from; the Rushmore technology *feeds* on indexes.

FoxPro does much of its data management using the indexed data and bitmapped images of the search results and goes to the actual database files on disk only when absolutely necessary. This is one of the core techniques. For example, when you specify a search value (`LOCATE ALL FOR product.type = "WIDGET"`), the "Widget" search value is transformed into a bitmap image. If "Widget" occurs in an indexed field, Rushmore will store a bitmap image of the index in RAM. If you follow the first query with a second, similar query, Rushmore will use the results of the first query and the bitmap of the index. This approach can have dramatic effects on the speed of successive retrievals.

The point is to build most of your queries one piece at a time and let Rushmore continue to create its bitmaps and figure out the best way to manipulate the search. Don't try to force Rushmore by setting indexes; you'll probably only make it work overtime. Actually, when you set an index, Rushmore must go back to the index file for a *non-ordered* bitmap image and construct a sorted list. This takes time. In all the FoxPro commands that use Rushmore—**SELECT-SQL** queries and those with **FOR** and **WHILE** clauses—you should avoid setting an index order before using them.

On the other hand, having appropriate indexes on hand will help Rushmore to optimize. That's because if Rushmore needs an index for a query but doesn't find one, it will create a temporary index. This is not a serious problem with small tables (less than 25,000 records), but for larger tables the wait to build an index can seem interminable. Although the query conditions for each table are different, a reasonable approach is to create single-field indexes to cover obvious search fields. Compound and complex indexes can also be used by Rushmore, but the rules governing their use are murky. Sometimes they work, and sometimes they don't.

RUSHMORE OPTIMIZATION

Rushmore loves to do its own thing with indexes, but for any search operation and especially for SQL queries, how does it choose which indexes to use (or create)? Selecting the best way to retrieve data is called *query optimization*.

Optimizers, the generic term for software that manages the query operation, are notoriously complex. Without going into the convolutions of how an optimizer works, its basic job is to determine which indexes and other resources are available, which logic should be applied, and how the search should be prepared. This task requires a heady mixture of search algorithms, RAM caching, bitmaps, and even artificial intelligence routines.

The Rushmore optimizer is a smart query cutter, but it's not infallible. For one thing, you can make it impossible for the optimizer to do its job. This is what Microsoft means when it says you must build "optimizable" queries. The prescribed format for an optimizable query looks familiar:

<index expression> <relational operator> <constant expression>

Example:

```
FIRSTNAME =                    "Mark"
```

This simple example contains the classic format. In this case, FIRSTNAME is a key field (all or the first part of an index key). Rushmore must find an index expression in the table that matches the query index expression. If it doesn't, it may decide to build an index. With character expressions, it must compare index keys against the **<constant expression>** values on a character-by-character basis, moving from left to right. If it had to search long concatenated keys, its speed would be drastically cut. This is also why you can't use the substring search operator, **$**, in an optimizable query.

The best queries are those that don't vary much from the classic format. Try to make the index expression match single-expression index keys. And keep your constant expressions simple. Although you can use functions that result in a constant expression, they take extra processing time.

NOTE

When you begin to program in FoxPro, you'll discover that nothing beats the speed of a direct **SEEK** into a table. Coupled with a **SCAN/ENDSCAN** loop, it also works well for retrieving a small set of data for an item of known value. For general data retrieval, you're better off exploiting Rushmore, especially using the Query and View Designers and the **SELECT-SQL** capacity.

APPLICATIONS AND SQL

Did you know that magazines publish SQL brain teasers, and people make a hobby of creating weird SQL constructions? That's because SQL can be fiendishly complex, subtle, and powerful—all at the same time. So, you might ask, if SQL and FoxPro's Query and View Designers are not the easiest tools for retrieving data, why are they included? This question is not rhetorical. Until 1990, they *weren't* included, and it's a legitimate question to wonder what's so special about SQL that FoxPro would choose to add it to the already bulging retrieval toolkit.

One reason (not necessarily the most important reason for everyone) is the capability of SQL to work with many different kinds of relational databases on many different kinds of computers. SQL evolved from an academic experiment with relational database theory into the common language of the database management industry. Put another way, SQL is everywhere. It has become standardized—shoehorned into almost every conceivable database product—and it's almost the only way to query relational databases that reside on different kinds of computers. By joining the SQL movement, FoxPro has rightly positioned itself to work with other relational systems, especially for client/server database management.

But that's not all SQL offers. It is a compact format for doing an enormous amount of database work, and it provided FoxPro with the opportunity to show off the Rushmore database engine, especially the query optimizer. Finally, either as a language or in the designers, SQL is a *database* tool. It's at its best when retrieving data from more than one table or even multiple databases.

Incorporating SQL data retrieval in your applications breaks down into those elements that may be visible to the user, such as the Query and View Designers, and those that are kept more or less invisible. The question becomes, how much SQL should be made available to the user? Here are two points to keep in mind:

- The Query and View Designers are not beginner-friendly. You would never unleash them on the average user in a crucial part of your application.
- If you plan to distribute your applications as self-running executable (EXE) files, you can't use the Query and View Designers. The designers are available strictly for interactive FoxPro and must be accompanied by a full copy of the program.

For these reasons, most developers shy away from presenting SQL to the end user of an application. Instead, it is used internally, often in the programming language format, or integrated with various user interface objects such as forms and reports. Many developers create, or buy, SQL query modules that put a friendly face on SQL. This type of module is very much part of an application framework, because it's a component that can be developed as a separate entity, tested, and then incorporated in any application that needs it.

Learning SQL with the Query Designer

The Query and View Designers are very similar. They use the same basic screen, and both of them use the same approach, creating a **SELECT-SQL** query to retrieve data. The similarity ends abruptly at the point where data is retrieved: a view allows data editing and can update the original tables, whereas a query is read-only and specializes in providing data for various methods of display (graphs, cross tabs, and so on).

A bit later in the chapter, I'll explain the differences between the two designers, but for an example we'll go through the development of a SQL query using the Query Designer. Actually, the emphasis of this chapter should not be on the designers, but instead on learning how to use **SELECT-SQL** directly. There are two good reasons: You need to understand the underlying command to make the designers work properly, and there are things you can do with the command that can't be done in the designers.

THE PARTS OF A QUERY

You've already seen how SQL commands can be used to do various kinds of database management tasks such as creating a table or deleting records. But first and foremost, SQL is what its name implies: a query language. It retrieves information from tables by formulating a query. The query, or more accurately the query statement, begins with the command **SELECT** and is followed by options from the rather formidable syntax.

Command syntax:

```
SELECT [ALL | DISTINCT] [TOP nExpr [PERCENT]]
    [Alias.] Select_Item [AS Column_Name]
    [, [Alias.] Select_Item [AS Column_Name] ...]
FROM [FORCE]
[DatabaseName!]Table [Local_Alias]
    [[INNER | LEFT [OUTER] | RIGHT [OUTER] | FULL [OUTER] JOIN
        DatabaseName!]Table [Local_Alias]
[ON JoinCondition]
[[INTO Destination]
    | [TO FILE FileName [ADDITIVE] | TO PRINTER [PROMPT]
    | TO SCREEN]]
[PREFERENCE PreferenceName]
[NOCONSOLE]
[PLAIN]
[NOWAIT]
[WHERE JoinCondition [AND JoinCondition ...]
    [AND | OR FilterCondition [AND | OR FilterCondition ...]]]
[GROUP BY GroupColumn [, GroupColumn ...]]
[HAVING FilterCondition]
```

[UNION [ALL] SELECTCommand]

[ORDER BY Order_Item [ASC | DESC] [, Order_Item [ASC | DESC] ...]]

```
SELECT usr.userid,usr.lastname,usc.activity,usc.access ;
  FROM user usr INNER JOIN usersec usc ;
   ON usr.userid = usc.userid ;
  WHERE usr.birthdate > {12/31/50};
GROUP BY usr.lastname ;
  HAVING COUNT(usr.lastname) > 2 ;
ORDER BY usr.lastname ;
INTO CURSOR tempname
```

Rather than explain all the clauses, let's stick with the essentials, which, believe it or not, can be expressed in (relatively) plain English: "Select a list of fields from the specified tables, where certain conditions are true. Then group the results of this selection by the values in certain fields, and select from these groups all records having met certain conditions. Then sort the final results and send them to the specified output destination."

If that is the basic description of a SQL query, here's a typical request for information: "Send the following information: a list of all the people in the company (please include the employee's last name, security group, and birth date) who have security clearances at or above level 4, showing how many in each security group are older than 57. Please sort by employee last name, and have the printed report on JR's desk by 8:30 AM."

This translates, roughly, into the following SQL query:

```
SELECT users.lastname, users.group, users.birthdate ;
 FROM utility!users INNER JOIN utility!usersec ;
  ON users.userid = usersec.userid ;
 WHERE usersec.access >= 4 ;
 GROUP BY users.group ;
  HAVING MIN(users.birthdate) < CTOD("01/01/40");
 ORDER BY users.lastname ;
 INTO TABLE secage.dbf
```

Some of this may look familiar from your work with FoxPro expressions, but the terminology may seem complex. Reduced to a basic format and rearranged a tad, this is the essential syntax:

```
SELECT <field list> ;
 FROM <table list> ;
 WHERE <join condition> ;
 GROUP BY <group field> ;
 HAVING <filter condition> ;
 ORDER BY <order item>
 INTO <output option> ;
```

This command language corresponds to seven steps for creating a query in the Query or View Designer:

1. **<Field list>** Select the fields to be output.
2. **FROM** Select the tables and the method for linking (joining) them.
3. **WHERE** Set the primary selection criteria.
4. **GROUP BY** Set any groups.
5. **HAVING** Set any secondary selection criteria based on the groups.
6. **ORDER BY** Set a sort order for the final output.
7. **INTO** Determine where the output should go.

We'll review the steps briefly and then demonstrate them in the Query Designer along with the underlying SQL statements.

Step 1: Select the fields to be output. This serves the same purpose as the **FIELDS** option in many FoxPro commands. You can select fields from the primary or any joined tables, and a number of calculated fields (Sum, Average) can also be included. You must select at least one field for output, or the query will not work.

Step 2: Select the tables from which to retrieve the information and the method for joining them. To start your query, all you need to do is to open a table. This first table is often called the *primary*, or *parent*, table, as seems appropriate for a system based on relational databases. However, what in FoxPro is a relation is called a *join* in SQL. The join performs like a FoxPro relation, but it's not created the same way. In the Query Designer, you open a table to add to the query, and FoxPro immediately asks you for a *join type*. The types are Inner, Right Outer, Left Outer, and Full. They're new with this version of Visual

FoxPro, although they've been part of the SQL specification for some time. Once you get over the strange terminology, you'll see that this is a major improvement.

NOTE

Although the Query Designer is great for working with multiple tables, you are not required to specify any joins. In some queries, only the primary table is used.

Step 3: Set the primary selection criteria. Criteria do not need to be based on fields, but typically they are the familiar `STATE="CA"` type of expression. If you've been practicing your logical expressions, you'll find that this part of using SQL is an extension of what you've been learning. Selection criteria are optional.

Step 4: Set any groups. This optional step works on all the records retrieved through the joins and selection criteria. A *group* is any repetitive pattern in the contents of a field. For example, in a STATE field the records for each state are grouped.

Step 5: Set any secondary selection criteria based on the groups. This step allows you to specify selection criteria to be applied to the groups you've defined. These criteria look exactly like the join expressions, because they must be based on the fields used for the groups.

Step 6: Set a sort order for the final output. You can use any (or even all) of the fields selected for output to specify a sort order for the records selected by the query. This is particularly useful when you're preparing output for reports. This step is optional.

Step 7: Determine where the output should go. By default, FoxPro sends query output to a Browse window. Other options include sending output to a report or label, a table (DBF), a screen (form), a chart (through the Chart Wizard), a cross tab, an array, or a cursor. The last two are primarily for programming.

Working in the Query Designer

To begin a query or a view, it's highly recommended (virtually mandatory) to start from the Project Manager. You'll find that accessing views is difficult any other way. In the **Data** tab of the Project Manager, expand until you can see the **Queries** line, and then select the **New** button.

The small New Query dialog box appears, giving you the option of using a

wizard or going directly to the Query Designer. FoxPro provides several wizards to get a query started, but they have important limitations that will be covered later in this chapter, so in this case choose **New Query**. FoxPro presents the Add Table or View dialog box for you to select the primary table for the query and then moves on to the Query Designer window.

The areas of the screen, illustrated in Figure 6.1, reflect the format of the **SELECT** command. Although the Query Designer interface hides the command language, FoxPro has provided a window where you can see the SQL statement as you build a query. Just click the **SQL** button in the Query Designer toolbar. You can't edit the statement in this window, but you can copy it and use it elsewhere in your code. Many developers use the Query Designer to start or prototype more complicated **SELECT** statements.

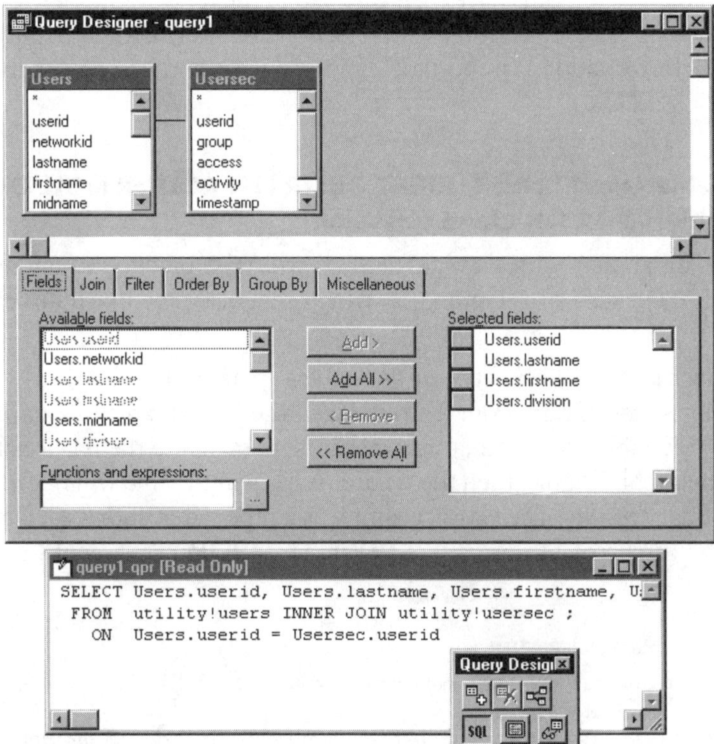

FIGURE 6.1 THE QUERY DESIGNER AND SQL.

Whenever you open or create a query, the **Query** menu option will appear in the menu. This option repeats everything that's available through the Query toolbar or buttons in the Query Designer window. The exception is the **Comment** option, which gives you a way to document the goals and strategy of your query.

STEP 1: TABLE SELECTION

The best approach is not to do any setup outside the designers and to **Add** tables as needed. The first table, which must be selected when you start, is the parent table from which joins (relations to child tables) are created.

JOINS

In Visual FoxPro 5.0, joins have their own tab in the Query and View Designers. They used to be lumped together with selection criteria (**Filter** tab), but that was before Microsoft added important new syntax—and great capability—to FoxPro's SQL **SELECT**:

FROM cTableName1 [INNER | RIGHT OUTER | LEFT OUTER | FULL OUTER] JOIN cTableName2 ON cJoinExpression

If you are unfamiliar with this language, it will take practice to understand it completely. Let's start with Figure 6.2, which schematically illustrates each type of join.

An *inner join* is a link between two tables (parent and child) in which the query returns results only from the records in the parent table that have matches in the child table. Put another way, if there's no match to the relational lookup in the joined (child) table, then the record in the parent table will not be included in the query results. The classic example is a report that shows each customer who made purchases in the previous year. The **FROM** clause looks something like this:

```
FROM customer INNER JOIN purchase ;
  ON customer.customerID = purchase.customerID
```

What about a report that shows customers who both did and *did not* purchase in the previous year—in other words, a list of all customers with perhaps a summary total of their purchases? In previous versions of FoxPro, this kind of query was possible but required a complicated query using the **UNION** clause. Now you can use the *left outer join*. A query with this type of join returns *all* the records in the parent table as well as data from the fields that match in the child table. The **FROM** clause would look like this:

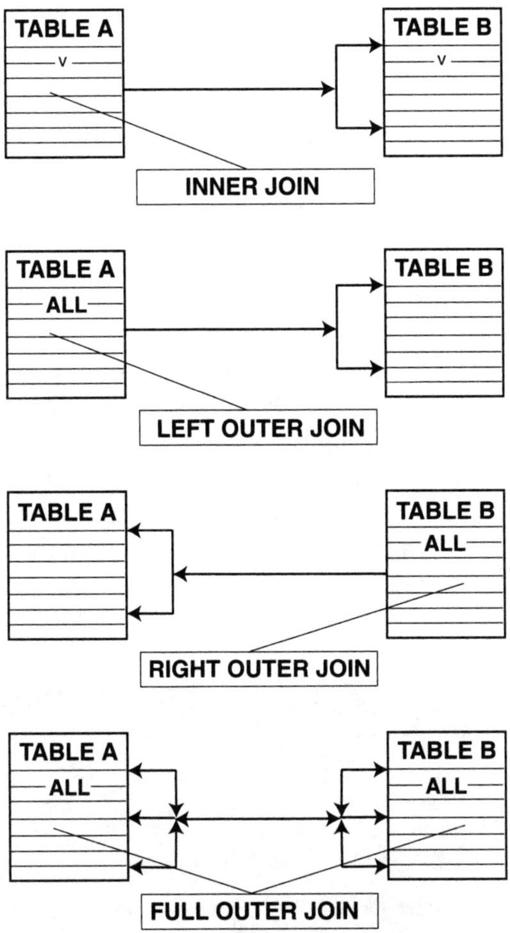

FIGURE 6.2 JOIN TYPES.

```
FROM customer LEFT OUTER JOIN purchase ;
  ON customer.customerID = purchase.customerID
```

Occasionally, you might also want a report that shows all the purchases along with some data from the customer table. This query would use a *right outer join*, which returns all the records of the child table plus matching information from the parent table. The basic clause looks like this:

```
FROM customer RIGHT OUTER JOIN purchase ;
  ON customer.customerID = purchase.customerID
```

Finally, there may be a time when you'll want records from both parent and child tables, even if it means, in effect, a cross product—records that match both ways—and potentially a huge number of records. This is a *full outer join*:

```
FROM customer FULL OUTER JOIN purchase ;
  ON customer.customerID = purchase.customerID
```

As you can see from the syntax, writing the joins is easy. Understanding when to use which type, and knowing the effects of stringing together more than one join, can require some serious noodling. We'll deal with many of the wrinkles in the chapter on advanced SQL and reporting (Chapter 20).

Joins are created in the designers starting from a number of places: choosing **Add** from the right-mouse shortcut menu, the Query toolbar, or the menu. The Add Table dialog box appears so that you can select tables. As you add more than one table, if FoxPro finds a persistent relation defined in the database file or an appropriately matching index, it will automatically suggest a join type and expression and will display it in the Join Condition window shown in Figure 6.3.

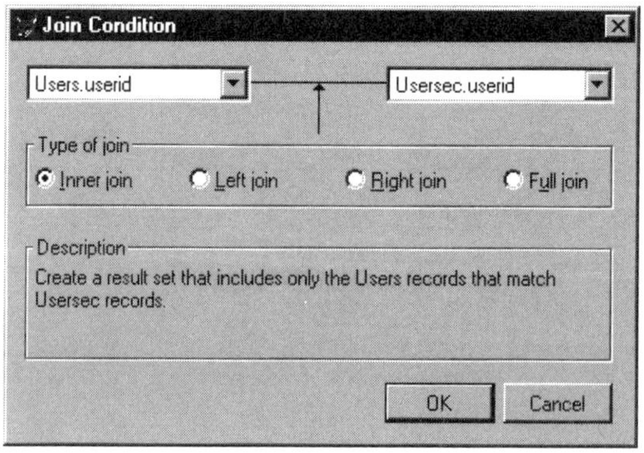

FIGURE 6.3 THE JOIN CONDITION WINDOW.

In this window are specified the field in the parent table, the linking operator, and the linking field name in the child table. This is the **ON** expression. You should note that the operators of the join distinguish SQL from the familiar **SET RELATION**. A standard FoxPro relation is based on a match (equality) between keys, called an *equi-join*, but in SQL you may use several other relational operators, which are expressed by an English equivalent, as shown in Table 6.1:

TABLE 6.1 SQL OPERATORS

FOX OPTION	SQL OPERATOR
Like	=
Exactly Like	==
More Than	>
Less Than	<

STEP 2: SELECT FIELDS

In queries in which you have joined multiple tables, the number of fields available to be displayed can be large; it may be too many for meaningful presentation. The Query Designer gives you a quick way to select fields simply by dragging a field name from a table box into the **Selected Output** area. By using the **Fields** tab of the Query Designer (Figure 6.4), you have more options for field selection.

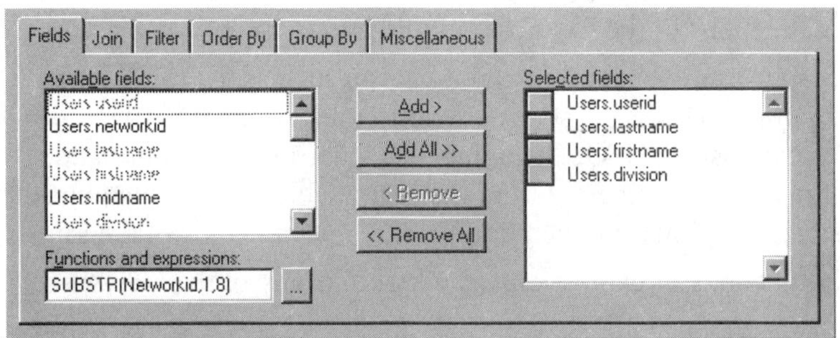

FIGURE 6.4 FIELDS TAB.

Most of the **Fields** tab is a variation of the standard Field Picker dialog box. You can select fields from the **Available Fields** list by double-clicking on them or by using the **Add** button. Similarly, fields can be deselected from the **Selected**

Output list by using the **Remove** or **Remove All** button or double-clicking on the fields.

NOTE

Fields that are used for criteria and joining are not required to be output selection fields, but as a rule they are included, if only to check the results of the query.

By whatever means in the Query Designer you use to select fields for output, it produces the **<select fields>** portion of the **SELECT** statement, such as in this example:

```
SELECT users.userid, users.networkid, users.lastname ;
  FROM users
```

In addition to the selection of fields, two options are available in the **Fields** tab that are quite significant.

SQL Field Functions and Expressions

In the **Fields** tab, under **Functions and Expressions** you can select from a list of SQL *field functions* such as **Count**, **Average**, and **Sum**, or you can create an expression (in the FoxPro sense) of your own. You can type an expression or field function in the entry area or use the standard Expression Builder dialog box. Earlier versions of the Query and View Designers had a funky but effective popup for displaying the SQL field functions. Now they are buried among all the other functions in the Expression Builder.

You can use any standard FoxPro function such as **SUBSTR( )**, as in the preceding example. However, such functions must work on a record-by-record basis. By contrast, the SQL field functions accumulate information from all records (or subsets of records) from the entire table. These functions, described in Table 6.2, are similar in operation to FoxPro commands of the same name.

Field functions or expressions may look like any of the following:

```
*This is like inserting a prompt into each line.
"Field Title"
*This uses a standard FoxPro function.
SUBSTR(users.lastname, 1, 20)
*This is a SQL field function with embedded qualifier.
COUNT(DISTINCT users.department)
```

TABLE 6.2 SQL FIELD FUNCTIONS

FUNCTION	DESCRIPTION
COUNT(<expr>)	Count all occurrences of a (non-empty) field or expression.
SUM(<expN>)	Sum all non-empty occurrences of a numeric field or expression.
AVG(<expN>)	Average all occurrences of a numeric field or expression, as before a combination of Sum divided by Count.
MIN(<expN>)	Return the minimum value found in a numeric field or expression.
MAX(<expN>)	Return the maximum value found in a numeric field or expression.
COUNT(DISTINCT <expN>)	Count all unique occurrences of a field or expression.
SUM(DISTINCT <expN>)	Sum all unique occurrences of a numeric field or expression.
AVG(DISTINCT <expN>)	Average all unique occurrences of a numeric field or expression.

Once you've constructed your field expression, use the **Add** button to put the expression into the **Selected Output** list. Any expressions or functions used here are added to the list of **<fields list>** following the **SELECT** statement:

```
SELECT "Field Title", SUBSTR( users.lastname, 1, 20), ;
  COUNT( DISTINCT users.department ) ;
  FROM users
```

In effect, you are creating additional fields or, as they are sometimes called, *calculated fields*. These "fields" have no existence outside the query but will be displayed in the output just as if they were a field.

In most cases, the argument of a field function will be a single field. However, they can work with other expressions, including standard FoxPro functions. For example:

```
MIN(ROUND(usersec.access))
```

You can remove a field function or other expression in the same way you would any other field: by highlighting the field in the **Selected Output** area and using the **Remove** button.

NOTE

In SQL, the asterisk (*) token means all (of something), depending on context. You can include all fields from all joined tables in the query by using the * (all fields) argument: `SELECT * FROM users, usersec`. A little more selectively, you can include all the fields from a particular table with this construction: `SELECT users.*, usersec.activity FROM users, usersec`. The asterisk can also be used with field functions to mean all records: `COUNT(*)`.

STEP 3: SELECTION CRITERIA (FILTER TAB)

As you might expect, selection criteria are used to specify which records you want retrieved from the tables. In the Query Designer, criteria perform the same function as the logical expressions in a typical **FOR** clause and are constructed in much the same way except for the "example" term on the right side of the relational operator.

Field Name (or Expression) **Criteria** (operator) **Example**

This is the Example as in Relational Query By Example, which is what the Query Designer was called in the previous versions of FoxPro. You might easily believe that this requires some sort of example or generic expression, but you really need to specify *exactly* what you want. You enter:

```
users.department     =     Sales Accounting
```

to get all the records that have Sales Accounting in the department field. If you use just Sales as the example, you'll get all the departments that begin with Sales. (Note that in the example entry area, you don't need quotes for character strings.)

By now you may have recognized that the example is often simply a constant or, as Fox would have it, a value expression. However, you can also use functions in the example or even complex expressions. What remains may scarcely be recognizable as an example but simply any valid FoxPro expression. And what is true for the right term, also applies to the left term. You can use either a field or any valid expression. In fact, buried way down at the end of the field list that pops up when you select the left term, you'll find the **<expression>** option. Selecting this option will bring up the familiar Expression Builder dialog box, and you can construct an expression just as you would in any other place in FoxPro.

Multiple criteria entries become additions to the **WHERE** clause, preceded by either an **AND** or, if there is more than one, an **OR**. The **AND** clauses are automatic when you add another criteria or join. The **OR** must be signaled explicitly by selecting the **Add Or** button at the bottom of the window. In addition you can select the **Not** button to put a **NOT** in front of your right side expression. All these logical operators behave as you would expect from your experience with building expressions. They are used to combine criteria into a complex conditional expression that might look something like this in a SQL statement:

```
SELECT users.* ;
  FROM users INNER JOIN usersec ;
  ON users.userid = usersec.userid ;
  WHERE (users.group = "TEAM1" ;
  AND NOT (usersec.access < 2 ;
  OR (usersec.access > 4)))
```

Notice that parentheses are used in the same way as in standard FoxPro expressions: to clarify the order of precedence.

The operators for criteria are the same as for joins, with two additions: **BETWEEN** and **IN**. The **BETWEEN** operator can take a range between two values separated by a comma. This works for numeric, date, and character values and is typed directly into the example area in a form like this: `BETWEEN 1,500` or `BETWEEN MN,MT`. **IN** is the list operator. Again, with any numeric, date, or character values, you can enter a list separated by commas: `IN 1,5,7,9` or `IN CA,MI,NY,NJ`, and so on. Here's a typical SQL statement using **BETWEEN** :

```
SELECT users.userid, users.birthdate ;
  FROM users ;
  WHERE users.birthdate BETWEEN {12/1/80},{12/31/80}
```

Criteria may use the **Case** option, located just to the right of the example area. This option toggles the use of the **UPPER( )** function (conversion of all characters to uppercase) to both left and right terms. For example, in SQL:

```
WHERE UPPER(users.lastname) = UPPER("Johnson")
```

This option is useful to ensure that the case of character expressions doesn't get in the way of making a complete selection, because "Johnson" doesn't match "JOHNSON."

Miscellaneous Options

The options in the **Miscellaneous** tab are not exactly criteria, but they do have the effect of limiting the records returned by a query. For example, the **No Duplicates** button will force the query to output only unique records, meaning that it will screen out records in which the values in every output field are the same. This option uses the **DISTINCT** clause of the **SELECT-SQL** command. Although the uses for this option are limited, you might want, for example, to see only the first member of a family in a table of family members.

The **Top** area in the **Miscellaneous** tab has two options that are new with Visual FoxPro 5.0, both very useful. By default, **All** is checked. When **All** is unchecked, you can use the **Number of Records** spinner to indicate how many records a query may return. In that way, when testing a query in a table of 399,789 records, if you specify the top (first) 100, you don't have to wait for an entire result set that may be quite large. This is an important feature for client/server development, in which the server may be much harder to control and the database may contain a large number of records.

The other option, **Percent**, answers a common complaint about FoxPro's **SELECT-SQL**, which didn't have the ability to easily deal with questions such as, "Show me the top 10 percent of salespeople by gross sales." Now you can do this and other similar "show the top x percent" queries, but only if you carefully structure the criteria to hinge on a numeric value that makes sense for a percentage return.

Step 4: Grouping

In a table of 3000 addresses from all over the country, a STATE field is bound to have some states with multiple entries. If you use this SQL option to *group* the table by state, then all the records from each state will be grouped together. This is, in effect, another kind of sorting. (In many systems you would need to sort the table before the groups could be used.) In SQL and the Query Designer, the **GROUP BY** clause performs the grouping of the data. Selecting the **Group By** tab displays the Group By window (shown in Figure 6.5), which uses the familiar field picker arrangement.

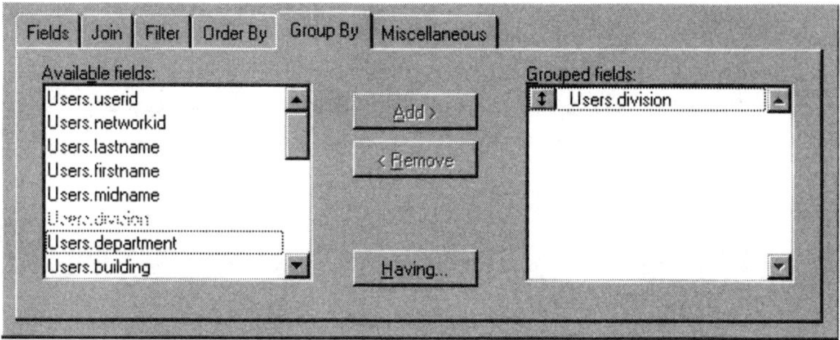

FIGURE 6.5 GROUP BY TAB.

When you're selecting grouping fields from the **Available Fields** list, be sure you understand how the values in the fields will group when sorted. The STATE field example is fairly obvious, but other fields may not produce the groupings you need. Also keep in mind that Query Designer and SQL will group only records that have already passed through any selection criteria you have established. More than a few people have tried to group values that didn't get that far.

Here's a **SELECT** statement using the **GROUP BY** clause:

```
SELECT users.lastname, users.group, users.birthdate ;
 FROM utility!users INNER JOIN utility!usersec ;
  ON users.userid = usersec.userid ;
 WHERE usersec.access >= 4 ;
 GROUP BY users.group
```

At this point, you might ask, "SQL will make groups. So what?" The answer lies in making selections from the groups.

STEP 5: SELECTING FROM THE GROUPS

Once you have established one or more groups based on a field, you can select records from those groups. Typically, this is some kind of summary information drawn from each group. For example, in a grouping by state you might sum the sales income, count the number of salespeople, and average their margin—but only where the state's total sales are greater than a certain amount. You place that condition on each group by using the **Having** option of the **Group By** tab (Figure 6.6).

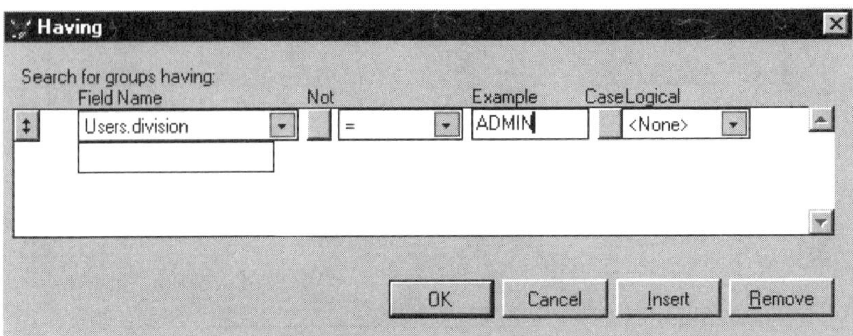

Figure 6.6 Group By tab, Having window.

Having is exactly like the selection criteria. Even the window is a copy of the criteria area of the main Query Designer window. However, whereas the selection criteria are applied to *all* records of a table, the **Having** conditions are usually applied to the records retrieved from the **Group By** fields. It is a characteristic of complex SQL statements that you can, in effect, specify layers of selection in the query. Layer 1 specifies the tables and fields. Layer 2 sets conditions so that only certain records are available. Layer 3 groups these records and provides for another selection based only on those groups.

NOTE

For the record, even if you don't specify a group and use **Having**, SQL will treat all records coming through the selection criteria as one big group. In other words, it will still work exactly like a selection criterion. Confusing? Maybe. Redundant? Definitely. But that's SQL.

Extending the example used for **GROUP BY**, here's the SQL statement so far:

```
SELECT users.lastname, users.group, users.birthdate ;
 FROM utility!users, utility!usersec ;
 WHERE users.userid = usersec.userid ;
  AND WHERE usersec.access >= 4 ;
 GROUP BY users.group ;
  HAVING MIN(users.birthdate) < CTOD("01/01/40")
```

The **HAVING** clause will cause this statement to show records from each security group that has at least one person born before 1940.

STEP 6: SORTING THE RESULTS

By any other name, **ORDER BY** is a sorting operation, and it works like all the other sorts in FoxPro. When you click on the **Order By** tab (shown in Figure 6.7), you'll see once again the familiar field picker approach.

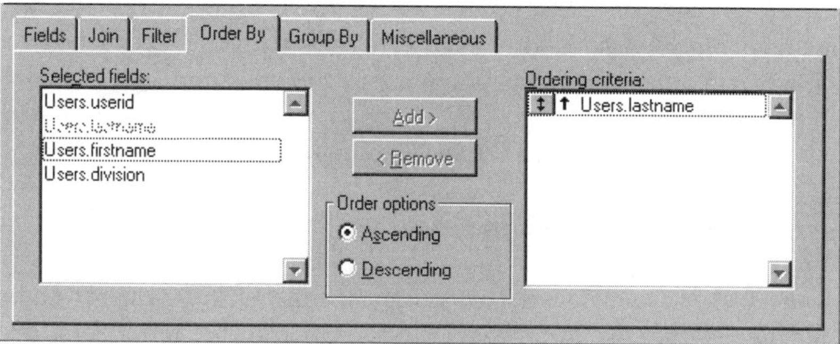

FIGURE 6.7 ORDER BY TAB.

You can move fields from a candidate list to a selected list—in this case, into the **Ordering Criteria** list. These are your sort fields, and the sort will proceed according to the order in which you list the fields. You also have **Ascending** and **Descending** order options, which can be applied individually to fields, and, as you'll notice, you can sort only on fields that are in the **Selected fields** list.

Putting all the steps together so far, we've done all the processing of data:

```
SELECT users.lastname, users.group, users.birthdate ;
 FROM utility!users INNER JOIN utility!usersec ;
   ON users.userid = usersec.userid ;
 WHERE usersec.access >= 4 ;
 GROUP BY users.group ;
  HAVING MIN(users.birthdate) < CTOD("01/01/40");
 ORDER BY users.lastname
```

Order By is very much an output clause. Its sole function is to organize the data that is to be delivered to an output option (file, report, and so on).

Step 7: Output Options

The default output for the Query Designer is a Browse window. This is the most useful way to develop and spot-check your query. However, when you're satisfied that the query is performing correctly, it may be time to turn to the other forms of output. The Query Designer has a rich assortment of options, and that is a distinguishing feature from the otherwise more versatile View Designer.

The query output destinations (as FoxPro calls them) can be reached with the Query toolbar, shortcut menu, or system menu and are summarized in Table 6.3.

Table 6.3 Query Designer Output Destinations

Destination	Description
Browse	The default output for the Query Designer and the most convenient way to scan the results of a query. However, the Browse window is read-only (cannot be edited), and once the table is closed the data is gone.
Cursor	One of the key concepts in FoxPro, a cursor (not related to a screen cursor), links the relational database system to object-oriented programming. In SQL jargon, a *cursor* is a somewhat shadowy temporary file. Depending on the Rushmore technology, a cursor may be an actual file on disk or else a table that resides in memory. In FoxPro, a cursor is essentially a table object with almost all the properties and capabilities of a standard table. You can index a cursor, set relations to it, and use a cursor as an input table for another SQL statement. A cursor can also be saved to a DBF file.
Table/DBF	This option creates a standard DBF file on disk. After choosing this option, you need to enter the file name into the **Name** text box, or use the File Selection dialog box to choose an existing file.
Graph	Connects the retrieved data with the Graph Wizard and then into Microsoft Graph, a subsystem included with many Microsoft products. Using a query and the Graph Wizard is the most common way to create graphs in FoxPro.

Screen Data retrieved in a query can be sent to provide data for a screen (now called a *form* everywhere else in FoxPro). This is usually done with a named cursor that is part of a form's data environment. This output option simply formalizes the connection between a specific query and a form.

Report Except for the Browse window, this is the most common way to use data retrieved through the Query Designer's queries. Selecting this option automatically channels the data into a FoxPro report (created in the Report Designer) or creates a quick report on the spot.

Label Similar to the **Report** option (actually a part of the same output screen), this outputs the data through a label form created in the FoxPro Label Designer.

If you've selected **Report** or **Label** from the output destination options, you'll see the Query Destination window expand to include a raft of options (Figure 6.8). Most of these options will make more sense after we've covered the Report Designer. You can use the **Wizard** button to reach the report wizards or choose **To text file** for simple output to a printer or file.

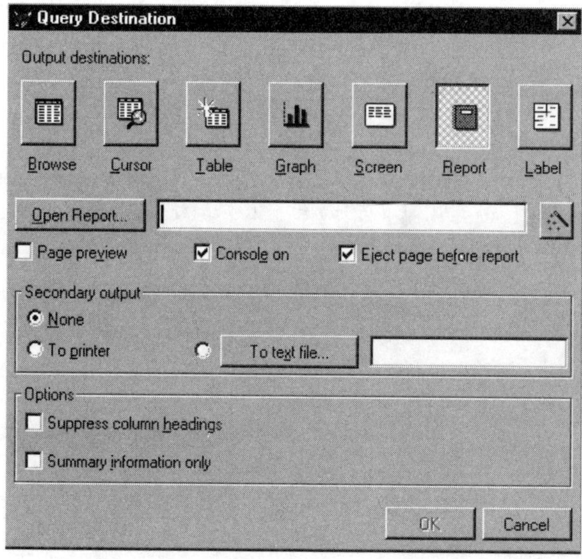

FIGURE 6.8 QUERY DESTINATION WINDOW, EXPANDED.

All the output destinations, as well as arrays, can be used in a **SELECT** statement. Here's an explanation of the relevant arguments:

Command syntax (output arguments):

INTO Destination You can use this to send output to an array, a cursor, or a DBF file. The **Destination** argument changes to:

ARRAY arrayname This output option is commonly used in programming, especially to provide data for FoxPro controls.

CURSOR cursorname Although used more extensively for views, a query cursor may also be useful in many programming situations when you need to reference a temporary data source.

TABLE|DBF tablename Creates a standard table from the query output.

TO FILE FileName [ADDITIVE] Output to an ASCII text file with the complete file name. The **ADDITIVE** clause will append all output to the text file.

TO PRINTER [PROMPT] Sends output to the currently selected Windows printer. If you use the **PROMPT** clause, the Windows Printer dialog box will appear to allow the user to select printer options.

TO SCREEN Output will be displayed in the currently active window or in the main FoxPro desktop.

PREFERENCE PreferenceName Use this option with the default Browse output (no **INTO** or **TO** specified); use the named Browse window specification.

NOCONSOLE For output to a printer, this disables display on the screen.

PLAIN Disables the display of column headers for printer and screen output.

NOWAIT For Browse window or screen output, this will cause program execution to continue after the window and data have been displayed. Used primarily in programming.

Examples:

```
SELECT * FROM users ;
 WHERE users.lastname = "SMITH";
 INTO TABLE newuser.dbf
*
SELECT * FROM users LEFT OUTER JOIN usersec ;
 ON users.userid = usersec.userid ;
 TO PRINTER PROMPT NOCONSOLE PLAIN
```

```
*
SELECT * FROM users INNER JOIN usersec ;
 ON users.userid = usersec.userid ;
 PREFERENCE newuser NOWAIT
```

Here's the completed **SELECT** statement for the one we've been building:

```
SELECT users.lastname, users.group, users.birthdate ;
 FROM utility!users INNER JOIN utility!usersec ;
   ON users.userid = usersec.userid ;
 WHERE usersec.access >= 4 ;
 GROUP BY users.group ;
  HAVING MIN(users.birthdate) < CTOD("01/01/40");
 ORDER BY users.lastname ;
 INTO TABLE secage.dbf
```

This completes the description of SQL query basics, from selecting the first table to deciding where to put the results. A **SELECT** statement can be far more complex, especially when you begin adding subqueries (**SELECT**s within **SELECT**s) and **UNION**s. But most of the steps are optional; in fact, the following statement is completely valid:

```
SELECT * FROM users
```

Of course, all it does is to take the data from the USERS file and put it into a Browse window. It wastes the SQL power to join with other tables, select specific records, group and select information from the groups, and then sort the output and send it to any one of eight different places.

SAVING AND REUSING QUERIES

Saving a query in the Query Designer requires nothing more than using **File**, **Save** (or **Save As**) from the system menu. If you started in the Project Manager, then the query will be registered automatically.

One of the more interesting aspects of FoxPro's SQL treatment (in addition to its being fully integrated with the programming language) is that everything is geared to the **SELECT** statement. When you click the **SQL** icon, you see the actual statement, and when you press the run button (!) in the standard toolbar, it executes that statement exactly as it finds it. When you save a query, creating a QPR file, the contents of the file are simply ASCII text of the SQL statement; when you open a QPR file, FoxPro uses the statement to perform the entire Query Designer setup. You can edit a QPR file (without even being in FoxPro), so if you have any problems with the SQL statement, you can often fix them before FoxPro tries to create a Query Designer setup.

The Query Wizards

FoxPro has several wizards for the query process:

- **Query Wizard**—A startup for a single table query.
- **Cross Tab Wizard**—Helps to create a query that will produce a cross tabulation.
- **Graph Wizard**—The only way to interactively step into a graph.
- **Pivot-table Wizard**—Will help to create a pivot-table in a Microsoft Excel spreadsheet using FoxPro data.

Like all wizards, these are not available for your applications (legally) and from a practical point of view, aren't designed for end users anyway. Whether you use them for development work is in part a matter of preference. For example, the Query Wizard can create a query only for a single table. Because most queries work with multiple tables (and that's the whole idea behind SQL), the Query Wizard is, at best, a startup device. On the other hand, the Cross Tab and Graph Wizards are almost indispensable for their specialized services.

Cross Tabs

The **Cross-Tabulation** button, tucked away in the **Miscellaneous** tab of the Query Designer, is easily overlooked. Yet it is the connection to powerful and useful FoxPro capabilities, including the Graph Wizard. A finished cross tabulation looks something like Table 6.4.

TABLE 6.4 CROSS TAB: SECURITY LEVELS BY GROUP, NUMBER OF MEMBERS

	LEVEL1	LEVEL2	LEVEL3	LEVEL4	LEVEL5
TEAM1	3	5	6	22	2
TEAM2	2	3	12	9	10
TEAM3	3	6	21	4	1
ACCOUNTING	1	3	4	2	1

This layout looks like the rows and columns of a Browse window, but in some ways it's closer to a spreadsheet layout. The far left column acts as the *y-axis*, the top row is the *x-axis*, and the data between is the result of the cross tabulation—a compilation of values related to the axes. Rather than rows and columns from a database table, Table 6.4 shows a summary of values generated with the Cross-Tab Wizard and the Query Designer.

The tricky part of using cross tabulation is the setup—specifically, visualizing the cross-tabulation arrangement. You need three fields that must be in the order corresponding to the x-axis, y-axis, and cross-tabulated content. The data in these fields should make sense for the purposes of cross tabulation. That's the hard part. How do you know that a certain three fields will work for a cross tabulation?

More often than not, you need two fields in conjunction with some kind of total. For example in one table you have a field for the names of salespeople. Another, related table has a field with the names of the district offices. Finally, you need either a field that contains the accumulated total of sales for each salesperson at each office or, more likely, a field that can be totaled by using a Query Designer field function such as **SUM**.

Using the Cross-Tab Wizard, which should be started from the Project Manager, you will be immediately asked to identify three fields from a table to use in the cross tabulation. One good thing about this wizard is that if you aren't sure which three fields will produce the results you want, you can experiment—stepping backward and forward in the wizard—until you find the field combination that works.

The screen that best illustrates what the three fields do is shown in Figure 6.9, the second step of the Cross-Tab Wizard.

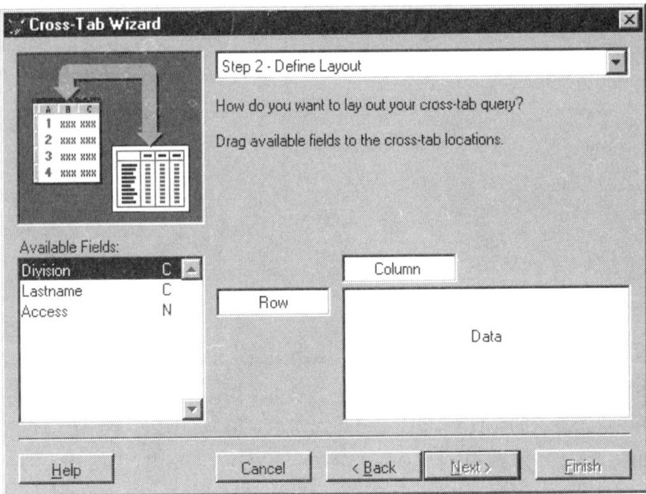

Figure 6.9 Cross-Tab Wizard, Step 2: Define Layout.

Here you assign the three fields to the x-axis (columns), y-axis (rows), and data area. The next window, Step 3, shows the Cross-Tab **Add Summary information** options, where you select from the SQL field functions: **Sum**, **Count**, **Average**, **Max**, and **Min** (see Figure 6.10). These functions will be applied to the field you've selected for the data area. In the final screen of the wizard, a liberal use of the **Preview** button will help you see whether you're getting the results you expected.

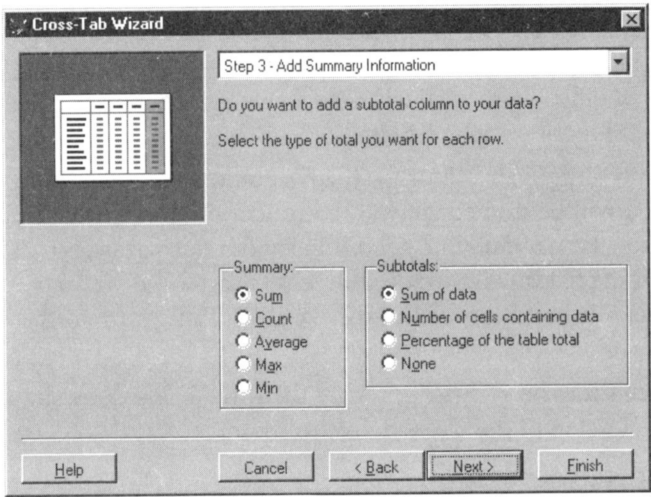

Figure 6.10 Cross-Tab Wizard, Step 3: Add Summary Information

Once you get the hang of it (it requires a kind of spreadsheet-think), creating a cross-tab query in the Query Designer is easy. Many times, the cross-tabulated table is all you need, but the payoff comes when you send the cross-tabulation data to the FoxPro Graph Wizard and then into Microsoft Graph. This subsystem, originally created for Microsoft's Excel spreadsheet, is now bundled with many of the Microsoft applications, including FoxPro.

THE GRAPH WIZARD

The Graph Wizard will guide you through a series of steps to produce a basic graph of the data in a cross tab. The program has few bells and whistles, but it's extremely easy to use, and the output is useful either on screen or in printed form.

You access the Graph Wizard either by starting a new query or by using the Query Designer. You must be using the **Cross-Tabulation** option from the **Select Fields** window. (This is done automatically if you use the Cross-Tab Wizard.) In other words, the Graph Wizard is expecting to be using data in its *datasheet* format, and the only way FoxPro produces that format is with cross tabs. As part of a cross-tab query, you can finish by specifying **Graph** as your output destination. When you execute the query (**Run** button), the cross tab will be generated and then you'll be in the Graph Wizard. After the initial screen, you be given a choice of graph types (Figure 6.11).

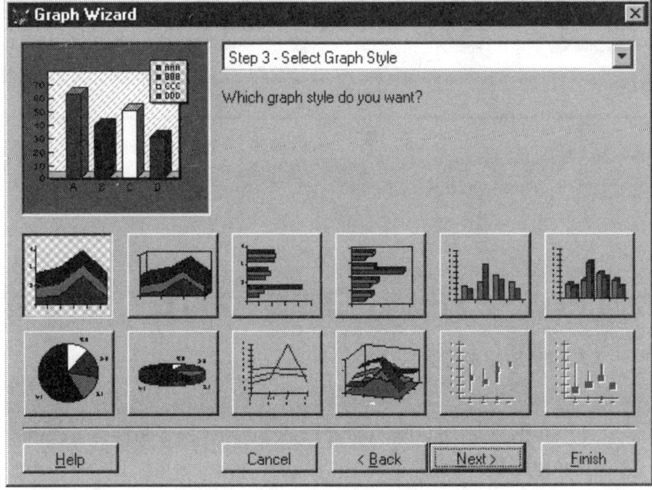

FIGURE 6.11 GRAPH WIZARD, STYLE GALLERY.

There are 10 types to choose from, and it may help to use the preview feature to make an appropriate selection. Once you have selected the type, press **Next** to move to the Title window, where you enter a title for the graph. Once this minor formality is completed, FoxPro will proceed to "call" Microsoft Graph (programmer-speak for one program running another program). Microsoft Graph creates the graph on the screen (Figure 6.12) and provides you with a number of ways to modify it. The graph can be viewed on screen, printed, and saved to a file.

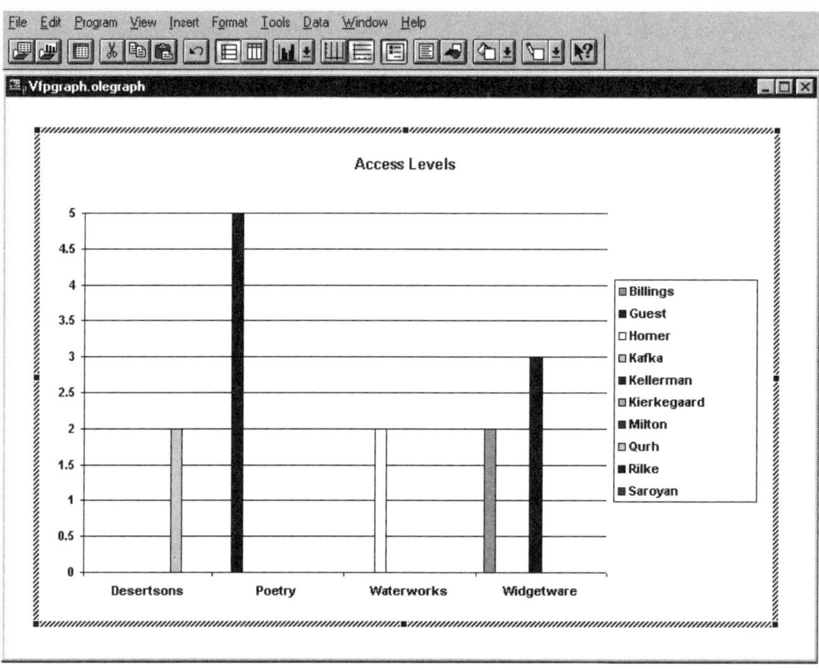

FIGURE 6.12 MICROSOFT GRAPH WINDOW.

USING THE VIEW DESIGNER FOR LOCAL VIEWS

Simply put, a SQL *view* is a query that retrieves data you can edit. To produce a view, you go through virtually the same steps as you take to create a query. Like a query, the view retrieves data for results which are often sent to a Browse window or a screen form. In either case, you can edit the data produced by the view, and the original tables will be updated with your changes. This makes SQL views one of the most powerful and important features in FoxPro's data management arsenal.

When you **USE** a view (the same as opening a table), FoxPro gathers the data from the original tables and automatically puts it into a *cursor*. (shorthand for CURrent Set of Records) The cursor becomes a live table, one that you can index, set relations to, and so forth. However, when you close the database associated with the cursor, the cursor vanishes with all its data. In the meantime, you can edit the cursor, and, when appropriate, FoxPro will update the original tables.

The SQL view draws much of its usefulness from the SQL ability to pull data from a wide variety of sources. In Visual FoxPro, as in few other database management systems, the SQL view has been expanded to include not only native FoxPro databases (called *local* data) but also data found in a wide variety of database systems, called *remote* data because of its non-FoxPro format and because sometimes it's not even located on the same network.

This ability to work with non-FoxPro data is another distinguishing feature of a SQL view, because a standard FoxPro query can work only with data in FoxPro tables. Given that a SQL view can reach more data, that the data is editable, and that you handle it just like a table, you might well ask, Why use a standard query?

Here are some factors to consider:

- Standard queries are often easier to create.
- The results of standard queries are automatically read-only, and that means the original data cannot be accidentally altered.
- Under certain circumstances, especially for feeding data to reports, there is no need for data updating, and queries are safer and perform slightly better.
- Views can't be selected for automatic output to graphs, cross tabs, reports, or labels (their range of output destination is limited.

Standard queries have their place, even as FoxPro continues to evolve into a more comprehensive SQL environment. On the other hand, the SQL view is more or less "the ultimate tool," and the more you work with it, the more you'll get out of it.

Working with the View Designer

Additional options and controls are associated with the updating process, but fortunately everything you've learned about the Query Designer works equally well in the View Designer.

Starting a View

To start a SQL view, you should be in the Project Manager and have an open database. The reason for this is simple. Unlike queries, views are not stored in their own files but rather in a database file (DBC). Without an open database, there's no place to store a view, and FoxPro won't even let you begin one. Without the Project Manager, it would be difficult to track the view, which in a sense is buried in the DBC file. It's important not to forget this aspect of FoxPro's views: They are tied to a specific database. In fact, it may be helpful to think of views as two different animals: the view as it exists in the DBC file (as a definition) and the active view that contains data (and acts like a table).

As with the Query Designer, you have two starting points: You can go directly to the View Designer window and start constructing a SQL view, or you can go through a wizard. There are two wizards for SQL views: the Local View Wizard and the Remote View Wizard. There is little or no difference between the Local View Wizard and the standard Query Wizard; neither one is very helpful. (The Remote View Wizard is another story, and we'll save it for a later chapter.)

Whether you choose the Local View Wizard or start the View Designer directly, you'll notice that the View Designer is almost a copy of the Query Designer window, with one important exception: the **Update Criteria** tab displayed in Figure 6.13.

Once in this window, you go about the business of completing a query—a view—as you have before, adding tables by creating joins, adding criteria if needed, defining groups (with any subcriteria in the Having clause), and determining the sort order.

NOTE

There is no **Output Destination** option for a view. In contrast to a standard query, in the View Designer views automatically display all output to a Browse window. To make other uses of the data, you must create an explicit link between a report or form in the same way you would link to a table.

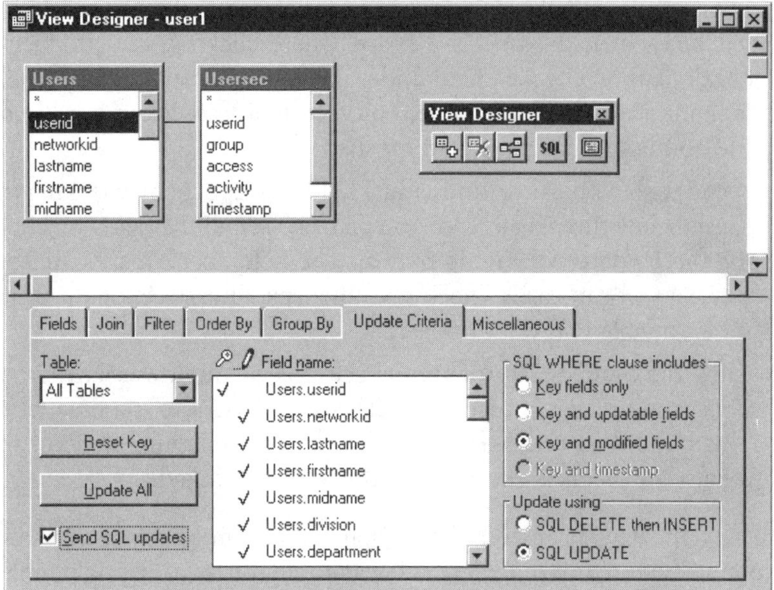

FIGURE 6.13 VIEW DESIGNER WINDOW.

Because the other tabs of the View Designer window are the same as those in the Query Designer (and work the same way), let's concentrate on the **Update Criteria** tab in Figure 6.13. Most of the options in this window apply only to remote views, but a few are also important for local views.

The most important point about table updating (writing changes to what FoxPro calls the *base tables*) is that it proceeds on a table-by-table basis. You can, however, select which tables will be updated and even which fields. On the left side of the **Update Criteria** window is the **Table** popup, where you can select each table involved in the view.

The second most important point is that when you first create a view *it has not been set to update the base tables*. Put another way, by default a view does not do updating. You need to explicitly set updating table-by-table or even field-by-field. Once you've done it, however, your settings are saved as part of the view definition and will be re-created each time the view is used.

In a new view, as you select each table for updating, the cardinal requirement is that the table have a unique (index) key for both the base table and the view. That's because FoxPro relies on the key values being unique for each table in order to make its updates. So step 1 is to set the index key for each table:

1. Look for the small key icon (see Figure 6.13). Below it and to the left of each field name is a space where clicking will produce a check mark. A checked field under the key icon means that the field is the index key for the table. For each table, set a key, usually on the normal primary key field for the table.
2. If you wish, you can set individual fields for update by checking the space below the pencil icon. You can also set all the fields by clicking the **Update All Fields** button. The field check marks are toggles, so you can easily check and uncheck your selections. Do this for each table you want updated.
3. Click the **Send SQL updates** check box in the lower-left corner. This action makes it official; updates will be sent to the base table. This check box acts as a master switch for updating. None of the other settings takes effect unless this box is checked.

Once these steps have been completed, you can edit in a Browse window with fields coming from many different tables as though it were a single table. The view produced in the View Designer is automatically saved with the database file when you close the view or database. Thereafter, every time you open the database, the view is available *exactly like a table*. You can **USE** the view to open it, set an alias, or whatever. Frankly, for something with such a complex background (especially with remote views), being able to handle a view in such a simple and familiar fashion is amazing.

Managing Views with Commands

Most of the time you'll create SQL views in the View Designer, but it's important to know that you can manage views by using commands in much the same way that you manage tables.

NOTE

For all the following commands (except **DISPLAY VIEWS**), the database that contains the view must be opened exclusively.

Before you create a view, it's a good idea to test the view's **SELECT** statements either with the actual command (for example, in the Command window) or in

the Query Designer. When you're satisfied that the statement gets the data you want, copy the text to the Windows clipboard and paste it into the **CREATE SQL VIEW** command.

Command syntax (partial):

CREATE SQL VIEW [ViewName] [AS SQLSELECT Statement]

Arguments:

ViewName The name of the view as it is stored in the database file.

AS SQLSELECT Statement This is the heart of the matter, a standard FoxPro **SELECT-SQL** statement to define all the elements of the view: tables, fields and so on.

Example:

```
CREATE SQL VIEW newusers AS SELECT * FROM users;
  WHERE users.birthdate > {12/31/80}
```

The degree of complexity of the **SELECT** statement is nearly boundless (limited only by your ability to comprehend what you're doing). However, keep in mind that one of the goals of a view is to bring together fields that can be updated. The use of complex expressions, a large number of field functions, or other non-updatable fields defeats this purpose, and your query would probably be better executed in a standard query.

Once views have been created and stored in the database file, you can get a listing of them (and their properties) using the **DISPLAY VIEWS** command.

The occasions to open the View Designer from a program are rare (and not available for EXE compiled applications). You can modify, rename, and delete a view using commands: **MODIFY VIEW ViewName**, **RENAME VIEW ViewName1 TO ViewName2**, and **DELETE VIEW ViewName**. In a program, where no interactive handling is desired, you can use a sequence of these commands to manage a view. For example:

```
OPEN DATABASE utility EXCLUSIVE
*Create the temporary view
CREATE SQL VIEW newusers AS SELECT *;
  FROM users WHERE users.employstat = "I"
*Open the view for business.
USE newusers ALIAS nu EXCLUSIVE
```

```
INDEX ON userid TAG userid
*Set the view to update
=DBSETPROP("Newusers","View","SendUpdates",.t.)
*Do some work on it.
REPLACE ALL nu.employstat WITH "D" ;
  FOR nu.birthdate >= {12/31/88}
*Flush the updates back to the original table
=TABLEUPDATE()
*Close the view
USE
*Remove the view from the database
DELETE VIEW newuser
CLOSE DATABASES
```

If you didn't spot them, there are two new functions in this code: **DBSETPROP( )** and **TABLEUPDATE( )**. They're needed because in the command mode, a view is not completely set for automatic updating. The first function, **DBSETPROP( )**, is one example of a (very large) family of uses.

```
DBSETPROP("Newusers","View","SendUpdates",.t.)
```

In this case, only the first argument, the name of the view, changes; the others remain fixed to enable view updating. **DBSETPROP( )** will be covered in great detail later, after you've had some exposure to object-oriented programming and object properties.

Similarly, the **TABLEUPDATE( )** function is used here to make sure that the changes are written to the original table. This is part of handling multiple tables in a multiuser environment, a topic that's covered in Chapter 19.

Customizing Views

If your application needs to use a view repeatedly, each time making minor changes to the value of a criterion—for example, changing the date range—then you might consider customizing your view so that it will ask the user to fill in the data that changes. This technique has the intimidating name of *parameterizing* a view, but it's not difficult. The strategy is this: In your view, you have criteria with some value (or values) that are changed almost every time you run the view. Typically, this value is a constant in the right-hand expression of a view criterion, such as `state = "CA"`. However, instead of a constant, you want to insert a variable that will be replaced with the value the user will enter as a parameter. To do this, change the expression to `lastname = ?pcLastName`. The question mark causes FoxPro to substitute the value found in the variable `pcLastName` for the usual constant in the expression.

Having added the variable, you next set the parameter: In the menu (with a view already open), select **Query**, **View Parameters**. This action opens the dialog box in Figure 6.14. Enter the name of the variable used in the view criterion (in this case, `pcLastName`) and save it by pressing the **OK** button. When you run the query, FoxPro will automatically create a View Parameter data entry dialog box, depicted in Figure 6.15. Here, you enter the value (as a parameter) that you want to have in the criterion.

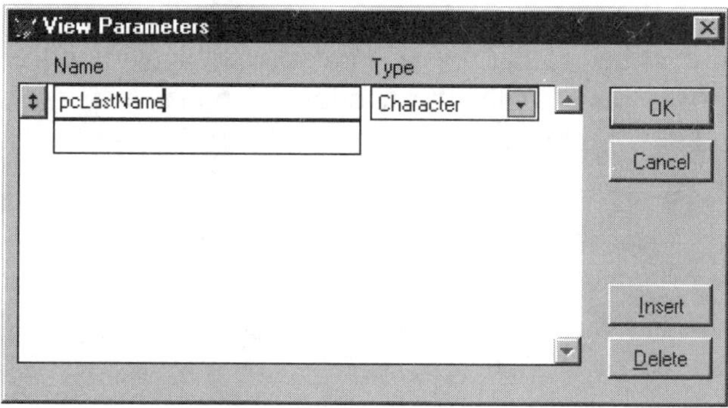

FIGURE 6.14 VIEW PARAMETERS DIALOG BOX.

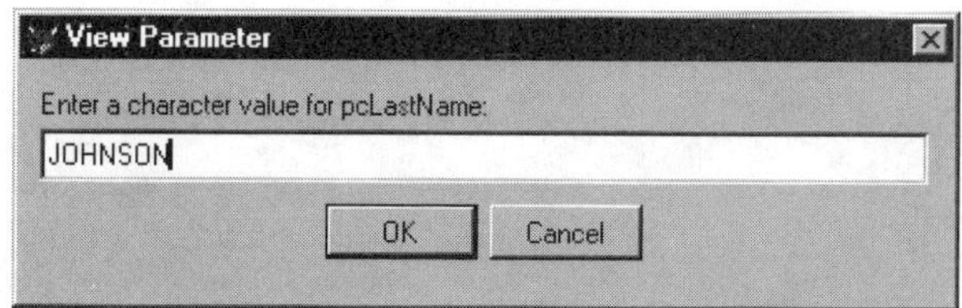

FIGURE 6.15 VIEW PARAMETER DATA ENTRY DIALOG BOX.

This isn't exactly a major feature of the SQL view, but it's a nice refinement for views that are used often, in or out of applications. It's also the basis of an important technique in which you feed parameters to a SQL view from variables in your program, something we'll cover in Chapter 20.

CHAPTER WRAP-UP

Even at this early stage, it's obvious that using SQL is one of the key skills in FoxPro. Queries provide data for reports, popup lists, and many other programming situations. Views provide data for forms and any situation in which queried data needs to be updated. Between the two, views may account for as much as 50 percent of the data management in your applications. It's highly recommended that you wean yourself as soon as possible from using the interactive tools (the Query and View Designers and especially the wizards), concentrating instead on the **SELECT-SQL** command language. You won't abandon the designers; they will remain a useful way to access SQL. However, advanced SQL features, such as sub-queries, are not available in the designers, and a language-level control over SQL will help you better understand what it can and can't do.

This chapter barely scratches the surface of SQL and what it can do for your applications, but we had to start somewhere, preferably without overload. We'll revisit many of the same topics throughout the book, in particular the Data Environments of FoxPro reports and forms.

CHAPTER 7

OUTPUT AND THE REPORT DESIGNER

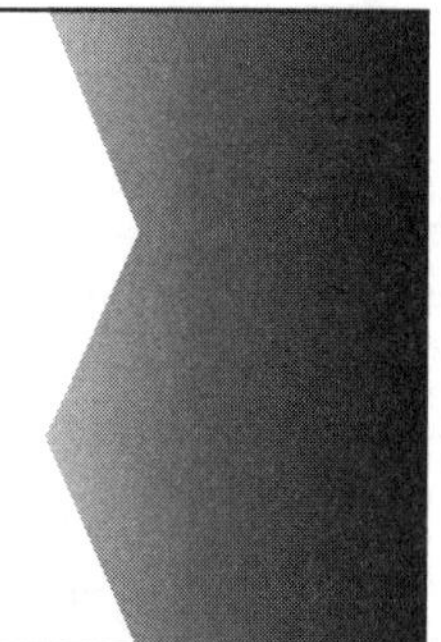

Previous chapters have shown you some of the ways to retrieve information for your applications. We've described the SQL approaches as well as the traditional Browse, **SET FILTER**, and **LOCATE** techniques. This chapter emphasizes the output options—the ways of presenting the information to the user—including the following:

- The Report Designer
- The Label Designer
- Summarizing commands such as **CALCULATE** and **TOTAL**
- File Output commands such as **COPY TO**
- Simple listings with commands such as **DISPLAY**

Although most of this chapter deals with creating reports, it's important to acquire a balanced view of output for an application. Printed reports are important, but they're not the sole means of output available to you. As you will see, some of the other methods work better in some circumstances.

OUTPUT FOR APPLICATIONS

Whether you do it at the beginning or (more typically) near the end of the development of an application, at some point you need to think about the ways to present the information captured in your application's database. We've covered the most important ways to *retrieve* the data, but you also need to consider how to deliver the output. When you're considering how to display information to users, here's a list of the options you might find useful. They're ranked in an order that's representative for most applications:

1. **Data entry and edit screen viewing:** These forms make up the main portion of the application's user interface. As a rule, they show one record at a time on the screen.
2. **Grid or Browse viewing:** These options are often associated with the forms part of the user interface but are also used solo. This is the screen format best adapted for scanning data rapidly.
3. **Printed reports:** These are often associated with the format of the data in the screen forms, but they take on many different forms. Reports are often a formal presentation of an application's information and may require considerable time to develop and refine.
4. **Reports in print preview mode:** In FoxPro, any report that can be printed can also be sent to the screen in preview mode. For quick lookups, this approach may be more useful than sending the data to a printer.
5. **Quick reports:** The only difference between these and other reports is the lack of formatting and other decoration. An alternative name, *data dumps*, conveys the correct flavor. This type of report is intended to present data quickly, whether in printed form or in print preview mode.
6. **Labels:** Some applications use label printing extensively, others not at all. Creating labels is a variation of reporting.
7. **Output to file:** Most commonly, this option uses commands such as **COPY TO** to send application data to a variety of file formats. Reports generated in the FoxPro Report Designer can also be sent to an ASCII text file. In either case, the usual reason for output to a file is to transfer the data to another program such as a word processor or spreadsheet.
8. **Screen prints:** Although it's seldom used, the ability to capture an image from the screen and send it to a printer is available under Windows and can be appropriate for some applications.

You'll notice that printed reports are not listed first. They can be important in some applications, but it's becoming common for users to spend more time with the information on their screens than they do reading paper reports.

One of the standard exercises for developing an application is to review each of the tables and screen forms and decide which of the many output options best serves the application. As a rule, it will be a mixture: some reports, forms, grids, and quick screens. But considering that each output item requires time and attention to develop, what you omit is as important as what you include. Applications often suffer from "creeping reportism," in which a handful of planned output forms and reports blossoms into dozens (if not hundreds) of instances.

As with printing, most data output is naturally read-only. In many applications where screen viewing is important, a distinction is made between data presented for update or maintenance and data intended strictly for viewing. Data that is available for editing usually requires explicit protection, depending on the environment (LAN and multiuser) and the level of security. In many forms and grids, you'll need to provide a way to distinguish between an editing mode and a viewing (read-only) mode.

As you begin to work with the user interface of your application—and output will definitely be part of it—you'll see that you must make another distinction between the user interface provided by FoxPro to you, as a developer, and the one you choose to provide in your application. The standard FoxPro user interface scatters output options over four menus and a dozen dialog boxes. You may want to consolidate some of these functions, or even build your own user interface for handling output. This is where the application framework comes in. Building components to handle various kinds of output is a standard part of developing an application framework. In Chapter 22, we'll explore this aspect of output in detail.

SIMPLE OUTPUT

Although FoxPro's SQL-based tools (queries and views) are the preferred methods for extracting data from tables, once in a while you may need just a quick look at your data. That's the purpose of simple output: basic commands that display, copy, and calculate, mostly from single tables. Although these commands are more useful to the developer, they may also find spot usage in applications.

LIST AND DISPLAY

These two commands have the identical syntax (except for the basic command, of course). **LIST** displays records in a table one after the other without pause.

DISPLAY does the same thing but pauses each time a new screen full of records is reached. **DISPLAY** is used mostly for viewing in the screen, and **LIST** for sending output to a printer or file.

Command syntax (abbreviated):

DISPLAY or LIST [[FIELDS] FieldList] [Scope] [FOR lExpression1] [WHILE lExpression2] [OFF] [NOCONSOLE] [TO PRINTER [PROMPT]|TO FILE FileName]

Arguments:

FIELDS FieldList Uses a comma-separated list of fields; otherwise, all fields will be included.

Scope Uses the standard scope clauses: **ALL**, **NEXT n**, **REST.**

FOR lExpression1 Uses the standard logical expressions of the **FOR** clause.

WHILE lExpression2 Uses the standard logical expressions with the **WHILE** clause.

OFF Normally, record numbers are displayed for each record. This command turns it off.

NOCONSOLE Does not echo output to the screen.

TO PRINTER Sends output to a printer.

PROMPT Displays the Windows Print Setup dialog box before printing.

TO FILE FileName Sends output to the named file.

Examples:

```
DISPLAY FIELDS lastname, firstname, birthdate
DISPLAY ALL FOR city = "Seattle"
LIST ALL FOR children > 2 TO PRINT PROMPT
LIST ALL TO FILE pieces.txt
```

These are two of the oldest commands in the Xbase language. They can't do sophisticated formatting, but they serve the job of delivering data quickly. Their greatest advantage is how easily they produce a printout, file, or screen without an elaborate setup.

Variations of the **DISPLAY** command are also used extensively for a quick look at the internal status of FoxPro. These forms are as follows:

DISPLAY CONNECTIONS to see the definitions of remote data connections.

DISPLAY DATABASE to display database information about tables and fields.

DISPLAY MEMORY to see the contents of the FoxPro memory, variables, windows, and so on.

DISPLAY STRUCTURE to see the field structure and definitions of a table.

DISPLAY STATUS to see the current status of tables, indexes, relations, and other settings.

DISPLAY TABLES shows a list of tables contained in a database file.

DISPLAY VIEWS provides information about the views stored in a database file.

These commands are occasionally used in applications to gather information for processing routines, an approach that requires some manipulation of files.

COPY TO AND EXPORT

COPY TO is the output side of **APPEND FROM**. In the era before SQL, it was the primary method of extracting data from one table into another DBF. These days, **SELECT-SQL** is usually preferred for this task, especially with multiple tables. However, **COPY TO** still has an active role to play as a method to export data to other file formats and for routine data transfer from one DBF to another.

Command syntax (abbreviated):

COPY TO FileName [FIELDS FieldList] [Scope] [FOR lExpression1] [WHILE lExpression2] [[WITH] CDX] [[TYPE] [FOXPLUS | FOX2X

Arguments:

FileName Specifies the name of the file to be created (including path if needed).

FIELDS FieldList Uses a comma-separated list of fields; otherwise, all fields will be included.

Scope Uses the standard scope clauses: **ALL**, **NEXT n**, **REST.**

FOR lExpression1 Uses the standard logical expressions of the **FOR** clause.

WHILE lExpression Uses the standard logical expressions with the **WHILE** clause.

WITH CDX Include this clause if you want the index file from the source table to be re-created for the new table.

TYPE FOXPLUS|FOX2X Specifies the file format of the new file (see Table 5.1 for options).

Examples:

```
USE users
COPY TO newuser FOR lastname = "SMITH"
COPY TO test FIELDS lastname, firstname, birthdate WITH CDX
```

During data maintenance there are innumerable occasions to copy a subset of data from one table into another table, do some manipulation to the table, and then append its data to yet another table or back into the original table. For this sort of job, **COPY TO** and **APPEND FROM** are more convenient (and often faster) than using SQL-based commands.

Just as **COPY TO** is the output side of **APPEND FROM**, so **EXPORT** is the output companion to **IMPORT**. This command is also available in the menu under **File**, **Export**.

Command syntax (abbreviated):

EXPORT TO FileName [TYPE] [FIELDS FieldList] [Scope] [FOR lExpression1]

[WHILE lExpression2]

Arguments:

FileName Specifies the name of the output file and path (if needed).

TYPE Specifies the type of file format to be created (see Table 5.1 for a list of formats).

FIELDS FieldList Uses a comma-separated list of fields; otherwise, all fields will be included.

Scope Uses the standard scope clauses: **ALL**, **NEXT n**, **REST.**

FOR lExpression1 Uses the standard logical expressions of the **FOR** clause.

WHILE lExpression2 Uses the standard logical expressions with the **WHILE** clause.

Examples:

```
EXPORT TO newuser TYPE XL5
EXPORT TO newuser TYPE WK3 FOR birthdate > {12/31/50}
```

There is considerable overlap between the four input/output commands. However, in general, **IMPORT** and **EXPORT** are used most frequently when you're creating non-DBF file formats, and **COPY TO** and **APPEND FROM** are used for DBF-to-DBF or ASCII file transfers. If you use **Export** in the menu, you are actually using the **COPY TO** command.

Some applications require the ability to select and extract data for use in other programs such as Microsoft Excel or Word. This capability could be either under program control (an automated procedure) or something users can select from a menu. If the tasks involved aren't too demanding, including the **Export** menu option in your application may do the job. Otherwise, you might need to program a more elaborate user interface and perhaps use a combination of **EXPORT** and **COPY TO**.

CALCULATION COMMANDS

The calculation commands—**COUNT**, **AVERAGE**, **SUM, CALCULATE**, and **TOTAL**—provide a way to extract statistics from your tables. Although the equivalents of these commands are more commonly used as functions in the Report Designer and the Query and View Designers, they are available in this form (especially in the Command window) for data maintenance and quick responses to queries such as, How many widgets did we sell last month? or What was the average sales total per salesperson? The greatest advantage of the calculation command is the simple setup: Open a table and run the command.

Use of these commands in applications is limited, but if you don't need many pieces of information at once and you're working with local tables, they may be sufficient to deliver certain statistics. You can link the commands with reports by having the results stored to memory variables, which are then picked up as expressions in the Report Designer, or in a similar fashion displayed in a screen form.

COUNT

COUNT is the most valuable of the summary commands because there are many situations, especially in data maintenance, when it's useful to get a count of how many records fit a criterion. **COUNT** is also one of the fastest of commands in FoxPro, at least on indexed fields.

Command syntax:

COUNT [Scope] [FOR lExpression1] [WHILE lExpression2] [TO MemVarName]

Arguments:

Scope Uses the standard scope clauses: **ALL**, **NEXT n**, **REST**.

FOR lExpression1 Uses the standard logical expressions of the **FOR** clause.

WHILE lExpression2 Uses the standard logical expressions with the **WHILE** clause.

TO MemVarName Stores the results of the count to a specific memory variable.

Examples:

```
COUNT ALL FOR EMPTY(lastname)
COUNT ALL FOR AT(",",lastname) <> 0 TO nComma
```

A count is nearly always used with a logical expression that defines what is being counted. Typically, this expression is a **COUNT FOR**. (Simply counting a field would get the number of records in a table, a figure easily obtained without running a count.) Although it is occasionally used in applications—for example, to provide an up-to-the-minute tally for an information screen—**COUNT** is used mostly during interactive data maintenance. Here's an example of how it can be applied:

```
*Open database
OPEN DATABASE utility
```

```
* Open table, note exclusive use for maintenance.
USE users IN 0 ORDER sysdate EXCLUSIVE
*Test to see if any outdated records exist.
COUNT ALL FOR sysdate <= {12/31/94}
* Assuming some exist
COPY ALL TO olddata FOR sysdate <= {12/31/94} WITH CDX
* Delete the old records
DELETE ALL FOR sysdate <= {12/31/94}
* Remove them from the table.
PACK
* Examine the new file.
* Mark records to put back in main table by deleting them.
USE olddate IN 0 ALIAS od
SELECT od
BROWSE
* Close the table
USE
* Re-integrate keeper records from the new table.
SELECT users
APPEND FROM olddata FOR DELETED()
* Remove deletion marks
RECALL ALL
* Clean up
CLOSE DATABASES
```

AVERAGE, SUM, AND CALCULATE

Like all the summarizing calculation options (except **COUNT**), **AVERAGE** and **SUM** require a numeric data field. **AVERAGE** is actually a combination of the sum and count commands: average = sum / count. This implies that before an average can be computed, FoxPro has already done a sum and count, and that is why in the **CALCULATE** command you can do all these summarizing functions at the same time. This is a case of one stone and many birds. **CALCULATE** can do counts, sums, averages, and standard deviation (**STD**), Minimum (**Min**), maximum (**Max**), net present value (**NPV**), and variance (**Var**). It can also do one or more of them at the same time.

Command syntax:

CALCULATE eExpressionList [Scope] [FOR lExpression1] [WHILE lExpression2]

[TO MemVarList|TO ARRAY ArrayName]

Arguments:

eExpressionList This is a comma-separated list of fields to be totaled.

Available expressions are **AVG()**, **CNT()**, **MAX()**, **MIN()**, **NPV()**, **STD()**, **SUM()**, and **VAR()**.

Scope Uses the standard scope clauses: **ALL**, **NEXT n**, **REST**.

FOR lExpression1 Uses the standard logical expressions of the **FOR** clause.

WHILE lExpression2 Uses the standard logical expressions with the **WHILE** clause.

TO MemVarList Stores the results in a named variable.

TO ARRAY ArrayName Stores the results in an array.

Examples:

```
CALCULATE MIN(birthdate), MAX(birthdate) FOR state="CA";
   TO dMinDate, dMaxDate
AVERAGE fees, credit FOR birthdate > {12/31/50};
  TO nAvgFee, nAvgCredit
SUM fees, credit FOR birthdate > {12/31/50};
  TO nSumFee, nSumCredit
```

CALCULATE is the command that provides true summary statistics from a table, and does it on a single pass and with a minimum of setup. It's easy to overlook this command, because the summary calculations are more commonly performed in queries or views, but it can be an efficient way to grab a handful of summary data for application use as well as during application development.

TOTAL

Although it also does summary field calculations, the **TOTAL** command is different from the other calculation commands. It sends its output to another DBF, and it is also dependent on the sort or index order of the source file. In many ways, **TOTAL** is a remnant of the days before SQL, which can do a similar job with more flexibility.

BASIC OUTPUT OPTIONS

There are three basic *destinations* (to use the FoxPro word) for output: printer, file, and screen. These options come in several variations; for example, you can hardly lump a multipage form with the print preview as a "screen" output. Most commonly associated with printing options are output to printer, output to a named file, and print preview.

PRINTED OUTPUT

The use of a printer is so pervasive that almost all software uses the word *print* in the menus when it really means *output*. FoxPro is no different in this respect. It jams printer options into the same dialog boxes as Clipboard and ASCII text file options. Sooner or later, most applications must answer the question of how much of this FoxPro user interface is used to provide printer options for the user. As I've mentioned, the FoxPro interface is largely designed for developers, and although some parts of it may work for users, other parts of it won't. For one thing, the print options are scattered all over the menu system:

- File menu, FoxPro **Page Setup**.
- File menu, **Print Preview**.
- File menu, **Print**.
- Standard toolbar, **Printer** icon.
- Print dialog box, **Windows Print Setup**.
- Query and View Designer windows, **Output**, **Report/Label**.
- Command window and programs, **TO PRINT** option for commands.
- Command window and programs, **PROMPT** option for commands.
- Command window and programs, print-related commands such as **SET PRINT ON**.
- View menu, **Preview** option.
- File menu, **Print Preview** option.
- Standard toolbar, **Print Preview** icon.
- Standard toolbar, run ! icon, for all reports and labels.

This dispersal of printing options is significant, because you almost certainly do not want to leave it this way for your applications. You can design an application's menus to include (or not include) most of FoxPro's options, and you can reorganize the menus to group logically related options. This chapter will outline FoxPro's output options, reviewing them from the perspective of how they may, or may not, fit an application. Chapter 22 will cover what you can do to reorganize and present these options with your own output manager.

Print Menu Options

As a developer, how you get something printed depends on what you are doing. Some of FoxPro's printing options are in menus that come and go with particular windows, or the options become enabled and disabled. The only printing access that is usually available is in the menu under **File**, **Print** (or by using **Ctrl-P** from the keyboard).

The Print dialog box (Figure 7.1) and its subdialog are versatile enough to handle 80 to 90 percent of your printing requirements. Having been reorganized for Visual FoxPro 5.0, the most important part of the dialog box must now be accessed through the **Options** button. This action opens the Print Options dialog box, which has a **Print what** area (with the drop-down list shown in Figure 7.2). The first selection in Print Options is what **Type** of printing is to be done. Your choices are **Report**, **Label**, **Command**, **File**, **ASCII file**, and **Clipboard**. If you select **Report**, **Label**, **File**, or **ASCII file**, you need to follow up and designate the file you want to print in the **File** entry area. The **Command** option lets you type a command in the Command window, and the output will be sent to the printer. The Clipboard option prints whatever is in the Windows Clipboard.

At this point, it's a good idea to ask yourself, "Of these options, how many will be easily understood and operated by the users of my application?" For example, consider the need to identify a particular report file. Do your users understand the Windows 95 and NT folder system? Can they distinguish between file types—for example, those with an FRX extension (reports)? Or from a slightly different angle, will your users be confused by seeing the Command window option? Most of the FoxPro printing tools require that users be fairly sophisticated. If that doesn't describe the typical user of your application, you need to consider alternative ways to organize output.

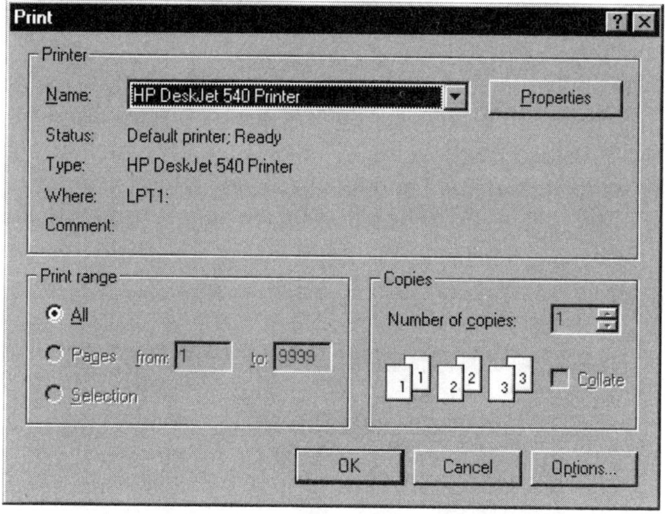

FIGURE 7.1 PRINT DIALOG BOX.

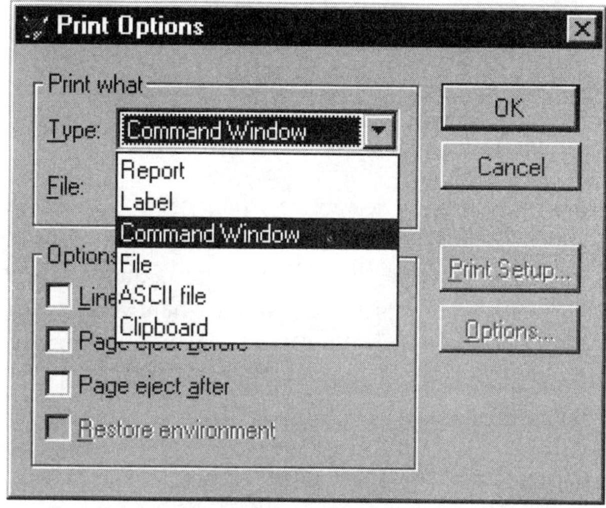

FIGURE 7.2 PRINT OPTIONS DIALOG BOX.

In the Print Options dialog box, depending on your selection in the **Print what** area, the other options in the dialog box become enabled or disabled. Sometimes available is **Print Setup**, which gives you access to the standard Windows Print Setup dialog box shown in Figure 7.3. This dialog box is also available under **File**, **Page Setup**. You go to these dialog boxes to select which printer you want to use (if there is more than one) and to specify any other printer characteristics. (Except for shifting between Landscape and Portrait printing orientation, most people make few changes.) The Print Setup dialog box is standard for Windows programs, so as a rule you can assume users will know what to do with it.

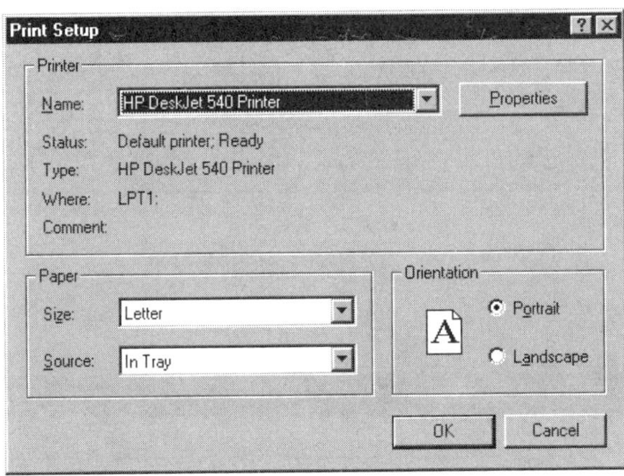

FIGURE 7.3 PRINT SETUP DIALOG BOX.

The **Print Options** button becomes active whenever you select **Report**, **Label**, **File**, or **Command** in Print Options. This dialog box, shown in Figure 7.2, has its own **Options** button, which leads to a tiny Criteria dialog box with the familiar **Scope**, **For**, and **While**. This is another point where you need to ask whether your users will know how to create FoxPro logical expressions. That will determine whether using this standard options dialog is satisfactory or whether you need to develop an alternative.

REPORT DESIGNER PRINT OPTIONS

The Page Setup dialog box changes completely when the Report Designer is open, and its specifications are always related to the current report. Whereas the Windows Print Setup dialog box is used to specify the size and orientation of paper for printing, the FoxPro Page Setup dialog box adds detailed specification for columns, print order, printable area, left margin, and the type of page dimensions. Both sets of instructions (Windows and FoxPro) will be used by the Report Designer to determine the dimensions of the printed area of the report.

While you're working in the Report Designer, there are three places to find **Print Preview**. The most obvious is in the Standard toolbar; another one is lurking in the View menu, the other is in the File menu. As you will see later, print preview is a good way to study printed output without using paper.

Most applications do not include the FoxPro Report Designer as an available option. There is no barrier to including it except that it takes a very knowledgeable user to be able to modify (or create) reports, and you will usually need to protect some reports from being modified.

NOTE

When you create a FoxPro application (as either an APP or an EXE file), virtually the entire capability of FoxPro—with the major exceptions of the View, Query, and Database Designers—is automatically compiled into the file, regardless of how many features your application actually uses. That's one reason the distribution files you make with Visual FoxPro are more than 1MB in size.

View and Query Designers Print Options

In the Query Designer, FoxPro provides you with the means of sending output to a report or label form (previously created) or to a Quick Report. When the query is run, the Report or Label window is displayed with the same options (but different layout) than the Print dialog box described previously. The View Designer, on the other hand, sends output only to an immediate Browse window. Most of the time, views are used to provide data for other output methods. Because neither designer is available for an EXE file application, it may not be a good idea to plan on using the designer anyway.

Printing in the Command Window

The print options you enter in the Command window are the same ones you would use in a program. **TO PRINT** can be added to nearly all the output type commands, such as **LIST**, **DISPLAY, TOTAL**, and even **REPORT FORM** (these commands will be introduced shortly). **TO PRINT** simply instructs the command to send the output to the printer. It's often combined with the **PROMPT** clause, which causes FoxPro to display the Print dialog box.

Whereas **TO PRINT** and **PROMPT** combine with other commands, **SET PRINT ON|OFF** is a command in its own right. This command enables output to a printer of any command that *echoes to the screen* or, put another way, any command that displays to a screen, such as **LIST** or **DISPLAY**. This option is not used often, because it is global: Once it is on, it works for all such commands. Most people would rather send output to the printer on a command-by-command basis using the **TO PRINT** clause.

Output to Screen

Output to screen, in this case, is not about specially constructed forms and grids but rather refers to the output options of reports and other commands. For most of the retrieval tools and commands, the screen is the default output: the place where information is displayed if you don't explicitly choose another output method. The Query Designer, for example, automatically displays results in a Browse window. Commands such as **LIST** simply scroll the information in the main FoxPro window.

This form of output, screen or window presentation, is useful for relatively short bursts of information. Most people can scan a few hundred records, which amounts to lines or rows on the screen. In some applications, this relatively short burst of screen data may be all that's necessary to review information. But when the number of records goes into the thousands, visual inspection wears people out. It's not that reading printed paper is much easier, but it seems more natural to put paper down and later pick it up. Most of us are accustomed to reading long documents in printed form.

Output to File

In some places in FoxPro where you can print, you will also have the option to send the output to a file. This requires nothing more than telling FoxPro the name of the file and which folder to put it in. It's important to understand that, in contrast to the **COPY TO** command, you have no choice of the file type for output. In all cases, FoxPro produces an ASCII text file.

In a way similar to the **SET PRINT ON** command, you can also instruct FoxPro to send all screen output to a file. This approach requires two commands and is available in the Command window or within a program.

Command syntax (abbreviated):

SET ALTERNATE TO <filename>

SET ALTERNATE ON | OFF

Example:

```
SET ALTERNATE TO guest.txt
SET ALTERNATE ON
<print something>
SET ALTERNATE OFF
```

The first command specifies the name of file to use for the output, and the second command enables output to the file. Thereafter, if you use a command such as **LIST**, the output will be echoed to a file (output displayed on the screen will also be sent to the file). The word *echo* is significant, because if you have **SET ECHO OFF** either from the Command window or in the **Options**, **View** tab, then results of commands will not be sent to the screen or to a file.

In the days before report generators (such as the Report Designer) let us produce reports with fonts and other fancy formatting, people often sent report output to a file.

APPLICATIONS AND REPORTS

Reports are a big chunk of almost every application. After you've learned how to use the FoxPro Report Designer, you'll be able to develop reports of almost any description with relative ease. But there is more to reports in an application than that. Consider this list for a moment:

- Users need a way to select reports to run.
- Some reports may require special processing before being run.
- Many reports require changes in data criteria—different dates and so on.
- Users may need to choose the method of output: file, printer, or screen.

- For printer output, the user may need to select the printer.
- You should provide at least minimal messaging to the user about the status of the run.
- Some reports may require special processing after being run.

Many of the items in this list require a dialog with users, when they want to run a report. These dialogs can become quite elaborate. Some reports also require fairly sophisticated data management operations before and after they run. The point is that your reports do not exist in a vacuum. You can't say, "I used the Report Designer and built the 20 reports needed by the application," and consider yourself finished.

It's a good exercise to think through each report from the user's point of view: getting started; needed information; printer options; status messages. Then consider the report from the data management point of view: data retrieval, processing operations, cleanup after the report has been run. We'll come back to these considerations. Meanwhile, as you learn to use the Report Designer, keep in mind that its product—a report file—isn't the end of the story.

Using the Report Designer

It's a rare application that doesn't need a battery of reports. For many users, nothing has happened with the application until the printed reports are done. Given the importance of reports, it's not surprising that attempts to make them easier to create are as old as computing. Fortunately, reports lend themselves to various kinds of automation, because they're basically repetitive and have well-understood components. The result has been a long history of *report generators*—programs that simplify the design and execution of reports. The FoxPro report generator, now called the Report Designer, is already in its seventh edition. With each succeeding version, it has matured, has acquired more features, and has become easier to use. The Visual FoxPro version approaches state-of-the-art in report generators, and that is saying a lot.

It wasn't long ago, 10 years or so, that microcomputer report generators were capable of only the most basic formats. Reports of any complexity usually had to be programmed—hard coded—one of the most nit-picking and time-consuming tasks in all of programming. Be thankful that you may never have to program a report. The FoxPro Report Designer isn't unlimited in capability, but it can handle more than 95 percent of all the reporting needed for applications.

The Report Designer wouldn't be half the tool it is without the powerful FoxPro database machinery, as well as the rich programming environment, behind it. Without the services of the Rushmore technology, SQL, and user-defined functions, the limitations of the Report Designer would be considerable.

If you are new to report generators, be prepared to wrap your mental powers around some new concepts for database reporting that are inherent to the Report Designer. This process won't be difficult, but on first exposure, terms such as *bands*, *groups*, and *report variables* seem strange. Even if you've done some of this before, it takes a while to get used to the Report Designer package.

REPORTS WHOLE, AND IN PART

Because a printed report is a visual object (something you can see), we'll approach a report as something you should be able to visualize, at least in the mind's eye. Start with an image of data tables, on the one hand, and a printed report on the other—something like Figure 7.4. The question is, how do you get from one to the other?

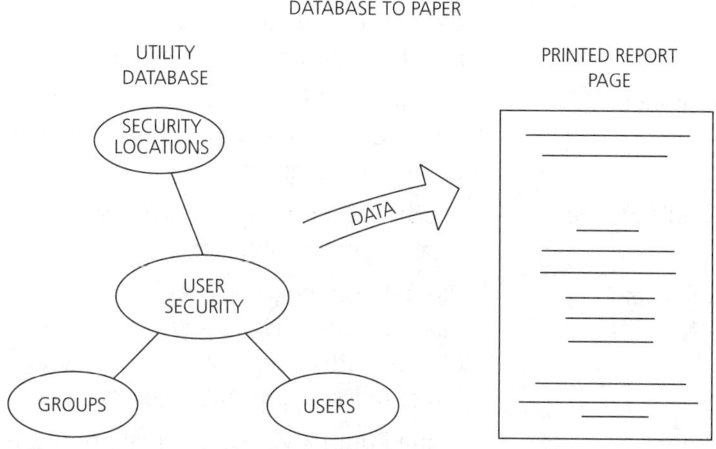

FIGURE 7.4 DATABASE TO PAPER.

A path leads from data to the printed page. It is complex at times, but if you get a feel for it, no report will be too great a challenge. Table 7.1 outlines the general steps for creating a report. These steps, like the steps to a query, are fundamental, but not all of them are required.

TABLE 7.1 STEPS TO CREATING A REPORT

STEP	DESCRIPTION
Analysis	Depending on the complexity of the report, analysis may simply be a quick copy of an existing report, or it may be a detailed study of the data, report layout, and processing requirements. Analysis should include whether any special user dialog boxes or data processing is required.
Data Setup	Creating the data environment for the report is usually a combination of SQL views and database tables, complete with relevant indexes and relations. It may also include incorporation of user input for report criteria.
Page Layout	Choosing all of the report layout elements, such as paper size, print orientation, page order, and placement of information on a page. This is usually a combination of printer capabilities and the requirements for display of the data.
Field Placement	Placement of table fields into a report sets not only the basic design but also many of the processing requirements.
Groups and Calculations	Specify report groups to organize a report and create report variables for summary calculations.
Design Objects	Placing text, boxes, circles, lines, and pictures into the report layout, plus enhancing report objects and layout for visual effect including fonts, styles, and possibly colors.
Run and Test	Using Print Preview and actual printing, examine layout, design, and calculations for appearance and accuracy.

Let's go through each of these steps in detail.

ANALYSIS: WHAT IS THIS REPORT?

Before you lay hands on the Report Designer, it's probably a good idea to stop and ask, What is this report? It's a simple question, although an easy one to fudge—at least until you get halfway into a report and realize it won't work. A formal preparation includes a study of data requirements and drawings of the report layout. This preparation is always a good idea, but under typical time pressure, reports often don't get done this way. Developers are always making trade-offs between what they can do in their heads, which is quick, and what they do on paper, which is usually more accurate. The more complex the report, however, the more need there is for homework.

NOTE

Visualizing reports is another of the "learned intuitions" that developers acquire. After you've done several (hundred), you begin to have a sense of how particular kinds of reports are constructed. This knowledge makes the job of creating new reports easier, but it doesn't necessarily make it faster. Much tedious detail work goes into complex reports, and there are precious few shortcuts.

The starting point for report homework is to determine the purpose of the report. What is it supposed to do: show profit and loss, highlight best-selling products, calculate sales commissions? Frequently the purpose is obvious, but you might be surprised by how many reports turn out to have no real purpose. (Then again, maybe you're not surprised.) Another basic consideration relates to who is going to use the report and the style it should follow: Is it a raw listing of data (a data dump), an executive summary, a report to the board of directors using fancy graphics, or a routine business report? All these reports are intended for a specific audience. To some extent, that dictates your approach, especially the report's presentation quality.

The next piece of homework is to determine which information is to be included in the report. For a variety of reasons, this isn't always clear. You can ask users of the report what they need, but people often have only a general idea of what they want, and they may have difficulty expressing their requirements. You must be something of a translator. Sometimes it won't become clear what people really want until you deliver the report. Then they can point to what they don't want or what's missing. Fortunately, the Report Designer makes it relatively easy to add or delete items from a report. Of course, it's still important to get a good list of required data.

NOTE

The examples in the remainder of this chapter are based on one of the utility subsystems included on the accompanying disk: Application Security. Briefly, the system assigns three values to security "gates" (which are user-defined functions) at various locations in the application, such as menu options and push-button controls. These values represent the security group for the gate and the access and activity levels. For example, a particular menu option for the accounting group may be set to an access level of 4 and an activity level of 3. Users of the application may have many security records, each with three assigned values: security group, access level, and activity level.

The analysis of the sample report goes like this: The boss stomps into the programmer's cubicle and says, "I need a report that lists all the security gates in the application, showing which users have clearance for them." (That's the purpose.) "It's for the boss, so the report needs to be neat but not fancy." (That's the style of report.) "And if it's not done by five o'clock today, your job's on the line." (That's the motivation.)

The selection of tables to use for a report is determined by the information required. Most reports consist of a *primary* table, possibly one *scan* table, and any number of *lookup* tables, as shown in Figure 7.5 for the example being used here.

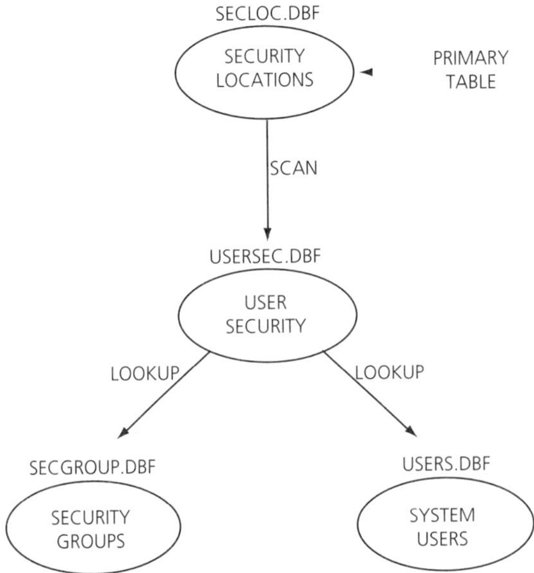

FIGURE 7.5 REPORT TABLES.

The primary table (for this example, the table of security locations) controls the processing of the report. Scan tables provide multiple instances of something related to the primary table, which in this case are the security assignments for each user. Lookup tables are used for record-at-a-time searches, typically to provide supporting information. In this example, information about a user and security groups comes from lookup tables.

The sort order—or, more likely, the index order of the primary table—is often extremely important for report grouping. In the example, the SECLOC (security locations) table is opened with a compound index on the MODULE+SECLOCID fields. The other tables will generally be ordered with indexes appropriate for setting relations. The USERSEC (user security) table is opened with the index GROUP, and SECGROUP is opened with the index GROUP. Reports may use relations extensively. Lookup tables have the basic relation, a record-at-a-time link. Scan tables will have the one-to-many relations in order to link with multiple records.

SETUP: CREATING THE DATA ENVIRONMENT

Once the analysis is complete and decisions have been made about the table data, you can move to FoxPro and begin to create the Data environment for the report. This process doesn't necessarily start with the Report Designer. In many cases, the report will be more efficient if you use the View Designer to create a view that does all the combining, selecting, and sorting of data before it goes to the report. (This also applies to the Query Designer.) The view you create is, in effect, a single table that can be passed to one of the five ways FoxPro gives you for starting a report. These options can be confusing, so here's a review of the pros and cons of each approach.

- **Report Wizard.** For reports that use only one table, this is an excellent start. You can easily select the desired fields, sort order, and even certain basic design aesthetics (which are defined as Executive, Ledger, and Presentation). FoxPro generally does a good job of providing a decent-looking report based on the simple requirements.
- **Report Designer Direct.** Going directly into the Report Designer is the most practical way to start if you are not using a view and if your report will use more than two tables. In this case, you're building a

report from scratch—table setup, basic layout, processing options, and visual design—and that takes time.

- **Quick Report.** The Quick Report is halfway between the "raw" Report Designer and the Report Wizard. For a single-table report, you can pick fields and a basic layout; but you're still left with making cosmetic improvements and usually rearranging the fields.
- **One-to-Many Report Wizard.** When your report needs two tables—one primary table and one for scanning—the One-to-Many Report Wizard performs the same role as the basic Report Wizard: It lets you pick fields, orientation, and one of three styles. However, because you need to set up the relations between the two tables before going into the Wizard, it doesn't save much time over going directly into the Report Designer.
- **Group/Total Report Wizard.** For reports from a single table that need to total on groupings (for example, fee totals by state), the Group/Total Report Wizard can be used to create up to three groups with totals and subtotals. Because it also does the other usual Report Wizard things, such as set fields, orientation, and layout, this Wizard can be a time-saver for grouped reports.

Although you can start and finish a report within each of the report wizards, they often work best as a way to jump-start a report to be enhanced and completed in the Report Designer. Keep in mind that all except one of the report wizards work only with a single table, whereas in a relational database system, reports should use multiple tables (three to five tables even for a simple report). That makes the approach of most of the wizards (at best) a start-up, leaving you with significant rearranging to do as you add the needed tables. That's true unless you are using a view, which can combine many tables into one (a cursor), thereby automatically overcoming the limitation of the wizards.

Except for using the Project Manager to start a new report (select **Documents**, **Reports** and then **New**), there is no best way to begin a report. The One-to-Many and Group/Total Report Wizards are specialists, and, if your report fits the limitations, they can be a help. If there is a general approach, one that will fit a large number of report requirements, it is to use the standard Report Wizard to get started, especially with a view, and then go from it into the Report Designer and Data Environment windows to add other tables and change the layout.

NOTE

The reason for using views instead of queries for the report's Data Environment is that a view's cursor can be automatically re-created whenever you run the report. You can also use query cursors, but they must be explicitly created (by you or a program) before you run a report.

By whatever route, you will eventually wind up in the Report Designer window, illustrated in Figure 7.6. Note that there are three possible toolbars: Report Controls, Report Designer, and Layout. You may not be able to keep all of them on the screen at one time unless you're using a 17-inch, or bigger, monitor.

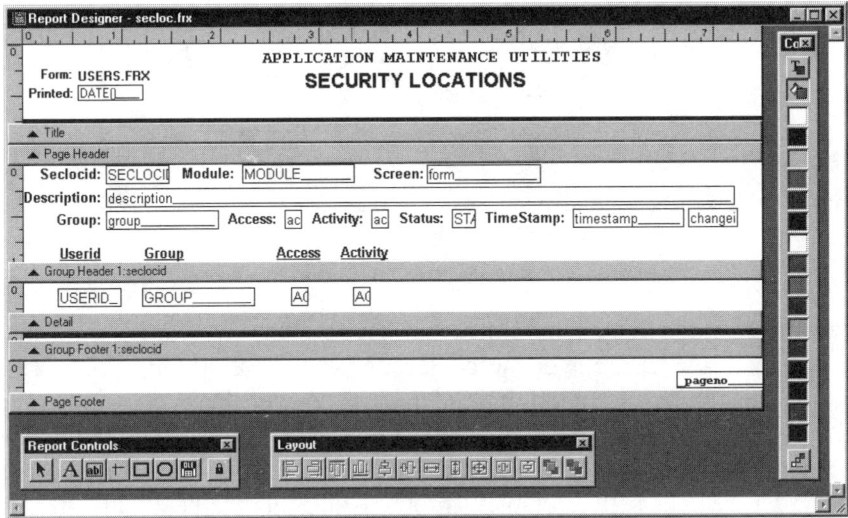

FIGURE 7.6 THE REPORT DESIGNER WINDOW.

It's highly recommended that unless you have saved the report in a wizard, you should immediately save the report using **File**, **Save**, which stores the report form in an FRX file. Save reports often—you never know when you may want to undo a bad design decision by reverting to an earlier version.

THE DATA ENVIRONMENT WINDOW

Once inside the Report Designer, you have access to its Data Environment, using either **View**, **Data Environment** or the **Data Environment** icon. The Data Environment is a major feature of Visual FoxPro and is used with both reports and screen forms to establish a unique data environment. As you can see in Figure 7.7, it has a visual approach very similar to that of the Database Designer.

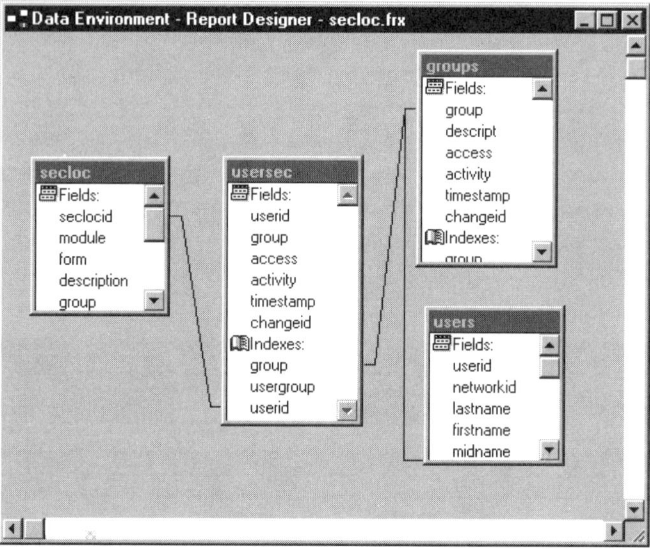

FIGURE 7.7 THE DATA ENVIRONMENT WINDOW.

If you arrived in the Data Environment (sometimes abbreviated as DE) from a wizard, it will already have one or more tables represented in it. Otherwise, use the right mouse button to summon the Add Table or View dialog box so that you can add tables to the DE. Each table (or cursor) has its own box, just as in the Database Designer. The fields in each table can be dragged and dropped into the report, and you can set relations between tables simply by dragging the field name from one table box to another (provided there are matching indexes). You can think of the Data Environment as an intermediary between the tables and the fields of the report, the place to specify and control access to data, as illustrated in Figure 7.8.

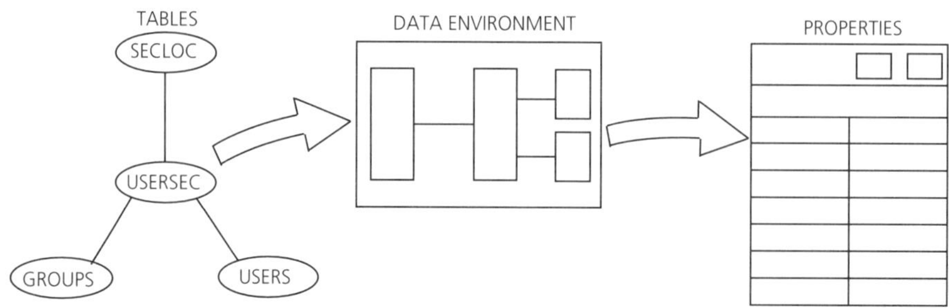

FIGURE 7.8 TABLES TO DATA ENVIRONMENT.

A significant part of the data specification is found in the Data Environment Properties window, which is the link between the data and FoxPro's object-oriented approach. We'll cover this window in much more detail later. For a brief introduction, open the Properties window by selecting **Data Environment** and using the shortcut menu (click the right mouse button) to select **Properties**.

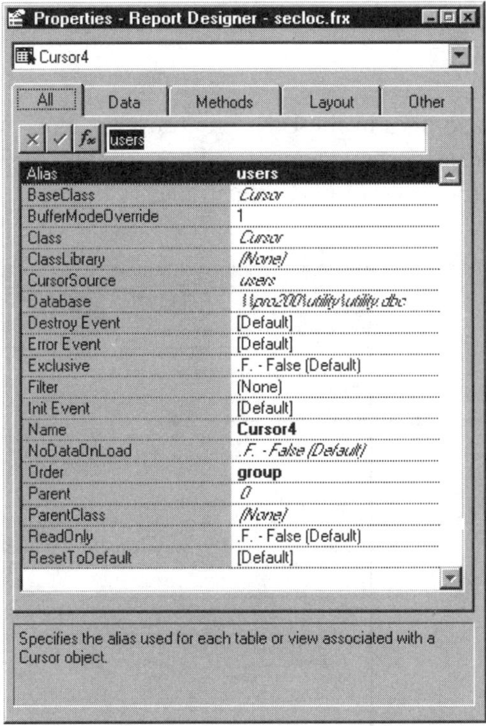

FIGURE 7.9 DATA ENVIRONMENT PROPERTIES WINDOW.

This window contains mostly object-oriented jargon and looks like a cross between the Project Manager and a mini spreadsheet. As you scroll up and down the properties list in the **All** tab, a few items may be familiar: **Database**, **Exclusive**, **Filter**, **Order**, and **ReadOnly**. These properties do what their command counterparts do: specify a database, set exclusive use, set a filter, set an index order, and set the table for read-only. For example, if you want to set a standard FoxPro filter on a table, select the **Filter** property; in the data entry area, enter any valid filter expression just as you would for a **SET FILTER TO** command.

NOTE

When you are working in a Data Environment, tables are no longer the center of attention; instead, the cursor becomes the focus. In part, that's because a cursor is considered an object by Visual FoxPro and, as an object, may have properties, events, and methods associated with it. It's also because a cursor is the image of a table's data held in RAM, where FoxPro does most of its work.

PAGE LAYOUT

Having set the data sources in the Data Environment, you can turn your attention to the large-scale design elements of the report: the page layout. This process starts with the order of pages illustrated in Figure 7.10.

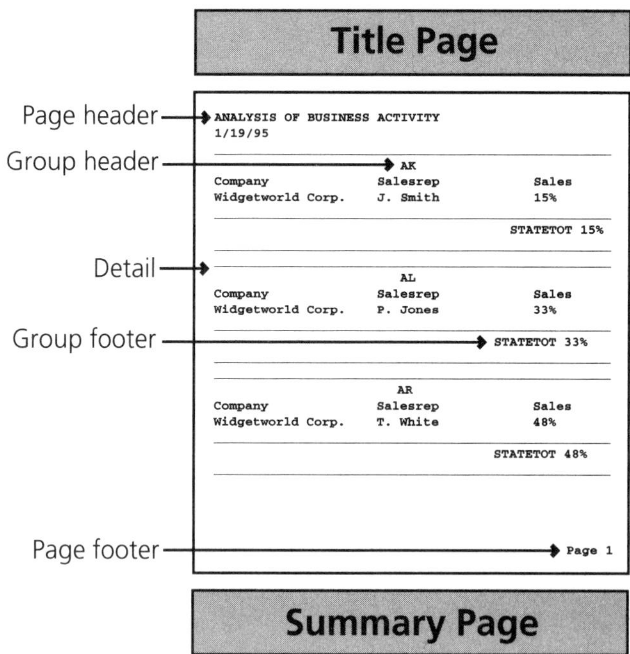

FIGURE 7.10 REPORT PAGE STRUCTURE.

Some reports, particularly the formal type, have a *title* page. This page is followed by the basic report pages, sometimes called the *body* of the report. Occasionally, there may be sections inside the body of the report, and these may have their own title pages. Finally, there may be a *summary* page, which typically is used for summary statistics and totals.

The main (body) pages of the report have their own structure. As they print from top to bottom, a *page header* is often used to identify the report and present other basic information. Many reports follow the page header with one or more *group headers*, which provide space for column headers and other identification associated with report groups. These headers are followed by the *detail* area, which contains the bulk of a report's information. After the detail come *group footers*, which may summarize information related to groups, and finally the *page footer*, which is often used for page numbers.

The illustration in Figure 7.6 shows a simple report that uses some of the bands available in the Report Designer. *Bands* are a visual representation of pages and page areas of a report: title page, page header, detail, and so forth. The Report Designer is said to be a band-oriented report generator, one that uses bands to control the structure of the report, the logic of processing, and the format of the printing. You can add or remove report space (measured as printed lines) from any of the band areas (the white space between band bars) simply by using the *band slider* button at the left of each band. Alternatively, you can double-click on the band buttons to pop up a Band window, where you can set the band size with precision.

The behavior of the bands at printing time is fairly straightforward, with the exception of the detail band. Whereas the title, headers, footers, and summary bands are fixed—they never print more lines than you've indicated in the designer window—the detail band can stretch, adding more lines as needed by the content of the data. This is why memo fields, which contain a variable amount of text, are best printed in the detail band. The same principle applies to graphics elements, particularly bitmap pictures. Only the detail band can accommodate the shaping of pictures to fit with a variable amount of printed text.

NOTE

The bands define the areas of a report and act as a guide for which data and design elements, such as pictures, might be used. But WYSIWIG this is not. To get a picture of what the output looks like, don't forget to frequently punch up **View**, **Preview** or the **print preview** icon in the main toolbar.

As part of visualizing how your report will look and creating the basic layout, you may need to set options such as the size of the paper, printing flow, and default font. It's a good idea to set these options as soon as possible so that your page setup will accommodate the data. Many of these layout options are found in the

Page Setup window, which is reached via the menu: **File**, **Page Setup**. This displays the Page Setup dialog box shown in Figure 7.11, which is quite different from the Print dialog box that shows up when you're not in the Report Designer.

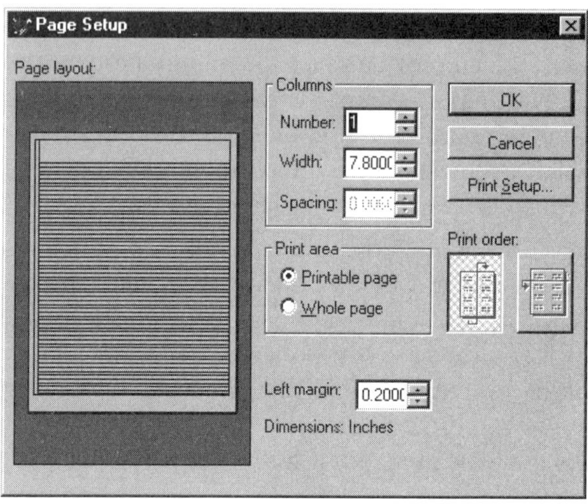

FIGURE 7.11 PAGE SETUP DIALOG BOX.

This dialog box is a grab bag of options ranging from printer setup to page layout. Most of the options are important.

- **Print Setup**. Clicking this button brings up the standard Windows Printer Setup dialog box. You can select portrait or landscape mode for page layout along with the size of the paper. You can also set the printer (or similar output device) for the report.
- **Print Order**. The icon button on the right is the standard print order: left to right across the entire page. The button on the left is column order, which enables printing in text columns (not the same as numeric reports printed in columns) and opens the door to many kinds of multiple column formats. Column order uses a snaking continuous print, proceeding from the column on the left, from top to bottom, to the next column in turn, from top to bottom.
- **Columns**. In the **Number** spinner, you can specify as many as 50 columns on a page. To make the columns work properly, you'll need to consider the width of data to be included and how it will fit inside a column. What you will see in the Report Designer window is what will

fit in *one* column. If you have more data than will fit in the column size you've selected, FoxPro will gray out those items that won't fit.

With a single column, only the left margin width can be adjusted. Once you have specified more than one column, then you can set the **Width** of the columns and the **Spacing** between columns (the gutter).

- **Print Area**. FoxPro lets you distinguish between the **Whole Page** or the **Printable Page**, which actually prints. This distinction applies to laser printers, which typically have a frame of 1/4 inch that does not print around each page.
- **Left Margin**. You can use this setting to create a left margin, typically used to allow for punched paper or binding.
- **Dimensions**. This option sets the unit of measurement for the report to inches or centimeters.

Other options affecting layout are found in the system menu. From the Report menu, use the **Default Font** option to display the Font Selection dialog box. This is a global setting, meaning that all text in the report will use the selected font, font size, and style. Font types and sizes can play a major role in the formatting of a report, so if you decide to use unusual fonts and sizes, be sure to print samples frequently.

In the Format menu you'll find the options **Set Grid Scale** and **Snap to Grid**. The former (see Figure 7.12) dimensions the ruler at the top of the design window. The ruler can be set to inches or pixels. **Snap to Grid** forces alignment with the grid lines and is used to ensure that a row or column of objects is in accurate alignment. This feature helps with large-scale alignment but can become a nuisance for small adjustments, so you may want to turn it off as the report progresses.

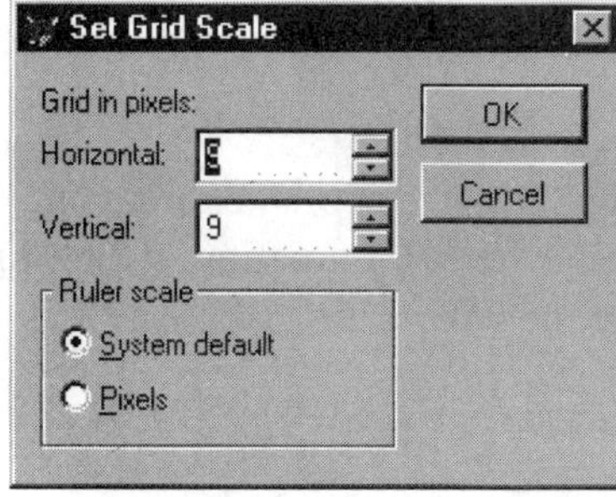

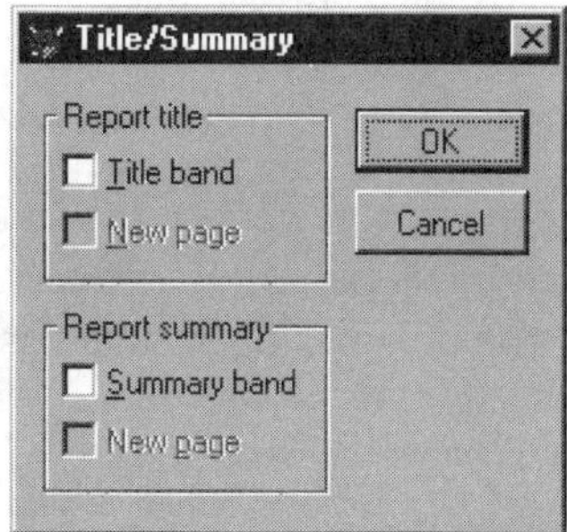

FIGURE 7.12 SET GRID SCALE AND TITLE/SUMMARY DIALOG BOXES.

The Title/Summary dialog box (Figure 7.12) is reached through **Report, Title/Summary** in the menu. There's not much to this: Selecting **Title** or **Summary** adds that band to the report. If you also select the page options, each item will be on a separate page.

REPORT EXPRESSION (FIELD) PLACEMENT

Fields in the report are, so to speak, the end of the pipeline that begins with the tables and travels through the Data Environment cursor into the bands and fields of the Report Designer, and finally onto the printed page. Figure 7.13 illustrates this connection. Even if you used Quick Report or a wizard to start your report, you'll still need to add or adjust the data fields. Here they aren't called fields—they're *report expressions*. This more generic term implies that they don't have to be fields from a table. That's true, although 98 percent of the time, report expressions are fields from a table.

Placing a field into a layout (on any page or page area) is a matter of selecting the field tool from the Report toolbar, creating a cross-hair cursor. You use this cursor to mark the area to be occupied by the field: Click on the upper-left corner of the area and drag the *marquee* (the dotted-line box) to the proper size. When you release the mouse button, the Report Expression dialog box appears (Figure 7.14).

If you know the name of the field, you can type it directly into the text box to the right of **Expression**. Otherwise, select the three-dot button; yet another instance of the Expression Builder dialog box will appear, ready for you to select a field or construct an expression. About 90 percent of the time, you will simply select a field. Another eight percent of the time, you'll combine a field with functions or other expressions:

```
TRIM(lastname) + "  ID:"+ networkid
```

The remaining two percent of the time will involve special expressions. The following example is based on a condition in the **IIF( )** function, which prints NOT ASSIGNED if the user has no security assignments:

```
IIF(EMPTY(usersec.userid), "NOT ASSIGNED", "" )
```

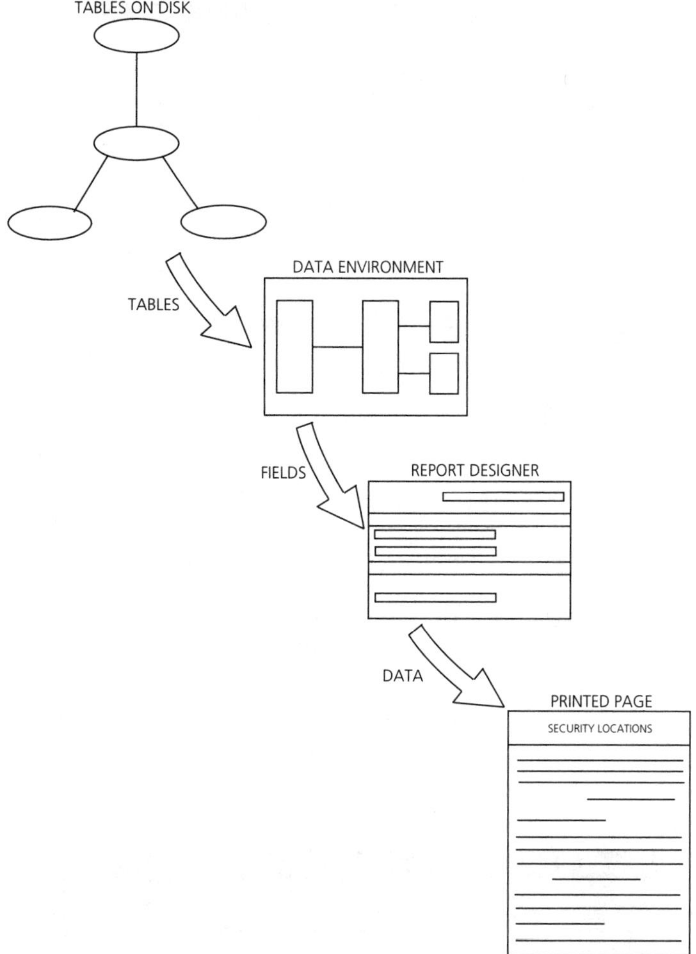

FIGURE 7.13 TABLES TO PAPER.

This example illustrates the flexibility you have in the Report Designer to define not only simple field expressions but also many other kinds of calculated or conditional expressions.

Once the expression object has been placed in the layout, other options in the Report Expression dialog box cover two main aspects of the expression's characteristics: format and printing.

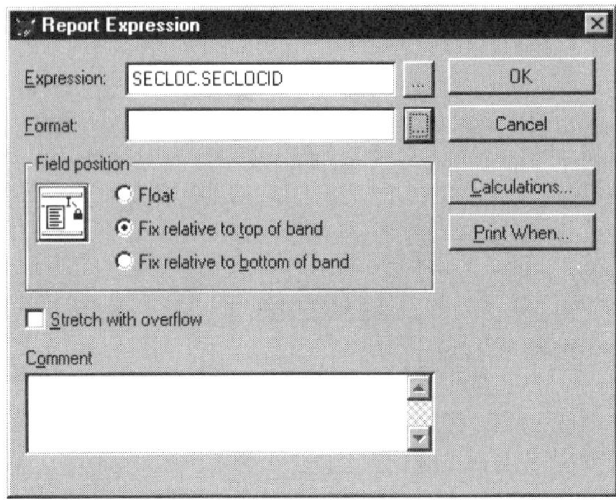

FIGURE 7.14 REPORT EXPRESSION DIALOG BOX.

EXPRESSION FORMATTING

Clicking on the **Format** three-dot button will display one of the three expression Format dialog boxes. Depending on the data type of the expression, you'll get Character, Numeric, or Date. (The character Format dialog is illustrated in Figure 7.15.) FoxPro will try to match the data type, but some expressions may not have a clear type, and FoxPro will get it wrong. Be sure to check the radio buttons below the format text box to see whether you have the correct data type.

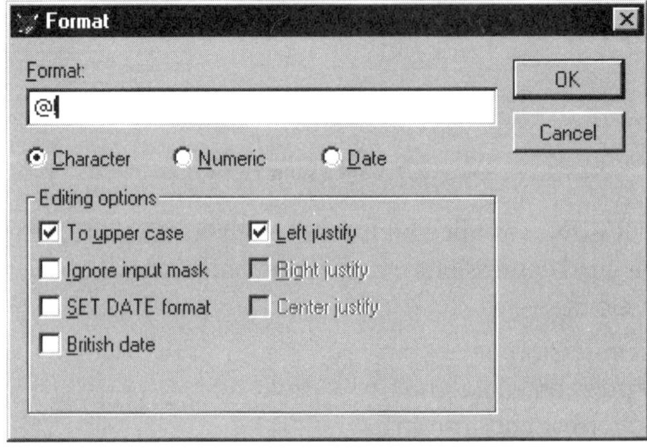

FIGURE 7.15 CHARACTER FORMAT DIALOG BOX.

Expression formatting lets you shape and control output. For example, if a field expression normally produces output in lowercase (johnson), but you want it in all uppercase (JOHNSON), there are two ways to produce this effect. Apply the **UPPER( )** function to the field in the expression definition or use the **To Upper Case** option in the Format dialog box. There are many other output effects, some created through formatting functions and others with format templates, and they are summarized in Tables 7.2 through 7.4. An asterisk marks those options that are most commonly used.

TABLE 7.2 CHARACTER DATA FORMAT FUNCTIONS

OPTION	CODE	OUTPUT AND EXAMPLE
Alpha Only	A	Display only alphabetical characters (no numbers etc.)
***To Upper Case**	!	All characters displayed in uppercase (all caps). `[ JOHNSON]`
R	R	Non-format characters displayed. `[(612) 454-6547]`
Edit "SET" Date	D	Edit data as a date using current SET DATE format. `[12/12/93]`
British Date	E	Use European date format. `[12.12.93]`
***Trim**	T	Remove all leading and trailing blank spaces.
***Right Align**	J	Align text on the right of the field. `[ JUSTIFIED RIGHT]`
***Center**	I	Center text in the field. `[ CENTERED ]`

*Most commonly used

TABLE 7.3 NUMERIC DATA FORMAT FUNCTIONS

OPTION	CODE	OUTPUT AND EXAMPLE
*Left Justify	B	Numeric data aligned with left side of field. `[1234    ]`
Blank if Zero	X	If the field output is zero, then nothing will be printed.
*(Negative)	(	Negative numbers placed in parentheses. `[  (3423)]`
Edit SET Date	D	Edit data as a date using current SET DATE format.
British Date	E	Use British date format.
CR if Positive	C	CR (credit) printed after number, if positive. `[    34CR]`
DB if Negative	Z	DB (debit) printed after number, if negative. `[    34DB]`
Leading Zeros	L	Print leading zeros before number. `[0000234]`
Currency	$	Prints a currency format. `[$20,220]`
Scientific	^	Displays numbers in scientific notation. `[   1.45E]`

*Most commonly used

TABLE 7.4 DATE DATA FORMAT FUNCTIONS

OPTION	CODE	OUTPUT & EXAMPLE
Edit Date	D	Edit field as a date in current date format. `[12/12/93]`
Edit British Date	E	Edit field in European date format. `[12.12.93]`

All these options are available at the click of a mouse in the Format dialog boxes. You may notice that after you click on the options, the code representation of your selection appears in the Format text box. You can enter the same codes directly into the box using the @ character to signify a format function, followed by one or more of the codes listed in the tables. For example, enter **@D** to have something output as a date, or **@T!** to have text trimmed and output in uppercase.

Format functions affect the entire content of a report expression. On the other hand, *format templates* impose patterns on individual elements (characters, numbers, and so on) of an expression. Suppose you wanted the first three letters of a field capitalized; you can use the format template: **!!!XXXXX** to accomplish it. These templates are called **PICTURE** template codes in the Xbase language, and *field masks* or similar terminology in other systems. They provide you with minute control over the output format. You'll notice in Table 7.5 that many of the options have an equivalent in the format functions except that here they operate on one character at a time.

TABLE 7.5 FORMAT TEMPLATE CODES

CODE	OUTPUT AND EXAMPLE OF USE
A	Allows output of only alphabetic characters. `[AAAAA]`
L	Allows output of logical data only. `[L]`
N	Allows letters and digits only for output. `[NNN]`
X	Allows any character. `[XXXXXXXX]`
Y	Allows Y,y,N,n only, with Y and N converted to uppercase. This code is used to print from logical fields. `[Y]`
9	With character data, allows only numeric output. With numeric data, allows all numbers and signs. `[$99.99]`

(Continued...)

CODE	OUTPUT AND EXAMPLE OF USE
#	Allows numbers (digits), blanks, and signs. `[###,###]`
!	Converts lowercase letters to uppercase. `[!!!]`
$	Displays current currency symbol. `[$ ##.## ]`
*	Displays asterisks in front of numeric values. `[***###]`
.	Specifies the decimal point. `[99.99]`
,	Comma separation for digits left of decimal point. `[$ ###,###,###]`

If you choose to enter function or template codes directly, be certain you include the @ symbol for any of the function codes. Don't use quotation marks for any of the entries. Function codes and picture templates can be combined. For example: `@B$ ###,###` is interpreted by FoxPro to format a number left-justified with a leading dollar sign, and with a comma between thousands and hundreds, like this: `$234,222`.

Using either format functions or templates is a way to fine tune a report expression. Their purpose is largely to properly shape the output of the report, and occasionally to correct for imperfections in the data (such as printing only numbers when fields may contain letters).

In the Report Expression dialog box, the **Field Position** area provides you with three options for placement of the expression in a line. **Float** aligns with the top of a line but allows the field area to expand (vertically) with the volume of text. **Fix relative to top of band** aligns the field with the top of a line and maintains its size. The **Fix relative to bottom of band** option aligns the field with the bottom of a line. All these options are best used to ensure uniform alignment across a line.

NOTE

If you are an inveterate mouser, you can get much more accurate placement of all report objects by dragging them into position with the mouse and then switching to the **Ctrl+** arrow keys for precise movement one pixel at a time.

REPORT GROUPS AND CALCULATIONS

Many reports are simply lists: lists of customers, lists of parts, and so forth. Such reports run from the first record of the primary table to the last record, printing record-by-record. But what if a list can be categorized, such as a list of parts by car model, and you want to highlight these categories? Or what if you need to get summary sales figures by state from a list of stores? That's when a simple report crosses into the territory of report *groups*.

The ability to create report groups is universal among report generators, and you may recall that the Query and View Designers also create groups. Groups are typically used to break data into types or categories within a specific field, such as a state field broken out by individual states. Groups allow you to separate different types of data visually on the page and for purposes of calculation. For example, in a report that groups by state, every time the state changes (say, from California to Colorado) there is an opportunity to print a group footer and a group header and to reset values depending on the state.

There's no secret to grouping, although it's common to find it mysterious at first. It's based on data in one or more fields being in a sort order so that like values are grouped. In fact, there's a law of grouping: If it isn't sorted on it, you can't group by it.

Most groups result from the sort order of the primary table. The sort order is often created by an index but can instead be accomplished with the **SORT** command or with the **Order By** clause of a SQL view or query. In the application security example, the sort order for this report is based on the index expression MODULE+SECLOCID for the primary SECLOC table. This expression has one sort order, by module, and can make one group. If additional groupings were needed—say by screen and then by department—the index would be an even bigger composite key : MODULE+SCREEN+DEPARTMENT+SECLOCID. These *cascade sorts* (or indexes) produce the ordering necessary to define three groups: module, screen, and department.

Once the correct sort order has been established, defining groups in the Report Designer is easy. From the menu select **Report**, **Data Grouping**. This action opens the Data Grouping dialog box seen in Figure 7.16.

The window displays a list of the existing group expressions, to which you can insert or delete. On **Insert**, all you need to do is to type the name of the sort field (or more complex expression, if there is one). If you need help, the three-dot button is available to invoke the Expression Builder.

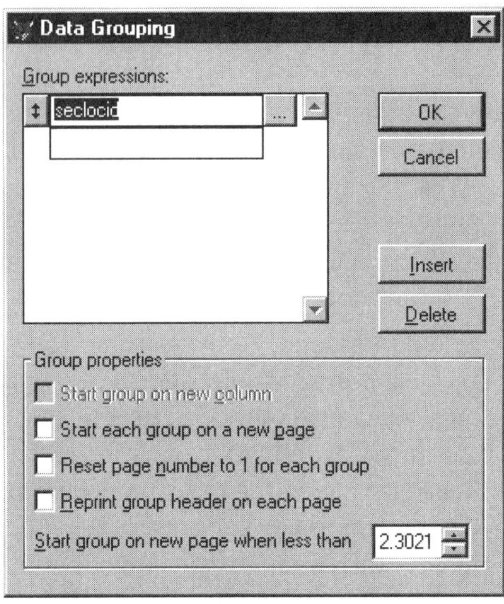

FIGURE 7.16 DATA GROUPING DIALOG BOX.

In addition to establishing the identity of a group, you can specify what happens when a group changes. These options are in the **Group properties** section and include **Start group on new column** (for a column-based report), **Start each group on a new page** (for page-based reports), with an option to **Reset page number to 1 for each group**). The column option works in concert with columnwise printing and provides some interesting design possibilities, particularly for multicolumn landscape reports. Another check box specifies **Reprint group header on each page**. This option can be very useful for repeating column headings and other visual alignment elements (lines, boxes). Finally, the window has what might be called a "widow/orphan" option for groups. If you specify the distance between a group header and the end of a page, **Start group on new page when less than**, FoxPro will force a page break rather than leave a group header without any subsequent content on the same page. This feature eliminates widows.

All these options give you control over the effect of a group and in particular what happens at a *group break*.; the point where one group item ends and another begins. As you will see, group breaks have a very important role in the use of report variables and calculated fields.

SUMMARY EXPRESSIONS (CALCULATED FIELDS)

In the Report Expression dialog box, clicking the **Calculations** button will open the Calculate Field dialog box (Figure 7.17). Here you'll see a list of options that look very much like the options of the FoxPro **CALCULATE** command (or the SQL field functions). These options transform the report expression, almost always a field, into a summary expression that is typically used to count or sum a particular field for the entire report or for a group in the report. The **Reset** popup is used to specify where a calculated field resets its stored value to zero. This is usually at the end of the report or at one of the group breaks.

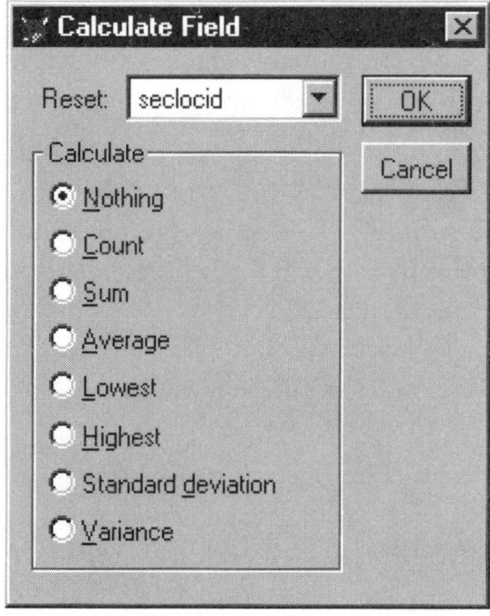

FIGURE 7.17 CALCULATE FIELD DIALOG BOX

NOTE

Calculated fields are less flexible than report variables. A field can't have more than one calculation, calculated fields can't be used inside other expressions, and the results of calculated fields can't persist beyond the running of the report. However, calculated fields are simple to use, and if you limit their use to group and summary bands, they'll do the job.

REPORT VARIABLES

Report variables are, first of all, just variables. Like all other variables in FoxPro, they can store values of any kind (character, numeric, or date). You can use a report variable anywhere in a report to hold values. As with regular variables, these values can be passed into user-defined functions and can persist beyond the run of the report.

Yet report variables seem different, because FoxPro provides a special window to define them and they can be linked with report summary calculations such as Sum and Count. This latter capacity makes report variables very similar to calculated fields, and that causes people to confuse report variables with calculated fields. On the whole, report variables, and to a certain extent their connection with report groups, are probably the most perplexing part of the Report Designer. But they're important, so let's attempt a simple explanation.

Using the ongoing application security example, Table 7.6 lists five fields that might be used with report variables. The first column shows the table fields, the second column the summary calculations, and the third column the report variables. The fourth column shows the reset break (group or report) associated with the variable.

TABLE 7.6 REPORT VARIABLES

FIELD	BREAK	CALCULATE	REPORT VARIABLE
SECLOCID	MODULE	Count	nSLocCnt
MODULE	REPORT	Count	nModCnt
SCREEN	REPORT	Count	nScrCnt
SEC1	MODULE	Average	nAvgSec1
		Min	nMinSec1
		Max	nMaxSec1
SEC2	MODULE	Average	nAvgSec2
		Min	nMinSec2
		Max	nMaxSec2

All the fields are from the primary table, SECLOC, which is indexed on MODULE +SECLOCID. The MODULE field is the only group. Using Table 7.6 as a guide, the SECLOCID is unique to each location, so a count of each ID will be made, totaled for each program module, and stored in the variable `nSLocCnt`. The MODULE field, which has the name of various modules of the application, is the most useful unit for grouping, but a count of modules *by module* will always be 1—so this report variable will hold a count for the entire report. In a similar vein, an individual module has only a few program screens, so a count of the SCREEN fields will be for the whole report. The two security level fields—SEC1 (Access) and SEC2 (Activity)—will be analyzed by module for average, minimum, and maximum values.

The use of a report variable in this example is dependent on the table being ordered by MODULE. To define the first variable for the SECLOCID, the place to start is in the menu: **Report**, **Variables**. This action brings up the Report Variables dialog box pictured in Figure 7.18.

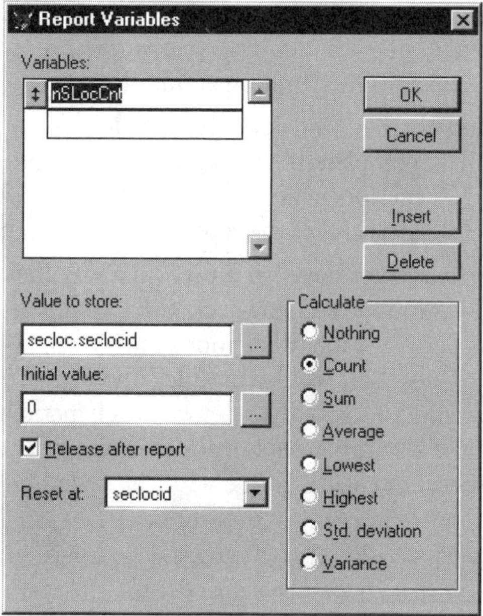

FIGURE 7.18 REPORT VARIABLES DIALOG BOX.

This dialog box exists because you have no direct access to the workings of a FoxPro report. In general programming, you can manipulate the code surrounding a variable, but in a report you can't tinker with the FoxPro code. So the definition dialog box gives you limited but still useful ways of inserting and manipulating a variable in a report.

The main purpose of report variables is to store the running values of summary calculations. In the case at hand, you want a running count of security locations by module. In the Report Variables dialog box, you enter a name for the variable, such as `nSLocCnt`, and indicate the **Value to store** to be `SECLOCID`, the unique location ID. Because there is no starting value for this variable, you can leave the default of **0** in the initial value box. Similarly, the default **Release after report** can remain checked to remove the variable from memory as soon as the report completes.

The crucial entry for this definition is the **Reset** option. Reset usually means reset to zero for summary calculations. You use this any time you want to have the calculations start over with a new grouping. In addition to the standard options (End of Report, End of Page, End of Column), each group that you have defined will also appear in the **Reset** popup. In this case, `MODULE` would be selected, because you want the security location count to be zeroed before starting a new module. The final step for defining this variable is to select the **Count** option so that it will contain the running count of the security locations field.

All the fields and their report variables are defined in the same manner. When the definition is completed, the variables based on the module group break can be placed in the footer area for that group (as a report expression). The variables that reset at the end of the report go into the report summary page.

So far, the report variables have been used in a way that may be duplicated with calculated fields. You could, however, use the report variables `nAvgSec1`, `nMinSec1`, and `nMaxSec1` to do some calculations for each application module. For example, `nMaxSec1 / nAvgSec1` would produce the ratio between the highest access level for that module and the average level; perhaps too high a ratio would indicate that the security gates for this module are not uniformly valued. This use of report variables can't be done with calculated fields.

NOTE

As the FoxPro manuals point out, you need to be careful with any report variable that contains another report variable as part of its definition. The order in which variables are listed in the Report Variables dialog box sets the order of calculation.

When to Print

The **Print When** options extend what can be placed in the bands of a report by making it possible to include objects or lines that do not print if there's nothing to print. This option opens the door, for example, to having lookups in multiple tables that print only when certain conditions are true.

The **Print When** button appears in all report object dialog boxes. When it is selected, it opens the Print When dialog box (see Figure 7.19). The uses of options here are not always obvious, but they are versatile.

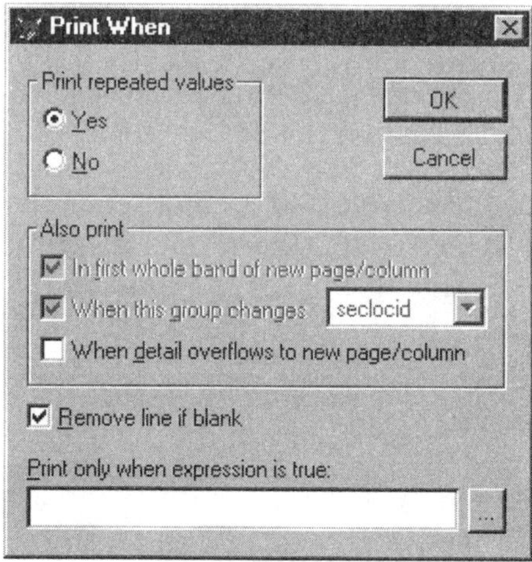

FIGURE 7.19 PRINT WHEN DIALOG BOX.

The **Print repeated values** option suppresses repeated printing of expressions in the detail band. The classic example is for a company name followed by a list of invoices. The company name is needed only once, so you would select **No** in the **Print repeated values** area.

The **Also print** area contains three options that are used mostly for printing of objects in and around page, group, and column breaks. **In first whole band of new page/column** is used to make sure that a field isn't printed until a complete new page or column is started. **When this group changes** will print a field only when a specified group changes. **When detail overflows to new page/column** will print a field when the detail band overflows. It is often used to print a "continued" message.

At the bottom of the Print When dialog box are two inconspicuous options—the two most important. **Remove line if blank** works to omit lines that are blank. With **Print only when expression is true**, all objects in the line should be set not to print unless they satisfy a condition. If they fail that condition, FoxPro interprets the line as blank and will not print it.

Selecting the three-dot button, the **Print only when expression is true** option uses the Expression Builder to create the logical expression that defines when the object should print. For example, in the detail band of the application security report, it might be desirable to print a line with the text "No security values assigned" if the current security location has no users assigned to it. To do this, you would create a new line in the detail band and define a report expression with nothing except the text "No security values assigned." Then, in the **Print only when expression is true** area, enter the following:

```
IIF(FOUND("USERSEC"), .f., .t.)
```

This uses the **FOUND( )** function to test each record in the SECLOC table for a match in the USERSEC table. If none is found, then "No security values assigned" will print; otherwise, it will not be printed.

NOTE

Remember that *every object* in a line must have the same Print When logic if you want the line not to print.

DESIGN OBJECTS

In addition to the basics—page layout, field (report) expressions, groups, and report variables—FoxPro provides a number of report elements, or objects, that can be used to enhance the appearance and readability of a report. These design-oriented objects include lines, text, shapes, pictures, and colors (relevant if you have a color printer). Although it is easy to visually overcomplicate a report, a judicious use of these design elements can make a big difference for a formal report intended for special audiences such as a board of directors.

THE FORMAT MENU

All report objects are design elements in the report layout and contribute to the visual presentation of the information. At some point in the creation of a complete report, you'll probably turn your attention to its visual layout and decorative aspects. In the process of refining these elements, you'll need to use the options in the Format menu. They can be put into two categories: positioning options (Table 7.7) and object characteristics options (Table 7.8).

TABLE 7.7 FORMAT MENU: POSITIONING OPTIONS

OPTION	USE
Align	If you select the **Ruler/Grid** option from the Report menu, you can use this object to force objects to align with the grid. This can be useful in the early stages of report design, when you want to make elements line up correctly and evenly. On other occasions, however, you'll need to turn the grid alignment off to allow for off-center and other precise positioning. The numerous variations of this option apply mostly to controls (pictures, fields, and so on) in the report.
Size	The next three options are most often used with a group of objects in a report. Sizing will change the relative size of all selected objects.
Horizontal Spacing	This option adjusts the horizontal space between selected objects so that they are equally distant from each other.
Vertical Spacing	Like horizontal spacing, this adjusts the vertical spacing between objects so that they are equidistant from each other.
Bring to Front	Any object or group of objects can be positioned on top of other objects. In effect, objects can be layered. This option lets you change which object is on top of a stack and completely visible. Using this option will put the selected object up front, visible above any other object underneath.
Send to Back	The opposite action from **Bring to Front**, this option sends an object (or group) behind other objects. In effect, it pushes it to the bottom layer.
Center	Automatically centers the selected object on the page between the left and right margins.

(Continued...)

OPTION	USE
Group	Either by using the mouse to draw a marquee around several objects or by using the **Shift** key with the arrow keys, you select two or more objects simultaneously. Then you choose this menu option, and all the objects become a single object as a group. This arrangement can make it much easier to move and reposition the objects. Typically, this option is used on lines of objects in the report.
Ungroup	Frequently, groups are created for the sole purpose of moving a large number of objects from one part of the report to another. Once the move has been made, it's usual to ungroup the objects for further adjustments.

TABLE 7.8 FORMAT MENU: OBJECT CHARACTERISTICS

MENU OPTION	USE
Font	Selecting the **Font** option brings up the Font window. Depending on your collection of fonts, you can apply almost any typeface, size, and style to your report text.
Text Alignment	Text can be aligned inside the text frame you have created. The options that appear here are **Left**, **Center**, **Right**, **Single** space, **One and a Half** space, and **Double** space.
Fill	**Fill** applies only to objects that have the space to take a fill pattern (hatching, lines, solid colors, and so on), most typically rectangles, circles, and so on.
Pen	Lines, text, box edges, and so on may all have one or more pen characteristics. These include width of pen (width of the line), which ranges from hairline to 6 points, and style of line (dots, dashes, dots and dashes, solid).

MENU OPTION	USE
Mode	In a related characteristic to **Front** and **Back** objects, the **Mode** determines whether an object is transparent or opaque. If you make an object opaque, nothing underneath it will be visible. If you make it transparent, portions of anything underneath will show through wherever "white space" occupies the transparent object.

TEXT, LINE, AND RECTANGLE OBJECTS

As objects go, the line and shape objects are simple to use. They are decorative elements used to highlight, segregate, and organize the visual elements of a report. Each of the objects is used by selecting the corresponding tool from the Report Controls Toolbar and applying it to the Report Designer window. Here's a brief rundown of each object.

Text objects are used for titles, descriptions, and explanations in the report. The most important thing about them is that they can become major design elements. That's because text can take on the attributes of **Font** and **Style**. Adding unusual fonts or styles (especially when combined with large sizes) can have a major impact on the appearance of a report. The Text window associated with text objects doesn't have many options: **Print When** (discussed previously) and **Position Relative To**, which refers to the positioning of text relative to the line it occupies.

The two geometric shape objects, which are actually four objects—squares, rectangles, lines, and circles—are similar. Rectangles (squares) and lines share the Rectangle/Line window. Like text objects, they can have a **Print When** condition and can be positioned at the top or bottom of a line. A rectangle or square can also be set to stretch with a band. This capability is particularly useful if you want to box a memo field and have it expand with the size of the text.

Round rectangles (and circles) have their own window. Here, you'll find similar options as in the Rectangle/Line window except that the **Style** choices represent various bevels for the corners. The selection on the far right, however, turns the rectangle into a circle. This is a curious way of presenting a circle shape, but presumably you don't use many circles in printed reports.

PICTURE OBJECTS

It takes a graphical user interface to make the presentation of graphics (pictures, icons, and so on) relatively easy. The Report Designer allows you to incorporate picture elements in a report, and the mechanics are simple. Most of your time will be spent with minor adjustments, sizing, and alignment to make the picture element fit properly in the report. Fortunately, the rest of the task, especially making the picture print properly, is the domain of FoxPro and Windows and not the person creating the report.

Like the other report objects, picture objects are best created with the picture tool from the Report Designer toolbar. You select the picture icon and then use the mouse to draw the outline of the picture frame in the Designer window. When you release the mouse button, the Report Picture dialog box will appear, as in Figure 7.20.

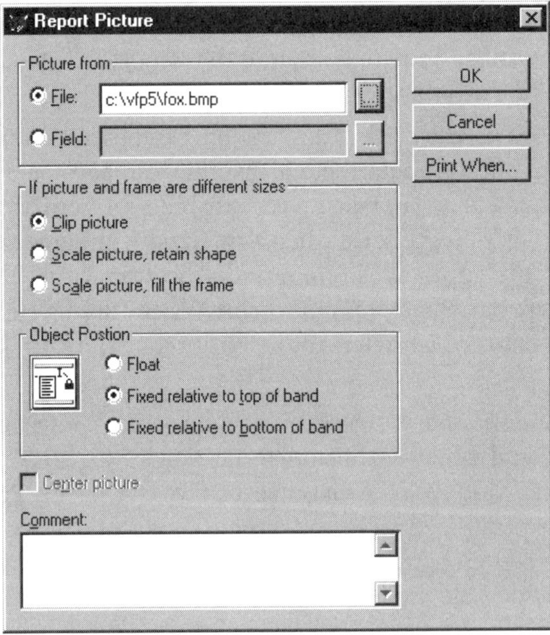

FIGURE 7.20 REPORT PICTURE DIALOG BOX.

The first step is to identify the source of the picture (pictures are never stored in the report). You have two options: a file on disk with a BMP extension (or at least any true *bitmap* picture file) or a General field in a table. If you select the **File** three-dot button, you'll get the familiar Windows File Open dialog box where you can select the file you want. As usual, this requires that you have an idea where to look for files. For this reason, it's usually a good idea to put all BMP files of a project in the same folder (subdirectory).

If you select the **Field** three-dot button, you'll get the Choose Field/Variable dialog box. The only choice that makes sense is, of course, a field. The field must be of the General data type and must contain something that is (or closely approximates) a bitmap image.

That's all there is to selecting the image. However, bitmap images tend to come in a wide variety of shapes and sizes, and they don't always fit neatly into the area you've selected in the report. So FoxPro gives you options for shaping pictures.

In the **If picture and frame are different sizes** box there are three options: **Clip picture** will handle pictures that are bigger than the frame you indicated. It clips the overlap of the picture and shows only the portion that will fit in the frame. If this option doesn't show what you had in mind, you need to go back to the picture's source (usually a drawing program of some kind) and edit the picture. **Scale picture, retain shape** allows you to resize the picture inside the frame without losing the proportions of the original shape. In effect, this option allows only exactly proportional changes to the picture size. **Scale picture, fill the frame**, on the other hand, will stretch the picture to fit the frame whether or not that distorts the picture.

In addition to the picture and frame options, you can select positioning options. **Float** allows the picture to center itself within the frame. (Bitmap files have a known size and will always fit the frame.) This option will automatically center the picture in the frame instead of in the default position in the upper-left corner. **Fixed relative to top of band** will always position the picture as close as possible to the top of the band, whereas **Fixed relative to bottom of band** puts it at the bottom.

Different pictures react differently to these treatments. You'll frequently have to experiment to find the right combination of frame, sizing, and alignment. Because of the sometimes peculiar behavior of pictures and the time it takes to print them, it's a good idea to be moderate with their use in printed reports.

RUN AND TEST

While you're creating a report and of when it's time to run it, FoxPro provides the run ! icon in the main toolbar (or **Run Report** in the Report menu.). Selecting either item will display the standard Print dialog box (the same as in Figure 7.1).

This dialog box has a few items buried under the **Options** button that leads to the Print Options dialog box (Figure 7.3). If you are working on a report form, the name of that report will appear in the **File** text box. Otherwise, you will need to select a report **Type** from a file on disk. Reports are stored in FRX files. To simplify locating them with the File Open dialog, it's a good idea to put them all in one folder (subdirectory), at least for development. As mentioned, for the user this arrangement may not be satisfactory.

The **Restore Environment** check box can be used if the report was created with the Data Environment enabled. If it was, FoxPro will open and restore all tables, indexes, and relations necessary to run the report.

Selecting the **Options** button brings up the familiar **Scope**, **For**, and **While** options. You can enter these options directly in their corresponding text boxes or use the buttons to summon the Expression Builder. These options are often used to selectively print data in the same way they are used to control other FoxPro operations.

A FoxPro report can also be run from the Command window (and in programs) by using the **REPORT FORM** command.

Command syntax:

```
REPORT FORM FileName1 | ?
    [ENVIRONMENT]
    [Scope] [FOR lExpression1] [WHILE lExpression2]
    [HEADING cHeadingText]
    [NOCONSOLE]
    [NOOPTIMIZE]
    [PLAIN]
    [RANGE nStartPage [, nEndPage]]
    [PREVIEW [WINDOW WindowName]
    [NOWAIT]]
    [TO PRINTER [PROMPT] | TO FILE FileName2 [ASCII]]
    [NAME ObjectName]
    [SUMMARY]
```

Arguments (abbreviated):

ENVIRONMENT Use the Data Environment stored with the report form.

HEADING cHeadingText Include a standard heading defined by **cHeadingText**.

NOEJECT Do not eject a page of paper before printing.

NOCONSOLE Do not echo the report output to the screen.

PLAIN Print page header only at beginning of report.

PREVIEW Send output to the Print Preview window.

TO PRINTER Send output to the printer.

PROMPT Before printing, display the Windows Print Setup dialog box.

TO FILE FileName2 [ASCII] Send output to a file.

Examples:

```
REPORT FORM users TO FILE users.txt
REPORT FORM usersec TO PRINT PROMPT FOR sysdate > {12/31/94}
```

As you can see, this command carries many options that can be used to change the output of the report and even some of the formatting. That's why, in some instances in applications, you might want to use this command rather than go through the standard FoxPro output dialog boxes.

NOTE

In almost all cases, printing moves from left to right and top to bottom. Although it is possible to make some printers back up, it's not commonly done and FoxPro doesn't give you any easy way to do it. This means that you can't have the printer go down the page, printing one piece of information, and then start over with another piece. In other words, you need to think of printing as continuous; if it can't be done in one pass, it can't be done. You can reprint a page, but alignment problems generally make this difficult and impractical.

Testing a Report

Unless you create many reports with the Report Designer, the logic peculiar to printed reports—the use of report variables, grouping, and so forth—conspires to make problems seem more obscure. When you study your reports for accuracy, *never assume*; check your logic and the calculations. If possible, run different sets of data through the report to see whether it accurately handles extremes. Still, you won't catch everything.

The most troublesome reports are often those that expand horizontally to include more field data, as opposed to those that are purely vertical. This means that reports with scans into subsidiary tables cause more problems than those that merely run vertically down the primary table. When you are testing and debugging a report, the interactions among lookup and scan tables, report groups, and summary calculations make for subtle errors. In many cases, only a sense of how these elements work together—and trial and error—will lead to a solution.

When looking at the overall task of creating a database application or similar projects, you should never forget that although simple reports take only minutes, other reports of devilish complexity may take days. And that's if you use the Report Designer—think of how long it would take if you had to code reports from scratch!

Creating Labels

One pedestrian but necessary task of many applications is to crank out mailing labels. This is another output variation for which FoxPro provides a specialized tool. The Label Designer could be called Report Writer Jr. It has a similar layout and set of options as the Report Designer. However, there are differences: The front end of the label creation requires you to select the type of label to be used, and in the Label Designer only the detail band has any output. When you start creating a label, you are making mailing labels—and that's all. Any other label application, such as making name tags or product labels, is done just as easily and more flexibly in the Report Designer.

To create a label, you can either use a Data Environment or open the needed table(s). If this process involves any indexes, sorts, or relations, these, too, should be done before you begin designing. After the label has been designed, you can save it to a file, which is automatically assigned the extension LBX.

As with creating all other files in FoxPro, you should start with the Project Manager. Because label creation is relatively cut and dried, it's usually best to use the Label Wizard to get started. This wizard will guide you through the process of selecting label formats and putting the appropriate data into the forms. When you arrive at the Label Designer window (Figure 7.21), 95 percent of the work has been done.

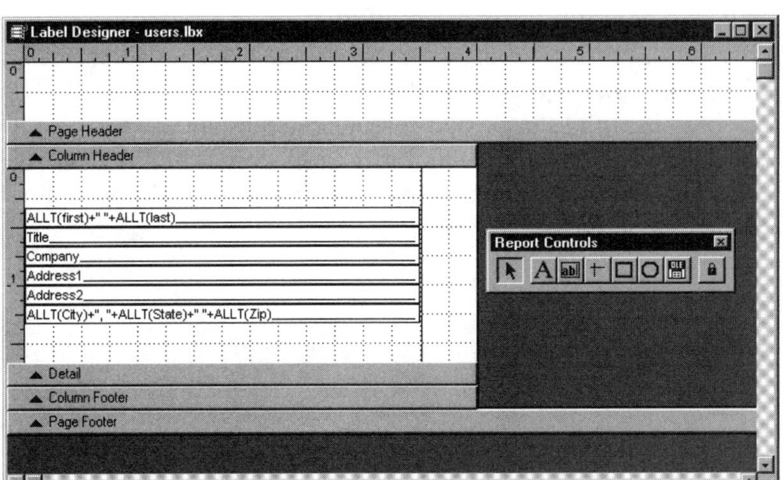

FIGURE 7.21 LABEL DESIGNER WINDOW.

After you make any desired minor alterations, the Label output uses the run icon or **Run**, **Label** from the Report menu. It also uses the same Print dialog as used with reports.

CHAPTER WRAP-UP

Although the Report Designer is the centerpiece of FoxPro's output capability, hopefully this chapter has also made it clear that other forms of output, such as file and screen display, also have their place in many applications.

It's important to distinguish between the way you use FoxPro's tools and the way you can expect the users of an application to use them. This is particularly crucial for the Report Designer. Very few users will be able to use this tool to modify (much less create) their own reports. The degree to which you allow the user of an application to access FoxPro's designers and other dialog boxes (such as the Expression Builder) is an important decision for many applications. Not only will it impact your program's ease of use, but also it may force you to provide services—that is, program them—that are normally provided by FoxPro. If you choose to program these services, you have to consider them part of an application framework and organize them like other components.

The Report Designer is not one of the easier FoxPro tools to master, although it is not nearly as complex as the Forms Designer. Still, it is a transition tool between the object-oriented programming of Visual FoxPro and the older way of doing things in FoxPro for DOS. It will pay you to experiment as much as you can with the Data Environment, especially with the Properties window. Sometimes the most difficult lessons of object-oriented programming will be learned by the simplest of examples.

SECTION 3

Good Old-Fashioned Programming

There is nothing facetious about the title of this section. Not many years ago, all programming in FoxPro (and most other languages) was accomplished with an ASCII text file and an editing program. The file was composed of a series of commands and other program structures that executed in a more or less linear fashion. This was called *procedural* programming. Then along came *object-oriented* programming (OOP), which, for the most part, executes in a nonlinear fashion, triggered by events (user-generated or otherwise). OOP is often characterized as *event-driven* programming. OOP applications are also structured quite differently, and that makes it natural to wonder whether procedural programming is obsolete.

The answer is unequivocally no. The techniques associated with procedural programming are fundamental to all languages, including OOP languages. Put another way, if you don't know how to use program control structures, create functions, manipulate arrays, and understand the scoping of variables, you won't be able to do object-oriented programming.

Like the data management commands, the elements of procedural programming are found throughout an application but don't provide many stand-alone components to an application framework. Remember that a framework isn't the same as the content of an application: for example, individual reports are not part of an application framework. Reports are created for a specific application as needed. However, the application framework might provide the means of organizing reports and presenting output options to the user, something that can be added to almost any application.

In a sense, as shown in Section Figure 3.1, we're working at the top of the application framework, where the material is fundamental but doesn't generate big plug-and-play chunks. There are a few exceptions. Some applications will use procedural code for data processing or special calculations. These components can be kept in program (PRG) files in much the way they've always been done in FoxPro. This group might also include MAIN.PRG, which is traditionally used to start an application. As I've mentioned, the Query Designer is often replaced by something more user-friendly or customized for an application. These components are small potatoes compared with the class hierarchy, but they serve to illustrate that an application framework in FoxPro is more than the parts created with OOP.

The three chapters in this section cover a lot of ground, essentially the basics of programming. We'll begin with the issues involved in preparing to program and end with the creation of stand-alone procedural programs:

- Chapter 8, "The Programming Environment" deals with the preparation for developing an application and programming in general. It covers hardware, operating system, and other software issues and explains the many ways to configure the internal environment of FoxPro.
- Chapter 9, "Programming Basics," introduces the basic FoxPro program file and describes how you use control structures, variables, and other programming elements to manage the flow of a program and its data.
- Chapter 10, "Procedural Programming," covers how to program database management routines and how to use standard FoxPro commands and functions to create programming elements that are used throughout the object-oriented part of FoxPro.

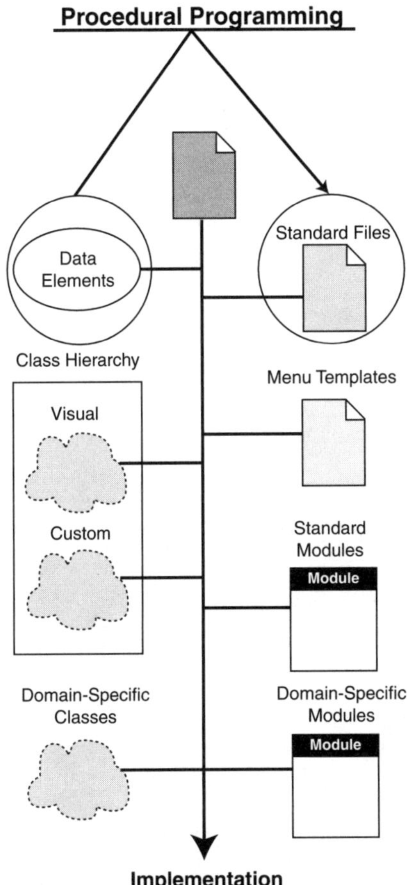

SECTION FIGURE 3.1 APPLICATION FRAMEWORK.

The goal of this section is not to teach programming but rather to introduce you to programming elements that you will use even when doing visual programming in the Forms Designer. The full picture of programming in FoxPro, which includes object-oriented programming, will be completed in Section 4.

CHAPTER 8

THE PROGRAMMING ENVIRONMENT

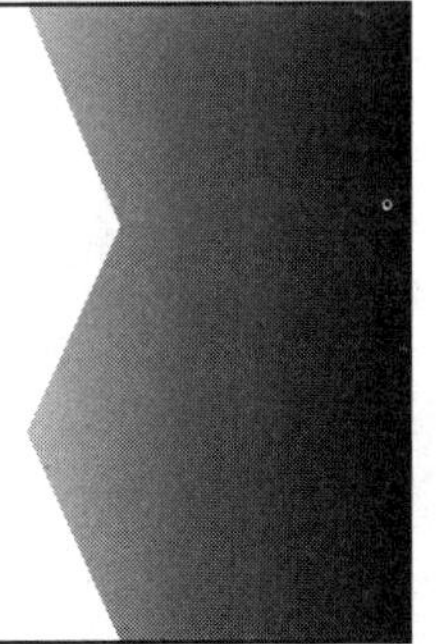

Getting your gear together, configuring your software, and working out your way of programming are all part of an essential first step in application development. These decisions are also very personal. It's helpful to see the programming environment as having two parts: the general computing environment *external* to FoxPro (hardware, operating system, and other software) and the *internal* environment of FoxPro while it's running (variables and option settings). This chapter will cover the highlights of configuring your computing environment, but it's impossible to describe how to set up an ideal environment, because you'll have to discover one for yourself.

That doesn't mean there isn't common ground among programmers. Application development imposes conditions—such as deadlines and budgets—that affect the working environment for almost everyone. Some projects can be done by the seat of your pants (they're a lot of fun, too), but developing an application of any size isn't one of them. There are too many pieces: databases, forms, reports, labels, help systems, maintenance routines, and so forth. Keeping track of everything is part of the challenge. So is getting the most out of hardware and software so that you can be reasonably efficient. Not that orderliness isn't a virtue in its own right, but the less time you spend wondering where things are and futzing with the details of your programming environment, the more time you have for the creative aspects of programming. The development process has enough distractions (necessary evils such as clients, employers, and users) that you don't need a helter-skelter working environment as part of the mix.

The topics in this chapter are the ones most obviously involved with configuring your programming environment:

- Hardware requirements and selection
- Operating system choices
- File management and directory structure
- FoxPro system options
- The FoxPro editor
- Keyboard macros

There are other, more subtle configuration issues, such as associating data types with visual controls, and we'll get to them as we go more deeply into object-oriented programming. For now, everything in this list represents something that can, and usually should be, customized by the developer. A note of caution: Don't go overboard unless you have lots of time for recreational swimming. Good tools (hardware and software) cost money, and establishing a comfortable working environment takes time. Up to a point, it's worth whatever resources you can spare.

The Programming Cycle

Although it's not quite as inevitable as death and taxes, the programming cycle is difficult to avoid . Even with modern GUI tools such as the Form Designer, the programming process remains in outline (and in Figure 8.1) what is has been for a long, long time.

1. **Create or edit.** First you create the original form, code, class, or procedure. Thereafter, you edit the programming. In Visual FoxPro, creating and editing programs is a mixture of writing lines of code, changing object properties, and positioning visual elements in one of the designers.
2. **Compile or build.** In one fashion or another, the programming is compiled by FoxPro so that you can run it. In a form, FoxPro compiles directly from the form (SCX) file when you save it. When you create an application, you use the Project Manager to do a build, which consists of compiling all the forms and other program elements and then putting them together in a single application file (APP or EXE).

3. **Test.** You run the code (either directly, as in a form, or as an application file) to test the programming. Testing usually leads to the discovery of errors.

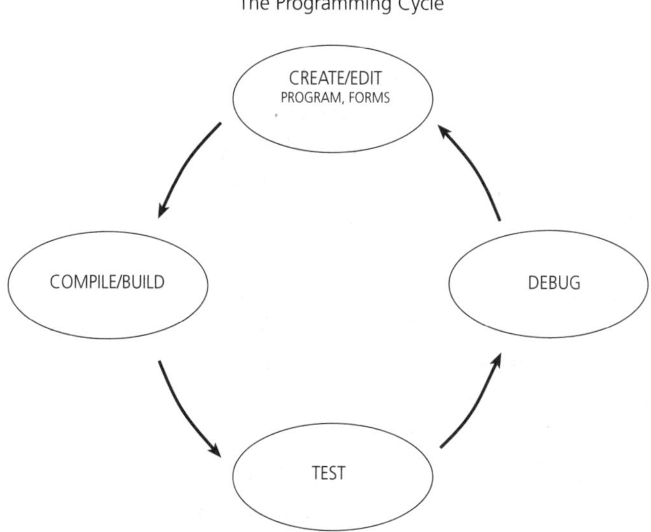

FIGURE 8.1 THE PROGRAMMING CYCLE.

4. **Debug.** You figure out what the errors are and then edit the code to fix the bugs, make changes, or enhance what you've written. Then the programming cycle starts again.

The programming cycle should not be confused with the *development* cycle, which includes much more than programming (such as application analysis and design) and takes place over a longer period of time. As an application developer, you go through the programming cycle many times every day. Because it is repetitive, much of what you do to configure your working environment should be aimed at making the cycle as efficient as possible.

NOTE

I'm assuming that, as with the rest of us, your application development will be under pressure from deadlines, short budgets, cranky clients, and all the other curves that life can throw (unless you have the luxury of programming for a hobby, and perhaps even then). Programming efficiently may be defined in different ways, but it still comes down to producing an application on time, on budget, and on spec.

External Configuration

The basic elements to be configured are the hardware and software needed to develop applications with Visual FoxPro. There are many options and decisions. Some of them you can change at any time, and others you'll have to live with for quite a while. As always, the iron triad rules: Good, fast, cheap—pick any two. For example, if you want good and fast equipment, it won't be inexpensive.

In hardware, many of the critical decisions are fairly obvious: CPU, RAM, disk drives, monitors, and backup devices. In software, you have choices for operating systems compatible with Visual FoxPro (Windows:95, NT), the choice of office applications (word processor, spreadsheet), and any third-party support software for FoxPro (class libraries, utilities).

The recommendations that follow make the probably false assumption that you are starting from scratch and that you have carte blanche to put together a premium system. Getting the best is a worthy goal, even though the reality is usually not so advantageous.

NOTE

It's important not to forget the distinctions between *your* configuration, which should be highly optimized, and the configurations where your application will be run. This chapter concentrates on the developer's perspective. The configuration for the users of an application may be quite different. For example, you may develop software on a computer that has 32 MB of RAM and everything runs with snap. When you install your application at the client site, you may discover that its 8MB systems are so loaded with other software that Visual FoxPro runs like a half-ton pig in a mud hole.

Hardware

Whether you receive your hardware as standard corporate issue or buy it piece by piece out of your own pocket, the same principle applies: Your time is worth money. The faster your computer can help you deliver good code, the more money you will save. Because of the amount of processing, data access, and screen manipulation involved in application development, it pays to get the best (meaning fastest) equipment you can afford. That's the common theme in all these recommendations.

- **CPU**. Your CPU choice is simple: Buy the fastest. Visual FoxPro 5.0 runs well on Pentium models and less than well on a 486 anything. Do you need a rationale for spending the money? Consider these points:

  1. When you build an application with the Project Manager, a complex internal process generates an output file and then compiles it.
  2. Depending on the size and complexity of the code you create, the generation and compile time can vary from a few seconds to several minutes. One thing is certain, however: The CPU, memory, and disks of your system receive a healthy exercise during these operations.
  3. Studies have shown that most programmers average between six and eight programming cycles per hour. That's 50–70 cycles in an eight-hour day. Simple math says that if you can shave a half minute off each cycle, you save around half an hour a day. That's a lot of thumb twiddling.

  All things being equal, as the economists say, the most effective way to shave time is to invest in the fastest CPU you can afford.

- **RAM**. Memory is the other place not to play cheapskate. Quite simply, if performance is an important criterion, give FoxPro as much memory as you can (as much as 64 MB). Microsoft has set the recommended level of RAM for Visual FoxPro 5.0 at 10 MB. By itself, this level doesn't mean much; the combination of memory and operating system is more important. In the 32-bit Windows environment—Windows 95 or NT—10 MB isn't enough, but at least with more memory these systems can run multiple applications. For all FoxPro programming, a more accommodating memory size is 16 MB on Windows 95 and 32 MB for NT 4.0.
- **Disks**. Because much FoxPro activity is disk-based, it also pays to have a big and fast hard disk. Fortunately, the price of fast two- or three-gigabyte hard drives is slipping toward $300 (as of this writing). If you've been around computing a while, you know that this price is mind-boggling. It's true that software has become more demanding of disk space; Visual FoxPro minimally requires 15 MB

(laptop) and will normally exceed 100 MB if you choose a typical developer's installation. Still, at these prices, no one should whine about not having enough hard disk.

- **Backup devices**. If you're developing applications on a network, your work is probably backed up routinely. For single computer development, you need some form of backup (not a wing and a prayer). If cost is a barrier, gauge the type of backup to the size of your projects. Small projects and even some medium-sized projects can be backed up to a floppy disk (with compression). Bigger projects may require tape backup. Complicated development, such as multiple large projects, might be better served by optical storage, especially CD-ROM, which can also be used as a distribution medium. Given the price of hard disks, it may also be practical to back up to another hard drive, although this concept seems strange to many people. In this case, synchronization software (which comes with some utility programs) can be convenient.
- **Monitors**. This is one of the important "electives." No, a 17-inch monitor is not required to program in Visual FoxPro. Yes, you absolutely need a 17-inch monitor (or bigger) if you want to keep any semblance of order on the screen. FoxPro spawns windows like guppies. Without a bigger screen real estate, there is often nowhere to put windows except on top of one another. Soon, manipulating windows takes up a healthy percentage of your time. As before, time being money, invest in a larger monitor. FoxPro is not a graphics-intensive program, so it doesn't require an ultra-high-speed, 3-D, or other sophisticated graphics adapter (although it won't hurt).

Other hardware, such as printers, plotters, fax boards, modems, and scanners, is either handled in a standard fashion by Windows or is a configuration issue only when related to the special needs of an application.

NOTE

Even if you're connected to a network, the requirements for an application developer's workstation don't differ much from those of a single computer except that the network may provide some disk space, reducing the need for space on the workstation.

SOFTWARE

In the Windows environment, no program is an island (although some programs act like it). In the first place, all programs are citizens of the operating system. Under DOS, this arrangement was very loose . Under Windows 3.1 and Windows for Workgroups, the union is tighter but not heavily enforced. With the 32-bit systems (Windows 95 and NT), software literally registers with the operating system and is mostly bound to the rules and regulations of working in that system.

This doesn't mean that all programs obey the rules (on any operating system). That's why, when you set up your working environment and, more important, when you set up the client's environment, you need to take into account *all* the software that FoxPro may encounter. This is especially true if you intend to use FoxPro in OLE automation. In this process, you use two or more Windows applications, such as FoxPro and Microsoft Excel, to exchange data and perform automated functions. How well OLE automation works, and how safely, is primarily a function of the operating system.

OPERATING SYSTEMS

The operating system picture is complicated by the number of active versions of FoxPro: FoxPro 2.6 for DOS, FoxPro for Windows 2.6, FoxPro for Macintosh 2.5, Visual FoxPro for Windows 3.0, Visual FoxPro for Macintosh 3.0, and now Visual FoxPro 5.0 for Windows. Theoretically, you can develop with any of these versions and deliver applications to their respective operating systems. What you can't do is easily move code back and forth between the versions. Microsoft provides some conversion software, but it is invariably one-way. You can convert upwards from FoxPro for Windows to Visual FoxPro, but not the other way around.

The choice of operating system may not be a choice. Very often you must go with what is used by the target systems for your application. In this case, you'd choose Visual FoxPro 5.0 because your target computers are all running Windows 95 or Windows NT 4.0. Microsoft has made a break with this version, saying, in effect, that 32 bits is the only proper way to run a GUI database manager.

NOTE

Microsoft is right. The 32-bit Windows 95 or NT 4.0 is the way to go for many reasons—speed, reliability, and ease of use—especially for Visual FoxPro. I know that this choice can meet with a great deal of resistance, because the upgrade requires substantial hardware investment. Upgrading isn't always possible, but if you have a choice or can influence the selection, favor the most robust system available. As I write this, a Pentium Pro 200-MHz computer with 32 MB of RAM, 2.5 GB of disk space, and Windows NT 4.0 costs less than $3,000 and provides an extremely comfortable system that won't be totally obsolete for at least five years—a long time in this business. That's the kind of thing you're shooting for.

Folder Structure

Day to day, the most important element of the external software configuration is the folder (directory) structure. FoxPro generates a huge number of files, hundreds for even a moderate application. If you are working on multiple projects, the quantity of files goes well beyond your ability to remember what they are and where they are.

Your main ally in the struggle against file glut is the Project Manager. It does much of the file location management automatically, but you must help it. Begin by starting FoxPro so that it uses the Project Manager files situated in the correct folder. As you add files, you may need to locate them for the Project Manager. It helps to know where to look, and that implies some sort of organization of file folders.

The first thought for organizing files may be to put them all in one folder. Here's why that's not a good idea:

- Throwing all files from all projects (or even one project) into one folder soon becomes ridiculous. You will have thousands of files, all of them similar, in a place where you can find nothing quickly, even in the Windows Explorer.
- Too many files in a single folder can affect FoxPro performance, because it needs to load and sort available files when it does many operations. Most developers try to keep no more than 200 files in a folder.
- Backup from an overloaded folder is unwieldy, because it will be difficult to segregate different elements of a project for selective backup.
- Your own file searches, which occur often in FoxPro, will take forever because there are so many files (and the file you want is inevitably near the bottom of the list).

A better way is to create a relatively modest folder structure that helps to categorize the files and minimize the number in any one folder. There are two approaches to this configuration: one for the stand-alone computer and another one for networked computers. It makes some difference if you are developing applications with a team of programmers for clients who will share data on network, but not as much difference as you might think.

This chapter will start with relatively simple and basic folder configurations (with room to grow), which you usually create before you start developing an application. One caveat: There are many ways to structure folders for FoxPro projects; the important point is to develop a reasonable structure and stick with it across all projects.

SINGLE-USER FOLDER STRUCTURE

When you installed Visual FoxPro, it automatically created a number of folders for itself. Starting with the home folder of \VFP, it spread out to other folders: \VFP\SAMPLES, \VFP\TOOLS, and so forth. Each branch is used to segregate work areas of types of files that belong together. When you create a folder structure for your applications, the same principle applies. The system might look something like Figure 8.2.

The project *home folder* (APP1, in this case), which may or may not be the application's home folder, is used to isolate the files of a programming module that is essentially compiled by itself. The utility folder system provided on the accompanying disk is like this. It contains programming that is relatively independent and can be developed and compiled by itself or can be incorporated later in the final build of an application.

The home folder contains the project manager files, the configuration file, and possibly a few other files that relate to the entire project, but that's it. Most of the working files are kept in folders under the home folder. By convention, these folders reflect the major file types used in FoxPro applications: DATA, FORM, LIBRARY, INCLUDE, PROGRAM, MENU, REPORT, and BITMAP. It's a good idea to keep these folder names short, because long ones often don't fit in the Windows file dialog boxes and it's a nuisance to type long path names.

If you develop more than one application, it's common to use a folder to contain code elements (programs and class libraries) that can be shared among all projects. In this case, there are separate folders for PROGRAM, LIBRARY, and FORM.

As a rule, an application's home folder is not part of the Visual FoxPro (VFP) folder system. This arrangement avoids confusion, keeps the home folder at the highest directory level possible, and accommodates any change in the version (and folder) of Visual FoxPro.

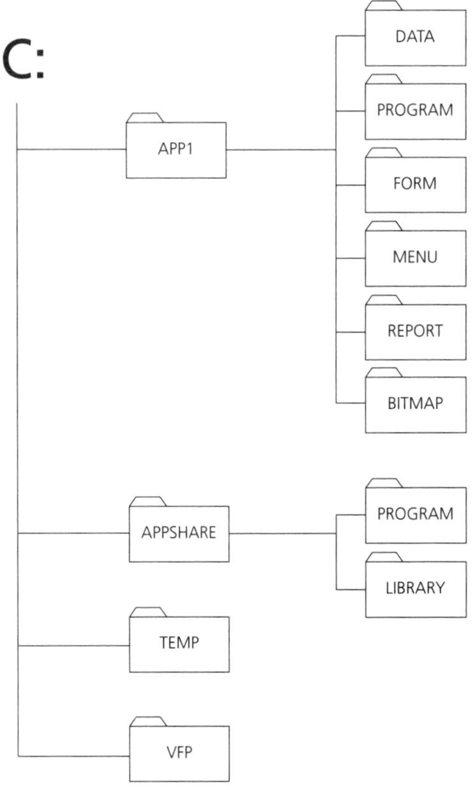

FIGURE 8.2 BASIC SINGLE-USER FOLDER STRUCTURE.

While FoxPro is running, it maintains a set of working temporary files to store data and code while it is being processed. You can specify where these working files are to be created, usually on your fastest hard drive and in a location you can easily check from time to time. As you will soon find out (if you haven't already), developing software inevitably causes crashes—in FoxPro, in Windows, and even in the whole computer. When this happens, FoxPro's temporary files, which are usually automatically erased when you leave FoxPro, are left stranded. In time, you may have quite an accumulation of files, and it helps to have a central location to go to for a little housekeeping.

MULTIUSER AND NETWORK FOLDER STRUCTURE

As you can see in Figure 8.3, the folder structure for a network application isn't very different from the single-computer version.

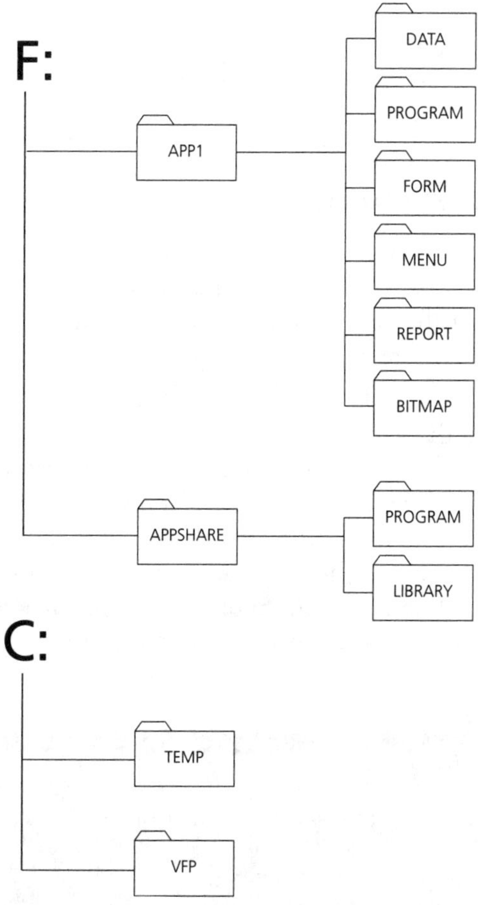

FIGURE 8.3 BASIC NETWORK FOLDER STRUCTURE.

The main difference is that, in the single-computer setup, the temporary files and FoxPro itself are located on a local hard drive, rather than on network drives. This arrangement usually improves performance if faster computers are being used. In networked development systems where more than one programmer is involved, it's important to create shared folders that contain common programming material.

In most cases, the network folders will need to be part of the general network security system. In Novell networks, for example, access to folders is usually assigned to specific security groups, and then files within the folders are flagged as shareable (or non-shareable) as appropriate.

NOTE

Keeping folder structure simple is always a good idea. Over the life-cycle of an application, the development, beta testing, and production phases often require their own folder system. They are usually a mirror image of each other but with a differently named home folder.

TEAM PROGRAMMING

By itself, FoxPro is not a particularly good team player as a development environment for more than one programmer. For example, the Project Manager, which is usually at the center of every development effort, cannot be accessed simultaneously by more than one programmer. In each session of FoxPro, Project Manager files are used exclusively; they are not shareable.

To get around this limitation, a simple, but flawed, approach is to break an application into discrete modules and use multiple copies of an application's project file, one module per file. Although only one programmer at a time can build (compile) the final application, this technique allows programmers to work on separate pieces of the project. Ultimately, the application must be synchronized across all copies of the project file. This may present housekeeping headaches, because the update to a master copy must be done carefully, with full knowledge of what has and has not been changed.

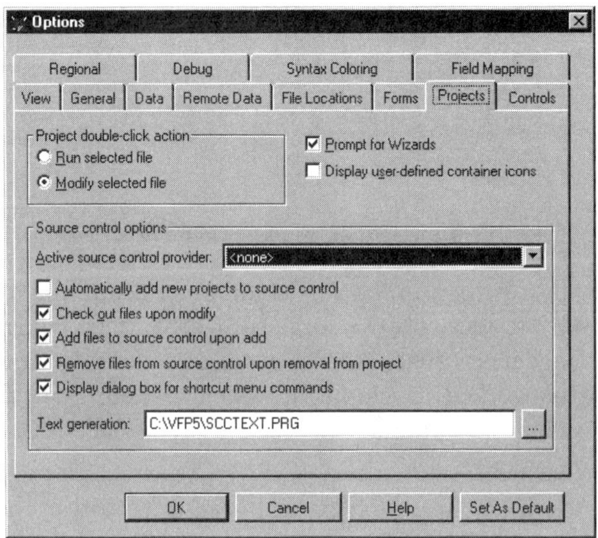

FIGURE 8.4 SOURCE CONTROL OPTIONS.

You can remedy this situation by using the hooks in Visual FoxPro 5.0 to another Microsoft product: Visual SourceSafe. This version control package can track the use of files (check in and check out) and give a programming team the tools to work on the same pieces of code without stepping on one another's work. If you look in the **Projects** tab of **Tools**, **Options** in the menu (Figure 8.4), you'll see that FoxPro provides explicit links to SourceSafe, including a shortcut menu and automatic file registry.

FoxPro Startup

Getting FoxPro up and running, especially with multiple projects, also touches on directory structure and file location. In a nutshell, a **FoxPro** icon, on the desktop or in the Start menu, has as one of its properties a command line that starts Visual FoxPro and tells it which configuration file to use. (We'll cover the details of the configuration file soon.) The configuration file then tells FoxPro, among other things, which folder and folder paths to use for a specific project. The specifics of creating this file vary slightly between Windows 95 and NT 4.0, but essentially it goes like this:

1. Create a copy of the **FoxPro** icon.
2. Open the icon's Property dialog box.
3. Change the icon's name to something related to your project.
4. In the **Target** line (**Shortcut** tab), make sure that you are starting the correct version of FoxPro and add the command switch `-t`, which tells FoxPro to skip the opening FoxPro logo.
5. Add to the **Target** line the command switch `-c` followed by the path to the FoxPro configuration file (CONFIG.FPW) for the project. The complete command line looks something like this: `C:\VFP\VFP.EXE -t -c:\myapp\config.fpw`.
6. In the configuration file, include the line `DEFAULT=C:\MYAPP`, which tells FoxPro the location of the application's home folder.
7. In the **Working Folder** line of the Properties dialog box, enter the home folder of your project, such as `C:\MYAPP`. This forces Windows to reset the active directory.

You can have as many of these shortcut icons as you need for your projects. It is also possible to shift projects while you're still in FoxPro, although many people consider it simpler to just exit and restart with a new configuration. That's because the configuration of a FoxPro session often involves more than references to the working folders.

Backup for a Project

A routine for saving your work—backup—is also part of configuring your environment. If you've been around computers for more than a short while, you know that the possibility for disaster is real. The only protection is regular backup. There are shareware programs that can read the FoxPro Project Manager and compress the files to floppy disks. You can do backup with nothing more than `XCOPY *.* /S` in a batch file. If you are developing many (or very large) applications, your backup schemes need to become correspondingly capacious. It's probably time to graduate to tape backup, optical storage devices, or another hard disk. What matters is not the technique but rather the unfailing execution. Wagging finger aside, remember that Murphy (of Murphy's laws) would have been a programmer if he'd lived that long.

Internal Settings

As you might imagine, the operation of Visual FoxPro is complex and entails a large number of internal settings, parameters, options, and status values. Most of FoxPro's inner workings are safely hidden from tampering, but as a developer you're given access to a fairly large number of internal settings and values, which you can monitor and modify for your own purposes. Most of these settings are situation-specific, such as **SET NULLDISPLAY**, which specifies what should be displayed in browses and reports when a table contains nulls. A few settings, such as **SET DELETED**, can have a major impact on programming in general.

Working interactively, you access most of the internal settings via the Options dialog box pages (found under **Tools**, **Options** in the menu). All these settings, along with a few others, can be executed with commands or functions in the Command window. The same commands are also used in programming, so it may be a good idea to learn them first rather than rely on the Options pages.

WARNING

Although manipulating internal settings is indispensable for application development, it carries a certain amount of responsibility and risk. Most of the time, your application will run with FoxPro's default settings. However, when you change a setting, there is always a possibility that you may forget to restore it; elsewhere, code that expects a default value will fail. This is a source of some of the nastier bugs. As you'll see, there are many ways to deal with this potential problem, but one rule applies: What you do going in, undo going out.

SET COMMANDS, OPTIONS, AND FUNCTIONS

There are three ways to change FoxPro's internal settings: by programming commands and functions (in code or the Command window), by using the **Options** pages, and by using the FoxPro configuration file.

In the Command window and in programs, you gain access to most of the internal environment through the **SET** commands. Here is a typical example of the syntax:

Command syntax:

SET TALK ON|OFF|WINDOW [WindowName]|NOWINDOW

Arguments:

ON|OFF Enables or disables processing messages (talk).

WINDOW Sends processing messages to a window.

[WindowName] Sends messages to a specific (already created, named, and activated) window.

NOWINDOW Sends talk to the main FoxPro window.

Examples:

```
SET TALK OFF
SET TALK ON WINDOW talkwin
```

In the FoxPro user interface, most of the options are, appropriately, found under **Tools**, **Options** in the menu. This series of tabbed pages covers all aspects of FoxPro operation. Of these tabs, **Data**, **Regional**, **General**, **View**, **Controls**, and **File Locations** contain most of the **SET** commands. The options in the **Remote Data**, **Projects**, **Debug**, **Field Mapping**, **Syntax Coloring**, and **Forms** tabs do not have **SET** equivalents; some are available only in the Options dialog boxes and others use different commands. In general, however, because programmers tend to go in and out of FoxPro frequently, it's often inconvenient to set the configuration interactively in the Options tabs. Most developers quickly learn to use the automatic (and application-specific) approach of the configuration file.

NOTE

You can determine the current values for some of the **SET** options by using the **SET( )** function with the name of the command (in quotes) as the argument, such as `SET("TALK")`. In a similar vein, there are a number of **SYS( )** functions (system functions) that either return the status of **SET**-related options or perform the same operation as the **SET** command.

Many of the **SET** commands are described in Table 8.1, which condenses the list to those most frequently used and puts them in a format for easy cross reference. All three ways of changing the option are presented, along with the **SET( )** or **SYS( )** function, if there is one. This may seem like a long list, but over time you will use every one of these commands as well as some of the *other* 50+ commands. It's a good idea to review the **SET** commands and options in the *Language Reference* to become familiar with the less frequently used commands. In Table 8.1, the Options tab pages are designated by a letter:

G = General, D = Data, V = View, F = File Locations.

Table 8.1 Common SET Commands, Functions, and Options

Command, Config file, Option, Function	Arguments, Default Value	Description
SET ALTERNATE TO, ALTERNATE = <File>, **SET(**"ALTERNATE",1**)**	**<File Name>**, No default	Specify the file to which out put should be sent. Must be done before setting alternate on.
SET ALTERNATE, ALTERNATE = ON|OFF, **SET(**"ALTERNATE"**)**	**ON | OFF**, OFF	Turn on or off sending output to file. This is strictly ASCII output.
SET BELL, BELL=, (G) **Warning Sound**	**ON|OFF**, ON, off/default	Enable or disable the bell, sometimes called the alert sound.
SET BELL TO, BELL=, (G) **Warning Sound**	**<frequency>**, 512, **<Wave File>**	Set the tone of the bell or change it to a wave file sound.
SET CARRY, CARRY=, (G) **Fill New Records with Current Values**	**OFF|ON**, OFF	Copies the values in all fields to the fields in a new record.
SET CLOCK, CLOCK=, (V) **Show Clock**, **SET(**"CLOCK"**)**	**OFF|ON**, OFF	Turn display of clock on or off.

COMMAND, CONFIG FILE, OPTION, FUNCTION	ARGUMENTS, DEFAULT VALUE	DESCRIPTION
SET CONFIRM, CONFIRM=, (G) Enter or Tab to exit fields	**OFF|ON**, OFF	When on, you can't exit a text edit box by just typing; a specific exit key (**Enter**, **Tab**, **Arrow**) must be used.
SET DEFAULT TO, DEFAULT=, **SYS(5)**, (F) Default Directory	**<drive>|<dir>**	Set the default drive or folder where FoxPro will begin searches for all files.
SET DELETED, DELETED=, (D) Ignore Deleted Records	**OFF|ON**, OFF	When on, deleted records are not available to commands.
SET ESCAPE, ESCAPE=, (G) Cancel Program on Escape	**ON|OFF**, ON	Enables or disables the **Esc** key during program execution. Often disabled for final application delivery.
SET EXACT, EXACT=, (G) SET EXACT	**OFF|ON**, OFF	For string comparisons, when on, two *unequal length* strings must match on a character-by-character basis.
SET EXCLUSIVE, EXCLUSIVE=, (D) Open Exclusive	**ON|OFF**, ON	Open all tables in exclusive (single-user) mode. Almost always set OFF for running applications.
SET LOCKS, LOCK=, **SYS(2011)**, (D) Automatic File Locking	**ON|OFF**, ON	Enables file locking for many table commands (COUNT, LIST, and so on).
SET MEMOWIDTH TO, MEMOWIDTH=	**<8 to 256>**, 50	Set the width of display for memo field lines (in windows or listings). Often varied for some applications.

COMMAND, CONFIG FILE, OPTION, FUNCTION	ARGUMENTS, DEFAULT VALUE	DESCRIPTION
SET MULTILOCKS, MULTILOCKS=, (G) Multiple Locks	**ON|OFF**, OFF	Enables locking for a set of records. Required for row **Multiple Locks**and table buffering. Often set ON in config file.
SET NEAR, NEAR=, (D) SET NEAR	**OFF|ON**, OFF	With near on, a failed search stops at the next nearest match. When off, the failed search goes to EOF
SET NOTIFY, NOTIFY=, (V) System Messages	**OFF|ON**, ON	Enable or disable display of system messages (which might confuse the user).
SET PATH TO, PATH=, (F) Search Path	**<path list>**	Set default path for FoxPro file searches. Usually in config file.
SET PRINT, **SET** ("PRINT"), **SYS(102)**, **SYS(13)**	**ON|OFF**, OFF	Send output to printer.
SET PROCEDURE TO, PROCEDURE=	**<file list>**, **ADDITIVE**	Open one or more procedure files containing functions and procedures. Often set in the config file or in the main program file.
SET REFRESH TO, REFRESH=, (D)Browse Refresh Interval, Table Refresh Interval	**<#1>,<#2>**, 0-3600, 0 , 5	Determines how many seconds between refreshing of data: #1 for Browses, #2 for tables. The first number is often set > 0.
SET REPROCESS TO, REPROCESS=, **SYS(3051)**, **SYS(3052)**, (D) Reprocessing	**<-2to32,000>**, **SECONDS**, **AUTOMATIC**, 0	Specifies the retry interval (in seconds or number of tries) for a failed lock. More on this in Chapter.

<table>
<tr><th>COMMAND, CONFIG FILE, OPTION, FUNCTION</th><th>ARGUMENTS, DEFAULT VALUE</th><th>DESCRIPTION</th></tr>
<tr><td>SET RESOURCE, RESOURCE=, (F) Resource File, check box, SET("RESOURCE"), SYS(2005)</td><td>ON|OFF, ON</td><td>Turn on or off the use of the FoxPro resource file. (See the section on the resource file in this chapter.)</td></tr>
<tr><td>SET SAFETY, SAFETY=, (G) Confirm File Replacement</td><td>ON|OFF, ON</td><td>Enable or disable warning for nonreversible file operations such as delete file. Usually set OFF in the config file.</td></tr>
<tr><td>SET STATUS BAR, STATUS BAR=, (V) Status Bar</td><td>OFF|ON, ON</td><td>Set display of FoxPro status bar on or off.</td></tr>
<tr><td>SET STEP</td><td>OFF|ON, OFF</td><td>Open trace window and put program execution in step mode. Used for debugging.</td></tr>
<tr><td>SET TALK, TALK=, SET("TALK"), SYS(103), (V) Command Results</td><td>ON|OFF, WINDOW name, ON</td><td>Display FoxPro processing messages either in the main FoxPro window or in a named window (already created).</td></tr>
<tr><td>SET TYPEAHEAD TO, TYPEAHEAD=</td><td>0 to 128>, 20 <</td><td>Set the maximum number of characters to store in the typeahead buffer. Often set in the config file or main program.</td></tr>
</table>

NOTE

If you want to save the current settings for use in a program file or form, here's a nifty trick: In an Options dialog tab, make your choice of settings and then hold down the **Shift** key while you press the **OK** button. This action will echo all the **SET** commands into the Command window, where they can be copied to the Clipboard.

SYSTEM VARIABLES FOR CONFIGURATION

In addition to the **SET** commands, FoxPro provides numerous *system variables*, which contain the current operating values for internal settings. For example, **_TALLY** contains the count from any command that queries or lists data from a table. Notice that the names of all these variables begin with an underscore (which is one reason you shouldn't use underscores to begin your own variable names). Many of the system variables related to printing are of limited use in the Windows environment. The system variables used for configuration are summarized in Table 8.2.

TABLE 8.2 SYSTEM VARIABLES USED IN CONFIGURATION FOR DEVELOPMENT

VARIABLE	VALUE	DESCRIPTION
_BROWSER	`<file path>`	Folder path to BROWSER.APP
_BUILDER	`<file path>`	Folder path to BUILDER.APP
_CONVERTER	`<file path>`	Folder path to CONVERT.APP
_GENMENU	`<file path>`	Folder path to GENMENU.PRG
_SCREEN	`.<property>, .<method>`	This variable makes an object from the FoxPro main window and can be addressed for dozens of properties and methods. Here's a typical example: `_SCREEN.caption="My App"`. This code sets the title of the main window.
_SPELLCHK	<file path>	Folder path to SPELLCHK.APP
_WIZARD	<file path>	Folder path to WIZARD.APP

Most of these variables are used in the configuration file, if at all. The system variables that take a file path are usually omitted except when the related file (BROWSER.APP) is located in a folder other than the Visual FoxPro home folder. They are also omitted when, in a delivered application, the programming-oriented variables are given a null string value, `_BROWSER=""`, which tells FoxPro not to look for the files.

THE CONFIGURATION FILE

As Visual FoxPro loads, the configuration file, CONFIG.FPW, is the first file FoxPro reads for instructions. It works something like the old DOS CONFIG.SYS file. CONFIG.FPW is not a program file, and only command lines with the correct format will execute. Most of the commands that can be used in the file are based on the **SET** commands (as in Table 8.1). A few others, unique to the configuration file, are listed in Table 8.3.

TABLE 8.3 OPTIONS UNIQUE TO THE CONFIGURATION FILE

COMMAND	VALUE	DESCRIPTION
TITLE =	**<Title Text>**	Use this to change the title of the FoxPro main window (same as `_SCREEN.caption`).
TMPFILES =	**<folder path>**	Specify the folder (with path) where FoxPro should create its temporary work files. Otherwise, use the next three options to specify where the work files go individually.
SORTWORK=	**<folder path>**	Specify the folder (with path) where FoxPro should create its files while sorting.
EDITWORK=	**<folder path>**	Specify the folder (with path) where FoxPro should create its temporary program editing files.
PROGWORK=	**<folder path>**	Specify the folder (with path) where FoxPro should create its temporary program files while running.

COMMAND=	**<command>**	You are allowed one default command that FoxPro will execute on startup. Here are some typical uses:
		`DO <startup program>`
		`MODIFY PROJECT <project file>`

Later in the development cycle, when you deliver the first prototype (or beta version) to the users of your application, you will probably change the options that are set in the configuration file and the first program file. For development, however, it's typical to use the configuration file the most. In contrast to program files, which must be edited and then compiled before changes take effect, settings in the configuration file can be edited in any text editor and take immediate effect when FoxPro starts. However, this flexibility can raise security issues, and that is one reason why the configuration file is de-emphasized or removed for the delivered application.

There are two schools of thought about how many configuration items should be in the developer's configuration file. One school says, "Include only the necessary options: those that are different than the default." The other school says, "As a matter of documentation, include all the important options, whether or not they have default settings." This is a philosophical difference, but when you're dealing with applications, it's probably better to come down on the side of doing as much documentation as possible. Here is an example of a more comprehensive configuration file for application development:

Sample CONFIG.FPW (Network version)

```
DEFAULT     = F:\MYAPP
PATH        = \MYAPP;\MYAPP\DATA;\MYAPP\FORM;\MYAPP\MENU;\MYAPP\PRO-
GRAM;
\MYAPP\REPORT;\MYAPP\BITMAP
AUTOSAVE    = ON
BLOCKSIZE   = 64
CLASSLIB    = F:\MYAPP\LIB\MYAPP.VCX
CONFIRM     = OFF
DELETED     = OFF
DEVELOPMENT= ON
ECHO        = OFF
ESCAPE      = ON
EXCLUSIVE   = OFF
FULLPATH    = ON
HOURS       = 24
KEYCOMP     = WINDOWS
LOCKS       = ON
LOGERROR    = ON
```

```
MARGIN      = 10
MEMOWIDTH   = 60
MULTILOCKS  = ON
NEAR        = ON
NOTIFY      = ON
ODOMETER    = 100
OLEOBJECT   = ON
REFRESH     = 0,5
REPROCESS   = ON
SAFETY      = ON
SYSFORMATS  = ON
TALK        = ON
TYPEAHEAD   = 50
SORTFILE    = C:\TEMP
PROGFILE    = C:\TEMP
WORKFILE    = C:\TEMP
EDITFILE    = C:\TEMP
COMMAND     = MODIFY PROJECT myapp
```

THE RESOURCE FILE

In user-friendly software, it's considered a nice touch to keep track of where users go, what they do, and how they do it. Then, when they come back to something, the software can configure itself just the way users left it. To do this, however, the user information (which can be sizable) must be stored somewhere on a permanent basis. In FoxPro, that's the main reason for the *resource file*, FOXUSER.DBF. As the user works with FoxPro, it stores the window configurations, color selections, option tab settings, and a number of other elements in the resource file. For example, if you open a Browse window, size it, and move it to a corner of the screen, the name of the window, its size, and its location are stored in the resource file so that the next time you open the same Browse window, it can resume its previous configuration. That's the meaning of the **BROWSE LAST** command, where the **LAST** refers to using the last configuration stored in the resource file.

Depending on how much interaction the user has with standard FoxPro windows, such as Browse windows, the resource file can accumulate information until it contains many megabytes of data. On a network, this is true in spades if you don't make separate resource files for each user. Consequently, for some applications it's necessary to keep an eye on the size of FOXUSER.DBF. Although it's rare, the resource file can also be the source of some intractable bugs in Visual FoxPro. One of the "last resort" options for user interface problems is to blow away the resource file and force FoxPro to create a new one from scratch.

For most applications, it's recommended that you create a separate resource file for the project and put it in the home folder. Do this with a line in the configuration file: `RESOURCE = C:\MYPROJ\MYAPP.DBF`, where `MYAPP.DBF` is the name you want to give the resource file. Also, when you design your application, you might consider whether each user should have his or her own resource file. Implementing this policy is not trivial, because it implies the need for login and security control as well as a designated directory and other file housekeeping. You might also consider a separate user tracking file to contain information, such as grid configurations, not kept by FoxPro. The FoxPro resource file could be used, but the mechanics are clumsy.

NOTE

In some ways the FoxPro resource file is a remnant of the DOS days, when it was used to contain information that has become irrelevant in the object-oriented world of Visual FoxPro—for example, printer information that now is handled by Windows. But the resource file is hardly dead. All the settings found in the Options tabs are stored in the resource file, making it lively indeed.

THE FOXPRO EDITOR

The program editor is a big part of a fully integrated development environment, and all major vendors provide their own editors while making it relatively inconvenient to use something else. This arrangement is, at best, a trade-off, because the built-in editors are rarely in the same league as those available from third-party vendors. However, Visual FoxPro stores most of the code in the memo fields of tables, and that makes it largely inaccessible to third-party editors. So we make the most of the FoxPro program editor, which isn't half bad. In fact, it's more than half good. Over the years, and especially for Visual FoxPro 5.0, there have been important enhancements:

- Drag-and-drop editing: the ability to select, copy, and move text using only the mouse.

- Indenting and unindenting of selected text for proper clegic display.
- The ability to change fonts, size, and line spacing.
- As of Visual FoxPro 5.0, different colors are applied to elements of syntax.
- Also new to VFP5, a specialized shortcut menu for editing options.

The last two items are not only cool but also useful. Colored syntax has more than an aesthetic effect; it makes it easier to spot errors and to organize segments of code. The kicker is the new shortcut menu (right-click in a text window), pictured in Figure 8.5, which has some welcome features summarized in Table 8.4.

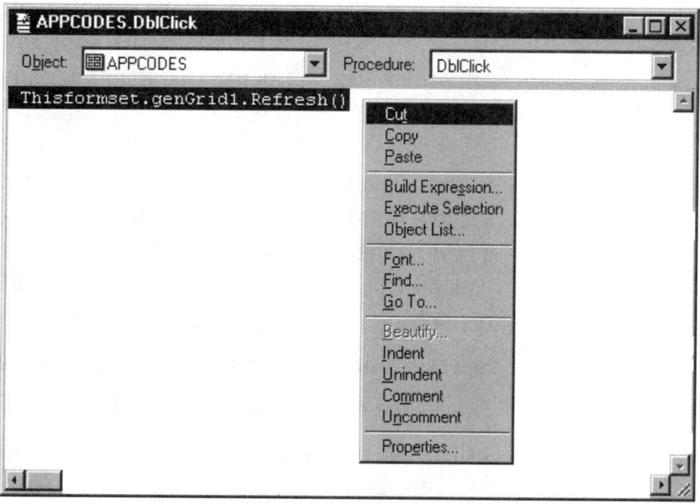

FIGURE 8.5 TEXT EDITING SHORTCUT MENU.

TABLE 8.4 FEATURES OF THE SHORTCUT MENU

OPTION	DESCRIPTION
Cut, Copy, Paste	The standard Windows functions for cutting, copying, and pasting text (via the Clipboard).
Build Expression	Selecting this brings up the Expression Builder dialog box, where you can create a complex expression, test it, and have it automatically inserted into your code.

(Continued...)

Option	Description
Execute Selection	If you highlight a segment of code in the editing window and select this option, FoxPro will execute (run) it. This is a great way to test code, especially code with loops and conditionals that can't be used in the Command window. Be careful, however, that the code doesn't reference variables, tables, or other objects that are not available. For obvious reasons, you'll get error messages.
Object List	Until you've done some object-oriented programming in FoxPro forms, you won't appreciate how important and wonderful this menu addition is. It provides the complete object reference sequence to a selected object relative to the object you are editing and inserts it into your code. For example, if you are in a button on a form and you want to reference a grid on the same form, select this option and it will generate something like `This.Parent.Grid1`. We'll come back to this gem in later chapters.
Font	Select a font for the current Editing window.
Find	Access the FoxPro Find/Replace dialog box.
Go To	Brings up a tiny dialog box to Go To a specified line number.
Beautify	There are ways to format FoxPro code, and then there are better ways. Beautify is a program that automatically converts your sloppy-looking code into neatly organized code. More on this after the section in Chapter 9 that covers coding conventions.
Indent	Select (highlight) a block of text, and this will indent the entire section by whatever number of spaces you've set for a tab.
Unindent	Reverse the indent on a selected block of code.
Comment	Select a block of text and this will insert comment markers (*) for every line, thereby removing them from active code. This technique is used all the time during development and debugging.

OPTION	DESCRIPTION
Uncomment	Remove the comment markers from a selected block of text.
Properties	Access the text editing Properties dialog box.

With an Edit window active, you can reach the configuration options for the FoxPro editor, shown in Figure 8.6, through the menu by using **Edit**, **Properties** or in the shortcut menu by using **Properties**. Table 8.5 summarizes the options.

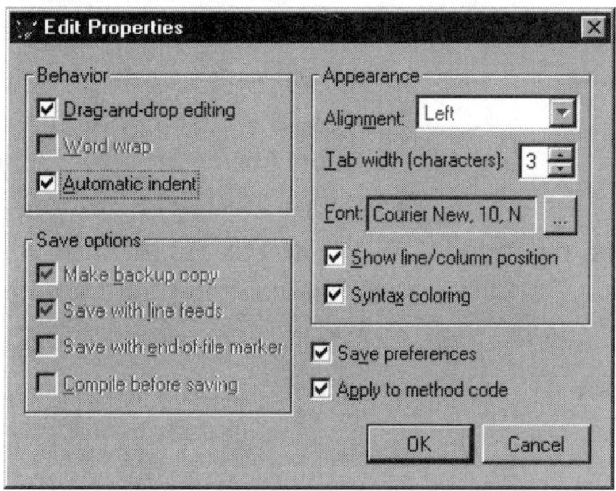

FIGURE 8.6 EDIT PROPERTIES DIALOG BOX.

TABLE 8.5 EDIT OPTIONS TAB

OPTION	DESCRIPTION
Drag-and-drop editing	*On. Enables standard drag and drop text editing.
Word wrap	Word-wraps lines within the editing window. Never turn this on for programming; it may create invalid command lines. Used mostly for occasional text blocks.
Automatic indent	*On. Automatically indents text according to the first line's indent. This does not affect how the text is saved. This is important for programming clarity.

(Continued...)

OPTION	DESCRIPTION
Alignment	Align text left, center, or right—rarely anything but left.
Tab width (characters)	*4. Specifies how many characters wide each tab is. The range is from 1 to 50 characters, but most programmers work with 3–5. Actually, there are many situations when the tab can cause problems in formatting, and spaces are preferred instead; but this is largely a matter of personal choice.
Font	Use the three-dot button to bring up the Font dialog box. The font set here will apply to all Edit windows.
Show line/column position	*On. Enables the display of line number and column position in the status bar.
Syntax coloring	*On. Why not?
Make backup copy	*On. Specifies that Visual FoxPro create a backup copy each time you save a file. This applies only to text files.
Save with line feeds	*On. Saves the file with line feeds. If not on, line feeds are removed when the file is saved. Always leave selected for programming (save with line feeds).
Save with end-of-file marker	Places a **Ctrl + Z** at the end of a file when the file is saved. This extra character saved with the file helps resolve the difference between normal editing activity and MODIFY MEMO activity.
Compile before saving	Compile the program and check for syntax errors when the file is saved. This option applies only to PRG files.
Save preferences	Saves preferences only for the current file.
Apply to method code	The current settings become the default for all new files of the programming type.

*Most often used

There are plenty of editing tricks that the FoxPro editor hasn't learned (text blocks by column, for one), but with ingenuity and keyboard macros (see the next section) you can make your own shortcuts. Even better, if you want to fully upgrade the editor, invest in one of the shareware programs for FoxPro such as the Cob Editor Extensions (CEE). These are available on the CompuServe FoxForum and various sites on the Web.

KEYBOARD MACROS FOR PROGRAMMING

To shortcut some of the lengthier command combinations, FoxPro provides a method for creating *keyboard macros*—recorded key combinations—which can be inserted into text or executed on demand. Macro recording is reached through the menu using **Tools**, **Macros** (see Figure 8.7). The essence of the technique is to plan a key or keystroke combination, assign it to a key (such as **F4**) for execution, record the sequence of keystrokes, and, if necessary, edit the results. (The recording is in the form of editable FoxPro **KEYBOARD** commands.)

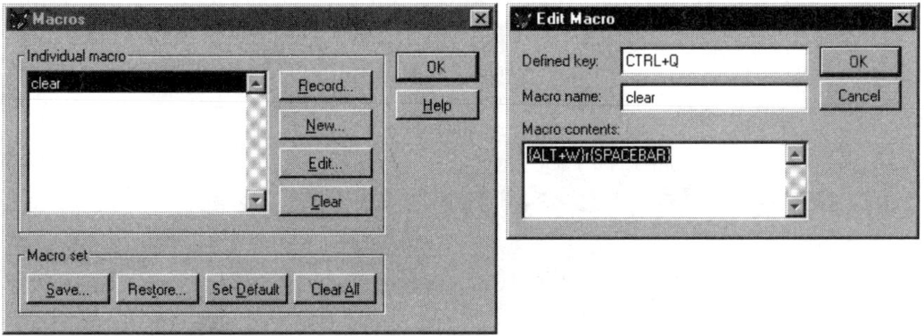

FIGURE 8.7 MACROS AND EDIT MACRO WINDOWS.

From the main Macros window (shown in Figure 8.7), you start a **New** macro, re-**Record** an existing macro, **Edit** a macro, and **Clear** a macro. The first set of macros is usually for the function keys **F2–F12** (**F1** is reserved for system Help).

You begin the recording process by selecting **New** or **Record** and then defining the trigger key or key combination (function keys, **Ctrl** + key, **Alt** + key, **Shift** + key). If the key combination isn't already assigned to a macro, recording begins immediately. Otherwise, you'll get the Overwrite Macro dialog box; normally, you'd choose to overwrite. Then recording commences with a message in the upper-right corner to remind you that selecting **Tools**, **Macro** will end the macro.

The macro recorder is literally a keystroke recorder—it records *only* keystrokes. Mouse clicks are not recorded and in fact can invalidate your entire macro. In practice, this means that all menu options must be chosen with keystrokes. You should exercise care in pressing keys so that they will record cleanly and in the correct order (although you can edit the macro later).

When you go to **Tools**, **Macro** to end recording, the Stop Recording Macro dialog box will be displayed. Here, you can add **Pauses** or **Literal** keyboard input or otherwise terminate the macro. Then you're finished. You should test the macro to make sure you didn't leave out a step. If there are problems, you can rerecord or edit the macro (the Edit Macro dialog box is shown in Figure 8.7).

The mechanics of creating macros are simple, but making the perfect macro is not easy. You may forget parts of the sequence, forget to turn off the recorder, or forget it can't read mouse clicks. And running macros *inside* programs doesn't work very well. (Leave the macro work for the Command window and the FoxPro editor.) Given the limitations of macros, some people dislike them, but others find them indispensable and create a library of macro sets. Fortunately, no mandate is involved; you can find your own best methods. The details of the procedures are found in the Visual FoxPro *User's Guide*. In assembling an application, you have much bigger fish to fry than messing with keyboard macros. But if you have a lonely weekend, why not indulge in this kind of configuration?

CHAPTER WRAP-UP

If you want to be a serious application developer (using that trendy, trite, and fuzzy word *serious*), it's important to spend some time setting up your working environment. You'd do this anyway, but it pays to be systematic. It starts with acquiring the best hardware you (or your company) can afford. On the professional level, if there is one activity that time and time again has a proven justification for maximum hardware, it's programming. The justification is simple: Time is money, and better (faster) equipment saves time.

Whether you are a professional developer or a serious amateur, you're looking for the best combination of CPU speed, RAM, and disk space to accommodate the operating system requirements and the number and size of application projects you are working on. This package usually includes access to backup equipment and printers, although these tasks may be handled by a network.

For software, configuration begins with all the programs you intend to run while developing applications. This process starts with FoxPro and may also include a word processor, a graphics program, and a number of utilities and third-party products that work with FoxPro. All these programs must have enough memory and disk space, and must be compatible with one another.

When you're running FoxPro, each application and often each project may have its own configuration. This has a number of elements:

- Defining a folder structure
- Configuring FoxPro startup options
- Using the FoxPro configuration file
- Using the Options pages
- Using the Command window
- Configuring the FoxPro editor
- Modifying the resource file
- Creating keyboard macros for programming

The goal is to establish a standard set of configurations involving all (or most) of these elements, options that can be varied to suit the requirements of an application. It will take time to develop this configuration. If you can work out your configuration elements so that you can easily clone them for a new project—copy the folder structure, files, macros, resource files, and so forth—it will save you a lot of time.

CHAPTER 9

PROGRAMMING BASICS

This chapter covers a number of fundamental building blocks for programming:

- Program files
- Control structures
- Variables
- Scoping
- Variable substitution
- Arrays

These commands and techniques, together with what you've learned about the FoxPro data management commands, let you create powerful programs that process data. We haven't yet arrived at the world of object-oriented programming and graphical user interfaces, but these basics are important in those areas, too.

For many people, the starting point for programming isn't the Form Designer and object-oriented technique. Instead, programming begins with the transition from doing interactive database commands (in the Command window) to writing commands in a program file. This is a good approach. The Forms Designer and OOP are complicated tools, and in the early stages of learning to program there are many basics that need attention more than learning the user interface. The simplicity of a program file or function makes it easier for you to concentrate on purely programming issues.

PROGRAM FILES

Using the Command window to enter FoxPro commands is part of programming, but there comes a time when the limitations of this approach are a problem. Perhaps you're tired of retyping frequently repeated commands, or perhaps you feel it's time to get on with real programming. That means it's time to create a program file to contain the sequence of commands you need. With a program file, you can begin to take advantage of control structures (loops and conditionals), and your work can be run as a program at any time (and by anyone).

There are many ways to start a program file: In the Project Manager, open the **Code** tab, select **Program**, and then select **New**. In the menu, select **File** (or the **file** icon), **New**, **Program**, and **New File**. From the Command window, you can use the command **MODIFY COMMAND <Filename>**, where the file name can include the complete path to the location of the new file. With the other two methods, you'll need to specify the file name and location when you save it, which you should do immediately using the **Save** icon or **File**, **Save** in the menu. FoxPro will automatically add the PRG extension to the file name. The important point is to save the file into an appropriate folder where you can easily find it later.

The open program file is nothing more than a text sheet, and you use the FoxPro editor to enter your commands in sequence. Your first efforts may be no more complicated than this:

```
*TEST.PRG
x=3
y=4
z=x+a
```

To run this program, you'd simply click the **Run** icon (!) or use **DO<program name>** in the Command window. FoxPro will ask you whether you want to save the changes to the file (or name the file if you haven't). After you answer **Yes**, the program will be compiled and run almost instantaneously. It will also stop at the line `z=x+a` with an error message—a bug. After you escape the error message dialog box, an editing window is opened, and FoxPro will highlight the line with the error in it (very convenient). Fixing this bug is easy, because you know where the error is located and all the relevant code is right before your eyes. In this case, FoxPro is complaining because you've introduced a variable, `a`, without assigning it a value.

A slightly more ambitious program, one containing database commands, might look like this:

```
* MAINT.PRG
OPEN DATABASE CUSTOMER
USE CUSTOMER ORDER CUSTID IN 0
USE ORDERS ORDER CUSTID IN 0
SELECT CUSTOMER
SET RELATION TO CUSTID INTO ORDERS
SCAN
IF STATUS="I" AND LASTORD<DATE()-365
DELETE
IF FOUND("ORDERS")
SELECT ORDERS
SCAN WHILE CUSTID=CUSTOMER.CUSTID
DELETE
ENDSCAN
ENDIF
ENDIF
SELECT CUSTOMER
ENDSCAN
```

In this case, the coding cannot be duplicated in the Command window because of the `IF..THEN` and `SCAN..ENDSCAN` control structures. Assuming you're not familiar with **IF..ENDIF** and **SCAN..ENDSCAN**, did you find them a bit difficult to pick out of the code? As small as this program is, it's difficult to follow, and that raises the issue of programming conventions.

Some Basic Programming Conventions

Contrast the following version of the MAINT.PRG with the preceding one:

```
* MAINT.PRG
* 1/25/95
* Locates and Deletes Order and Customer records, where
* the account is no longer active.
```

```
OPEN DATABASE customer
USE customer ALIAS cus ORDER custid IN 0
USE orders   ALIAS ord ORDER custid IN 0
SELECT cus
SET RELATION TO custid INTO ord

*Customer File Processing Loop
SCAN
  * Delete only customers who are inactive, "I", and who
  * have not ordered in more than a year.
  IF cus.status = "I" AND cus.lastord < DATE() - 365
    DELETE
    *Check order file
    IF FOUND("ord")
      SELECT ord
      *Order File Processing Loop
      SCAN WHILE ord.custid = cus.custid
        DELETE         && Remove all
      ENDSCAN
    ENDIF
  ENDIF
  SELECT cus
ENDSCAN // cus loop
```

It's the same code but with a few additions: indented lines and a liberal use of the ***** (full line) or **&&** (partial line) comment markers to enter documentation. This code is not polished, but the shape of the program is visible. Shape? This is form as a guide to content. It's what helps you distinguish between a command, a function, and a variable or to ascertain where the program loops begin and end.

Programming conventions are established to create a consistent pattern that can be instantly recognized. If all your code is structured consistently, it will be easier to read. And if you follow a few generally accepted conventions, other people will be able to read it, too. For example, conditional structures and control loops are indented to show that they are nested, one inside the other. For example:

```
SCAN
  IF <test>
    DO WHILE
      <do something>
```

```
    ENDDO
  ELSE
    <do something>
  ENDIF
ENDSCAN
```

The use of indentation, called *clegic display*, is one of the more obvious programming conventions. There are many others, some of them quite subtle. The following annotated version of the program example describes a few of the more common FoxPro conventions:

1. Identify a program with as much information as needed to understand what it does, who wrote it, and when it was written.

   ```
   * MAINT.PRG
   * 1/25/95
   * Locates and Deletes Order and Customer records, where
   * the account is no longer active.
   ```

2. Segments of code with different purposes are separated by blank lines or some other visual separator.

   ```
   * Open files.
   ```

3. FoxPro commands are all capitals (uppercase). Fields, variables, and aliases are lowercase.

   ```
   USE customer ALIAS cus ORDER custid IN 1
   USE orders   ALIAS ord ORDER custid IN 2
   SELECT cus
   SET RELATION TO custid INTO ord
   ```

4. Significant segments of the program are annotated.

   ```
   *Customer File Processing Loop
   SCAN
   ```

5. Logic or processing that is not self-evident should be explained.

   ```
     * Include only customers who are inactive,"I", and
     * who have not ordered in over a year.
   ```

```
IF cus.status = "I" AND cus.lastord > DATE() - 365
  DELETE
```

6. Consecutive program structures, such as ifs and loops, are indented.

```
*Check order file
IF FOUND( "ord" )
  SELECT ord
  *Order File Processing Loop
  SCAN WHILE ord.custid = cus.custid
    DELETE
  ENDSCAN
ENDIF
```

7. Annotate the ends of structures that are not easily connected to their beginnings.

```
  ENDIF // status = i
  SELECT CUS
ENDSCAN // cus loop
```

If you're the only one who will ever read your code, you may legitimately wonder why you should bother with all this formatting. On the other hand, if your programs need to be shared with other people or if you'd like to understand what you were doing six months ago, then conventions that make your code more legible and better documented are more than worth the effort.

There is no one true way to document and format FoxPro programming. There are some common approaches, many of them drawn from Microsoft's manuals and the experience of expert developers. But even these approaches vary. The point is to establish a set of conventions you can remember and stick with them. Many of these conventions will be highlighted as the book goes along. None of them is difficult or time-consuming if you make them automatic—a habit. They become a habit simply by doing them.

Control Structures

A few programs may execute every command without stopping, figuratively running line by line from top to bottom. But when you create an application (or most programs), you need to be able to control the flow of program execution—starting, stopping, and changing direction. That's the purpose of the control structures.

They're called *control structures* because they have the ability to turn, direct, change, cycle, and corral the execution flow of a program. Control structures are similar to events and menu selections, but control structures are purely programmatic; no human interaction is involved. There are three types: conditionals, loops, and calls. The *conditionals* are the traffic cops, making logical decisions to channel program flow as well as performing other testing chores for a program. The *loops* capture the flow of a program and force it to repeat. The *calls* are programming commands that start programs, forms, procedures, and functions, moving the flow in other directions and sometimes bringing it back.

CONDITIONAL STRUCTURES

The two conditional structures provide the logical framework for programming, and they exist in similar syntax for every modern programming language.

THE STANDARD IF STRUCTURE

IF you want a million bucks, THEN you'll write a great piece of software, or ELSE you'll sell newspapers. The English syntax works quite well when formulating a FoxPro **IF...ENDIF** statement. In some languages, IF/THEN/ELSE is the actual syntax. In FoxPro, the formal syntax is a little different:

Command syntax:

IF lExpression
Commands
[ELSE
Commands]
ENDIF

Arguments:

lExpression A logical condition that controls the execution of true or false.

Commands Any and all valid FoxPro commands, including whole programs.

Example:

```
IF customer.state = "CA"
    DO statetax WITH nTaxPercent
    DO fedtax WITH nFedRate
ELSE
    DO notax
ENDIF
```

You've already met the **IF...ENDIF** construction in the form of the in-line IF, **IIF( )**; **IF...ENDIF** is the original format. Giving a loose translation to the syntax, the command structure works like this:

> IF < some logical test that is either true or false >
> The test was true, do something here.
> ELSE (control structure separator)
> The test was false, so do something else here.
> ENDIF (marks the end of the control structure)

You already know that the logical test for the **IF** can be almost anything:

Very simple	`IF 1+1 = 2`
Relatively simple	`IF cWorldPeace = "InterNet"`
Sort of complex	`IF SUBSTR(cus.company, 1, 3 ) = "IBM"`
Moderately complex	`IF MIN(ACOS(nRoof)/30,4.35) > SQRT(ATAN(nRoof)/60)`
Complex	`IF wYesNo("Are you sure.?" , 8, .t., "GR+/R,W+/B")AND cus.ytdpurch > 1000`
Very complex	`IF SEEK("Home","CUS")AND NOT(MONTH( DATE())=12 OR nOverDue<IIF(inv.due>100,inv.due, 0))`

The only requirement is that the statement evaluate to true or false. If the logical expression is true, then program control goes first to the code between the **IF** and the **ELSE** (or if there is no **ELSE**, then the **ENDIF**). Once the code inside is completed, program control resumes at the first line beyond the **ENDIF**. If the logical expression evaluates to false, in the preceding example, control drops immediately to the line beyond the **ENDIF**. If there is an **ELSE**, however, control is passed to the code between the **ELSE** and the **ENDIF**.

The **IF**, **<logical expression>**, and **ENDIF** are required. Everything else depends on what the program requires for a conditional test, or *branching*, as it is sometimes called. When branching, the **IF** is used to redirect program flow, usually with a program call, as in the previous syntax example. You can also *nest* the **IF** statements:

```
IF nYrTotal > 1000
   SELECT cus
   SEEK cno
   IF cus.ytdpurch > 500
      SELECT inv
      SEEK cno
      IF inv.itotal > 250
       cAward = "We have a winner!"
      ENDIF
   ENDIF //cus.ytdpurch
ENDIF //nYrTotal
```

Some observations about this example might be helpful:

- This example could not be constructed with a single logical expression in the first **IF**, because it was necessary to execute a command to get the information necessary for the next **IF** condition.
- The **//** slashes following the **ENDIF**s are an element of documentation style. Actually, the FoxPro compiler will ignore any commentary following keywords such as **ENDIF**. No special markers are required, but the slashes visually reinforce the structure of the **IF/ENDIF**, and the notation of the logic will relate the **ENDIF** to the original **IF**. This example spans only a few lines and presents no problem, but some **IF/ENDIF** structures run to hundreds of lines and many nested levels. Without detail formatting like this, you can waste a lot of time trying to figure out which **ENDIF** belongs to which **IF**.
- The indentation convention used is three spaces. There is no standard for this except that it is highly recommended not to use tabs; they have a way of printing and formatting badly. Three's a good number. It helps to keep program lines inside the boundary of a standard 80 characters (screen and paper width). If you use a deeper indentation, you can quickly get nested structures that push lines outside the area.

THE CASE STRUCTURE

All conditional logic is *bifurcating*, meaning that it potentially splits program flow in two directions. You know, however, that there are often more than two ways to go. In many cases, the logic isn't either/or but rather a series of possibilities. In programming, this kind of logic is implemented as a list of conditions, only one of which is true. It is expressed in FoxPro by the **DO CASE...ENDCASE** structure. Here's the syntax:

Command syntax:

DO CASE
CASE lExpression1
 Commands
[CASE lExpression2
 Commands
...
CASE lExpressionN
 Commands]
[OTHERWISE
 Commands]
ENDCASE

Arguments:

lExpression A logical condition that controls whether a **CASE** will execute.

Commands Any and all valid FoxPro commands, including whole programs.

Example:

```
DO CASE
CASE cMenuChoice = "Add"
  DO AddOne
CASE cMenuChoice = "Edit"
  DO EditOne
CASE cMenuChoice = "Delete"
  DO DeleteOne
CASE cMenuChoice = "Quit"
  CANCEL
```

```
OTHERWISE
  WAIT "Please make a selection." WINDOW NOWAIT
ENDCASE
```

Program flow starts at the first **CASE** and works its way down. If a **CASE** condition is true, the ensuing code is executed, after which program flow drops to the next program line after the **ENDCASE**. If none of the cases is true, the optional **OTHERWISE** can be included to provide a response. Because of the top-down, one-hit-only approach of the **CASE** structure, you must be careful with the logic so that all the choices are actually possible. Here's an example of one that doesn't work:

```
DO CASE
CASE nCount <= 500
CASE nCount <= 300
CASE nCount <= 100
ENDCASE
```

The last two cases will never fire. This is an obvious example, but it's easier than you might think to create a similar, if more sophisticated, mistake.

LOOPING CONTROL STRUCTURES

Loop control structures do what their name implies: cause program execution to repeat. Loops are said to have a top and a bottom, with program code in between that is executed every time the program cycles inside the loop. There are three main loop control structures in FoxPro: **DO WHILE...ENDDO**, **FOR...ENDFOR**, and **SCAN...ENDSCAN**. Each type has its own characteristics, typical uses, and peculiarities. However, some things are common to all the loops, as illustrated in Figure 9.1.

In FoxPro, the primary logic that sustains the loop is located at the top. These conditions or counters determine whether the loop should continue or drop out to the first line beyond the end of the control structure. Curiously, the Xbase language has no loops that test for an exit at the bottom of the loop. However, the **EXIT** clause causes program flow to immediately drop out of the loop at the bottom. The **LOOP** clause causes an immediate return to the top of the loop.

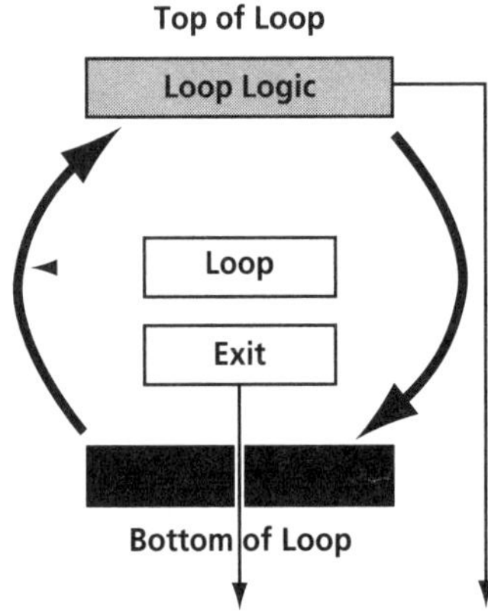

FIGURE 9.1 LOOP CONTROL STRUCTURES.

DO WHILE...ENDDO: THE GENERAL LOOP

The **DO WHILE...ENDDO** is the grandad of Xbase loops, being the one and only loop in the progenitor, dBase II. These days it's used sparingly, mostly where you might want a pure loop: one not tied to a table (compare with **SCAN..ENDSCAN**) or one not tied to a counter (compare with **FOR..ENDFOR**). The syntax is simple:

Command syntax:

DO WHILE lExpression
Commands
[LOOP]
[EXIT]
ENDDO

Arguments:

lExpression A logical condition that controls whether the loop will continue executing.

Commands Any and all valid FoxPro commands, including whole programs.

Example:

```
DO WHILE .t.
   DO CASE
```

```
    CASE USED("cus")
      BROWSE FIELDS <customer fields>
      DO CustFix
    CASE USED("inv")
      BROWSE FIELDS <invoice fields>
      DO InvFix
    CASE USED("det")
      BROWSE FIELDS <detail fields>
      DO DetFix
    OTHERWISE
      EXIT
    ENDCASE
ENDDO
```

If the logical expression at the top is true, the loop continues. If it is false, the loop exits at the bottom without executing any further code inside the loop. The preceding example is a *permanent loop*, because the logic at the top is always true. The escape hatch must be somewhere else in the code and use the **EXIT** clause. Here's a more typical **DO WHILE...ENDDO** with a conditional expression that actually tests for something:

```
*Gas Chromatograph Input Loop
*Run until outside of test parameter.
nSpike  = 0
nNorm   = 0
nTest   = 0
DO WHILE MAX( nSpike, nNorm, nTest ) < 100
  nSpike = GCHigh()
  nNorm  = GCTable( nSpike, 2.1)
  nTest  = GCTest(nSpike, nNorm, "EC")
ENDDO
```

The Counting Loop

The **FOR...ENDFOR** loop is used whenever a loop needs to run a specific number of times. This loop can be emulated with **DO WHILE...ENDDO**, but the **FOR** is specifically designed for the task and executes more quickly. The key part of the syntax is the unique **FOR** condition:

Command window:

FOR MemVarName = nInitialValue TO nFinalValue [STEP nIncrement]
Commands
[EXIT]
[LOOP]
ENDFOR | NEXT

Arguments:

MemVarName A variable to store the current count of the loop.

nInitialValue The starting value for the loop.

nFinalValue The stop value for the loop.

nIncrement The numeric increment to be used for counting.

Commands Any valid FoxPro commands.

Examples:

```
FOR x = 1 TO 10
   x = x + nNewX
ENDFOR
*
nStop = customer.balance
FOR i = 1 TO INT(nStop) STEP 10
  nValue = IIF( nTotal/i > 100, nTotal, 0)
  IF nValue > nStop
    EXIT
  ENDIF
ENDFOR
```

Translated, the syntax reads like this: Continue looping **FOR** as long as the value of the counting memory variable is between the starting value **TO** the ending value. Count in **STEP**s of the increment size. Most of the time, the counting is by addition, and the progression is from a lower value to a higher value; however, the loop can also go in the other direction. For example:

```
FOR i = 10 TO 1 STEP -1
   x = x - nValue
ENDFOR
```

In this case, the optional **STEP** clause is used to indicate the subtraction in the count. Otherwise, **STEP** has a default value of 1. Although it's most common to use constants for the **nInitialValue** and **nFinalValue** values, they can also be any kind of expression. For example:

```
nCount = 1
FOR k = dStartDate TO dEndDate+365 STEP 7
  aWeekIncome[nCount] = WeekLook()
  nCount = nCount+1
ENDFOR
```

NOTE

New Visual FoxPro 5.0 is a variation of the **FOR...ENDFOR** loop: **FOR EACH <variable> IN <array or container>...ENDFOR**. This version is limited to looping through arrays and object containers (e.g. show all controls in a form sort of thing), but it's specialization makes it both fast and convenient

THE TABLE LOOP

The only task of the **SCAN...ENDSCAN** loop is to scan a data table, traversing record-by-record from top to bottom. This replaces the old **DO WHILE...ENDDO** construction:

```
DO WHILE NOT EOF()
  SKIP
ENDDO
```

In effect, **SCAN...ENDSCAN** has the **SKIP** command built-in at the bottom of the loop and will execute 10 15 percent faster than the **DO WHILE...ENDDO**. It's by far the preferred way to move through a data table. Here's the simple syntax:

Command syntax:
SCAN [NOOPTIMIZE]
[Scope] [FOR lExpression1] [WHILE lExpression2]
[Commands]
[LOOP]
[EXIT]
ENDSCAN
Arguments:
Scope Uses the standard **NEXT** and **NEXT n** expressions.
FOR lExpression1 The standard control expression.

WHILE lExpression2 The logical control expression commonly used with this loop.

Commands Any valid FoxPro commands.

Example:

```
SELECT cus
IF SEEK( cus.cno, "inv")
  SELECT inv
  SCAN WHILE cus.cno = inv.cno
    IF inv.itotal > 500
     cAward = "We Have a Winner!"
    ENDIF
  ENDSCAN
ENDIF
```

Notice that **SCAN...ENDSCAN** has the hallmarks of a table command: **SCOPE, FOR, and WHILE**, the familiar data table clauses that determine which records will be included in the **SCAN**. Otherwise, this loop looks like and works like a normal loop.

In the example, a **SEEK**, **SEEK( )**, or **LOCATE** is used to find something in a table; then **SCAN** is used to run through the records that still match the initial search condition. This is an extremely common use of **SCAN...ENDSCAN**. In this connection, notice the use of the **WHILE** clause, as is customary in a table in which the pointer is already located on the desired starting record.

To indicate the flexibility of a **SCAN** loop, here's a construction that's not typical:

```
SELECT cus
SET ORDER TO lastdate
SEEK dYearEnd
SCAN FOR cus.state = "CA" ;
     WHILE dYearEnd <= cus.lastdate ;
     REST
  IF cus.ono <> "1"
    nCustTotal = nCustTotal - cus.ytdpurch
  ELSE
    nCustTotal = nCustTotal + cus.ytdpurch
```

```
    ENDIF
  ENDSCAN //cus.state = "CA"
```

This loop starts with the record pointer on the first record that matches the `dYearEnd` value—for example, 1/31/94. It then scans forward while that value is less than or equal to the last date of customer activity. However, it will include only those records of customers whose state is California.

NOTE

SCAN loops are one of the most useful of all control structures. General table commands such as **SUM**, **TOTAL**, and **REPLACE** are one-trick ponies compared with **SCAN**. It gives you the opportunity to work with a table on a record-by-record basis, inserting within the confines of the **SCAN...ENDSCAN** construction almost any kind of logic, table updating, or conversions.

PROGRAM CALLS CONTROL STRUCTURE

A program call isn't precisely a control structure, but it definitely involves controlling and changing program flow, so the term's appropriate. The word *call* is old programming jargon for invoking a named subroutine within a program—for example, making a *function call*. The word isn't used very often in object-oriented programming (a *method call*?), but it still applies. There are three kinds of calls in FoxPro:

- Procedures, forms, and program files, which are called with the **DO** command.
- Functions, whether called with **<function>,** nested in another command, (`IF SEEK()`), or called by assignment (`cDrive = CURDIR()`).
- Methods, which are called by reference to their object: `oObject.Refresh()`.

The most important aspect of any call is that it is made from one environment into another. By "environment," we mean all the things mentioned in Chapter 8, including the internal status of FoxPro, the configuration of files and tables, and the scope of variables (which you'll encounter soon in this chapter). A program call usually invokes another piece of programming (a function, method, or procedure), which does its thing and then returns program control to the calling program. It's the programmer's responsibility to see that the environments of both the calling routine and the called routine aren't disrupted or changed in a way that causes an error. This sounds like a simple and sensible rule, but in practice it's one of the most difficult and pivotal aspects of programming.

NOTE

From personal experience, I would say that more programs founder from the transition between programming elements than from any other cause. It's incredibly easy to lose track of variables, table conditions, or environmental settings and do something that will cause the program to crash—often far from the place where the mistake originates.

The difficulty of managing program calls is complicated by the object-oriented approach and the so-called modeless type of program. Traditionally, users moved from one part of a program to another in a more or less controlled fashion: Make a menu choice, go into a module, make other selections to call functions, and then return to the menu. All very linear. In the *modeless* approach, aided when you work with objects, users can jump more or less at will between program elements, often leaving many of them active on the screen at the same time. For developers of applications created with many (sometimes hundreds) of objects, the mechanisms for managing program calls become extremely important. They're also a significant part of what an application framework is all about.

We'll tackle this facet of programming repeatedly throughout the rest of the book, but let's start with something simple you can do anywhere: Highlight the transitions between program elements with documentation. Whenever your program calls something other than a FoxPro function or method—your procedures, methods, functions, and so on—mark it and add notes if there is anything unusual or important about the transition. Here's a typical example for the **Click** method of a CommandButton object in a form:

```
*Create variable to hold returned value.
LOCAL lcUserPick
lcUserPick = SPACE(9)

*===============> SELECT A USER

DO FORM usr1pick NAME usr1pick LINKED TO lcUsrPick

*<============= RETURN A SELECTED USER IF ANY

* Check for USERS table being open.
IF NOT USED("USERS")
```

```
  USE main!users IN 0 ORDER userid
ENDIF
SELECT users
SET ORDER TO userid
* Look up the selected matrix and update the form.
IF SEEK(lcUsrPick,"users")
  qcUserId = users.Userid
  This.Parent.bctTextBox5.Value = TRIM(user.lastname)
  This.Parent.BctTextbox5.Refresh()
ENDIF
```

VARIABLES

Someone once wrote, "Variables are to programming as corpuscles are to blood; they carry vital materials throughout the system." Without taking this analogy too far, it's a useful notion that variables are containers that can "flow" throughout a program, carrying data. This section explores the relationship between variables and programming, including some of the more difficult aspects such as variable scoping and variable substitution.

Recall that a variable is a named space in RAM that may contain data of any type. Creating a variable is simple:

```
cVariable = "Item"
```

This line assigns a name to a variable and then loads it with a specific item of data. In this case, because the data is a character string, the variable becomes a character variable. It is highly recommended that every time you create a variable, you document what it is used for:

```
cVariable = "Item"                && Sample variable
```

An alternative form for creating and storing values in variables is sometimes useful, because you can create more than one variable at a time:

```
STORE 0 TO nStart, nFinish, nCount
```

Once a variable contains data, it can be used in the code to deliver that data to functions, equations, statements, and commands. For example, the following lines store numbers into three variables and then use the variables to do some math:

```
nSolution1   = 8.00             && percent solution
nSolution2   = 12.00            && percent solution
nRequiredMl = 0.00              && Amount required in Ml.
*Calculate required milliliters of solution, given
*input percentages of solution.
nRequiredMl = (nSolution2*20 - 160)/(8-nSolution1)
```

In this example, all the lines of code, including the ones that create and load the variables, are in the same place. It is more typical for the variables to be created or loaded (or both) in a location different from the lines that use them. In fact, this is the main reason for variables: to deliver data from one part of a program to another. Sometimes this takes place within a single function, method, or procedure. At other times, variables may carry data between different objects or even between modules of an application.

Using the same example, suppose the three variables are created and given initial values in the opening file of the program:

```
*LABMAIN.PRG
nSolution1   = 0.00             && percent solution
nSolution2   = 0.00             && percent solution
nRequiredMl = 0.00              && Amount required in Ml.
```

Then the variables are assigned working values in a testing form:

```
*LABTEST.SCX
nSolution1   = 8.00             && percent solution
nSolution2   = 12.00            && percent solution
```

Finally, they are used in a third instance to provide data to a method:

```
*olab.CalcPctSol()
nRequiredMl = olab.CalcPctSol( nSolution1, nSolution2 )
```

Passing data between procedures is possible because variables can persist in memory until deliberately released or the program terminates. This capability, although vital, is not without pitfalls. Suppose, for example, that the person who programmed the LABTEST form inadvertently used the following line of code before the CalcPctSol() method is called:

```
nSolution1 = IIF(nSolution1 > 0, 12.02, "NA")
```

Can you see why this code will cause problems? Most of the time it will substitute 12.02 for 12.00 percent, causing the calculations to be subtly inaccurate. This is a data value error. Once in a while, the CalcPctSol( ) function will simply produce a FoxPro error message, because the data type for "NA" is character, and the function requires a numeric value. This is a data type error. In large programs and sometimes even in small ones, such programming mistakes can be a source of bugs.

SCOPING, PART I: VARIABLES

The concept of *scoping* for variables is dry as toast, but it is important. As your application moves in and out of forms and other objects, you will create many variables to contain information. The question is, of all these variables, which are active? In FoxPro, variables may take on any kind of value anywhere in a program, leading to both data value errors and data type errors.

Because of the potential difficulty of tracing these errors, the programming world has developed a near paranoia (the flip side is obsession) about controlling variables. There are several approaches, three of which are used by FoxPro:

- Variables are scoped to control how long they are active and when they can be used.
- Objects have their own way of controlling variables, including the use of properties.
- Programmers are encouraged to *pass* variables and values as parameters between objects and other program elements.

Nearly all programming languages provide ways to scope variables; the *scope* defines how long and in what way variables are active. FoxPro supports four types of variables relative to scope: default, public, private, and local. Objects also support a type of variable, as a property, that has a scoping pattern similar but parallel to the conventional variables. We'll cover that part of the story in Chapter 11, in a section called "Scoping, Part II: Properties." The third approach, passing variables and values as parameters, will be covered in Chapter 10. All three approaches are used in a typical application, with object-oriented and procedural variables often working side by side. This can be confusing, but once you learn a few rules of thumb, the confusion usually resolves itself through experience.

The Default Scope

When you create a variable by assignment, it has two scoping characteristics by default:

- It remains in memory (persists) as long as that program or object is active. As soon as a procedure is terminated or an object is released, the variable and its contents are released.
- The variable is available (visible) to all procedures or objects below the originating procedure or object.

As illustrated in Figure 9.2, programmers typically talk about program execution occurring "above" or "below" a sequence of procedures or objects during the running of a program. Traditionally, procedures are called one after another and it's assumed that most of the time the sequence will be reversed until program control winds up back at the original procedure. It's easy to see how one procedure can be characterized as above or below another one.

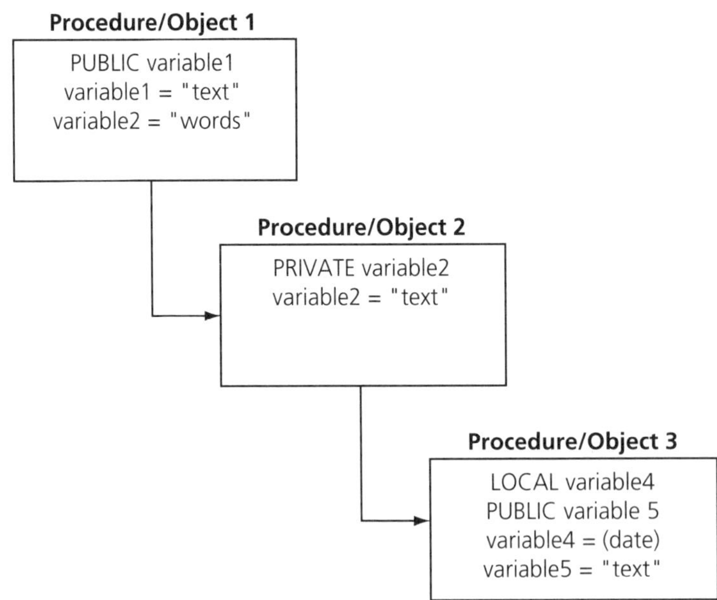

Figure 9.2 The scope of variables.

In object-oriented programming, *above* and *below* still have meaning. This sense of vertical positioning is obvious within a class hierarchy and also applies in the sense that program control is passed from one object to the method of another object and is returned. But given the ability of events to move program control in any direction, even sideways (so to speak), what can be said is that a variable created with a default scope in one object is available for use only by objects that are called *after* the original object.

If you create a variable in procedure 1 by assignment (`variable2 = "text"`), it will persist as long as procedure 1 is active. FoxPro will automatically release the variable as it exits or terminates the procedure. In this way, FoxPro takes care of much of the housekeeping for variables. The second default characteristic means that all variables created in procedure 1 are visible (can be read) and available (can be changed) by any procedure called in sequence from procedure 1. In this way, variables initialized in the very first program file are, in effect, globally available for all the procedures that follow.

This default scoping is convenient because you let FoxPro do the work of releasing the variable. But it can also be risky. What if you don't want a variable created in one part of an application to be available to other parts? Or what if you want to create a variable somewhere other than the first file that will persist both above and below the procedure in which it was created? For such needs, FoxPro supports three commands to create types of variables: **PUBLIC**, **PRIVATE**, and **LOCAL.**

PUBLIC VARIABLES

As soon as it is created, a public variable will be visible and available to *all* other procedures (above and below the current procedure). It will persist until explicitly released or until FoxPro execution is stopped through a **QUIT**. Public variables persist even when you cancel the running of a program. Public memory variables are created using the following syntax:

Command syntax:

PUBLIC <variable list>

Example:

```
PUBLIC nCount, cTable
nCount = 0
cTable = "NEWTABLE"
```

NOTE

It's important to note that *declaring* a variable (giving it a variable type with one of the commands) creates the name of the variable and assigns it the value of .f. (logical false). It's customary to immediately assign the variable its appropriate value.

In Figure 9.2, VARIABLE 1 and VARIABLE5 are declared public. VARIABLE1 is available throughout the run of the program, whereas VARIABLE5 becomes available only after procedure 3 has been run but will also be available throughout the remaining run of the program.

Most programmers use public variables to contain generic information that is used throughout a program—for example, the name of the current user, the active date, or an important status marker, as in the following:

```
* Initialize global variables.
PUBLIC cUserName, dActDate, cWorkFlag
cUserName = SPACE(20)          && for current user
dActDate  = DATE()             && active date
cWorkFlag = SPACE(1)           && work in progress flag
```

WARNING

The standard advice about public variables is use them sparingly, if at all. Because they hang around for so long, they present a greater opportunity for data errors. Object-oriented programmers would say that there's no reason ever to use a **PUBLIC** variable, because you can create persistent variables as properties of objects. Also, be careful not to declare the same variable **PUBLIC** more than once. Doing so will generate a Syntax Error message that may be difficult to interpret.

PRIVATE VARIABLES

Whereas public variables are available everywhere, private variables are restricted in availability. Their scope is the same as a variable created by default: active in the procedure in which they are created and any procedure subsequently called below it. However, a variable declared private has one unique property: It can have the *same name* as an existing variable. (Doing this with a public variable creates a syntax error.) The new private variable *hides* the original variable so that its contents can be neither read nor changed.

The syntax for the **PRIVATE** command is similar to that of **PUBLIC**:

Command syntax:

PRIVATE <memvar list>

Example:

```
PRIVATE nCount, cTable, cFirstName
```

In Figure 9.2, VARIABLE2 is created in procedure 1 and then declared **PRIVATE** in procedure 2. While in procedure 2, VARIABLE2 is independent in scope and content from the original VARIABLE2. When the program returns to procedure 1, the VARIABLE2 of the second procedure is released and VARIABLE2 resumes its original value.

LOCAL VARIABLES

Local variables are the most stringent in scope. They can be used and modified only within the procedure, function, or method in which they are created. This also makes them the safest and, in many ways, the most useful. Local variables are created in the same fashion as the other variable types:

Command syntax:

LOCAL Variable List

Example:

```
LOCAL nType, cName
```

In Figure 9.2, the local variable (VARIABLE4) is declared in procedure 3 and is available only in that procedure. In contrast to the private variables, you can't use a **LOCAL** variable name that is already created. FoxPro will release the local variables as soon as the program exits the procedure.

If you're serious about not allowing variables to cause bugs in your programs, then you'll name them so that you can tell which data type they use. You'll also follow the Golden Rule of scoping: Limit the scope of variables as much as possible. In FoxPro, this rule translates in practice to using parameters as much as possible, using **LOCAL** variables in almost all other situations, and only when absolutely necessary create a default, **PRIVATE**, or **PUBLIC** variable for special circumstances.

Variable Naming

In Chapter 3, where variables were first introduced, the naming of variables was discussed along with the idea of using a lowercase prefix for each variable based on the abbreviation for its data type: c = character, n = numeric, y = currency, b = double, i = integer, l = logical, d = date, and t = datetime. Now it's suggested that you also prefix variable names with a lowercase letter for its scope: g = global, l = local, p = property, r = private, and t = parameters. In this scheme, which is fairly common practice, variables look like this:

```
glIsSecure  = .T.
lcUserName  = "JOHNSON"
This.pdStartDate = {12/01/97}
rtTimeStamp = DATETIME()
```

By using these conventions, you make it possible to tell at a glance the data type and scope of a variable, and that makes it much easier to identify if it contains the wrong kind of data or is active in the wrong place. This convention will be especially helpful in the debugging windows, where it's not always easy to see the complete context of a variable.

NOTE

It is sometimes suggested that the data type conventions be applied to field names. That's probably not a bad idea except when field names are coded into a program and you change the field's data type and hence the name in the table. You'd have to track down every instance of the old field name.

Saving, Removing, and Restoring Variables

Removing variables from memory can often be left to FoxPro, because by default it releases variables whenever the procedure in which they were created is terminated. You can also help FoxPro by deliberately removing variables from memory when they are no longer needed. The command options are as follows:

Command syntax:

RELEASE <memvar list>

Example:

RELEASE nCount, cTable, cFirstName

Command syntax:

RELEASE ALL [LIKE <skel> | EXCEPT <skel>]

Examples:

```
RELEASE ALL
RELEASE ALL LIKE nCount*
RELEASE ALL EXCEPT aStat*
```

You can include placeholders (* and ?), which are similar to the DOS wildcards, to indicate any lettering allowed before or after a variable. This technique makes it possible to remove only a specified category of variables. The explicit release of variables has a secondary value: It's self-documenting. You'll know that the listed variables no longer exist.

There are times when you may not want to lose all (or some) of the working variables, instead just putting them away for a while. FoxPro can do this, too:

Command syntax:

SAVE TO <file> | TO MEMO <memo field> [ALL LIKE <skel> | ALL EXCEPT <skel>]

Examples:

```
SAVE TO taxvars ALL LIKE nTx*
SAVE TO MEMO comment ALL LIKE cNote*
```

Command syntax:

RESTORE FROM <file> | FROM MEMO <memo field> [ADDITIVE]

Examples:

```
RESTORE FROM taxvars.mem ADDITIVE
      RESTORE FROM MEMO comment ADDITIVE
```

The **SAVE TO** command puts all or selected variables and their contents into a memory variable file (with a MEM extension) or into a memo field of a table. Later, you can put them back into a program using the **RESTORE FROM** command. When restoring, be sure not to forget the innocuous **ADDITIVE** clause. If you forget, you can kiss all the existing variables good-bye.

NOTE

What's the difference between saving variables to a file and saving them to a memo field? For practical purposes, there's not much difference. But another rule of thumb for application programming is to limit the number of associated files (of all kinds), because applications with hundreds of files become unwieldy and prone to file-related errors. In larger applications, a common approach is to save variables to a memo field in a single system table, similar to the FoxPro resource file, that contains many kinds of operational information.

SYSTEM VARIABLES

FoxPro has a set of system variables that provide information about values stored for internal use. For the most part, these variables behave like ordinary variables; you can read and change them. However, if you try to release them, FoxPro politely ignores the command.

As summarized in Table 9.1, system variables fall into four categories: printing, programming, versions, and setup. All of them have their in programming, but only **_SCREEN** is used with regularity. Table 9.1 does not list those system variables that are obsolete or remain for backward compatibility.

TABLE 9.1 VISUAL FOXPRO SYSTEM VARIABLES

SYSTEM VARIABLE	T	DEFAULT	DESCRIPTION
Printing			Many of these variables are used extensively in the DOS version. In Visual FoxPro, only the variables used in the Report Designer are of interest.
_ASCIICOLS	N	0	Returns the number of columns in a file generated by running a report TO FILE ASCII.
_ASCIIROWS	N	0	Returns the number of rows in a file generated by running a report TO FILE ASCII.
_MLINE	N	0	Returns specific lines from a memo field.

SYSTEM VARIABLE	T	DEFAULT	DESCRIPTION
PAGENO	N	1	Useful for putting page numbers into reports.
Versions			These variables are used to identify the platform (type of computer) and version of FoxPro currently running.
_DOS	L		.T. if FoxPro for MS-DOS.
_MAC	L		.T. if FoxPro for Macintosh.
_UNIX	L		.T. if FoxPro for UNIX.
_WINDOWS	L		.T. if FoxPro for Windows.
Setup			These variables contain the path to FoxPro support files and are placed in the CONFIG.FPW file if they are located anywhere except the default FoxPro directory.
_BROWSER	C		Path to BROWSE.APP.
_BUILDER	C		Path to FoxPro Builders.
_GENMENU	C		Path to GENMENU.PRG.
_SPELLCHECK	C		Path to SPELLCHK.APP.
Programming			
_CLIPTEXT	C	Null	Contains the contents of the Windows Clipboard.
_DBLCLICK	N	0.5	The amount of time to measure between mouse clicks.
_SCREEN	O		This is actually an object and can be referenced for all the properties of the properties and methods active in the main FoxPro window.
_SHELL	C		If **_SHELL** contains any command to run a program (**DO <program>**), it prevents all access to the Command window.

SYSTEM VARIABLE	T	DEFAULT	DESCRIPTION
_TALLY	N	0	The count of records returned from a SQL query, a **COUNT**, or any other command that returns a record count.
_TEXT	N	-1	Text merge output.
_TRIGGERLEVEL	N	0	Indicates the current level of nesting within the DBC triggers.
_THROTTLE	N	0	Sets the speed with which program text is displayed in the Trace window.

VARIABLE SUBSTITUTION TECHNIQUES

Making code generic so that it can be reused is one of the touchstones of object-oriented programming. Variable substitution plays a role in making your code more generic, so it's an important topic. But it will take practice and insight to understand how it works.

Let's start with some code that is not generic at all. Suppose you open a table like this: `USE f:\lab\dbf\labstaff IN 0`. The path to the file is highly specific and the file must exist there. When you compile and distribute a program that contains this line of code, no matter where the program runs there must be a file named LABSTAFF located in a folder path of F:\LAB\DBF. In programming jargon, this file path is *hard-coded*. If the location of the file is moved to another folder, you will have to find and manually edit each instance of this code. This may not be a problem for a small program, but what if your application has hundreds of file opening commands? On the other hand, if you use one of the variable substitution techniques—in this case, something called a name expression—you can make a generic file opening command that can open many different files:

```
cFileName = "F:\LAB\DATA\LABSTAFF"
USE (cFileName) IN 0
```

The parentheses around the variable CFILENAME tell FoxPro, "Substitute the variable name with the contents of the variable." In this way, FoxPro will execute the command using the file and its path rather than take the variable literally. Anywhere in the program, the variable CFILENAME can be loaded with a new file path (perhaps from a table), greatly easing the maintenance of these file-opening statements.

There are thousands of other uses for the variable substitution techniques, some of them astonishing. The three techniques available are name expressions, the **EVALUATE( )** function, and macro substitution. They are all *run-time* substitutions, because they occur at the time you run your programs, and not during design or compilation. This means that they allow you to alter the content of commands (and even the commands themselves) as the program is running.

NAME EXPRESSIONS

Whenever you encounter a command that can be read as **COMMAND <name of something>**, you can probably use a name expression. The **<name of something>** is always the name of a FoxPro object: a file name, a table name or alias, a variable name, a window name, a project name, and so forth. To use a name expression requires a variable (as do all three techniques). First, you assign a variable with the name of something. Then, using parentheses, you include the variable with the command. Here are some common examples:

- Tables:
```
cTableName = "customer"
USE ( cTableName )
```
- Programs:
```
cFileName = "taxcount.dbf"
DO ( cFileName )
```
- Fields:
```
cFieldName = "customer.lastname"
REPLACE ( cFieldName ) WITH cLastName
```
- Aliases:
```
cOldAlias = ALIAS()
SELECT ( cOldAlias )
```
- Indexes:
```
cOldOrder = ORDER()
SET ORDER TO ( cOldOrder )
```

Name expressions are ubiquitous in well-written programs. They can be used in myriad places where there is changeable content for a command or command clause. Here's an example that is used in almost every function, method, or procedure:

```
* Initialize environment variables
cOldAlias = ALIAS()
cOldOrder = ORDER()

…
*> Cleanup
*Restore original file/index (trap for no file/index).
IF NOT EMPTY( cOldAlias )
  SELECT ( cOldAlias )
  IF NOT EMPTY( cOldOrder ) AND ORDER() <> cOldOrder
    SET ORDER TO ( cOldOrder )
  ENDIF
ENDIF
```

The variables and name expressions (`cOldAlias`)and (`cOldOrder`) make this routine generic by storing and restoring any file and index tag that comes along.

Using EVALUATE( )

Whereas the name expression simply passes the content of a variable, as a character string, to a command, **EVALUATE( )** processes (evaluates) the expression stored in the variable. The function is commonly abbreviated to **EVAL( )**, probably because it sounds like something from the C++ language. The expression used for the function's argument must be a character string or a character variable, and it must be something that can be evaluated, such as a formula:

```
nTotal = 50
? EVAL( "nTotal" )
```

Returns: `50`

```
? EVAL( nTotal )
```

Returns: `! Invalid function argument value, type, or count.`

```
cValue = "2+2"
? EVAL( cValue )
```

Returns: `4`

```
cDateLine = "{12/01/96}-{12/01/95}"
? EVAL( cDateLine )
```

Returns: `365`

```
cLogic = "nTotal > 100"
? EVAL( cLogic )
```

Returns: `.f.` or `.t.`

There are no rules for when to use **EVALUATE( )**, except that it's faster than a macro substitution for any expression that needs to be evaluated before being passed to a command. It's also overkill (both computationally and as a matter of typing) for situations that can use a name expression. Its best use is in places where an evaluated substitution must be repeated often, as in loops such as the following:

```
nTotal = 0
FOR i = 1 TO 10,000
  IF EVAL("nTotal > 500")
    EXIT
  ELSE
    nTotal = GetTotal()
  ENDIF
ENDFOR
```

MACRO SUBSTITUTION

Macro substitution is the granddaddy of all the variable substitution techniques and has been used and abused more than any other special feature of the language. The macro substitution operator looks harmless enough: **&** , the simple ampersand. If you put this in front of a variable, FoxPro will substitute the contents of the variable into the command or expression being executed. For example:

```
cFileName = "f:\lab\data\labstaff"
USE &cFileName
```

This works exactly like a name expression. But a macro substitution can do more:

```
cValue = "2+2"
? &cValue
```

Returns: 4

This is just like **EVALUATE( )**. The macro substitution will also evaluate an expression stored in the variable as a character string. It can do still more:

```
cCommand = "USE labstaff ALIAS stf ORDER lastname"
? &cCommand
```

The macro substitution will execute this entire command! This is possible because FoxPro is, in essence, an *interpreted* programming language. This means that commands are executed one at a time, as if the program were being run sequentially one line at a time. A result of this approach is that when you're working in the Command window, FoxPro immediately executes your commands.

One might think that compiled programs behave differently. However, FoxPro always has an interpreted component, even when programs are compiled. There is always a run-time processing engine that acts as the interpreter. Some parts of your code will bypass this run-time interpreter and thereby execute faster. A macro substitution, however, always invokes the interpreter. It works something like this:

In a procedure:

```
cCommand = "USE labstaff ALIAS stf ORDER lastname"
? &cCommand
```

In the run-time interpreter:

Pass 1: **USE** "USE LABSTAFF ALIAS STF ORDER LASTNAME"

Pass 2: **USE** LABSTAFF **ALIAS** STF **ORDER** LASTNAME

On the first pass, FoxPro unloads the variable, pulling out its contents. On the second pass, it evaluates (in this case, parses) the contents and includes the result with the current instructions. This two-pass approach is what makes macro substitutions powerful. It also makes them slow. Because of all the machinery necessary to load the interpreter and run two passes, macro substitution is one of the slowest operations in FoxPro.

Whether it's slow or not, you can do some amazing things with macro substitution, and only with macro substitution. Like all the other substitution techniques, it is used to make code generic. A classic example involves reports. A high percentage of reports need to vary a selection criterion (the **FOR** clause). For example, you may run the same report over and over, changing only the date range for records to be included. It would be cumbersome, or impossible, to program every possible combination of date ranges.

Sooner or later, almost every FoxPro programmer discovers that report parameters can be manipulated generically using macro substitutions, as in this abbreviated example:

Procedure 1:

```
*Get the user's input on the dates to report (in a form).
PUBLIC dStartDate, dStopDate
dStartDate = {}
dStopDate  = {}
```

Procedure 2:

```
*Compose the FOR expression, note date brackets.
cFor = "lab.startdate >= {"+DTOC(dStartDate)"} ;
  AND lab.stopdate <= {"+DTOC(dStopDate)+"}"
SELECT lab
*Get a count needed for the report.
COUNT ALL FOR &cFor TO nCount
*Run the report with macro substitution.
REPORT FORM lablog FOR &cFor TO PRINT
```

NOTE

FoxPro takes it's share of knocks for being an interpreted language, because it's self-evident that any language that isn't truly compiled must be slow. There's some truth to that, but for most applications the difference in speed is not great enough to matter. On the other side, programmers who have worked with macro substitution know how much it helps to make code generic and reusable—the whole point of object-oriented programming.

Using Arrays

An *array* is a series of indexed variables. Arrays look like this:

```
aState[1]
aState[2]
aState[3]
```

Each variable, called an *element* of the array, has an index value, the *subscript*, which is enclosed by brackets (or parentheses). In its simplest form, as shown next with a single subscript, an array is like a column of memory variables, each in sequence. What distinguishes one element from another element is the value of the subscript. Because the subscript is a number and can be represented by a variable containing a number, it's possible to scan a series of array elements in a way that's impossible to scan individual memory variables:

```
FOR i = 1 TO 50 FOR EACH cState IN aState
  IF aState[i] = "TEXAS"
    EXIT
  ENDIF
ENDFOR
```

Thinking of an array as an indexed series of memory variables, usually containing related data, can be helpful in understanding how to use them. Arrays are a convenient way to store and manipulate related items of information.

Arrays don't look like regular variables, and they're not created in the same way variables are created. Arrays can't be created by assignment; they must be explicitly created by either one of two commands:

Command syntax:

DECLARE ArrayName1 (nRows1 [, nColumns1]) [, ArrayName2 (nRows2 [, nColumns2])] ...

DIMENSION ArrayName1 (nRows1 [, nColumns1])[, ArrayName2 (nRows2 [, nColumns2])]

Examples:

```
DECLARE aState[51]
DECLARE aCounty[36], aCity[1000]
DECLARE aState[51,4]
```

```
DIMENSION aState[51]
DIMENSION aCounty[36], aCity[1000]
DIMENSION aState[51,4]
```

When used to create an array, the numbers in brackets define the number of elements in the array. If there are two numbers separated by a comma, the array is two-dimensional. Typically, you follow the creation of an array by initializing it to a data type. This can be done with a single command:

```
STORE SPACE(30) TO aState, aCounty
```

It is also common to immediately load (by assignment) the elements of an array with specific data:

```
DECLARE aState[5]
aState[1] = "TEXAS"
aState[2] = "VIRGINIA"
aState[3] = "RHODE ISLAND"
aState[4] = "CALIFORNIA"
aState[5] = "FLORIDA"
```

You may have noticed that the basic syntax of the two commands that create an array is identical. Why, you may ask, are there two of them? The duplication is a nod to history. One previously popular form of the Xbase language (Clipper) uses **DECLARE** and other programming languages use **DIMENSION**. FoxPro decided to allow both commands. You can also use parentheses instead of brackets to enclose the subscript, again a bow to other programming languages.

Making the best of a redundancy, some people like to use **DECLARE** to create an array and **DIMENSION** to redefine it, but it matters not a bit to FoxPro.

There are three things about arrays in FoxPro that are well worth remembering:

- An array may have one or two dimensions.
- Arrays can be redimensioned at any time.
- Arrays can contain data of almost any kind in any element.

Speaking like a mathematician, two-dimensional arrays are the same as a matrix, and a one-dimension array is a vector. A one-dimensional array is a column of memory variables. A two-dimensional array is a table. Suppose you declare an array like this:

```
DECLARE aState[5,4]
```

This means that there are five element *rows* and four element *columns*. You can visualize a two-dimensional array like this:

```
aState[1,1]="IA"
aState[1,2]="IOWA"
aState[1,3]="Des Moines"
aState[1,4]="Midwest"
aState[2,1]="ID"
aState[2,2]="IDAHO"
aState[2,3]="Boise"
aState[2,4]="West"
```

That is the way programs must view it. Or, you can picture it like this:

```
aState    1]      2]          3]               4]
  [1,     IA      IOWA        Des Moines      Midwest
  [2,     ID      IDAHO       Boise           West
  [3,     IL      ILLINOIS    Springfield     Midwest
  [4,     IN      INDIANA     Indianapolis    Midwest
```

Does this remind you of a data table? That's another important feature of arrays: They can mimic a data table. Moreover, because they are RAM based, you can perform some database-like actions on an array more rapidly than from a table on disk. FoxPro gives you three commands that support the array-as-table concept. One of them moves data from a table into an array:

Command syntax:

COPY TO ARRAY <array> [FIELDS <field list>] [FOR <expL1>] [WHILE <expL2>]

Arguments:

<array> The name of the array.

[FIELDS <field list>] A list of fields to be included—the columns of an array.

[FOR <expL1>] The standard **FOR** clause with a logical expression.

[WHILE <expL2>] The standard **WHILE** clause with a logical expression.

Example:

```
COPY TO ARRAY aState FIELDS state.abbrev,;
        state.name, state.capital, state.region
```

The second command returns data from an array into the fields of a table:

Command syntax:

APPEND FROM ARRAY <array> [FIELDS <field list>] [FOR <expL>]

Arguments:

<array> The name of the array.

FIELDS <field list> A list of fields to be included—the columns of an array.

FOR <expL1> The standard **FOR** clause with a logical expression.

Example:

```
APPEND FROM aState FIELDS state.abbrev, state.name
```

The third command, probably the most used, involves **SQL-SELECT**, shown here in abbreviated format:

Command syntax:

SELECT...INTO ARRAY <array>

Example:

```
SELECT DISTINCT state.abbrev ;
      FROM state ;
      ORDER BY state ;
      INTO ARRAY aState
```

If you specify more than one field (or default to all fields), these commands automatically produce a two-dimensional array with as many columns as there are fields and as many records as are in the original table (or in the subset you create with the **FOR**, **WHILE**, and other options in the **SELECT**). Before using any of these commands, you should remind yourself that a 1000-record database with 50 fields is an enormous amount of data. You may not have enough RAM to accommodate an entire table.

In FoxPro, an array can be redimensioned at any time, for the most part without losing content. There are some commonsense rules for redimensioning. Suppose you start by creating a 10 by 4 array (10 rows, 4 columns) and load it with blanks using the **STORE** command:

```
DECLARE aName[10,4]
STORE " " TO aName
```

Over time the elements become filled with data (names of people), and you decide that 10 entries (rows) isn't enough. You need a couple more columns and many more rows. Adding them is simple:

```
DIMENSION aName[100,6].
```

FoxPro will add the new elements (all 90 x 2 of them) without disturbing the data in the original 40 elements. However, now you can't initialize the array with the **STORE** command, because it would overwrite the first 10 rows of original data. You need a loop that starts at the 11th row and initializes the rest of the array:

```
FOR i = 11 TO 100              && outer loop for rows
  FOR j = 1 TO 6               && inner loop for columns
    aName[i, j] = SPACE(3)
  ENDFOR
ENDFOR
```

Next, suppose this array fills with no more than 60 names, and you decide to trim the size a bit to conserve memory:

```
DIMENSION aName[50,6]
```

This is a mistake. You will lose 10 array rows containing data. You need to exercise caution in reducing the number of elements in an array.

One final aspect of arrays is they can contain elements with any data type except General. An array such as the following is perfectly acceptable, even useful, because it packages a set of related information:

```
DECLARE aPerson[10,6]
STORE " " TO aPerson
aPerson[1,1] = "Johnson"             && last name
aPerson[1,2] = "Herbert"             && first name
aPerson[1,3] = "M."                  && midinit
aPerson[1,4] = {09/22/36}            && birthdate
aPerson[1,5] = DATE()- aPerson[1,4]  && age
aPerson[1,6] = "999-00-9999"         && social sec.
```

THE ARRAY TOOLKIT

Plain and simple arrays are useful as a quick and convenient way to store related data. They're also essential for working with List and ComboBox controls. For these and other purposes, FoxPro includes a number of functions that increase the usefulness of arrays. Many of these functions perform tasks that are similar to those of a data table, such as sorting and searching.

ALEN( )

In many situations, most frequently when a SQL query returns results to an array, you need to know how many rows were returned. There is a slightly different syntax depending on whether it is a one- or two-dimensional array.

Command syntax:

ALEN(ArrayName [, nArrayAttribute])

Arguments:

ArrayName The name of the array.

nArrayAttribute 1 returns the number of rows, 2 returns the number of columns.

Examples:

```
DECLARE aState[52,4]
? ALEN( aState )
```

Returns: 204

```
? ALEN( aState,1 )
```

Returns: 52

```
? ALEN( aState,2 )
```

Returns: 4

The **ALEN** function, which returns the "length" of an array, illustrates how FoxPro views an array as a continuous stack of elements. If you omit the **<expN>** qualifier, you will get the total number of elements. This function is frequently used to control a **FOR... ENDFOR** loop that massages the data in an array:

```
FOR i = 1 TO ALEN(aState,1)
  FOR j = 1 TO ALEN(aState,2)
     aState[i,j] = SPACE(12)
  ENDFOR
ENDFOR
```

AINS( ) AND ADEL( )

It's not uncommon, particularly for arrays bound to a ComboBox control, to add or delete elements (rows). FoxPro provides a function for each operation—**AINS( )** and **ADEL( )**—but they have some behavior that makes them somewhat difficult to use:

Command syntax:

AINS(ArrayName, nElementNumber [, 2])

Arguments:

ArrayName The name of the array.

nElementNumber [, 2] The location of the row to be inserted. With a 2, the column to be inserted.

Examples:

```
DECLARE aState[48,4]
=AINS( aState, 3)  && Inserts a row before row 3
```

Returns: 1, if successful.

```
=AINS( aState,2,2) && Inserts a column before column 2
```

Returns: 1, if successful.

It's important to remember that **AINS( )** does not make the array bigger. If you insert 10 elements into a 20-element array, the last 10 elements get pushed out of the array—that is, lost—and you lose all the data in them. When you want to expand the array, you need to first make room for the insertion, as in this example:

```
DECLARE aState[48,4]        && an array of states
DIMENSION aState[51,4]      && redimension by 3 rows
=AINS( aState, 1)           && insert rows for 3 states
=AINS( aState, 1)
=AINS( aState, 1)
aState[3,1] = "AK"          && load new rows
aState[3,2] = "Alaska"
aState[3,3] = "Juneau"
aState[3,4] = "Western"
```

Command syntax:

ADEL(ArrayName, nElementNumber [, 2])

Arguments:

ArrayName The name of the array for deletion of elements.

nElementNumber [, 2] The location of the row to delete. With a 2, the location of the column to delete.

Examples:

```
DECLARE aState[51,4]
=ADEL[ aState, 3]                && Deletes row 2
=ADEL[ aState, 3, 2]             && Deletes column 2
```

Returns: `1`, if successful.

As the reverse of **AINS( )**, the **ADEL( )** function deletes array elements. The principles are similar. Deleting elements, rows, or columns does not change the size of the array. It simply fills the gap by causing the array elements to be moved up from the bottom of the array into the space (element, row, or column) being deleted. In a one-dimensional array, the **<expN>** indicates the element to be deleted. In a two-dimensional array, it indicates the row. And if you want to delete a column, add the **2** option.

AELEMENT( ) AND ASUBSCRIPT( )

One of the realities of arrays is that even though you can visualize them as two-dimensional, internally FoxPro treats them as one-dimensional. An array declared as [5,4] doesn't really have five rows and four columns. It has 20 elements, numbered 1–20. That's why several functions require that you provide the element number of the array to work on, and they won't accept dual subscripts. This is no problem with one-dimensional arrays, because there is only one reference number. But with two-dimensional arrays, it isn't as easy. So FoxPro provides you with a couple of functions to make conversions: **AELEMENT( )** and **ASUBSCRIPT( )**.

Command syntax:

AELEMENT(ArrayName, nRowSubscript [, nColumnSubscript])

Arguments:

ArrayName The name of the array to use.

nRowSubscript The row subscript.

nColumnSubscript The column subscript.

Example:

```
DECLARE aState[51,2]
= AELEMENT( aState, 10, 1)
```

Returns: 19

Command syntax:

ASUBSCRIPT(ArrayName, nElementNumber, nSubscript)

Arguments:

ArrayName The name of the array to use.

nElementNumber The element number.

nSubScript Use 1 to return a row subscript, 2 to return a column subscript.

Examples:

```
DECLARE aState[51,2]
= ASUBSCRIPT( aState, 19, 1)      && row subscript
```

Returns: 10

```
= ASUBSCRIPT( aState, 19, 2)      && column subscript
```

Returns: 1

This bookend pair of functions tells you the element number from a given subscript (**AELEMENT( )**) or the subscripts from a given array element (**ASUBSCRIPT**). Only their two-dimensional syntax is useful.

ASCAN( )

Similar to the **LOCATE** command, **ASCAN( )** performs a sequential search for a match to the **<expr>** you've specified. If the search is successful, it will return the number of the element found; otherwise, it returns 0. The returned element can be used to directly reference an array, because FoxPro accepts both an element and subscripts:

```
aState[20,1] = aState[19] = aState[ASCAN(aState,"IL")]
```

Command syntax:

ASCAN(ArrayName, eExpression [, nStartElement [, nElementsSearched]])

Arguments:

ArrayName The name of the array to scan. Can be a literal ("astate") or a variable expression.

eExpression The expression of any data type to be located in the array.

nStartElement The starting array element to begin searching. The default is element 1.

nElementsSearched The number of elements to search. The default is all elements.

Examples:

```
DECLARE aState[51,2]
=ASCAN( aState, "AK")
```

Returns: 3

```
=ASCAN( aState, "IL", AELEMENT(aState,10,1))
```

Returns: 19

It's important to keep in mind that **ASCAN( )** by default searches *all* the elements. It knows nothing about rows and columns. Even if what you're looking for must be in the second column (the "state name" column, for example), there's no way to make **ASCAN** search only that column. Two-dimensional arrays can mimic data tables, but you don't have the same depth of tools for working with arrays.

ASORT( )

Arrays are usually sorted in preparation for display of the data in one of the List controls or ComboBoxes. The syntax is similar to that of the other array functions.

Command syntax:

ASORT(ArrayName [, nStartElement [, nNumberSorted [, nSortOrder]]])

Arguments:

ArrayName The name of the array to sort.

nStartElement The element or row to begin sorting.

nNumberSorted The number of elements or rows to sort.

nSortOrder The sort order; 0 = Ascending, and 1 = Descending.

Examples:

```
DECLARE aState[51,2]
= ASORT( aState )
```

Returns: `1` if successful; otherwise, `-1`.

```
= ASORT( aState, AELEMENT(aState,10,1),30)
= ASORT( aState, 1, -1, 1)  && Sort array descending order
```

Arrays are flexible, and they're more memory-efficient than regular variables, so why not use them for everything? There are good reasons to limit your use of arrays, but they don't become obvious until you've overworked an array in some way. For one thing, data in arrays is relatively anonymous. You might be clear what is being stored in an array at the time you create it, but six months later when you look at code such as `aStatus[60,4]`, will you know what's in it without constantly studying the documentation (presuming there is documentation)? Code filled with hundreds of anonymous array elements makes readability almost impossible. Also, as you may have noticed with the array functions, manipulating two-dimensional arrays can be difficult. Arrays are great tools, but don't try to substitute them for regular memory variables.

CHAPTER WRAP-UP

If you have done some programming before, most of the material in this chapter probably was familiar. However, if you weren't familiar with Visual FoxPro, you may have noticed some variations (or deviations), particularly the macro substitution capability. Whether you're experienced or not, it's highly recommended that you practice with all the elements introduced in this chapter. Using the Command window and a simple program file, you can experiment with the variations in syntax and start the process of learning when and how to apply control structures, variables, variable substitution, and arrays.

These elements are such fundamental building blocks for programming (not just for FoxPro) that you need to make their use automatic. Later, when we start to work with object-oriented programming in detail, you'll need to use all of these elements within the class definitions and methods.

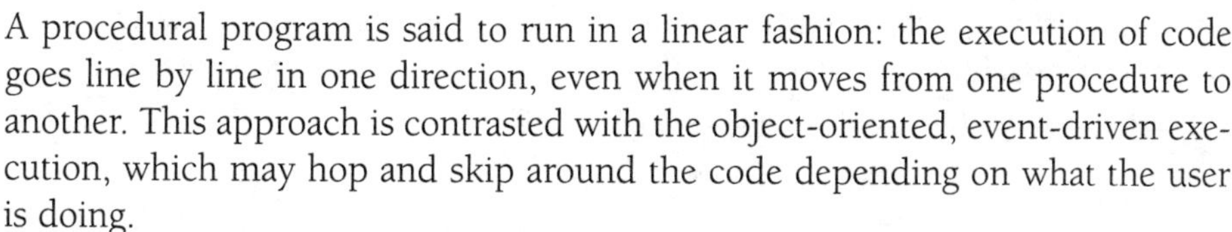

CHAPTER 10

PROCEDURAL PROGRAMMING

A procedural program is said to run in a linear fashion: the execution of code goes line by line in one direction, even when it moves from one procedure to another. This approach is contrasted with the object-oriented, event-driven execution, which may hop and skip around the code depending on what the user is doing.

Chapter 9 introduced most of the fundamental building blocks necessary for procedural programming. This chapter explains how those building blocks and FoxPro's database management command language are integrated into your own procedures, functions, and methods. Some new FoxPro commands and functions will also be introduced to round out the necessary toolkit. We're heading toward an important use for procedural programming: FoxPro's database management with field and record validation, triggers, and stored procedures.

In the olden days (about two years ago) when FoxPro programmers began to make the transition to object-oriented programming, I used to emphasize procedural programming as a kind of isolated facet of programming in FoxPro. No more. Procedural programming doesn't go away, but instead becomes tightly woven into the structure provided by objects and classes. This is another way of saying that you'll be writing all kinds of procedural style code side-by-side with purely object-oriented code. You might as well get used to it.

Program Files and Procedures

For the most part, procedural programming in Visual FoxPro flows from database management. For some applications, there is also a need for procedural code to execute traditional kinds of calculations, text manipulation, and similar algorithms. Not long ago, FoxPro applications were built by writing code in program (PRG) files and stringing them together with menus and screens. All that changed with object-oriented programming, and today some developers will tell you that you don't need standard program files at all. Others will say that you don't need them often but you should know what they are and how to use them.

You could do without program files entirely, but there are at least four places where a program file approach is either required or makes sense from a packaging point of view: the startup file for an application (MAIN.PRG), procedure files, pure data processing procedures, and stored procedures for FoxPro databases. So it's worthwhile to know about program files and to understand fundamental approaches to structuring not only program files but also other kind of FoxPro code, including the object-oriented kind.

Program Files

Do you remember the application framework? It's been a long time since we visited the *raison d'être* for this book, mostly because the chapters have been dealing with low-level building blocks and not the larger components that go into a framework. Now we come back to the framework and begin the process of describing what it is and what goes into it.

You may want to look at the illustration that begins Section 3, where you'll see that along with data elements there's a representation for standard files in the application framework. These files are mostly program files and may include the application startup file, one or more procedure files, and header files (sometimes called include files), which have an H extension. Each of these file types will be explained in various chapters. The emphasis here is on the generic program file or, more precisely, the structure of a generic procedure.

You were introduced to program files in Chapter 9. They're nothing more than text files with a PRG extension in which you write lines of commands and commentary. Of course, there's more to a program file than just stuffing it with code. The structure common to program files also appears in procedures, functions, and object methods. The typical structure is illustrated in Figure 10.1.

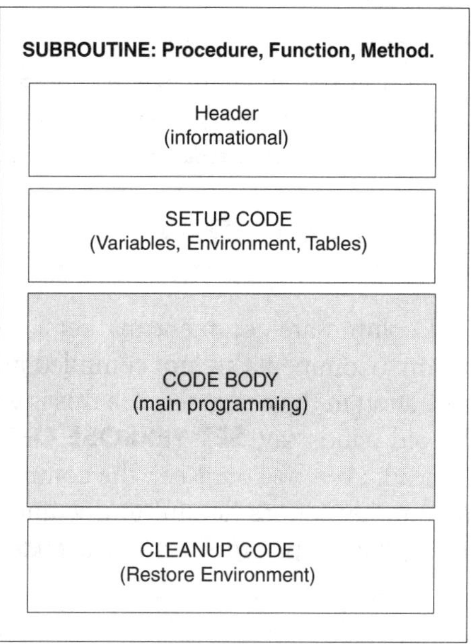

FIGURE 10.1 PROCEDURE STRUCTURE.

There are no tricks or complications here. Identify what the procedure is about. Set up the working environment. Do whatever the procedure is supposed to do. Clean up the environment before leaving. The important part of this simple format is that it be used systematically—every procedure uses the same format. That makes it possible to quickly scan a procedure, because you know where everything is. It also reinforces the idea that each procedure is responsible for its own environment: Whatever it changes on the way in should be restored on the way out.

HEADER

Just like the header in a report, a procedure's header usually conveys basic information about the procedure: the file's name (if there is a file), what the procedure does, who made it and when, and possibly a log of changes. The following format is merely a suggestion, but it keeps things simple and reasonably clear.

```
*******************************************************

* PROCEDURE..... DUPECHEK

* DESCRIPTION... CHECKS FOR DUPLICATES IN CHARACTER FIELDS

* CREATED....... 12/12/96
```

```
* PROGRAMMER.... NK
* Notes: A generic program to search any data table for
* duplicate values in a character field (where duplicates
* are not allowed but you don't want primary or candidate
* indexes). Table and field names are passed as parameters.
* Revision History:
* 3/31/97  Corrected SCAN loop problem. NK
**********************************************************
```

The asterisks in the left column are comment markers. FoxPro will ignore the lines that begin with them. (Comments are not compiled into a program.) Never be stingy with documentation in the code, because this is where it does the most good. However, as the old hands say, **SET VERBOSE OFF**. Wordy documentation probably won't be read, even by you. Keep the commentary terse, accurate, and relevant. In a program header, it's helpful to document the purpose of the procedure and any tricks, quirks, or problems in the code.

Setup Code

Most procedures reserve a section at the beginning to set up the working environment. This chore may include declaring variables and arrays, recording FoxPro **SET** values, opening tables, and setting relations. There's no standard way to do a setup, but a typical approach looks something like this:

```
LPARAMETER tcTableName, tcFieldName
*---------------[ SETUP
* Initialize local variables
LOCAL lcOldValue, lcDeleted, lcExact, lcOldAlias
lcOldValue = ""          && assuming a character field

* Save Environment
lcDeleted  = SET("DELETED")
SET DELETED OFF          && important for this routine
lcExact    = SET("EXACT")
SET EXACT OFF
lcOldAlias = ALIAS()

* Open table to be checked
* (Name substitution with parameter table name)
USE (tcTableName) ALIAS work IN 0
```

```
SELECT work
* Make a table based on the original to hold duplicates
COPY TO dupes STRUCTURE
* Open table to hold duplicates
USE dupes IN 0
* Reset work table
SELECT work
GO TOP
```

This example is minimal, but the purpose is the same—to prepare the programming environment for the main body of code. What helps most is to be consistent with the placement of setup elements so that you become accustomed to seeing them in the same place.

CODE BODY

There is no such thing as a typical code body, of course. It could be a data processing loop (such as this example), a math algorithm, or almost anything else.

```
*——————————[ SCAN LOOP TO FIND DUPES
SCAN
  *Compare current field value with stored value.
  IF lcOldValue = &tcFieldName
    * If values match, process a duplicate
    * Store current record to m. variables
    SCATTER MEMVAR
    * Put the record with duplicate into dupe table
    INSERT INTO dupes FROM MEMVAR
    * Mark current record for removal
    DELETE
  ENDIF
  * Store current field value
  lcOldValue = &tcFieldName
  SELECT work
ENDSCAN // end of dupe check loop
```

There are many ways to do this duplicate checking routine. This particular approach shows off FoxPro's variable substitution techniques and the use of temporary tables to hold data. It also makes use of what was an important command, **SCATTER MEMVAR**, before the days of buffered tables (more on this later). The command creates "m." variables of the same name as the fields, and that makes it easy to create a record in the temporary table using the **INSERT INTO** command.

Cleanup Code

The cleanup section does all the housekeeping necessary before leaving the procedure: closing tables, releasing variables, and resetting environmental values.

```
*————————————[ Cleanup
* Close tables
SELECT dupes
USE
SELECT work
USE
* Restore previous table, if any.
IF NOT EMPTY(lcOldAlias)
  SELECT (lcOldAlias)
ENDIF

* Reset environment
SET EXACT(cExact)
SET DELETED(cTalk)
```

The presence of specific sections for setup and cleanup code is all about the responsibility of any application component (program file, form, report, or object) to maintain its own integrity while not affecting the integrity of other components.

User-Defined Functions, Methods, and Procedures

Before you get too far into learning the difference between functions, methods, and procedures, you should know that to the FoxPro compiler they're all handled in the same way, with one exception: Functions may return a value. Most of your programming will be done in methods that are associated with objects and classes. Of these, event methods are provided by FoxPro, as you define the rest. Methods can be defined as either procedures or functions.

NOTE

Over the years, this aspect of FoxPro nomenclature has driven programmers nuts. We've seen procedures emphasized, then user-defined functions (UDF), then snippets, and now methods. All along, however, it didn't really matter which term was used. These terms were merely names for containing a discrete unit of code, and the only difference among them was whether or not they returned a value. As a kind of proof of this, you'll never see the keywords **FUNCTION** or **PROCEDURE** in a FoxPro designer. However, there are times when you will specifically want to create procedures and functions, and for that you need to know the difference between them.

- Procedures begin with the keyword **PROCEDURE** followed by a name having as many as 254 characters.
- Functions begin with the keyword **FUNCTION** and then a name (maximum 254 characters).
- Both procedures and functions take a **PARAMETER** or **LPARAMETER** statement to receive values from the calling program.
- The function usually has a **RETURN <value>** at the end. A procedure may have a **RETURN,** but it's not required.

Here's what they look like:

Procedure:

```
* Call a procedure
DO CountIt WITH "CA",1000

*Sample Procedure
PROCEDURE CountIt
LPARAMETER tcState, tnCount
LOCAL lnStateCount, lcStateTable

SELECT customer
COUNT FOR customer.state = tcState TO lnStateCount
IF lnStateCount > tnCount
  lcStateTable = tcState+"CUSTOMER"
  COPY TO (lcStateTable) FOR state = tcState
ENDIF
```

Function:

```
* Call a function
=CountIt( "CA", 1000 )

*Sample User-Defined Function
FUNCTION CountIt
LPARAMETER tcState, tnCount
LOCAL lnStateCount, lnTopCustomer, lnNationalRatio
SELECT customer
COUNT FOR customer.state = tcState     TO lnStateCount
COUNT FOR customer.ytdpurch > tcCount TO lnTopCustomer

RETURN lnNationalRatio = lnStateCount/lnTopCustomer
```

These examples illustrate a common practical distinction between procedures and functions: Procedures do some kind of processing, often with tables, but don't need to communicate about what was done. Functions are used whenever explicit information is needed as a result of what the function does, typically either a returned value (as in the preceding calculation) or a .T. or .F. to signal whether or not the function worked.

Building Functions

Functions can be used everywhere—in simple program files, in forms, in class definitions, in event methods. In a typical application you may create dozens of functions. Just like the built-in FoxPro functions, user-defined functions operate with a *function call*:

[=] <function name>(<argument list>)

Just as in the C programming language (the mother of function-based programming), the FoxPro function call has *arguments*, and the function structure itself has *parameters*. FoxPro allows as many as 27 arguments and parameters in a function, although you'd be foolhardy to create one that complex.

The structure of a function is the same as that of any other procedure, complete with a header, setup, body, and cleanup, to which it adds the return.

```
*********************************************************
* FUNCTION...... Markup()
```

```
* DESCRIPTION... CALCULATES A PERCENTAGE MARKUP
* CREATED....... 12/15/96
* PROGRAMMER.... NK
* Notes:
*******************************************************
FUNCTION MarkUp
LPARAMETERS tnCost, tnPrice
RETURN ((tnPrice - tnCost) / tnCost) * 100
```

Sometimes, almost all there is to a function is the return.

FUNCTION NAME AND PARAMETERS

The function header is immediately followed by two of the three official function clauses:

> **FUNCTION <function name>**
>
> **PARAMETER <parameter list>** or **LPARAMETER <parameter list>**

You are allowed as many as 256 characters for a function name, although you would have to be a manic typist to use that many. By convention, function names should be as mnemonic (memory-jogging) as possible and written in mixed case, Microsoft C programming style: `PriceCheck()`, `CalcCost()`, `FeeLook()`. This practice helps to distinguish user-defined functions from FoxPro's own functions, which are all uppercase by convention. Some programmers also like to data type their functions in the name (`nCalcCost()`, `cNameFind()`), using the same convention as for variables.

The two optional parameter statements create different variable types: **PARAMETER** creates private variables (available in the function and anything called by it), and **LPARAMETER** creates local variables (available only in the function). Unless you have an explicit reason for making the parameters available to other functions, it's best to standardize on **LPARAMETER**.

You may have already gathered that the **LPARAMETER <parameter list>** has a correspondence to the **<function name>([argument list])** of the function call. For the most part, this is a one-to-one linkage. Argument 1 is said to be *passed* to parameter 1:

```
=YourFunction( arg1, arg2, arg3, arg4 )
FUNCTION YourFunction
LPARAMETER parm1, parm2, parm3, parm4
```

Stop a moment, however, and ask yourself, What is being passed? That might lead to an even better question: Why do we use parameters?

It's another approach to scoping. One of the more positive reasons for functions and procedures is to isolate their operations and information (variables) from the rest of a program. This relative independence is what makes it possible for the same function to be used in a variety of different places. The theory is that a function shouldn't care about the environment of the function call; it should only accept the information it needs and then go about its business without affecting anything around it. You'll see exactly the same rationale used for objects.

Parameters are normally part of *encapsulation*. Instead of a function needing to know about variables that exist in the calling program, it gets a specific list of variables. All other variables that it needs are created for local use and disappear when the function returns. However, the encapsulation is relative. A function that requires data that is specific to a particular calling program is said to be *tightly bound*, and a more generic function is *loosely bound* or, in fact, not bound at all.

Another aspect of binding answers the question, What is being passed? Parameters of functions may be passed *by value* or *by reference*. The default is by value. If <argument 1> of the function call is a variable with assigned value of 2, the receiving <parameter 1> of the function will also be assigned the value of 2. For example:

```
nCount = 2
= CalcCount( nCount )
...
FUNCTION CalcCount
LPARAMETER tnCnt
? tnCnt
```

Returns: 2

No matter what happens to the parameter variable in the function, the value of the originating variable will remain the same.

When a parameter is passed by reference, something quite different happens. The receiving parameter gets the memory location (instead of the value) of the variable in the calling argument. The receiving parameter is a *reference* to the argument variable. This means that when any new value is assigned to the parameter variable, the value of the original variable is changed.

```
nCount = 1
SET UDFPARMS TO REFERENCE
= CalcCount( nCount )
SET UDFPARMS TO VALUE
? nCount
```

Returns: 3

```
...
FUNCTION CalcCount
LPARAMETER tnCount
tnCount = 3
RETURN
```

The **SET UDFPARMS TO REFERENCE | VALUE** in the preceding example is the command that switches the method of passing for function parameters. In practice, passing variables by reference is used selectively. Especially in object-oriented programming, a method that expects variables by reference depends on the calling (message-sending) object to actually create the variables.

In FoxPro, you need not have all the arguments for all the parameters. For example:

```
= MakeWindow("Continue Entering?", 8, "Y")
...
FUNCTION MakeWindow
LPARAMETER cTitle, nAtRow, cDefault, cWithColor
```

Here, there are three arguments and four parameters. The last one is not used but FoxPro won't complain. With Visual FoxPro, you can even omit parameters in the middle as long as you leave the commas in place, and it still won't complain. If you're careful with placement of the argument, this feature allows for future growth of a parameter list. Adding more arguments doesn't necessarily affect older function calls that have fewer arguments.

NOTE

Procedures, programs, and forms may also take parameters and use the same **PARAMETER** or **LPARAMETER** statements, but they can take parameters only by value and not by reference.

Function Setup

As usual, the function setup is the place where you define variables, set tables, and do other housekeeping before launching into the main part of the function. You may also need one piece of business that is special to *subroutines* (another name for functions, procedures, and methods) that take parameters. You may need to test to make sure which parameters have been given values or a reference. Here's an example:

```
*——————————————————[ SETUP
LPARAMETER tcTableName, tcFieldName, tlis_ok

*The first two parameters are required by the function
IF PCOUNT() < 3
  * Trapping for bad parameters
  DO CASE
  CASE EMPTY( tcTableName )        && must have a name
    RETURN .F.                      && if not, bug out
  CASE EMPTY( tcFieldName )
    RETURN .F.
  ENDCASE
ENDIF
```

In this typical example, the first order of business is often to decide whether the function should execute. If some needed precondition is missing, there's no point in going through the rest of the code. In the preceding example, a **RETURN** is used to abort the function. In some programming circles, this practice is considered *verboten*, and the rule is, Thou shall have one and only one **RETURN**. On the other hand, the use of **RETURN** to shortcut an improper call is clear, requires no additional code, and has no side effects.

NOTE

The function **PCOUNT( )** is used to determine how many parameters were actually passed. This function is reliable only when you're not using Visual FoxPro's ability to omit parameters by using a comma placeholder. If you're using this feature, you must test each parameter individually to make sure it is valid.

Return of the Function

Contrary to the practice in C, FoxPro does not require a **RETURN** either in a function or a procedure. However, if you want the function to return a value, which it usually does, then you must include the **RETURN** command followed by an expression that produces the value to be returned. Some programmers also think that always including a **RETURN** makes it clear where one function or procedure ends and another begins.

Because functions return values, they are often used to trigger something in the calling routine. This principle applies to your own functions and methods just as much as to the FoxPro functions. Frequently, if you're not returning some data value, the function should at least return a .T. or .F. (true or false) to indicate whether the function performed successfully. That gives the calling routine the option of dealing with a failed function.

COMMANDS AND FUNCTIONS FOR PROGRAMMING

FoxPro has a whole class of functions and commands that are used primarily for things related to the mechanics of programming: starting a program, stopping a program, compiling a program, and so on. Some of these you will use mostly in the Command window, and others are useful in general programming.

COMMANDS FOR PROGRAMMING

In FoxPro the vast majority of commands are related to data management. Another fairly large group have something to do with the user interface, although most of them have been made obsolete by the object-oriented approach. There are a few others that you will need at some point in your programming, whether it's procedural or object-oriented.

The first three of these commands—**SUSPEND**, **RESUME**, and **CANCEL**—are often used in the debugging process. They are also useful in limiting the run of a program to specific sections of code.

Command syntax:

SUSPEND

RESUME

CANCEL

Example:

```
* Test whether it's OK to continue
IF NOT FOUND("CUSTOMER")
  WAIT WINDOW NOWAIT "Customer not found."
  CANCEL
ELSE
  SUSPEND
ENDIF
```

SUSPEND stops the execution of a FoxPro program. All memory variable contents, data table pointers, and environment settings are completely unchanged, and you can use other tools, such as the **SET( )** function or **DISPLAY MEMORY**, to get a reading on the conditions. Exercise care that you don't change important values or table positions if you want to use **RESUME** to continue execution of the program (at the line of code where it stopped). When the FoxPro Debugger stops program execution at a breakpoint, you'll see that **SUSPEND** is echoed to the Command window, and you can use **RESUME** to start again.

CANCEL terminates program execution and releases all local and private memory variables. It's important to realize that it does not release many of the other elements of a FoxPro program, and that may or may not be a good thing. In quitting an application or its modules, it's more customary to use one or more of the following closing commands:

- **CLEAR** removes all text from the current window. It doesn't close windows.
- **CLOSE ALL** closes all open tables, databases, and project files.
- **CLEAR ALL** closes all tables and releases all variables, menus, and windows. In short, this is the one to use if you want to go back to scratch.

There are many more related commands, and it's worth your time to look them up in the on-line help. They are usually object-specific, such as **CLOSE WINDOWS**, and so are used only in specific situations.

SYS( ) Functions

The FoxPro **SYS( )** functions are an odd lot. They've grown up with the FoxPro language, and many of them have become obsolete. Others were thrown in to cover gaps in other functions or to provide an odd function here and there to complete the language. The useful ones get reincarnated into functions with more memorable names; **SYS(2003)**, for example, became **CURDIR( )**. Table 10.1 summarizes a few that are used with some frequency.

TABLE 10.1 FOXPRO SYS() FUNCTIONS

FUNCTION	DESCRIPTION
SYS(3)	Legal file name. Use `SUBSTR(SYS(2015), 3, 10)` to create a unique, legal, eight-character file name.
SYS(5)	Returns the name of the default disk drive.
SYS(2003)	Current directory or folder. Same as **CURDIR( )**.
SYS(2011)	Current lock status.
SYS(3050,nType [,nBuffMemSize])	Sets buffer memory size
SYS(3051[,nWait])	Sets lock retry interval for wait in milliseconds.
SYS(3052,nFileType [,lHonorReprocess])	Overrides SET REPROCESS locking.
SYS(16,nProgLevel)	Executing program file name.
SYS(2015)	Unique procedure name.

NOTE

Because of the numeric reference, **SYS( )** functions can be hard to remember. Fortunately, only a few of them are used regularly. All you need to remember is that a certain function exists, and then use the on-line help or *Language Reference* to come up with the name and appropriate syntax.

CONVERSION FUNCTIONS

In addition to the two data conversion functions already introduced—**VAL( )** and **STR( )**—other functions are useful for moving data from one format and data type to another, a common programming task. The most important of these functions is **TYPE( )**, which returns the data or object type from a given expression. This function is heavily used to test whether an object has been instantiated.

Command syntax:

TYPE(cExpression)

Argument:

cExpression The name of the item to be typed, as a character string.

Example:

=TYPE("nStart")

Returns: **N**, the data type as a letter.

```
oGenData.CREATEOBJECT("GENDATA")
IF TYPE("OGENDATA") <> "O"
  ...
ENDIF
```

TYPE( ) currently recognizes 10 types: C=character, N=numeric, Y=Currency, L=logical, D=date, T=DateTime, M=memo, O=Object, G=General, and U=undefined. The argument of this function is really a name expression that does a lookup in a FoxPro internal memory variable table to determine the type. A common use of **TYPE( )** is to check a parameter list of functions and procedures, as in this example fragment:

```
FUNCTION CheckPart
LPARAMETER tcPartId, tnOnHand, tdPurch

IF TYPE("TCPARTID") <> "C"
  WAIT "Invalid Part ID" WINDOW NOWAIT
  RETURN .F.
ENDIF
IF TYPE("TNONHAND") <> "N"
  WAIT "Invalid On Hand Count" WINDOW NOWAIT
  RETURN .F.
ENDIF
IF TYPE("TDPURCH") <> "D"
  WAIT "Invalid Purchase Date" WINDOW NOWAIT
  RETURN .F.
ENDIF
```

It's typical of conversion functions to come in pairs to convert one way and then back. You've already seen some of the more common ones: **DTOC( )**, and **CTOD( )**, **VAL( )** and **STR( )**; and **TTOC( )** and **TTOD( )**. Here are a few others:

CHR(nExpression)

Converts an ASCII number value (0–255) into its equivalent in the IBM PC character set. For example, this will put a check mark in a field: `REPLACE flag WITH CHR(251).`

ASC(cExpression)

Converts an ASCII character from the IBM PC character set to its ASCII number.

ISALPHA(cExpression)

Returns: a .T. if the first character of the **cExpression** is a character.

ISDIGIT(cExpression)

Returns a .T. if the first character of the **cExpression** is a number.

MTON(yExpression)

Converts a currency expression to a numeric expression.

NTON(yExpression)

Converts a numeric expression to a currency expression.

MIN(nExp1,nExp2,...)

Returns the minimum value from a list of values.

MAX(nExp1,nExp2,...)

Returns the maximum value from a list of values.

You should always be on the lookout for ways to extend the FoxPro functions to cover new territory. For example, the **ISALPHA( )** and **ISDIGIT( )** functions work only on the first character of a string expression. What if you want to test the entire expression? Write yourself a user-defined function such as this one:

```
*________________________________________
* FUNCTION.....AlphOrNum(<expC>)
* DESCRIPTION..DETERMINES IF A STRING IS ALPHA OR NUMERIC.
* CREATED......1/23/95
* PARAMETERS...cWord = Any valid character expression.
* NOTES: This checks every character. If all of them are
* numeric then false is returned. Otherwise this will be
* called an alpha, even if it contains some numbers, and
```

```
* will return true (.T.).
*________________________________
FUNCTION AlphOrNum
LPARAMETER tcWord
LOCAL i
* Loop to test each character
FOR i = 1 TO LEN(ALLTRIM(tcWord))
  * If one character is alpha the whole thing is.
  IF ISALPHA( SUBSTR(tcWord, i,1))
    RETURN .T.
  ENDIF
ENDFOR
RETURN .F.
*
```

DATABASE PROGRAMMING

Visual FoxPro gives you three ways to do database programming: the Command window, a PRG file, and the Database container (DBC) file. As you will see, each approach has its place. The Command window is great for quick and interactive data manipulation. A program file is always easy to trot out for extended processing. The capabilities of the Database Container—validation, triggers, and stored procedures—extend the control and flexibility over data in many important ways.

NOTE

By now you've probably realized that this chapter is amassing many details about programming: formats, functions, and commands. There's much more to come. I learned the hard way that much of programming has nothing to do with blazing fast commands and snazzy user interface designs. Much of it is bit-fiddling: conversions, maintenance, data checking, and many routines that require close attention to detail. The slightest error in this level of coding can create subtle but significant program errors. I'm also saying you gotta like this aspect of programming, or you'll find nothing but frustration.

MANIPULATING RECORDS AND FIELDS

Before exploring the new ability to program in the Visual FoxPro database file (and other kinds of database programming), let's look at a number of functions that are used in this type of work. Most of them are used to extract information about the database, tables, indexes, and other data-related elements.

MORE DATABASE FUNCTIONS

The many database, table, and index-oriented functions (some of which you've already seen) are specialists but are used fairly often in maintenance and other data routines. Typically, they give you information to check on something: Does a table exist? Is it open? How many indexes are there? Before executing a routine, you need to know whether the conditions are right.

ADATABASES(ArrayName)

Places the names of all open databases and their paths into the named array

AFIELDS(ArrayName [,nWorkArea|cTableAlias])

Places information about the structure of the current table into an array and returns the number of fields in the table

AUSED(ArrayName [,nDataSessionNumber])

Creates an array and loads it with the names (or aliases) of open tables.

CANDIDATE([nIndexNumber] [, nWorkArea | cTableAlias])

Returns true (.T.) if an index tag is a candidate index tag; otherwise, returns false (.F.)

CURDIR([cExpression])

Returns the current drive letter.

DISKSPACE()

Returns the number of bytes available on the default disk drive.

FCOUNT([nWorkArea | cTableAlias])

Returns the number of fields in a table.

FILTER([nWorkArea | cTableAlias])

Returns the table filter expression specified in **SET FILTER**.

HOME()

Returns the name of the directory that Visual FoxPro was started from.

ISEXCLUSIVE([cTableAlias | cDatabaseName])

Returns true (.T.) if a table or database is opened for exclusive use; otherwise, returns false (.F.).

ISREADONLY([nWorkArea | cTableAlias])

Determines whether a table is opened read-only.

LUPDATE([nWorkArea | cTableAlias])

Returns the date when the table was last updated.

Basic Character Functions

Because many of the fields in a table are of the character or memo type, it makes sense that there are a large number of functions to manipulate and test character data. (Keep in mind that functions work on variables and constants as well as on fields.) In the Command window and throughout your applications, you will often do various kinds of editing and programming tasks with character fields and variables.

NOTE

It's not glamorous, but I consider string manipulation one of the most important fundamentals of programming. That's based on the amount of time spent doing it and on how important it can be to most programming.

To illustrate how character data is manipulated, let's start with a representative character string as it might be found in a field:

```
"  My dog, Spots, has fleas    "
```

The leading and trailing blanks are intentional. For a variety of reasons, character strings in data fields and variables often have these spaces, and dealing with them is very much a part of data manipulation. As a matter of shorthand (so that it won't need to be written out every time) and because it's a common practice, we'll store the string to a memory variable:

```
cText = "  My dog, Spots, has fleas    "
```

Position in Character Strings

The most common task in manipulating character strings is to count *positions* in the string. Each letter occupies a number position counting from left to right. For example, here are the positions for the sample text:

```
"  My dog, Spots, has fleas    "
 12345678901234567890123456789
          10        20
```

The text begins at 1, a blank; the dog's name, Spots, begins at position 11 and ends at position 15; the string has a total length of 29 characters, and so forth. Position numbering is important, because many of the FoxPro functions that work with character strings use them. For example, to pluck a substring from a character string, the function might begin at position 3 and end at position 10.

You will seldom have the opportunity (or time) to lay out every text string for the kind of visual analysis just illustrated, and in programs you have no chance at all. So FoxPro provides a number of functions to help locate and position things within an expression. These functions in turn are used with other functions that change the character expression. We'll start with functions that do the position locating:

Command syntax:

AT(cSearchExpression,cExpressionSearched[,nOccurrence])

RAT(cSearchExpression,cExpressionSearched[,nOccurrence])

Arguments:

cSearchExpression The character expression to search for.

cExpressionSearched The character expression to be searched.

nOccurrence Specifies the occurrence of the search expression to return a position.

Examples:

```
? AT( ",", "  My dog, Spots, has fleas    ",2)
```

Returns: 16

```
? RAT(",", "  My dog, Spots, has fleas    ",2)
```

Returns: 9

In both the preceding examples, the function is supposed to return the position of the second comma in the search string. **AT( )** searches from left to right, counts from the left, and returns 16. **RAT( )** searches from right to left, also counts from the left, returning 9. Most of the time, people use **AT( )** because we are accustomed to counting from left to right. But sometimes, counting from the right is the shortest distance or makes the most sense. Then you would use **RAT( )**.

In the context of character expressions, **LEN( )** is used to get the end position of a character string.

Command syntax:

LEN(cExpression)

Arguments:

cExpression The character expression to be measured.

Example:

```
? LEN(cText)
```

Returns: `29`

MODIFYING CHARACTER STRINGS

The second group of functions is used to change the shape and content of a character string. This is the business end of string manipulation and also the trickiest. To make your routines work, you need to understand position calculation and gain insight into the mechanics of pulling and pushing characters within a string.

THE TRIMMING FAMILY OF FUNCTIONS

You may have noticed that the text sample contains spaces at the beginning and the end. These spaces are called *leading* and *trailing* blanks. In some cases they are harmless, but most of the time unwanted spaces cause problems. For example, if you wanted to add to the basic example text " — and ticks," you'd get " My dog, Spots, has fleas — and ticks." The extra spaces don't help the readability. To get rid of them, you can use **ALLTRIM( )** or one of the **TRIM( )** variations.

Command syntax:

ALLTRIM(cExpression)

Arguments:

cExpression Any character expression.

Example:

```
? ALLTRIM("  My dog, Spots, has fleas    ")
```

Returns: `"My dog, Spots, has fleas"`

As the name implies, this function trims leading and trailing blanks from a character string. One school of thought says to use **ALLTRIM()** all the time. It covers all the bases. Another school says that **ALLTRIM()** wastes processing time, and it's not clear what you want trimmed. Clarity of intention is one of the cardinal virtues of good programming.

Command syntax:

TRIM(cExpression) and **RTRIM(cExpression)**

Arguments:

cExpression Any character string.

Example:

```
? TRIM(" My dog, Spots, has fleas   ")
```

Returns: `" My dog, Spots, has fleas"`

Both functions do exactly the same thing: trim off trailing blanks. Why are there two of them? The answer, as usual, reflects the function's history. **TRIM()** was there from the beginning of Xbase, when there was no **ALLTRIM()**, **RTRIM()**, or **LTRIM()**. When left and right trim were added (following the tradition of the Basic language), **TRIM()** stuck around for reasons of continuity. Although using indicators such as left and right is clearer, **TRIM()** and the concept of trimming remain ingrained in Xbase manuals to this day.

Command syntax:

LTRIM(cExpression)

Arguments:

cExpression Any character string.

Example:

```
? LTRIM(" My dog, Spots, has fleas   ")
```

Returns: `"My dog, Spots, has fleas   "`

This function lops off leading spaces.

THE PADDING FAMILY OF FUNCTIONS

Let's say you want to make the sample text the title of a paper (it's crazy, but it happens). Now you need to put it into the title page, neatly centered. You could count the width of the page, usually 80 characters, count the characters in the string, subtract that from 80, divide that by two, and add that many spaces to the front and back of the text. Or you could use one of the padding functions, in this case **PADC()**.

The padding functions work on any character string by adding a character (any character) at the left, right, or both left and right. They are used most often to do things such as pad serial ID numbers (such as `"00000123"`) and amounts in checks (such as `SUM OF ********1.00`) .

Command syntax:

PADL(eExpression,nResultsize[,cPadCharacter)

PADC(eExpression,nResultsize[,cPadCharacter)

PADR(eExpression,nResultsize[,cPadCharacter)

Arguments:

eExpression The expression to be padded, which can be of any type except logical or General.

nResultsize The total number of characters, after padding.

cPadCharacter An option character to use for padding. Blanks are the default.

Example:

```
? PADC("  My dog, Spots, has fleas   ",10," ")
```

Returns: `"              My dog, Spots, has fleas                 "`

The first argument, **eExpression**, is anything you want padded. The second argument, **nResultsize**, is the total length of padding, and the third, optional argument is the character you want to use for padding. Spaces are used by default, but for clarity it doesn't hurt to show the character.

The **REPLICATE( )** function takes any character or text, **cExpression**, and repeats it **nTimes** (number of times). It's best used in long character fields where you want to add something to a replacement string but don't want to type 100 asterisks or whatever. For example:

```
REPLACE ALL TITLE WITH "Not available "+REPLICATE("*",50);
      FOR STATUS = "Inactive"
```

Command syntax:

REPLICATE(cExpression, nTimes)

Arguments:

cExpression Any character expression.

nTimes The number of times to replicate the character expression.

Example:

```
? REPLICATE( cText, 2)
```

Returns: `"  My dog, Spots,has fleas My dog, Spots,has fleas  "`

In a similar vein, the **TRANSFORM( )** function is used to convert numbers (either as numeric or character data) into nicely formatted character strings.

Command syntax:

TRANSFORM(eExpression, cFormatCodes)

Arguments:

eExpression Any numeric or character expression.

cFormatCodes The picture template to be used. Same as for report expressions.

Examples:

```
=TRANSFORM( 2343235, "$###,###,###")
```

Returns: `$2,343,235`

```
=TRANSFORM( "Modem256   ","@R !!!!!###")
```

Returns: `MODEM256`

The important part of this function's work is that it automatically takes the significant digits, characters, or date elements from the target item and maps them from left to right into the symbols in the template (mask). For example, a variable containing the number 2334 will map into a template such as `"(#,###)"` as 2,334. In forming the picture template, you have at your disposal most of the **PICTURE** functions (**@B,@R**) that you encountered with the Report Designer.

THE CASE FAMILY OF FUNCTIONS

Whether text is uppercase (capitalized), lowercase, or mixed case can make a difference in a number of computer operations, particularly searches. The issue of *case sensitivity* is too broad to cover in detail here, but suffice it to say that from time to time you will need to adjust data in tables to particular case requirements. FoxPro gives you five functions to do the job, and three are detailed here. The other two—**ISUPPER(cExpression)** and **ISLOWER(cExpression)**—are used to test whether the first character of **cExpression** is in uppercase or lowercase.

Command syntax:

UPPER(cExpression) or **LOWER(cExpression)**

Arguments:

cExpression- Any character expression.

Examples:

```
? UPPER(cText)
```

Returns: `"  MY DOG, SPOTS, HAS FLEAS    "`

```
? LOWER(cText)
```

Returns: `"  my dog, Spots, has fleas    "`

Converting from uppercase to lowercase (and the reverse) is common for all kinds of data manipulation. **PROPER( )**, on the other hand, is associated mostly with names.

Command syntax:

PROPER(cExpression)

Arguments:

cExpression Any character expression.

Examples:

```
? PROPER(cText)
```

Returns: `"  My Dog, Spots, Has Fleas    "`

Because **PROPER()** converts the first letter of every word in a character string to a capital, it is frequently used to change an all-lowercase name field to a mixed-case field.

Unfortunately, its operational rule doesn't know what to do with names such as "mcdonald" (McDonald), so people have created their own functions for capitalizing names.

Command syntax:

SPACE(nExpression)

Arguments:

nExpression Any numerical expression as the number of spaces to return.

Examples:

```
? cText + SPACE(10)
```

Returns: `"  My dog, Spots, has fleas            "`

The **SPACE()** function has many uses. In most cases, as just shown, it's used as a specialized **REPLICATE()** function to add blanks to character strings. It's used more often in programming as a shorthand for *initializing* (storing the first value of) character variables, because `cFirstName = SPACE(24)` is both more precise and clear than

```
cFirstName = "                        ".
```

The *substring* function, as **SUBSTR()** is called, is probably the most heavily used function for character strings, and possibly the most used of any function for general table maintenance. Its ability to pluck a string from another string is used in data conversion, field-to-field transfer, and many other instances of character manipulation. You'll find that a large part of data maintenance involves rearranging text fields, and **SUBSTR()** will be one of your principal tools.

Command syntax:

SUBSTR(cExpression, nStartPosition[,nCharactersReturned])

Arguments:

cExpression The character expression from which to extract a substring.

nStartPosition The starting position of the substring to be extracted.

nCharactersReturned The number of characters to be extracted.

Example:

```
? SUBSTR("  My dog, Spots, has fleas   ",11,5)
```

Returns: `"Spots"`

The first argument, **cExpression**, is any character string, and it is often a variable or even a complex expression that produces a character string. The arguments **nStartPosition** and **nCharactersReturned** are the boundaries of the string to be extracted, as if the instructions were as follows: Starting at character position # from the first character on the left, take # characters to the right.

The trick to using **SUBSTR()** is to master the art of determining the **nStartPosition** and **nCharactersReturned** positions. In the preceding example, the character position of "Spots" is known: It starts on the 11th character from the left and ends five characters to the right. But what if you don't know the precise position and length of a substring? That's when you call on the services of other functions, such as **AT( )**, **RAT( )**, and **LEN( )**, to help determine various character positions. Here are some typical examples:

```
REPLACE dogname WITH SUBSTR(cText, AT("Spots",cText),5)
```

In this case, the substring is known but not its position, so that is provided by the **AT( )** function. What if you know the position but not the substring? This case is a bit more challenging:

```
REPLACE dogname WITH SUBSTR(cText,11,AT(",",cText,2)- 11)
```

By adding the third argument to the **AT( )** function (the second occurrence), it determines the position of the second comma in the string, which is at the end of the name. The fact that two commas exist as brackets to the name must be known. Subtracting the position of the first character in the substring (already known) will get the length of the substring for the **SUBSTR()** function.

As you can see, manipulating character strings can be painstaking work. That's why even experienced programmers often use the Command window to prototype and test such expressions.

The next two functions—**STRTRAN( )** and **STUFF( )**—are complex and high-powered string manipulators.

Command syntax:

STRTRAN(cSearched,cSearchFor[,cReplacement][,nStartOccurrence] [,nNumberOfOccurrences])

Arguments:

cSearched The string to be searched.

cSearchFor The substring to search for.

cReplacement The string to replace the search substring.

nStartOccurrence The first occurrence to search for (optional, by default the first one).

nNumberOfOccurrences The number of occurrences to replace (also optional).

Example:

```
? STRTRAN("  My dog, Spots, has fleas   ", "Spots", "Fluffy", 1, 1)
```

Returns: `"  My dog, Fluffy, has fleas   "`

Usually pronounced "stringtran," this function replaces one substring in text with another substring. Among its uses are to change or fix substrings in fields. For example, say you have a field called COMPANY, which in several hundred records has the company name `"MyDogs Inc."` Then the company changes its name to `"MyPuppy, Inc."`. One way to change it would be to use the following command in the Command window:

```
REPLACE ALL COMPANY WITH ;
  STRTRAN(COMPANY,"MyDogs","MyPuppy,");
  FOR "MyDogs" $ COMPANY
```

Command syntax:

STUFF(cExpression, nStartReplacement, nCharactersReplaced, cReplacement)

Arguments:

cExpression The character expression to be stuffed (the stuffee).

nStartReplacement The starting position of the substring to be stuffed.

nCharactersReplaced The ending position of the substring to be stuffed.

cReplacement The character expression to stuff (the stuffer).

Example:

```
? STUFF("  My dog, Spots, has fleas   ",1,2,"Gosh! ")
```

Returns: `"Gosh! My dog, Spots, has fleas   "`

In many ways, **STUFF( )** is more difficult to use than **STRTRAN( )**, but it is also more precise. With **STUFF( )**, you need to know, or test for, the exact position and exact length of the substring you plan to replace. This is not always easy, and you may need to use complex expressions using **AT( )** to get the information.

The name *stuff* is a good clue as to what this function does. By adjusting the **nCharactersReplaced** argument, you can change the number of characters to be replaced. A zero (0) will not remove any characters and will "stuff " the new string into place. The **cReplacement** argument can also be set to a null string (""), and then the number of characters indicated by **nCharactersReplaced** will be removed from the current string. Both options are useful, as in the following examples:

```
cText = STUFF( cText, 1, 2, "")
```

Returns: `"My dog, Spots, has fleas    "`

```
cText = STUFF( cText, LEN(TRIM(cText)), 0, ".")
```

Returns: `"  My dog, Spots, has fleas.   "`

Character position manipulation is not a black art, but it does take practice.

Logical Searching in Strings

The functions in this group are similar to the **AT( )** and **RAT( )** family, because they search for a character expression in other character expressions. However, instead of returning a position number, they return either true or false (.T. or .F.)

Command syntax:

cSearchFor $ cSearchIn

Arguments:

cSearchFor The string to search for.

cSearchIn The string to be searched.

Example:

```
"Spots" $ "  My dog, Spots, has fleas   "
```

Returns: `.T.`

As odd as the dollar sign may seem, the substring operator is one of the most frequently used for character work. It tests whether the first string can be found in the second string or, put another way, whether the first expression is *contained in* the second expression. The test is case-sensitive, so you must be careful that you're not comparing uppercase apples with lowercase oranges, so to speak. Here's a simple example of its day-to-day use that takes into account a possible difference in case:

```
COUNT ALL FOR "DOG" $ UPPER(title)
```

This gets a count of all the records where DOG (note the capitals) is contained in a field called TITLE. Note the use of the **UPPER( )** function to be sure that the search string and the search field have the same case.

The substring operator **$** lends itself to logical expression conditions such as those of the **FOR** and **WHILE** clauses, but be warned: A **$** expression is not optimizable by the Rushmore technology. Whenever you use this operator, you'll get a sequential search from one end of the table to the other.

INLIST( ) is a general-use function, because it can work with any kind of expression. Most commonly, however, it's used for character strings.

Command syntax:

INLIST(eExpression1, eExpression2 [, eExpression3 ...])

Arguments:

eExpression1 The expression (any data type) to search for.

eExpression2[,eExpression3...] A list of expressions (separated by commas) to search in. All expressions must be of the same data type as **eExpression1**.

Example:

```
? INLIST("dog", "Spots", "fleas", "my", "dog")
```

Returns: .T.

When working in data tables that have fields with a single character or character string (a character, word, or phrase), you can use **INLIST( )** to test whether the string is in a specific list. For example, in a field that's supposed to contain nothing but certain codes, you could run these commands:

```
COUNT ALL FOR NOT INLIST(codefield,"A","C","E","F","Z")
LIST ALL FIELDS RECNO(), lastname, codefield ;
  FOR NOT INLIST(codefield, "A","C","E","F","Z") TO PRINT
```

The first command line gets you a count of how many codes in the CODEFIELD are not legitimate. If there aren't too many, the second command line is used to print the offending records with the record numbers and the last name. In large tables, it's usually a good idea to know the size of your problem before you print a list—unless you don't mind spitting out a ream of paper.

Command syntax:

LIKE(cExpression1, cExpression2)

Arguments:

cExpression1 The character expression to be matched, including wildcard symbols.

cExpression2 The character expression to test.

Example:

```
? LIKE( "dog", cText )
```

Returns: `.F.`

This functions returns a true (.T.) only if all the characters in the first expression exactly match all the characters in the second expression. If this were all it could do, **LIKE( )** would be very limited in use, because exact matches can be tested in other ways. The kicker is that in the first expression you can use *wildcard* symbols, such as those used in DOS file wildcards: ***** matches anything, and **?** matches any single character.

If you're familiar with DOS file searches, then you'll understand how **LIKE( )** can be used to determine whether a certain word or phrase fragment exists in another character string. This technique will almost always be used with an operational command, something like this:

```
COUNT ALL FOR LIKE( "Spot*", name )
BROWSE FOR LIKE( "flea?" , insecttype )
```

The first command will get a count of all names (records) in which "Spot" is the first four letters. Matches might include such names as "Spotlein" and "Spotrunner" but not "Polkaspot." The second command will display in a browse window only those records in which the insect type begins with "flea" and any single letter after that. Matches would include "fleas" but not "flease."

PUTTING CHARACTER MANIPULATION TO WORK

At this point, we've looked at enough character related functions to do some work. First, let's fix the sample text, "   My dog, Spots, has fleas   ".

```
cText = ALLTRIM("   My dog, Spots, has fleas    ")
```

Returns: "My dog, Spots, has fleas"

```
cText = cText + "."
```

Returns: "My dog, Spots, has fleas."

```
cText = STRTRAN( cText, "fleas", "a beautiful tail" )
```

Returns: "My dog, Spots, has a beautiful tail."

In fact, let's fix it all in one command:

```
? STRTRAN(ALLTRIM("   My dog, Spots, has fleas   ")+;
  ".","fleas","a beautiful tail")
```

Returns: "My dog, Spots, has a beautiful tail."

Here's a more realistic example: In the process of building a customer database, a number of temporary data entry people were hired to input names, addresses, and phone numbers of customers, working from old sales slips. Unfortunately, they were not schooled on some of the finer points of data entry, and there was no standardization on the correct way to enter "Mr. and Mrs.". Consequently, the NAME field of the CUSTOMER table now contains numerous variations:

```
Mr. and Mrs. Johnson
Mr and Mrs Works
Mr. John J. and Dora Whitely
MR., MRS. HARRY CLAUSS
Mr. & Mrs. Brotelli
Mr. Bruce T. and Mrs. Martha Timmer
MR./MRS. FINLAYSON
```

Worse, extra spaces have been inserted into some of the character strings. All this might have been relatively harmless, but the owner of the company has decided that a uniform salutation is mandatory because she wants to target husband and wife customers. She also wants to make sure that the first names are kept separately for husband and wife so that gender-targeted mailings can be made.

The resident data management guru, who happens to be one of the data entry people, decides to use the powers of FoxPro like this:

```
USE customer ALIAS cus ORDER firstname EXCLUSIVE
MODIFY STRUCTURE
```

Add the fields:

```
SALUTATION C 10
HUSBAND C 12
WIFE C 12
```

Make a count of the problems:

```
COUNT ALL FOR "MR" $ UPPER(name) AND ;
("AND"$UPPER(name)OR"&" $ name OR "/"$ name OR "," $ name)
```

If you check the examples, this formulation will catch all husband and wife listings without including miscellaneous entries. The **COUNT** also tests a **FOR** condition that will be similar to one used for making the changes:

```
REPLACE ALL SALUTATION WITH "Mr. and Mrs." ;
 FOR "MR" $ UPPER(name) AND ;
("AND"$UPPER(name)OR "&" $ name OR "/" $ name OR "," $ name)
```

This takes care of loading the salutation field. But now it's necessary to get rid of the various Mr. and Mrs. combinations and parse out the first names, if any. Now things get tricky. First are the scans for Mr. and Mrs. with first names:

```
REPLACE ALL HUSBAND WITH ;
 SUBSTR(name,AT("MR",UPPER(name))+2 ,;
   AT( "AND", UPPER(name)) -2) ;
   FOR "MR" $ UPPER(name) AND ("AND" $ UPPER(name));
   AND LEN( SUBSTR( name, AT("MR",UPPER(name))+2 , ;
   AT( "AND", UPPER(name)) -2)) > 2
```

This is where prototyping in the Command window becomes invaluable. The character string logic is tricky (and picky). The first **SUBSTR( )** function will extract any name lying between the period of MR. and the space before an AND. The **LEN( )** function is used to screen out instances of a MR not followed by a name. (Two spaces between the MR and the AND might contain an initial, but that's not likely.) This example is only for the "AND" case. A similar construction is used for the "&", "/", and "," cases in turn.

Now to do the Mrs. part. Guess what—you can't do the Mrs. part. There is nothing between the MRS and a last name on which to anchor a function. FoxPro can't tell the difference between a last name and a first name. You might try to use the spaces. There are two of them where a Mrs and a first name exists, but there could be many exceptions. Sometimes it's better to eyeball the table and make corrections based on the insight of the human brain. In that case, you should leave the original field untouched until the visual proofing has been completed.

In any case except eyeballing, the entry of `Mr. John J. and Dora Whitely` will fall through the cracks, along with names in which the `Mr.` `and` are separated by more than two spaces but contain no names. This real-world example has a few terse lessons:

- Lesson 1: Design the table right in the first place. If there had been SALUTATION, HUSBAND, WIFE, and LASTNAME fields, most of this problem would have been eliminated.
- Lesson 2: Some things are impossible for FoxPro. It's not an artificial intelligence program.
- Lesson 3: As a corollary to lesson 2, some complex character manipulation may be possible, but, compared with the efficiency of human vision, it's not very practical. The bigger the table, the less practical it is to check the data visually.

DATA INTEGRITY PROGRAMMING

Almost everything you've learned so far can be brought into focus with data integrity programming. Maintaining *data integrity* (the validity of the data) is one of the most important elements of a database management system. Without it, a database system can't be trusted for critical work. Improvements in this area are some of the most important changes in Visual FoxPro. To understand how important they are, a little background will help.

One of the concepts mentioned earlier is business rules, a fuzzy, generic term for the various rules and procedures relating to data. Here's an example: An ORDERS table contains information on each product purchased. A PRODUCTS table contains basic product information. The two relevant fields for this example are ORDERED (how many of the product are ordered) and ONHAND (how many are available); the latter is in both the ORDERS and PRODUCTS tables. For these two fields, there might be three business rules:

1. For each product ordered, at the time of entry, calculate the remaining stock on hand, using the formula PRODUCT.ONHAND - ORDERS.ORDERED.
2. If the level of on-hand product drops below a specified limit (individually set for each product), notify the manager.
3. If the level of on-hand product drops below 0, notify the person making the entry. If that person accepts the entry, complete the transaction and flag the product as being on backorder.

These typical inventory rules could be quite important for some businesses, and the rules need to be enforced somewhere in the application. The question is where they should be enforced.

Traditionally, a FoxPro developer would apply the logic of these rules in a data entry screen, a form. Normally there would be two choices of when to apply the rules, both of them were tied to what are now called *events* (specific things that can happen in a program). One event—leaving a field—was called *field validation,* and the other event—leaving the record—was called *record validation*. Both events were triggered by the user's actions, such as tabbing out of the ORDERED field in the form or using a **Save** button to finish editing a record.

Typically, developers would attach a small program routine (sometimes called a *snippet*) to the ORDERED field. This snippet would take the value of the ONHAND field in the PRODUCTS table, calculate the new ONHAND, and then test that against the stocking level rule for having less than 0. Depending on the results, it would update the PRODUCT file and perhaps notify the person making the entry. When the user selected the **Save** button, the ONHAND entry would be checked by another snippet for the rule about stock being less than a certain value. (It was done here so that the person making the data entry would have the opportunity to make corrections or changes without triggering this rule.)

This set of rules is not particularly complicated, but it does involve other tables, the user, other people, and both field and record validation. All the programming would have been done in the screen form. But this approach has drawbacks:

- An application's business rules become scattered over every form in an application and, more often than not, aren't documented.
- Any change in a business rule would require hunting down all the occurrences of that rule in the screen forms and then rebuilding the application.

In client/server jargon, the business logic of the traditional FoxPro approach is located in the client instead of in the database server. But the server is the preferred location, because the rules can be centralized, easily maintained, and applied uniformly to any form, view, or other database operation.

Visual FoxPro is not a database server program, but the rationale behind a database server is also valid for FoxPro's database engine (at least for business rules). So Visual FoxPro has added several features to its system that are direct counterparts to a database server: field and record validation, triggers, and stored procedures. We'll go through each of these features in the following sections.

Most of the action in data integrity programming is found in the Table Designer, and the code stored in the database (DBC) file. As you will see, the key to all data validation is your ability to express business rules (or other rules) as FoxPro expressions and command routines (functions or procedures). You create the business logic in the database; when any form, browse, or view accesses the database, these rules are automatically applied to all transactions, just as they would be in a database server. This approach applies both to interactive uses of FoxPro (Command window, and browses) and to the programmed application.

NOTE

You are not required to use the database file for data validation. Although it's often the best place, there are times when putting the business logic in the data entry forms may make more sense, such when a lot of specialized processing is associated with a particular form. There is one other consideration: Loading a database with a lot of validity checking early in the development cycle can complicate your life. To FoxPro, the rules you build into the database are strictly an either-or proposition. If they exist, they're applied. Sometimes they're applied so that you can't open a table, close a table, or leave a form—even if there's an error. As a result, it's usually better to wait until table and form designs have jelled before you load most of the database validation.

FIELD VALIDATION

Access to the database validation routines normally occurs through the Project Manager, into the Database Designer, and then into the Table Designer. As shown in Figure 10.2, there are several places to go for the various types of validation.

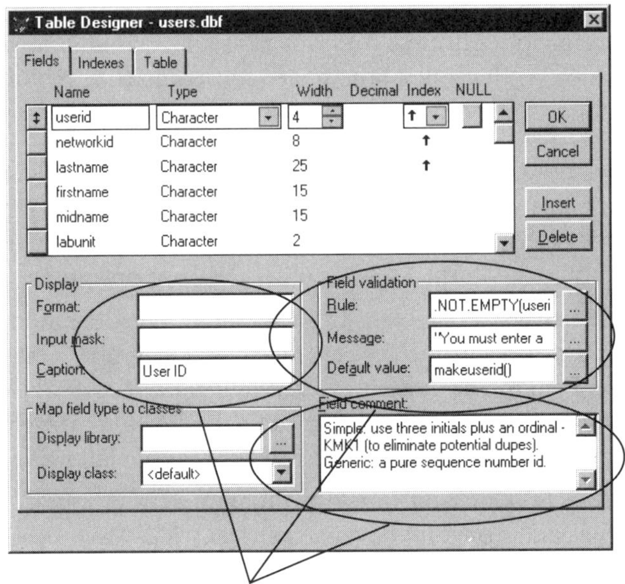

FIGURE 10.2 TABLE DESIGNER, VALIDATION ACCESS.

DEFAULT VALUES

One of the simplest ways to avoid data validity errors is to provide an initial (default) value. An obvious example is to load the day's date into a login date field. The Table Designer window provides a **Default Value** entry for each field in a table (see Figure 10.2).

Typically, you study your fields and decide which ones will be helped by providing a default value. In the **Default Value** area, you enter the default expressions, often in the form of constants: `"CA"`, `.T.`, `9999`. Alternatively, the three-dot button on the right of the **Default Value** provides access to the Expression Builder, where you can create any kind of FoxPro expression. Of course, all expressions must provide an appropriate value for the field; you can't have a numeric default value for a character field and so forth.

Whereas the default value is pre-entered into a field, the next two topics discuss validation techniques that occur after the data has been entered.

FIELD VALIDATION RULES

Field validation rules are also entered in the main Table Designer window (refer again to Figure 10.2). This time you have two entry areas: **Validation Rule** contains the logical expression that will test the data (the expression must return a true or false), and **Validation Text** holds the message to be displayed if the test is failed.

NOTE

In Visual FoxPro, validation rules (and text) can be entered only as an expression. You can't enter a sequence of commands (such as a snippet); instead, you put them into a user-defined function, which is then used in the validation expression.

Let's return to the example of the ORDERS table. The required code will be in a function called OnHandValid( ). The function is called from the **Validation Rule** for the ORDERED field. The function definition might look like this:

```
FUNCTION OnHandValid
LOCAL lnNewOnHand
* Do lookup in product table
IF SEEK( orders.productid, "PRODUCT")
  * Business rule calculation: 0-4.1
  lnNewOnHand = product.onhand - orders.ordered
  IF lnNewOnHand < 0
     * Execute user notification procedure
     IF WarnStockOut(lnNewOnHand)
        * If backorder accepted
        REPLACE product.onhand WITH lnNewOnHand ;
          IN product
        REPLACE orders.status WITH "BACKORDER" ;
          IN orders
     ELSE
       *Backorder rejected, user adjusts amount.
       RETURN .F.
     ENDIF
  ELSE
     * Update the product count
     REPLACE product.onhand WITH nNewOnHand;
```

```
        IN product
    ENDIF
  ELSE
    * Just in case the product isn't listed
    DO BadProdRef WITH orders.productid
    RETURN .F.
  ENDIF
  RETURN .T.
  *
```

This example assumes that the appropriate tables are open and set to the correct index. (If it's not the case, some additional table setup and cleanup will be necessary.) You may have noticed several user-defined functions in the example: OnHandValid(), WarnStockOut(), and BadProdRef(). Where are the function definitions stored? They're stored in *stored procedures*, which are part of a FoxPro database container file for functions and procedures used in database expressions. More on this in a bit.

WARNING

Validation rules have an important side effect: Users can't leave a field that contains an invalid entry. They're given an error message and allowed to make changes, but they are stuck in the field if they can't find a correct value. By "stuck," I mean that they must reboot the computer or end FoxPro as a task. If correct values aren't obvious, you'd better provide necessary information in the error message (or by some other means) or let the user back out gracefully.

The possibilities for field validation are endless, but remember, you are not required to use them. If a lot of data must be validated (such as when you're using **REPLACE**), marginally useful validation can slow the processing measurably.

Record Validation

The only difference between field validation and record validation is that the latter occurs when the user leaves a record instead of a field. Typically, this validation expresses business rules that require values from two or more fields. Presumably, entry into the fields is completed if the user is moving to the next record. Record validation rules are entered in the Table Properties window (shown in Figure 10.3) of the Table Designer.

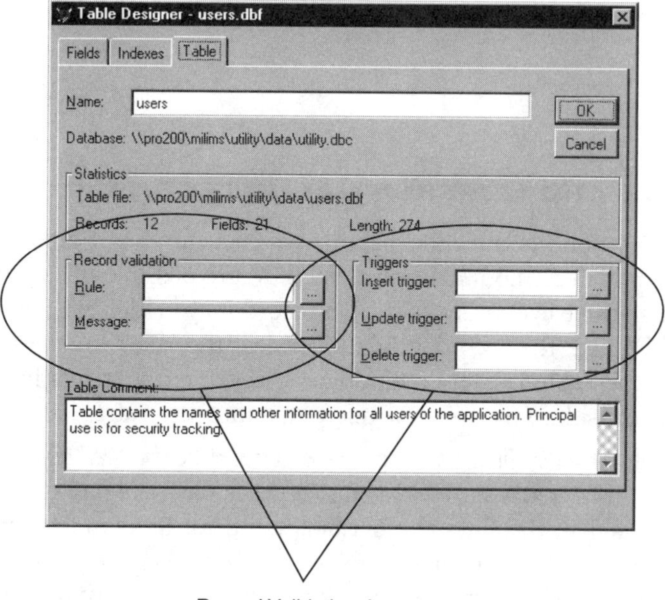

FIGURE 10.3 TABLE PROPERTIES WINDOW, RECORD VALIDATION.

This area looks similar to the field validation entry areas. It should, because the **Validation Rule** and **Validation Text** areas have exactly the same function. There is the usual provision to access the Expression Builder for each validation.

In our example, a UDF called OnHandRecordValid() is used to validate the user's entries of product on hand for the record:

```
FUNCTION OnHandRecordValid
* Do lookup in product table (does not assume it's
* already been done)
IF SEEK( orders.productid, "PRODUCT")
  IF product.onhand < product.reorderlevel
     * Execute notification procedure
     =WarnStockLow(product.productid)
  ENDIF
ELSE
  * Just in case the product isn't listed
```

```
    DO BadProdRef WITH orders.productid
ENDIF
RETURN .t.
*
```

Triggers and Referential Integrity

Visual FoxPro supports three database *triggers* that fire when a record is inserted (added), updated (modified), or deleted. Many possible business rules may apply to these three events, such as, "No record may be deleted that is less than 90 days old." Like the record validation rules, the rules for these events are entered into the **Table Designer** window. However, in the trigger fields you may need to first consider FoxPro's new referential integrity rules.

Maintaining *referential integrity* (perhaps better described as "relational" integrity) is vital for relational database systems, because they rely on being able to link values in one table with values in other tables. If those links are broken—by deletions, changes in values, or index problems—then many records in tables can become disconnected, in effect lost from the system. These lost records are classified by the colorful term *orphan* records. In databases that contain tables with a one-to-many relationship (for example, customer-to-invoice), sometimes the parent records are lost or deleted, leaving records in the child file with no reference.

Until Visual FoxPro, this was one of the most difficult data integrity problems to handle. It usually required a considerable amount of programming and was often left undone. Enforcing referential integrity still requires a high level of programming, but, thankfully, FoxPro provides the Referential Integrity Builder, which does the programming for you.

NOTE

Although it's rare, the reverse of the orphan record (a *widow* record) occurs when there are parent records but no child records even though there should be. This might happen if someone deletes all the child records. FoxPro does not support this kind of referential integrity enforcement.

Using the Referential Integrity Builder

FoxPro recognizes three database events that may require referential integrity treatment: insertions, updates, and deletions. These events correspond to three SQL commands are **INSERT**, **UPDATE**, and **DELETE**. The equivalent standard Xbase commands: **APPEND**, **EDIT**, and **DELETE**. The most common use of triggers is to allow the Referential Integrity Builder (RI Builder) to create the complex programming that enforces relationships between tables.

The easiest way to reach the RI Builder (Figure 10.4) is to begin with the Database Designer window open for your project. Select a relationship line (the lines between table boxes that indicate a relation) and use the right mouse button to bring up the shortcut menu to select **Referential Integrity**. (You can also reach the RI Builder through the menu: **Database**, **Referential Integrity**.)

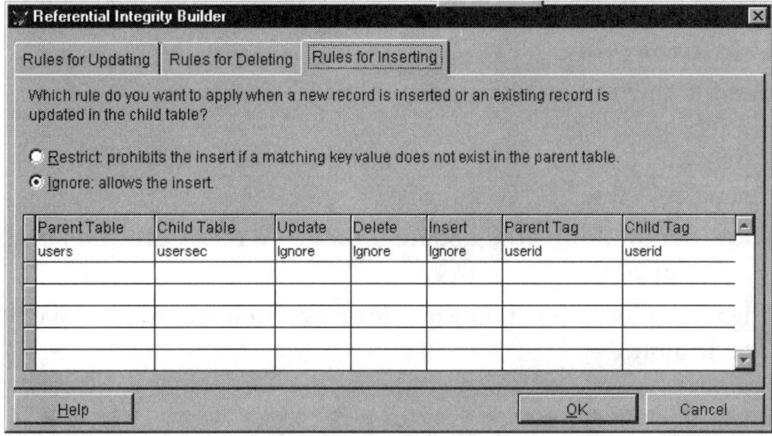

FIGURE 10.4 RI BUILDER, INSERT TRIGGER.

The Referential Integrity Builder window is split in two parts. In the top half are the current referential integrity rules (summarized) for all the tables in the database. The bottom half contains the available rules and the selected option for the current table.

As you'll notice, there are three tabs (**Rules for Inserting**, **Rules for Updating**, and **Rules for Deleting**) and as you will see, the rules change for each of them.

In the **Parent Table** column you can see the list of tables from the utility database that currently have persistent relations defined with tables in the **Child Table** column. If you highlight these relations with the mouse, the values in the rule portion of the window will change correspondingly. The **Update**, **Delete**, and **Insert** columns summarize the rules being applied (if any) for each relation. The last two columns—**Parent Tag** and **Child Tag**—indicate which indexes are involved in the relation.

RULES FOR INSERTING

The business end of the RI Builder is the lower portion of the window, where you select which rules (if any) should be triggered for each event. For inserting, only one rule may be applied when a record is added or changed in the child table: **Restrict: prohibits the insert if a matching key value does not exist in the parent table**. This rule says that you can't add records or change the index key value of the child table unless there is a matching value in the parent table—no orphans. The alternative is **Ignore: allows the insert**. This selection would be typical for relations used in a data lookup, where matches may or may not be found.

RULES FOR UPDATING

The **Rules for Updating** tab (Figure 10.5) has three options:

- **Cascade: updates all related records in the child table with the new key value**.
- **Restrict: prohibits the update if there are related records in the child table**.
- **Ignore: allows the update and leaves related records in the child table alone**.

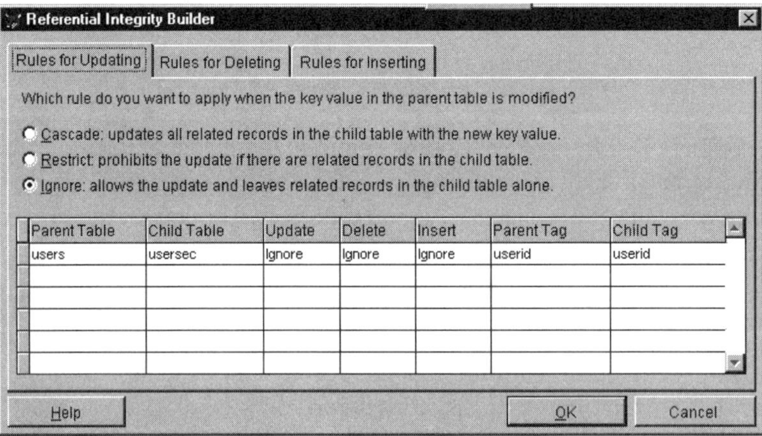

FIGURE 10.5 RI BUILDER, UPDATE TRIGGER.

The **Cascade** option (so named because of the one record after another—cascading—update) is used in one-to-many relations, where maintaining the link between one parent record and any number of child records is paramount but

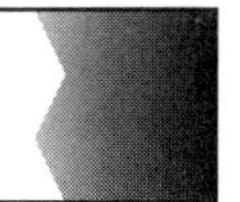

where, for various reasons, it is necessary to change index key values. This arrangement is rare, but it could happen in situations (such as product codes) when it may be necessary to change the entire coding system from time to time.

The **Restrict** option is the most commonly used, because when orphan records are not permitted, you also do not want index key values to be changed. However, with this rule, if there are no related records in the child table, it's perfectly harmless to change the index key value.

The **Ignore** (do-nothing) option allows changes in the parent table's key values. This option seldom applies, because it disconnects any related records in the child table. This might be acceptable if another integrity routine is run to test for orphan records and delete any that are found (a job for **COUNT** and the **DELETE** command).

RULES FOR DELETING

As you can see in Figure 10.6, the three options for deleting deal with the possibility of leaving orphan child records because of deletions in the parent table.

- **Cascade: deletes all related records in the child table.**
- **Restrict: prohibits the deletion if there are related records in the child table.**
- **Ignore: allows the deletion and leaves related records in the child table alone.**

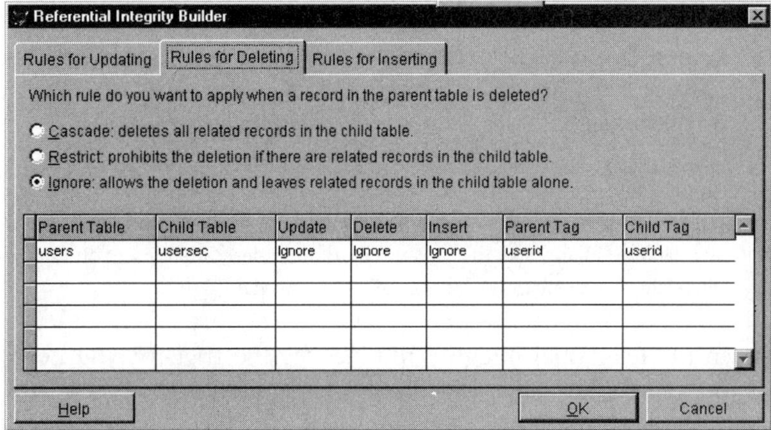

FIGURE 10.6 RI BUILDER, DELETE TRIGGER.

Similar to the update rule, the **Cascade** option ensures that if the parent record goes, all the child records go. This option might also be called the "purge" rule; under most circumstances, the deleted records would soon be permanently removed from the table.

The **Restrict** rule simply says that you can't delete the parent record if there are any child records. This situation might occur when you want to maintain a record of relations even after the relation has been changed or dissolved. For example, you might have the parent table define a code (such as a product code) that then becomes attached to a number of child records. Then one day, the code is no longer used, but you want the system to continue to store the old code and all the old related child records. (There might be a new code and a whole new set of child records.)

The do-nothing rule (**Ignore**) is applied to situations in which the relational link is dynamic—expected to change—and it is not unusual to delete a parent record and then (for example) reassign the child records to another parent. This might be the case in an agency when an employee's set of clients is reassigned when the employee leaves. This requires a reassignment routine to change the child records to reference a new parent record.

When you're finished selecting RI rules and press the **OK** button in the RI window, FoxPro generates the appropriate programming, which will be permanently attached to your database. From this point, every time you open the database (or one of its tables), these RI rules will be applied.

NOTE

It might be instructive to see what FoxPro does with the rules it generates. In the Database Designer, select **Database**, **Stored Procedures** from the menu. This action opens an Edit Text window in which you will see many lines of FoxPro programming code that do the job of maintaining referential integrity.

WARNING

Any changes you make to the structure or relationships of your tables need to be reflected in the referential integrity rules. It is important to run the RI Builder after any database changes so that it can rebuild the rules. Otherwise, you may see some interesting (and unhappy) consequences in your data.

Having seen the referential integrity routines for the triggers, you need to be careful if you want additional routines to be run on the same triggers. They must coexist with the same expression used for the RI functions.

STORED PROCEDURES

Stored procedures typically hold the FoxPro referential integrity routines along with any routines (functions and procedures) you add for field and record validation. However, the concept is very general; any procedure or function that logically belongs with the database can be stored there. It need not be something that is used in data integrity checking.

Stored procedures are part of a database file and are automatically opened when the database is opened. You can edit the stored procedures in the database by going through the menu: **Database**, **Edit Stored Procedures** (with the database open). You can also use **MODIFY PROCEDURE** in the Command window.

It's also possible to edit the stored procedures while the application is running. This intriguing capability is made possible by the fact that the code for stored procedures isn't part of the application's code but rather belongs to the database—a separate file and program entity. In practice, this means that you can extract the stored procedures using **COPY PROCEDURES TO cfilename** to create a text file that can be modified programmatically. Then you put it back into the DBF file with **APPEND PROCEDURES FROM cfilename**, close the database, **COMPILE PROCEDURES cDatabaseName**, and then open the database to make them active. Modifying the text file in a program would not be easy, but this capability means that you can add new procedures or modify existing ones based on some conditions in the application. For example, you could execute an automated change in security algorithms or data encryption routines that would be difficult to decipher or duplicate.

CHAPTER WRAP-UP

Having covered the new data integrity programming features of Visual FoxPro (field and record validation, triggers, and stored procedures), you've also completed the basics of FoxPro procedural programming. Because it includes most forms of database programming, procedural programming is a significant chunk of FoxPro and will usually be an underpinning of your applications—controlling the integrity of the data and business rules with the database container, providing the queries, views, and tables on which form and report Data Environments are built, and giving you numerous tools to monitor and manage the data.

Figure 10.7 is a diagram of the complete Visual FoxPro data management system. At this point, you have enough background to understand how most of it works. Some pieces are more advanced: data buffers, ODBC connections, and SQL remote views will be covered in later chapters. But as you can see, from this perspective the database file is the center of FoxPro's data management, around which the traditional Xbase an FoxPro commands and the SQL commands are used to provide data to other FoxPro objects, especially the forms and reports.

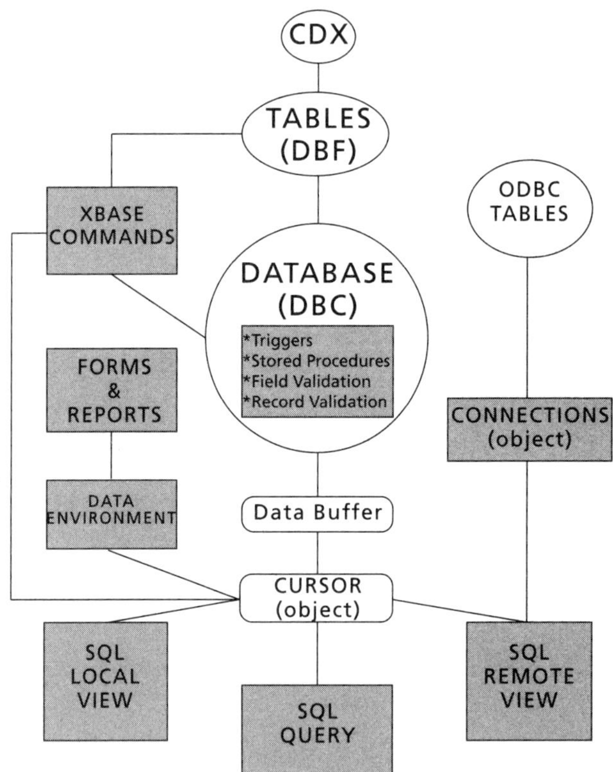

Figure 10.7 The complete FoxPro data management system.

A few chapters from now, when you are deep into the object-oriented approach to programming, much of this procedural programming will seem almost old-fashioned. It is, in some ways, but it still contributes many basic concepts to the object-oriented techniques (such as control structures, functions, and procedures).

On occasion, you will also need to write purely procedural code to do certain kinds of database processing. Procedural programming isn't like the old soldier, just fading away. Instead, it has evolved into more of a blend of programming approaches.

SECTION 4

OBJECT-ORIENTED PROGRAMMING

You've been introduced to object-oriented programming, reviewed the tools available for data management, and covered the basics of procedural programming. Now we come back to OOP, where you put everything else into practice—objects, data, and programming—for the majority of your applications. Referring to the application framework context (Section Figure 4.1), we're beginning to work on the principal elements of the class hierarchy, itself a major portion of the framework.

In this section, as you make the transition from database and procedural programming to object-oriented programming, you will be spanning a leap the computer industry has been attempting for more than 10 years. It is far from finished. This is also true for Visual FoxPro, which not only is new to OOP but also is still in transition itself (Section Figure 4.2).

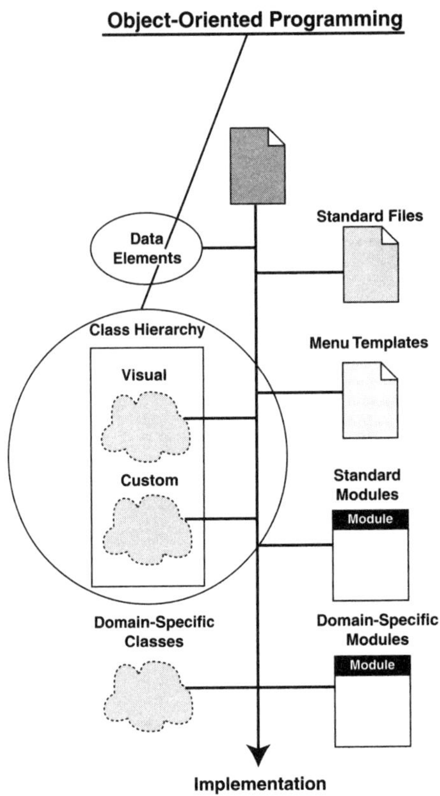

SECTION FIGURE 4.1 APPLICATION FRAMEWORK.

As you can see from the diagram, only some of these elements are truly object-oriented. However, by and large Visual FoxPro has tied all the pieces together within the major object-oriented programming concepts: classes, objects, methods, and properties. The three chapters of this section complete the introduction to OOP and show you how to use the new Visual FoxPro Debugger.

- Chapter 11, "Understanding OOP, Part II: Classes"
- Chapter 12, "Events and Methods"
- Chapter 13, "Debugging"

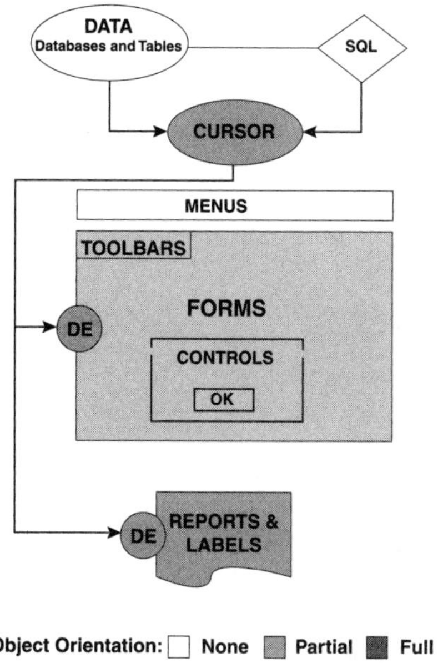

SECTION FIGURE 4.2 APPLICATION ELEMENTS AND OBJECT ORIENTATION.

CHAPTER 11

UNDERSTANDING OOP, PART II: CLASSES

Object-oriented classes were introduced in Chapter 2. You may recall that classes are the blueprint that creates objects. Perhaps you got the impression that classes are important. Let's reinforce that impression: Classes are used to create 99 percent of your application user interface and about 70 percent of the data processing and business rule management, and they will account for roughly 90 percent of a FoxPro application framework. By the numbers, classes are obviously important. But in a more philosophical sense, developing classes is the heart of object-oriented programming.

So why don't they call it class-oriented programming? That's a good question. The answer is that as an end product of classes, objects have a life of their own. When you download an ActiveX *object* from the Internet, you can be blissfully unaware of any class (or class hierarchy) that produced it. The objects produced by classes in Visual FoxPro aren't as independent, because they need to have the FoxPro run-time interpreter available. Still, Visual FoxPro objects are independent enough from the classes that spawned them to be modifiable even while the program is running. The world and programming are full of objects, and not classes, so *object-oriented* programming it is.

None of this belies the importance of classes, especially in FoxPro. Consider this chapter an introduction to the tools for managing classes. Later chapters will deal with how they're applied to specific elements of an application framework. We'll go through the various aspects of classes and explore how they are created:

- The concept of a class hierarchy and how it affects an application framework.

- Visual base classes and their limitations.
- Creating your own subclasses in the Class Designer.
- Creating custom (nonvisual) subclasses.
- Commands and functions for developing classes.
- Using the FoxPro Class Browser to study your classes.

NOTE

Along the way, I hope you will begin to pick up not only the how-to of classes but also the why and wherefore. Just as programmers have developed a sense for how functions can be made generic (and then reused), there is a similar sense for generic classes and how they can be modified by subclassing into a class hierarchy.

Understanding the Class Hierarchy

It is possible to program an entire application without creating a single class. By pulling together FoxPro base class forms and controls, hooking up with a database, and perhaps adding a procedure file and something to initialize the whole thing, you'll have an application. Almost none of it will be reusable without major surgery, but if you have the Dr. Frankenstein impulse, your creation might suffice. On the other hand, if you want to be able to create the next 10 applications with minimum hassle and maximum speed, you'll want to take full advantage of the greatest tool in object-oriented programming: *subclassing*, or creating your own classes.

Gaining a Little Inheritance

To start this chapter, we'll create a type of form that almost everyone uses these days: a tabbed dialog box. If you need an overworked example, check out the FoxPro Options dialog box (**Tools**, **Options** in the menu). This type of dialog box is a variation of the **Form** class that should be in every developer's application framework and class hierarchy. It can be quickly rolled out for those situations when a controlled but fairly complex dialog is needed with the user.

You'll start by combining two Visual FoxPro base classes: **Form** and **PageFrame**. Both classes are containers, so you'd expect to fill them with controls, but for this example we'll leave out the details so that basic points are

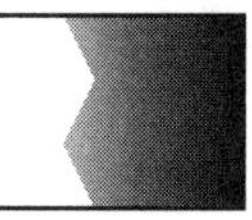

clearer. To make this easier, you might want to haul out the exercise material from Chapters 1 and 2.

As usual, things begin with the Project Manager (see Figure 11.1). Select the **Classes** tab and then click the **New** button. This action brings up the New Class dialog box (also in Figure 11.1). You need to give the class a name. In later chapters we'll cover the many naming conventions for classes, but for now it can be anything. Let's use TESTFORMFRAME. This class will be based on the FoxPro base class **Form**, which you need to hunt down and select from the **Based On** drop-down list. You'll notice that FoxPro requires a file in which to store the class. For now you can create any file name (such as TEST), probably in the LIBRARY folder (if you have one). This will create the class library file, with an extension of VCX.

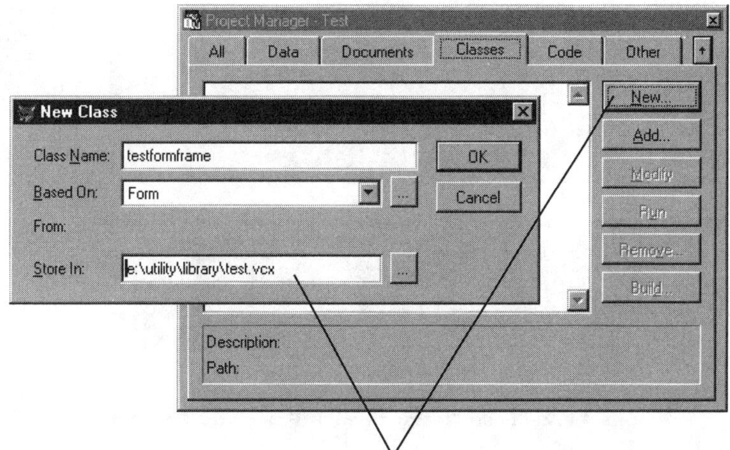

FIGURE 11.1 PROJECT MANAGER AND THE NEW CLASS DIALOG BOX.

Once you click **OK** in the New Class dialog box, FoxPro grinds the disk and comes up with the Class Designer (Figure 11.2). You should also see one or more toolbars appear. (If it does not, you should open at least the Form Controls and Form Layout toolbars from the **View**, **Toolbars** menu.)

At a glance, the Class Designer window looks just like the Form Designer window. Visually there is no difference, but there are differences, including class-oriented captions and an output file. Before adding the **PageFrame**, let's change a property of the form to prepare it to become a modal dialog box. If the

Properties window isn't visible, click inside the Class Designer and then use the shortcut menu (right mouse button) to select **Properties**. In the Properties window, locate the **WindowType** property under the **All** tab and change it from the default (0 = modeless) to 1 (modal). As a modal dialog box, our form won't let the user activate any other window.

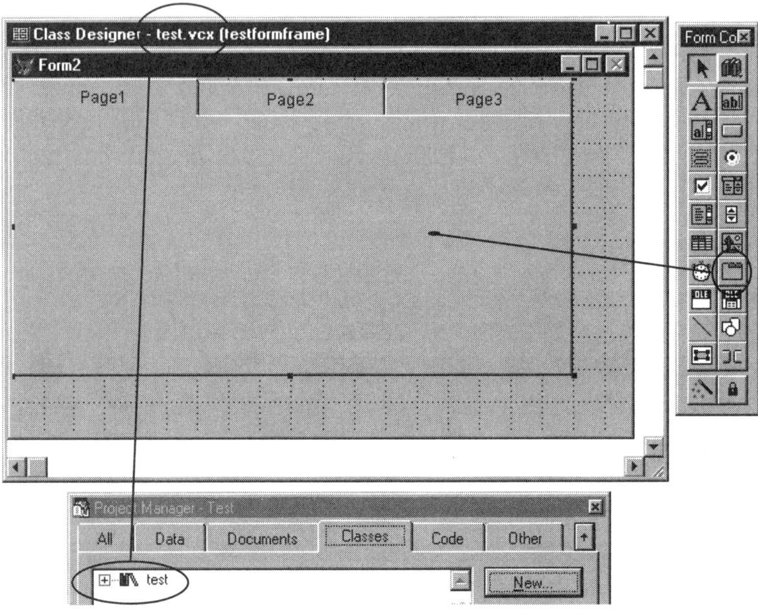

FIGURE 11.2 CLASS DESIGNER WITH FORM AND PAGEFRAME.

On the Form Control toolbar, locate the **PageFrame** icon and select it. Using the marquee in the Class Designer window, draw the area inside the form where the page frame should be created (as in Figure 11.2). Unlike the form, a *page frame* is not a stand-alone object; it must be placed in a form before it can exist. By default, the **PageFrame** class has two tabs. Let's change that to three tabs. Make sure the page frame is selected in the Class Designer. The name PageFrame1 should be showing at the top of the Property window. In the Property window, find the **PageCount** property and change it from 2 to **3**. The third tab will instantly appear in the Class Designer window. Save the class and close it.

Now we're ready to test the class. But how? There's no **Run** icon or menu option for the Class Designer. Unlike forms, classes must be explicitly instantiated within a program before you can run them. This is where your program shell from Chapter 1 may come in handy. It had a startup program file, probably called MAIN.PRG. Use the Project Manager to open it for editing and enter the following commands:

```
SET CLASSLIB TO test
oTest = CREATEOBJECT("TESTSFORMFRAME")
oTest.Visible = .T.
```

The code in MAIN.PRG looks something like this:

```
PUSH MENU _MSYSMENU
DO main.mpr

SET CLASSLIB TO test
oTest = CREATEOBJECT("TESTSFORMFRAME")
oTest.Visible = .T.

READ EVENTS

POP MENU _MSYSMENU
```

The new commands tell FoxPro to open the library file TEST, and they instantiate the form by assigning the variable OTEST to it as a name. Thereafter, you can use OTEST to refer to the object, and that is just what the next line does. It makes the form *visible*. If you can get your form running—don't be discouraged if you run into some snags—play with it a bit and try sizing the window. You'll see that the window can be sized, but the page frame doesn't size with it. That's not exactly a desirable behavior. In fact, it's hard to think of a tabbed dialog box in which you wouldn't want the tabs to follow the size of the form. Aha! This calls for a generic behavior, something you put into a class at or near the top of a class hierarchy so that all the subclasses inherit it.

To improve the page frame behavior, reopen the TESTFORMFRAME class from the Project Manager. Be sure that the form is selected and not the page frame (this is an easy mistake to make). In the Property window, switch to the **Methods** tab and locate the **Resize** event method. Open its editing window and enter these two lines:

```
ThisForm.Pageframe1.Width  = THIS.width
ThisForm.Pageframe1.Height = THIS.height
```

These lines synchronize the width and height properties of the page frame with those of the form. Because they're in the **Resize** event, every time the size of the form is changed, this event will fire and **PageFrame** will follow suit.

If you've never done any object-oriented programming, the construction of these lines may look strange. There's more referencing than command. One of the cardinal rules of OOP is that all behavior—properties, methods, and events—must be referenced to specific objects. Referencing can sometimes be as simple as using the name of a variable; you've seen that previously. Other times, because of objects being contained in other objects, a long trail of **object.object.object** may be necessary to reference something accurately. In this case, a couple of shortcuts are being used: **THIS** and **THISFORM**. These methods let you reference an object generically, because you don't need to know the actual name of the current object (THIS) or of the form (THISFORM). More on referencing shortly.

Save the class and run the program to verify that the **PageFrame** will resize with the form.

Making a Subclass of a Subclass

Now that TESTFORMFRAME has a couple of useful generic properties, we'll make a subclass of it. This arrangement leaves the generic class open for additional generic features, and the subclass can be used to add less generic, or even application-specific, features. From the Project Manager, in the **Classes** tab, highlight the **TEST** library and click **New**. Give this new class a name; something like TESTFORMFRAMENEW would help to indicate the parentage of the class. The important step is to use the three-dot button to summon the file select dialog box so that you can select the TEST library and TESTFORMFRAME as the class to be subclassed.

NOTE

It's possible that somewhere during this exercise you asked yourself why you should make changes in different subclasses. Why not make them all in one subclass? Unfortunately, to keep things simple, the example for this exercise can't illustrate the necessity of subclassing. Later, when you're creating your own classes and loading them with special properties and methods, you'll see that making changes incrementally through subclasses helps to organize the hierarchy. Essentially, additional subclasses are used to separate generic classes from those that are successively less generic and more tied to a specific application. This is the key element in class hierarchy design, a major topic in Chapter 15.

When you've completed the New Class dialog box, the Class Designer window appears again. You could do many things in this new class, such as adding colors and controls, but let's say you decide you want this class to have only two tabs instead of three. So you go to the **PageCount** property of the **PageFrame** and enter **2**. You'll get an error message: `Member PAGE3 is a class member.` FoxPro won't let you reduce the number of tabs. Why?

The **PageCount** is one of those properties that create a *member*, an object in its own right. **ColumnCount** in a grid is similar. Members (objects) defined in containers of a previous class cannot be removed in a subclass. You'd have to go back to TESTFORMFRAME and remove the third tab there. That's no problem—if that class hasn't been used in other subclasses or forms. What happens, however, if you've created a number of forms in your application based on the three-tab class and suddenly it has only two tabs? FoxPro will not stop you from doing this.

ANOTHER LOOK AT INHERITANCE

Inheritance is one of the key concepts in object-oriented programming, and it provides a powerful framework for developing applications. However, it comes with its own set of complications. As an illustration, let's start with an analogy.

This case concerns manufacturing and selling a custom dune buggy. The primary manufacturer provides the chassis, engine, and drive train. A secondary manufacturer adds the body, wheels, and internal components (seats and dashboard). Then the vehicle is turned over to a dealer, who may add appointments such as a radio or body decals. At each level, the work is supplementary, and everyone counts on the previous step having done what is expected. In that way, changes up the line have minimal impact down the line. However, what happens if the secondary manufacturer decides to turbocharge the engine? If one level decides to modify another level's components, there are only two choices: Replace it entirely or try to add functionality without disrupting the original. Even so, there's always some danger that the "enhanced" or replacement component won't work properly. And what if the primary manufacturer decides to change or remove the component?

In the class hierarchy, the primary manufacturer is the base class—for example, a **Form**. In FoxPro, the base class form can't be modified, so it's common to create an immediate subclass and, like the secondary manufacturer, add a number of essential features. Then the new subclass is ready for use in an application with the kind of relatively minor modifications that a dealer might make. In general, properties are not redefined, although you can certainly change their values. If you choose to redefine a method, you must either completely override the original or use the original intact and add some different functionality.

Put in more specific terms, once you establish a class hierarchy, it's relatively easy to create a subclass that stomps on code in a higher class. There is no technical fix for the problem. There is only good documentation and the admonition, "Know thy hierarchy."

NOTE

One of the best ways to learn about a class hierarchy (except for building one) is to pick a control or form in someone else's hierarchy and follow its subclasses all the way back to the FoxPro base class. The Visual FoxPro examples (Tastrade and Wizard) can be used to do this, as can the utility classes that accompany this book.

Creating Your Own Subclasses

Creating your own subclasses is a big subject—it covers almost the whole of the application framework. We won't try go through everything in one push. This section deals with some of the basics and introduces you to the underlying code of all classes.

In Visual FoxPro, creating your own subclasses starts with the base classes. Of these, there are two kinds: custom classes and everything else (visual classes). Subclassing most of the visual classes seems like a fairly obvious thing to do. The majority of these classes can stand some enhancing, and the containers (forms and grids) cry out for combination into other useful classes. Custom classes play a less obvious role than visual classes. They may have no connection to the user interface and are often used for data processing, business rules, and application management. It needs to be emphasized that creating both kinds of classes is important for developing applications and the application framework.

The Class in Code

As a rule, classes are created in the Class Designer. A few may be created in the Form Designer (as form classes); seldom will you define classes in a program or procedure file. Still, because the same code is generated by all approaches, it doesn't hurt to understand what constitutes a FoxPro class definition in code. It will also provide a guide to compare against the somewhat fragmented coding arrangement in the Class Designer.

Creating a class definition outside the Class Designer (or Form Designer) is simply a matter of opening a program file and entering the code. Here's the original syntax:

Command syntax:

DEFINE CLASS ClassName1 AS ParentClass [OLEPUBLIC]
[[PROTECTED | HIDDEN PropertyName1, PropertyName2 ...]
[Object.]PropertyName = eExpression ...]
[ADD OBJECT [PROTECTED] ObjectName AS ClassName2 [NOINIT]
[WITH cPropertylist]]...
[[PROTECTED | HIDDEN] FUNCTION | PROCEDURE Name
[NODEFAULT]
cStatements
[ENDFUNC | ENDPROC]]...
ENDDEFINE

Jammed together this way, the syntax appears to be complicated. It's not. Here's the syntax broken out into a code shell, using <> as placeholders for the arguments of the structure:

```
DEFINE CLASS <> AS <>
  *———————— PROPERTIES
  *> Public properties
  <> = <>
  *> Protected properties
  PROTECTED <>, <>
  <> = <>
  *> Hidden properties
  HIDDEN <>, <>
  <> = <>
*———————— OBJECTS
  *> Public Objects
  ADD OBJECT <> AS <> NOINIT
   WITH <>, <>, <>, <>
```

```
  ADD OBJECT <> AS <>
   WITH <>, <>, <>, <>
  *> Protected Objects
  ADD OBJECT PROTECTED <> AS <>
   WITH <>, <>, <>, <>
  *——————— METHODS
  *> Public methods
  FUNCTION <>
    ...
  ENDFUNC
  PROCEDURE <>
    ...
  ENDPROC
  *> Protected and Hidden methods
  PROTECTED FUNCTION <>
    ...
  ENDFUNC
  HIDDEN PROCEDURE <>
    NODEFAULT
    ...
  ENDPROC
ENDDEFINE
```

Most of the sections are optional; the only required element is the **DEFINE CLASS/ ENDDEFINE** structure. A class isn't required to have properties, methods, or added objects. There is also an important distinction between working with classes derived from visual base classes and working with those from the **Custom** base class. The visual classes come with an extensive set of properties and events; you can change property values or create event methods, and you can create new properties and methods of your own. The custom classes have very few properties and methods, and you will have to create most of the class functionality with your methods and properties.

Class Code and a Visual Class

Let's take a tour through a class definition, not of a custom class, which would be the most common use for code, but rather of a visual class (one that follows the basic format). Our purpose is to emphasize the relationship between code and all the classes. The example creates the object pictured in Figure 11.3, a container with a spinner control allowing selection of records from a table (similar to the VCR button controls but in a different context).

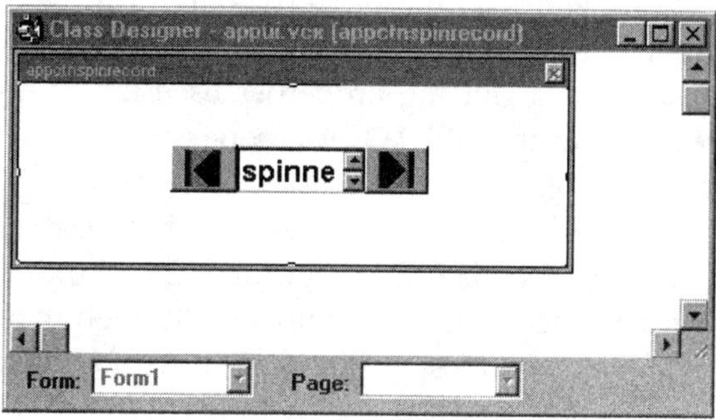

FIGURE 11.3 THE APPCTNSPINRECORD CLASS IN CLASS DESIGNER.

For the sake of simplicity and brevity, the example here doesn't contain every line of code, but the final product is in the APPCTN class library on the accompanying disk:

```
DEFINE CLASS appCtnSpinRecord AS Container
```

The name of the class follows a convention that annotates its parentage. In this case, **appCtn** is an abbreviation for the application container class category. The new class is basically a spinner control, so **Spin** is part of the name; and because it changes the display of records, the final piece of the name is **Record**. This is only one of many possible naming conventions for classes. It doesn't matter much which one you use, only that it make some kind of sense, and above all, that you use it consistently.

The code begins by defining properties, which are primarily used as variables dedicated to the object created from this class.

```
*——————— PROPERTIES
*> Public properties
pnLastRecord = 0
*> Protected properties
PROTECTEDpnMaxValue, pnMinValue
pnMaxValue = 999999
pnMinValue = 0
*> Hidden properties
```

```
HIDDEN pnTotalValue
pnTotalValue = pnMaxValue+pnMinValue
```

The properties section defines all the property values (in the standard format) that are needed by the class to do its work or that you want the class to make available to other objects. In general, properties used only within the class are declared **HIDDEN** (equivalent to the **LOCAL** scope), because they are not needed by any other class or object and you don't want to expose them to potentially damaging changes. If you want to make the properties visible to classes lower in the hierarchy, use the **PROTECTED** keyword. Those properties that other objects may freely access are considered "public," although there is no keyword to that effect. Like regular variables, they're created without declaration.

NOTE

I've adopted the convention of labeling properties with a prefix of `p`, plus the usual data type prefix: `pnMaxValue`. In most other naming schemes, `p` is used for private variables, however, it's my belief that properties are much more important (because of OOP), and deserve the `p` designation. In this scheme, private variables are denoted with `r`: `rcMaxValue`.

Although property definitions look like standard variable declarations (which, of course, they are), a property is handled differently. Properties are always associated with a specific object and often are linked to a particular characteristic (such as color or size) for which the property contains the current controlling value. When you are programming, you can simply *use* a variable: `cText = "Dog"; cBigText = UPPER(cText)`. You *reference* a property:

```
THISFORM.cmdButton1.Caption = "Dog"
THISFROM.cmdButton2.Caption = UPPER(This.cmdbutton1.Caption)
```

In application building, the majority of properties you create will be associated with a form or a class derived from a **Form** or **FormSet**. When you reference these objects you need to use either the exact name of the form or the more generic `THISFORM`. Forgetting the `THISFORM` is an extremely common mistake.

All container classes (**Container**, **Form**, **Grid**, and **PageFrame**) are so named because they contain one or more objects, typically controls. In code, they're added this way:

```
*———— OBJECTS
*> Public Objects
```

```
*none
*> Protected Objects
ADD OBJECT PROTECTED appCtnSpinner AS bctSpinner NOINIT
  WITH THIS.enabled = .T.
ADD OBJECT PROTECTED appCmdButton1 AS appCommandButton
  WITH THIS.enabled = .F.
ADD OBJECT PROTECTED appCmdButton2 AS appCommandButton
  WITH THIS.enabled = .T.
```

In this case, the parent class is a subclass of the **Container** base class. Into it go the three operative objects: a spinner and two command buttons along with associated properties defined in the **WITH** clause. The **NOINIT** option allows you to specify that an object's **Init** event method is not executed when the object is instantiated. This is used mostly to prevent some nongeneric code from being run.

NOTE

The meaning of **PROTECTED** and **HIDDEN** is the same for properties, objects, and methods. In Visual FoxPro, a protected member is available only to its own class subclasses. (This is very much like a **PRIVATE** variable.) It is not available (*visible* is the alternative term) to objects in other hierarchies or to superclasses of its own hierarchy. **HIDDEN** is visible only to its own class. Remember that "visible" in this sense means that you can reference the property with its object name: `oObjName.MyMethod()`.

Now we come to the business end of a class: methods. In the Class Designer or in code, methods can include both the native event methods and the methods you define for the class. As you'll notice in the following example, methods can be either functions or procedures.

```
*———————— METHODS
*> Public methods
FUNCTION BottomRecord
  GO BOTTOM
  IF RECNO() = RECCOUNT()
    This.pnLastRecord = RECNO()
    RETURN This.pnLastRecord
  ENDIF
  RETURN 0
ENDFUNC
*> Protected methods
```

```
  PROTECTED PROCEDURE DownClick
    NODEFAULT
    IF NOT EOF() AND this.value <= RECCOUNT()
     GO this.value
    ELSE
     GO TOP
    ENDIF
    Thisform.Refresh()
  ENDPROC
  PROTECTED PROCEDURE UpClick
    NODEFAULT
    IF NOT BOF() AND this.value >= 1
      GO this.value
    ELSE
      GO BOTTOM
    ENDIF
    Thisform.Refresh()
  ENDPROC
ENDDEFINE
```

The methods segment of a class definition is usually the lengthiest, most complicated, and potentially most troublesome portion. It's not complicated in the structural sense. Methods are either functions or procedures, and the only differences between them and "normal" functions or procedures are the keywords **PROTECTED** and **NODEFAULT** along with the use of the **PROCEDURE/ENDPROC** and **FUNCTION/ENDFUNC** control structures.

Methods become complicated in relation to other objects and especially in their relation to the class hierarchy. Event methods, in particular, can be troublesome, because their names are the same regardless of which class level or hierarchy they are in—a practice known as *repeated polymorphism*. The **Init** event method always has an `INIT()` method in code (although in the Class Designer you don't see it that way). This is one place where the use of **HIDDEN** can be extremely important to avoid unwanted execution of methods.

A simple example (similar to the one in the *Developer's Guide*) is clear enough. Define a subclass of a FoxPro base class:

```
DEFINE CLASS myButton AS COMMANDBUTTON
```

Create a **Click** event method in the class:

```
PROCEDURE Click
  Thisform.this.caption = "More"
  Thisform.datasession = 2
  Thisform.buffermode = 1
  Thisform.Refresh()
ENDPROC
```

Subclass this class:

```
DEFINE CLASS myNewButton AS myButton
```

Create a new **Click** method in this class:

```
PROCEDURE Click
  IF lExitOk
    Thisform.this.caption = "Quit"
  ELSE
    =DODEFAULT()
  ENDIF
ENDPROC
```

At this point, there are three class levels (COMMANDBUTTON, myButton, and myNewButton), and the **Click** event method in myNewButton overrides the **Click** event method in myButton. However, the second method is written so that under a particular condition it executes the parent CLICK method, using the **DODEFAULT( )** function (which largely replaces the scope resolution operator of Visual FoxPro 3.0).

OTHER CLASS LANGUAGE ELEMENTS

Visual FoxPro has provided a number of functions and commands that help with the management of classes (and objects). These elements are used from time to time within a program to build methods (or functions) that manipulate classes and class libraries. They can also be used in the Command window to do class library housekeeping chores.

Class Functions

The first two are bookend functions: **ACLASS( )** and **AINSTANCE( )**. The former can tell you an object's parents (the class hierarchy), and the latter reports how many objects have been created from a class.

ACLASS( ) loads an array with the parent (and other ancestors, if any) of an object.

Command syntax:

ACLASS(ArrayName, oExpression)

Arguments:

ArrayName The name of the array in which to place the class name (and superclasses).

oExpression The name of the object as expression, reference, variable, or array element.

Returns: an array of parent class names.

Example:

```
=ACLASS(aFrmOrders, "NEWORDERS")
```

AINSTANCE( ) loads an array with the instances of a class (the objects created from it) and returns the total number of instances.

Command syntax:

AINSTANCE(ArrayName, cClassName)

Arguments:

ArrayName Name of the array in which to place instance names.

cClassName Name of the class.

Returns: the number of objects created by the class.

Example:

```
IF AINSTANCE(aFrmOrderForm,"ORDERFORM") = 2
  WAIT WINDOW "Sorry, no more than two orders at a time."
ENDIF
```

This function is most useful as part of a control mechanism for the number of allowable instances of an object. For example, as in the preceding example, it can be used to limit the number of times a user can open a form.

You've already seen **CREATEOBJECT( )** many times, because it is one of the vital elements in the Visual FoxPro scheme of OOP. In programs (often) and in the Command window (occasionally), it's used to create an object from a class definition or an OLE application.

Command syntax:

CREATEOBJECT(ClassName[,eParameter1,eParameter2,...])

Arguments:

ClassName Name of the parent class or OLE object.

eParameter2... Optional parameters that can be passed to the Init method of an object.

Returns: an object reference.

Examples:

```
oOrderForm = CREATEOBJECT( "ORDERFORM" )
oNewCar = CREATEOBJECT("MAKECAR",cCarModel,nType)
DECLARE aFldList[10]
DECLARE aFldLength[10]
oGridPick = CREATEOBJECT("GRIDPICK",@aFldList,@aFldLength)
```

It's standard practice to assign the return value of **CREATEOBJECT( )** to a memory variable. (An array element can also be used, but this is less common.) From then on, the name of the variable can be used to reference the object. Note that the variable is not automatically released if the object is released.

An important issue at the time you use **CREATEOBJECT( )** is how it finds the class. It's good programming practice not to tie your code to specific external conditions, such as a path to a file, so you need to take advantage of the sequence in which FoxPro will search for the location of class libraries (VCX files):

1. Visual FoxPro base classes.
2. User-defined class definitions in memory in the order they were loaded.
3. Classes in the current program.
4. Classes in VCX class libraries opened with **SET CLASSLIB**.
5. Classes in procedure files opened with **SET PROCEDURE**.
6. Classes in the Visual FoxPro program execution chain.
7. The Windows Registry (for OLE objects).

The one thing FoxPro won't do is to look for specific classes. For classes created in the Class Designer, the appropriate thing to do is to use **SET CLASSLIB** to open the appropriate library file (see the next section). If you wrote your own class definition code, include it either in the relevant program file or as part of a procedure file.

CLASS LIBRARY MANAGEMENT

Although class libraries can be manipulated in both the Class Designer and the Class Browser, the command alternatives can be useful for direct maintenance in the Command window and occasionally in programs.

SET CLASSLIB opens a VCX visual class library that contains class definitions.

Command syntax:

SET CLASSLIB TO ClassLibraryName [ADDITIVE] [ALIAS AliasName]

Arguments:

ClassLibraryName Name of the class library to open.

AliasName Name of the alias.

ADDITIVE Library contents should be added to memory.

Examples:

```
SET CLASSLIB TO MyClass ALIAS MyCntrls
mMyButton = CREATEOBJ('MyCntrls.MyButton')
```

If you forget to use the **ADDITIVE** clause when there are already open libraries, FoxPro will unceremoniously dump all the other libraries from memory, usually with negative results in your program. This is one of those self-policing programming errors that never get as far as the user.

The following six class library commands are variations of standard FoxPro commands that apply to many kinds of files and objects. The file-oriented commands work best if the files are located on the FoxPro path, but you can also use complete paths in the command itself.

To remove a class from memory:

CLEAR CLASS ClassName

Example: `CLEAR CLASS appGridPicker`

To remove a class library from memory:

CLEAR CLASSLIB ClassLibraryName

Example: `CLEAR CLASSLIB appBase`

To create a new, empty class library in a VCX file:

CREATE CLASSLIB ClassLibraryName

Example: `CREATE CLASSLIB c:\appdemo\appBase.vcx`

To close a VCX visual class library that contains class definitions:

RELEASE CLASSLIB ClassLibraryName

Example: `RELEASE CLASSLIB appBase`

To remove a class definition from a VCX visual class library:

REMOVE CLASS ClassName OF ClassLibraryName

Example: `REMOVE CLASS appGridPicker OF appBase`

To rename a class definition contained in a VCX visual class library:

RENAME CLASS ClassName1 OF ClassLibraryName TO ClassName2

Example: `RENAME CLASS myOldGrid OF appGridList TO myNewGrid`

The final command, **ADD CLASS**, is used to add a class definition to a visual class library:

Command syntax:

ADD CLASS ClassName [OF ClassLibraryName1] TO ClassLibraryName2 [OVERWRITE]

Arguments:

ClassName Name of the class to be added to a library.

ClassLibraryName1 Name of library where class already exists.

ClassLibraryName2 Name of library where class is to be stored.

OVERWRITE Overwrites an existing class of the same name.

Examples:

```
ADD CLASS appGridLookup TO appGridBase
ADD CLASS appFrmOrder OF appOrders TO appFormBase
```

The second example, using **OF ClassLibraryName1**, is the same as using a copy command. Using the format of the first example, without specifying the source library, requires that the class definition be somewhere in the search sequence (see **CREATEOBJECT( )**).

THE CLASS DESIGNER

The most obvious characteristic of the Class Designer is that it looks like the Form Designer. There are many similarities. Even when you create a nonvisual, custom class, you get what looks like a form in the Class Designer window (see Figure 11.4), and that often confuses people at first.

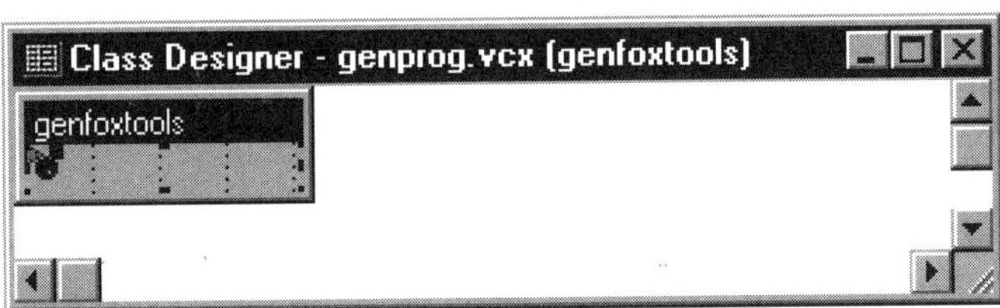

FIGURE 11.4 CUSTOM CLASS IN THE CLASS DESIGNER.

However, you can use the Class Designer to build classes not based on a form, including nonvisual custom classes, something you can't do in Form Designer. On the other hand, if you want a stand-alone form—one that is not a class—you must use the Form Designer. This raises an important question: Why would you want a stand-alone form stored in an SCX file instead of as a class in a class library? Shouldn't every object in an application be created by a class?

In the case of forms, they're always *based* on a form class. But when you've finished modifying the form in the Form Designer, you have the option to save it as a form (SCX) or as a class. This option would be only of academic interest except that a form created in the Class Designer has no Data Environment. To most people's thinking, this would be too much to give up, although some developers consider the Data Environment difficult to control.

NOTE

When you create a form as a class, it becomes a form object in your program with the standard approach: `oObjVar=CREATOBJECT("OBJECTNAME")`. With a form created in the Form Designer, a different approach is used:

```
DO FORM formname NAME oObjectName LINKED oObjectName
```

There's more to the command, but you can see that to make a form behave like an object, this **DO FORM** is quite different from the familiar **DO** command.

Whether or not you choose to create stand-alone forms, you'll still create classes with forms in the Class Designer. These form classes can then be used by the Form Designer—with Data Environment attached—to create stand-alone forms.

USING THE CLASS DESIGNER

Earlier in the chapter you were introduced to the Class Designer. Let's return to it now and go through a more detailed description.

Using the New Class dialog box (Figure 11.1) accomplishes the same as the `DEFINE CLASS <> AS <>` portion of the FoxPro code. Once you give the class a name, specify the class it's based on, and indicate in which class library it's to be stored, you are in the Class Designer window.

It's a good idea to arrange any toolbars you might need, specifically the Form Control, Form Designer, Layout, and Color Palette. Also, be sure to open the Project Manager to the **Class** tab or, better still, "tear off" the **Class** tab (as you see it in Figure 11.5) and place it with the toolbars. You'll can use this tool to drag and drop classes from your libraries into the Designer and marvel at how easy object-oriented programming can be. (Of course, first you must create the classes.) If you have the Professional Edition of Visual FoxPro, you can even go the Project Manager one better by using the Class Browser, (see the last section of this chapter for details).

Unless you are creating a nonvisual class, you'll go about your work just as you would in the Form Designer by, for example, dragging needed controls onto the form (or other container). This is exactly the same as specifying added objects in the code:

```
*———————— OBJECTS
*> Public Objects
```

```
ADD OBJECT <> AS <>
ADD OBJECT <> AS <> NOINIT
*> Protected Objects
ADD OBJECT PROTECTED <> AS <>
```

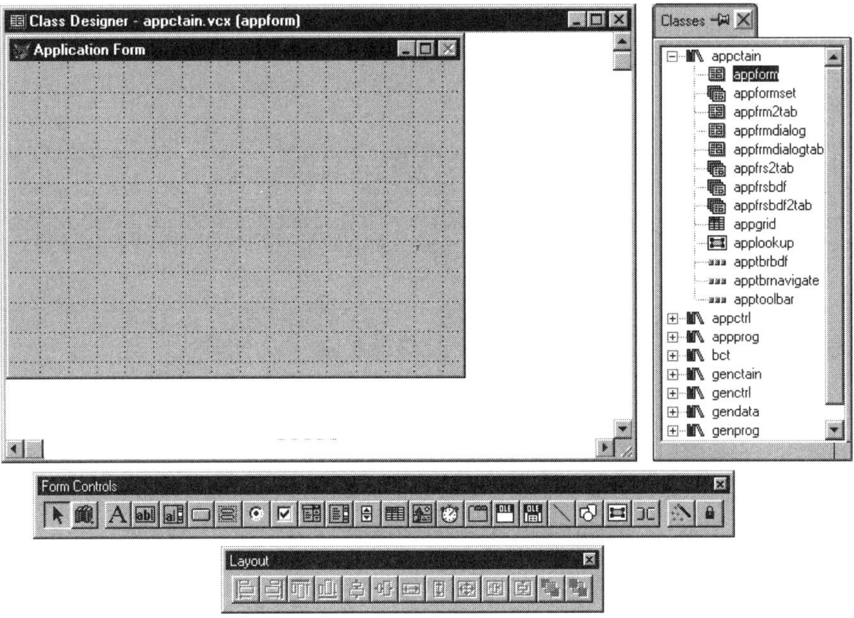

FIGURE 11.5 CLASS DESIGNER WINDOW WITH TOOLBARS.

Once you've assembled the visual elements, you can start to define the properties and methods that go with them.

There are two kinds of property and method definitions: those associated with events or properties of the FoxPro base classes; and those you create yourself. We'll get more into the *why* of creating new properties and methods in later chapters; here, mechanics are the main point. For a new property, with the Class Designer window activated, select **Class**, **New Property** from the menu and use the New Property dialog box (Figure 11.6).

This accomplishes the property definition as in the code, except for the values:

```
*> Public properties
<> = <>
*> Protected properties
```

```
PROTECTED <>, <>
*> Hidden properties
HIDDEN <> = <>
```

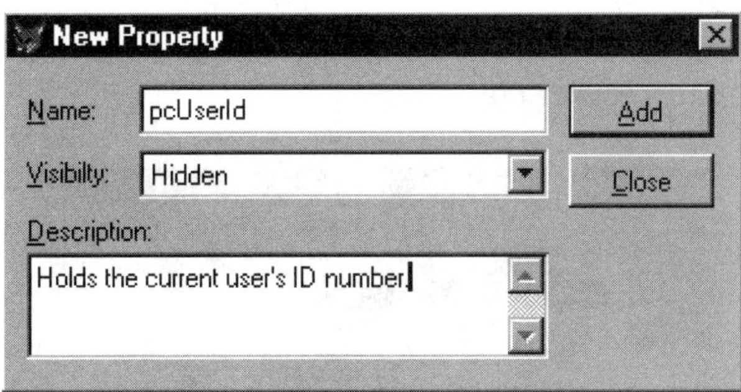

FIGURE 11.6 NEW PROPERTY DIALOG BOX.

Remember that values for properties are entered in the Property window. These values initialize the properties, the first thing that happens when an object is instantiated.

Methods start out like properties. Select **Class**, **New Method**. In the New Method dialog box (Figure 11.7), give the method a name and specify whether it's protected, hidden, or public.

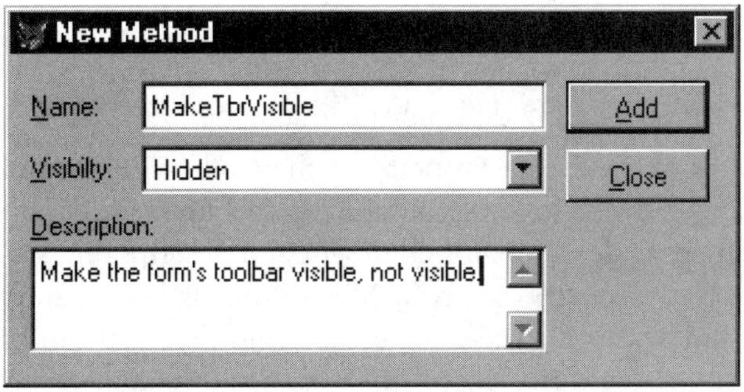

FIGURE 11.7 NEW METHOD DIALOG BOX.

In effect, when you've completed the dialog box, FoxPro has created the FUNCTION/ENDFUNC or PROCEDURE/ENDPROC portion of the code definition. As with properties, you do most of the work—in this case, writing code—by going to the method in the Property window and opening a Code window.

EDITING IN THE CLASS DESIGNER

After you've created your properties and methods or whenever you want to access any of the FoxPro versions, you are editing in the Class Designer. Editing has its own menu option: **Class**, **Edit Property/Method**, which brings up the Edit Property/Method dialog box

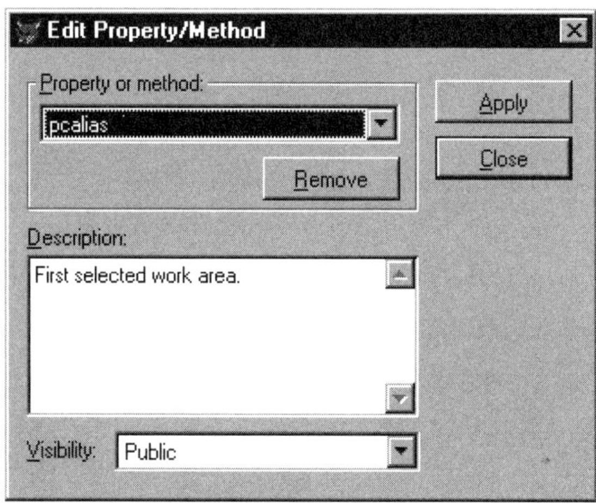

FIGURE 11.8 EDIT PROPERTY/METHOD DIALOG BOX.

This is the place where you remove or rename a property or method, something that can't be done in the Property window. On the other hand, you can't assign values to properties or edit code from this dialog box.

As you work in either the Property or the Code window, remember to do yourself and anyone who follows you a favor: Document what you do. FoxPro has thoughtfully provided areas for comment and description; you saw a couple of them in the New Property and New Method dialog boxes, and there are others. If you missed describing the class at the beginning, you can go to the menu and use **Class**, **Class Info** to access the Class Information tabbed dialog box, shown in Figures 11.9 and 11.10.

The **Class** tab has a space for a description of the class. You can also set the icons for the Form Control toolbar and a container if you choose to register your class with the Form Designer (more on this later). This is also the spot to declare your class available to other OLE-enabled programs. The **Members** tab has information on all the objects, methods, and user-defined properties in your class. This is occasionally useful for reference.

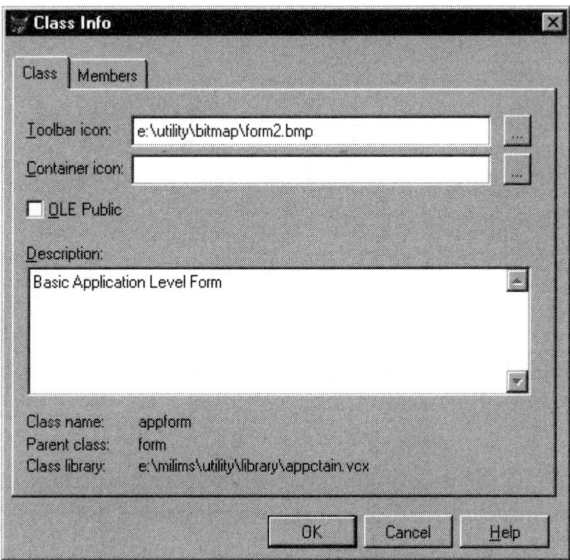

FIGURE 11.9 CLASS INFORMATION WINDOW, CLASS TAB.

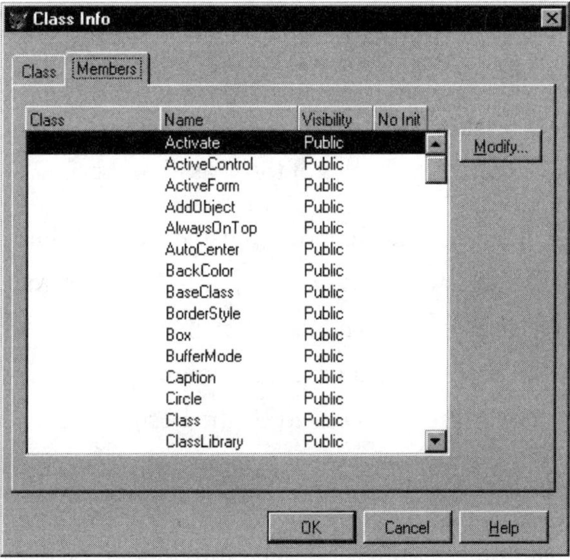

FIGURE 11.10 CLASS INFORMATION WINDOW, MEMBERS TAB.

NOTE

You can go through the members list to access the Edit Properties/Methods dialog box. Here, you can change the scope of FoxPro methods and properties to public, private, or hidden, something you can't do if you come to the dialog box from the menu. Although it's rarely used, this capability lets you protect—make invisible outside the class—key FoxPro methods such as **Init** and **Load**.

THE CLASS BROWSER

The Class Browser is an object-oriented programming tool included with the Professional Edition of Visual FoxPro. To make good use of it, you need to have a fairly extensive set of class libraries and classes. That will happen quickly as you build a class hierarchy and application framework.

As the number of user-defined classes increases, and the number of objects in an application mounts, one of the most serious problems of object-oriented programming is the need to keep track of what came from what and the difficulty of understanding the interactions between objects. That's where the Class Browser comes into play. It has many roles, but perhaps the most significant—day in and day out—is to help the programmer track and manage class hierarchy relationships. To do this, a good browser works not only while you write a program in the Designers but also when the program is running. This latter capability is necessary because objects don't become real until the program runs, when they become instantiated. It can be hard to debug nonexistent objects when a program isn't running.

Here are the primary capabilities of the Class Browser:

- Create, edit, copy, remove, move, rename, and redefine classes.
- Drop classes into the Form Designer and Class Designer.
- View the class hierarchy and list all members.
- Work with classes while a program is running.
- View the FoxPro code generated by the Designers.

The Class Browser is not a stand-alone class manager; it works in tandem with the Designers. However, like the Project Manager and the Command window, it's one of the tools you typically leave open throughout a working session.

NOTE If the Class Browser was available with the standard edition of FoxPro, I'd recommend using it as a matter of course. Although you can use the Project Manager to manipulate classes, the Class Browser gives you more tools and a far better presentation of the class hierarchy. Because a class browser is considered an integral part of object-oriented programming and should be in every developer's toolkit, Microsoft should include it with all versions.

The FoxPro Class Browser (itself written in Visual FoxPro) picks up where the Project Manager **Class** tab ends and goes many steps beyond. There are two ways to start it: From the menu, select **Tools**, **Class Browser**. In the Command window, use `DO (_BROWSER)`. The FoxPro system variable `_BROWSER` should contain the path to BROWSER.APP (normally located in the VFP folder). Depending on where you were when you started the program, the Class Browser will ask you to identify the class library to be browsed, or, if you were on a selected object, it will immediately show you the object's ancestry. This works whether you're in a designer or a running form.

The Class Browser window, seen in Figure 11.11, has been rearranged in Visual FoxPro 5.0. The interface is less crowded, and a large number of functions have been put into the Class Browser shortcut menu (also in Figure 11.11).

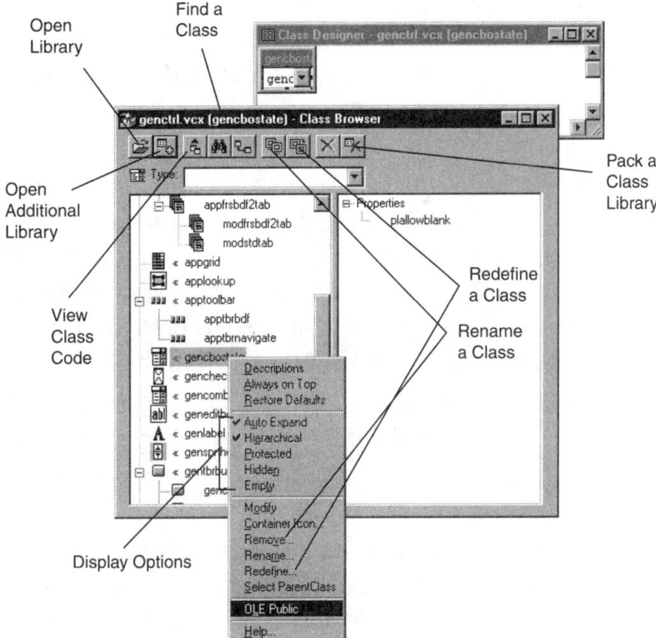

FIGURE 11.11 THE CLASS BROWSER WINDOW AND SHORTCUT MENU.

You'll probably find yourself using the shortcut menu much of the time, and that demonstrates the usefulness of shortcut menus for your own applications. Most of the Browser options break down into two groups: search and maintenance. Search means the ability to group classes a variety of ways or to find a particular class. This capability becomes valuable when you have enough classes to make visual searching difficult. The maintenance options are the most important. You'll use them often to do the class library housekeeping chores.

Housekeeping in the Libraries

As the class library grows, either by your own hand or from importing classes from elsewhere, you'll need the services provided by the Browser:

- **Create a subclass**. Start by opening a class library, selecting the class to be subclassed, and choosing the **Add Subclass** icon. This action will automatically add the new class to the current library.
- **Copy classes between libraries**. Open two copies of the Class Browser. In the second Browser window, highlight the library to receive the class. From the first window, drag the icon of the class to be copied to the second window (a plus sign indicates you are on target). You can also copy multiple classes by filtering the source class list and then dragging the entire library file icon to the target library.
- **Delete a class or class library**. Open the class library and select the class, library, or form you want to delete and then choose the **Remove** icon or shortcut menu option. Libraries and forms are immediately deleted from the disk; classes are marked as deleted in the VCX file and removed by using **Clean Up Library** from the Class menu.
- **Rename a class**. After opening the class library, select the class you want to rename, and then choose the **Rename** icon or shortcut option.
- **Change the parent class**. You can redefine the inheritance of a class by opening the class library, selecting the class you want to redefine, and choosing the **Redefine** icon or shortcut options. There are some rules: The new parent must be derived from the same base class as the original. You can redefine a grid as another class of grid, but you cannot redefine it as a form.

WARNING

Almost all these operations, especially delete, rename, and change parent, may have far-reaching repercussions if any of the classes or subclasses has already been used in applications. You should be certain that these changes won't leave sections of your programming without a class or, worse, with a class that is only partially functional.

In addition to these file and class-oriented tasks, the Class Browser can access member descriptions:

- **Change a class description**. In the Class Browser, select the class to change. In the edit box in the lower left, enter or edit the description.
- **Change a method or property description**. Start by selecting the class to change. Then, in the tabs, select **Method** or **Property**. Highlight the member to change and then use the edit box.
- **Change a class icon**. Select the class to change and right-click the class icon (above and to the left of the display area). In the open file dialog, select a new icon bitmap.

IMPORTING CLASSES AND CLASS LIBRARIES

All the housekeeping tools described in the previous section can be used to move and adapt classes from other class libraries. This is an important capability and not one to be taken lightly.

One of the central issues of building an application framework is how much of it you should code yourself and how much you can absorb, incorporate, and graft from other sources. At issue is the trade-off between expediency and comfort level. It can be expedient to use classes developed by someone else. Some types of classes (the more generic, the better) are fairly easily transferred. On the other hand, importing classes can leave you without an understanding of how they work. Consequently, when something breaks, you may spend an enormous amount of time hunting down the problem. Some programmers feel uncomfortable with this black box approach.

When you work with ActiveX controls, you will be dealing mostly with black boxes. You may know something about the exposed properties and methods, but you won't have access to the original code or any private methods. With ActiveX that's OK, because ActiveX objects are treated as *components*. They're part of an application framework perhaps but are not part of your FoxPro class hierarchy.

Incorporating FoxPro classes is another matter. The major complication is the class hierarchy itself and the chain of inheritance from class to subclass. It can be exceedingly difficult, even impossible, to slip other people's classes into your hierarchy without disrupting either the inheritance of your own classes or that of the imported class. Often, importing classes means taking them apart and rewriting them to fit. This task can be time-consuming, but it has the advantage of forcing you to understand the imported classes.

Another approach that usually works is to adopt entire class libraries, or even a class hierarchy, from another source and treat it as a separate component of your application framework, making no attempt to mix it with your own classes. This technique may create a certain amount of redundancy—classes with overlapping features—but if you have good documentation, you should be able to keep apples from becoming oranges.

VIEWING THE HIERARCHY

You can view the class hierarchy of a class or object either from a static or running program. The left portion of the Class Browser window by default shows the hierarchical relationships between classes. (You can also use the **Hierarchical** shortcut menu option to toggle to a list of classes displayed in alphabetical order.) Whether the view is alphabetical or hierarchical also affects the display of a filtered list. The right portion of the window gives you subset lists of class members based on objects, methods, properties, and instances. Instances are visible only with a running form or program.

If there comes a time when you have so many classes that scrolling through them becomes a chore, you can use the **Type** combo box to create a filter for the classes. You can use any of the wildcards or token characters shown in Table 11.1

You can also use the shortcut menu to select **Protected** (protected members), **Hidden** (hidden members), or **Empty** (members with nothing in them). These criteria act as filters for the classes.

TABLE 11.1

WILDCARD	DESCRIPTION
*	The asterisk is the wildcard for trailing characters in a class name. For example, use **APP*** to find all classes beginning with APP.
?	The question mark is the wildcard for any specific character in a class name (just as it is in DOS). For example, `myButton?` will match myButton1, myButton2, and so on.
%%	Bracketing with two percent signs signals a "contained in" search. For example, `%GRID%` will find all class names with GRID in them.
,	You can have multiple filter criteria by separating them with a comma. For example, `myButton?, %FORM%`.

VIEWING CLASS CODE

Working in the Class Designer or Form Designer, you don't see the structures that wrap around the properties and methods you define. One of the unique features of the Class Browser is its ability to display classes in the native FoxPro code. Some programmers, particularly if they come from a nonvisual programming background, find this a good way to proof their code and to get a better sense of how FoxPro is implementing the classes and methods.

To view class code, select the desired class in the left pane of the Class Browser and click the **View Class Code** icon in the Browser toolbar. A window titled Classbrowser.export appears with the code. You can cut segments of this code and paste them elsewhere, but you can't edit code in the window.

THE ACTIVE CLASS BROWSER

The Class Browser can play an active role in programming and debugging forms and other containers. Just as you are able to drag and drop classes from the Project

Manager class list to a working form, you can drag them from the Class Browser (but the Browser is much better at helping you find the right class). Here's how:

- **Adding an object to an open form.** Open the form in either the Form Designer or Class Designer. In the Class Browser, select the class to be added and drag its icon to the form. The class name in the hierarchy pane can't be dragged; instead, use the icon next to the **Type** box.
- **Adding an object to a running form.** This requires a little more setup, but it's a good way to test new classes as objects (short of creating a fully running program). In an open form, add the following code to the form's **Drag and Drop** event method:

```
LPARAMETERS oSource, nXCoord, nYCoord
LOCAL oNewObject
oNewObject = oSource.Parent.FormAddObject(THIS)
```

  Then save and run the form. You can drag and drop classes from the Class Browser to the running form. This technique is so useful in testing classes that many developers create special forms as a test bed. You can also reference the newly added object using the `oNewObject` variable, which is useful for gathering information about the object.

As you can see, the Class Browser is versatile, although you should be aware that it is not bulletproof. Any OOP program that allows you to tinker—if that's the word—with the internals of the class structure is also vulnerable to lockups and odd behavior. It's not necessarily the fault of the Class Browser but rather of the complex environment in which it must operate.

Chapter Wrap-Up

A taste of the class hierarchy and a rundown of class management tools does not a class hierarchy make. You need additional pieces: specifically, more information about creating methods within the classes (event management), designing a class hierarchy, and the details of implementing the visual classes. However, I hope that this introductory chapter gives you enough information about the tools to make you dangerous. Go forth and experiment.

CHAPTER 12

EVENTS AND METHODS

This chapter expands the introduction of classes and objects to include more details about events and methods, primarily by cataloging and explaining the built-in FoxPro methods. Much of this programming relates to creating the user interface, but for the time being we'll generally ignore interface design issues and concentrate on how events and methods work together.

As you may recall, an *event* in modern programming jargon (events are not exclusive to OOP) is an action taken by the user or a program that can be trapped (intercepted). Typical events are mouse clicks, keyboard presses, and window movement. When you click the right mouse button, it sends an electrical signal to a serial port of your computer. The signal is interpreted by the serial input/output handler and then by the mouse-handling code of the operating system. From that point, Windows sends a message to FoxPro, identified as "right mouse click." Because this is an event FoxPro recognizes, it checks the object currently running or in focus to see whether it has a **RightClick** method. If it does—most controls and the forms do—FoxPro then checks to see whether this particular object has any code in the method. If there is some code, such as commands to open a shortcut menu, FoxPro executes it. That's how event-driven programs work. Most of the time they are responding to events.

The fact that an object can respond to particular events has no significance in a program until you provide it with code that does the responding. In fact, this is the central issue of event-driven programming: which event methods should have code and how they should interact. But before you get to this thorny subject, it's important to understand the main topics of this chapter:

- The context of events and methods
- FoxPro's events and the methods that respond to them
- FoxPro's non-event methods
- Creating your own methods

NOTE

A significant part of the user interface is provided by the classes in your libraries (and components built from them), and they in turn are a significant part of an application framework. I've also found that even after completing a class hierarchy and application framework, I spend most of my time adjusting and expanding the event and method code in forms and controls. In a practical, day-to-day sense, event-driven programming is the beef in object-oriented programming.

THE EVENT MODEL

When you're describing the *event model*, one question that often arises is, Why is it such a big deal? It didn't used to be. In the days before graphical user interfaces, people communicated with a computer only through keystrokes. In effect, there was only one kind of user event—the keystroke—and only a few kinds of software devices to collect user keystroke events: menus, data entry areas, and function key options. Then, too, programs were linear. You started in one place and progressed back and forth from a sequence of program options, always along a fixed path. In this environment, there was no need to emphasize events.

Then along came the mouse, a harbinger of change in the user interface. Suddenly, the types and number of user events increased dramatically. On the Apple Macintosh, the mouse heralded another massive change: the graphical user interface (GUI). With it emerged an even more radical idea: People could select the paths between functions of a program in a nonlinear fashion. To interpret keystrokes and mouse clicks, the GUI used a multitude of ways, including a raft of new software devices for gathering user events: check boxes, scroll lists, radio buttons, and more. The GUI also allowed users to jump from one section of a program to another almost at will. This is what the FoxPro manuals identify as *modeless* operation. Users need not be in a specific mode (such as editing mode) to accomplish something; they can do pretty much what they need to do when they want to.

Even in the GUI's earliest days, there were dozens of user events, all needing interpretation and response. It was time for an event model or system.

If you study the typical office application, such as a word processor in the environment of Windows 95, you'll quickly understand how complicated the user event sequences have become. Soon, we'll be adding voice and pen input to the mainstream of user events. If you think the user interface is complicated now...

The ability of object-oriented programming to handle events is one of its major strengths. The object model provides a way to structure and harness the events. Instead of having events occur at random throughout the running of a program—making interpretation a nightmare—events are always associated with objects. Because objects are defined entities, it makes interpreting what the events are and what the response should be much easier (not easy; easier).

The object model also lends itself to the hop, skip, and jump open-endedness of a modeless user interface, because moving program execution between objects (or whole modules composed of objects) is an integral part of the system. Without object-oriented programming, you would have a difficult time allowing a program to become fully event-driven and not lose control.

EVENT SEQUENCES

First on the list of nitty-gritty topics is the *firing sequence* of events: the order in which events trigger (fire) during the creation or destruction of objects and as the user moves through the objects of a program. There are many such sequences. The major ones are the instantiation and destruction of a form and the entry and exit sequences for data entry controls.

A simple example involves a TextBox control, the one used to gather most of the typical character and numeric data in a form. As the user attempts to enter and then exit this control, the sequence of events goes like this: **When**, **GotFocus**, **KeyPress**, **InteractiveChange**, **Valid**, **LostFocus**. At each event you have the option of using code in the event method to check on the user, validate the entry, and so forth.

Some knowledge of firing sequences needs to be in the back of your mind when you're programming event methods. If you don't keep an eye on the sequence, it's easy to program a method and then discover that it never fires or it fires in such a way as to make your code useless. A faulty sequence is also the source of some sneaky bugs and explains why Visual FoxPro includes an Event Tracker in the new debugging system (more on this in Chapter 13). Event firing sequences will be mentioned often in this and later chapters.

THE FOXPRO EVENTS

For the umpteenth time, let's reiterate: FoxPro classes and the objects created from them recognize certain events. Each event has an associated event method. Although the method exists and you can bring it up in a Code window, by default it contains no code and will not fire. By putting code into an event method, you make the event execute the method.

In terms of syntax, all the Visual FoxPro event methods are written this way:

PROCEDURE Object.MouseWheel
LPARAMETERS [nIndex,] nDelta, nShift, nXCoord, nYCoord

This code indicates that the events will trigger a method of the same name; the method has the construction of a procedure and can take certain parameters if any. With the exception of the **Init** event method, the parameters (or arguments) are not user-definable. Most of the time you will create event methods in the Class Designer or Form Designer, but they can also be created in a program file with ordinary code.

NOTE

You don't have to wait for an event to trigger the event methods. You can call them at any time (like this: `oObject.Click()`) just as you would any other method. This capability can be useful when you don't want to proliferate a piece of code, such as in a particular control's **Click** event method. You can call it from wherever you need it.

The following listing provides an overview of the Visual FoxPro events and their syntax. They're grouped by the objects most associated with them, although some of them, such as **Init** and **Error**, are part of all objects. I've attempted to give you the practical flavor of each event—how it fits into day-to-day programming—and also to rank the events in terms of importance and frequency of use.

It's tempting to assume that all events are equal and that you should strive to employ as many as possible. Resist the temptation. Experience will teach you that only a few of the events are used repeatedly, and they often contain a minimal amount of code. The other events are useful in specialized situations. You need to know they're available, but there's no point in using them until necessary.

What are the key event methods? The list will depend on who's putting it together. In part, it's a matter of coding style and the type of class hierarchy. The FoxPro manuals describe a subset of core events: **Load**, **Unload**, **Init**, **Destroy**,

Click, **DblClick**, **RightClick**, **GotFocus**, **LostFocus**, **KeyPress**, **MouseDown**, **MouseMove**, **MouseUp**, **InteractiveChange**, and **ProgrammaticChange**. The following listing of all the FoxPro events amends Microsoft's suggestions. Key events are marked with an asterisk (*).

EVENTS FOR CONTROLS

DownClick

Trigger: The down arrow key is used in a spinner. This event and **UpClick** work only in Spinner controls when either the Spinner arrows or arrow keys are used. Rarely used event.

DropDown

Trigger: The list portion of a ComboBox drops open. Rarely used event.

RangeHigh

Triggers: Spinner and TextBox on losing control. Fires before **Valid**, but it's better to use the **Valid** event to check user high or low entry for Spinners and TextBoxes.

RangeLow

Triggers: Spinner and TextBox on losing control. See **RangeHigh**.

UpClick

Trigger: User presses up arrow key or Spinner arrow up. See **DownClick**.

*Valid

Trigger: A control is about to lose focus. This holdover from older versions of FoxPro is still quite important. It's used in several controls, notably TextBoxes, to validate the user's entry (hence the name). In a TextBox (and not necessarily in other controls) if the **Valid** contains code, FoxPro will fire this event whenever **Enter**, **Esc**, **Tab**, or a mouse movement is used. In short, there is no way for the user to avoid the validation. If you return .F. or 0, users won't be able to leave the control. The **Valid** event method can be the gateway to a large number of data checking and user support mechanisms.

When

Trigger: A control is about to receive focus. If the **When** succeeds, the **GotFocus** event fires. Along with **Valid**, this is one of the last holdovers from the old FoxPro **READ** event structure. **When** is occasionally used to deny access to TextBoxes and other controls. It's different from using the Enable and Disable properties, because it can be selective about what is allowed in.

EVENTS FOR DATA ENVIRONMENTS

AfterCloseTables

Trigger: After the tables of a data environment have been closed and before the **Destroy** event. This event is associated only with Data Environments and isn't used very much. It's not the last event to fire on the exit sequence from a report or form, and most cleanup routines are put into the **Destroy** events of either the DE or the form.

BeforeOpenTables

Trigger: A data environment's tables have just been opened but the process is not complete. Occurs before a form's **Load** event, but not before the **OpenTables** method (which automatically loads a Data Environment's tables). This is one of the first user-accessible moments in the loading of a Data Environment (either report or form) and is sometimes used to implement environment settings that need to be in place before the tables are fully open.

EVENTS FOR ERROR TRAPPING

*Error

Parameters: **nError** (number of error), **nMethod** (method name), **nLine** (line number).

Trigger: A run-time error in the code. Returns the FoxPro error number, the name of the offending method, and the program code line number. All classes, including custom classes, have this event. It is an integral part of any application error-trapping system, which we'll cover as part of an application framework.

ErrorMessage

Trigger: **Valid** event returns false; **ErrorMessage** allows an error message to be sent. It's easy to set up a reboot situation with this one, so don't use it. Instead, use a more comprehensive error and validation trapping approach .

EVENTS FOR FORMS AND PAGES

*Load

Trigger: A Form or FormSet is about to be instantiated. A FormSet is loaded first. This event occurs after the Data Environment is instantiated but before any part of a Form is instantiated. Because a Form's controls connect to their data before the Form's **Init** event, the **Load** event method is often used to do data management setup needed by the form. This includes executing SQL **SELECT**s to fill arrays and establishing relations not set by the Data Environment.

*Unload

Trigger: A Form or FormSet is unloaded from memory. This event tends to be used as a bookend with the **Load** event. Anything you do in the **Load**, such as open tables or set environment variables, is undone here. This is also the method to use in Forms to return a value to the calling program.

*Activate

Trigger: A Form, FormSet, or Page object is activated or a ToolBar is shown. This event method is used primarily to make sure that the working environment of an object (typically a form or page) is correct. This task often includes checking the tables and enabling or disabling controls.

*Deactivate

Trigger: As a Form, FormSet, Page, or ToolBar loses focus. Although not used as often as the **Activate** event method, this event can be used to make sure that the environment is reset or that something is checked (such as a valid data entry) before the user leaves a form or page.

Paint

Trigger: A Form or ToolBar is repainted. This event fires often, so be cautious about putting code in the method. It could affect performance.

***QueryUnload**

Trigger: A Form is about to close because of a click in the window close box or a program command. Does not trigger if the Form is **RELEASED**. You can use this event method to make sure the form should be closed. A user dialog box might be appropriate. If the form shouldn't be closed, use the **NODEFAULT** command, which prevents the form from closing. Some developers use this event method to coordinate with the **ON SHUTDOWN** command, which prevents the user from closing FoxPro without first deciding whether the forms can be closed.

UIEnable

Trigger: Whenever a Page in a PageFrame is activated or deactivated. This is one of the more inscrutable events. Put as simply as possible, the event fires in each control of a page as the page is activated or deactivated. What would you use it for? Possibly to make sure that a critical control (or a temperamental one) such as a ComboBox has the correct data.

Events for Grids

AfterRowColChange

Parameter: **nColindex** (number of the new column).

Trigger: A user moves from one column or row in a Grid to another. Follows **GetFocus** and **When** events. This event can be used to execute changes in the grid's appearance based on the focus (and cursor) being in a particular column. Some of the Dynamic properties of the grid come into play here. You might also use this one to do some data management in the background.

BeforeRowColChange

Parameter: **nColindex** (column number).

Trigger: A user changes row or column in a Grid and before the **LostFocus** event. In a sense, this event can act like the **Valid** event of other controls, allowing you to check the user or the grid's condition before the user is allowed to move to another row or column.

Deleted

Parameter: **nRecNo** (current record number)

Trigger: A user clicks in the delete column of a grid (either delete or recall). This event can be used to react to deletions and sometimes as a simple way of letting the user "mark" a record (users don't have to know it's a deletion).

Scrolled

Parameter: **nDirection** (direction of scroll)

Trigger: Scroll bars of a Grid are clicked or moved, either by user or with **DoScroll** method. You could do some rearranging of the grid based on the user scrolling, but it's unclear exactly what that would be.

EVENTS FOR THE KEYBOARD

KeyPress

Parameter: **nKeyCode** (code of key pressed)

Trigger: A user presses and releases a key. The object with focus receives the event. There are older FoxPro functions that do similar things (**INKEY( )**, **READKEY( )**, and **LASTKEY( )**). As much as possible, especially within objects, favor the **KeyPress** event method instead. It's not that the old ways don't work; they're just—well—old.

EVENTS FOR THE MOUSE

*Click

Trigger: The user clicks the mouse button over a control, or a program command simulates the event. This is probably the most used event method in FoxPro. It's available to do something when the user selects an object (which usually requires clicking on it). With CommandButton and toolbar controls, it's used to initiate actions and call routines, among many other things. It's not uncommon for the bulk of an application's programming to be tied to **Click** event methods. It's important to note that FoxPro fires the **Click** event for more than mouse clicks. Under certain circumstances, it's also triggered by **Spacebar** and **Enter** key presses. In short, any kind of user selection action in or around objects that have a **Click** event will fire it.

***DblClick**

Trigger: The user double-clicks the left mouse button. If you've paid any attention to how commercial programs handle mouse clicks, or if you grew up with a Macintosh, you'll know that a double-click is used for a "confirmed" user selection. How you implement its use in your applications is up to you, but it's a good idea to have a convention and stick with it.

***RightClick**

Trigger: The user clicks the right mouse button. Once upon a time, this was an orphan button. (It was even taboo on an Apple computer.) Now we have shortcut menus triggered with the **RightClick**, and in Visual FoxPro 5.0 you should standardize on this click for that purpose.

MiddleClick

Trigger: The user clicks the middle mouse button. This event was never used much, and now that we have the **MouseWheel** on the newest Office 97–enabled mice, that's probably where you should put your code.

MouseDown

Parameters: **nButton** (1 = left, 2 = right, 4 = middle), **nShift** (state of keys), **nXCoord**,**nYCoord** (position coordinates).

Trigger: A user presses a mouse button. This event distinguishes between mouse buttons and can be used in combination with the **Shift**, **Ctrl**, and **Alt** keys.

MouseMove

Parameters: **nButton** (1 = left, 2 = right, 4 = middle), **nShift** (state of keys), **nXCoord,nYCoord** (position coordinates).

Trigger: The user moves the mouse over a control or other object. This event can trigger continuously, raising havoc with the internal registers of FoxPro. Use with care.

MouseUp

Parameters: **nButton** (1 = left, 2 = right, 4 = middle), **nShift** (state of keys), **nXCoord**, **nYCoord** (position coordinates).

Trigger: The user releases a mouse button. Same type of behavior as **MouseDown**.

MouseWheel

Parameters: **nDelta** (change in position), **nShift** (state of keys), **nXCoord**, **nYCoord** (location of mouse).

Trigger: The user scrolls up or down with the wheel. This is the newest of FoxPro's events and won't become a factor in user interface design until Microsoft Office 97 becomes widely used. Its day will come, though, because the zoom capability of the wheel is compelling.

DragDrop

Parameters: **oSource**, (source object), **nXCoord**, **nYCoord**, (location of mouse).

Trigger: A drag-and-drop operation is completed. Event is triggered by the object receiving the dragged object. Drag and drop is a wonderful, although specialized, capability. You'll use this and the **DragOver** event to implement it. See Chapter 18 for details.

DragOver

Parameters: **oSource**, (source object), **nXCoord**, **nYCoord**, (location of mouse), **nState**, (number of transition state).

Trigger: A control is dragged over a target object. The type of drag is in **nState**, where 0 = control in range of target, 1 = control moving out of range, and 2 = control over the target.

EVENTS FOR OBJECTS IN GENERAL

*Init

Parameters: **parm1**, **parm2...**

Trigger: After an object is created, this is the first event. In a container, especially a form, it means that all the form's controls and other objects have been created before the form's **Init** fires. This event method is distinguished by being the only one that can receive user-defined arguments and parameters. (All the others have event parameters fixed by FoxPro.) That makes **Init** indispensable for passing information into an object. It's also the location for a lot of code dealing with properties and other environmental management. It's used less often for data management, because the form's controls already connect to data before **Init** fires.

Destroy

Trigger: An object is released. This is the "sayonara" event method, sometimes used to clean up the environment and perform other housekeeping before an object is completely released. However, because of the use of **Load** and **Unload** to handle the data setup and cleanup, many developers prefer to keep all that kind of code in those two event methods.

DoCmd

Parameter: **cCommand** (specifies the FoxPro command to execute).

Executes a Visual FoxPro command for an instance of the Visual FoxPro application automation server, ApplicationObject.DoCmd(cCommand).

***GotFocus**

Trigger: An object receives focus by user action or in code. Can be used to test where the user has moved among many objects. Unlike the **When** event, **GotFocus** can't be used to prevent the user from accessing an object.

***LostFocus**

Trigger: An object loses focus. Only when Enabled and Visible properties are .T.. Like **GotFocus**, this event can be used to test whether a user is leaving an object. It is particularly useful in controls in which the **Valid** event doesn't always fire: ComboBoxes, ListBoxes, and Spinners.

***InteractiveChange**

Trigger: A user changes the value in a control with either the mouse or the keyboard. This event can be invaluable in monitoring changes—not accidental access—to data. It gives you a way to do things that should happen only if the user changes a value. It's a powerful capability, but you should be aware that in controls such as a TextBox, where the user enters keystrokes, the event will fire with each key.

ProgrammaticChange

Trigger: The value of a control is changed during the run of a program. In the same vein as the **InteractiveChange** event, this one can be used to monitor changes to values based on program commands.

Moved

Trigger: An object has been moved or a container's position has been reset by program. This is used mostly to monitor the movement of forms.

***Resize**

Trigger: An object is resized either by a user or with code. Chapter 11 showed an example of how this event is used to synchronize a PageFrame size with a form. Many similar uses are common, and this event usually gets built into a high level of the class hierarchy.

EVENTS FOR TOOLBARS

AfterDock

Trigger: A ToolBar object has been docked, either by a user or with a dock method. All three toolbar events are used to monitor and adjust toolbar positions.

BeforeDock

Parameter: **nLocation** (location of docking position).

Trigger: A ToolBar is about to be docked. Used to change ToolBar before it is docked.

UnDock

Trigger: A ToolBar is moved from its docked position.

EVENTS FOR THE TIMER CLASS

Timer

Trigger: The number of milliseconds in the **interval** property has elapsed.

Several events are used only when Visual FoxPro converts older FoxPro programs: **ReadActivate**, **ReadDeactivate**, **ReadShow**, **ReadValid**, and **ReadWhen**. These events are provided for backward compatibility only. That's equivalent to saying, "Don't use them."

Many events have the **nIndex** parameter, which passes the number of the currently active control. This parameter was originally designed to help programmers identify controls in a control array, but the scheme was never fully implemented by Microsoft. For that reason, it's not listed here as one of the parameters.

NOTE

In the previous edition of this book, I included a massive table showing which events were associated with which objects, but in practice there's no time and little point to using it. People learn the associations they need—a rather limited set—by using them. It will probably do you more good to simply review the **Methods** tab of the Properties window as you create classes and forms.

The "Missing" Events

As inclusive and powerful as the Visual FoxPro event list is, it doesn't cover everything. Two significant kinds of events—events for data management and menu selection—are not part of the official event list. This omission is indicative of the partial implementation of the object model in FoxPro. The data management part may never be fully object-oriented, because it's not an object-oriented data system. Menus should be part of the object model, but they're not. That bothers purists, and there are a couple of schemes that bypass the Visual FoxPro menu system to make menus more object-oriented, most notably the one in YAG's (Yair Allen Griver) *Visual FoxPro Codebook*.

Using the FoxPro menu system "as is" works, but in designing your applications you need to keep in mind that menus are an important source of user events that trigger all kinds of program activity. The same goes for much of data management, where processing goes on outside the FoxPro object-oriented event system. Even error trapping for data management is different from the one associated with objects. Instead of the **Error** event, you need to rely on the old FoxPro error trapping "event," which is monitored by the **ON ERROR** command.

The Role of Events

As important as events are, it's necessary to put their role in perspective. Here is a small scenario: A developer is creating a UserLogin object with the purpose of acquiring the name and password of the user to see whether her or she has the rights to enter the program. To accomplish this, a **UserLogin** class has these features:

- Variables to hold the name and password of the user.
- A form to get information (name and password) from the user.
- The ability to detect when the user has entered a name and a password.
- The ability to search a table to find a match for the user's name and password.
- The ability to respond to the user if no match is found.
- The ability to remove the form and object.

Which of these features are related to FoxPro events? Here's the analysis:

- Variables to hold the name and password of the user (**Properties**).
- A form to get information from the user (**a screen form programmatically started**).
- The ability to detect when the user has entered a name and a password (**Valid event with event methods**).
- The ability to search a table to find a match for the user's name and password (**non-event method**).
- Respond to the user if no match is found (**non-event method for a dialog box**).
- Remove the form and object (**programmatic event with event methods**).

In this typical configuration, about two-thirds of the scenario involves methods, but only half (or less) of them are user events. Events are important, but they're not the only thing happening in objects.

METHODS, EVENTS, AND OBJECTS

In this section, we'll take a look at all three types of methods: built-in FoxPro methods, event methods (method code that you write), and user-defined (non-event) methods. Although all methods are constructed in a similar way, the type of method affects how they are written and used.

BUILT-IN FOXPRO METHODS

For all practical purposes, the built-in FoxPro methods are just another set of FoxPro functions, with one caveat: They must be associated with an object. That object is always a Visual FoxPro base class or one of its subclasses. You can't use a method like this: `SetFocus()`. It must include an object reference: `gridObject.SetFocus()`.

Most of the methods are clustered in a few categories based on function: control management, display and graphics, data, grids, list controls, object management, and toolbars. As you build an application, you'll use quite a few of these methods, especially when working with controls, forms, and grids.

Table 12.1 lists all the methods along with their arguments and a brief description. To keep the table from being even longer than it is, the following abbreviations for reference objects are used: **o.** = object, **f.** = Form, **s.** = FormSet, **c.** = control, **a.** = container, **g.** = Grid, **t.** = ToolBar.

TABLE 12.1 VISUAL FOXPRO METHODS ARRANGED BY USE

METHOD	ARGUMENTS	DESCRIPTION
CONTROLS IN GENERAL		
c.Drag([nAction])	**nAction**: number for action to perform.	Control drag action: 0 = cancel drag, 1 = (default) Begin dragging, 2 = End dragging (drop).
c.SetFocus( )		Assigns focus to a control. Control must be enabled and visible.
DISPLAY AND GRAPHICS		
o.Box(nXCoord1, nYCoord1, nXCoord2, nYCoord2)	**nXCoord1**, **nYCoord1**: starting point of box. **nXCoord2, nYCoord2**: endpoint of box.	Draws a rectangle (box) on a form.
o.Circle(nRadius, nXCoord, nYCoord [,nAspect])	**nRadius**: radius of circle. **nXCoord**, **nYCoord**: center of circle. **nAspect**: aspect ratio.	Draws a circle or ellipse on a form. **nAspect** = 1.0, circle; > 1.0, vertical ellipse, < 1.0, horizontal ellipse.
o.Cls( )		Clears graphics and text from a form.
o.Draw( )		Repaints a form.
o.Hide( )		Sets Visible property to `.f.` and hides the specified object.

METHOD	ARGUMENTS	DESCRIPTION
o.Line(nXcoord2, nYCoord2)	**nXcoord1, nYCoord1**: starting coordinates. **Xcoord2, nYCoord2** **n**: ending coordinates.	Draws a line on a form.
o.Move(nLeft [,nTop [,nWidth [,nHeight]]]	**nLeft**: column coordinate. **nTop**: row coordinate. **nWidth**: width in columns. **nHeight**: height in rows.	Moves an object either in a form (for controls) or on the screen (for forms). Use the 0,0 format for positioning.
o.Point(nXCoord, nYCoord)	**nXCoord**: horizontal. **nYCoord**: vertical.	Returns the color of a specified point as an RGB value.
[s].o.Print[(cText)]	**cText**: character string to print.	Displays (prints) a character string on a form.
[s].o.Pset(nXCoord, nYCoord [, nColor])	**nXCoord**: horizontal. **nYCoord**: vertical. **nColor**: RGB value.	Sets a point on a form to a specific color (RGB value such as 255,210,255).
[s].o.Refresh( )		Repaints form or control and refreshes all values.
[s].o.Show([nStyle])	**nStyle**: 1 = modal, ` 2 = modeless (default)	Displays a form and optionally sets as modal or modeless.
[s].o.TextHeight, (cText)	**cText**: text string. ScaleMode units.	Returns test height in current
[s].o.TextWidth, (cText)	**cText**: text string.	Returns width of text expression in current ScaleMode units.
o.Zorder, ([nOrder])	**nOrder**: 0 = front of z-order (default), 1 = back of z-order.	Places specified object at front or back of its graphical level.
DATA		
o,DataToClip ([cTable] nRecords] [, nClipFormat])	**cTable**: source table. **nRecords**: number of recs . **NClipFormat**: delimiter.	Copies records from a FoxPro table to the Windows Clipboard.
d.CloseTables( )		Closes all tables and views of a data environment.

METHOD	ARGUMENTS	DESCRIPTION
GRIDS		
g.ActivateCell (nRow, nCol)	**nRow,nCol**: row and column to activate.	Activates a cell in a Grid column.
g.AddColumn (nIndex)	**nIndex**: column position to add a column.	Adds a column to a Grid. Other columns move 1 right.
g.DeleteColumn (nindex)	**nIndex**: order number of column in grid.	Removes a column from a Grid.
g.DoScroll (nDirection)	**nDirection**: scroll direction as a number.	Scroll Grid control: 0 = up, 1 = down, 2 = page up, 3 = page down, 4 = left, 5 = right, 6 = page left, 7 = page right.
LIST CONTROLS		
c.AddItem (cItem[, nIndex][, nColumn])	**cItem**: character expression to add. **nIndex**: order position. **nColumn**: column position.	Adds an item to a ComboBox or ListBox with or without index. **nIndex** is for the order of items and does not move with an item for insertions or deletions.
c.AddListItem (cItem [, nItemID] [, nColumn])	**cItem**: character expression to add. **nItemId**: unique ID for an item. **nColumn**: column position.	Adds an item to a ComboBox or ListBox; used with **nItemId**, the unique and persistent ID for each item. Use with RowSourceType > 0.
o.Clear( )		Clears the contents of a ComboBox or ListBox with RowSourceType = 0.
c.IndexToItemId (nIndex)	**nIndex**: position number of an item in the control.	Returns an item ID for a given item index.
c.ItemIDToIndex (nItemID)	**nItemId**: ID number of item in a control.	Returns a position number for an item ID.
c.RemoveItem (nIndex)	**nIndex**: position number of item in control	Removes an item from the specified control.
c.RemoveListItem (nItemid)	**nItemID**: unique ID of item in a control	Removes an item from the specified control by its ID.

METHOD	ARGUMENTS	DESCRIPTION
c.Requery( )		Refreshes the row data source for ListBox or ComboBox.
OBJECTS		
o.AddObject (cName, cClass [, cOLEClass] [,ainit1,ainit2...])	**cName**: name of object. **cClass**: class of object. **cOLEClass**: OLE class. **ainit1,ainit2**: init event parameters.	Adds an object (usually a control) to a container at run time.
o.CloneObject (newName)	**NewName**: name of the new object.	Completely duplicates an object.
o.DoVerb[Verb]	**Verb**: either the name of an OLE verb (play) or a numeric index value.	Executes an OLE verb for the specified object. Use index values to denote verb.
o.Eval(cExpression)	**cExpression**: data type.	Used to execute a FoxPro expression in OLE automation.
o.Quit( )		Quits an instance of Visual FoxPro in OLE automation.
o.ReadExpression (cPropertyName)	**cPropertyName**: name of property to return expression from.	Returns the value (expression) of the specified property. Design time only.
o.ReadMethod (cMethod)	**cMethod**: name of the method.	Returns the code from a specified method.
o.Release		Releases FormSet or Form.
o.RemoveObject (cObjectName)	**cObjectName**: name of object to remove.	Removes a specified object from its container.
o.ResetToDefault (cPropertyName cEventName I cMethodName)	**cPropertylcEventNam elcMethodName**: name of what is to be reset.	Resets the value of properties and methods to their original value (when they were created).
o.SetVar (cVariablename, vValue)	**cVariableName**: name f the variable. **vValue**: o initial value.	Creates an OLE automation variable.

Method	Arguments	Description
o.SaveAs(cFileName [,oObjectName])	**cFileName**: name of SCX file to use or create. **nObjectName**: name of object to be filed.	Save named object as an SCX file. Class of named object must already exist in a VCX file.
o.SaveAsClass (ClassLIbName, ClassName [,Description])	**ClassLibName**: name of the VCX file. **ClassName**: nameof class. **Description**: optional description.	Saves an object (instance) as a class definition in a VCX file. The object must already belong to a class with a VCX file.
a.SetAll(cProperty, Value [,cClass])	**cProperty**: property to set. **Value**: setting value. **cClass**: class name.	Assigns property settings to all or various controls in a container.
o.WriteExpression(cPropertyName, cExpression)	**cPropertyName**: name of property to write to. **cExpression**: value to write into property.	Writes a value expression into a specified property. Available at design time only.
c.WriteMethod (MethodName, MethodText)	**MethodName**: name of method. **MethodText**: code.	Writes text (code) to the specified method. Available at design time and for existing method only.
Toolbars and Timer		
t.Dock(nLocation [,X,Y])	**nLocation**: docking location. **X**: x coordinate. **Y**: y coordinate.	Docks the ToolBar at specified location.
Timer.Reset		Resets the timer to 0.

Creating and Using Methods

Of the two kinds of methods that are user-definable (event methods and user-defined methods), the event method is the most used. Most applications are built from FoxPro classes, and the majority of the operative code is located within event methods such as **Click** and **Activate**. However, for the same reasons programmers have developed user-definable functions, you'll also create a fair number of your own methods, ones not associated with an event.

Both kinds of user-definable methods are often confused with standard functions and procedures, probably because they *are* functions and procedures; only the object-oriented context makes them different. Methods are associated with specific objects and are active only when the object has been created (instantiated). This is as true of event methods and user-defined methods as it is of the built-in FoxPro methods. Here's the basic syntax for using a method:

Command syntax:

Parent.Object.Method([eExpression1, eExpression2,...])

Arguments:

Parent The parent object (usually a container) or any chain of objects sufficient to identify the primary object of the method.

Object The immediate object associated with the method.

eExpression1... The arguments of a method that will take parameters.

Examples:

```
frmNewMembers.grdFeesPaid.ACTIVATECELL(3,4)
cmdQuit.SETFOCUS()
oNewScreen.PRINT("SELECTIONS")
```

Parentheses are required for methods that return values (they are functions) but should be used on all methods as a matter of convention. Many developers also put parentheses at the end of event methods so they are clearly visible: `Init()`, `Click()`.

You may have noticed that two of the examples for the names of objects being referenced had prefixes such as txt and cmd. This is a convention, widely adopted but certainly not required, that object names are prefixed with an abbreviation for their base class. In this way, you can tell at a glance what type of object is being referenced. Table 12.2 lists are the suggested prefixes.

TABLE 12.2 OPTIONAL OBJECT REFERENCE PREFIXES

BASE CLASS	OBJECT PREFIX	EXAMPLE
CheckBox	chk	chkWantList
Column	grc	grcPrimary
ComboBox	cbo	cboNewName
CommandButton	cmd	cmdQuit
CommandGroup	cmg	cmgMain
Container Object	cnt	cntChoices
Control Object	ctl	ctlBoxMenu
Custom	cus	cusMyFave
DataEnvironment	den	denOpenFile
EditBox	edt	edtOldNotes
Form	frm	frmFileOpen
FormSet	frs	frsOrderEntry
Grid	grd	grdMaster
Header	grh	grhPrimary
Image	img	imgEmployee
Label	lbl	lblOneMail
Line	lin	linStripes
ListBox	lst	lstTypes
OLE Bound Control	ole	oleAccessBox
OLE Container Control	olc	olcExcel
Option Button	opb	opbVote
OptionGroup	opg	opgProducts
Page	pfp	pfpSports
PageFrame	pgf	pgfNewPaper
Shape	shp	shpSunBurst
Spinner	spn	spnRecords
TextBox	txt	txtCustomerName
Timer	tmr	tmrLateAgain
ToolBar	tlb	tblLayout

Some confusion about methods may also arise from the various ways FoxPro provides to create methods for an object:

- **Class Designer Menu: Class, New Method**. This approach accomplishes the same thing as defining a method in a program file, but the form of the output is hidden behind the Class Designer user interface, so you don't see constructions such as **DEFINE PROC/ENDPROC**.
- **Form Designer Menu: Form, New Method**. Functionally identical to using the Class Designer.
- **Form Designer, Method tab, double-click method (or event)**. This route is used to access any method associated with an object, and it is the easiest way to create and edit event methods.
- **Program file, DEFINE CLASS**. In a PRG file you define methods as part of the class definitions using **DEFINE FUNC/ENDFUNC** and **DEFINE PROC/ENDPROC**, which look suspiciously like normal function and procedure definitions.

If you create your own object with a class definition, all four ways of adding (or editing) a method are available. Base classes are not directly editable, but you can modify some of the property values and methods when a base class is used in creating another class or subclass.

No matter where you are creating or editing a method, the approach is exactly the same as the one you would use to create a standard function or procedure, with the exception of the variations in function and procedure declarations. You still use parameters, usually with the **LPARAMETER** keyword in procedures or the new parameter approach (see the following example) for functions; if it's a function, you use **RETURN <value>**. Here's a typical example, in this case in a class definition:

```
DEFINE CLASS spnRecords AS Spinner
    *<Other class code>

  *---------- METHODS
  *> Public methods
  FUNCTION RecExist(nRecNo)
    RETURN IIF( nRecno <= RECCOUNT(),.T.,.F.)
  ENDFUNC
ENDDEFINE
```

NOTE

The optional format `FUNCTION functionName( parameters )` is rapidly becoming the standard convention for this type of method. Not only does it make it clear that this function takes arguments, but it also specifies those arguments, and they are automatically turned into local parameters.

The reasons for creating methods in an application are as diverse and unlimited as they are for creating functions and procedures. There are recognizable types based on functionality, including the following: event methods (which respond to events), property methods (which return a property value or act on a property), processing methods (typically used in database work, but also might involve calculations), management methods (those that help manage objects), and user interface methods (which help manipulate the UI objects). In the later chapters on implementing an application framework, you'll see many more examples of different types of methods.

Chapter Wrap-Up

This chapter serves to introduce the built-in FoxPro events and methods, putting them into context with the event model. Even when it comes to creating your own methods, there's nothing particularly difficult about the mechanics; most programmers with FoxPro experience will immediately recognize the similarities between methods and functions or procedures. The correlation between events and methods is an OOP fundamental. FoxPro handles it in its own way, and it should be easy enough to understand as a concept. You can expect to encounter complications in managing the user interface of an application, but that's a subject for Chapters 16–18.

CHAPTER 13

DEBUGGING

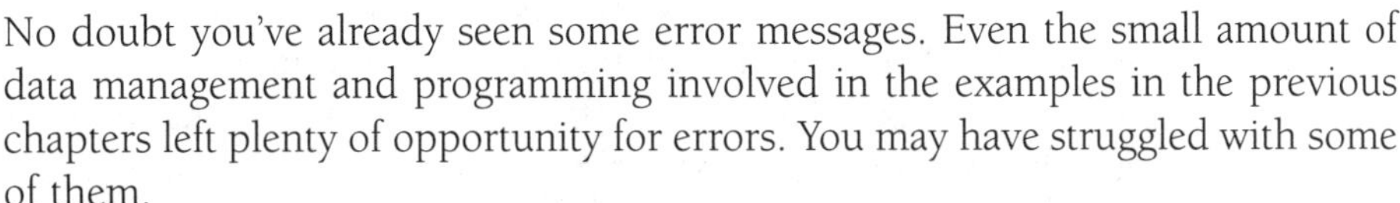

No doubt you've already seen some error messages. Even the small amount of data management and programming involved in the examples in the previous chapters left plenty of opportunity for errors. You may have struggled with some of them.

Wisdom says: It's not that you make mistakes—we all do—what counts is how well you learn from them and how fast you can recover. Like many wise observations, this one is easy to say and not easy to do, especially when it comes to debugging. Visual FoxPro 5.0 provides a new and powerful set of tools for debugging, and we'll spend most of this chapter explaining how to use them. But they won't be enough. Good debugging, which includes not only finding and fixing problems but also doing it fast, is a function of experience. There is no substitute for having been there and done that.

Much of the difficulty in debugging comes when you encounter a kind of misdirection—something like magicians use—that easily fools you into thinking the problem is one thing when it's really something else. No manual, book, or journal article can tell you how to recognize a misdirection. You simply have to have seen it and worked through it. The next time it happens, you will recognize the signals and solve the problem much more quickly. Keep this in mind as you become immersed in the details of setting up the Visual FoxPro debugger.

Related to the misdirection problem is the difficulty of the initial step of debugging: finding the bug's location in the code. Sometimes you'll need to find the general location, which provides you a context, before you can begin to understand what the bug is. Other times you'll want to go to the source of the problem as directly as possible. Either way, you must deal with the elaborate arrangement of classes and objects that make up a typical application and particularly with the need to track errors through both the class hierarchy and the containership hierarchy.

CONTAINERSHIP

It's a dual hierarchy, that's what it is. You've already learned about the class hierarchy, which is created by subclassing the FoxPro base classes and using inheritance to pass the capabilities of one class to another. Now we come to yet another hierarchy: *containership*, one object inside another object, inside another object, and so on. A FormSet contains a Form, a Form contains a Grid, a Grid contains Columns—this is the typical chain or hierarchy of containership that you will encounter in object-oriented programming. It's significant in two crucial ways: First, all objects must be referenced by their position in the containership hierarchy. Second, when you debug a program, you must track errors through the levels of containers. It would not be unusual if you occasionally mix up the two hierarchies, although with practice you'll come to see how different they are.

REFERENCING OBJECTS

One area of terminology that is crucial to the use of methods (and properties) is object referencing. The *Developer's Guide* does a good job of explaining how objects can be nested and how they are referenced. To explain it from a slightly different angle, Figure 13.1 shows the potential relationships of a container hierarchy.

In relative terms, the hierarchy—nesting of containers and objects—goes like this:

_SCREEN

FormSet

Form

PageFrame

Page

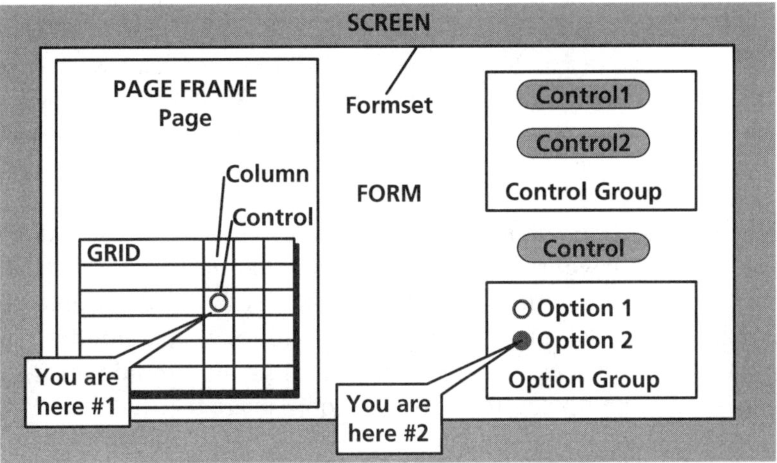

FIGURE 13.1 OBJECT REFERENCING.

All visual objects exist in the screen, not just of your monitor but, in the FoxPro sense of an object, the **_SCREEN**, which is a FoxPro internal variable. Although FormSets and Forms reside in the screen, **_SCREEN** is not part of the referencing scheme. However, it can be used to determine important information about objects that exist in the screen. This capability is frequently used when you're debugging. FoxPro provides three properties of the **_SCREEN** object, which can return the properties of the current control, form, or page:

_SCREEN.ActiveControl

```
lCtrlSeen = _SCREEN.ActiveControl.Visible
```

_SCREEN.ActiveForm

```
cFormName = _SCREEN.ActiveForm.Name
```

_SCREEN.ActivePage

```
nControls = _SCREEN.ActivePage.ControlCount
```

NOTE

It may seem strange that a FoxPro variable, **_SCREEN**, is an object. Actually, it illustrates an important capability: an *object reference*. You can make object references simply by doing this: `oNewPage = CREATEOBJECT("INFOPAGE")`. here, `oNewPage` is a variable that receives the return from the `CREATEOBJECT()` function. From then on, the program can refer to `oNewPage` as if it were the original object; for example, `oNewPage.caption`. Once an object has been instantiated, there is no need to continue making copies throughout the program. Instead, it is much more compact and generic to use an object reference. In a way, **_SCREEN** behaves just as if you had used the command: `_SCREEN = CREATEOBJECT("FOXPROSCREEN")` except that FoxPro has done it for you internally.

Inside the FoxPro screen is the **FormSet**, which contains **Forms**, and forms in turn may contain a **PageFrame** with two or more **Pages**. There is also the **Grid**, **Column**, and **Control** container hierarchy, which can be placed into either a form or a page. That's also true for any control group, option group, or control. FoxPro has a number of container classes (including the **Container** class itself), which are used to group controls. The final objects are usually controls, which are placed inside one of the containers.

The FoxPro frame of reference begins with a FormSet, if there is one, or a Form. As you've no doubt noticed, the references are placed from left to right, with a period—dot operator—separating each level:

FormSet.Form.PageFrame.Page.Grid.Column.Control

This is the absolute reference for "You are here #1" in Figure 13.1. To be precise with an instruction—for example, to change the status of the **Control**—you would include the name of each object in this hierarchy (or address). This is rarely done, not only because typing such long references is a nuisance but also because using relative referencing is equally accurate, shorter, and more generic. For example, the reference for the object at "You are here #1" is THIS.**Control**. THIS is the reference to the immediate object. You can also identify the form (THISFORM), the FormSet (THISFORMSET), and the immediate container of the object (**Parent**).

Notice that all these references are generic in the sense that you don't need to know the name of the current Form, FormSet, or container. So the reference to "You are here #2" relative to "You are here #1" is THISFORM.**Option Group**.**Option2**. This also illustrates the crucial part of referencing: It's always relative to where you are and what you want to reference. In programming terms, it means that a reference must accurately place the target of a reference in the container hierarchy relative to the active object.

NOTE

Bear in mind that all the relative referencing keywords (THIS, THISFORM, THISFORMSET, and **parent**) are valid only in a method. You can't use them in the Command window or as plain code in a program file. And to reiterate a point, all references must be to existing objects.

If the object is in the same container hierarchy, then THIS, THISFORM, THISFORMSET, and **parent** work well. If the object is in another hierarchy—a different Form, for example—then you may have to fall back on absolute referencing, using the actual names of the form and control. The goal in all cases is the shortest unambiguous reference, although that may be difficult to accomplish in complex FormSets.

NOTE

You don't usually have to waste time figuring out an object reference while you're programming in the Code window. Click the right mouse button in the window at the line where you want the reference, and use the **Object List** option. In the dialog box, select the object you want to reference. Presto! The correct reference code is inserted into the Code window.

BASIC DEBUGGING

Even if you're not a programmer, you already know what is meant when someone says that a piece of software has a bug. What is not generally understood is that *all* software has bugs. Shrink-wrapped commercial software, for which people pay good money, is buggy. The software cranked out by corporate programmers is buggy. Your code is buggy. This can be said not only with confidence but with conviction, because it is the nature of the software beast.

However, there is an important qualifier: How buggy? The degrees of buggyness can be classified by two criteria: How bad is the bug, and how often do bugs occur? The spectrum can be represented by Table 13.1. Pick one from each column.

TABLE 13.1 HOW BUGGY IS IT?

HOW BAD	HOW OFTEN	THE CONSEQUENCES
Causes system crash.	Every time it's used.	Programmer or staff is fired, disgraced, or flogged.
Program crashes.	Several times a day.	Program is discredited, abandoned, or ignored.
Program causes data errors.	Once or twice a day.	Program is used but disliked or distrusted.

(Continued...)

How Bad	How Often	The Consequences
Program fails to perform some function.	Couple of times a week.	Program is marginally acceptable.
Program has nonfatal errors.	Once in a while.	Program is OK but could use polishing.
Program has harmless but irritating glitches.	Happened only once.	Program is great. Fix problems as they crop up.

This table may appear light-hearted, but there is pain within it. People—users and makers—have bad experiences with buggy software. The point, however, is that although all software has bugs, it's important to decide what level of buggyness is acceptable. Major commercial software (such as Visual FoxPro) is often shipped not because it is bug-free, but because there are no (or few) detectable *showstoppers*: fatal bugs that cause system or program crashes.

The line between "acceptable" and "what you can get away with" is very fine, and it raises a number of interesting ethical and practical questions that we'll go into a little more in Chapter 21. The issues are there for all application developers, because time is always limited and the bugs always exist.

Classifying Bugs

To understand the debugging process, you can start by classifying software problems in two broad categories: design problems and programming errors. The first category is usually not considered part of debugging, although it's every bit as important. It includes missing functionality, difficulty of use, bad documentation, ugly appearance, and so forth. However, programming errors—the immediate cause of bugs—are the focus here.

Under the category of programming errors, there are three types:

- Syntax errors
- Run-time errors
- Functional errors.

Syntax errors are mistakes in the mechanics of programming: typos, missing clauses, command structure errors, and so on. Most but not all syntax errors are caught by the FoxPro compiler. Then there are the errors that don't show up until you run the program: the *run-time* errors. They can be many kinds but are exemplified by problems with variables: bad data types, missing data, and so on. The third type, *functional* errors, are things that run OK (they don't stop the program) but don't do what they're supposed to do, such as calculation errors and missing data.

When you debug a program, you must regularly deal with all three types of errors. It's a challenge to be good at debugging software, and a it's necessary skill. The better you are, the better your software is likely to be and the less time you will have to spend dealing with bugs.

Unfortunately, there is no magic formula or college course in how to become an expert in debugging. Debugging is one part setup—the tools you have at your disposal for analyzing and fixing bugs—and one part knowledge and experience. Often, the cause of a bug is not what the error message says it is, but it takes experience to recognize that. Sometimes you fix a bug not by finding it but by doing something a different way. Every programmer has also encountered the situation in which you fix a bug and then two more bugs are caused by what you changed. If you've done very much debugging, you'll understand why it can be said that all software is buggy.

THE EDIT/COMPILE/DEBUG CYCLE

There are many cycles in programming, but few have more impact on the life of a software developer than the edit/compile/debug cycle. The reason is simple:

Edit/Compile/Debug Cycle = TIME = $

It takes time to create and edit a program; time to compile it; and a lot of time to debug it. It's a cycle, so you do it over and over again: Write some code; compile it; run it; encounter bugs; fix bugs; write some more code. In an eight-hour day, a programmer working at an average pace (if there is such a thing) probably goes through this cycle 50–70 times a day.

The two worst thieves of time in programming are simple modifications and debugging. Programmers sometimes get improvement-happy and are forever tweaking their code. They can also become mired in a seemingly endless process of debugging. On projects that require working with users, it's estimated that program modification and debugging take as much as 60 percent of the project time. Of that, easily half is debugging. Anything that takes 30 percent of your programming time is worth a good hard look.

Dealing With a Bug

What happens when you encounter a FoxPro error message? You can respond on any of several levels:

- Level 1: Rely on the error message, experience, and a look at the code.
- Level 2: Use one or more of the FoxPro debugging tools.
- Level 3: Set up a complete debugging session.
- Level 4: Quit looking for the bug and program around it.

This sequence is predicated on the fact that programmers don't like to do any more work than they have to, a common trait. It takes time to set up a debug session of any thoroughness. So the first-level technique is to read the error message and go looking in the code for the problem.

Level 1 Debugging

From the standpoint of saving time, what you want is for all bugs to fall into the level 1 category. That's because all you need to do is to read and interpret the error message, go into the code, find the relevant area, and fix the bug. If it's a simple error, one pass into the code will be enough.

NOTE

It's been my experience that with good object-oriented programming practices—tightly built classes and good documentation—and keeping applications as modularized as possible, an important part of debugging becomes much easier: You can find the location of the problem code much more quickly. If this practice helps avoid rolling out the heavy machinery, such as the Visual FoxPro Debugger, so much the better.

Syntax errors are usually the easiest to deal with, because most of them are caught immediately by the FoxPro compiler and are fairly obvious. And until you fix them, your program probably won't run. There are many possible syntax errors (they become more bizarre as deadlines approach and the hour gets late), but they fall into some recognizable types:

- Simple typos or misspelling a command. Everyone commits these errors from time to time.

- An actual error in the syntax of a command or function, such as forgetting a required clause.
- Invalid use of a command, method, or property, such as referencing the wrong object type for a property.

The good news is that the more you program, the more often your syntax errors will fall into the level 1 category, because you become better at interpreting and finding errors. Experienced programmers make rather few syntax errors.

A run-time error occurs during the execution of the program (or object) and typically involves problems that occur with data or the use of program commands inappropriate for their context. Here are some common types:

- Data errors lead the list, with wrong field types, bad or inappropriate data, and trouble with variable types being most frequent.
- Table relation and index errors, such as the wrong index selection or an invalid index for a particular relation.
- Bad or missing programs, methods, functions, or objects—any reference to something that either doesn't exist or isn't locatable by FoxPro.
- Environmental errors, such as running out of memory or having the wrong setting for a printer.

Run-time errors can be far more difficult to overcome than syntax errors are. For one thing, you must run the program (or object) in order to encounter them and rerun it to make sure they're fixed. Run-time error messages are helpful but not always accurate. Sometimes they are wrong or, worse, misleading.

You'll quickly learn that bugs may produce symptoms that are reported by an error message that only hints at the underlying cause. To find the cause of a bug, you may need to carefully scrutinize the program's condition at the time the bug occurred: the program file or object that was executing, the properties or variables being used, the status of tables and indexes, and so on—there may be dozens of pieces of information that could help to lead to a diagnosis. What you need is more information, which the FoxPro error message doesn't give you.

NOTE

Provided in the accompanying disk is the form GENERROR.SCX in the UTILITY\FORM folder. When your program generates an error, the **ON ERROR** command can call this form to display much more information about the condition of the program: tables, indexes, variables, error messages, line of code, and procedure name. You can also view the complete listing of variables and system status. The form gives you several options: stopping and clearing out the program, a simple **CANCEL**, or continuing. You can install this form in your application testing shell:

```
ON ERROR DO FORM GENERROR WITH ERROR(),MESSAGE(),;
  MESSAGE(1), SYS(16), LINENO(1)
```

This window is not a substitute for the FoxPro Debugger. Rather, it's designed to provide you immediate information about an error situation, information that could also be gleaned from the Debugger. The advantage is that this window is automatic for most kinds of errors.

Debugging in the Project Manager

One of the benefits of using the Project Manager is the ready access it gives you to generator and compiler errors. All compiling and generating, whether started from the Command window, menu, or the Project Manager, produces an error log (a file with an ERR extension). However, the first two don't automatically show you the log or even provide a way of calling it. The Project Manager can do both. The Build Option dialog box has a check box you can set to automatically **Display Errors**. And if you'd rather do it yourself, there's the **Show Errors** option in the Project menu.

Either way, you get a listing in an Edit window showing syntax errors and reference errors. Most developers hate to have errors in the Project Manager build and work like mad to remove them. That's not necessarily because they seek perfection, but because FoxPro stops the build and requires the programmer to press a key or two, and that means the programmer can't go out for coffee (input or output).

Syntax errors are mostly the result of typing dyslexia (a condition that accelerates after 2 AM), memory lapses, or overeager cutting and pasting. Most syntax errors can be dispatched quickly. Reference errors are calls to files or objects that the Project Manager can't locate. Most of the time, you'll track down the references and locate the missing procedures.

Occasionally, however, the Project Manager will complain about references that it thinks are missing program files but are really arrays or variables. The cure for this and other reference errors is to use the **EXTERNAL** directive. The main candidate for **EXTERNAL** is a reference to a procedure, report, or form via a macro or a name expression. For example:

```
cProgName = "F:\UTILITY\FORM\APPERR"
DO (cProgName)
```

The FoxPro compiler has no way of knowing what to put into the macro expansion or name variable, so it thinks the file is missing. The solution is to put the **EXTERNAL** in the same procedure where the hidden call is being made:

```
EXTERNAL PROCEDURE APPERR
cProgName = "F:\UTILITY\FORM\APPERR"
DO (cProgName)
```

EXTERNAL, followed by the clause that identifies the type (**ARRAY**, **CLASS**, **FORM**, **LABEL**, **LIBRARY**, **MENU**, **PROCEDURE**, or **REPORT**), is placed immediately after the beginning of the routine or menu code where the offending reference occurs.

The error information provided by FoxPro is static—a slice of the program's condition at one (halted) moment. If this doesn't give you enough of a picture to locate or diagnose the problem, that's when you move to level 2 debugging and the Visual FoxPro Debugger.

The Visual FoxPro Debugger

For generations FoxPro developers have worked with debugging tools that were offered piecemeal. Some we had to create ourselves. Visual FoxPro 5.0 ends (most) of that with the new Debugger. This is a major upgrade that can give you both a better picture of the inner workings of your programs and the ability to track bugs. It's a massive piece of machinery with its own learning curve and difficulties. It can also be overkill, which is why "Level 1" debugging should always be the first avenue of approach.

Setup for the Debugger

Now that the Debugger is its own entity, it has its own page in the FoxPro Options dialog box. Select **Tools**, **Options**, **Debug** (tab) from the menu, and you'll see the page in Figure 13.2.

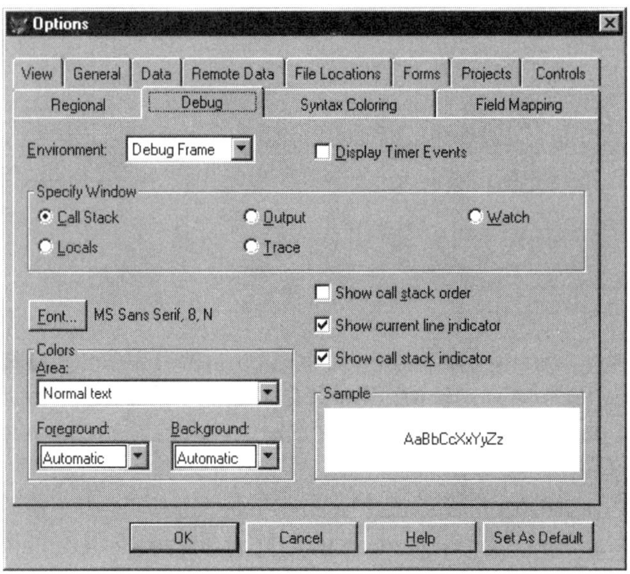

FIGURE 13.2 DEBUGGER OPTIONS.

We'll come back to this illustration to discuss options relating to individual windows of the Debugger, but first let's look at a few general options. The most important option is the selection of whether you want the Debugger to appear as a separate window within the FoxPro window or as an independent window (like a separate Windows program). This is the **Environment** option with its pull-down combo box. Most of the time it's more convenient to run the Debugger as a separate window; the Debug Frame can be docked in the Task Bar and floats independently of the FoxPro window.

The **Display Timer Events** check box is not used except when you're debugging a Timer process. When a Timer is running, the events may come fast and furious. You can also customize the font and colors of the Debugger text, although the default is adequate for most uses.

LEVEL 2 DEBUGGING

When simple analysis of an error message and inspection of code don't reveal what's wrong, it's time to move to level 2 and the Visual FoxPro Debugger. Level

2 debugging is the way to get dynamic information about the program, because you can see values changing and watch the code go by, line by line, as the program runs. Most of the FoxPro Debugger is designed to provide this kind of information. Here's what it offers:

- **Trace window**. Displays the code from your programs and highlights each line of code as it is executed.
- **Watch window**. You can specify variables and other FoxPro expressions, which are evaluated as the program is running.
- **Locals window**. An Explorer-like window where you can view the current values of variables, arrays, and properties.
- **Call Stack window**. Presents a hierarchical view of each routine called by a program as it executes.
- **Debug Output window**. Displays the output from error trapping code you put into the program.
- **Set Breakpoint dialog box**. Provides many sophisticated ways to pause the execution of a program.
- **Event Tracking**. Displays the firing of selected events as the program executes.

What the Debugger brings to the party is a number of ways to see what your code is *actually* doing, as opposed to what you think it's doing. The Debugger can expose wrong values, inappropriate commands, unexpected jumps between events, tables out of sync, improper environment settings, and much more. Of course, it won't do any better than your ability to see these things. In fact, some of them can't be seen unless you configure the Debugger's windows to show them. That's where both creativity and experience come in. You have to try things, experiment, and learn. Go forth and let the bugs multiply.

STARTING THE DEBUGGER

To activate the Debugger before you begin running the program, use **Tools, Debugger** from the menu. You might want to do this to get the program configured. Occasionally, it's necessary to prestart the Debugger if the bug is near the beginning of the program. However, running the Debugger can significantly slow execution, so most programmers choose to invoke the Debugger so that it appears only in strategic places in the code. There are several ways to do this.

The simplest way is to put the following command into the code: **DEBUG**. The older FoxPro commands **SET TRACE ON** and **SET DEBUG ON** will also work, but stick with the newer version. In the standard debug mode, the program continues execution after the Debugger window is open. **SET STEP ON** opens the Debugger in step mode, where one line is executed after another only on command from the user. This is the mode most often used for debugging. You can also have the Debugger halt the program in a variety of situations, but we'll cover that in the section on the Breakpoint dialog box.

NOTE

If you choose to use the GENERROR.SCX form provided with this book, it has an option to start the Debugger from the point where the error occurred.

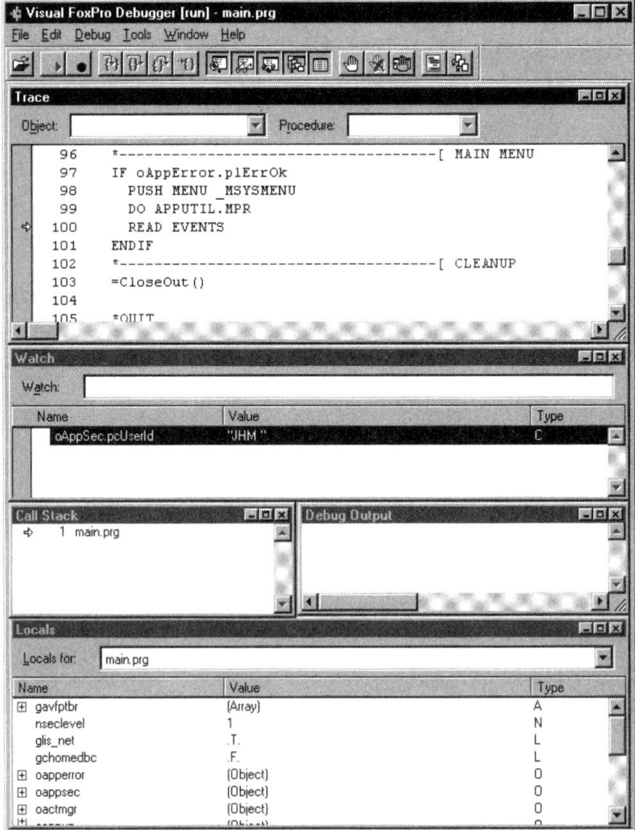

FIGURE 13.3 FULLY LOADED DEBUGGER FRAME.

When the Debugger starts, it will display whatever windows were in its last configuration. Typically, this will include at least the Trace and Watch windows. Figure 13.3 shows the Debugger frame with all five windows. This configuration takes up a lot of screen real estate, although you can dock the frame. (Add to your list yet another argument for a big monitor.)

The Debugger toolbar, shortcut menu, and standard menu have the options for opening or closing each window. Which of the five windows you have open depends on what kind of information you're after. The whys and wherefores will be clearer after we've described each window.

THE TRACE WINDOW

The Trace window is code in motion. This pane of the Debugger displays your code as it executes, highlighting one line at a time. It's impressive to watch hours of your coding zip by like a train at high speed. It's useless too, because at that speed you can't read it. The purpose of the Trace window is to allow you to inspect the code as it goes by, looking for the flaws that might be causing a bug. The Trace window is most often used in tandem with Watch window (see Figure 13.3) to examine lines of code as the values of problem variables change. From looking at that information, you might be able to detect some kind of false interaction with a table or a calculation that has gone astray.

There are two speed options: throttle or step mode. The execution throttle is the speed at which the lines of a program are executed through the Trace window. This can range from 0 (full speed) to a delay of 5.5 seconds. The best speeds for legibility are between 0.35 and 0.6 seconds. You can set the default throttle speed in the Debug Options dialog box: Select **Tools**, **Options**, **Debug**, specify the **Trace** window, and set the **Pause between line execution** option. In the Debugger you'll find the Execution Throttle in the Debug menu under **Debug**, **Throttle**.

Step mode moves through the code one line at a time under manual control. To make the program continue, you must click on the **Step** icon of the toolbar or in the menu. There are four step options:

- **Step Into**. Moves program execution one line at a time.
- **Step Over**. Causes program execution to perform subroutines (methods and so on) without tracing through them. This option can be a great time-saver, but you must be alert to use it.
- **Step Out**. Seldom used because it signals for program execution to continue until it returns to the calling routine.

- **Run to Cursor**. After you mark a line with the cursor, this option causes program execution to continue until that point.

Once the program is halted, you can use the **Cancel** option (toolbar or menu) to terminate the program or **Resume** to continue program execution at speed. If you've found the bug, cancel and go fix it by selecting **Debug**, **Fix** from the Debug menu. This drops you into the offending line (or region) in a Code window.

As you'll see, it takes a lot of time to flow code through the Trace window. Because good debugging is also the art of not wasting time, you can do a couple of things to reduce the amount of time spent in the Trace window. One approach is to use *breakpoints*: places where programming execution is told to halt. You can set breakpoints in the Trace window (when execution is suspended) by clicking with the mouse on the breakpoint bar to the left of the highlighted line or by using the **Spacebar** or **Enter** key. A red bullet will appear in the breakpoint column. When you've set the breakpoints, program execution will stop at each one, allowing you to inspect variables or whatever. You can continue with **Resume** or one of the step options.

If you don't want to see all the code between the breakpoints, use the Debugger shortcut menu to toggle **Trace Between Breaks** off. Because you must individually select each line to be a breakpoint, this option can be time-consuming if many lines of code need to be marked. That's when you might turn to the Breakpoints dialog box.

SETTING BREAKPOINTS

The purpose of the Breakpoints dialog box (Figure 13.4) is to provide several ways of stopping program execution, ideally so that you can pinpoint problem areas without scrolling hopelessly through hundreds of lines of code.

Use the Debugger menu to select **Tools**, **Breakpoints**. The Breakpoints dialog box is a sophisticated tool that will take some practice to master, but it can be a great time-saver. Some of what you can do in the Breakpoints dialog box overlaps with the Trace and Watch windows; in fact, breakpoints set in those windows show up in the Breakpoints dialog box. This gives you a central location for all breakpoints and works well if you have many of them. You can construct four types of breakpoints:

- **Break at location**. Select this form of breakpoint in the **Type** combo box. In the **Location** field, enter the name of a procedure, program file, method, or other routine. You can specify a particular line by including the line number with the routine: `MAIN,11`. In the **File** field, enter or find the file that contains the routine. Being location-specific requires that you know which routine is involved or else have the routine in the Trace window so that you can set the breakpoint there and edit it in the Breakpoints dialog box.

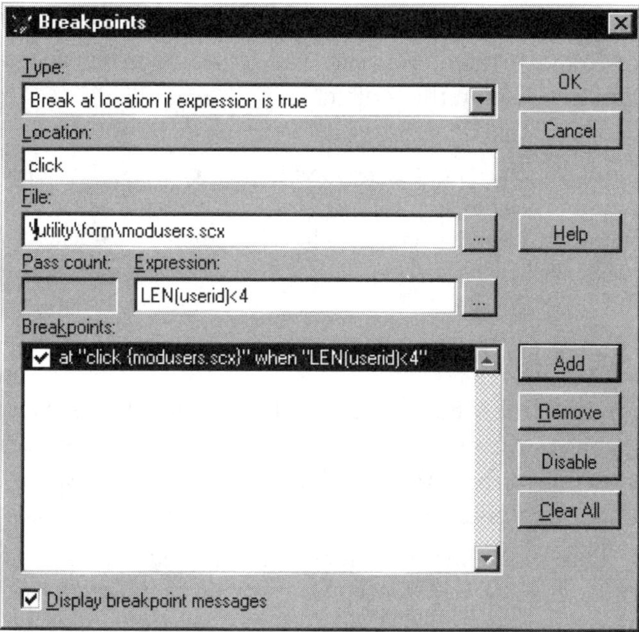

FIGURE 13.4 BREAKPOINTS DIALOG BOX.

- **Break when expression has changed**. Select this type of breakpoint to use expressions such as `PROGRAM()` or `oObject.TextBox1.value`, which trigger a break when their values change. These are single-valued expressions and not conditionals. Enter them into the **Expression** field or use the ubiquitous Expression Builder button. Click the **Add** button to enter this expression into the list. This type of breakpoint is often set in the Watch window.
- **Break when expression is true**. This is the conditional type of expression—for example, `RECNO()>10 or oObject.appForm.Left < 3`. Enter the expression in the **Expression** field and click the **Add** button to put it in the breakpoint list. This option can create some of

the most generic breakpoints, those that are likely to appear in many places throughout an application.

- **Break at location if expression is true**. This option requires both location information (**Location** and **File** fields) and a conditional expression. It sets a relatively narrow criterion for the breakpoint and is useful for breaking within fast-moving event methods.

Having set breakpoints, you can use this dialog box to **Disable** (temporarily deactivate) or **Remove** them. You can also toggle them on and off using the **Toggle Breakpoints** icon in the toolbar.

WARNING

A word of caution: Don't go overboard with breakpoints. If you have too many, it becomes difficult to keep track of what's doing what. In addition, it takes time to construct useful breakpoints. The object is to get into the neighborhood of problem code as quickly as possible—and not to display how clever you are with breakpoints.

USING THE WATCH WINDOW

The main purpose of the Watch window is to allow you to see the changing values of expressions as the program executes. Again, these are expressions in the broad FoxPro sense of the term: variables, functions, and logical expressions. You can enter any expression you think would be helpful to isolate a problem.

There are a many circumstances for an error and just as many approaches to using the Watch window. Here's a typical example to illustrate the flavor of the process. Suppose you receive the following error message:

```
! Invalid function argument value, type, or count.
```

This message indicates that a FoxPro function has been passed an invalid argument. It's most likely that a parameter is receiving the wrong data type, but at this point you don't know that for sure. There might be something wrong with several parameters.

If you're using the GENERROR error trapping window, you'll see that the currently executing procedure is a form, INSPECTOR.SCX, and the offending line of code is as follows:

```
REPLACE ALL inspector.district WITH ;
   STUFF(cDistrict, cOld, cNew, nStart, nTimes)
```

The offender is the FoxPro **STUFF( )** function, and you have five parameters that could be wrong—but which one? It's time to turn to the Watch window and have a look at these variables as they change before the function call. (You can copy the names of the variables to the Watch window expression field and break them up there.)

Open the Debugger (**Tools**, **Debugger**) and enter the five variables in the Watch window's **Watch** field. At the moment you enter them, the value area should evaluate to null or empty values if the program has stopped execution (unless some of the variables were Public). Before you run the program again, there's one more step you can take.

The Watch window can be used to set breakpoints. In the case of the example at hand, you might want to enter a breakpoint expression such as this one:

```
PROGRAM()="INSPECTOR" AND LINENO()=34.
```

When this statement evaluates to true, you'll be at the line in the program where the original error message was generated. Then you run the program in the normal way until the breakpoint is triggered. When the program execution hits your breakpoint, the program will stop (but not cancel), and you can examine the values in the five argument variables as displayed in the Watch window (Table 13.2).

TABLE 13.2 FIVE ARGUMENT VARIABLE DISPLAYED IN WATCH WINDOW

VARIABLE	VALUE
gcDistrict	"West South"
lcOld	"South"
rcNew	324
rnStart	6
rnTimes	1

If you have followed the convention of indicating the data type of variables in the second letter of the variable name, you will spot that `rcNew` should be a character but instead has a numeric value. Otherwise, you'd have to remember that the third argument of **STUFF** is a **cExpression**.

Now you know the offending variable, but you still need to find out where it's being set to the wrong value. In real life, you'd probably open the form at this point and go right to the method where this variable takes on a value. But let's say that `rcNew` takes on several values along the way to the function call, and you don't have any idea which one is the source of the error. Now you can remove the other variables from the Watch window and set a breakpoint at `rcNew` so that the program will stop whenever the value changes. Rerun the program and watch for the point where the variable takes on the incorrect value.

NOTE

In the preceding example, you could take advantage of a new capability: changing values in the Watch window. You can assign a new value to variables and watch the effect on the program. However, this approach can easily be a two-edged sword and cause more errors. Use it with care.

Using the Locals Window

Entering the name of old-style variables in the Watch window is easy; all you need is the variable name. It's not so easy with properties or variables associated with objects, because you need the entire object reference chain. This is one time when the containership of objects tends to make debugging more difficult. It's also why you'll occasionally want to use the Locals window of the Debugger.

This window, shown in Figure 13.5, works something like the Windows Explorer except with variables, properties, arrays, and objects instead of files. Use the **Locals for** combo box to select a procedure from the call stack; the pane below will display the name, value, and type of all visible elements. The Locals window isn't the Watch window, so you can't create expressions here. You can edit the values, and, less dangerously, you can drag and drop variables from here into the Watch window. This technique not only saves typing but also gets the object reference correct.

Locals

Locals for: main.prg

Name	Value	Type
oappsec	(Object)	O
baseclass	"Custom"	C
class	"Appsecure"	C
classlibrary	"\\pro200\milims\utility\library\appprog.vcx"	C
comment	""	C
controlcount	0	N
controls	(Collection)	A
height	22	N
helpcontextid	0	N
left	0	N
name	"appsecure"	C
objects	(Collection)	A
pagroup	(Array)	A
pagroup[1,1]	"GENERAL "	C
pagroup[1,2]	5	N
pagroup[1,3]	5	N
parent	(none)	

Figure 13.5 Locals window.

USING THE CALL STACK WINDOW AND OUTPUT WINDOW

There's not much to say about the Call Stack window. If you display it, it will show you where you are in the application—that is, which routine (program file, form, and so on) is currently executing and where it sits relative to other routines that have been called.

There's even less to say about the Output window except that it needs to be open for event tracking or using **DEBUGOUT** if you want them to display to the screen.

SAVING A DEBUGGER CONFIGURATION

In older versions of FoxPro, it was possible to go through an elaborate debugging session—complete with Debugger windows, breakpoints, and expressions—and then believing that you found the bug, to quit FoxPro, only to find that the bug wasn't gone, and your debugging session was lost. Few things were more frustrating. But that scenario is no more. The Visual FoxPro 5.0 Debugger lets you save debug sessions. From the Debug menu, select **File**, **Save Configuration** (or use **Alt+F2** from the keyboard). Use **F2** or **File**, **Load Configuration** to bring the session back.

LEVEL 3 DEBUGGING

When you hit a bug, you always hope it can be fixed by inspection (level 1) or at least by rolling out some of the Debugger tools such as the Trace and Watch windows (level 2). Once in a while, however, you hit a bug that stumps you. You know it's not something obvious, such as a variable with a bad value or a misplaced command, but maybe you're not sure where the problem is occurring or whether it's being caused by a flaw in the setup of a routine. Now you may need to become more proactive and you put something in the code to help locate the problem. That's the definition of level 3 debugging. This level is characterized by the use of code within the program to produce output for the Debugger.

The obvious disadvantage of this approach is that you must go back and clean up when you're finished. None of the methods for tightly controlling a debugging environment is quick and easy, but then you wouldn't be getting this deep into the mechanics of debugging unless you're dealing with a devil of a bug.

The first of the tools for insertion into your code is **DEBUGOUT**.

Command syntax:

DEBUGOUT eExpression

Argument:

eExpression Any valid FoxPro expression that can be evaluated and displayed.

Examples:

```
DEBUGOUT "Starting the data process."
DEBUGOUT "Ending the data process"
DEBUGOUT IIF(ALIAS()="USER","In USER.","UNKNOWN TABLE")
```

As you can see, this command is primarily informational. It doesn't stop the program, change a variable, or affect processing in any way, but it can give you important information about where the program is operating. The information generated by the command will be displayed in the Debugger's Output window if it's open.

An alternative to **DEBUGOUT** is to use the **WAIT WINDOW** command. It, too, can be placed in your code at strategic points, but its output goes to a small window (no doubt you've seen it) and can harmlessly halt the program until a key is pressed. For example: `WAIT WINDOW "About to enter the User module"`. If you don't want to stop the program, use this variation: `WAIT WINDOW "Done" NOWAIT`.

Similar to **WAIT WINDOW**, FoxPro also offers the **ASSERT** command.

Command syntax:

ASSERT lExpression [MESSAGE cYourMessage]

Argument:

lExpression A logical expression.

Examples:

```
ASSERT PCOUNT()=1    MESSAGE "We're missing a parameter!"
ASSERT nValue <> 20  MESSAGE "The calculation is off."
```

When **ASSERT** fires, it produces a dialog box that gives you the opportunity to Cancel the program, continue, or bring up the Debugger. In other words, it provides an opportunity to evaluate the condition being tested by the **ASSERT**.

The obvious difference between this command and **WAIT WINDOW** is the evaluation of the logical expression. **ASSERT** is conditionally triggered, and you can put it into your code anywhere there might be a problem. This is a proactive debugging technique, because it can be used before there is a bug. The **SET ASSERT ON|OFF** command is used to turn it on or off, so you can use it at will during development. There is some speed penalty if you have many **ASSERT**s , so it's best to remove them before an application is shipped.

Because these three commands are placed within the code, you can be very specific in placement—something that's harder to do with breakpoint expressions—and you can keep the program rolling while you observe the information.

NOTE

This so-called level 3 approach is not a substitute for using the Debugger. It's a supplement, something you do along with tracing code and watching variables.

DEBUGGING BY CODING AND COMMENTING

You can try a couple of other proactive strategies when other approaches fail. One technique is to remove code that may be causing a problem. The simplest approach is to open the appropriate Code window, select the lines in question, and use the shortcut menu to **Comment** out the selection. A related approach is to insert alternative code for something that seems not to be working. Usually, you'd comment out the original code in case it wasn't the problem and you need to restore it.

The worst debugging problems are usually caused by something in the program's environment or by something wrong with the structure of the program. Environmental bugs arise from conflicts and interactions of elements outside your program, such as the subtle effects of running short of memory or trouble that originates in other programs and third-party class libraries. There are also bugs and anomalies in Visual FoxPro itself as well as problems with Windows or other Windows programs. These bugs are also bad because they have normal symptoms and error messages but you can never find the source, because the problem isn't in your program.

The deeply procedural bugs are those that arise from the structure of your program, the interaction of variables, or the way your program handles the tables (among the most common occurrences). Switching between program modules—the hallmark of event-driven programming—is notorious for side effect bugs. Correcting some of these problems can take hours while you narrow options, test theories, and try fixes. Sometimes, you simply have to throw up your hands and say, "I don't know what's causing the problem; I'll work around it." That's when you've reached level 4 debugging.

NOTE

Using alternative code or repackaging your code (such as using a new form or different container) can be an important strategy in Visual FoxPro, because from time to time you will encounter weird behavior. It might be something you did, but it might also be the way FoxPro works, or worse, a real bug in FoxPro. I once had an ugly afternoon when the program continually crashed and FoxPro itself died without warning and without remedy. I knew it had to be something fundamental and that it was something that had just started, so I was probably the culprit. Six hours later, I broke the program into smaller, independent pieces and discovered that Visual FoxPro was blowing up trying to compile multiple forms in a FormSet that used the same original classes. I still don't know what in the code triggered this bug, but at least the alternative approach worked.

Event Tracking

Before we wrap up this chapter, let's look at a couple of additional debugging features introduced with Visual FoxPro 5.0: event tracking and coverage analysis.

One of the debugging wrinkles introduced by object-oriented programming is the ability of the user (or the program itself) to jump around from object to object, usually through triggering events. Theoretically, objects are self-contained, and this kind of program execution hopscotch is harmless. Unfortunately, objects in real programs are dependent on information being passed to them and on the environment in which they operate. In other words, they are vulnerable.

Roughly 90 percent of the coding you do will be associated with events, either directly in the event methods or by classes and methods associated with events. That makes events, and event methods, extremely important. It also makes the order of their firing significant for debugging. Although the sequence of events is known for some actions, such as the instantiation of a form, the ad hoc sequences found in most applications are unpredictable. That's why the Event Tracker can be helpful; it can show which events are really firing and in which order.

The Event Tracker is managed through a dialog box (Figure 13.6) summoned in the Debugger menu with **Tools**, **Event Tracking**.

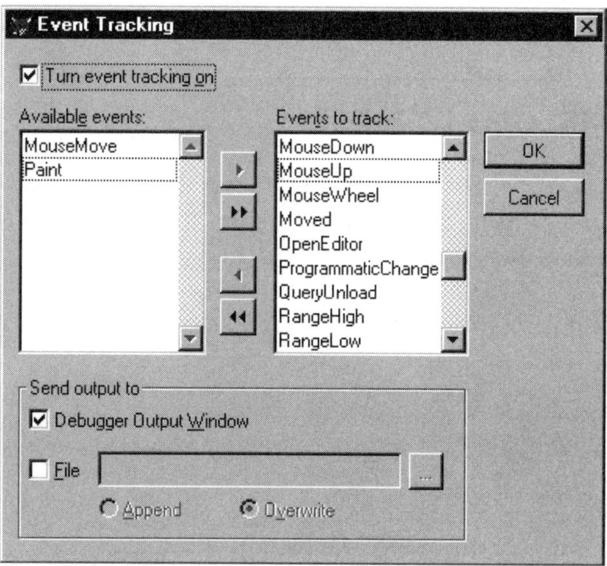

FIGURE 13.6 EVENT TRACKING DIALOG BOX.

Clicking the **Turn event tracking on** check box will cause Visual FoxPro to record each event listed in the **Events to track** window and will send the output to either the Output window of the Debugger or to a file of your choosing. There are a couple of important operational points:

- Try to be as selective as possible with the events to track. By default, all events are in the tracking list. Don't leave the list this way unless you want your program to crawl. At a minimum, remove the **MouseMove** and **Paint** events from the list, because they fire constantly during normal operation of a program but rarely contain code.
- Sending output to the Output window is fine if you've cut the events list to a minimum and have restricted the amount of code to run. Otherwise, the window will be flooded and you'll have no chance to read it effectively. Output to file makes more sense if you need an extensive profile of event firing.

In general, unless you are studying event patterns between modules of an application, the more tightly you focus the event list and control the sections of code that are run, the more useful the tracking will be, especially for debugging.

Coverage Analysis

Although you start coverage analysis from the Debugger, it is not exactly a debugging feature. Coverage analysis is a report for each line of code run by a program. It gathers the following:

- How long each line took to execute (in seconds).
- The class the line belongs to, if any.
- The method or procedure of the line.
- The line number.
- The file that contains the code.

You can use this information to see which lines of code are executing the most, how long it takes them, and whether there are any performance bottlenecks or places where efficiency could be tuned. Reading coverage analysis reports can be a subtle business and is very much tied to the language.

Coverage analysis is started by selecting **Tools**, **Coverage Logging** in the Debugger menu. You need to specify the output file in the Coverage dialog box. The default file extension is LOG, and the output is strictly ASCII text. To help interpret the data, you can transfer the file output to a table. There you can apply filters, queries, and reports to give you specific analytical information. The code for this technique is in the *Developer's Guide*.

Chapter Wrap-Up

Despite the emphasis in this chapter on debugging techniques and the Debugger machinery, the fact is that most debugging goes very quickly (thank goodness). Ironically, you'll spend much time sniffing through code and the Debugger windows, only to find something you can fix in a minute (or less). The analysis and information-gathering part of the process is key, and it explains why there's no substitute for experience. In time you'll be able to dispatch "routine" bugs quickly, using a variety of Debugger techniques that you'll customize for yourself.

Some bugs and other kinds of coding problems are not dispatched so expediently. Head knockers or wallbangers, I call them. Sometimes they are caused by your being too familiar with the code; you can't see the problem even though it may be staring you in the face. If you've been at a bug for hours, it might be a good idea to get a second opinion. Similarly, debugging when you're tired is usually not productive. Like original coding, good debugging is a creative activity, combining analysis and choice of tools in creative ways—something that is hard to do when you're stone tired.

SECTION 5

PLANNING AN APPLICATION

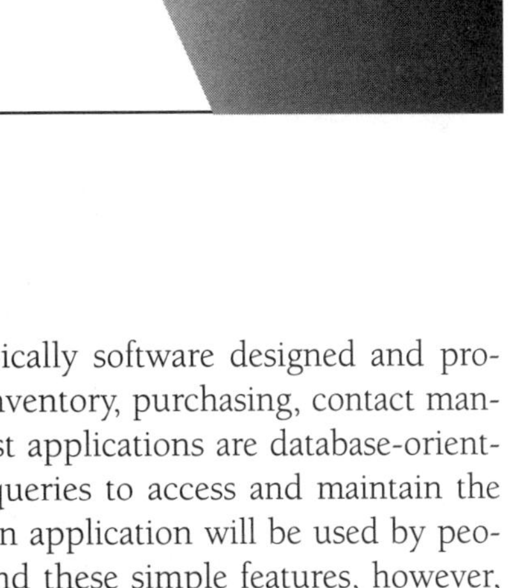

In the FoxPro context, an *application* is typically software designed and programmed to do some kind of work or job: inventory, purchasing, contact management—the list is endless. In FoxPro, most applications are database-oriented and use data entry forms, reports, and queries to access and maintain the data. In most cases, it is also assumed that an application will be used by people other than the developer—clients. Beyond these simple features, however, an application is one of those concepts that everyone generally understands, but a precise description becomes tangled in all the possibilities. So how do you plan an application?

In this book, the major theme is that the best way to plan an application is to start by building an application framework. However, despite the application framework's importance, it's not the whole story. The difficulty of defining the concept of an application reflects something important in the real world: You'll have to define each application you build. There's no universal template that says, "This is how to build every application." There are similarities between applications—if there weren't, the object-oriented approach would be useless and so would an application framework—but it's still necessary to define each application on its own terms before you can start combining objects from a framework (Section Figure 5.1).

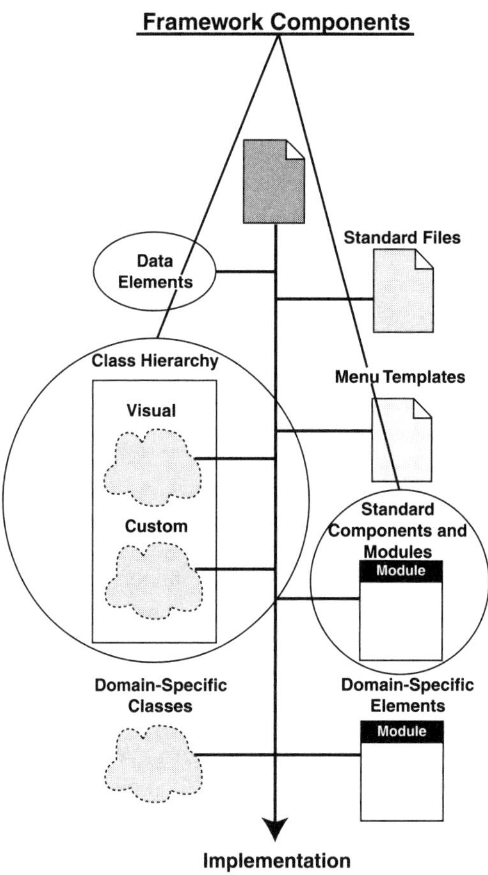

SECTION FIGURE 5.1 APPLICATION FRAMEWORK.

This points up a separation, at least in the beginning, between *what* needs to be done and *how* it's going to be done or, to use jargon, the difference between analysis and implementation. The classic advice is, "Study and analyze the application without reference to the method of implementation." This is supposed to be true whether you're doing database analysis or using object-oriented techniques. It's good advice but not very realistic. Developers think about how they're going to build an application in their development system of choice, even when they're doing the most basic analysis and design. That's because one of the first big questions about a project, faced by almost every developer, is, What's it going to take to build this application?

There are only so much time, resources, and ability to go around. This means that it's important to determine the scale of an application, especially if it is a professional commitment. Naturally, a developer tries to figure out what's required by an application and how the tools available can be brought to bear on it. So, the first part of planning an application is to get its measure (analysis), figure out what it will take to build (components from an application framework), and then design it. This section covers all these aspects of application planning, concentrating on the application framework but putting it into context with the analysis and design of an application.

- Chapter 14, "Application Analysis," introduces some of the key techniques used to analyze the need for an application and how it should be constructed. These approaches include data analysis, object-oriented analysis (especially scenarios), and functional analysis.
- Chapter 15, "Application Design," uses the information gathered during analysis and turns it into a database schema, class hierarchy, and application framework.

These two chapters return us to the cycle of application development outlined in Chapter 1. To this point, we've covered the basics of data management, procedural programming, and OOP; now we'll start more directly down the road that produces an application and an application framework.

CHAPTER 14

APPLICATION ANALYSIS

We're back at the beginning—the beginning of the software development cycle outlined in Chapter 1. Analysis, the generic name for getting to know your application before you build it, means different things to different developers. In some institutional settings—large corporations, government, and so on—the traditions of mainframe software place high value on analysis and design, as well they should when applications require months or years to develop and cost hundreds of thousands, if not millions, of dollars. In that context, what's a month or two for analysis and design?

On the personal computer side, the approach has tended to be more relaxed. The beauty of PCs is their responsiveness to the individual. If you want to write software, you don't need to get on-line time from someone or have a degree in computer science. All you need is a PC, a vision of what you want, and the perseverance to create it. Sooner or later, you'll get what you want.

The sense of immediacy is still characteristic of PCs, and in fact with visual programming tools such as those in FoxPro, it may be more true now than ever before. In the meantime, our vision of what you can do on a PC has grown. In 1981, it was great fun to produce a database program cataloging a stamp collection with dBase II. Today, many PC developers are contemplating applications that will run a company. Visions of snazzy multimedia interfaces dance before our eyes, and we think nothing of tables with 100,000 records.

Such large-scale programming and database management wasn't simple in the days of the mainframe, and it isn't simple in the days of the PC. True, many large applications may no longer require years to write or cost millions of dollars, but they still take a lot of time, effort, and money. As long as that is true, some of the mainframe traditions remain valid—including analysis and design. It usually pays to know what you want to do before you do it.

So it becomes a question of how much front-end work is necessary. What's the right balance between formal analysis and the impulse to do it on-the-fly? These questions are even more relevant because of the move to object-oriented programming, which has added its own analysis and design requirements to the mix.

Although there are half measures—for example, doing an analysis but not doing extensive research or interviews—if you're going to do analysis formally, you usually do it with all the standard steps and techniques. Otherwise, you do it informally and cut as many corners as you like. The appropriate words are *due diligence*: You put in as much work as required by the scale of the application. If that means doing a formal analysis, you try to be systematic and thorough.

There are no formulas, but to frame your decision making, here are some rules of thumb. An application needs formal analysis and design if any of the following applies:

- It's a totally new application, for you at least, and especially if it's new to the client.
- It has four or more developers or programmers working on the project.
- It has five or more people who are users and managers with responsibility in the area of the application.
- The project involves information critical to some aspect of the company.
- The volume of information or transactions is demanding of hardware resources.
- The speed of response for information is a high priority (real-time systems).
- The application has two or more modules.
- The application's data, processing, user interface, or reporting are inherently complex.

It would take separate chapters to fully explain how each of these factors impacts an application, but broadly speaking they fall into two categories: the use of analysis and design to communicate with people about the project and to avoid technical problems. Unless you've written the application before (or one very much like it), each new application has many unknowns. Formal analysis and design is, at the very least, a way to become familiar with the application and find the comfort zone for making decisions.

Having said all this to emphasize the idea that formal analysis and design are good, we now turn to some of the specific elements—and immediately run into a couple of problems. First, there are so many approaches that they can't all be covered, and the ones we cover can't be covered in depth. (There are many books on almost every approach.) Second, it's difficult to pick a representative application to illustrate the process. If the example is too generic, it may not seem real, and if it's too specific, it may be difficult to understand.

This chapter will outline four approaches: functional analysis, object-oriented analysis, data analysis, and business rules analysis. For most part, it avoids academic discussion and tries to remain generally descriptive. You are strongly encouraged to consult books that expand on the outlines. In particular, many of the concepts and ideas come from a seminal work in object-oriented analysis: Grady Booch's *Object-Oriented Analysis and Design with Applications*. For an example application, we'll use an application called a laboratory information management system, or LIMS for short. As you will see, this example is closely related to a generic manufacturing program, but it has enough wrinkles to make it interesting.

ANALYZING AN APPLICATION

Even the most trivial application arises from someone's need to computerize something. This means that all applications have a context: a conglomeration of ideas, needs, personalities, schedules, relationships, money, equipment, and communications (among other things). It would be tidier if banging out a perfect application were simply a matter between you and FoxPro, but the context of application development is seldom tidy. You should not be surprised that the context (life in disguise) will intrude on your application development process.

For one thing, unless you are developing applications strictly for yourself, there are always other people who have an interest, perhaps a stake, in what you create. The computer industry tends to lump these other people into a broad category: *users*. You will know them as customers, clients, employers, colleagues, or friends. Much of the time you will even know them by name, and their wishes are often what start the application in the first place.

In short, applications are developed for someone and are supposed to do something. These are touchstones that interact, because the people who use the application will ultimately determine whether it does what they want. Also, the number of people who will use the application and the complexity of what it does will largely determine the scale of the project.

Organizing application development has three components: you, the application, and the users. To do the work, you need to get yourself organized, including the setup for programming covered in Chapter 8, your understanding of how application development works, and the management of your resources (your time and energy, if nothing else). Organizing the application entails a continual process of analysis and design so that all the necessary elements come together during development, especially given the way object-oriented applications are constructed. Organizing the users, although not exclusively the role of the developer, includes management of expectations, communications, and often complex scheduling.

THE START OF AN APPLICATION

It might be a phone call, a visit from a client, or a memo from your boss. Perhaps you won a bid. The start of an application is exciting. (If it isn't, you're in the wrong business.) It represents a new challenge—a challenge to your powers of analysis, your skill with people, your judgment, and your programming acumen. I'm speaking of the process as if it were a personal project, although you might be part of a development team, or even its leader. It's the same process but you might have different parts of the responsibility.

It's always interesting to compare your impression of an application on the first day you hear of it with your concept of it on the day it's delivered. The beginnings are usually fuzzy and often consist of nothing more than some general information. For the LIMS project, it was something like this:

- **The job at hand:** Develop a laboratory information management system that tracks samples from the moment they are received at the laboratory until they are tested, recorded, reported, and finally disposed of.
- **The client and users:** The client is an environmental laboratory that tests water, soil, food, and other materials for pesticides and other contaminants. The users are mostly degreed technicians, many of them experienced with computers. However, there has never been a lab-wide software program, and a centralized approach such as a LIMS may not appeal to all employees.

- **The hardware and software:** The project will be done with Visual FoxPro on Intel-based computers (Pentium 100s and better) running Windows 95 or NT 4.0 and on a Novell LAN.
- **First impression:** Tracking samples looks like a manufacturing process, with testing being the value-added activity. The variety of samples is large and could be difficult to characterize. It's a good bet that many procedure and policy decisions need to be made for a LIMS, a major complication for both analysis and implementation.
- **First step:** Go talk to someone, preferably the person who is paying for the project. We'll assume the estimated time-line is too short and the budget barely adequate, but these real-world considerations are outside the scope of this book.

RESEARCH AND INTERVIEW

The first phase of analysis is usually very active, as you try to gather information about the application in as many ways as time allows. Much of your best circumstantial information will come from meetings or interviews with the people involved. The main task is to get a good description of what people do in their work: the procedures, flow of information, daily routines, communications, and so forth.

At the same time, you're also probing their desires (and fears), knowledge (and ignorance), and general opinion about the project. On the one hand, you're trying to get a list of needs relevant to the application from as many people as possible. On the other hand, you're trying to assess the "political" environment—attitudes and relationships that may affect the application development process.

For the LIMS application, interviews covered all the main groups of employees: administrative, technical, and support. The LIMS is an intrusive program in the sense that almost every employee will have some part of his or her job affected by a requirement to use the software. Therefore, there was a need to acquire information about most employees and certainly all major job categories.

At the same time you interview, you start collecting stuff—*information artifacts*, in the jargon of the analysis trade. You ask for any relevant reports, forms, documents, publications, computer programs, memos, notes, and so forth that have a bearing on what the application is supposed to do and how the employees do work that is related to the application. You need to convey the idea to people that you want to see everything with a minimum of selectivity.

In most cases, it's also valuable to observe people doing the work involved in the application, whether it's filling out forms, processing phone calls, or, in the case of the LIMS, their testing procedures and other laboratory practices. If time and practicality allow, it might even be a good idea to do some of the work. As an application developer, you will rarely be an expert in the all the work areas covered by the application, but there's no defense for being an ignoramus about them.

As all this information comes flooding in, you start to analyze it. That's where the four analytical approaches mentioned earlier come into play. They are certainly not the only ways to view the information, but they're mainstream approaches and provide a reasonably comprehensive framework for analysis.

FUNCTIONAL ANALYSIS

The term *functional analysis* is something of a catch-all, encompassing any kind of analysis that attempts to model how systems function. Mostly, it is about what people do in their work—the discrete events of their job.

The word *function* sometimes gets in the way of understanding the approach; it's so overloaded with different meanings that people think too hard about it. It's best to keep the concept as simple as possible: In their work people do specific things. A lab analyst prepares a sample, tests it, derives results from the tests, and reports the results—these are all functions of the job. Functional analysis is mostly about noting these various actions, and steps—events—as a framework for a program.

In the case of the functions for the lab analyst, most (but not necessarily all) will play a role in a computer application. Certainly the results of the tests will be entered in a computer screen, and quite possibly the calculations from which the results are derived will be computer routines. However, the goal of functional analysis is not to match functions one-to-one with program elements, but rather to provide an abstract, albeit concise, description of the sequence of events involved in the system as a whole.

NOTE

The term *system* in this context includes all the things relevant to the area in which the computer program is to be applied. If you're building an inventory application, you analyze the client's inventory system. In this sense, systems include people (with their job category and the events of their work) and also the activity of computer programs, communications, or many other kinds of events (with or without human involvement) associated with an area of work.

As you begin to list and refine the functions, you may turn to a number of different diagramming approaches, including dependency diagrams, Jackson diagrams, and functional flow charts (as in Figure 14.1) to represent the analysis. Most people find the diagrams easier to understand than detailed listings.

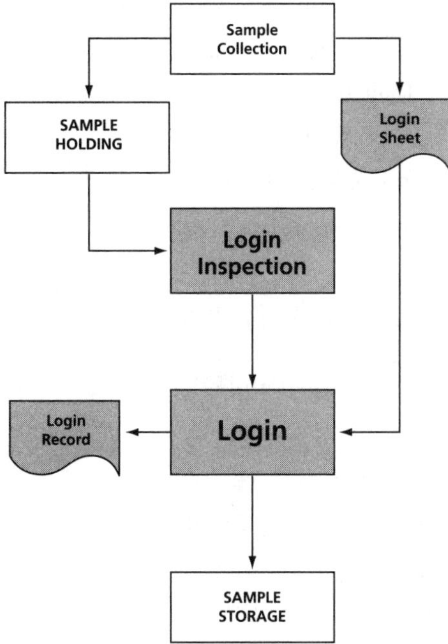

FIGURE 14.1 A FLOW CHART OF FUNCTIONAL COMPONENTS.

On the other hand, the detailed listings of functions can help you derive two useful techniques for analysis: function points and scenarios.

FUNCTION POINT ANALYSIS

Function points, as a concept, were first described by Allan Albrecht in 1979 to denote "one end-user business function" or, more generally, the outwardly observable and testable behaviors of a system. In this case, "system" means computer software; "observable" means that the user can see what the program does; and "testable" implies that the results of the computer operations can be verified; for example, a report accurately calculates its information.

Function points are usually derived from the detailed list of functions compiled during earlier analysis. Here, for example, are the functions (events) involved in the process known as sample login for the LIMS application:

1. The samples are placed in the holding area.
2. A login sheet is prepared.
3. The login sheet is delivered.
4. The login sheet is received.
5. The login sheet is examined.
6. Basic information is logged and a sample batch created.
7. Each sample is logged.
8. A batch record is created.
9. A batch is marked as logged and approved.
10. Samples are moved to appropriate storage.

And here are the items in this list that can be considered function points because they involve computerization in the application:

1. Basic information is logged and a login batch created.
2. Each sample is logged.
3. A batch record is created.
4. A batch is marked as logged and approved.

This isn't all that a login program should do, but these are some of the "outwardly observable and testable" functions that people will expect it to perform (or support). One of the benefits of using function points is their close relationship with complexity: The more points, the more complex the application. In some cases, function points can also be used as the basis of specifications or testing metrics (measuring the success or failure of a project), but for the purposes of working with Visual FoxPro, function points are most useful as a gateway to object-oriented analysis.

OBJECT-ORIENTED ANALYSIS

Fortunately, the starting point of object-oriented analysis (OOA) isn't much different from that of most other kinds of analysis. It tends to be based on the functions involved in a system (application) and usually draws on familiar sources of information for data items, descriptions of people's work, and other business processes. What's different about OOA is the outcome: candidate classes and their potential relationships.

Rather than dwell on functions, OOA moves on to look for things in function points that may constitute objects. These elements may include the following:

- Things (samples, lab instruments, bottles)
- Places (storage room, refrigerator, bio-lab)
- People or roles (chemist, biologist, administrator)
- Events (testing, alarms)
- Concepts (quality control, batches)
- Organizations (lab units, client companies)

The most generally recommended route to deriving objects is through scenarios.

USING SCENARIOS

There are some similarities between movie scenarios and object-oriented scenarios: They're both abbreviated stories about a situation or event. Object-oriented *scenarios* describe the system functions of an application. In practice, this means that they are usually based on function points. Here's an example:

> **Function point**: Basic information is logged and a login batch created.
>
> **Scenario**: The registrar enters the basic login information (source, type, client) and creates a login batch.

The scenario fleshes out the function point with people, places, events, times, and other details that not only enhance the understanding of the function point but also provide the basis for object-oriented analysis. Here are all the LIMS login function points translated into scenarios:

1. The registrar enters the basic login information (source, type, client) and creates a login batch.
2. The registrar logs each sample and, depending on the sample type, may check for specific login conditions that may result in a sample rejection (for example, a dairy sample being above 4 degrees centigrade).
3. A record of the batch is presented to the client for approval.
4. If approved by the client and the registrar, the batch is marked as logged.

Scenarios can be drawn up with users, experts in the domain of the application, and the developer(s). Then each scenario is analyzed, essentially by expanding the description to include any and all relevant details—the people, places, and things—and then converting these details into classes, the relationships between classes, and the operations that objects of these classes perform on one another. For example, for the first scenario, we might derive the following classes: **aRegistrar**, **aClient**, **loginInfo**, and **loginBatch**. The relationships might be represented like this:

	aRegistrar	loginInfo	aClient	loginBatch
Registrar enters basic login information	——————>	enters		
If the client is known				
data is filled in		fill	<———	
else				
registrar creates new client entry	——————>	—————>	create	
A **loginBatch** is created by the program			————>	creates

As in this example, the scenarios are often expanded to include rules and exceptions (called *secondary* scenarios). From analysis of the scenario, patterns and relationships may suggest more abstract or generalized scenarios or may more directly evolve into class diagrams that show the relationships among the key objects (see Figure 14.2 for an example). This class diagram becomes the representation of the candidate classes (with some of their methods) for the portion of the application covered by the scenario.

NOTE

In another similarity with movie scenarios, object-oriented scenarios are often developed and analyzed in brainstorming sessions complete with storyboards and walk-throughs. Not only is this a more interesting way to do software analysis, but also, if handled well, it never loses sight of what's important: systematically capturing the real (and relevant) events.

For all the login scenarios, this diagram was a listing of candidate classes: **aRegistrar**, **aClient**, **aSample**, **loginBatch**, **loginInfo**, and **sampleCollectionInfo**. If you're well organized, the results of each scenario analysis are logged (perhaps to a development data dictionary). When all the scenarios are completed, the candidate classes can be analyzed for consolidation, finer definition, and more-precise relationships. There's nothing particularly mysterious about this process, but in a

large application it can become complicated simply by the sheer numbers of scenarios and the resulting horde of classes and objects they may suggest.

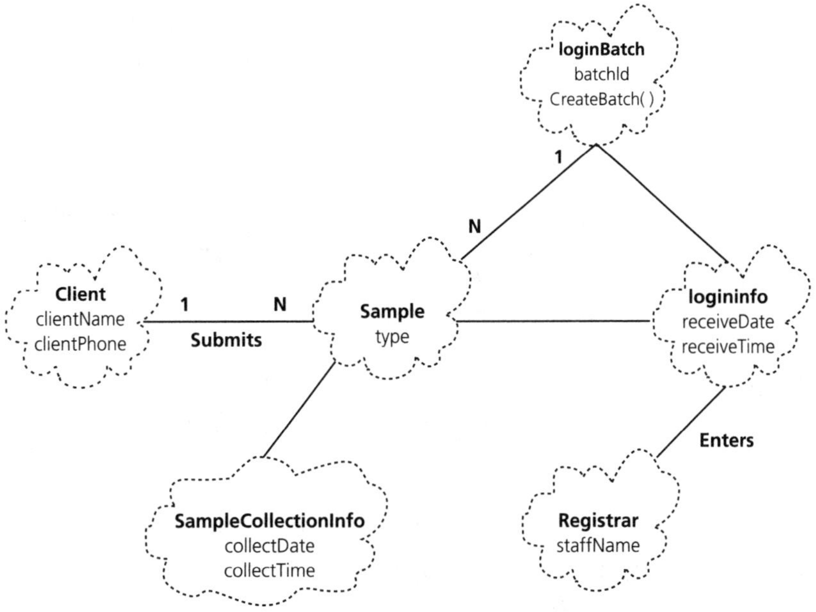

FIGURE 14.2 CLASS DIAGRAM FOR A LIMS LOGIN SCENARIO.

NOTE

It's important to note that to this point, no mention has been made of any Visual FoxPro classes or of any relationship between FoxPro's object-oriented implementation and the results of the analysis. This is the classic approach: Analysis is about what the application should be and not how it should be done. On the other hand, it may be helpful to note that almost all these classes, if they become implemented, will be custom classes and not based on visual classes. They're often referred to as business classes.

DATA ANALYSIS

Whereas the functional aspects of a system are mostly discovered by working with people (and that is why the scenario approach is effective), data analysis usually proceeds from working with the information artifacts: reports, memos, computer programs, and so forth. Just as you think through scenarios to uncover the abstractions (objects and methods), you scan through the information artifacts for *data items*: discrete pieces of information that may (or may not) become fields in a table.

Existing reports are invaluable as a starting point, because they indicate in a formally organized way what people wanted for information in the context of the application you're analyzing. You can expect a percentage of data in the reports to be useless, and there will be new data items not in the reports, but it's not unusual for the majority of the data in current reports to show up in a new system.

In doing analysis for a LIMS application, there was no lack of a paper trail. Laboratories generate reams of report data daily. The problem was that the reports came from many sources: typewritten, stand-alone PCs, networked PCs, and even a large mainframe located at a state agency. None of the reporting was coordinated, of course, so each piece had to be analyzed in its own context and then (hopefully) the data items pooled with those of other sources.

As you study the various information sources, you are usually doing three things:

1. Collecting data items and giving them a quick definition.
2. Aggregating data items that appear to be related.
3. Attempting to identify relationships between aggregates of data.

In abbreviated and crude form, the process looks something like the following. First, a collection of data items (definitions are omitted) gleaned from the many sources of data might look like the list in Table 14.1.

TABLE 14.1 LIMS APPLICATION: CANDIDATE DATA ITEMS

ITEM	ITEM	ITEM	ITEM
login date	rejection criteria	sample collection date	test requested1
login time	rejection description	sample collection time	test requested2
login registrar name	rejection approval	sample collector name	test requested3
login location	sample disposition	sample collection site	test requested4
login temperature	login batch number	sample condition	special handling
login storage	login condition	sample packaging	handling specs
sample receive date	transported by	sample sealed	billable sample
sample receive time	transport date	sample split	bill-to name

ITEM	ITEM	ITEM	ITEM
sample receiver name	transport time	sample matrix type	bill-to address
sample rcv.location	transport method	sample matrix	bill-to phone
client company	client report by date	client sample number	sample hazard
client address	client report to name	sample type	sample disposal
client primary phone	client report to phone	sample description	sample safety
client contact	client description	sample container	sample EPA number
client contact title	client site number	sample	sample label

Because the items came from various documents, they were already grouped to a certain extent, an arrangement that is helpful but sometimes misleading. Overall, the LIMS project identified more than 2,200 potential data items. Because of the large number, there was plenty of room for redundancy, fuzzy definition, and gaps in coverage, all of which needed to be cleaned up during analysis. The preliminary list in Table 14.1, covering login only, has had some weeding and feeding (culling redundancies and adding standard items), but only enough to help categorize the data. Again, this is analysis of what's known and not the creation of a design for final computerization.

The next step is to *aggregate* the items: to group them by some kind of categorization. This process usually starts with some tentative but often fairly obvious groupings. For example, using the collection of data items suggested the following groups:

- Samples
- Clients
- Tests
- Batches
- Billing information
- Login information
- Lab staff

As you look at the list, you may wonder, "Why these?" Perhaps you think there's a Transport group, because several of the data items are labeled that way. Actually, they are slightly mislabeled, because what is being transported are samples, and so these items are really part of the samples group. In this same way, the seven groups cover all the data items, but they're all subject to revision with more analysis, especially in the design phase.

These groupings are candidate tables, and their constituent data items are candidate fields; but we're still quite a way from being able to make that transformation. The relationships among these groups can best be shown with a simple diagram (Figure 14.3).

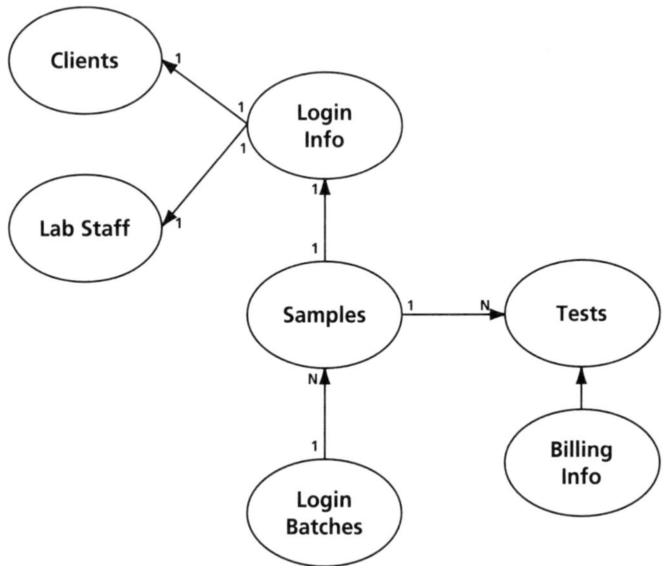

FIGURE 14.3 CANDIDATE DATA GROUPINGS AND THEIR RELATIONSHIPS.

Compare this diagram with Figure 14.2 for the classes and their relationships. Notice any similarities? You should, because (happily) the results of object-oriented analysis and data analysis have considerable overlap. However, in a sense, data analysis is a subset of OOA; it covers only the data portion of an application, whereas OOA covers not only data but also the user interface and other kinds of processing.

Theoretically, a thorough object-oriented analysis should arrive at a set of classes that map directly to tables. This is jargon expressing the following rules of thumb:

- Each class is represented as one or more tables.
- Each many-to-many association between classes is represented in a table.

- Each one-to-many association between classes maps to a table, or one class becomes a foreign key in the other class—a foreign key field in a table.

The correlations between classes and tables do not imply that a relational database design and an object-oriented analysis lead to the same thing. In the design phase of an application, there are many specific considerations for relational design that are only tenuously connected (at most) to object-orientation. Similarly, there are many aspects of object-oriented design that will not relate directly to the underlying database structure. This is especially true of Visual FoxPro's implementation, which tends to compartmentalize the relational data handling from the object-oriented user interface.

NOTE

There is some controversy among developers about whether analysis should start with an object-oriented or a data-oriented approach. This is something of a strawman argument. Each kind of analysis has its place, and it matters very little which one is done first.

BUSINESS RULES ANALYSIS

As covered briefly in Chapter 10, there are rules, written or unwritten, for every job and task in business. When you set about building an application to computerize one or more of these tasks, you'll need to embed these rules in your program. They can be as simple as rules for calculation (formulas). For example:

Rule: All temperatures in Fahrenheit must be converted to Celsius.

Code: `nCelsius = (5*(nFahrenheit-32))/9`
Or they can be as complicated as a series of **IF, ELSE** conditions. Using a LIMS example, a particular decision rule to reject a sample at login might be expressed this way:

Rule: Any dairy sample that has a temperature of greater than 4 degrees C at the time of login, and has a temperature of greater than 2 degrees C at the time of collection or has been in transport for longer than four hours, cannot be accepted for login without approval from a supervisory biologist of the microbiology unit.

Code:

```
IF sample.type = "DAIRY" AND lnCelsius > 4
  IF log.CollectTemp > 2 OR
    (log.logtime - log.collecttime) > 240
     * Signal Lab for supervisor
     SELECT log
    SCATTER TO ARRAY laLabCall
     = LabCall("TEMP08","MICRO",@laLabCall)
  ELSE
    * Notice of potential violation in sample log.
    =UpdateLog("WARN003")
  ENDIF
ELSE
  *Normal update to sample log
  =UpdateLog("NORMAL")
ENDIF
```

Business rules are attached to fields, records, and tables on the data side. They may also be attached to processes between objects, to part of a class's methods, or to one of the properties of an object. The latter is especially true for business rules that are part of Visual FoxPro forms.

Traditionally, in most PC programming (and elsewhere), business rules have been incorporated on-the-fly. They have been added as they became necessary and too often have been embedded (hidden) in the code in ways that make it extremely cumbersome to make changes. Although client/server techniques and capabilities, such as FoxPro's triggers, make it possible to store business rules in a more coherent and maintainable fashion, the only way to be truly organized is to make business rules an explicit part of the analysis process.

Implementing this policy will not be easy for two reasons: First, business rules are often not explicit, and considerable effort must be expended to detect their existence and then clarify them. Second, the attempt to make rules explicit may trigger policy debates and raise other organizational issues. This may be healthy for the organization, but it usually contributes only headaches and delays to the development effort.

Unfortunately, there is no good "one approach fits all" technique for business rule analysis. There are a number of books on the subject, and they espouse elaborate methodologies. If your application is rule-intensive or simply so big that it contains many rules, it may be worthwhile to investigate the formal methodologies. Otherwise, a few commonsense procedures will probably be sufficient for most applications.

As you perform the other elements of analysis (interview, research, functional analysis, OOA, and data analysis), be alert for business rules, either those explicitly documented (this happens occasionally) or those you sense are present. Be especially aware of rules in data items dealing with money, counts, and codes. In object-oriented analysis, look for rules as part of the operations that objects perform on each other. For example, the client object updates a login form; what does that "update" mean, and when is it permissible? Then document the rules you find, perhaps using the following guidelines:

- Devise or adopt a standardized notation for rules.
- Attach a unique identifier to each rule.
- Log each rule in a table (perhaps as part of a data dictionary).
- As the application is designed, attempt to incorporate in classes rules that are not part of a database, so that each instance can be more readily tracked. (FoxPro has the capability of displaying every instance of a particular object.)
- Log the location of each rule as you program.
- Fully explain each rule, including a general description and the complete rationale.

The process of logging business rules will continue throughout the development cycle. Modifications will also be common. In fact, one of the reasons to complete an organized analysis of business rules is to use the analysis to guide clients into dealing with issues that must be settled for the application. The more clearly you can document and present the known rules, the better chance you will have of getting problems resolved—if they can be resolved enough for computerization.

The business rules of the LIMS application were voluminous, a set of binders eight inches thick just for the laboratory standard operating procedures. Even at that, many of the most complicated rules and procedures (especially for lab administration) existed only in the heads of key people. In some cases, it took nearly six months of effort before programmers and lab staff understood the rules well enough to computerize them. In fact, there were some business rules so complex they could not be reasonably computerized. An artificial intelligence program of some size and sophistication might have been able to handle it; but no one was willing to pay for such a thing, so the best choice was simply to let people do it. (This is often the best choice anyway.)

A Sample Format for Business Rule Documentation

If there is a problem with business rules, it's documentation. In the spirit of showing that it can be kept fairly simple, here's a format used for the LIMS documentation:

```
CATEGORY: TEST RESULTS ENTRY

RULE NAME: PARAMETER ASSIGNMENT: SPECIFIC ANALYTE

OBJECT REFERENCE:
tstcode.appForm.bctPageFrame1.Page5.bctOptiongroup1.Option1

CLASS: MODFRSBDF2TAB (MODFORM.VCX)

FORM:  TSTCODE.SCX

RULE:  Results entry parameters may be assigned to a specific analyte.

IMPLEMENTATION: By selecting Option1, the Results Entry module does a
lookup by method TSQ and analyte ID. If a match is found, the parame-
ters are applied.
```

The CATEGORY identifies the area of the program or function that is involved. The RULE NAME provides an easily readable handle for the rule. In applications that have several hundred rules, it's probably a good idea to load them into a FoxPro table. At that point, the text NAME won't be enough to provide a reliably unique identifier for the rule and you may need to add a RULEID field.

The OBJECT REFERENCE is filled in when the rule is coded into the application. It identifies the exact object reference of the rule location. Similarly, the CLASS and FORM (if any) of the rules location are listed after the rule is coded. The RULE itself is expressed in English, as clearly as possible. IMPLEMENTATION explains how the rule was expressed in the FoxPro language including any data management, variable expressions, calculations, or other algorithms involved.

As simple as this format is, it's still a major headache to maintain. That's why considerations of the cost of finding and changing rules must be weighed against the cost of documentation. The more important the rules and the more likely they are to need changing, the more it pays to do this kind of detailed documentation.

NOTE

One of the more important trends in client/server application development has been *partitioning*, a technique for separating not only client software (on the PC) from server software (on the LAN server) but also from the business rules, which may have their own server. Separating the business rules into a third layer makes it much easier not only to track and document the rules but also to ensure that they are regularly maintained at a central point. It also adds a major degree of complexity to application design as well as a certain level of performance headache. Unless you get very creative (and have the time), Visual FoxPro does not support this kind of partitioning, so perhaps it's a moot point. Still, you might want to explore some of the concepts of business rule partitioning if your application is heavily rule-oriented.

CASE Tools for FoxPro

All the forms of analysis covered so far can be approached through specific analysis *methodologies*, which tends to be a fancy word for diagramming. Diagrams can be wonderful. At their best, they communicate complex ideas quickly and clearly, even to non specialists. Diagrams can also be a nightmare. Creating them can be extremely time-consuming and frustrating, and the result can be an unintelligible hodgepodge of boxes, arrows, and arcane symbols. The best diagrams are usually the result of practice, commitment to the diagramming technique, and a CASE tool (or tools).

The two major approaches to CASE (computer-assisted software engineering), are usually referred to as upper CASE and lower CASE. Upper CASE is about software analysis and design. Lower CASE is about code generation from design tools—the sort of thing that FoxPro's Designers can do. But FoxPro has nothing to offer for upper CASE, and, although it may seem odd, there are as yet no third-party CASE products that marry relational database design with object-oriented analysis and design.

It's odd because in the past 10 years or so, the rush to find the perfect CASE tool has been a computer industry Holy Grail, and just as unattainable. For one thing, most of the comprehensive CASE implementations were designed for and by mainframe people. Their products are so complex and expensive that none of these CASE tools is widely used, much less in a position to solve all the major problems of PC software development. For another thing, the mainframe-based and minicomputer-based CASE systems have been hard-hit by the sudden drop in sales (and interest) in those hardware platforms. These CASE companies think nothing of charging $5,000 to $50,000 for their products, the norm in mainframe circles, and can't even contemplate making money selling to the PC crowd.

For the user of database management systems, especially an Xbase product such as FoxPro, the world of upper CASE has until recently paid them scant attention. Few of the CASE programs know anything about DBF files or the operational syntax of an Xbase application. That may be changing, slowly. Software such as EasyCase, by PineTree Systems, and xCase for FoxPro, by Neon Software, runs on standard Windows hardware and not only is more in the range of a PC pocketbook but also directly supports DBF files. As more of these PC-based products come to market, they're worth considering. They may even make the work of formal analytical methodologies more palatable.

How much CASE you use is directly related to how much formal analysis and design you believe is necessary in building your application. Many programmers cringe at the thought of spending days interviewing and researching and then more days tweaking diagrams. Other developers find the methods useful, and still others believe that they can't do their job without them. It all depends on the nature of the applications and on personal preferences.

NOTE

For smaller applications, it may be practical to produce analytical and design diagrams using popular drawing tools such as Corel Draw or Visio. As tools, these products contribute little to the overall process; unlike real CASE tools, they don't generate code or provide a framework of methodology. But they are relatively easy to use and can be customized to present many kinds of software diagrams. Visio has an inexpensive set of software development "templates" (premade symbols and connectors) for a variety of techniques, including both Booch and Rumbaugh notation for object-oriented analysis.

Chapter Wrap-Up

At the end of the analysis phase, you should have in hand at least four related but different kinds of information:

- A clear picture of the functionality required for the application, usually as a list of function points accompanied by diagrams.
- A listing, description, and diagrams of the key abstractions, usually expressed as candidate classes.

- A listing and diagrams of candidate data items, grouped by functionality or object-oriented principles into candidate tables (or databases).
- A listing of business rules involved in the application.

The amount and level of detail required depends on the application. The goal is to understand the application and the environment in which it works, including what is called *domain*-related knowledge, or the area of work covered by an application—for example, laboratory practices for a LIMS, accounting principles for an accounting application, and so forth. Also related to the application's domain is the knowledge of the people who will be using the application as well as their needs and the workplace politics. All of this can affect the development of an application.

CHAPTER 15

DESIGNING AN APPLICATION

If you've done your fieldwork (analysis), it's time for the homework (design). You should have a good idea what the users want and how the application should (or perhaps should not) reflect the way people do their work—sometimes called the *behavior* of the system. Whether formally or informally, you should have acquired listings of candidate classes and data items along with ideas about how they can be grouped or categorized. All these elements will be converted during the design process into something you can do with Visual FoxPro: the implementation.

In large part, the increasing flexibility of the programming tools has made rapid prototyping possible and has enhanced the ability to "fix" applications as they are built. Still, it's fair to say that more applications are made or doomed at the design phase than at any other. This does not mean that design is the most important phase, but, as the focal point for analysis and the blueprint for implementation, its role is pivotal.

The essential guide for application design is the *overview*: the ability not only to envision the class structure or data structures but also to develop a vision of the whole. An overview includes the following elements:

- Class structure and hierarchy
- Database design
- User interface design
- Required components

An overview isn't easy to acquire; it takes both experience and effort. But the successful design of a complete, full-scale application may require a sense for *architecture*, a structural view of the whole. Smaller applications can be developed without such a grand vision. Often, an abbreviated approach, keeping only the basic elements, can be effective for smaller projects.

Most of this application architecture—especially those elements that are built for all applications and can be used repeatedly—can be developed using an application framework. In this chapter we'll cover basic design considerations in a relatively abstract way, including the application framework. In later chapters, most of the same elements will be taken up in the implementation of various FoxPro classes, and that should help make the abstractions more realistic.

Designing an Application Framework

As we have been developing the theme throughout the book, an application framework is a way of organizing program elements, ideally in an easily repeatable and reliable fashion. What it organizes generally falls into three categories:

- Structural elements that are standard for most applications: Form, FormSet, Toolbar, Grid, data management, application management classes, and so on.
- Components that are standard for most applications: security system, error trapping, network management, and so on.
- The elements that are specific to the domain of the application.

In Figure 15.1, you'll notice that most of the elements are either classes or completed application modules. That's because the classes are already a blueprint that's used during programming to create most of the application, and the modules are designed as plug-and-play units to work with the rest of the framework. A framework specifies which classes and modules are available for a more or less generic application, how they fit together, and how other elements (the domain-specific material) are integrated.

The framework is composed of the following:

- **An architecture document**. In the formal development of an application framework (it's tempting to say *serious* development), an architecture document is created that describes how an application is constructed using the application framework. The document spells out the generic components and classes and describes how they work and how they are integrated with other elements. This information is mostly programming documentation, but its focus should be on the whys and wherefores of the generic elements.

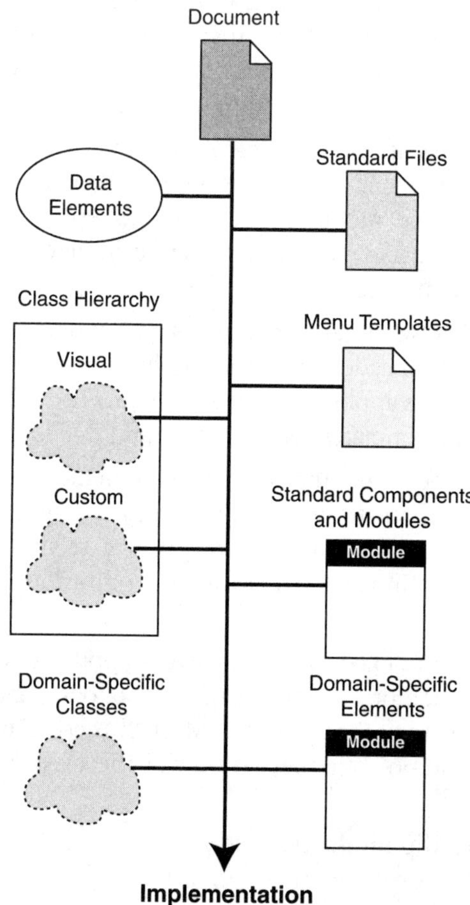

FIGURE 15.1 AN APPLICATION FRAMEWORK.

- **The data elements**. Virtually every FoxPro application involves data management. The design and implementation of the database system are extremely important, although in most respects they are the least "reusable" elements of the application framework.

- **The class hierarchy**. The most important part of the application framework is the creation and documentation of subclasses of the Visual FoxPro base classes. Because the base classes can't be modified, the generic subclasses are created to provide flexibility and a high degree of customization. For example, application frameworks have subclasses of the base classes that add functionality with new methods and properties. From that, you create a hierarchy of subclasses, usually grouped into *class categories*, that cover the basics of an application from error trapping to most of the user interface.
- **Standard application modules**. As outlined later in this chapter, many components of an application lend themselves to becoming fully encapsulated modules—for example, error trapping systems and report management. The application framework specifies how these components are used.
- **Standard files**. Many applications use a standard initialization file and one or more header (.H) files to define constants, variables, and other items of the application's environment. The application framework provides templates for these files and documents their use.
- **Menu templates**. Like the standard files element, menu templates are neither difficult to create nor of special importance, although every application has menus. You need a relatively small set of basic menus—templates—that can be modified as needed for each application.
- **Domain-specific classes**. Almost every application creates classes to deal with the domain-related specifics of data management, user interface, and logical processing. Most of these classes are unique to the application, but they use all of the class hierarchy as the foundation.
- **Domain-specific modules**. A few applications may need application modules (or components) that are unique to the application but are used in several different instances within the application. These domain-specific modules are handled in much the same way as the standard modules—again, as specified by the architecture document.

Over a period of time and a number of applications (if you intend to build several), you can continually refine and augment an application framework. For some people, it will become an elaborate and formal system; for others, it will combine a few tried and true elements as required by an application. There are many ways to implement a framework. The best way is the one you will actually maintain.

WARNING

Some of the worst applications—that is, failures—are products of avid object-oriented developers who create mountains of classes, either by design or by the seat of their pants, without considering whether the accumulation of classes is appropriate or how the classes interact. It should be stressed that most successful OOP applications grow incrementally, with experience, from a relatively small number of classes.

With that cautionary note in mind, let's get started with the most important part of an application framework: the class hierarchy.

OBJECT-ORIENTED DESIGN

Object-oriented design is (or should be) one of the most important steps in developing applications in Visual FoxPro. There are two main aspects of object-oriented design: the short-term consideration of designing and implementing a particular application, and the long-term desire to develop and reuse classes and objects. The first aspect takes the work done during analysis and devises the appropriate class structure to reflect the application at hand. The second aspect is architectural (concerned with the overall structure of an application) and involves being alert for ways to organize applications in a generic fashion, especially with a class hierarchy—in short, to evolve an application framework.

DESIGNING A CLASS HIERARCHY

By now you're familiar with inheritance and the way classes can be subclassed to share methods and properties. You start with basics, the Visual FoxPro base classes, and subclass them to add more functionality. Although you can subclass more or less willy-nilly, there will probably come a time when it strikes you that organizing the subclasses might be a good thing. There are many ways to structure classes in a hierarchy. Figure 15.2 shows the arrangement used in this book.

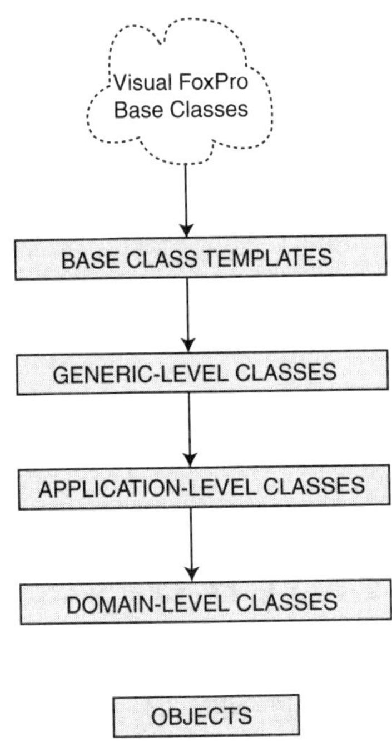

FIGURE 15.2 CLASS HIERARCHY DESIGN.

CLASS LEVELS

In this scheme, both visual and custom FoxPro base classes are used to create a class category (stored as a VCX class library) of *base class templates*: modified and augmented base classes. Creating base class templates gets around the inability to modify the methods or properties of the FoxPro base classes. For all practical purposes, you forget about the FoxPro classes and build everything else with the base class templates. This level is the top of the hierarchy.

The next level down in the chain of inheritance makes use of the base class templates to create a *generic* level. At this level, the base class templates (grids, forms, and controls) are combined, and that immediately distinguishes the generic classes from the base class templates. The generic classes may also be enhanced (using new method code and properties) but only with the most generic features. The idea is that a generic-level class could be used even in a quick-and-dirty program the doesn't need the software machinery of a complete application. This level is clean enough—free of complications—to use as a test if something isn't working with the levels further down the hierarchy. A good example is a simple base class template Form combined with a base class template Toolbar to make a generic FormSet.

The *application* level takes the generic classes and adds programming to make them suitable for a full-scale application. For example, if you decide that application windows should be opened where the user last put them, you need a table to store the locations and code to manage the window positions. A considerable amount of program machinery is involved, and it shows up in every Form class. This feature must be formally initialized when a program is started, and you'd expect it to function throughout the application. The same is true for LAN and multiuser enhancements, security systems, help systems, and a number of other, more or less standard features of applications. What you don't have, at this level or the generic level, is much attention to cosmetic differences such as colors or shapes.

The application and generic classes can be used in virtually any application, but as soon as you need to attach application-specific tables or create methods (especially custom methods) that are useful only within the application, you don't want them in the application level. The same goes for color schemes, font choices, and a host of user interface design features. That's when you shift to the *domain* level.

At the domain level are two characteristic types of classes: forms customized for a particular application, and custom classes to implement the business rules, data processing, and specialized routines of the application. Whenever possible, these classes are kept generic enough to be reused within the application itself.

The class levels are the fundamental organization of the class hierarchy and are designed primarily to fit the way developers put together applications with OOP components. Most of the application is built with things from the bottom levels of the hierarchy, but the entire hierarchy is fair game depending on what's needed.

CLASS CATEGORIES

The levels of the class hierarchy structure are composed of class categories: groups of related classes that are stored in a class library (VCX) file. Figure 15.3 illustrates an arrangement of these categories.

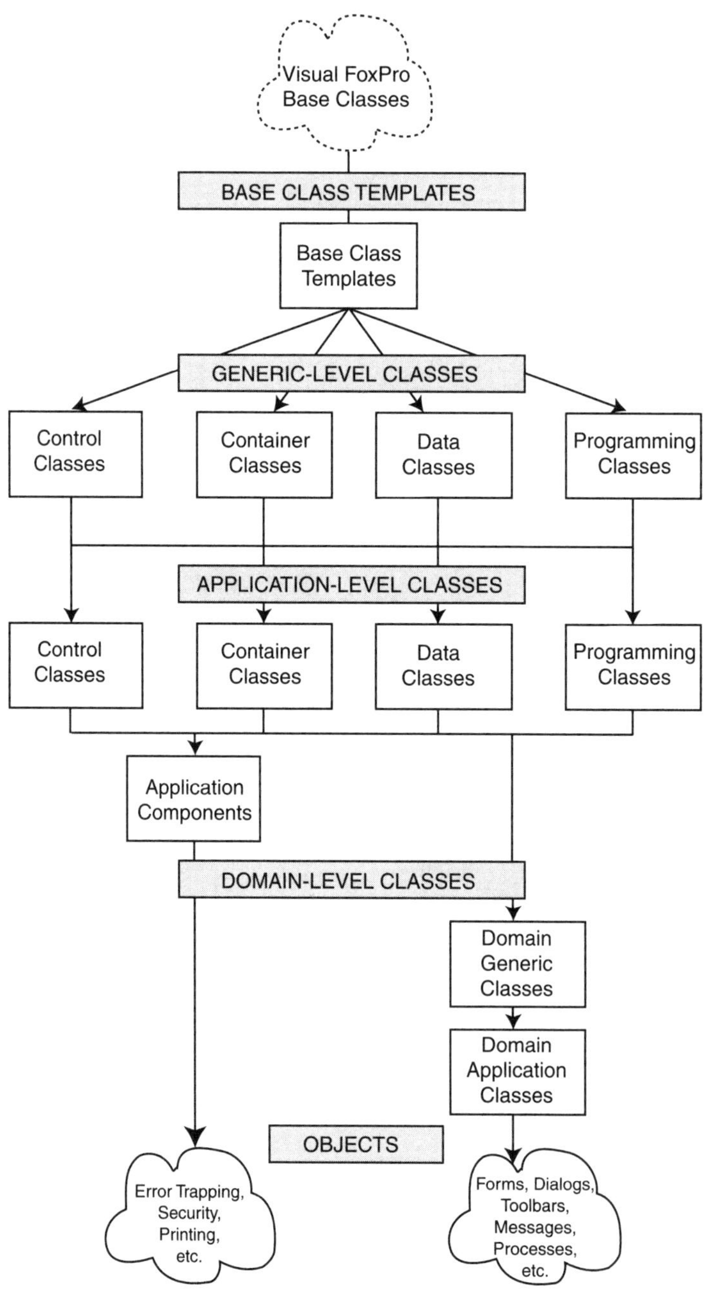

Figure 15.3 Class hierarchy, class categories.

The base class templates occupy one category of their own and one class library file (for example, BCT.VCX). To keep the structure simple there are only four categories—control, container, data, and programming—and they are repeated in the generic and application levels. The control category includes the control classes—those built from the visual base class template controls—such as **genTextBox**, **genSpinner**, and **appTbrButtonTop**. You'll notice that there's a naming convention at work. We'll get to that in Chapter 16.

The container class category at the generic level has enhanced visual containers (**genForm**, **genGrid**) and combined containers (**genFormSet**, **genCmdMore**). These basic forms and grids have been given enhancements such as automatic sizing of a grid within a form. The combined containers are the beginnings of useful classes, such as a FormSet, but they don't have any methods or properties that require special setup. That's easily contrasted with the container classes at the application level: **appGridPick**, **appFormSet**. These descendants of the generic classes have added methods and properties for automatic window location, application security, and multiuser data entry (among other things).

The data classes handle often-used data management routines, such as opening the database and adding new records. Most of these classes are at the generic level, because they can be applied to a large number of situations: **genTable**, **genField**. The programming category has the most complex classes at either the generic or application level. The generic classes, such as **genFoxTools** and **genSound**, handle enhancements to FoxPro commands and functions. The application programming classes, such as **appError** and **appSecure**, are the engines for major functions such as error management and application security.

This arrangement of class categories separates visual from nonvisual classes and attempts to put classes into useful groups. It generally implies that one class category has an inheritance link to the category of the same name in the next level down, such as from generic controls to application controls. This is basically true, except that the further down the hierarchy you go, the more likely it is for the classes to contain inheritance from classes in categories either from above or on the same level.

CLASS INHERITANCE

What, exactly, is inherited in a class hierarchy like this one? To begin with, everything built into the FoxPro base classes is inherited, especially properties and methods. Also inherited are event methods that contain code, user-defined methods, and all user-defined properties. Figure 15.4 shows how classes inherit and can be combined within the class categories.

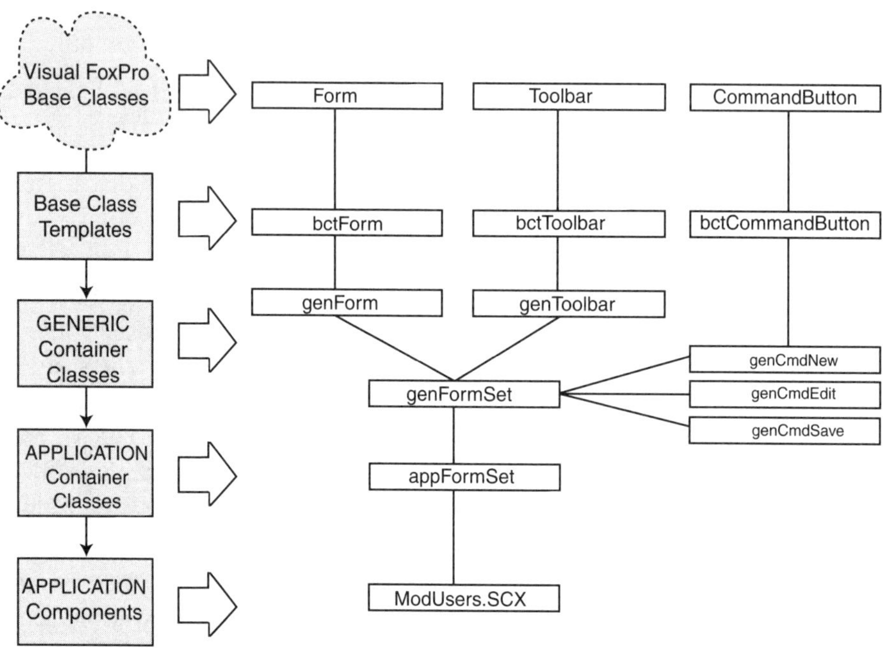

FIGURE 15.4 CLASS INHERITANCE IN THE HIERARCHY.

Combinations are usually a matter of containership—for example, with PageFrames, Grids and similar classes being added to Forms. Custom classes start as nonvisual, but they often define methods that use visual containers. That's how inheritance can become complicated in a large hierarchy.

The complications don't matter once you get a class thoroughly tested and debugged, but if something goes wrong or you introduce a new class, the lines of inheritance become vulnerable. For example, you might put some generic code in the **Resize** event method to automatically resize a PageFrame (as we did in Chapter 11). Suppose that at the application level you decide to put code in the **Resize** method that will dock a toolbar. When you open the Code window on the **Resize** method, it's empty, because the inherited code is back up in the generic level. So you blithely enter the new code. You've just canceled the execution of the inherited code, and suddenly your PageFrame stops adjusting to the size of the form.

There are ways around this problem; the **DODEFAULT( )** function is available to force FoxPro to execute inherited code. But you won't use this function unless you know there is code somewhere up the hierarchy that you want executed. That's where documentation comes in.

DOCUMENTING CLASSES IN THE HIERARCHY

In the documentation included on the accompanying disk, which covers a fairly extensive class hierarchy, here's the notation used to help overcome the problem of tracking inheritance:

```
TREE: ToolBar
      ➢ bctToolBar Init
      ➢ genToolBar Init*::
      ➢➢(genUserPrf) appToolBar
```

Each class has a class tree that begins with the Visual FoxPro base class and ends one subclass below the current class (if any). The "tree" is nothing more than a stack of each class, from top to bottom, on its own line. The ➢ symbol is used to indicate direct (single) inheritance. (Purists may eschew the graphic chevron in favor of the humble >.) In some cases, FoxPro containers may have objects from more than one class—a kind of multiple inheritance. These objects are annotated with the double arrow followed by the secondary superclass(es) in parentheses: ➢➢ `(genUserPrf)`.

It's important to list all event methods that contain code. If a subclass overrides a superclass event method, it's marked with an asterisk (*). If it also calls a superclass method, it's marked with the scope resolution operator (::). Here's a complete class entry:

genFrmDialogTabs

```
PARENT CLASS (LIBRARY): genFormDialog (GENCTAIN.VCX)
CATEGORY (LIBRARY): Generic Container (GENCTAIN.VCX)
TREE: Form
      ➢bctForm
      ➢genForm
      ➢genFrmDialog Init*::,Destroy,Unload
      ➢genFrmDialogTab (bctPageFrame)
          (bctCommandButton:Click)

PARAMETER: None
DESCRIPTION: A MODAL dialog form with two tabs.
USAGE: This can be used to create tabbed dialogs in a simple program
or application. At this level, it contains the minimum machinery nec-
essary to center and manage the dialog. There is a Close button. The
class returns a value to the calling program.
METHODS:
```

Click( ) Releases the dialog.

```
PROPERTIES: None
```

Maintaining this level of detail requires discipline, but it's probably some of most useful information you can have for an OOP system. Fortunately, after you experience the initial chaos of building a class hierarchy, classes stabilize and upkeep on this kind of documentation diminishes.

Is It Worth the Work?

Why go to the trouble of structuring classes in this or any similar way? Here are five good reasons.

- A structure makes it easier to understand the path of inheritance.
- Being systematic helps prevent overlapping functionality.
- The structure is, to a certain extent, self-documenting.
- Formal documentation tends to be easier and more consistent than informal documentation.
- It's easier to figure out what you have—and don't have.

If you have only a handful of classes, this elaborate structure might be counterproductive. On the other hand, class hierarchies tend to grow as you develop more applications. You start with the most basic and obvious classes, but over time you acquire specialized classes that also need a place in the hierarchy. It doesn't take long to acquire 100 or more classes, at which point keeping them organized becomes a necessity for most people.

NOTE

I suppose you're either into organized programming or you're not. I will say this, though: Because of the complex relationships set up by inheritance, object-oriented programming can be devilishly difficult to debug. An organized class hierarchy—one that you fully understand—is the best way to prevent problems and to solve them if they occur.

Other Approaches to a Class Hierarchy

The demonstration application Tasmanian Traders, supplied with FoxPro, is well worth your time to study. Open the TASTRADE project and look at the **Class** tab.

You'll see that class libraries have been created that loosely fit into the class structure described in this chapter: The **About** and **Login** libraries are typical application components; **Main** is the application-level initialization class category; **Orders** is a domain-specific class category; **Tsbase** contains the base class templates; and **Tsgen** has mostly generic-level utilities.

A contrasting approach can be found in *Visual FoxPro Codebook* (Yair Alan Griver, Sybex Inc., 1995). Here the classes have been structured on a functional basis; class library files that contain classes are grouped as interface, application behavior, and business. Except for deriving a "one-off" subclass of the Visual FoxPro base classes, most of the class libraries don't reflect layering. They're collections of classes around a central theme, such as CCustFrm for custom forms or Cbehavior for data behavior. The *Codebook* approach is all-encompassing, especially in its way of making objects from menus and Data Environments, elements that are not purely object-oriented in FoxPro.

NOTE

I'm bringing in these other approaches to illustrate that structuring a class hierarchy is not a radical idea and that there are many ways of doing it. As I said in Chapter 1, this book presents *a way* and leans in the direction of giving you enough information to go out and create your own. For a variety of reasons, that's not appropriate for everyone, so you may want to consider a number of approaches and even third-party class hierarchy products.

DOMAIN CLASSES

In the best of all possible OOP worlds, the entire application is built by instantiating generic classes. This ideal virtually never happens because most applications have more than enough unique data, specific user interface design requirements, and other peculiarities to require extensive programming at the domain level. Remember that classes in this level are built from classes taken from the hierarchy, inheriting, for example, multiuser and security behavior.

Many of the domain classes are built around the content of the domain: handling the data management, calculations, business rules, and special functions associated with a particular application. A good example can be found in the LIMS candidate classes that were uncovered during the analysis of the sample login scenarios: **Registrar**, **Client**, **Sample**, **loginBatch**, **loginInfo**, **sampleCollectionInfo**, and so on. Let's use the class **Sample**, because it involves both data collection and user activity.

Sample is supposed to handle the information about each sample. Because samples are the most important object in the LIMS, the **Sample** class will be called upon many times in the application under a variety of circumstances. Sometimes all that is needed is access to information about a single sample or a set of samples. Other times, a user display form is required, and still other situations call for ways to select and modify sample data. We need not only a **Sample** class but also a class category with its own file and a hierarchy of subclasses, each of whose classes are instantiated multiple times in the application.

If the analytical homework was thorough, there would be many scenarios covering various uses of a sample or sample-related activity; these scenarios would be our guide to designing a class structure. In FoxPro, class structures of this type are usually custom classes that use methods to capture the functionality of a class. An initial class structure, located in a domain data class category, might look like Table 15.1.

TABLE 15.1 SAMPLE DOMAIN CLASS STRUCTURE

CLASS	METHODS	DESCRIPTION

Sample	`GetSample()`
	`GetDetail()`
	`SetStatus()`
		Provides information on one sample and related data. Includes other generic methods for manipulating a sample.

SampleSQL	`GetView()` `ViewParms()`	Returns a view (cursor) with a number of specific properties.
SamplePick	`PickForm()` `OnColPick()`	Uses `GetView()` to pull data and then displays a list for selection.
SampleList	`SampleGrid()` `SetSort()`	Uses `GetView()` to fetch data and then provides a grid display.
SampleUpdate	`SampleForm()` `PageHandler()`	Creates a multipage display of both data and sample status information.

The final LIMS class structure for **Sample** had 10 subclasses and nearly 70 methods. It didn't look much like this example, because over time it evolved.

Designing application-specific classes is usually one of the trickiest (and most interesting) aspects of using object-oriented design. We've just touched on the subject here, but with more detail in Chapter 16 you should be able to distinguish between classes used for applications in general and those that are specific to one application.

DATABASE DESIGN

Many factors enter into your decisions about which databases and tables to create, which data items to put into them, how they should be indexed, and how they are related to other tables. Data integrity is usually a high priority for most databases, as is performance; but sometimes these two factors require a tradeoff: a little slower performance for intensive data validation. Let's review the design elements for data management.

NORMALIZATION

Normalization is the process of designing tables to eliminate redundant data and data not related to the primary key. There are practical and theoretical reasons to normalize a database, chiefly potential problems with maintenance and data integrity. Normalization also helps to categorize data into logically consistent units (database: ADMINISTRATION: tables: CLIENTS, LOCATIONS). This arrangement helps maintenance by making it easier to change table structures, because each table has a dynamic life of its own—without compromising any other table—as long as the relational links are maintained.

On the other hand, normalization is not without cost. The maintenance of a complex network of relations may carry a performance penalty. Depending on hardware and the type of use, FoxPro may show considerable performance degradation when maintaining more than three or four active relations during an operation. There are situations in which deliberate (emphasis on deliberate) violations of normalization rules are necessary to maintain acceptable performance.

The example LIMS was designed to meet a variation of the third normal form called the BCNF (Boyce-Codd Normal Form), a fairly rigorous approach. But for performance reasons, this level of normalization was occasionally compromised.

COMPLEXITY

Relational database systems tend to sprout files prolifically. It's not unusual for an average application to have 50–100 data-related files (DBC, DBF, and CDX). If most of the tables have multiple relations with other tables, the design of a schema quickly begins to look like the web of a mad spider. As the complexity level rises, so, too, do problems with maintenance, concurrency, performance, and data integrity.

The operative rule is not to create more files than you need. Of course, some applications are complex, and your design will reflect that fact. Sometimes, extra tables may help to simplify the content of a design even while they add to the complexity of the structure. For example, in the LIMS it was noted that most of the clients had at least two and often three or more associated addresses and phone numbers: for the main office, branch offices, warehouses, and so on. To keep all these addresses in the CLIENT table would mean many dead fields for some client records, so it was decided to create a LOCATION table to contain nothing but address-related information. This arrangement simplified the content of the CLIENT table considerably, but it added another permanent relation and two more files to the system.

PERFORMANCE

Performance has always been a signal feature of FoxPro. In fact, Visual FoxPro represents a monumental effort to coax speed from an operating system not noted for extreme performance, even in Windows 95. But there is more to a database than raw processing speed. When it comes to your application, you need to put performance into perspective with all the other factors.

Not all applications need blazing speed. Many applications should trade performance for security, data integrity, and other requirements. On the other hand, most FoxPro applications have active users, and although users don't generally sit in front of their computer with a stopwatch (if they do, you're in trouble), they have a subjective notion of the difference between fast and slow response.

Designing a database for performance usually means balancing many of the other factors. Almost all of them may contribute to diminishing performance; for example, too many relations and a complex file structure may have a performance penalty. Heavy multiuser activity diminishes performance. As a rule, the need for speed is not uniform throughout an application. Most users will wait minutes for a report to print—they know that printers are slow anyway—but they may become impatient waiting more than five seconds for a screen to refresh. If reading data is a factor, you may need to try all kinds of tricks to squeeze extra performance for certain situations and, at least in that operation, sacrifice some of the other requirements.

Characteristically, the LIMS had only a few spots where snappy response was a requirement, all of them dealing with the user interface, data being pulled from multiple tables, and the expectations of the users. The most difficult such area was a form that displayed the current status of a sample in many possible configurations. This form had to be redesigned three times to get adequate performance.

STORAGE SPACE

In theory, it is supposedly not desirable to consider physical factors, such as storage space, and performance, when you're designing tables and the database schema. To that, most relational designers say, "Get real." Hardware considerations are important. A database system that is underpowered, especially with an inadequate hard disk, will have performance problems and is more likely to have data integrity and concurrency problems.

As mentioned in Chapter 8, the storage space capacity of a database system is no longer the issue it was only five years ago. One-gigabyte hard drives now cost less than $200. A quick computation will show you the potential size of a database that will fit in a 1 GB drive, given a record size of 500 bytes (that's 20 fields of 25 characters): 1,000,000,000 / 500 = 2,000,000 records. Although space is never unlimited, cost is no longer much of a problem for a normal FoxPro database. This is not to imply that a database design can simply ignore data storage, but if you need 50 characters in a field, you don't usually need to cut back to 30 characters and force the users to make do.

NOTE

In terms of performance, the number of records in a table is more significant than the amount of data stored per record or in the table. Even with FoxPro's vigorous database engine, at some point many database operations become lengthy simply because there are so many records in the table. This point varies somewhat with the hardware, but 100,000 records is a rule of thumb.

The LIMS databases (ultimately there were four) were affected by the need to store the output of scientific testing equipment (mass spectrometers and gas chromatographs), which generate enormous volumes of data on a daily basis. The databases involved with that type of equipment store 20–50 gigabytes of data, while routinely dumping archival material to tape and optical storage.

CONCURRENCY

Concurrency is a fancy name for sharing files. It's safe to say that most applications will be run on LANs or some other form of multiuser system. As soon as more than one person needs simultaneous access to a table, you have a concurrency issue. This big subject is a major part of Chapter 19. In database design, consideration for multiuser operation may influence a number of decisions, including the distribution of tables—for example, the use of local files (files located on the hard disks of workstations rather than on network servers)—and the careful management of the FoxPro data buffers.

Concurrency also has an impact on data security, data integrity, and performance. The more people who use a system, the more opportunities exist for the data to be compromised. Protecting files against unwanted access, sudden hardware failure, and esoteric concurrency problems, such as the *deadly embrace* (in which two users lock each other out of a required table or record), need to be part of the design and utilization plan for the system. In a multiuser system, you need to ask yourself a number of questions about each table: How many people will need to access this? How often will it be accessed? How important is it too keep the table available?

In the LIMS, it was expected that 10–15 people would almost constantly be working with overlapping segments of tables. This is not a high degree of concurrency, but it's enough to make it necessary to review every table from the point of view of how it would be shared on the network and how the sequencing of record edits should be handled.

DATA INTEGRITY

In most databases the tolerance for bad data is very low. If a database system introduces data errors or allows users to create them, it won't be trusted for long. However, all data systems acquire errors, and some errors are more important than others. For example, currency and numeric field errors in an accounting system are probably more serious than errors in descriptive text fields. The type of application often determines how much data integrity programming is required. Fortunately, FoxPro's database integrity features (triggers, field validation, and record validation) help a great deal in planning and implementing most data integrity measures.

SECURITY

Data security means access control. There are many levels of security, ranging from single password control (or no control) at the beginning of an application to completely encrypted data files. If you're working with a network multiuser application, network security plays an important part in the physical location and distribution of a database schema. The more extreme security measures, such as complete file encryption, have definite performance consequences. Distribution of data tables and control over the rights to folders and files add to the complexity of a system. Also, as far as the user is concerned, the tighter the security, the less user-friendly the system.

Because the example LIMS processes information that impacts public health, it is in an interesting position in relation to data security. On the one hand, information about samples, tests, and results is highly confidential to the client and is especially sensitive while the results are still incomplete. On the other hand, most of the information ultimately becomes public and is subject to various disclosure laws. During the course of sample testing, a flexible and comprehensive (table, record, and field) security capability was required. This aspect of the application required a long time to define, ratify, and design.

MAINTAINABILITY

Overall, the design of the database and the structure of the individual tables need to be extremely well documented. Most of the maintenance of an application is applied to the data tables, indexes, and other files in the system. Badly designed or badly documented systems (or both) make maintenance much more difficult by obscuring important fields or indexes. Overnormalized systems require many data maintenance routines, and the use of too many consolidated files tends to result in huge files that take a long time to process and maintain. Although it usually isn't appropriate to design a database for maintenance purposes, keeping an eye on this requirement during the design process is a good idea.

NOTE

The client/server environment tends to magnify difficulties for most of the database design elements. Two things can complicate the trade-offs: accessing data that resides in physical locations you can't immediately reach and on systems (hardware and database software) that may not be under your control.

This review of design elements is intended to sensitize you to the dynamics involved in a typical database. Throughout an application, you will need to make design decisions that involve compromises: to gain speed but lose simplicity or to provide data security while giving up convenience. When you work with the next topic, relational design, you need to keep these factors in mind.

Relational Design

Your design of the application's database, sometimes called the *database schema*, has repercussions throughout the rest of the application. Most of your forms, reports, and other application components are dependent on the database and table design.

Relational database design has a reputation for being mysterious and difficult. It certainly is a barrier for the nontechnical users of database products. The industry has been trying to bypass the relational concepts for years. But as an application developer, you need to confront the rules of normalization with all the rest of the jargon and just get on with it.

You start with the lists of candidate data items and the preliminary data groups developed during analysis. By a process of normalization, balanced by the other design factors just covered, you develop the databases, tables, fields, indexes, and relations of your application. The design should capture all the information needed by the application and at the same time do it efficiently and accurately.

To put the cart before the horse for a moment, Figure 15.5 shows what a relational database schema looks like when it's finished.

Each ellipse in this bubble diagram is a table (a DBF file), and each table contains data related to the title of the bubble. This overview, simplified to keep things neat, depicts the functional dependencies between tables for the login portion of the LIMS program.

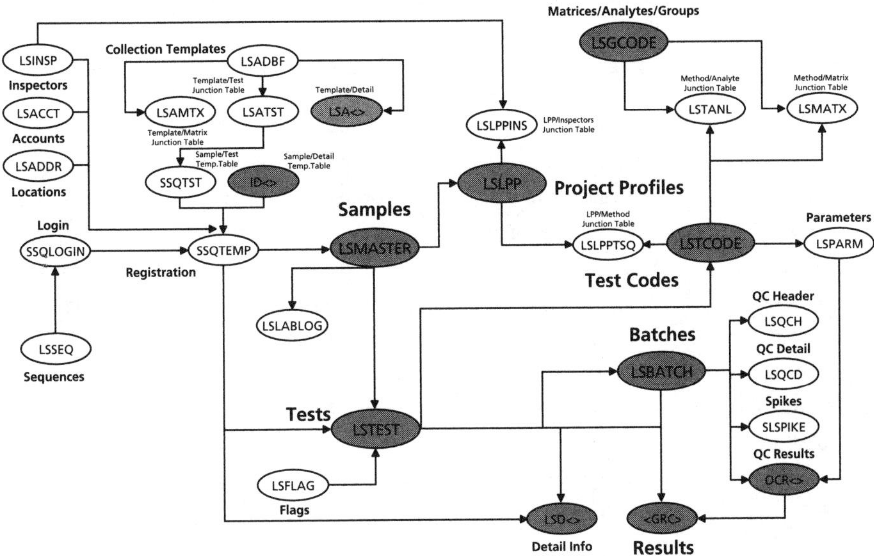

FIGURE 15.5 RELATIONAL DATABASE SCHEMA.

Now it's time to put the horse back in front of the cart. Whether you've been gathering information about your application for two hours or two months, the time comes when you take all that you have—the data, intuitions, observations—and turn it into one or more tables.

NORMALIZATION

The formal terminology of relational design—normalization—can be daunting. Your applications probably don't need the level of relational sophistication that uses descriptions like this: **R1=({A,B,C},{AB->C,B->C})**. But a rule of thumb or intuitive description of the relational approach should be helpful and won't require a six-month course of study.

There are five rules of normalization, but in most cases the first three will suffice. You'll hear the expression, "The table's in third normal form" which simply means that the database has been designed following the first three rules.

The starting point for normalization and table design is the list of candidate fields and their preliminary grouping into candidate tables from the analysis phase. Once again, we'll use the example of the LIMS login operation and the candidate fields in Table 15.2.

TABLE 15.2 LIMS APPLICATION: CANDIDATE DATA ITEMS FOR LOGIN MODULE

ITEM	ITEM	ITEM	ITEM
login date	rejection criteria	sample collection date	test requested1
login time	rejection description	sample collection time	test requested2
login registrar name	rejection approval	sample collector name	test requested3
login location	sample disposition	sample collection site	test requested4
login storage	login batch number	sample condition	special handling
sample receive date	login condition	sample packaging	handling specs
sample receive time	transported by	sample sealed	billable sample
sample receiver name	transport date	sample split	bill-to name
sample rcv.location	transport time	sample matrix type	bill-to address
client company	transport method	sample matrix	bill-to phone
client address	client report by date	client sample number	sample hazard
client primary phone	client report to name	sample type	sample disposal
client contact	client report to phone	sample description	sample safety
client contact title	client description	sample container	sample EPA number
	client site number	sample	sample label

During analysis, groupings of these items were suggested by the forms and reports associated with the login data:

- Samples
- Clients
- Tests
- Batches
- Billing information
- Login information
- Lab staff

As an example of the normalization process, as well as consideration of other factors, let's look at two candidate tables: SAMPLES and LOGIN-INFORMATION. During analysis these two tables were considered because one was for the objects arriving at the laboratory (the samples) and the other was for the information necessary at the time of login, essentially for a batch of samples. Now it's necessary to separate data items into candidate fields for each table, as in Tables 15.3 and 15.4:

TABLE 15.3 CANDIDATE TABLE: SAMPLES, NOT NORMALIZED

ITEM	ITEM	ITEM
Sample receive date	Sample collection time	Sample label
Sample receive time	Sample collector name	Test requested 1
Sample receiver name	Sample packaging	Test requested 2
Sample rcv.location	Sample sealed	Test requested 3
Sample type	Sample split	Test requested 4
Sample description	Sample matrix type	Rejection criteria
Sample container	Sample matrix	Rejection description
Sample status	Sample hazard	Rejection approval
Sample disposition	Sample disposal	Special handling
Sample condition	Sample safety	Client sample number
Sample collection date	Sample EPA number	Handling specs

TABLE 15.4 CANDIDATE TABLE: LOGIN, NOT NORMALIZED

ITEM	ITEM
Login date	Transport date
Login time	Transport time
Login registrar name	Transport method
Login location	Client report by date
Login storage	Login condition
Login batch number	Client site number
Transported by	Sample collection site

For this first pass, only simple criteria were used, *not* based on the labels (such as login labels go in the LOGIN table), but instead based on whether the item was about the sample itself or about some condition *for all samples*. Put another way, if the item could be simultaneously applied to all samples, it was put in the LOGIN table. If it applied only to one sample at a time, it went in the SAMPLE table. This is an example of both semantic and functional criteria.

Once the two tables have been tentatively identified, it's time to make an inspection pass to consider what are sometimes called prenormalization rules. These rules are distinguished from normalization, because they don't dictate the creation of new tables:

1. Add any items that might be required by the mechanics of the application (see Table 15.5).

TABLE 15.5 MECHANICAL REQUIREMENTS

ITEM	DESCRIPTION
RecordStatus	Indicates the status of the record, most often A = Active and so on.
RecordFlag	The *action flag*, or marker to do something to this record.
Systemdate	Automatic dating of the record upon adding or modification.
Systemtime	Automatic time of record being added or modified.

2. Add any other items that appear to be needed to complete a picture of the information in the table. For example, it was known that dairy samples had special information attached to them (see Table 15.6).

TABLE 15.6 SPECIAL INFORMATION (DAIRY SAMPLES)

Temp. at collection C.	Temp. at login C.	Pull date	Container type
Dairy type	Butterfat %	Volume	Volume Unit

3. Remove derived (calculated) data (see Table 15.7).

TABLE 15.7 DERIVED DATA

Temp. at collection Celsius	Temp. at login Celsius
Temp. at collection Fahrenheit	Temp. at login Fahrenheit

One pair of these data items need not be stored in a table, because it can be easily calculated from the other pair. In general, computers do calculations much faster than disk accesses, so storing derived data not only is unnecessary but also may hinder performance. There are exceptions, however, particularly for storage of historical data that will be viewed frequently; it may be more efficient to simply store totals once to a table rather than recalculate them endlessly.

4. Examine all items that may contain data aggregates and decide whether they should be separated or left in that state. The classic example shows up in the candidate items for the LIMS: the sample collection site. What, exactly, is meant by "site"? It could be a city, in which case it's a single item; but it could also be an address, so that the item might look like this:

   Mayer Dairy
   RR 2
   Wayzata, MN 55391

   You could store this data in a memo field, format and all, but you need to be sure that this is the most useful way to store the address. In a memo field you wouldn't be able to sort by city or even conduct a fast search for a value. If there is any need to organize data by the information contained in the address, most designers will break it into the standard address fields: COMPANY, ADDRESS1, ADDRESS2, CITY, STATE, and ZIP.

5 Establish the primary key for each candidate table. This step is the most crucial of the preliminary steps, because most of the normalization rules can be derived from a relationship to the primary key. As mentioned in Chapter 4, choosing the right key isn't always easy. It must be a field (data item) or combination of fields that can contain only unique values. It must serve to identify the contents of the table. In the case of the two-example table, the answer was the database designer's old friend: the generic sequence number or ID, one unique number for each record in the field. For the SAMPLE table, it was Sample ID, and for the LOGIN table: Login Batch Number.

These are guidelines rather than rules, but they consider what's missing or what should not be included in a table. The result is usually an augmented table with un-normalized data items, as in Tables 15.8 and 15.9 (new items in italics).

TABLE 15.8 CANDIDATE TABLE: SAMPLES

ITEM	ITEM	ITEM
KEY: *Sample ID*	Client sample number	Test requested 1
Sample receive date	Sample condition	Test requested 2
Sample receive time	Sample collection date	Test requested 3
Sample receiver name	Sample collection time	Test requested 4
Sample rcv.location	Sample collector name	*Temp. at collection C.*
Sample type	Sample packaging	*Temp. at login C.*
Sample description	Sample sealed	*Pull date*
Sample container	Sample split	*Dairy type*
Sample status	Sample matrix type	*Butterfat %*
Sample disposition	Sample matrix	*Container type*
Rejection criteria	Sample hazard	*Volume*
Rejection description	Sample disposal	*Volume unit*
Rejection approval	Sample safety	*Record status*
Special handling	Sample EPA number	*Record flag*
Handling specs	Sample label	*Record DateTime*

TABLE 15.9 CANDIDATE TABLE: LOGIN

ITEM	ITEM	ITEM
KEY: Login batch number	Transport time	*Site city*
Login time	Transport method	*Site state*
Login registrar name	Client report by date	*Site zip*
Login location	Login condition	*Record status*
Login storage	Client site number	*Record flag*
Login date	*Site name*	*Record Date-Time*
Transported by	*Site address1*	
Transport date	*Site address2*	

At this point, the candidate tables are ready for normalization—and they need it.

FIRST NORMAL FORM

First normal form. Even the name sounds stiff, like something out of an English grammar school. But it's the result of the first step of normalization, and it's vital to the design of relational databases. Here's the rule, paraphrased and shortened:

First Rule of Normalization: Eliminate repeating groups.

The classic example of repeating groups is a field for customer and six fields for customer orders in the same table. The orders fields are repeated one or more times for each customer, and that means they share the same basic customer data redundantly. The remedy is to make a separate table of the repeating fields and give it a primary key that can be related to the original table.

In the example candidate tables, there is one glaring instance of repeating field groups:

Test requested 1 Test requested 2 Test requested 3 Test requested 4

These candidate fields imply that for each sample there may be one to four tests requested by the client (actually, there may be many more than that). In a relational database design, these fields are moved out, probably to a TEST table, and are joined to the SAMPLE table by the Sample ID. The primary key would be Sample ID + Test ID.

A table from which all the repeating groups of fields have been removed is said to be in first normal form. This is not an arbitrary goal. For example, in the SAMPLE table there might actually be 100 tests that can be requested (for a single sample). To accommodate those tests in a single table would mean carrying 100 x the number of record field spaces, most of them blank. It's also difficult to run summary reports for this arrangement, because most reports do calculations from record to record and not from field to field.

The two tables we started with are now a part of a schema that looks like Figure 15.6.

SECOND NORMAL FORM

First normal form often produces the most obviously necessary tables. Second normal form is a little more subtle. Here's the rule:

Second Rule of Normalization: Eliminate redundant items.

The hallmarks of redundancy are values that depend only on part of a compound key. For example, with a key of CUSTOMERID+PARTID, a PART-DESCRIPTION field is dependent only on the PARTID field, and all its values will be appear repeatedly (and redundantly) in the table.

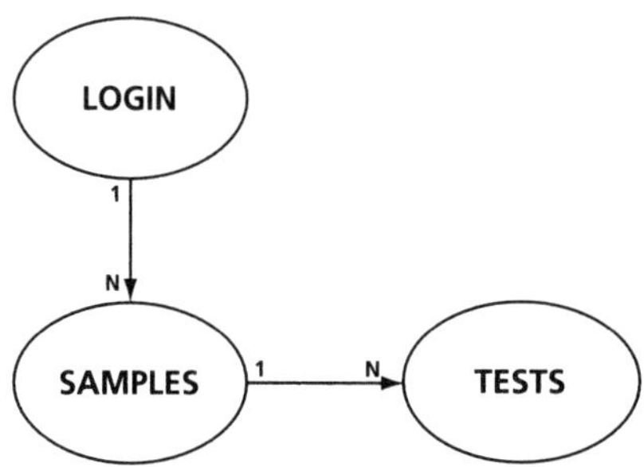

FIGURE 15.6 FIRST NORMAL FORM SCHEMA.

Knowing some of the motivations for this rule may help you spot its instances. In the PART-DESCRIPTION example, what if you need to change the description of several parts? You would need to find and change every record that contains those specific descriptions. If you miss a few, you've introduced update anomalies into the database. Likewise, if the last record that contains a particular part description is removed from the database, there would be no more record of that part, a condition sometimes called a *deletion anomaly*.

If you move the redundant candidate field to its own table, usually accompanied by the creation of a code or ID field to act as the linking index, its value can be changed at any time without affecting the content of the related records.

There are two examples of redundant candidate fields in the SAMPLES table:

Rejection description   Sample matrix type

Because the reasons for rejecting a sample will often be repeated, to include the description field in each record adds redundant data. So you can move the description to a separate table, joined with SAMPLES by a new field (and foreign key)—REJECTION-CODE—which is the primary key for the new table. The new table might be called REJECT, but large systems may have scores of such lookup items, mostly based on codes. In such sdystems, rather than proliferate tables, you collect them in a standard CODES table for easy maintenance. This arrangement works nicely for rejection codes, because there aren't many and very little other information is associated with them.

This solution, however, doesn't work for the candidate field, Sample matrix type. Although this information, too, is often redundant in the SAMPLES table, putting a matrix code in a CODES table has major problems: There are thousands of matrices, and they have a great deal of associated information. Therefore, a new table, MATRICES, is created with a primary key of Matrix ID. The resulting schema looks like Figure 15.7.

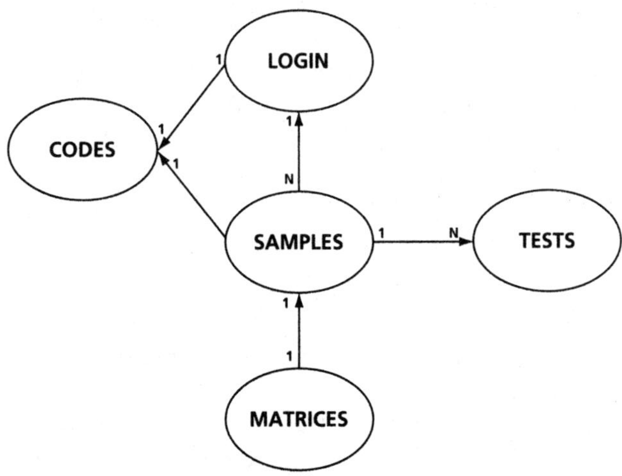

FIGURE 15.7 SECOND NORMAL FORM SCHEMA.

THIRD NORMAL FORM

Now that we have moved candidate fields that repeat or are redundant, there is one more table design issue covered by normalization. It is summarized in the third rule:

> Third Rule of Normalization: Eliminate items that are not fully dependent on the primary key.

This rule puts the focus on the primary key and the relationship of each candidate field to it. If the candidate field isn't fully dependent on the primary key—meaning that it does not contribute to a description of the key—then we remove it to its own table.

To spot this kind of candidate field, scan the field list for each table and ask yourself a question patterned on this one: "Does a client site (candidate field) in any way describe a sample (primary key)?" If the answer is no, then the candidate field should be removed.

Fields of this type are a relatively common occurrence. The candidate tables have several examples (see Table 15.10).

TABLE 15.10 THE LOGIN TABLE

Client site number	*Site address1*	*Site city* *Site zip*
Site name	*Site address2*	*Site state*

Clearly, client sites and all the information related to them don't describe a sample and should be removed to a SITE table with SITE-ID as a new primary key. A little less obvious are the candidate fields in the SAMPLE table that describe a milk sample (see Table 15.11).

TABLE 15.11 THE SAMPLE TABLE

Temp. at collection C.	*Pull date*	*Butterfat %*	*Volume*
Temp. at login C.	*Dairy type*	*Container type*	*Volume unit*

For these fields to be in normal form, the primary key would have to be SAMPLE-ID+SAMPLE-TYPE, because they are valid only for a particular type of sample. But the key is only SAMPLE-ID, so these fields are redundant for all but milk samples.

For the LIMS project there were more than 50 different types of samples, so the list of fields unique to each type actually totaled more than 400—far too many to include in one table. As a result, it was necessary to define a class of tables, called DETAIL files, to contain type-specific information—for example, MILK-DETAIL. The final schema, after going through the process of normalization, looks like Figure 15.8.

NOTE

Throughout the process of normalization, the design goal is to have tables without redundant data. The approach is to work toward a relatively simple rule: Tables should store facts only about their primary keys.

The pattern of normalization is beginning to emerge. You start with a conglomeration of data items and sort them progressively into functionally coherent candidate fields and into groups that suggest candidate tables. Then each of the tables is subjected to close scrutiny, first for the five preliminary conditions and then by the rules of normalization. What may have started as one or two tables may often finish with five or six tables.

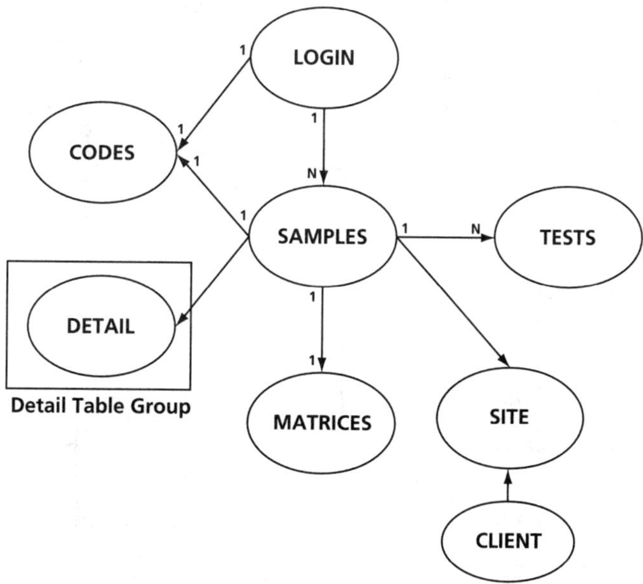

FIGURE 15.8 THIRD NORMAL FORM SCHEMA.

BINDER DIAGRAMS

There are many ways to represent a relational system of tables as a schema. The approach we'll illustrate was chosen because of its suitability for FoxPro development. It's called a Binder diagram, after Robert V. Binder. In the slightly modified form used here, it contains additional information about the names of tables and aliases. The only thing that's missing is a complete file structure; including it would make the diagram unwieldy. The example in Figure 15.9 is from the LIMS login group, about one-fifth of the full LIMS schema. Figure 15.10 shows the legend for the diagram.

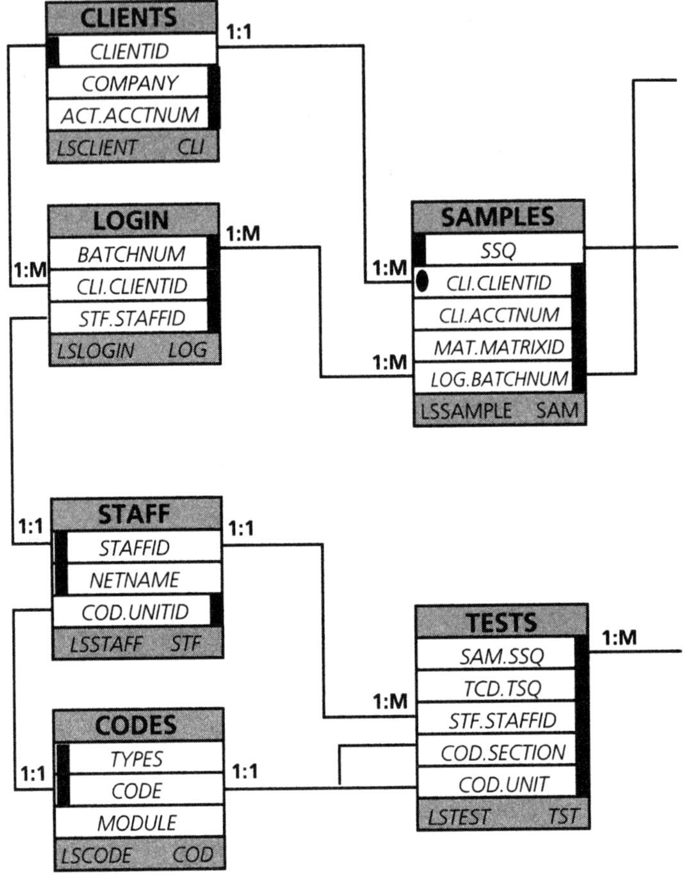

FIGURE 15.9 BINDER DIAGRAM.

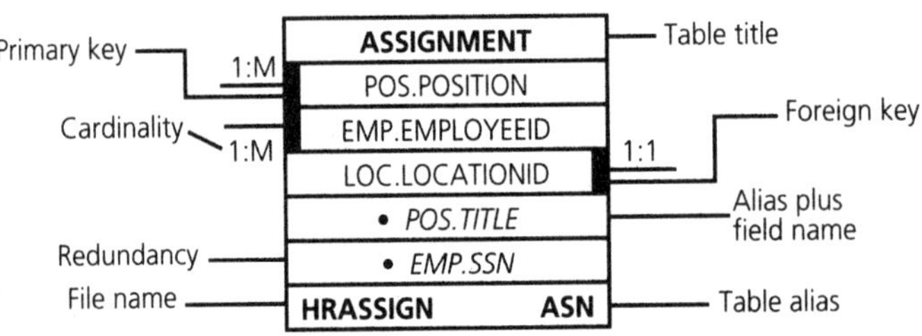

FIGURE 15.10 BINDER DIAGRAM LEGEND.

The Binder diagram is also notable for documenting redundancy (the dot in front of the CLIENTID field in the SAMPLES table). It acknowledges that real-world relational systems often include redundant fields that should be explicitly noted in the diagram. Overall, this diagram provides a good road map to a database schema. It leaves out details, and not all the relational links are included, but the point of a diagram such as this is to clarify the underlying data structure and not to catalog the details. It summarizes the table design in a compact format.

The end game of database design is to arrive at something you can turn into FoxPro databases, tables, and fields. This version of a Binder diagram includes the actual file names and aliases to be used in an application.

FROM DESIGN TO IMPLEMENTATION

The Binder diagram is one place to indicate the transition from a generic design (which should, in theory, be applicable to almost any database management program) to the actual implementation in FoxPro. Once the candidate fields and tables have been settled, almost all that's left is to convert them into the file names and field definitions you will enter into FoxPro's Database Designer and Table Designer (covered in section 3). For the two tables in the LIMS example, see Tables 15.12 and 15.13.

TABLE 15.12 TABLE: SAMPLES

FIELD NAME	TYPE	WIDTH	NULLS	DESCRIPTION
SSQ	C	8		Sample sequence number
SAMPLETYPE	C	2		Sample type, code
MATRIXID	C	8		Matrix ID number
SAMPLEDESC	C	40		Sample description
RECVDATE	D	8		Date received
RECVTIME	C	6		Time received
RECVSTAFF	C	6		Staff ID of receiver
RECVLOC	C	4		Location where received
CONTAINER	C	3		Container code
PACKAGE	C	3		Packaging code

FIELD NAME	TYPE	WIDTH	NULLS	DESCRIPTION
LABEL	C	20		Description of label
SEALED	L	1		Sample seal OK, Y/N
HAZARD	L	1		Sample hazardous, Y/N
CLIENTID	C	8		Client ID number
CLIENTSID	C	12		Client's sample ID number
COLLDATE	D	8		Collection date
COLLTIME	C	6		Collection time
COLLNAME	C	25		Collector's name
CONDITION	C	40		Condition of sample at receiving
SPLIT	L	1		Sample can be split, Y/N
SPECIAL	C	60		Special handling instructions
STATUS	C	1		Status of the sample
REJECTCODE	C	2		Sample rejection code
REJECTOK	C	4		Rejection approval, employee ID
DISPOSAL	C	1		Disposal code
RECSTATUS	C	1		Status of record
RECFLAG	C	1		Action flag for record
RECDATTIME	T	10		Record DateTime

TABLE 15.13 TABLE: LOGIN

FIELD NAME	TYPE	WIDTH	NULLS	DESCRIPTION
BATCHNUM	C	10		Login batch number
LOGDATE	C	2		Date batch logged

FIELD NAME	TYPE	WIDTH	NULLS	DESCRIPTION
LOGTIME	C	8		Time batch logged
LOGSTAFF	C	40		Staff person for login, ID
LOGLOC	D	8		location of login, code
TRANSBY	C	6		Batch transported by, company.
TRANSDATE	D	8		Date batch transported
TRANSTIME	C	6		Time batch transported
TRANSTYPE	C	3		Transportation method
CLIENTID	C	8		Client ID number
CLIENTSITE	C	4		Client site number
CLIREPDATE	D	8		Client report by date
LOGSTORE	L	1		Batch is completely stored
RECSTATUS	C	1		Status of record
RECFLAG	C	1		Action flag for record
RECDATTIME	T	10		Record DateTime

Once the database and tables, along with their indexes, have been created, you're ready to set the permanent relations and enter any of the business rules that apply to either the tables or the fields. You don't need to do the complete database design and implementation at one go. It's typical to refine and modify data structures and business rules up to and through the time of delivery. From the development perspective, once you have the tables in place, the next step is to load the tables with enough data to be useful for prototyping and testing the user interface.

USER INTERFACE DESIGN

As you contemplate the prospect of building an application, kick back in your chair with your eyes closed and visualize what it will look like. What's the user going to see? Windows float by your mind's eye, full of color, shapes, and even textures. Maybe you see pictures, icons, and toolbars. You know that FoxPro has all kinds of visual controls such as forms, buttons, grids, and combo boxes, and perhaps you see these in your screens. Welcome to user interface design.

It seems to be true that issues concerning the user interface are becoming paramount. Commercial application developers now say that for a typical application, 60–70 percent of their time is spent doing user interface work. Object-oriented programming is probably changing that ratio, because you can now do so much more with the user interface than even five years ago. The tendency is to spend even more time with the user interface, not because you necessarily should but because you can.

User interface design is challenging, and, although there are emerging standards, you have a great deal of latitude. The ways in which a computer program interacts with the user—mouse clicks, keystrokes, colors, flow of modules, windowing, menu options, and information support, to name a few—are some of the most interesting and creative aspects of programming. And an application with a well-designed user interface has a much better chance of success.

There are many issues in user interface design; this book can cover only a small fraction of them, and most of that will be in the how-to chapters that follow. But for building applications, you need to make a few important user interface decisions in the design phase. These decisions can be boiled down to three topics: designing visual classes, shifting between a modal and a modeless interface, and cross-platform development.

Visual Classes

Because you are working with Visual FoxPro for Windows, you've already made one major commitment to user interface design: Windows. As you are probably well aware, there is a Windows way of doing things. Although Microsoft doesn't enforce the user interface conventions with as much zeal as Apple does, you need to think twice before wandering very far from Windows conventions in your designs.

Actually, it's hard to stray from the conventions now that Microsoft has provided Visual FoxPro with a set of forms, toolbars, and controls that are standard for most Windows programs. The FoxPro base classes define these forms and controls and thus define the behavior for the majority of the user interface. On the other hand, when you subclass these user interface classes, you have ample opportunity to change the composition, color, shape, fonts, and even containership. If you like, you can wreak havoc with the standard interface, or you can improve upon it.

Although most applications will avail themselves of most of the standard containers and controls, a few important user interface decisions remain:

- **Toolbars**. Do you want toolbars in your application? If so, how many? Some applications have a program-level toolbar and then one toolbar for each form. Implementing toolbars isn't very difficult, but controlling them in a complex system can be tricky.
- **FormSets**. If you choose to have toolbars, you'll have FormSets by default. Otherwise there are some benefits and drawbacks of gathering forms into a FormSet. It can be difficult to control many forms, and multiple FormSets provide serious challenges.
- **PageFrames and Pages**. Tabbed pages, which are Forms with PageFrames and Pages, are all the rage in Windows interface design. Microsoft tends to reserve them for dialog boxes, but many programs now use this format for primary application windows. If you choose to have tabbed pages, you'll probably need to build some application-level or domain-level classes to standardize how they work and what they look like.
- **Menus and shortcut menus**. The standard Windows menu at the top of the screen is hard to avoid. Users expect it. Shortcut menus are relatively new. They're not necessarily required by every application, and they take some effort to implement. They are, however, a powerful addition to the user interface toolkit.
- **Mouse or keyboard**. The Microsoft ethos says that everything you can do with a mouse should also be doable with the keyboard: menu choices, toolbar selections, editing, and so on. Many people prefer to use the keyboard, and it's been shown many times that professional data entry people are much quicker with keystrokes than random mousing. On the other hand, scrupulous duplication of all mouse options with keyboard alternatives is difficult and time-consuming.

In the next three chapters, we'll go into the details behind most of these decisions. If you're not very familiar with the classes involved (Forms, FormSets, and PageFrames), it's important to get some experience, even on an experimental basis, before you make some of the UI decisions for an application.

Modal vs. Modeless

A major issue in user interface design can be expressed as the question, Who is in control of how a program runs? If the answer is the user, then you understand the power of the Macintosh and all that has come after it. If the answer is the company (meaning the requirements of an employer), then you understand what MIS has been doing almost forever. If you answer the programmer, then you understand self-preservation mixed with delusions of grandeur. The truth is that most applications are a mixture of control principles, usually applied at different places.

Control in an application usually means what the user is allowed to do and when. The words that are most often used to describe the two approaches are *modal* and *modeless*. A modal approach puts limits on what the user can do: In edit mode, only editing is allowed; the user can't run another program, do a calculation, or play Solitaire. In the modal approach, users can follow only certain predetermined paths through a program, typically guided by a menu. The modeless approach says, in effect, that the user is king. Users may choose any option, run any program, and overlap functions as much as they want. Years of argument, going all the way back to the early 80s, have attended the introduction of modeless user interfaces. In some circles, the positions held are almost religious in fervor.

In practice, most applications employ a mixture of modal control and modeless freedom. The question really is, how much freedom do users have and when do they have it? These major design decisions are far more demanding of your programming skills than designing a form or creating a report. Designing a truly modeless environment, even if only in selected parts of an application, can be tricky.

Your decision about shifting between approaches depends a great deal on the requirements of the application. An accounting system does not need, and probably shouldn't have, the wide open accessibility of a graphics program. The need for security, efficiency, and similar factors may increase the use of a modal approach. In the more relaxed direction, applications that provide information from various sources (for example, an executive information system, or EIS) will lean strongly toward a fully modeless approach.

The use of modal techniques is characterized by maximum use of menu control, forms that don't allow activation of other forms, and barriers to running simultaneous modules or programs. It involves both user interface design and application design. It's programming with an attitude, to use the colloquial expression. For modeless techniques (multiple modules and forms availability, flexible menu structures, hypertext-like ability), the spontaneity allowed the user can be orders of magnitude more difficult to program in spite of Visual FoxPro's event handling capability.

CROSS-PLATFORM INTERFACE DESIGN

FoxPro is positioned in the database application development market as a cross-platform product. It is possible to write one set of code and use it on DOS, Windows, Macintosh, and Unix platforms. If you're a commercial developer or are building applications for a company that supports more than one of these platforms, you'll probably find the cross-platform capability a decisive factor in choosing FoxPro.

Unfortunately, to the degree that FoxPro is a cross-platform product, it is at the expense of the user interface. Problems of moving between versions of FoxPro aside, the standard interfaces of these different platforms preclude moving that type of code from one to the other, at least in any complete fashion. There is some compatibility at the user interface level between Visual FoxPro for Macintosh and Visual FoxPro for Windows, but even that is hedged with all kinds of problems associated with the different metrics used for monitor display. With the other platforms and Visual FoxPro 5.0, there is no interface compatibility at all. You can transfer basic processing code—primarily data management code—but that's about it. Given that 80 percent of a modern application is in the user interface, this is a major limitation.

Transportability with the Macintosh is real, but until version 5.0 is available for that platform, you'll be in the difficult position of removing version 5.0 code from anything you do and still making the many necessary adjustments to the user interface. With careful planning, it can be done, but exactly how is beyond the scope of this book.

APPLICATION ARCHITECTURE DESIGN

The final portion of application framework design concerns the structure of the application itself: how the various pieces are packaged and how they run. What you are attempting to do is to pin down the components of an application, the files involved, the order of execution, and the interaction of objects, broken down in a way that supports the programming effort. Typically, this means organizing an application by components and modules.

Application Elements

During analysis we tend to focus on the needs of the users, the elements (objects) of the application domain (the area of work involved in the application), and the vocabulary used to describe the application. But when it comes time to plan and design the implementation, you quickly realize that, as a piece of computer software, an application has its own requirements. Applications need help systems, configuration routines, maintenance capability, and so forth. These features may be required by the programming or simply because applications are expected to have them.

People (including programmers) are often surprised by all the elements that go into a complete software application. Many of them are discrete units, or components. Others are distributed throughout an application. In either case, they usually require extensive programming or at least specific work by a programmer or data manager. Luckily, not all the elements are needed for every project, but many of them are part of a full-scale application. Table 15.14 lists all the elements, some of them basic, others highly specialized. When you plan your application, you need to make a checklist (mental or otherwise) of how many of them you will need.

Table 15.14 Elements of Full-Scale Applications

Component	Description
Archiving	The ability to archive and retrieve data as off-line access. This is a more formal and long-term arrangement than daily backup and restore systems.
Backup and Restore	Routine (daily) data backup and restoration capability, usually in conjunction with a tape backup device or other similar storage capability.

COMPONENT	DESCRIPTION
Business Rule Management	FoxPro programs have always had business rules, but they were usually buried in the code. Now, with the use of the database file, it is possible to centralize all or most of the business rule management. However, to do this conveniently will require special access forms and programming.
Charts and Graphs	The ability to create charts and graphs within FoxPro is available from the Graph Wizard (for nondistributed applications) and can be added with third-party products.
Class Libraries	One of the goals of working on an application in Visual FoxPro is to develop classes (and class libraries) that can be used in other applications. This is a crucial part of an application framework.
Communications	Some applications require communication services—for example, a simple modem-to-modem hookup or an elaborate download of information from on-line services such as CompuServe or the Internet. This is a rapidly expanding area in FoxPro applications, and there are many third-party programs to help you implement various aspects of communications.
Configuration	Configuration is the external and internal setup for starting the application. This includes CONFIG.FPW as well as specific startup routines for the application.
Data Conversion	Many applications require loading of databases or conversion of existing data before they can be used. Identifying and managing conversion issues can be important.
Data Encryption	In rare cases, entire tables or even databases need to be encrypted for security purposes. This is difficult to do properly, but a number of third-party solutions exist.

COMPONENT	DESCRIPTION
Data Transfer	A common component of many applications is the transfer of data, usually via files, to and from other systems over LAN, direct cable, telephone connection, or floppies.
Database	Virtually all FoxPro applications use a database system to manage the underlying data. Analyzing and designing database elements is one of the key tasks in application building.
Distribution	For applications that will be run in locations other than the site of development, a distribution scheme may be required that covers not only the format of distribution (EXE or APP file) but also issues such as installation, configuration, and remote service.
Error Recovery	Almost every application needs a system for a more user friendly error reporting system than the default provided by FoxPro. In many situations, the user must helped to recover from errors, and serious errors must be automatically logged and reported.
Forms	In Visual FoxPro, forms (screens) are the backbone of the user interface and of the object-oriented programming. Forms development may be the single most time-consuming element in developing a FoxPro application.
Help System	All good applications destined for distribution and user work have some sort of on-line help system. It needn't be fancy, but it should be available.
Installation	This includes routines for first-time installation and other application setup. Special routines may be needed for remote distribution of an application.
Internet Connection	This is a relatively new area for FoxPro (as it is for all the application development systems), but it is growing rapidly in importance. Your application may be called up to deliver and retrieve data from a Web site. Tools are available, but it's not a simple process.

COMPONENT	DESCRIPTION
Labels	Some applications need the ability to produce mailing labels or other personal labels. This capability is related to report printing but has a few wrinkles all its own.
Mail Merge	FoxPro provides a Mail-Merge Wizard for interactive connections with Microsoft Word. Because this wizard can't be distributed, you may need to develop your own routines for applications that require mail-merge capability.
Maintenance for Programming	Unless the application is a solo effort, some system for upgrading and tracking software versions is often a necessity.
Maintenance in the Application	Unless the application is a custom operation from start to finish, it will require some kind of maintenance facility to allow the user or administrator to perform routine data and application maintenance.
Menus	Most applications have a menu system present in nearly all forms and screens. This is not part of the OOP system and must be developed as a separate entity and then integrated into the application.
Multimedia Data	To a certain extent, the ability to handle multimedia data (sound, music, images, voice, and so forth) is built into FoxPro, but only at a very primitive level (mostly storage capability). An application that requires sophisticated use of one or more multimedia data will probably need third-party software or sophisticated programming.
Multi-User Operation	The majority of applications will require routines for multiple users (typically on a local area network).
ActiveX Components	Visual FoxPro is capable of incorporating components developed for the ActiveX-based OCX controls (a new version of the OLE controls). These components can include complete systems for spreadsheet software, word processing, and other specialized tasks that you would be crazy to try to develop for yourself.

COMPONENT	DESCRIPTION
ODBC Connections	Now as a standard Visual FoxPro capability (Pro version), many applications will use ODBC to establish external connections with other databases. Handling of ODBC connections usually requires special programming.
OLE Automation	The ability to manipulate Windows applications with OLE automation is just beginning to be part of FoxPro applications. Because of its potential (and newness), use of OLE automation will be a major undertaking.
OLE/DDE	Connection to other Windows software via object linking and embedding (OLE) or dynamic data exchange (DDE) is becoming common in FoxPro applications. With Windows 95 and NT 4.0, the trend should accelerate.
Peripheral Input	Input from bar-code devices, scanners, and scientific equipment occurs in many specialized applications and usually requires special programming.
Printer Management	Control and access to multiple printers and print forms is generally handled by Windows. However, in a few applications it may be necessary to use special printer drivers or direct manipulation of a printer, requiring special programming.
Processing Routines	Many kinds of applications have special processing and table management routines that are developed independently of the user interface. These routines are often extremely complicated and require a high level of programming skill.
Program Documentation	Programming documentation is specifically for the programmer and includes the use of the Documentation Wizard, system diagrams, analytical notes, business rules, and other forms of system documentation.

Project Management	Although it's not a component of an application, you don't produce an application of any size without some kind of project management. The bigger the project, the more people are involved and the more important this becomes.
Queries	Queries from the Query Designer and SQL-SELECT may be run independently of printed reports. This might also include the Graphics Wizard except where the application is to be distributed.
Report Management	Because the average application may have dozens, if not hundreds, of reports, a method is required for user selection of reports and various output options. This may also include classes for standard report dialogs and report processing.
Reports	Printed reports, which come in all shapes and sizes, are standard for virtually all applications. Creating a half-dozen reports is no problem; creating 100 reports is a massive undertaking and not at all uncommon.
Security	At the simplest level, almost all applications have some kind of user login for application security. Depending on requirements, the security system can range from basic to something that would satisfy the Pentagon. Many applications require at least a moderately comprehensive security system.
System Codes	Most applications have data that is stored in the form of codes. Larger programs may need a data table and management system for handling all codes used in the application.
System Parameters	Operational parameters, such as system date, name of owner, addresses, and so forth that are used to set up and operate the application may require a separate table and access form.
Tables	The usual complement of data tables, indexes, and memo files that form the underlying database of the application.

User Documentation	There are many possible formats, but usually the documentation consists of manuals or procedure books to explain the application and support the user.
User Support	This is support of the user in case of emergencies, debug situations, and other assorted crises common to custom application development. It can be handled informally or may require formal telephone and on-site service.
User Training	User training in the operation and use of the application may come in the form of classes, individual sessions, and even the use of video taped, CBT (computer-based training) for large, mission-critical applications.

Taken as a whole, the list is daunting. Is there any wonder it costs so much to produce good software? Decisions about which elements to include are often critical. Put more accurately, the key decision is how much effort will be made to produce the application. For example, user documentation might consist of 10 8 1/2 x 11 sheets stapled together or a professionally produced book of some 400 pages. What does a particular application need? User requirements, competitive pressures, and available resources all play a role in such decisions.

The list of elements is not a cookbook. There is no formula that says, "If you have five forms, six reports, three queries, and two databases, the application will take 10 days to program." Only experience will teach you how long it takes to produce certain things. And over time, you will learn important shortcuts, especially those provided by object-oriented programming and an application framework. Most people who do application development (professionally or otherwise) create their own standard components as part of the application framework.

As an approximate guide, almost all FoxPro applications will have these elements: database, tables, processing routines, forms, menus, queries, and reports. A quick and simple application (essentially for a single user) won't have much more than this. An application that will be distributed to other people and needs to be robust will probably add these elements: configuration, report management, multi-user operation, system parameters, system codes, a help system, maintenance routines, program documentation, error recovery, and user documentation.

An industrial-strength application, such as the LIMS program, may add security, printer management, installation, data conversion, user training, and user support.

Most of the other elements in the list depend on the nature of the application and may blend into some of the application-specific elements. For example, ActiveX and OLE Automation are gateways into other Windows programs. They might be part of a complex data transfer scheme or simply a way to put graphics into a database. If, for example, capturing artwork is a requirement, you might have a graphics component tailored specifically for that application.

The point of considering both general and application-specific components early in the process is to isolate areas that will require special attention (and presumably extra work). For example, in the LIMS, the peripheral input component had two significant requirements: bar coding and interfaces to testing equipment. Both of them required special planning, and the test equipment interfaces needed some tricky programming.

MODULE DESIGN

The *modules* of an application are a kind of high-level description of functionality, biased toward the programmer's point of view. It's not the same as the data structure, class hierarchy, or a collection of components, although they're a big part of it. With FoxPro, modules will typically be one or more forms used in combination with menus, reports, processes, and data environments. Some of them might be the components described in the previous section; others will be specific to the application. Breaking an application into modules is often part of managing software development so that you can say, "This week we're working on the such-and-such module."

Once you've decided on the modules for the application, you can design the programming elements that go into them. As illustrated in Figure 15.11, modules may seem to be redundant with the visual classes, but you'll notice that they include menus and other elements that are not part of FoxPro's object model.

These are the basic elements: forms (data entry, edit), processes (calculations, table updating), retrieval and output (reports, labels, queries), and menus. How specific you choose to be in a written description or diagram depends on how much there is to do, who must do it, and how long it is expected to take. The point of this part of the design is to make things clear for the developer or programmer. If you're doing the work yourself, you may need only enough notation to maintain a work outline. If other people are involved, and especially if a client needs to be informed, then the required level of documentation escalates.

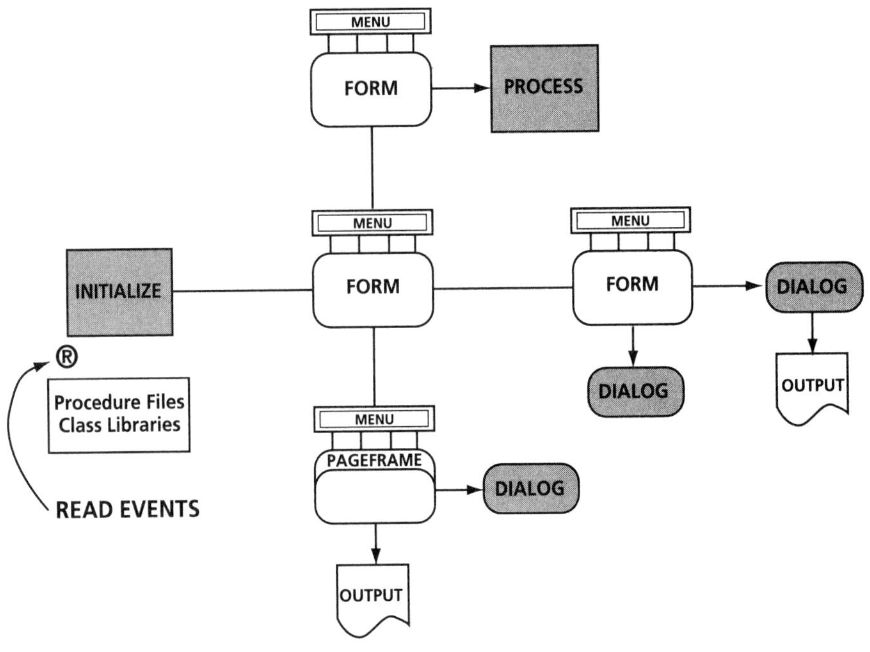

FIGURE 15.11 MODULE AND PROGRAMMING ELEMENTS.

CHAPTER WRAP-UP

The material in this chapter could easily fill dozens of books, or even a sizable library. Obviously, this chapter is an overview. Designing applications either as one-shot projects or as part of an application framework is probably the most challenging aspect of modern programming. Object-orientation has made it almost imperative that some time be spent on design, and you'll find that for applications of any size, you'll be creating many of the design elements described in this chapter whether or not you're conscious of them.

Because there are so many big pieces, here's a brief table (Table 15.15) that attempts to put the design of an application and an application framework into perspective.

TABLE 15.15 THE RELATION OF APPLICATION DESIGN TO AN APPLICATION FRAMEWORK

AN APPLICATION...	AN APPLICATION FRAMEWORK...
Is largely composed of objects created by classes.	Has a class hierarchy that organizes and documents the classes used to create an application.
Has a database schema: databases, tables, and the relations between them.	Provides guidelines for how the data is integrated with the classes and other elements of an application.
Has a user interface.	As part of the class hierarchy, has many visual classes that are used to construct the user interface.
Typically has a number of standard elements (such as menus, help system, and security).	Has a number of reusable standard components (such as menu templates, help system, and security classes) and explains how to integrate them with an application.
Is programmed as a number of modules.	Provides finished components as modules or as elements of modules.

Designing an application is not the same thing as designing the application framework, but the goal is to have the framework provide as much material as possible for the application.

SECTION 6

Building an Application Framework

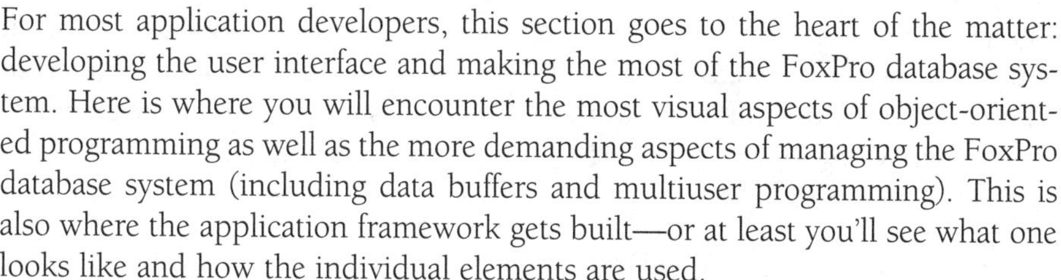

For most application developers, this section goes to the heart of the matter: developing the user interface and making the most of the FoxPro database system. Here is where you will encounter the most visual aspects of object-oriented programming as well as the more demanding aspects of managing the FoxPro database system (including data buffers and multiuser programming). This is also where the application framework gets built—or at least you'll see what one looks like and how the individual elements are used.

When people first go deeply into object-oriented programming and the mechanics of piecing together the elements of an application framework (forms, menus, toolbars, and data), they seem to encounter many dark corners—places where things don't seem to work. Even for experienced programmers, who certainly know how to construct a function and code an algorithm, inside the framework of object-oriented programming things seem different.

Things are different, and that is why the chapters in this section (especially Chapters 16–18) spend a great deal of time covering the setup and links between various parts of an application.

- Chapter 16, "Working on the Framework," provides an overview of the principal application framework elements and concentrates on the locations (usually in objects) where the various elements are connected.
- Chapter 17, "Developing the User Interface," describes the main elements of the user interface, in particular the Visual FoxPro controls and how they are used within the various containers, such as Forms, PageFrames, and Grids.
- Chapter 18, "Mastering Forms," covers the whole environment of a form, including network and multiuser issues, the basic data entry form, grids, FormSets, PageFrames, and drag-and-drop techniques.
- Chapter 19, "Mastering the Database," picks up from the beginning chapters of the book and goes into the details of OOP data management, multiuser programming, transaction processing, memo fields, and OLE.
- Chapter 20, "Advanced SQL and Views," explores some of the more complicated uses of SQL Select. It also covers some of the basic topics involved in client/server applications: ODBC and remote views.

There's a lot of material in these five chapters, more than could be covered by a couple of books. In addition to reading the Visual FoxPro *Developer's Manual*, you would be well served to seek out books and magazine articles devoted to object oriented programming. But the main thrust should be to create an application framework of your own or at least something with most of the basic application elements.

CHAPTER 16

WORKING ON THE FRAMEWORK

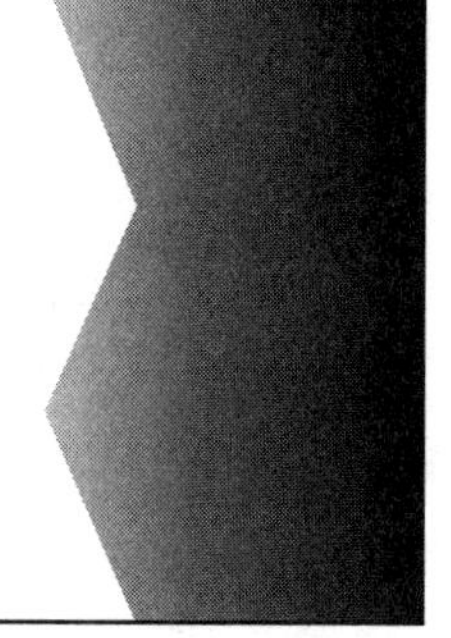

We're here to answer two questions in this chapter: What, exactly, goes into an application framework, and how do you make one? There's been a lot of preparation getting to this point: data management, procedural programming, object-oriented programming, and application analysis and design. Frankly, there's a lot more to follow. But when you're finished with this chapter you should understand, at least in outline, what an application framework is about. You'll also learn more about the structure of a typical application, because application frameworks are designed to parallel the way an application is constructed.

APPLICATION STRUCTURE AND THE APPLICATION FRAMEWORK

In Chapter 1 and again in Chapter 11, we dabbled with a few elements of an application: a startup program (MAIN), a menu (MAIN.MPR), and one form with a few properties and methods. Now we go for the whole enchilada: the elements of a complete application. Figure 16.1 illustrates the most common elements in an application structure, although some applications may have less and many of them will have more.

Let's run through each element briefly. (More detail will come a bit later.)

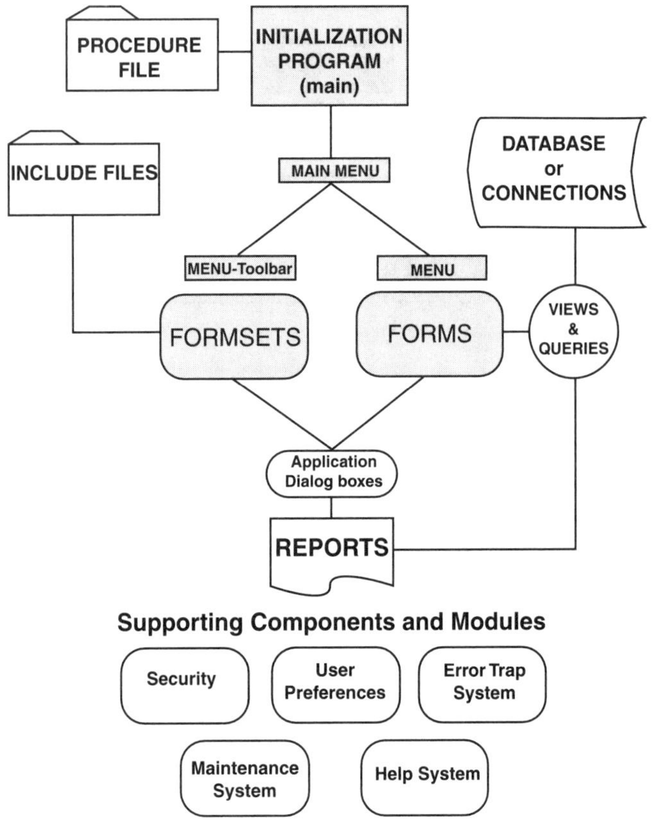

FIGURE 16.1 ELEMENTS OF A FULL-SCALE APPLICATION.

- **Initialization program**. All applications need a way to get started. It has become traditional in Visual FoxPro to use a program file named MAIN.PRG (a tip of the hat to C++) to perform the ceremony. Some developers also use the MAIN program to instantiate and initialize many of the objects used globally in an application. Probably more developers do this within a single APP object.
- **Procedure file**. Depending on your attitude, the procedure file is a vestige of the Old FoxPro or a convenient place for functions, procedures, and custom classes that don't belong in the Class Designer. Later in this chapter, you'll see an example of a generic custom class—in raw code—that is a candidate for a procedure file.

- **Main menu**. Most applications begin with a main menu that allows the user a choice of accessing the primary functions of the application as well as the official option for exiting the program.
- **Include files**. Most programmers take advantage of FoxPro's preprocessor directives to incorporate constant definitions (such as `#DEFINE pi 3.1416`). These definitions are stored in *include* files (they have the extension H, another C++ tradition).
- **Database or connections**. One way or another, most FoxPro applications use a database.
- **Views and queries**. Using SQL views and the occasional query has become an integral part of FoxPro programming. Many forms have views in their Data Environment.
- **Menus and toolbars**. It's customary, although by no means required, for every primary form to have its own menu. Toolbars are also optional, although they're ubiquitous in commercial Windows 95 and NT programs.
- **Forms and formsets**. In terms of the user interface and as containers for most of your programming, **Form** and **FormSet** classes are the center of activity. Most applications have numerous Forms or, if you use toolbars, FormSets.
- **Application dialog boxes**. Most applications need a battery of dialog boxes to handle messages, user information-gathering, and process management. Dialog boxes are created with forms, usually in their modal state.
- **Reports (and labels)**. Could an application exist if it didn't have reports?
- **Supporting components and modules**. These elements are sometimes stand-alone modules (such as a file maintenance system) or components created from classes that have their methods used throughout an applications (such as security, user preferences, error trapping, and help systems). Chapter 15 outlined a list of these elements that are common to most applications.

It's not a very big a list. Some of the elements, such as forms and reports, may be numerous. Others (such as include files) are permanent residents of the application framework, and you simply connect them to each application. That brings us to the relationship between application elements and the framework (Figure 16.2).

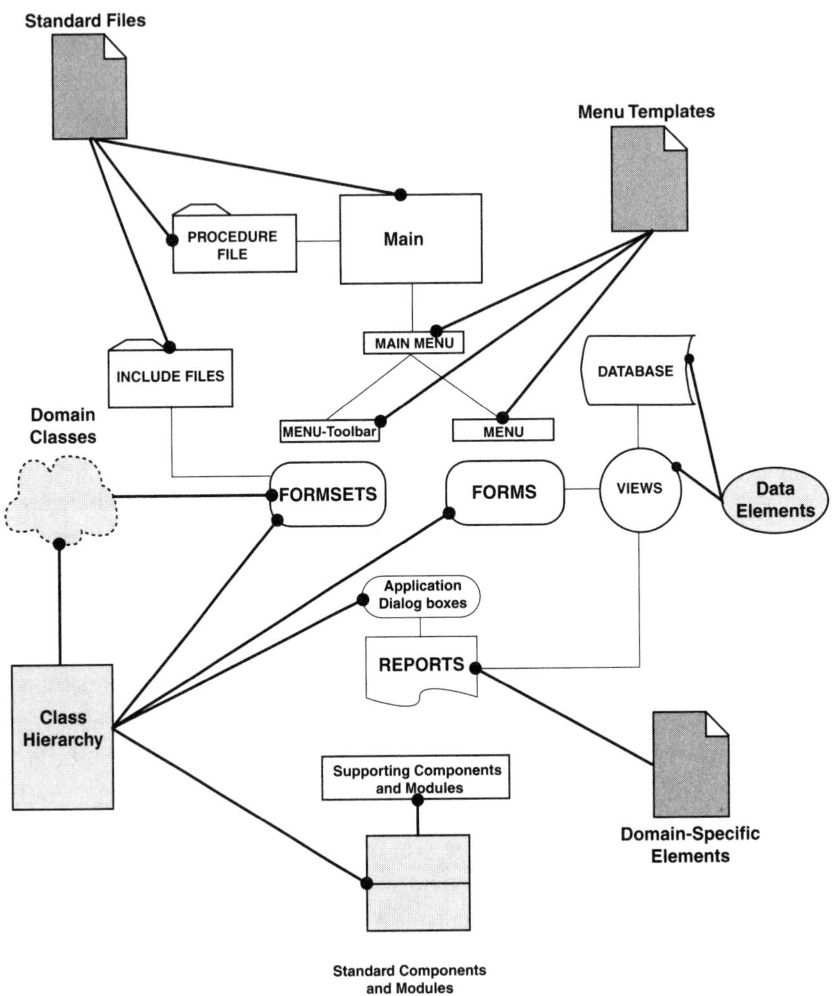

FIGURE 16.2 THE RELATIONSHIP BETWEEN APPLICATION ELEMENTS AND THE APPLICATION FRAMEWORK.

In each section of the book, you've seen diagrams of the application framework. Now it's applied to all the elements of an application. Remember that a framework is a set of files in a Project Manager, a concept, and a set of documentation; it provides an organizational framework along with documentation of the elements and how they are used:

- **Standard files**. For the application framework, you create one MAIN.PRG, which is copied and modified as needed for each application. There is usually only one procedure file (if any), which is loaded by each application that uses it. The same applies to include files, which are created once and used throughout applications.
- **Menu templates**. The framework usually contains three or four menu templates of different kinds: menu programs that have standard menu options that you add to or modify for use in specific applications. Toolbars are generally not part of the menu templates, because they are associated with FormSets. However, if you use an application toolbar (one that is associated with the application as a whole), you might create a template for it.
- **Data elements**. Most elements of the database structure and management are customized for each application and are therefore poor candidates for reuse in a framework. However, there are a fair number of tables (and a database or two) that handle application utilities and support modules; these tables and databases can easily be documented and used repeatedly. Views and queries are even more application-specific, again with the exception of those used with support modules.
- **Domain-specific elements.** For the most part, this means reports and labels. Most of these items have no use beyond a particular application. An exception is reports used with application management modules such as security and file maintenance. One component, report management, is often documented in this part of the framework because it's used in many applications but operates with a specific application's reports.
- **Class hierarchy**. This structure is the mother of the application framework, providing the classes that are used in almost every aspect of an application. It's used to create the supporting components and modules (security, error trapping, user preferences, and so on). Sometimes its classes are used directly within the application, particularly for application dialog boxes, and they're used to create the domain classes.
- **Domain classes**. Derived from the class hierarchy, these classes are specific to an application. When possible, the application framework contains **Forms** (or **FormSets**) and other classes that are reusable within the same application. Otherwise, the framework documents the standalone Forms (SCX or classes) that are used within the application.

- **Standard components and modules**. There's potentially a long list of modules and components that can be used in multiple applications. Some are more "standard" than others, such as security, error trapping, and file maintenance. Except for the class hierarchy, developers spend more time with these elements than with any other part of the application framework. As usual, the framework document explains each component and describes how it is used within applications.

In the beginning it's enough to create a framework that's capable of building a test application. Standard files and menu templates can be knocked off quickly. The class hierarchy is another matter. It may take a couple of weeks—or many months—and you're never really finished. Building the standard components and modules is a long-term project. If your current application needs a component, such as security, you build the security component (or appropriate the one that comes with this book) and document it for the application framework.

The Project Manager and Applications

Before going into the details of application framework elements, we need to stop at the Project Manager and cover its relationship to applications. You've been introduced to the Project Manager as the place to coordinate all the files used by an application. The second task of the Project Manager is to *build* an application: the process of compiling all the elements of a project and creating a file that can be executed—run—by the operating system. (In the world of C programming, the Project Manager performs the *Make* function.) The Project Manager will track all the files needed by your application, check to see whether they have been updated, and, if they have, compile them into an application file (APP), an OLE executable (DLL), or an executable file (EXE). Normally, these are the forms of your application that you distribute to the site of the project.

Using the Project Manager

One of the requirements for building applications with the Project Manager is that you identify a *main program* (use **Project**, **Set Main** in the menu), the program that starts all other elements of an application. This is the same one as the MAIN.PRG of the application framework. Beginning with the main program, the Project Manager follows the chain of execution—the succession of program calls from one element to another—until it tracks down everything (such as a file, class, procedure, or whatever) that is apparently required by the current project. In this process, the Project Manager will automatically add any file not already in its list. If it can't locate a file (or a procedure), it will ask for your help.

BUILDS

Among themselves, developers talk like this: "Hit a couple of weird bugs. Had to build that sucker 10 times before I found the problem." Doing a build is easy. Just use the **Build** button in the Project Manager window to open the Build Options dialog box (Figure 16.3).

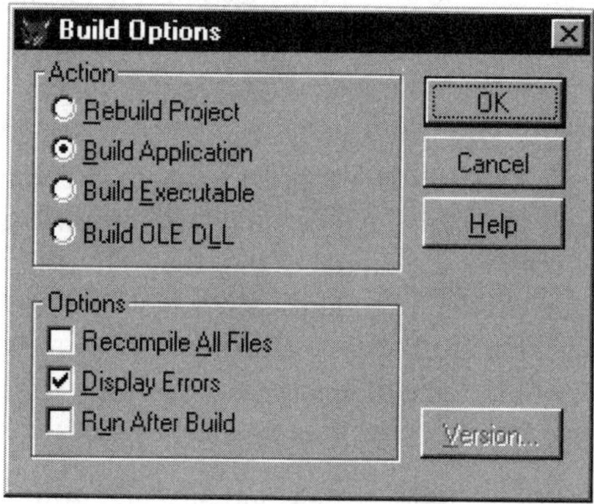

FIGURE 16.3 BUILD OPTIONS DIALOG BOX.

You can select **Re-build Project** (to make sure everything will compile), **Build Application**, **Build Executable**, or **Build OLE DLL**. You also have the option of having FoxPro **Recompile All Files** during the build (normally it works only with changed files), **Display Errors** (vital), and **Run After Build** (usually). After that, the Project Manager does a lot of work on your behalf:

1. It tracks the location of all listed files and the location of all references in the programming: function and procedure calls, array declarations, API library calls, or calls for special files such as memory (MEM), report (FRX), bitmap (BMP), and query (QPR). If files are missing or there are references the Project Manager can't find, the

errors will be displayed (if you left **Display Errors** checked) and logged to the project error file (ERR).

2. It compares the date and time (the *time stamp*) of each file on disk against the date and time stored in the Project Manager file. If the file has been updated or changed, it will be generated or compiled (or both), if appropriate, and incorporated into the project. Then the Project Manager dates and times are updated.
3. Menus are generated and then compiled. Program files are compiled. This produces an *object code*, which is stored in the memo file of the Project Manager (FPT). The memo files tend to become very large. You may notice from time to time that FoxPro will do some housekeeping, alerting you with messages such as "Packing Memo File." You can also do this housekeeping on command using the **Clean Up Project** option in the Project menu.
4. FoxPro scans the code for syntax or other compiler errors and creates a log file for your information.
5. If you have specified **APP**, **EXE**, or **DLL** the Project Manager will draw from the object files stored in its memo fields and will produce a composite file of object code. In the case of the APP, this file becomes the application file (APP). To build the executable file or DLL, you must have the Visual FoxPro Professional Edition. The Project Manager will hand off the object code to a *linker* that comes with the Professional Edition, which produces the final executable file (EXE).

The Project Manager is remarkably quick and efficient. Still, depending on your hardware, it takes time to build a large application. That's why developers like to work with smaller modules that can be built and tested independently. Throughout much of the development cycle, you can avoid doing builds by selecting **MAIN.PRG** in the **Code** tab of the Project Manager and then selecting **Run**. This approach works well, provided that you've generated any menus before running. Menu generation is the one thing that FoxPro can't do on-the-fly.

The Project Manager and an Application Framework

The most convenient way to build an application framework is to start a project for it. Call it APPFRAME or something similar, and use it as the repository for

all the files associated with the framework, including the application framework documentation. This technique gives you a single access point to the working files, which can later be dragged and dropped from the APPFRAME Project Manager window into the Project Manager tabs of a new application.

STANDARD FILES

Before we get to MAIN.PRG and a full initialization, we need to cover a couple of other standard file types that are part of the application framework: include and procedure files.

INCLUDE FILES AND PREPROCESSOR DIRECTIVES

Let's say that in an application you need to use the value 12.342432 in many places for a standard calculation. Every time you run across the value in a formula, you need to type this bunch of numbers, a chore that is a nuisance and prone to typing errors that could lead to difficult bugs. Such problems led compiler designers to develop a *preprocessor* capability. In essence, it works like this: You first create a *preprocessor directive*.

```
#DEFINE FACTOR1  12.342432
```

Then, in your code, whenever you need to use this number, use the word instead:

```
nNewValue = nTestValue * FACTOR1
```

When the program is compiled, the compiler will substitute the value for the defined word. This preprocess has no effect on a running program, although it has a minimal effect on the speed of compilation.

WARNING

Don't use FoxPro keywords for constant names or use system variables in the expression to be substituted. You might get odd results if you do something like `#DEFINE BROWSE GRAZING`. System variables, the ones beginning with an underscore, are not evaluated until run time, so using them in preprocessor directives will also have unpredictable results.

Although you can place **#DEFINE** preprocessor directives anywhere in FoxPro code, it's become traditional to put them in *header files*, separate program files that are included when the main program files are compiled. By convention (from the C language), these header files have an H extension, such as FOXPRO.H. The FOXPRO.H file is a real file (located in the \VFP folder) and is used in almost all the Visual FoxPro example programs. You should examine it, not only as an example but also because it should be a standard item in the application framework—and no work for you!

You can continue to add **#DEFINE**s to FOXPRO.H or perhaps augment it with a header file of your own (add that to the application framework, too).

MAKING CONNECTIONS: INCLUDE FILES

Add your include files to the **Other** tab of the Project Manager (APPFRAME project or an application's project) under the **Text Files** category. In FoxPro, the include files (header files) can be incorporated in two ways:

- **In code**: Use the **#INCLUDE** preprocessor directive. For example: `#INCLUDE FOXPRO.H`. This command can be used in an initialization file, a form, or even in a header file.
- **In the Form Designer and Class Designer**: From the menu, select **Form** (or **Class**), **Include File** and follow the dialog box to enter the name of the file to be included.

It's important to understand that FoxPro uses include files only *per program file*—that is, within the confines of a single program, class, or form file. There is no such thing as a global header file. This means that header files must be declared for every program, class, and form where you want to use preprocessor constants.

PROCEDURE FILES

In the days before FoxPro supported object-oriented programming, the procedure file was *the* place for reusable code, usually in the form of generic functions and procedures that could be used in a variety of applications. Although classes and class libraries have now usurped the majority of usefulness in a procedure file, there may still be a need for generic functions and procedures—sometimes called *free* functions or procedures—which are more convenient to call without the object-oriented machinery.

NOTE

You can also define classes in a procedure library. Some developers prefer to do this for nonvisual classes, because they are constructed with more traditional programming and because the visual approach of the Class Designer might be considered an impediment. This form of nostalgia makes OOP adherents cringe.

MAKING CONNECTIONS: PROCEDURE FILES

Create or transfer procedure files in the **Code** tab, **Programs** category of the Project Manager (APPFRAME or application's project).

Procedure files are regular program files. Procedures and functions are entered in sequence with the usual **PROCEDURE name** and **FUNCTION name / RETURN** format. Put them into the **Code** tab of the Project Manager under **Programs**. To load a procedure file in a program, use **SET PROCEDURE TO cFileName**. For example: `SET PROCEDURE TO stdproc.prg`. If procedure files are already open, use **SET PROCEDURE TO cFileName ADDITIVE.**

As a rule, procedure files are loaded into memory at the beginning of an application (because the routines are so generic) as part of an application's initialization routines.

INITIALIZATION

It has become traditional to initialize a FoxPro application with MAIN.PRG. This program file might do nothing more than get other things started, or it can contain a large portion of the code used for initializing an application. The one thing it must have is the **READ EVENTS** statement to set up the event loop that runs the application.

NOTE

If you've been following the bare bones testing shell that's been developing in several chapters, you might want to haul it out again. It's time to put it on steroids.

Although an initialization file for a testing shell is deliberately kept small and simple, initialization for an entire application can be voluminous and complicated. That's why there's no general agreement on the best way to do it. Some programmers prefer to put all their eggs in the one MAIN program basket, and others prefer to create a custom class that handles most of the initialization code. It doesn't matter to FoxPro unless there's something wrong with the coding or the sequence of initialization.

NOTE

OOP purists object to using any kind of procedural structure in an application and would naturally choose to put all initialization into one or more custom APP classes. This works. However, I figure it's a shame to make the MAIN.PRG nothing more than a ceremonial vestige, so I load it with most of the working startup code. This works, too. Moreover, I like coding in a text file. Label me old-fashioned.

In most respects, where you put initialization elements is less important than covering all the bases. Because code in the Class Designer can't be easily displayed, we'll use an example with a MAIN.PRG as the initialization file.

Initialization: General Environment

Use the **SET** commands to create the general operating environment. It's a good idea to make important default conditions explicit. For example, you might specify `SET EXACT OFF` even though that's the default, because you want to document the policy for the application. From this point, `SET EXACT ON` must be used explicitly and then returned to `SET EXACT OFF`. The **SET** commands also include **SET PROCEDURE**, which loads the program file containing a library of procedural routines, if you have one, and opens the library files of the class hierarchy.

```
*------------------[SET GENERAL ENVIRONMENT
* SET commands
SET TALK OFF                  && Applies only to program
SET SAFETY OFF                && At your own risk
SET BELL OFF                  && Make noise explicit
SET CONFIRM ON                && Exit TextBox on Enter
SET DELETE ON                 && Note: Troublemaker 1
SET EXACT OFF                 && Note: Troublemaker 2
SET MEMOWIDTH TO 50           && Default value
SET ESCAPE ON                 && Default
* PROC & CLASS LIBS
SET PROCEDURE TO STDPROC
SET CLASSLIB TO bct.vcx,genctrl.vcx,genctain.vcx,gendata.vcx
SET CLASSLIB TO appctain.vcx,appctrl.vcx ADDITIVE
SET CLASSLIB TO genprog.vcx,appprog.vcx ADDITIVE
```

The network setup, discussed in Chapter 19, depends on which network the program will run and may include third-party software to beef up the network awareness. The example setup presumes a Novell network. **SET REFRESH** can put a heavy load on a busy network. The fastest refresh (**0,0**) means the most network traffic. Reduce this value accordingly.

```
*————————————————-[ NETWORK SETUP
*DOS variable USERNAME set by Novell System or Login Script
*DOS SET USERNAME="%LOGIN_NAME"
IF NOT EMPTY(GETENV("USERNAME"))
  SET EXCLUSIVE OFF                    && Files are shared
  SET REFRESH TO 0,0                   && Fastest refresh
  SET REPROCESS TO 3 SECONDS           && Timing for retries
ENDIF
```

INITIALIZATION: DEFINE VARIABLES

Most applications of any size make it possible for the users or system administrators to set some of the operating parameters. The initialization routine checks to see whether application parameter data is available in a system table. If it is not, the routine calls the system setup routine so that anything critical can be entered. In some cases, it might be better if only a warning message is shown and the program terminated. All this depends on the environment of the application and the complexity of the setup.

```
*————————————————-[ DEFINE VARIABLES
#DEFINE DEVELOP = .T.          && DEVELOPER VERSION OF APP
* Variables Defined:
* dFYEnd  = Fiscal Year End
* cDDFile = Location of data dictionary
* cOrg    = Name of Organization
* cOrgSt1 = Address: Street 1
* cOrgSt2 = Address: Street 2
* cOrgCsz = Address: City,State ZIP
IF NOT FILE("SYSTEM.DBF")
  DO FORM SYSPARMS.SCX NAME SYSPARMS LINKED && Call setup
ELSE
  USE system IN 0 ORDER sysid
  SELECT system
```

```
  IF SEEK "APPVARS"
    RESTORE FROM MEMO vars1 ADDITIVE && Load parameters
  ENDIF
ENDIF
```

The following section loads the global variables used by the application, if any. It's a good idea to keep **PUBLIC** variables to a minimum and to be explicit about where they are used.

```
* GENERAL USE PUBLIC VARIABLES
PUBLIC gcFullName, gcUserName, gcOperator
gcFullName = ""                  && User's full name
gcUserName = ""                  && User's network name
gcOperator = ""                  && User's Operator ID
```

Initialization: Screen Display

The screen setup section takes care of anything required by the basic FoxPro screen. You may want to clear any old images and activate the status bar. Depending on your approach to color, this section may be empty or elaborate.

```
*———————————————————[ SCREEN SETUP
CLEAR
* Change the Main FoxPro screen caption
_SCREEN.Caption = "THE NAME OF THE APPLICATION"
SET STATUS BAR ON              && Default
SET MESSAGE TO                 && Default to statusbar
* Change the SCREEN CURSOR.
_SCREEN.MousePointer = MOUSE_HOURGLASS
```

The next piece of code takes care of hiding various FoxPro toolbars, primarily the Standard toolbar, under the assumption that you'll have no toolbars (other than your own). Later, in cleanup, another routine reverses this procedure.

```
*> Hide FoxPro Toolbars
LOCAL  i
PUBLIC gaVFPTbr
DECLARE gaVFPTbr[11,2]
gaVFPTbr[1,1]  = "Form Designer"
gaVFPTbr[2,1]  = "Standard"
```

```
gaVFPTbr[3,1]  = "Layout"
gaVFPTbr[4,1]  = "Query Designer"
gaVFPTbr[5,1]  = "View Designer"
gaVFPTbr[6,1]  = "Color Palette"
gaVFPTbr[7,1]  = "Form Controls"
gaVFPTbr[8,1]  = "Database Designer"
gaVFPTbr[9,1]  = "Report Designer"
gaVFPTbr[10,1] = "Report Controls"
gaVFPTbr[11,1] = "Print Preview"
*> Loop and hide
FOR i = 1 TO 11
  *Save status of toolbar
  gaVFPTbr[i, 2] = WVISIBLE(gaVFPTbr[i, 1])
  IF gaVFPTbr[i, 2]
    HIDE WINDOW (gaVFPTbr[i, 1])
  ENDIF
ENDFOR
```

INITIALIZATION: ERROR TRAPPING

Error trapping is a standard component of the application framework. Notice that this is the first object created by the application (in this setup, anyway). APPERROR is a class, defined in the class hierarchy, that manages all forms of error trapping.

```
*-----------------------[ ERROR TRAPPING
#IF DEVELOP
  *Development error trapping.
  *>Error trapping Class
  oAppError = CREATEOBJECT("APPERROR","DEV")
#ELSE
  * Substitute a user-oriented error trapping system.
  *>Error trapping Class
  oAppError = CREATEOBJECT("APPERROR","USER")
#ENDIF
```

The structure of the error trapping section (using the preprocessor directives) is designed to handle two systems: one for the developer and one for the user of the final product. At some point during the development cycle, the developer's version is turned off in favor of a system that is less technical and more user-friendly.

The preprocessor directive in this example has a construction that looks familiar yet strange:

Command syntax:

#IF nExpression | lExpression
<statements>
[#ELIF nExpression | lExpression
<statements>
...
[#ELIF nExpression | lExpression>
<statements>]
#ELSE
<statements>
#ENDIF

Essentially, this is a **DO CASE..ENDCASE** construction, although it looks like an **IF..ENDIF**. Here's a comparison:

```
                              DO CASE
#IF   nVersion = 2           CASE nVersion < 2
#ELIF nVersion = 1.5         CASE nVersion = 1.5
#ELIF nVersion = 1.0         CASE nVersion = 1.0
#ELSE                         OTHERWISE
#ENDIF                        ENDCASE
```

This construction segregates sections of code by using conditionals to tell the compiler which section to compile; in the preceding example, that's the directive section. In the initialization file example, a directive is used to distinguish code for development from production code.

Initialization: Application Objects

This section of the initialization is the one most often moved to an APP class, because it instantiates a number of application-oriented objects. Notice in this

example that a property of the APPERROR class, `plErrOk`, is used to signal that initialization of the objects succeeds or fails. The following example is abbreviated:

```
*>Basic Data Form command manager
IF oAppError.plErrOk
  oActMgr  = CREATEOBJECT("APPACTMGR")
ENDIF
*>User Tracking System
IF oAppError.plErrOk
  oAppUP  = CREATEOBJECT("APPUSERPREF",oAppSec.pcUserId)
ENDIF
*> FoxTools Wrapper Class
oGenFT = CREATEOBJECT("GENFOXTOOLS")
```

INITIALIZATION: STARTING THE APPLICATION

As you've seen before, the **READ EVENTS** starts the program after a main menu has been opened. In this example, that won't happen if there has been a problem with something up the line (using `plErrOk` as the trigger).

```
*————————————[ MAIN MENU & EVENT LOOP
IF oAppError.plErrOk
  PUSH MENU _MSYSMENU
  DO APPWORK.MPR
  _SCREEN.MousePointer = MOUSE_DEFAULT
  READ EVENTS
ENDIF
```

CLOSING THE APPLICATION

When the user terminates the program or the developer has placed code to quit the program, some sort of routine is needed after the **READ EVENTS** to do cleanup. In this example, a procedure, CLOSEOUT, handles the duties.

```
*————————————[ CLEANUP
#IF DEV
   DO CloseOut
#ELSEIF
   DO CloseOut
```

```
  QUIT
#ENDIF
```

Also defined in MAIN.PRG (in this example), the CLOSEOUT procedure can be called from anywhere in the program. It reverses the hidden toolbars and takes care of resetting FoxPro to the condition before the application started.

```
******************************CLOSEOUT
PROCEDURE CloseOut
EXTERNAL ARRAY gaVFPTbr

*>Close Main Toolbar, if any.
IF TYPE("OAPPTBR")<>"U"
  RELEASE oAppTbr
ENDIF

*> Loop and close forms
nFrmClose = 1
FOR i = 1 TO _SCREEN.FormCount
  IF TYPE("_SCREEN.Forms(nFrmClose)") == "O"
    *Release open forms, if any.
    IF _SCREEN.Forms(nFrmClose).QueryUnload()
      _SCREEN.Forms(nFrmClose).Release()
    ELSE
      _SCREEN.MousePointer = MOUSE_DEFAULT
      RETURN .F.
    ENDIF
  ELSE
    nFrmClose = nFrmClose + 1
  ENDIF
ENDFOR

*>Restore previous toolbars
FOR i = 1 TO 11
  IF gaVFPTbr[i, 2]
    SHOW WINDOW (gaVFPTbr[i, 1])
  ENDIF
ENDFOR

*>Reset main menu
```

```
SET SYSMENU TO DEFAULT

*> Other cleanup
_SCREEN.MousePointer = MOUSE_DEFAULT
MODIFY WINDOW SCREEN    && Restores original screen caption
SET MESSAGE TO
SET CLASSLIB TO
RELEASE ALL
ON KEY
ON ERROR
CLEAR ALL
```

An initialization routine can contain a good deal more than what's in this example. You might take a look at the one that comes with the UTILITY project of this book. Also look at the FoxPro example application, TASTRADE, to see how the same type of initialization can be done in a class. However you do it, MAIN program or a separate APP class, it's a part of the application framework that you put into the Project Manager for every project and then tweak according to the needs of the application.

MAKING CONNECTIONS-INITIALIZATION FILE OR CLASS

Create or transfer MAIN.PRG in the **Code** tab, **Programs** category of the Project Manager (APPFRAME or application's project). Alternatively, create an APPINIT (or similarly named) class in the **Classes** tab of the Project Manager.

To use them in an application, MAIN.PRG is selected as the main program. APPINIT would be instantiated somewhere in MAIN.PRG with **CREATEOBJECT( )**.

DATA ELEMENTS

In FoxPro, you don't get very far without using databases and tables. In most applications, they are the first things created. Not only do you need the tables, but it's also important to load them with enough data to provide a reasonable test of data management within your application.

If you've done the data analysis and design, then creating the database is mostly a matter of going into the Database Designer and entering the specifications for each table (including indexes). As a refresher, here is the general sequence:

1. Create the database from within the Project Manager.
2. Define each table, including fields and indexes.
3. Define permanent relations between tables.
4. Define default field values and validation rules.
5. Define record validation rules.
6. Define relational integrity rules in the RI Builder.
7. Load test data, either manually or by using **APPEND** or **IMPORT**.
8. Create standard views of the data.
9. If the views require access to remote data, define the needed connections.
10. Create any additional stored procedures relevant to the database or its remote connections.

For the application framework there are often a number of tables that can be associated with any application. These tables can be grouped into a single database, UTILITY.DBC, which is then incorporated into a Project Manager list. The UTILITY database contains tables such as the following:

- SYSTEM.DBF: System parameters and configuration information.
- USERPREF.DBF: Information about the preferences of individual users.
- USERS.DBF: A table of registered users for the application.
- USERSEC.DBF: A table of the security rights of each user.
- REPORTS.DBF: A table of all the reports used in the application.

Most of these tables (and many others) are associated with standard modules and components.

Making Connections: Database Elements

All data elements are created in the **Data** tab of the Project Manager and can be dragged and dropped from the application framework project (for example, APPFRAME) into the same tab of a new project. Using data within an application has many points of connection. Here are some of the most important:

- **In programming anywhere:** You have the use of FoxPro data management commands that can be used on any accessible table at any time in a program. This applies whether you are working with a program file, a menu file, or a form file (but not a report file).
- **In classes:** In general, you can use standard database programming techniques in the methods of your classes. At times, it may also be useful to encapsulate database information in an object.
- **In a query:** Use the Query Designer to create a read-only selection of data from one or more tables.
- **In a view:** Use the View Designer to create local or remote views from multiple tables. These views may be used as a readable data source or can be updated by the user (or programmatically), with changes posted to the base tables. Views are stored in the database and can be used in almost all respects as if they were a single table.
- **In a FormSet:** The key feature for data in a FormSet is the ability to establish either a shared or private data session for each form in the set. As the default, all forms share the same data session. If you set the **DataSession** property to **2**, then each form may have its own private data session. This means that it can have its own Data Environment, a unique set of tables and views.
- **In a Form:** Create a Data Environment by dragging and dropping tables or views from the Project Manager **Data** tab. Then define relations, if any, between the tables. To put the fields into the form, drag the field name from the Data Environment onto the form surface. The type of field determines the control that will be created: A logical field results in a check box, a Memo filed results in an edit box, a General files, an OLE bound control, and all other fields a text box.
- **In a Grid:** As befits one of the most complex objects in FoxPro, the Grid can handle data in a variety of ways. You can create a grid by dragging a table icon from the Data Environment onto a form.
- **In controls:** For those controls that can take field values (all except containers and command buttons), use the **ControlSource** property. This is usually a reference to the table and field, such as `test.sampleID`.
- **In a report:** Create a Data Environment the same way it's created in a form.

TOOLBARS AND MENU TEMPLATES

Virtually all applications have menus, if only because a program without a menu would be branded as a nonstandard Windows program. More important, users expect menus, and they provide access to options that are not well served by icons in a toolbar. In addition, many users prefer keyboard access to options, and toolbars don't provide that.

Chapter 17 covers the mechanics of creating both standard and shortcut menus. As you will see, in terms of object-oriented programming, menus are the odd man out; they're not objects, and, unlike forms, menu files must be explicitly generated and then compiled. When you attach a menu to a program, you call a program file—an MPR—instead of the container table file (MNX) as you do with forms.

When it comes to building menu templates for an application framework, a simple way to start is with a set of three:

- MAIN. Create one template for a main menu, the one that comes up immediately after the application is started. There's not much to the template, only the options **File**, **Help**, and **Quit**. Even these three are debatable, but that's a subject for another chapter. This menu gets filled with options for a specific application, usually access to various modules.
- APPMENU. Create one standard menu that could be attached to any primary form or form set. This menu usually includes **File**, **Edit**, **Control**, **Window**, **Help**, and **Close**. These options are geared to the actions needed by many forms. They include table navigation, window management, and user help.
- MODAL. Create one simple menu that is used with modal dialog boxes. It usually has only one option: **Close**.

MAKING CONNECTIONS: MENUS

Menu templates are created in the **Other** tab, **Menus** category of the Project Manager (APPFRAME project, in this example).

The standard approach for using menus is to replace one menu with another one or, in other words, to execute different menu programs. As a matter of mechanics, this task is simple: Use the command **DO MenuName.MPR**. If you wish to preserve the previous menu so that you can quickly return to it on exiting an object, the setup looks like this:

```
PUSH MENU _MSYSMENU
DO newmenu.mpr
...
POP MENU _MSYSMENU
```

TOOLBARS

Toolbars, as an element of an application, are attached to form sets. "Attached" is almost the wrong word, because usually you create a toolbar by dropping it from a class library onto a form, and that immediately turns it into a **FormSet** class. With a toolbar, the trick is to provide the appropriate control over its button activity—a topic for Chapter 18.

THE CLASS HIERARCHY

As the cornerstone of an application framework (and applications, too, of course), the class hierarchy requires a systematic effort to create. To be solidly trite: If Rome wasn't built in a day, then neither is an application framework. There is (or should be) a big difference between building your first application with Visual FoxPro and building your third application. If you've taken object-oriented programming to heart, have done your design homework, and have built a reasonably generic class hierarchy, the third application should be much easier than the first one. Why the third application? Because it usually takes that long to establish a good class structure and develop some of the other major components.

What's in a complete class hierarchy, one suitable for a comprehensive application framework? That depends, in part, on the design of your hierarchy. However you structure it, the design should suggest systematic development. It's something like filling in a big puzzle; you know the general outline and a few key pieces, and you figure out the rest as you go along.

How do you decide what goes into the hierarchy? Some of it is "standard" in that every application has forms, grids, and controls. Some of it is a result of your most basic design decisions: **Toolbars**, **FormSets**, and **PageFrames** are all classes that are expanded if you choose to use them. Many of the controls can be specialized; for example, you can create an intelligent date entry text box. A large number of custom classes can be built around data management (such as table and database objects), and an equally large number of classes deal with the mechanics of an application, such as a navigation toolbar for moving among records in a form. Some of this can be laid out in a systematic way, and you can see where the blanks need to be filled in with classes. Other times, the idea for a class just comes along. Let's look at an example.

Suppose you're working on a time and billing program for an ad agency. The program has date and time manipulation all over it, and you conclude that the DateTime data type is ugly and hard to use. It occurs to you that instead of trying to remember all the various conversion functions and their peculiar results, you could build a class to organize and simplify DateTime management. Indeed you can. In the class hierarchy design of this book, it's a generic data class, and it goes into the GENDATA.VCX library file. It might look like this in code:

```
*******************************************************
*  CLASS:   genDateTime CUSTOM CLASS
* CREATE:   oDT = CREATEOBJECT("genDateTime",DateTimeValue)
*  USAGE:   genDateTime.Init(DateTimeValue)
*******************************************************
DEFINE CLASS genDateTime AS CUSTOM
  *-----------PROPERTIES
  pcStdTime    = SPACE(8) && Time as HH:MM:SS character
  pnHourNum    = 0        && Hours as number
  pnMinuteNum  = 0        && Minutes as number
  pnSeconds    = 0        && Seconds as number
  pcLongDate   = ""       && Date as: Thursday May 12,1995
  pdDate       = {}       && Standard FoxPro date
  pnYearNum    = 0        && Year as number: 1995
  pcYearChar   = ""       && Year as character: 1995
  pnMonthNum   = 0        && Month as a number: 12
  pcMonthChar  = ""       && Month as a character: June
  pcMonth3Char = ""       && Month as 3 character: Jun
  pnWeekNum    = 0        && Week as number: 32
  pnDayNum     = 0        && Day as number: 4
  pcDayChar    = ""       && Day as character: Thursday

  *-----------METHODS
  PROCEDURE Init
```

```
    LPARAMETER yDateTime
    THIS.pcStdTime     = THIS.StdTime(yDateTime)
    THIS.pnHourNum     = HOUR(yDateTime)
    THIS.pnMinuteNum   = MINUTE(yDateTime)
    THIS.pnSeconds     = SEC(yDateTime)
    THIS.pcLongDate    = THIS.LongDate(yDateTime)
    THIS.pdDate        = TTOD(yDateTime)
    THIS.pnYearNum     = YEAR(yDateTime)
    THIS.pcYearChar    = ALLTRIM(STR(YEAR(yDateTime)))
    THIS.pnMonthNum    = MONTH(yDateTime)
    THIS.pcMonthChar   = CMONTH(yDateTime)
    THIS.pcMonth3Char  = SUBSTR(CMONTH(yDateTime),1,3)
    THIS.pnWeekNum     = WEEK(yDateTime)
    THIS.pnDayNum      = DAY(yDateTime)
    THIS.pcDayChar     = DOW(yDateTime)
  ENDPROC
  FUNCTION StdTime PROTECTED
    LPARAMETER yDt
    RETURN SUBSTR(TTOC(yDt),11,8)
  ENDFUNC
  FUNCTION longdate PROTECTED
    LPARAMETERS yDt
    LOCAL cLongDate, cCentSet
    cCentSet=SET("CENTURY")
    SET CENTURY ON
    cLongDate = CDOW(yDt) + ', ' + MDY(yDt)
    SET CENTURY &cCentSet
    RETURN cLongDate
  ENDFUNC
ENDDEFINE
```

This class can be used in programming this way:

```
oDT = CREATEOBJECT("genDateTime",DATETIME())
_SCREEN.ActiveForm.Caption = oDT.pcYearChar
```

In many ways, **genDateTime** behaves like the generic functions that used to be created and placed in a procedure file. What the class does that's unique to object-oriented programming is to wrap a number of related functions, some from FoxPro and others user-defined, in a protective shell. It's often called a *wrapper class*. It also defines some internal variables (as properties) that can be shared among the internal methods; a few of these variables are exposed for use by other objects. With this approach, you can feed the **genDateTime** object a single value and have immediate access to all the conversions as properties.

A Class Hierarchy Described

To re-create the layout and details of a comprehensive class hierarchy would require another book (the APPCLASS.DOC file that goes with this book prints to more than 80 pages), so what you see in Table 16.1 is a simplification. For each level of the hierarchy, as described in Chapter 15, and for each class category (library file), the classes are listed by name, a brief description, and status. They've also been grouped, in columns, by whether they could be considered standard (likely to be used in every class hierarchy), elective (something you do if you design your applications that way), and special (not used often but sometimes necessary).

TABLE 16.1 A SAMPLE CLASS HIERARCHY

STANDARD	ELECTIVE	SPECIAL
Base Class Templates		
(BCT.VCX)		
All Visual FoxPro Classes		
Generic Level		
Generic Containers		
(GENCTAIN.VCX)		
genForm: a modeless Form.	**GenToolbar**: generic toolbar without buttons.	**genGridPick**: a grid used for selecting records.
genFormSet: generic FormSet	**GenFrmDialogTabs**: a modal form with a PageFrame and tabs.	
genFrmDialog: a modal form.	**GenMessage**: various user messaging formats in a container.	
genGrid: generic grid	**genCmdMore**: a button container with text and button.	

STANDARD	ELECTIVE	SPECIAL
Generic Controls (GENCTRL.VCX)		
genCheckBox: enhanced CheckBox.	**genTbrButton**: toolbar button without icon.	**genCboState**: ComboBox with list of all states.
genComboBox: enhanced ComboBox.	**genCmdCancel**: toolbar button with icon and code.	**GenTxtDate**: special date entry TextBox.
genTextBox: enhanced TextBox.	**genCmdClose**: Toolbar button with icon and code.	**GenTxtPhone**: phone entry TextBox.
genEditBox: enhanced EditBox.	**genCmdDelete**: toolbar button with icon and code.	**GenTxtZipcode**: ZIP code entry TextBox.
genLabel: enhanced Label.	**genCmdEdit**: toolbar button with icon and code.	**GenSpnHour**: Hour selection Spinner.
	genCmdFind: toolbar button with icon and code.	
	genCmdNew: toolbar button with icon and code.	
	genCmdSave: toolbar button with icon and code.	
Generic Data (GENDATA.VCX)		
genDbc: database handler.	**genMoreGetDir**: enhanced Get Directory dialog box.	**genDateTime**: Date and Time methods.
genField: field handler.	**genMoreGetFile**: enhanced Get File dialog box.	
genRecord: Record handler.		
genTable: Table handler.		
genSelect: Work Area management.		
Generic Programming (GENPROG.VCX)		
genFoxtools: Wrapper class for FoxTools utilities.	**genSound**: Sound methods.	

STANDARD	ELECTIVE	SPECIAL
genSet: environment manager.	**genVideo**: video methods (under construction).	**genObjMgr**: object manager (under construction).
Application Level		
Application Containers (APPCTAIN.VCX)		
appForm: enhanced form.	**appFrm2Tab**: form with PageFrame and two Tabs	**appLookup**: ComboBox for selection and Label for lookup results.
appFormSet: enhanced FormSet.	**appFrmDialog2Tab**: modal dialog form with PageFrame and two Tabs.	**AppMover**: Move selections from one ListBox to another.
appFrmDialog: enhanced dialog box.	**appFrs2Tab**: FormSet with toolbar and Page-Frame with two Tabs.	**appFrsBdf**: Basic Data FormSet (BDF), used for table access.
appGrid: enhanced Grid (under construction).	**AppFrsBdf2Tab**: Basic Data FormSet with Page-Frame and two Tabs.	
	AppToolbar: main application toolbar	
	appTbrBdf: toolbar for Basic Data FormSet	
	appTbrNavigate: Toolbar with navigation buttons.	
Application Controls (APPCTRL.VCX)		
Most application-level controls are in containers.	**appTbrButtonNew**, **appTbrButtonEdit**, **appTbrButtonSave**, **appTbrButtonCancel**, **appTbrButtonDelete**, **appTbrButtonPrint**, **appTbrButtonFind**, **appTbrButtonClose**: toolbar buttons with code.	

STANDARD	ELECTIVE	SPECIAL
Application Data (APPDATA.VCX)		
Under construction		
Application Programming (APPPROG.VCX)		
appError: methods for trapping and managing application errors.	**AppActMgr**: methods for managing application activity, primarily toolbars.	
appSecure: methods for handling application security.	**AppUserPref**: methods for managing user preferences.	

NOTE

You're probably going to look at Table 16.1 and say, "This isn't very comprehensive. And look at those names—I could do better than that." I hope so. I could do better myself if I could find the time. But there's the rub. It takes lots of time to fix, enhance, and add to a class hierarchy. The point is, though, that when it's laid out like this you can see more clearly where the holes are and where names and features (among other things) could stand some rationalization. That's much of what this exercise in organization is about.

A Naming Convention

When you create classes, you're free to name them as you will, but even a cursory glance at the class hierarchy table leaves the impression that there is a naming convention at work. Many class naming schemes are in current use. For this one, three-letter prefixes represent the level of class category: bct (base class template), gen (generic), app (application), and something for the domain (such as lim, pay, and inv). This convention makes the class levels instantly identifiable and makes it easier to segregate them in the Class Browser or in debug screens. (The more general convention, used by Microsoft, prefixes all classes with a simple "C." This practice is easy but not very informative.)

After the prefix, the name of the base class or its abbreviation is used to identify the basic visual shape of the class. Custom classes don't use this convention, because they have no visual presence. Following the class identification, any combination of class names or words can be used to help describe, as briefly as possible, what the class is about. As usual, long names can be nicely descriptive but they cause problems with typing and screen display.

The Class Hierarchy and Application Programming

Having described a class hierarchy, let's step back a minute and see how it goes together to build an application framework. Here are the steps:

1. Define base class templates.
2. Build generic classes.
3. Construct application classes from generic classes, especially containers.
4. Build modular application components, mostly with the application classes.

This part of a class hierarchy can be used in almost any application. Next, you subclass these classes for a specific application:

1. Build domain-specific classes; many of these are custom classes.
2. Create domain-specific forms for the user interface of an application.

The last step—creating forms (with SCX files) from **Form** classes—is somewhat controversial. Some developers don't do it, because it's not pure OOP. However, this policy sacrifices the use of Data Environments and a few other form attributes that most developers would rather keep. Clearly, Microsoft agrees with keeping the SCX form, or it wouldn't have bothered with this approach except for backward compatibility.

Forms

The central role of forms in the structure of an application is confirmed by the fact that users spend nearly 100 percent of their time working in forms, and the application developer spends at least 75 percent of development time in and around forms creation (if you count **Form** class development). Forms are the basis of the user interface. Visual FoxPro also supports FormSets, which stand at the top of the container hierarchy and hold multiple forms, or any Form and Toolbar combination. Some developers standardize their primary screens on FormSets.

Forms are more than containers for controls; they are also the repository for most of the programming in your application (again, only if you include forms developed as classes). They contain not only virtually all of the programming related to the user interface but also a large proportion of the processing, data management, and program control is associated with forms.

NOTE

For programmers familiar with FoxPro 2.x, it's important to understand that with the FoxPro Designers, you no longer have an output file (except for the Menu Designer). Compilation takes place directly from the SCX file. This means that there is no program file (SPR) to edit. This also means, in effect, that you do almost all your user interface programming in the Form Designer or Class Designer.

There is a tendency to think of forms only as large containers—typically a data entry screen with many fields, text boxes, and other controls. However, there is another category of forms, user dialog boxes, that are at least as numerous as the primary forms. Dialog boxes come in every conceivable size (as long as they are rectangular), although most of them are small. They generally are thematic in content—for example, a report dialog box, a file opening dialog box, or an application-specific dialog box (a Test Procedure dialog box in the LIMS). They are distinguished from user messages by requiring more interaction, such as multiple data entry or selections.

Like every other form, dialog boxes are constructed in the Form Designer or Class Designer, although they lend themselves to becoming a set of generic classes. For example:

- Dialog box with a single **Done** command button.
- Dialog box with a list and add/delete capability.
- Dialog boxes that incorporate standard FoxPro dialog boxes such as color selection and file opening.

Unlike most of the major data entry forms, dialog boxes tend to be modal (setting the **WindowType** property to **2**). Once the dialog box appears, the user is not allowed to shift focus to any other window or object until the dialog box has been closed.

MAKING CONNECTIONS: FORMS AND FORMSETS

Forms (and form sets) of any kind are connected to the application either as objects or as a form program. This is an important distinction, because the handling of a form is somewhat different for each of them. Here are the points of connection:

- **Form or FormSet as a program:** The main approach is a to make an object of a form:

  DO FORM FormName NAME cName LINKED WITH arguments list.

  ```
  DO FORM sample NAME sample LINKED WITH cTestname, cSampleId
  ```

  If you use the arguments, you'll need to handle parameters for the **Init** event method of the form.

- **Form as a class:** If you've defined a form as a class (using the Form Designer or Class Designer), you use the form like any other object in the program. For example:

  ```
  SET CLASSLIB TO appCtain ADDITIVE
  oSample = CREATEOBJECT("SAMPLE",cTestName,cSampleID)
  oSample.SHOW()
  ```

DOMAIN CLASSES

Although it's easy to understand the class structure of the visual classes, nonvisual classes present something of a problem. They are, almost by definition, more abstract than visual classes. And because they have no initial visual interface, they must be created and manipulated the old-fashioned way—by programming.

On the other hand, there are as many reasons for writing nonvisual, custom classes as there are for subclassing visual classes. As you already know from Chapter 15, a large portion of your application may hinge on concepts or functional areas from the domain of the application—for example, from the LIMS application, **Test** and **Sample**. Such concepts (analytical objects) can be turned into relatively large nonvisual classes containing all the relevant properties, methods, and data access the concepts require and possibly without any user interface elements whatsoever (although a nonvisual class may have some visual elements within it).

Here, for example, is an abbreviated class definition for **Sample**, which encapsulates the information needed to manipulate a single test sample. (Recall the LIMS application from Chapters 14 and 15.) This class could be created in a program file (that is how it will be represented here); more likely, it would be done in the Class Designer and added to a domain class library.

```
DEFINE CLASS sample AS CUSTOM
  *————-PROPERTIES
  pcOrder        = ""
  pcSampleID     = SPACE(8)
  pcMatrix       = SPACE(10)
  pdRecvDate     = {}
  pdCollectDate = {}
  pnBufferMode  = 0
  PROTECTED cOk
  pcOk = SPACE(1)

  *————-METHODS
  *Event Methods
  * Setup
  PROCEDURE Init
    *Assumes correct sample has been located.
    SELECT test
    pcOrder = ORDER()
    *Set buffer mode to pessimistic
    IF SET("MULTILOCKS")<>"ON"
      SET MULTILOCKS ON
    ENDIF
    pnBufferMode = CURSORGETPROP("Buffering")
    =CURSORSETPROP("Buffering",2)
  ENDPROC
  * Cleanup
  PROCEDURE Destroy PROTECTED
    IF NOT SuperOk()
      REPLACE test.status WITH "I"
    ENDIF
    IF NOT EMPTY(cOrder)
      SET ORDER TO (cOrder)
    ENDIF
```

```
    *Restore previous buffering
    =CURSORSETPROP("Buffering",sample.nBufferMode)
  ENDPROC

  *User Defined Methods
  *Supervisory approval ok, only access is here.
  FUNCTION SuperOk
    pcOk = test.ok
    RETURN IIF(test.ok="Y",.t.,.f.)
  ENDFUNC
ENDDEFINE
```

Even this stub shows a few characteristics of custom classes:

- Custom classes have only the minimum three events: **Init**, **Destroy**, and **Error**.
- These classes usually make careful distinctions between information that is or is not available within the class (or its subclasses), and they make liberal use of PROTECTED and HIDDEN elements. If a protected property needs to be referenced, a special method is created to provide access.
- The class handles most of the relevant data fetching and checking (at least at this level of the hierarchy).
- The class often has a clutch of methods that specifically handle calculations, processes, and simple user interfacing for the information of the class.

NOTE

It's not uncommon to use **ADDOBJECT( )** to incorporate visual classes in a nonvisual class definition. However, it's tempting to make individual nonvisual classes handle too broad a spectrum of tasks—such as user interface, processing, and calculation—that might be better served in separate classes. As a rule of thumb, smaller is better in the world of classes; it is the way to leverage inheritance.

This **Sample** class would be added to the class hierarchy at the domain level. Unlike most visual classes, there is no form at the end of the hierarchy; you simply use these classes directly in a program. For example:

```
oSample=CREATEOBJECT("SAMPLE")
IF oSample.superok()
  DO FORM UPDATE NAME oUpdate
ENDIF
```

MAKING CONNECTIONS: CLASSES

You can create (define) classes with code in a program file, and they can be saved to a library or used directly within the program. You can also create classes in the Class Designer or the Form Designer and save them to a library. As part of the application framework, the library files are added to the **Classes** tab of the Project Manager in the APPFRAME project.

- **In program files**. Classes defined in a program, for example in a procedure file, can be used in an application with the standard **CREATEOBJECT()** approach. Keep in mind that whatever the program file, it must be loaded first, either with **SET PROCEDURE TO** or as a currently running program.
- **From class libraries:** In addition to using **CREATEOBJECT(),** classes stored in a class library can be used in forms in a couple of ways:

1. Open the **Classes** tab of the Project Manager, expand the appropriate class library (provided it's already been added to the project list), and drag the name of the desired class onto the form.
2. Register the class library to display the classes in the Controls toolbar. Select **Tools**, **Options** from the menu and display the **Controls** tab. Choose the **Add** button, and, in the dialog box, select the appropriate class library (VCX file). In a form, choose the **View Classes** icon from the Control toolbar and click the name of the class library you added. This action replaces the icons in the standard toolbar with the icons from that class library.

DOMAIN-SPECIFIC ELEMENTS

Most domain-specific elements—parts of an application that are unique to it—are mostly reports and labels along with their data elements such as queries and views. These elements are not part of an application framework. What is part of the framework are the ways in which reports, labels, and other output are managed within an application.

Most applications have reports with a variety of setup requirements: user-defined parameters, output destination options, network printer selection, and summary report variations—to name a few. Add these complications to the fact that you may have scores, if not hundreds, of reports, and you can see why producing not only reports but also queries, graphs, charts, e-mail, faxes, and other forms of output can become a major factor in the development process.

In larger or more complex applications, reports and other types of output are usually controlled by a program or form that allows users to select what they want, followed by another dialog box containing standard output options; then the report form itself is called. This constitutes a report management module, which is covered in detail in Chapter 22.

STANDARD COMPONENTS AND MODULES

As you may recall from the list of potential application components and modules in Chapter 14, there are more than a few subsystems that can be added to your list of projects for development. How many you choose to construct depends on the scale of your application, the time available, user expectations, and so forth. If you continue to develop applications, sooner or later you will need to provide all of the so-called user support elements: a help system, error trapping, user configuration, system security, and a data maintenance system.

Fortunately, most of these systems can be developed as independent units (modules), tested, and then plugged into your application. As part of an application framework, the file for each module becomes part of the APPFRAME project.

MAKING CONNECTIONS: STANDARD COMPONENTS

Some of the supporting modules will be in the form of an APP, a program unit that is invoked by your application just like any other program file:

```
DO config.app.
```

Support components, such as security and error trapping, may have stand-alone portions for management and data access, but they also must have part of their code scattered throughout an application. Security systems, for example, usually have method calls attached to menu options, command buttons, and any other place where a check of the user's access rights is appropriate. Error trapping systems rely on FoxPro internal events as well as **ON ERROR command** for the general running of a program and the **Error** event common to nearly all the FoxPro base classes. These events are often used to trigger a centralized error handler, a single program or form that handles the content of the error and provides the user with information.

CHAPTER WRAP-UP

Most applications are developed incrementally, one element from an application framework at a time. After the analysis and design, you create a new project in the Project Manager and begin adding files, grabbing as many as possible from the application framework project: a MAIN.PRG, an include file, possibly a procedure file, and a main menu. All along, you build or modify classes in your class hierarchy, working your way toward the domain classes and elements. Then you spend the bulk of your time working on the user interface and database management of the application. As time allows, you also work on the supporting modules and components. This process can be a very long one, especially for the first few projects, when you're learning object-oriented programming and developing your class hierarchy. Eventually, you will be able to drag and drop significant portions from the application framework into any application, and they will require little or no modification. At that point, you will begin to reap the benefits of the object-oriented programming approach and an application framework.

I've been workin' on the framework, all the live-long day...

CHAPTER 17

DEVELOPING THE USER INTERFACE

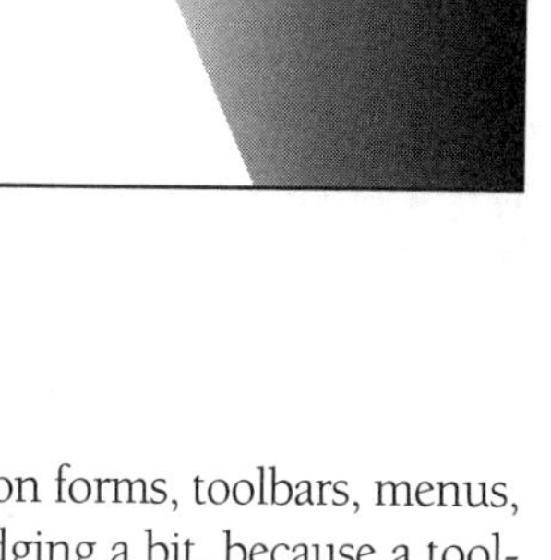

The visual user interface of a FoxPro application is based on forms, toolbars, menus, and a status bar. That's it—just four things. And that's fudging a bit, because a toolbar is just another kind of form under the skin and the status bar is trivial. If you're running FoxPro right now, take a good look at what is displayed. These are the four things you'll find. Of course, three of them come in different shapes and sizes. *Forms* is another word for windows, and they range from huge windows to tiny dialog boxes. Menus come in standard (fixed at the top of the screen) and shortcut formats. Toolbars can be free-floating or docked. These various guises obscure the fact that there are still only four user interface elements.

Everything else you associate with the user interface—grids, tabbed pages, spinners, command buttons, and so on—are all things that fit inside a form or a toolbar. For all practical purposes, the master container is the form and the **Form** class. When you build your initial application framework and class hierarchy, your first priority should be the **Form** class and related classes: **FormSet** and **Toolbar**. A close second for the application framework are the two menu types: standard and shortcut.

This chapter and the next one focus on the most important element of the user interface—forms—and the elements involved with them: form sets, menus, toolbars, grids, and controls. In the object-oriented scheme of things, the relationship between controls and forms (including the other form-related containers such as form sets and page frames) can be complicated. Because forms have their own properties and methods—often some of the most important ones—forms must interact with the properties and methods of the objects. Managing these interactions is one of your most important responsibilities as a programmer.

The technical difficulties of managing controls and forms are the focus of Chapter 18. This one concentrates on introducing the elements of the user interface, including non-object things such as menus and keyboard activity, and imparting a sense of the design considerations that lie behind an application's user interface.

BASIC FORMS AND CONTROLS

In Chapter 1, when you created your first form, what class was used? By default, Visual FoxPro uses the **Form** base class. Now that you're building a class hierarchy and have one or more subclasses of the base class form, how do you get FoxPro to use the one you want? This is not an idle question, and many a developer has wandered around the menus and manuals trying to figure it out. It's not difficult, just somewhat obscured. It's one of several things you need to do in preparation for working with forms in the Form Designer or Class Designer.

SETTING UP THE FORM DESIGNER

Most of the setup for the Form Designer is located in the Options dialog box, **Form** tab. Use **Tools**, **Options** from the menu to get to this point (illustrated in Figure 17.1).

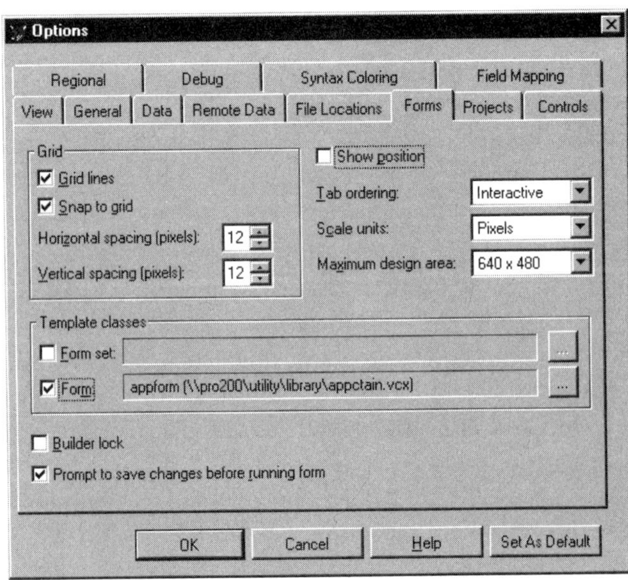

FIGURE 17.1 OPTIONS DIALOG BOX, FORMS TAB.

Look for the area marked **Template classes**. Here, you tell FoxPro which **Form** and **FormSet** class to use when you create a new one. Most class hierarchies have several kinds of forms (dialog boxes, standard forms, and so forth), so you'll be coming to this spot fairly often. Use the three-dot button to get to the Form Template dialog box (Figure 17.2) and locate the name of the class library in the LIBRARY directory. Select the library file that contains the **Form** class you want (APPCTAIN.VCX in the illustration), and FoxPro will display each class it contains. Choose your **Form** class and click **OK**. You're not finished—don't forget to click **Set As Default** in the Options window. If you just click **OK** in that window, the selection won't be saved.

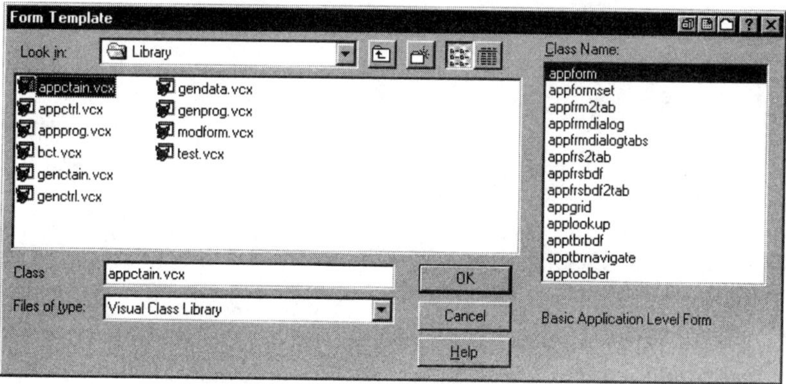

FIGURE 17.2 FORM TEMPLATE DIALOG BOX.

Don't quit the Options window just yet. There are several things here that you may want to configure. For example, one of the first considerations for using the Form Designer is the size of the screen in which the program will be run. This is more than a question of whether the application's users have 14-, 15-, or 17-inch monitors; it's also a question of whether they are running at the same resolution. The typical resolution is still 640 x 480 (pixels), but the trend for Windows computers is clearly toward 15-inch to 17-inch monitors with graphics boards running 800 x 600 or 1024 x 768. This consideration is extremely important in sizing your forms, because FoxPro does not automatically scale a form to the resolution.

If you do your own work at a higher resolution—say, 1024 x 768 on a 17-inch monitor, and then run the program, as is, on a 14-inch monitor using 640 x 480, your forms will be fatally chopped. On the other hand, if you design for a 640 x 480 screen and deliver the application to people using 17-inch monitors at a higher resolution, they may complain about the tiny windows in your application.

Visual FoxPro has provided a partial solution. Before you start designing, set the maximum design area for a form by selecting from the **Maximum design area** box (Figure 17.1) the pixel values for the design area you want (640 x 480, 800 x 600, 1024 x 768, or 1280 x 1024). However, if you must deliver your application into an environment where monitors and adapters come in mixed resolutions, you still have a problem. Your choices are to design to the lowest common denominator (640 x 480), build two or more versions of the program with different sizes (a maintenance nightmare), or construct very elaborate triggers and sizing routines to automatically detect the resolution and adapt the forms. None of these options is ideal.

Configurations of the Form Designer in the **Form** options tab also apply to the Class Designer.

Now let's take a look at the other options in the **Form** tab:

- **Grid lines**. Displays grid lines in the Form Designer and Class Designer. Helpful at the start.
- **Snap to grid**. Aligns objects with the nearest grid lines. Leave on for initial placement of objects but is often turned off for fine tuning.
- **Horizontal spacing**. The horizontal space between grid lines as measured in the current scale unit setting (pixels by default). Make this setting smaller for complex, crowded forms; otherwise, leave it at the default value.
- **Vertical spacing**. The vertical spacing between grid lines.
- **Show position**. The position of active objects is displayed in the status bar.
- **Tab ordering. Interactive**. Set control tab order with the mouse (**Shift**+Click); **By List:** Use the Object Order dialog box to set tab order.
- **Scale units**. Screen scale mode for Designers. By default, it's pixels. Foxels are for cross-platform (Macintosh/DOS) designing.
- **Builder lock**. When this is checked, Visual FoxPro will display the appropriate control builder when you drag a control onto a form.

You can alter most of these options while working in the Form Designer, but the next time you start FoxPro they will reset to the values entered here.

STARTING A FORM

Having made arrangements with FoxPro to use a particular **Form** class, you start a new form through the Project Manager. Go to the **Documents** tab, highlight **Forms**, and click the **New** button. Alternatively, for a **Form** class, go to the **Classes** tab, highlight the library where you want the new class to be stored, and click **New**. This time you'll go through the New Class dialog box (see Chapter 11) to create the **Form** class.

USING CONTROLS

Once you have the Form Designer or Class Designer open with a new form, you have a virtually blank palette. If the form was derived from a **Form** class in the class hierarchy, it may have inherited code but that won't be visible. It's ready to be populated with *controls*: Microsoft's term (now almost universal) for objects placed in a form.

You are given a good starter set of controls in the Visual FoxPro base classes, and, if you're enterprising, you'll build many more by subclassing. You can also use Microsoft ActiveX controls, formerly OLE controls. Some ActiveX controls come with Visual FoxPro Professional version, and others are widely available as freeware, shareware, or third-party products.

In Visual FoxPro, almost all the controls are data-related. In one way or another, they get or display data, most often in connection with tables. Before we can run down the list of control classes, you'll need to put a table in the Data Environment (DE) of a form. There are many wrinkles to this, and they will be covered in Chapter 18. Here, we'll keep it simple: With the Form Designer open in a new form, select **View**, **Data Environment** from the menu. This action opens the Add Table or View dialog box (covered in chapter 7) where you can select a table to add to the DE. Close or minimize the DE window, and you're almost ready to start adding controls that connect to this table for data—almost.

ADDING CONTROLS TO A FORM

There are three ways to put controls into a form. All three ways involve drag and drop (or a variation thereof): from the **Classes** tab of the Project Manager, from table boxes in the Data Environment, and from the Form Controls toolbar. If you drag and drop a control class from the **Classes** tab, you'll automatically get the right type of control, even one that you've customized, but it won't automatically be attached to data. If you drag and drop a field from a table in the DE, you'll get attached data but not necessarily the correct control, much less from a customized class. Using the Form Controls toolbar might get the right class, but it, too, isn't attached to data. So what do you do? Head for the Options window again (**Options**, **Field Mapping** tab).

As shown in Figure 17.3, you can use the **Field Mapping** tab to associate types of fields with specific control classes. This is new in Visual FoxPro 5.0.

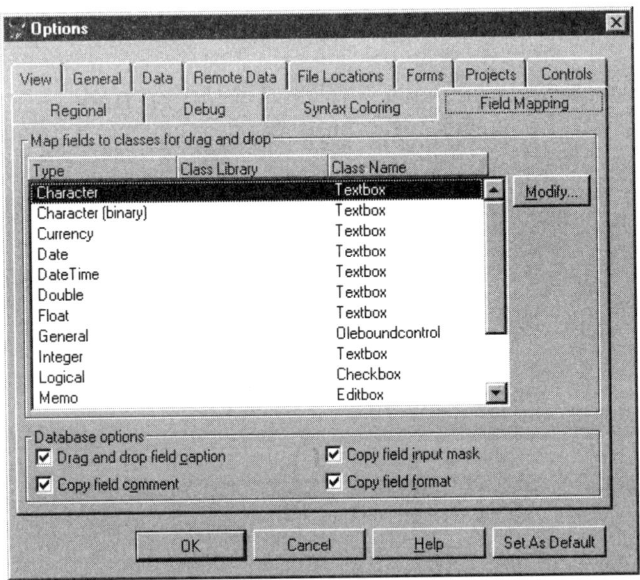

FIGURE 17.3 OPTIONS WINDOW, FIELD MAPPING TAB.

Highlight the field data type that you want to map and click the **Modify** button. In the Modify Field Mapping dialog box (Figure 17.4), select the library that contains the control you want and then pick the control name. Click **Apply** if you want to remain in this dialog box to do several mappings. (You can change the data type at the top.) When you map a control class to a field type, you not only get the right class when you drag and drop from a table in the DE or from the Form Controls toolbar, but you'll also get values from the database container: field captions, field comments, field input mask, and field format.

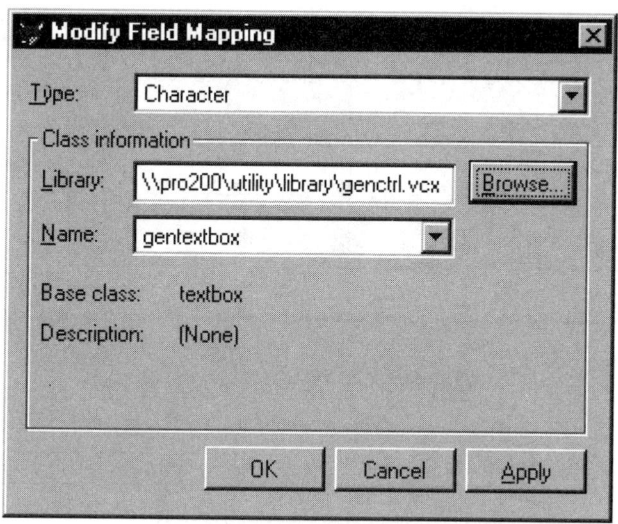

FIGURE 17.4 MODIFY FIELD MAPPING DIALOG BOX.

Notice in Figure 17.3 that the database information can be turned on or off.

You should go through the mapping procedure every time you create an appropriate class in the class hierarchy. Then you can use the DE drag and drop whenever you want a specific field attached to a control, the Form Control toolbar when you just want the control, and the **Classes** tab when you want a specialized control that isn't mapped. FoxPro gives you many options, and it's quite slick.

THE MOST BASIC CONTROL: TEXT BOX

In most data entry forms, about 80 percent of the controls will be TextBoxes. A TextBox, shown in Figure 17.5, is derived from the **TextBox** base class. It has a somewhat inappropriate name, because it's the primary control for numeric, date, and character data. Probably because it is called upon to do so much data gathering, the TextBox is one of the most versatile and complicated of all the controls. Figure 17.6 illustrates the events and other factors that come into play with a TextBox.

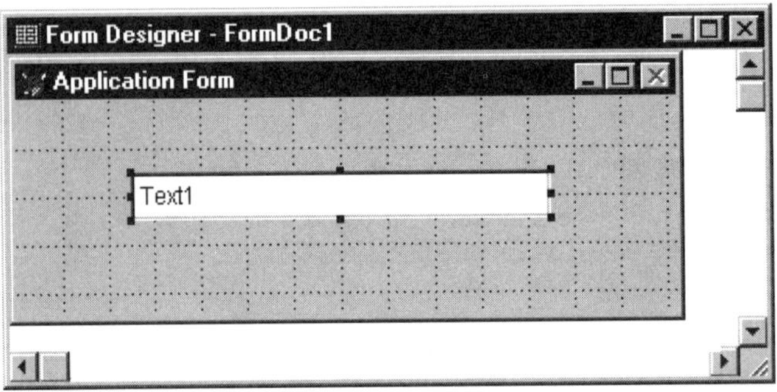

FIGURE 17.5 TEXTBOX CONTROL.

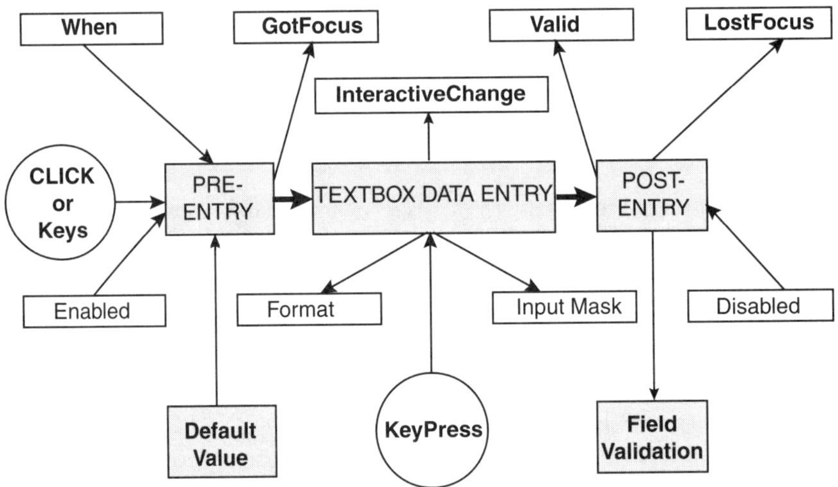

FIGURE 17.6 ANATOMY OF TEXTBOX DATA ENTRY.

Yes, there's a lot going on here, but most events and properties are not used every time on every TextBox. It's also an important representation of the many issues that are involved with data entry and display.

Data entry into a TextBox has three phases: preentry, entry, and postentry. The preentry phase is mostly concerned with whether users can or cannot enter the box, and what happens as they do. The entry phase is used to monitor the user's data entry. The postentry phase, arguably the most important, is used to validate the user's data. Let's go through each phase to describe the devilish details.

NOTE

It's a good idea to drag a TextBox control onto a form at this point so that you can see the Properties window and follow the references to various methods and properties. As you put TextBox controls into a form, learn to ask yourself this question: Of the many ways FoxPro gives you to monitor and control the user in and around a TextBox, which are appropriate.

PREENTRY PHASE

Even before a user gets to a particular Text Box, you can set the **ToolTip** property to identify what should go into the box. You can also assign a default value in the table definition for the field, and this value will appear if no other entry has been made.

The user gets into a TextBox either with the mouse or by using a key (**Enter**, arrow, or **Tab**). To prevent this, you can either set the **Enabled** property to false (`.f.`) or put code in the **When** event that returns false. **Enabled** tends to be used by other controls to manage access into dependent controls. For example, until it contains an entry, a MONTH TextBox might disable a DAY TextBox. **When** is used more often as an on-the-spot validation of whether the user can enter the TextBox—for example, as a check of the user's security clearance.

Once the user has access to the TextBox, you can monitor the mouse **Click** event or the **KeyPress** event if you need to do something related to those actions. (Unlike some other controls, data entry is usually a keyboard-driven process, so you can expect many users to arrive in a TextBox via a keystroke as well as with a mouse click.) For a TextBox, the **GotFocus** event is the place to create a method for arrival. It might be used for code that triggers an informational message or dialog box or perhaps disables other controls until entry is completed.

NOTE

Focus is the widely used term for a control becoming activated. It's generally associated with a change in the control's visible state (highlighting) and the ability of the control to accept user input. Controls are always said to *get focus* and *lose focus* during the use of a form, giving rise to the **GetFocus** and **LostFocus** events.

As a TextBox gets focus, its **StatusBarText** property can be used to display a message (or instructions) in the status bar. At that point, finally, the user is in the entry phase.

ENTRY PHASE

The **Format** and **InputMask** properties are largely carryovers from older versions of FoxPro, but they may still be useful to control entry of data in a text box.

Tables 17.1 (formats) and 17.2 (input masks) list the options. The **Format** property affects all input in the text box; the **Input Mask** affects individual entries.

TABLE 17.1 ENTRY FORMAT OPTIONS

OPTION	CODE	OUTPUT & EXAMPLE
Alpha Only	A	Allow only alphabetical characters (no numbers and so on). There are a few data entries that must be letters only, such as state abbreviations.
Display Mask Only	R	This format allows you to create an entry mask, but the mask characters will not be stored to the field; only the characters or numbers actually entered will be stored. This option is sometimes used to save disk storage space.
Multiple List	M	Create a comma-delimited list of values (characters only), something like this: `"Active,Inactive"`. If the field is not initialized to one of the values, the first value will become the default. Users can use **Spacebar** or enter the first letter of values to move between values and use **Enter** to select one.
Select Edit Region	K	Automatically selects the editing region, as if you'd marked a selection with the mouse or keyboard.
Edit Date	D	Edit field or variable as a date in current date format. This is the automatic mask for dates: mm/dd/yy. It ensures that only legitimate dates will be entered.
British Date	E	Edit field or variable in European date format: dd/mm/yy.
Leading Zeros	L	Display leading zeros before numbers. The zeros will not be stored with the variable or field.

TABLE 17.2 ENTRY INPUT MASK OPTIONS

CODE	DESCRIPTION
A	Allows only alphabetic characters, per position: AAA.
L	Allows logical data entry only, meaning that only T / t, F / f, Y / y, or N / n are accepted. All valid entries are converted to .t. or .f. for fields.
N	Allows letters and digits only, meaning it excludes diacritical marks and things such as #$%. Can be used only with character data.
X	Allows any character whatsoever.
Y	Allows Y,y, and N,n only, with y and n converted to uppercase.
9	With character data, allows only numeric entry. With numeric data, allows all numbers and signs.
#	Allows numbers (digits), blanks, and signs. This is often mixed with the "9" option to control entry of numeric values.
!	Converts lowercase letters to uppercase.
$	Displays current currency symbol.
*	Displays asterisks in front of numeric values. This is a check-writing option.
.	Specifies the decimal point (numeric data only).
,	Comma separation for digits left of decimal point (numeric data only).

With the **KeyPress** and **InteractiveChange** events, it is possible to closely monitor almost everything a user does in a text box. For example, you could write a method for the **KeyPress** event that checked every keystroke for invalid keys or did immediate spelling correction. The **InteractiveChange** event can be used when the value in the TextBox has changed, giving you the opportunity to validate the date even before it gets to the postentry phase. This kind of micromanagement isn't needed often, but it can be important when it is needed.

POSTENTRY PHASE

On the way out of a text box, a number of things can happen. It begins with the user pressing any of the exit keys (Table 17.3).

TABLE 17.3 TEXT BOX EXIT KEYS

KEY	DESCRIPTION
Tab, Shift-Tab	Move between controls without activating the **Valid** event. This depends on the status of the **TabStop** property.
Enter	Depending on the status of **SET CONFIRM**, will exit a region and trigger a **VALID** check. (**SET CONFIRM ON** requires an **Enter** to exit a control.)
Right or Left Arrow	If at the beginning or end of a control, will exit and trigger a **Valid** event.
Up or Down Arrow	Will move forward or backward one control and will trigger a **Valid** event.
Ctrl-S	Save without exiting.
Ctrl-W	Quit editing and save.
Esc	Quit editing without saving.

In a few cases, it may be desirable to trap the use of **Esc**, **Ctrl-W**, and **Ctrl-S** with the **KeyPress** event method.

After the exit key is pressed, program control passes through the **LostFocus** event and then the **Valid** event. If you want to prevent the loss of focus (perhaps because some other activity is in progress), you can use a method in this event. Normally, however, the **Valid** event is where most of the data checking (validation) takes place—if you have chosen not to have field validation defined in the database table.

The issue of whether to validate data at the form level or at the database level becomes extremely important in the client/server use of FoxPro. The decision is part of the partitioning of responsibilities between client program and a database server (or of middleware such as ODBC), and it's based on the need for immediate response to a user, the performance of the server, and the desire to centralize business rules at the server. The factors can be complex and will be discussed more thoroughly in a later chapter.

In most cases, when the user has completely left the text box, data resides in the data buffer waiting for an update function such as **TABLEUPDATE( )** or **TABLEREVERT( )**.

At this point, perhaps you are beginning to see that controlling data entry can be elaborate, although (thankfully) most TextBoxes have few, if any, of these options in use. Generally, the number of events trapped for a particular TextBox rises with the importance or confidentiality of the data. A TextBox that contains executive salaries might have many of these options to provide security and data integrity, but most TextBoxes in a form have only **ToolTips**, **StatusBarText**, and **Enabled** as the standard settings.

SELECTION CONTROLS

After TextBoxes, the next most common controls are those which offer the user a selection from a list of items or options (see Figure 17.7).

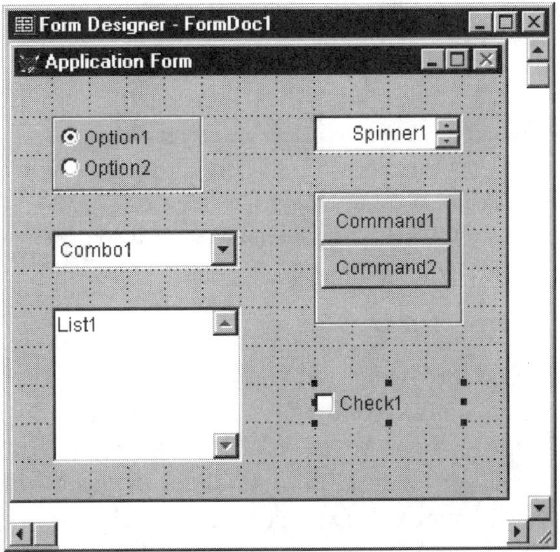

FIGURE 17.7 SELECTION CONTROLS.

Many of these controls (OptionGroup, CommandGroup, ListBox, and ComboBox) have a Builder, such as the one shown in Figure 17.8, to step you through the setup options. Builders are particularly useful for these selection controls because of their elaborate data source and formatting options.

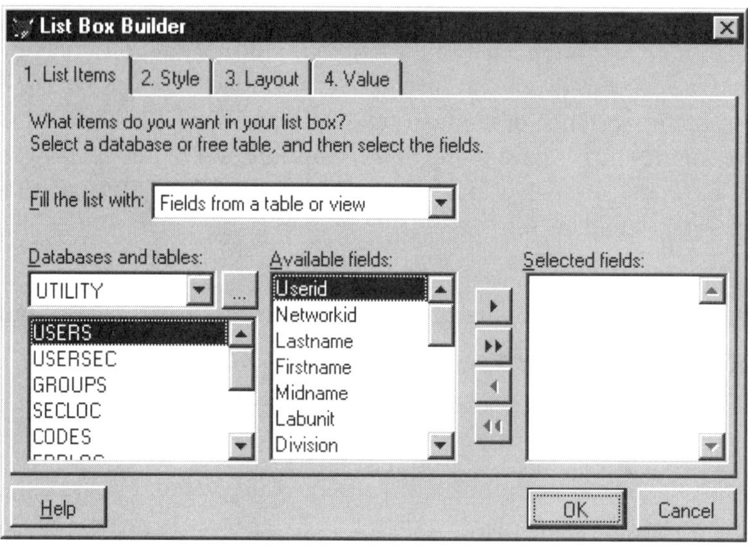

FIGURE 17.8 LISTBOX BUILDER

NOTE

Many controls (option buttons, command buttons, and check boxes) can serve as both a means for data entry and as a way of operating the program. For example, the command button can be used to provide data for a table but, much like a menu, is most often used to allow the user to make a selection to do something.

ComboBox Control

The ComboBox is used for selection from a list, sometimes combined with direct entry. The ComboBox control got its name from having two styles: drop-down combo box and drop-down list box. The drop-down combo box allows the user to make an entry as if using a TextBox, or click on the drop-down button to use a list. The drop-down list box allows selection from the list only. You can select the type in the ComboBox Builder or use the **Style** property (0 = drop-down combo, and 2 = drop-down list).

The advantage of either style is compactness; unlike the ListBox or Grid, the ComboBox takes up no more space on the form than a standard TextBox. Because managing the space on a form is an important consideration, the ability to hide the nonselected items is useful.

The most common use of either type of ComboBox is the selection of codes or items from relatively short lists. For example, most applications use codes that are abbreviations of longer identifications, such as *ml* for milliliter or *cm* for centimeter. However, because the user may not be familiar with all the codes, it's good user interface design to present a list with only the full identification and then translate into the code for storage in a table. The drop-down combo box is particularly good for this purpose, because it can contain both the description and the code but pass only the code to the table. It also allows the user to type in the code, and that may be quicker than searching through a list.

For searching a ComboBox list, you can enable the **IncrementalSearch** property, which searches on the letters a user enters. **B** finds all *Bs*, **BE** finds all words beginning with *BE*, and so forth.

Within their specialty (lists), ComboBoxes are quite versatile. You can use the **ColumnCount** property to display more than one item in the list, such as both code and description at the same time. The **MultiSelect** property allows the user to select more than one item at a time. This option requires special handling after selection but is an important variation. Similarly, the **MoverBars** property allows the user to move items in the list up and down so that you can derive user-sorted or prioritized listings.

If you're looking for a place to start learning about making template classes from visual base classes, creating classes from ComboBox variations (multiple column, multiple selection, and code translation) is a perfect exercise. It's highly recommended that you study the examples and options presented in Chapter 10 of the *Developer's Guide*.

LIST CONTROL

Almost the only difference between a List control and a ComboBox control, is that a List doesn't pop up; it remains on the screen as a fixed-size display. This is a subtle emphasis for the user interface: It makes the list itself seem at least as important as the current selection. In all other respects—data handling, properties, and methods—the List control is operated like the ComboBox control.

OPTION BUTTON GROUPS

Option buttons are used to select one of a set of options. Option buttons always come in groups of two or more (when there is only one option, a CheckBox or CommandButton is appropriate). This old Macintosh screen device (also called a *radio* button) is handy for representing a set of choices, all of which need to be constantly visible. When you select one, any other selected button is deselected. It's just like punching up radio stations on an old-fashioned car radio.

Unless you set the number of buttons in the Builder, you can use the **ButtonCount** property to specify the number of buttons in the group. Consequently, FoxPro references the individual buttons by the **Buttons** property, and that has important uses:

- `object.Buttons(4)` refers to the fourth button in the option group.
- `object.Buttons(2).Caption = "No Choice"` sets the caption for the second button.
- `THISFORM.object.Buttons(THISFORM.object.Value)` is the number of the button selected by the user.
- `cChoice=THIS.Buttons(THIS.Value).Caption` passes the caption of the selected button to the variable `cChoice`, which in turn can be used in a **DO CASE** statement to interpret the selection.

SPINNERS

The Spinner offers an alternative method for entering numeric values. The Spinner can be used for any situation in which the user enters a numeric value: numbers, dollars, a date, and so on. Its principal value is that it allows mouse-only selection of numbers by dialing with the **Up** or **Down** buttons. The Spinner also allows direct manual entry. In general, a Spinner works best with relatively small numbers—days of the week or month, choices from 1 to 10, and so on.

The range of values in a Spinner can be controlled by a set of properties:

- **SpinnerHighValue**. The highest value allowed for clicking the **Up** button.
- **SpinnerLowValue**. The lowest value allowed for clicking the **Down** button.
- **KeyboardHighValue**. The highest value allowed for user entry in the text box.
- **KeyboardLowValue**. The lowest value allowed for user entry in the text box.
- **Interval**. The increment or decrement value for each click of the **Up** or **Down** button.

Normally the **Interval** is set to 1, and the **Spinner** and **Keyboard** values are the same.

CHECKBOXES

Check boxes are used for a **Yes** or **No** (true/false) selection. Each CheckBox is a single data item (unlike most of the other controls, which often present more than one option at a time). A checked box is selected, unchecked is not selected, and the receiving variable is returned with either `.t.` or `.f.` (1 or 0 if initialized with a number). CheckBoxes are used either to represent values in a Logical data field or to get a yes or no (true or false) judgment from the user. The **Value** property is used to set or read the current value of a CheckBox:

- `THISFORM.chkbox1.Value = .f.`
- `REPLACE order.instock WITH THIS.chkbox2.Value`

COMMANDBUTTONS AND GROUPS

Command buttons are most often used for action selection. Because of their default button shape, command buttons are usually associated with the user's selection of some kind of action; something happens after the button has been pressed. Command buttons are used as an alternative form of menu, as gateways to subsystems, or as a way to shift to different pages. Like any other button, they can also be used to select items of information.

You can create individual command buttons or use command button groups. With both types, the **Click** event is the usual location for code. You can use the returned **Value** property to monitor the user selection (just as you can with the Option group). For example:

```
IF THISFORM.cmdMenu.Value = 3
  DO FORM FindName.SPR
ENDIF
```

It's also common to use bitmap images for the command buttons rather than the default text. This is easily done by using the following properties:

- **Picture**: Specifies the name and path for the basic BMP picture to be displayed on the button.
- **DisabledPicture**: Specifies the BMP picture to use when the button is disabled.

- **DownPicture**: Specifies the BMP picture to use when the button is pressed (clicked).

TEXT EDITING

Although you can enter as many as 254 characters in the standard TextBox, this number may not be sufficient (or convenient) for text entry, so FoxPro provides two additional approaches. The standard approach is the EditBox control, which is a permanent fixture in a form. The second approach uses the **MODIFY MEMO** command.

EDITBOX CONTROL

The EditBox takes up a considerable amount of screen real estate. This is its principle drawback and explains why the various popup approaches, such as **MODIFY MEMO** or an editing dialog box, are often used.

The **ControlSource** property, as usual, is used to connect to the source of text to be edited, most often a Memo field. Because tabs are sometimes used in editing, you need to decide whether tabbing is allowed in the edit area; otherwise, a **Tab** entry will move the user to the next control. The **AllowTabs** property is set to `.t.` if tabbing is allowed, and the users can use **Ctrl-Tab** to move to the next control. You can also make the entire edit area read-only by using the **ReadOnly** property, or you can hide the text of an unselected Edit Box with **HideSelection**.

One of the more useful approaches to the EditBox is to create a **Page** class (for a form's PageFrame), which contains the editing area, a command button to save and exit, and other code to manage the editing.

You can use **MODIFY MEMO** to edit a memo field directly. The basic syntax is simple: **MODIFY MEMO <field name> WINDOW <windowname>**.

NOTE

Among controls, only the EditBox can be used to edit Memo fields, character fields, character variables, character array elements, and text files. Using **MODIFY MEMO** is helpful if you want a separate window for editing, but it does not behave or look like part of the form-based system.

LABEL, IMAGE, AND DECORATIVE CONTROLS

The ability to add pictures and decorative objects to the screens of your application opens new dimensions in design. One of the nice surprises of FoxPro is how easy it is to display pictures or add shapes and lines to the form (see Figure 17.9).

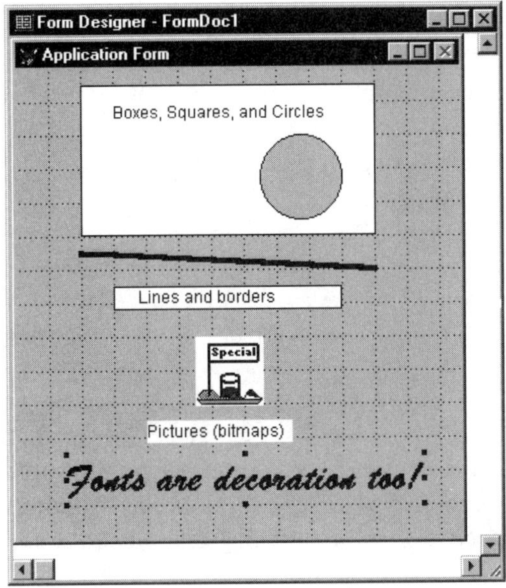

FIGURE 17.9 PICTURE AND DECORATIVE CONTROLS.

LABELS

Labels, which were formerly called *prompts*, are the text associated with controls or any kind of text in the form that conveys information to the user. Because you can vary the font, font size, color, and other properties of a label, it may be the single most important decorative element on the form. It's also the easiest to abuse. Keep in mind that professional layout designers rarely use more than two or three fonts in a single frame.

In Visual FoxPro, you typically use the Label tool to mark the area for the text and then go immediately to the Properties window to set **Caption**, **AutoSize** (which keeps the text the same size as the label box), and various font properties. You can also use the usual color properties (**BackColor**, **ForeColor**), **WordWrap** (if your text gets long), and **BackStyle** to set the label box as transparent or opaque.

NOTE

If you precede a character in the Label caption with \<, it becomes a *hot key* (using **Alt**+key) that will move focus to the next control beyond the label in the tab order. Because the data entry controls don't have hot keys, this can be a useful way of allowing users to get to specific controls in a form. It's also keystroke-oriented, something that's good for people who don't use a mouse.

IMAGES

With an Image control, the effect is much like that of a window fill except that this one has no frame or other window characteristics. You're simply laying down a bitmap image on a specific part of the form. Use the **Picture** property to specify the BMP file, The **Stretch** property, usually with the value 2, stretches the image to fit the frame size.

NOTE

With the General field in an OLE control, you can display an image created by another program and placed into a general field, an OLE operation. This technique is somewhat different from handling bitmaps, and it's more flexible.

All images on the screen are subject to the current font and font size of the area. This arrangement can sometimes have strange effects on the shaping of screen pictures. You also need to pay close attention to the resolution quality of the images being displayed. Some bitmaps may not take to kindly to enlargement.

SHAPES AND LINES

You can add a great deal of polish to your screens by taking the time to add boxes, lines, fills, and colors. In addition to the Line and Shape controls, FoxPro provides five methods that will produce graphics on a form: **Circle** (draws a circle or arc), **Cls** (clears graphics), **Line** (creates a line), **Pset** (sets a point), and **Print** (prints a character string). These tools are somewhat unusual and will require considerable experimentation to become useful. They are excellent candidates to be incorporated in a drawing class.

One side effect you may encounter with shapes, especially larger ones, is that they cover other controls. You'll need to use the **Send to Front** or **Send to Back** option of the Format menu to position them in the so-called z-order stack. A **Zorder** method is sometimes used to work with this condition.

PICTURE BUTTONS

Three controls support picture images: command buttons, option buttons, and check boxes. In each case, you specify a file with either an ICO (icon) or BMP extension, and FoxPro will create a button with the image from the file. The button will not look like an option button, check box, or command button; they all look like icons.

Although picture buttons may look different, they operate in the same way as their basic control: Command buttons and option buttons return a number for the button selected. The option buttons will always have one (and only one) button selected. The check boxes will return either `.t.` or `.f.` depending on whether or not they've been selected.

The size of the button plays a role. Images in an ICO file are limited to 32x32 pixels. If you enlarge a button beyond that size, FoxPro automatically increases the size of the button frame but the image size remains the same. All picture buttons have three visual states: UP (selected), DOWN (unselected), and DISABLED. Depending on the image used, the size of the button, and the background colors, these states are not always easy to distinguish (leading to a fourth state called confusion). If you want visible button behavior, you'll need to exercise considerable care in the choice of image, .

Traditionally, the images in an ICO file are icons: symbolic or suggestive images that are most suitable for picture buttons. Bitmap images, on the other hand, have largely been used as fill or wallpaper designs and were meant to be spread evenly over a surface of any size. However, the traditions are now rarely followed. You'll find many bitmap images that have the same design characteristics as icons. The result will almost inevitably be a large and growing collection of both kinds of files. (Don't forget to organize them in the Project Manager, and use the ImageEdit program that ships with FoxPro to edit the bitmaps.)

MENUS

Sometimes menus seem like holdovers from mainframe computing—Follow the menu!—but they provide necessary points of access for an application. The top of the screen menu is standard for Microsoft Windows software, and now you can also create right mouse button–activated shortcut menus. The mechanics aren't difficult, especially if you create a few template menus for the application framework.

ELEMENTS OF A STANDARD MENU

There is one and only one *menu bar*. You cannot move or shape the system menu bar, and its coloration is modified, if at all, through the Windows Control Panel. You can modify the content of the menu, beginning with the *pads*, which are the options of the menu bar. The Menu Designer labels them generically as Prompts.

With few exceptions, every Windows menu begins with the File pad. After that, there is little consistency, although the Edit pad is also very common. The FoxPro main menu consists of the pads File, Edit, View, Format, Tools, Program, Window, and Help. All these can be modified or removed at your discretion.

All the standard pads have an associated *popup menu*, which the Menu Designer calls a *submenu*. The popup, which is actually an old-style FoxPro popup list, contains one or more *menu options*. You've probably noticed that menu pads are usually short, single-word prompts. Menu options can be fairly lengthy and are often more than one word. There is a reason for this configuration. Long or multiword pads would quickly fill the visible menu bar and disappear out of sight on the right end. FoxPro can accommodate this, but it's poor user interface design because "out of sight is out of mind." Menu popups, on the other hand, are free to expand horizontally as well as vertically, and that means you can have longer prompts (within reason).

Although most Windows menu operations presume the use of the mouse, it's long been a hallmark of good Windows design to have much of the menu system also available to keyboarding. This takes one of two forms (and sometimes both): a hot key and a keyboard shortcut.

By convention, all menu pads and many menu options have a hot key that can be used in a sequence (usually beginning with **Alt**) to select menu items. You create a hot key in the Menu Designer by inserting the **\<** combination before the hot key letter. This shows up in the menu pad or option as an underline of the letter: for example, **File**.

The other keyboard method is the *keyboard shortcut*: a specific key combination that will cause immediate execution of a pad or option—for example, **Ctrl-x** to cut text. Shortcuts are defined in the **Options** area of the Menu Designer.

There are two even smaller details in a standard menu. You'll notice that many options, such as **Tools**, **Options...**, are followed by an ellipsis (the three dots). The ellipsis is a cue that selection of the option will bring up a dialog window. The other visual cue is a right pointer, which indicates that another popup menu (submenu) will appear. Neither detail is explicitly part of the Menu Designer. It's up to you to continue the convention.

Programming Options for the Standard Menu

In terms of programming, it's helpful to think of the FoxPro menu system as software machinery that manages menus and that can be turned on or off as needed. The system menu has a menu manager routine. It uses the menu instructions you provide, stores them in a special memory area, and controls their presentation and operation. Unlike other objects or program elements, the menu manager is always loaded; it just takes on different configurations.

The name of the menu manager is **SYSMENU**. Whenever you issue a direct instruction to the menu manager, it is by that name: **SET SYSMENU**. Several commands of this type are used to control the menu manager's operation.

SET SYSMENU ON activates the menu manager. When you start FoxPro, the system menu is **ON** and remains that way unless you issue the command **SET SYSMENU OFF**. In a running program (not the Command window), this command shuts off the menu manager and removes the system menu from the screen. Although it's seldom used, there are occasions—for example, in modal dialog boxes—when you might want to disable the system menu.

SET SYSMENU AUTOMATIC officially invokes the system menu as both visible and active. When running in automatic (which it does by default), the menu manager will add, remove, enable, and disable pads, popups, and options as appropriate.

SET SYSMENU TO DEFAULT restores the system menu to a default condition, usually the FoxPro original definition. You can modify the default definition with **SET SYSMENU SAVE**, which will make the current menu the default menu. This default does not remain in effect after you quit FoxPro.

The **SET SYSMENU TO** command is very selective. It removes all pads from the screen except those immediately involved with the current activity. If you're in the Command window, it removes all the pads except Format, because that's what's normally available in the Command window.

SET SYSMENU NOSAVE is the true reset for the system menu. It will always return the menu definition to the FoxPro original configuration, whereas **SET SYSMENU TO DEFAULT** returns it only to the last defined default condition.

NOTE

Running the system menu doesn't necessarily involve using any of the preceding commands. **SET SYSMENU ON** and **SET SYSMENU AUTOMATIC** are the defaults and should be enough for many applications. However, if you change the default definition, turn off the system menu, or create your own menus, you should at least close your program with **SET SYSMENU NOSAVE** to restore FoxPro to the original configuration. That's true, unless you're quitting FoxPro, when it doesn't matter.

MAINTAINING THE STANDARD MENU ENVIRONMENT

As a rule, from the very beginning of your application you'll be creating menus that redefine the system menu. As explained earlier, the system menu can always be restored using **SET SYSMENU NOSAVE**, but as you progress further into your application, several menus later what happens to the previous menu definitions?

Without a mechanism to save and restore menus, you would need to redefine the menu each time you entered and exited a new form (presuming you change the menu). That mechanism is the role of **PUSH** and **POP MENU**. These two commands manipulate a *stack* of menu bar definitions. As your application moves from one menu to another, it can *push* one menu definition after another onto the menu stack and, as it returns, *pop* the menus back. **PUSH** and **POP** both require the name of a specific menu bar, which is **_MSYSMENU** for the FoxPro menu. Although you can name your own menus, it's much simpler to use the system menu name. It works like this: **PUSH MENU MenuName** (`PUSH MENU_MSYSMENU`). When you push a menu definition onto the menu stack, that menu is not cleared from the screen and remains active. However, it's now safe for you to redefine and activate a new menu by calling a menu program created in the Menu Designer: `DO newmenu.mpr` When you leave this menu, you can then restore the previous menu with: **POP MENU MenuName**, `POP MENU _MSYSMENU`.

Using the Menu Designer

The Menu Designer automates the creation of menu code, either standard or shortcut, based on your definitions. We'll first cover how to make a standard menu and then look at shortcut menus. Starting or modifying a menu is best done from the Project Manager. When you've created some template menus for the application framework, you open one of them, rename it, and then modify it for the application.

Although it is quick and easy to make additions and changes to your definition in the Menu Designer, if you have a large application (and many menu options), it's probably a good idea to sketch the menu tree on paper before building it. It might look something like this:

- Main menu bar:
  - File, Edit, Login, Registration, WorkList, Reporting, Maintenance
- Menu popup options:
  - File. Use system default and then remove all except **Page Setup**, **Page Preview**, and **Print**.
  - Edit. Use system default.
  - Login. Submenu. **Quick Log**, and **Log Rejection**.

- Registration. Call registration module directly.
- WorkList. Submenu. **Testing**, **Results Entry**, **QA/QC**, and **Supervisory**.
- Reporting. Calls report manager directly.
- Maintenance. Submenu: **Data**, **Reports**, **Users**, **Codes**, **Security**, and **Configuration**.

As much as possible, try to keep the pad names short and use unique first letters (for hot keys). Translating this kind of design into a menu takes five easy steps in the Menu Designer window, as illustrated in Figure 17.10.

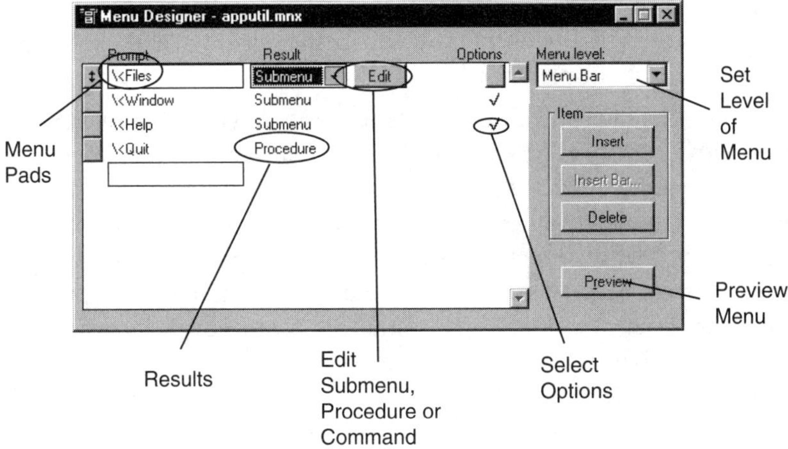

FIGURE 17.10 CREATING A MENU IN THE MENU DESIGNER.

Starting at the level of the main menu bar, follow these steps:

1. Enter a menu name for each pad (or option) in the **Prompt** area. Use the **\<** before the first unique letter as a hot key.
2. Enter the type of **Result** that should follow from selection of the prompt: **Submenu** to continue with options; **Command** for a single FoxPro command; **Procedure** to write a subroutine to be executed; and **Pad Name** to use one of the FoxPro internal pad or option names.
3. If the **Result** entry is **Command**, enter the FoxPro command to be used in the result edit area. If you selected **Pad Name**, enter the FoxPro pad or option name. For **Procedure** and **Submenu**, double-click the **Edit** button to enter the code or additional menu options.

4. Click the **Options** check box to add any desired menu options (more on this later).
5. If you want to see how the menu is shaping up, the **Preview** button will simulate the menu in operation.

Repeat this procedure for each main menu pad, and then go on to the submenus and define all the options under each pad. You can use the **Menu Level** list box to select which level of menu to edit.

The majority of menu entries will be related to starting something: a program module, a form, or a dialog box. If there isn't any complex transition between where the program is at the moment and where it's going through the menu option, then entering a simple **Command** may work: `DO FORM myform.scx NAME myform LINKED`. If there's more to do before or after a program call, use **Procedure** to edit multiple lines of code.

When you save your work in the Menu Designer (**File**, **Save**), it is stored in two files with extensions MNX and MNT. In contrast to other parts of Visual FoxPro, once you've created the menu you must generate the menu code, usually by doing a build through the Project Manager or from the menu (**Menu**, **Generate**). The menu generation program (`GENMENU.PRG`) creates a program file with the extension MPR, which is ready to be compiled like other program files but with the extension MPX. (This multistep procedure is how the Form Designer used to work.)

MENU OPTIONS

The FoxPro menu system supports a fairly large number of options, all of which can be programmed: option procedures, shortcuts, skip-fors, menu setup, menu cleanup, and general menu procedure.

WARNING

It's tempting to over program in menus. After all, doesn't FoxPro give you many ways to enter code? The problem is that menus (and menu programs) don't behave like anything else in Visual FoxPro. They're not objects, and they're not standard programs. Most programmers who have loaded menus with important code have sooner or later been bitten by unusual side effects. In addition, programming in menus is not consistent with the object-oriented model and, at least as a matter of policy, is a poor approach for the future.

PROGRAMMING MENU PADS AND POPUP OPTIONS

Procedures are created in the Menu Designer under the following guidelines: You should not use **PROCEDURE**, **FUNCTION**, or **PARAMETER** to start the procedure, and a **RETURN** is not necessary (although it's harmless). In the style of FoxPro for Windows 2.6, these procedures are called code *snippets*. In practice, most programmers use only direct object, procedure, and function calls in the menu option procedures. Control of menu options and menu modification commands are sometimes applied in the setup and cleanup code of the Menu Designer.

Each pad or menu option can have one or more options. These options appear in the Prompt Options dialog box (see Figure 17.11) when you click on the **Options** check box.

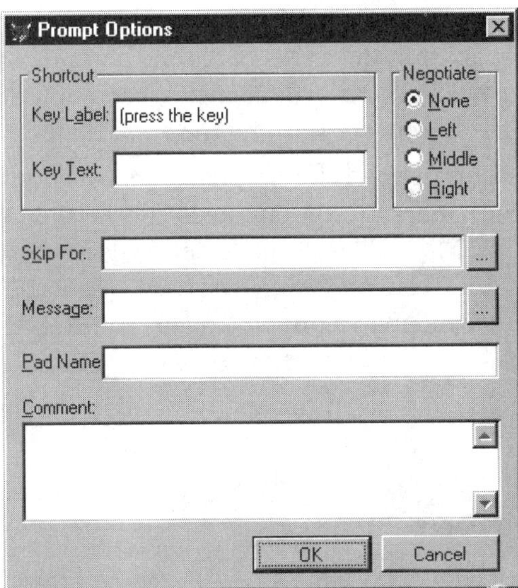

FIGURE 17.11 PROMPT OPTIONS DIALOG BOX.

The options are as follows:

- **Shortcut.** Most of the menu pads and popup options of the system menu have keyboard shortcuts. When you create your own pads and options, you should decide which of them are used often enough to warrant a keyboard alternative.

- **Skip For.** The way to disable and enable menu pads and options. It's used to toggle options—for example, alternating between **Delete** and **Recall** options depending on the status of a record. It is also one of the most important elements in an application security system, because denying access to various menu options is one way of establishing security control in parts of a program.

  You use a logical expression to trigger whether or not a menu option is available—for example, `m.security < 5`. If the logical expression is true, the menu item will be disabled; it will be enabled if the expression is false. The logic of a **Skip For** may be slightly confusing unless you say to yourself, "Skip this menu item when the logical expression is true."
- **Message.** This option is easy to overlook, but the message you enter here—as a text string ("The message is..") or any character expression—is displayed in the status bar at the bottom of the screen and cures the complaints about anonymous menu options. It's a helpful touch for people who are learning the application.
- **Pad Name.** This option is for programmers who don't like the cryptic procedure names created automatically by the Menu Designer with **SYS(2015)**. The usual code for pads comes out like this: `DEFINE PAD _qdi03itu1 OF _MSYSMENU PROMPT "\<System"`. If you specify a name for a pad in this option, you get something like `DEFINE PAD mypadname OF _MSYSMENU PROMPT "\<System"`.
- **Negotiate.** The options in this group position the menu relative to the menu of an incoming OLE application.

General Options

The General Options window (Figure 17.12) is reached through the View menu when the Menu Designer is open. This is the place to put code that affects the entire menu rather than any particular bar, pad, or option.

There are four options:

- **Procedure**. This general procedure, if you choose to create one, executes on every menu selection if there is no other procedure, command, or bar for that selection. In other words, this is the **OTHERWISE** of a **CASE** statement. Typically, this procedure is used to handle menu options that are not yet implemented and have nothing to execute. A simple `WAIT "This option not yet available." WINDOW NOWAIT` or something similar suffices.

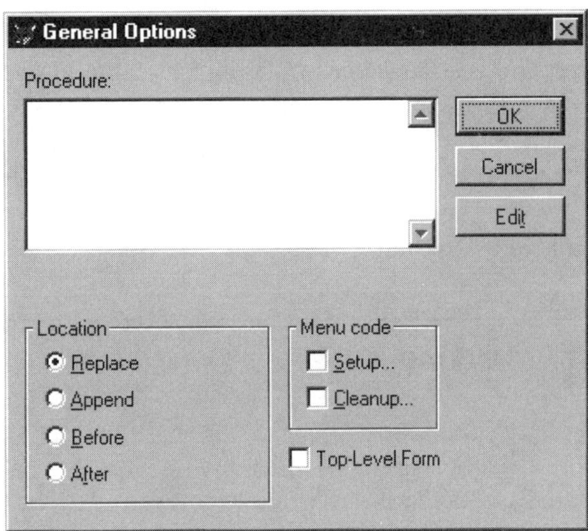

FIGURE 17.12 GENERAL OPTIONS DIALOG BOX FOR MENUS.

- **Setup....** Menu setup handles the definition of any variables used in the menu and any other environmental settings that affect the way the menu operates. Although you can put almost anything in the menu setup, including file openings and variable processing, the best advice is, don't. This also applies to using **PUSH MENU** in the menu setup. You can't use **POP MENU** in the cleanup, because it executes at the same time as the setup code. This means that your pushed menu gets popped—a nullifying effect. That, in turn, means that the **POP MENU** usually must go in the **Destroy** or **Unload** event of a form.
- **Cleanup....** Cleanup in menu code is a misnomer; if you programmed to clean up what was done in the setup, you would wind up with nothing, because the two code segments execute consecutively. By convention, what goes into the cleanup is code that arranges any special effects in the menu, such as marking, enabling, or disabling.
- **Location**. With this option you can insert your menu **Before** some option, **After** some option, or **Appended** at the end of all options, or you can use **Replace** all options. The tendency is to create an entire menu bar and **Replace** the existing one. This approach requires no mental bookkeeping. The other approaches are used mostly when the Menu Designer is creating menu stubs: bits and pieces of menu code to be inserted in other parts of a program to modify a menu on-the-fly.

MENU OPTIONS

These options perform the same role as the procedure and name options of the General Options window except that here they apply to a particular menu pad or popup menu. The Menu Options window appears in the View menu under **Menu Options**. Code in the procedure snippet will execute when any option in the bar or popup menu is selected, and that makes it useful for programming that affects options in that popup.

SHORTCUT MENUS

Shortcut menus are a relatively new item for the user interface (the concept was developed by Borland in the early 90s), but since the arrival of Windows 95 they have become virtually a standard for Windows software. There are good reasons for this success: They're effective and users like them.

Behind the scenes in FoxPro, a shortcut menu uses the same language as the popup portion of the standard menu. You can generate a shortcut menu in the Menu Designer, producing a menu file (MPR). When this file is run, Visual FoxPro 5.0 will recognize the shortcut menu and automatically produce the menu popup where the cursor is located. It's this "on location" aspect of the shortcut menu—the close association of its options with what the user is currently doing—that gives it so much appeal.

There is only one difference between creating a shortcut menu and creating a standard menu. In the Project Manager, select the **Other** tab, highlight **Menus**, and click the **New** button. This time, select **Shortcut** in the New Menu dialog box. This action puts you in the Shortcut Designer window, which is functionally identical to the Menu Designer. Create the menu in the same way you would a standard menu and save it.

To use a shortcut menu, you place a **DO cMenuName** command in the **RightClick** event method of any object that has one. This could be in a form, grid, page, or even specific controls. Typically, shortcut menus are used to provide access to functions or information for large objects, such as a page or grid.

NOTE

Because creating a shortcut menu is exactly like creating any other menu and invoking them is so simple, you'll find that they're one of those user interface elements that present almost all gain for the user and no pain for the developer.

USER MESSAGING

User messaging is a minor user interface topic that isn't really minor. Many people, including some developers, are oblivious to the number of user messages in commercial software. It can be said, almost unequivocally, that a good program keeps up a constant chatter with the user. "Chatter" doesn't mean orally (at least not yet). It means a host of signs, signals, dialog boxes, and other devices for notifying the user what the program is doing and which options are available.

There are many books that cover this aspect of user interface design, but to keep things compact, you can think of user messages in four basic categories:

- **Status**. Most status information is along the lines of, "You are here" and "This is what's happening." Keeping the user informed about the status of operations is standard practice. The FoxPro status bar is an example.
- **Procedural**. Procedural information is most likely to be popup signs and dialog boxes that inform the user about what to do next and which options are available. In some cases, such as the FoxPro Graph Wizard, it can be a series of dialog windows that guide the user through a complex process.
- **Cautionary**. Warnings, alerts, and other cautionary messages are almost always popups, often accompanied by user-selectable options.
- **Error**. There are several kinds of errors: software problems (including bugs), procedural errors (the user made a wrong choice), invalid entry errors, and hardware errors (disk full). In most cases, your program must provide responses to errors as well as the messages themselves.

One of the reasons for categorizing user messages is to decide how you want your application to deal with them. You have at your disposal a number of specific message elements:

- Dialog box forms
- **WAIT** windows
- **MessageBox( )** windows
- Window and form captions
- A status bar
- A message line

- Text labels
- ToolTips

You match one of these elements with the type of message to be presented, something along the lines suggested in Table 17.4:

TABLE 17.4 USER MESSAGING ELEMENTS

ELEMENT	DESCRIPTION	USE
Dialog window	The all-purpose message and response interface. These come in an almost unlimited number of forms because they are often tied to specific content (a files dialog box, a help dialog box) There are a few built-in dialog boxes, but most are programmer constructed.	As the name implies, a dialog with the user. There is both message information and response input. This may be as simple as a yes or no, to a number of questions in a sequence of entries. **Types:** Procedural (often), sometimes cautionary and error.
Wait window	This is a standard FoxPro element, a popup message in a window in the upper right of the screen. Although limited to one line, it can handle several kinds of messages.	Generally used for quick, no response, messages, or process status reporting. The big advantage is the convenience of a native command. **Types:** Status (often), sometimes cautionary or error.
MessageBox()	This function produces the familiar Windows messages, including the specific icons for Information, question mark, and so forth. The user can leave the message only with a command button.	Like the Wait window, used for quick popup messaging, but without the one-line and other restrictions. It can also take user choices. **Types:** All types.

ELEMENT	DESCRIPTION	USE
Status bar	A fixed position information source at the bottom of the screen. It is either on or off. **(SET STATUS BAR)**	Not needed at times, but in most cases where tables are open, or the user is manipulating data, should be left on. **Types:** Status.
Message line	Almost all controls support a user message to describe what the control does. **Status Bar Text Property**. The line is-displayed in the bottom row of the status bar.	If you use the Status bar text in a Text box, you'll be doing lots of them. But users find them helpful, at least in the beginning. **Types:** Procedural
Text label	Messages can be simply displayed as text on the screen. Sometimes popup boxing of areas, color changes, and other highlighting can be very important messaging.	Modify or augment text label controls to guide the user or reflect changes. **Types:** Procedural, status.
ToolTips	Most controls and all toolbar icons support the now standard Microsoft ToolTips—the little yellow information box that pops up after a mouse remains over a target control for a few seconds.	It's becoming standard practice to include ToolTips as part of the routine messaging for all controls or at least those that have ambiguous functionality. **Types:** Procedural

It's generally agreed that different kinds of messages should look different but that each class of message should be consistent within itself. FoxPro itself uses a mixture of standard Windows message elements—dialog boxes, file browsers, a status bar, and error messages—along with a set of old standard FoxPro messages. If you build your own set of messaging elements, it seems reasonable to use first the tools provided by FoxPro and Windows and then to invent those that are missing or needed specifically by your application.

MESSAGEBOX( )

One of the simplest and most versatile of the messaging elements was added to this version of FoxPro: the **MESSAGEBOX( )** function. It can handle variable-length messages and take limited user selection, and it is extremely simple to implement. Figure 17.13 shows a typical example, followed by the syntax.

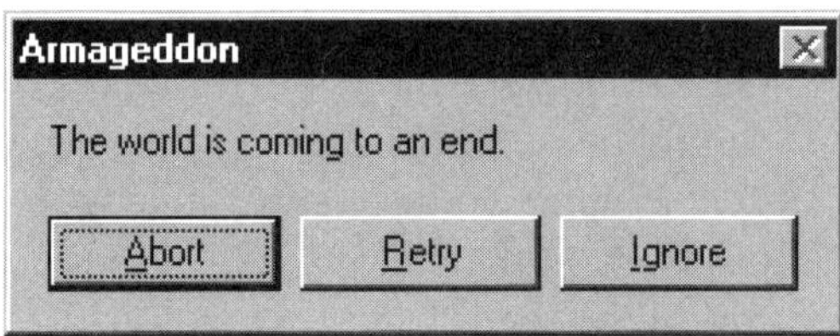

FIGURE 17.13 TYPICAL MESSAGEBOX.

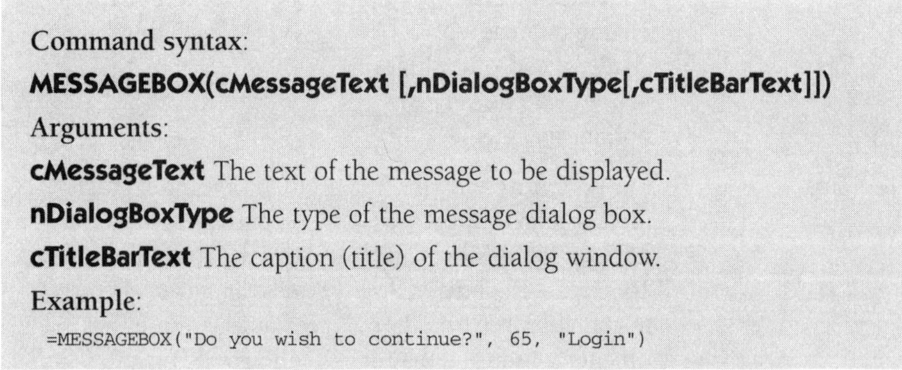

Command syntax:

MESSAGEBOX(cMessageText [,nDialogBoxType[,cTitleBarText]])

Arguments:

cMessageText The text of the message to be displayed.

nDialogBoxType The type of the message dialog box.

cTitleBarText The caption (title) of the dialog window.

Example:

```
=MESSAGEBOX("Do you wish to continue?", 65, "Login")
```

The key part of using **MESSAGEBOX( )** is the **nDialogBoxType** argument, which uses a peculiar code to specify how many (and which) buttons will be in the dialog box, what kind of message icon will be used, and which button will be the default. There are four message icons: stop sign, question mark, exclamation point, and the information **I** icon. The command buttons range from a single **OK** to **Abort**, **Retry**, and **Ignore**.

There are many combinations, but in practice developers use only a few. The simplest way to handle the options is to make preprocessor directive constants from the option values:

```
#DEFINE MB_OK                0    && OK only
#DEFINE MB_OKCANCEL          1    && OK and Cancel
#DEFINE MB_ABORTRETRYIGNORE  2    && Abort, Retry, Ignore
#DEFINE MB_YESNOCANCEL       3    && Yes, No, Cancel
#DEFINE MB_YESNO             4    && Yes and No
#DEFINE MB_RETRYCANCEL       5    && Retry and Cancel
#DEFINE MB_ICONSTOP          16   && Critical message
#DEFINE MB_ICONQUESTION      32   && Warning query
#DEFINE MB_ICONEXCLAMATION   48   && Warning message
#DEFINE MB_ICONINFORMATION   64   && Information message
#DEFINE MB_DEFBUTTON1        0    && First button default
#DEFINE MB_DEFBUTTON2        256  && Second button default
#DEFINE MB_DEFBUTTON3        512  && Third button default
#DEFINE MB_SYSTEMMODAL       4096 && System Modal
#DEFINE MB_APPLMODAL         0    && Application modal
```

These commands would be used in the function as the **nDialogBoxType** argument:

```
nOk=MESSAGEBOX("Continue with entry?",;
    MB_YESNO+MB_ICONQUESTION+DEFBUTTON1,;
    "Select")
IF nOk = 6
  DO MOREDATE
ENDIF
```

WAIT WINDOW

In both procedural and status messaging, there is a heavy use of spot messages: quick popups that give the user a piece of information before the program continues. At one time, there were few options except the obtuse **WAIT** command, which paused the program with a prompt: "Press any key to continue." In Visual FoxPro, however, the **WAIT** is more useful, something you might gather from the syntax:

Command syntax:
WAIT [cExpression] [TO memvarName] [WINDOW [NOWAIT]] [CLEAR] [TIMEOUT nExpression]

Arguments:

cExpression Any message that will fit in one line on the screen.

TO memvarName If the user presses a key to exit the **WAIT**, including this clause with a variable will save the keystroke to the variable. This can be used to monitor a response to questions in the wait message.

WINDOW Including this clause places the message inside the standard FoxPro message window. It will automatically be sized for the message (one line only) and will clear itself as soon as the user presses a key.

NOWAIT If you don't want the program to pause while the message is being displayed, use this clause. (It works only inside a program.)

CLEAR While a program is executing, you can clear a wait message with `WAIT CLEAR`.

TIMEOUT nExpression Wait windows are often put on the screen to notify the user that a process (printing, updating, and so on) has been completed. There are times when you'd like the program to continue after a reasonable time, whether or not the user presses a key. **TIMEOUT** will serve this purpose. It can be set to any number **nExpression** of seconds.

Examples:

```
WAIT "Press any key to continue."
WAIT "Press Y if you are happy." TO nHappyDay
WAIT "And that's the way it is." WINDOW NOWAIT
WAIT "The Printing Has Completed" WINDOW TIMEOUT 200
```

WAIT used without any other clauses is still the ancient Xbase command. It will pause the program and display the text "Press any key to continue." on the screen or currently active window. Using **WAIT WINDOW** puts the "Press any key..." message into the standard FoxPro message window.

Although **WAIT** can capture a keystroke—for example, **Y** or **N**—it's not a mouse-enabled option, so **MESSAGEBOX( )** is preferred for interactive messages.

NOTE

You might be interested in looking at the **genMessage** class in the GENCTAIN.VCX library file that comes with the accompanying disk. This classic wrapper class handles several forms of user messaging, including **MESSAGEBOX( )** and **WAIT**.

DIALOG BOXES

If ever there is a catch-all user interface element, it's dialog boxes. These windows pop onto the screen, contain some informational text, and provide space for the user to make entries or selections. Like a message box, some dialog boxes are largely informational and may ask the user only for a signal to continue or cancel. Others may be part of a series of steps in a procedure and might require data entry or other specific information from the user. There are no set rules. Even in Windows itself, there is only a shred of uniformity. Not even the shape of the dialog window is standard.

A certain amount of standardization is usually welcomed by the user. Being able to identify what a dialog box is about and what the user is expected to do is part of giving uniform visual cues. For example, if it's customary to provide dialog options such as **More** and **Cancel**, then they should always be **More** and **Cancel** and not sometimes **Continue** and **Quit.** To accomplish this uniformity takes either a little foresight and planning in design or a considerable amount of time later in the development cycle to proof all dialog boxes for consistency.

Another issue often raised about dialog boxes is whether they should be modal. The majority of dialog boxes are intended to be displayed only temporarily and are frequently only steps in a procedure or a momentary request for information from the user. As a rule, there is little or no reason for the user to do anything except view the dialog box and respond. Hence, dialog boxes tend to be modal—they don't allow the user to move to another window or menu choice. However, under some circumstances, you may find that having a number of dialog boxes open on the screen may be a useful technique. It becomes the responsibility of the programmer to manage the open windows (forms), the user input, and the sequence of events so that the program doesn't trip over itself.

NOTE

No application framework would be complete without at least two or three different kinds of dialog boxes ready for plug-and-play in an application. These may be limited to basic forms (usually modal) with and without tabs, but over time there are many variations.

BUILT-IN DIALOG BOXES

In addition to the **MESSAGEBOX( )** function, FoxPro provides other complete dialog boxes that you can use in your applications. Be aware, however, that these dialog boxes are not objects; you may find it useful to create wrapper classes for them. They are presented briefly here. You should check out the complete syntax in the *Language Reference*.

SELECT DIRECTORY DIALOG BOX: GETDIR

This function brings up the Select Directory standard dialog box. The user can navigate the disk directory tree and select an appropriate directory. If the user selects **Cancel** or uses the **Esc** key, a null string ("") is returned.

Command syntax:

GETDIR([cDirectory [, cDialogCaption]])

Examples:

```
cDir = GETDIR()
cDir = GETDIR("F:\SALES\","SELECT A SALES DIRECTORY")
```

Returns: `f:\sales\ron` The name of a directory as a character string.

OPEN FILE DIALOG BOX: GETFILE

The standard Windows Open File dialog box has been opened up a wee bit to allow you some leeway in controlling a user's file selection.

Command syntax:

GETFILE([cFileExtensions] [, cDialogCaption] [, cOpenButtonCaption] [, ButtonType])

Examples:

```
cFile = GETFILE("DBF")
cFile = GETFILE("PRG;SPR;MPR","Edit Program","Edit",1)
```

Returns: `f:\sales\ron\totals.spr` Path and file name if selected. Otherwise, a null string.

LOCATE A FILE: LOCFILE

LOCFILE is a sort of two-stage **GETFILE**. First, there will be a search for the file in **cFileName**. If a file is not found, the Open File dialog box will be invoked. The order of search goes first to the default directory (the one currently selected) and then to the FoxPro path. If the specified file isn't located, FoxPro will use the file extensions listed in **cFileExtensions**, if any, and will retry the path search for each of them. If that search fails, the Open File dialog box is called, and **cFileExtensions** becomes the list of files to be displayed. (See **GETFILE** for details of file extension lists.)

Command syntax:

LOCFILE(cFileName [, cFileExtensions] [, cDialogCaption])

Example:

cFile = LOCFILE("CUSTOMER.PRG","PRG;SPR","Customer File")

Returns: `e:\sales\customer.prg` Path and file name if selected; otherwise, a null ("").

SAVE AS DIALOG BOX: PUTFILE

The standard Save As dialog box is called by this function. It allows the user to select a file to be saved or to create a new file and file name.

Command syntax:

PUTFILE([cDialogCaption][,cFileName][,cFileExtensions])

Example:

```
= PUTFILE("Program Files","Customer.prg","PRG;SPR;MPR")
```

Returns: `e:\sales\customer.prg` The file name selected or entered; otherwise, a null ("").

EXPRESSION BUILDER: GETEXPR

You've probably seen the Expression Builder dialog box so many times that you might be somewhat surprised to learn it's available for use in your applications. The Expression Builder is a complex tool to unleash on the user, but, when circumstances warrant, it's a useful support mechanism.

Command syntax:

GETEXPR [cCaptionText] TO MemVarName [TYPE cExpressionType [; cErrorMessageText]] [DEFAULT cDefaultExpression]

Examples:

```
GETEXPR "" TO aCarType TYPE "C"
GETEXPR "Create Fruits Expression" TO cFruit ;
   TYPE "L;You must have your fruit." ;
   DEFAULT '"APPLE" $ fruit.name'
```

Retrieve a Picture File: GETPICT

This is a dialog box you might use for yourself to weed through the hundreds of BMP files you're likely to acquire. Because it has a preview image feature, it is a handy way to see the image in a file.

Command syntax:

GETPICT([cFileExtensions] [, cFileNameCaption] [, cOpenButton Caption])

Arguments:

cFileExtensions A list of file extensions to match files, usually BMP and ICO.

cFileNameCaption The caption for the file name window, by default "File Name."

cOpenButtonCaption Change the name of the **OK** button.

Examples:

```
cBmp=GETPICT("","Open bitmap")
```

Windows Font List Dialog Box: GETFONT

GETFONT( ) opens the FoxPro Font dialog box and allows the user to select a font from the Windows font list. The name of the font is returned.

Command syntax:

GETFONT( )

Example:

```
cNewFont = GETFONT()
```

Windows Print Setup Dialog Box: GETPRINTER

This command summons the standard Windows Print Setup dialog box so that the user can select a printer, which is returned as the value for the function.

Command syntax:

GETPRINTER( )

Example:

```
cNewPrinter = GETPRINTER()
```

PROPERTIES: COLOR

In code and in the Designers, FoxPro gives you two (not obsolete) choices for representing color: as a pure number value or as an RGB value. The number value is the most direct; colors are represented as values from 0 (black) to 16,777,215 (white). This is called *full color* in the video business, and you need a full-color adapter to be able to display the full spectrum. However, most of the gradations in color are not detectable (from one to the other) even with that kind of adapter. On VGA or SuperVGA monitors supporting 256 colors, most of the 16 million options default (more or less) to the nearest color. In the direct number approach, you can set the value of a property by providing the color number like this: `myControl.ForeColor = 16,777,215`.

The RGB approach uses the three most basic colors of light (the primary colors)—Red, Green, and Blue—and allows you to mix them. You have 256 levels of intensity for each primary color (0–255), with 0 being an absence of the color (black) and 255 being the brightest (white). The gradation of each primary color occurs in terms of *shading*, the amount of black, so you can expect each color to lighten as you go up the scale toward 255. At the lower end, about 100 and less, the colors will be dark and muddy, even gray. Around 200, each of the colors will be closest to what people would call its true color. At the top end, they will be bright but less intense (less saturated).

When you mix the three colors, your palette extends to the fullest. At the bottom end, with each color set to zero (`0,0,0`) through (`32,32,32`), you get black. From (`33,33,33`) through (`64,64,64`) will be gray. From (`65,65,65`)through (`191,191,191`) will be white. And finally, with all three colors at (`192,192,192`) or above, the colors become high intensity. Mixing with all three colors changes the *hue* (mixture of white) in the color.

NOTE

Don't expect these gradations between colors to be precise. Color selection is extremely hardware-dependent, and if your color adapter doesn't handle 16 million colors, it will substitute the nearest shade, which might not be very near. If you're trying to be creative with color but don't want unpleasant hardware surprises, avoid the lower end of the settings.

With the RGB approach, you typically use the **RGB( )** function to set up a color—for example, `myControl.ForeColor = RGB(255,255,255)`. The **RGB( )** function converts the three numbers into the single color number. That's why, in the reality of dealing with FoxPro colors, it's a good idea to avoid these unnecessary conversions and stick with the tools available: the Color Palette toolbar and the **GETCOLOR( )** function.

THE COLOR SYSTEM

The shift to object-oriented programming has left the FoxPro color capability with remnants of three older systems still functioning (although they're usually labeled as "included only for backward compatibility"). Unfortunately, when you run across references to color pairs, color schemes, and the like, not all of them are as clearly labeled as they should be: obsolete.

In a visual programming system—when you're working in any of the Designers—as much as possible you will be using the interactive color capabilities. With the Color Palette toolbar open (Figure 17.14), select the object you wish to color, select the color in the Palette (foreground or background), choose **OK**, and the color automatically changes. This technique works only for foreground and background colors, but there are six other color properties (depending on the object):

- `BackColor`. Background color of an object.
- `ForeColor`. Foreground color, typically of text.
- `BorderColor`. Color of a border.
- `FillColor`. Color on the inside of a shape.
- `DisabledForeColor`. The foreground color when the object is disabled.
- `DisabledBackColor`. The background color when the object is disabled.
- `SelectedForeColor`. The foreground color when the object is selected.
- `SelectedBackColor`. The background color when the object is selected.

While programming in a Code window, you won't necessarily have access to a Properties window to get color values. Here's a useful trick:

1. In the Command window, enter and execute this statement to bring up the Color Picker dialog box and save your selection to the Windows Clipboard:

   ```
   _CLIPTEXT = ALLTRIM(STR(GETCOLOR()))
   ```

2. Choose your color and close the dialog box with **OK**. At this point, the selected color number, expressed as a string value, is in the Windows Clipboard.

3. In the Code window, paste (**Ctrl-V**) the value wherever you need a color. For example: `THISFORM.backcolor = 12632256`

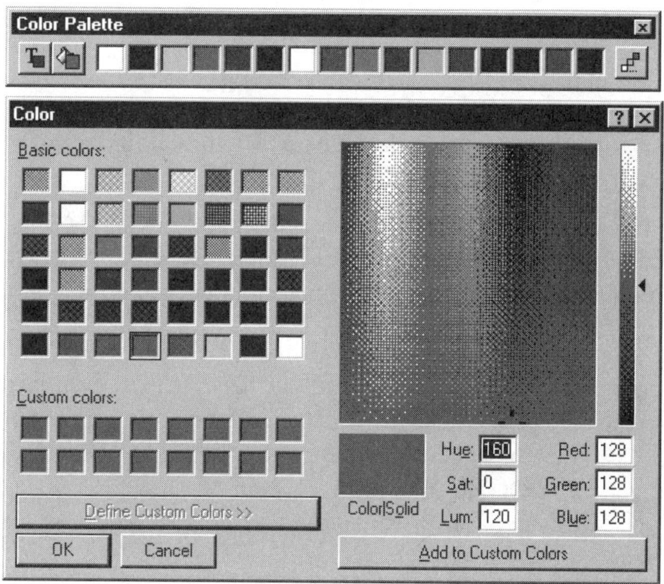

FIGURE 17.14 COLOR PALETTE TOOLBAR AND COLOR PICKER.

Alternatively, you can use constants created by preprocessor directives:

1. Create a color include file (header file), such as the following COLOR.H, or put the values into another include file.

```
COLOR.H
#DEFINE WHITE          16777215
#DEFINE BLACK          0
#DEFINE GRAY           12632256
#DEFINE DARK_GRAY      8421504
#DEFINE RED            255
#DEFINE DARK_RED       128
#DEFINE YELLOW         65535
#DEFINE DARK_YELLOW    32896
#DEFINE GREEN          65280
#DEFINE DARK_GREEN     32768
```

```
#DEFINE CYAN         16776960
#DEFINE DARK_CYAN    8421376
#DEFINE BLUE         16711680
#DEFINE DARK_BLUE    8388608
#DEFINE MAGENTA      16711935
#DEFINE DARK_MAGENTA 8388736
```

2. When creating a form, select **Form**, **Include File** from the menu and enter the name and path to the include file.
3. In your code for the form and its controls, you can use the defined words instead of the numbers: `myButton.BackColor = DARK_MAGENTA`. This technique has the important advantage of being self-documenting.

You can be much more sophisticated with the color scheme outlined by the defined directives, enough so that you might have an entire application's standard colors. Incidentally, you can also include the Color dialog box in your applications at any point where user selection of color is needed. For that, the simple syntax is **GETCOLOR( )**:

DESIGNING WITH COLOR

With screen colors, the gospel according to the experts is, "Less is more." The possibility of using millions of colors doesn't mean that you should have them all in one screen or that they should all be the brightest, flashiest available. In fact, what you have is the possibility to use subtle coloration. Naturally, beauty is in the eye of the beholder, and in matters of taste there is no dispute. This does not mean that good color selection and coordination are totally relative. It simply means that not everyone would do it "your way."

If you're not a trained graphics artist or designer, you might wish for a short course in how to pick colors for software. There is no such course, but there are a couple of good starting points. First, guide the eye to the most important things in the screen. As a rule, color shouldn't be used to draw attention to decorative elements. Instead, use it to highlight the important—functional—elements. That's why using bright colors for things such as borders is usually poor design.

The second guideline is to consider color on the basis of regular use. Too often, screens are designed with colors that make them look flashy and attractive, but with daily use they become distracting and even irritating to the user.

It's hard on the eyes to do hours of data entry on a screen filled with screaming yellow and eye-popping pink.

Even with these simple guidelines, the selection of colors for many different objects on a form can be complex. The windows in FoxPro tend to become layered, sometimes three or four deep, and color can play a role in making these layers clear (or confusing) to the user. Sometimes colors are chosen to identify a type of window or the module to which a form belongs. There a many legitimate reasons for applying color schemes. The only real test, however, is how the user actually perceives them. This is difficult to measure, but it's worth your time to consider.

Design Elements: Text and Fonts

In a broad sense, a large percentage of the visual material on the screen is text. Data entry is text, push-button prompts are text, messages are text, titles are text, and instructions are text. With the advent of toolbar icons and picture buttons, there are other options for decorating a screen, but text remains a major design element of the user interface.

The choice of font, size, and style makes the presentation of text even more of a design element. The availability of inexpensive TrueType fonts has turned font-mongering into a hobby for some people, and there are now thousands of fonts to choose from. However, you can make very few assumptions about the fonts available in other computer systems. When Windows encounters a font that it does not have in the local repertoire, it will make a substitution—a best guess as to which of the available fonts is closest to the one that's requested. The guess, based on point size, serif, and pitch, is usually not very accurate.

It is possible to test for active fonts using either **WFONT( )** or **FONTMETRIC( )**. Both functions return information about the currently active window font. (They won't help you with other types of screen objects.) Presumably, you could check to see whether the font you specified is the one actually used, but your corrective opportunities are limited. The point is this: Don't use fancy fonts unless you plan to ship legal copies along with your application.

Keyboard Events

Not all of the user interface is visual: the keyboard has a role to play. (And someday there will also be pen and voice input for Visual FoxPro.) Although the Windows

GUI environment seems to be moving away from function keys and other keyboard shortcuts, don't forget that a whole generation of computer users grew up with the expectation that they can use keystrokes to accomplish commands.

KEYSTROKE FUNCTIONS

Although monitoring most keyboard activity will be handled through the **KeyPress** event, FoxPro offers a number of commands and functions that are more active.

SET FUNCTION is the oldest Xbase function key command. This one-trick pony allows you to assign a macro or a string of commands to a function key or key combination. Its greatest value is usually to the programmer, who can short-cut routine commands. But from time to time, it can help users by putting common data entry values into function keys.

Command syntax:

SET FUNCTION nFunctionKeyNumber | KeyLabelName TO [eExpression]

Arguments:

nFunctionKeyNumber The number of the function key—F = 2 and so on—to be assigned a command macro.

KeyLabelName As an alternative form, you can use any valid key label (see **ON KEY LABEL** for details) to be assigned a macro.

eExpression A command macro or a string of commands using a semi-colon (;) to execute individual commands within the macro.

Examples:

```
SET FUNCTION 1 TO "DO CLEARSCR"
SET FUNCTION F2 TO "USE customer;BROWSE"
SET FUNCTION CTRL-F3 TO "MODIFY COMMAND MYPROG"
```

The use of **ON KEY LABEL** has become so popular that a piece of jargon has been coined for it: **OKL**s. Setting an **ON KEY LABEL** assigns a command to a key or key combination.

Command syntax:

ON KEY [LABEL KeyLabelName] [Command]

Arguments:

KeyLabelName Any of the 28 supported key labels—for example, HOME, F2, TAB, and ESC. (See the *Language Reference* under **ON KEY LABEL** for a listing.)

Command Any legitimate FoxPro command, most commonly **DO**.

Examples:

```
ON KEY LA=BEL F3 DO WorkList
ON KEY LABEL F4 DO LISTING.PRG
ON KEY LABEL CTRL+HOME  GO TOP
ON KEY LABEL INS BROWSE LAST PREFERENCE worklist
```

In some respects, using an **ON KEY LABEL** is dangerous. Because it is outside the OOP event loop, it can be like a loose cannon within a program. You must be very careful when you turn on and turn off any key assignments. Several commands are associated with **OKL**s, **PUSH KEY**, **POP KEY**, **ON KEY**, and the **ON( )** function. It's recommended that you shy away from using **OKL**s enough to need them.

The **KEYBOARD** command is the way to stuff the keyboard buffer with any string of values that can be executed. In short, it's the way to fake keyboard input.

Command syntax:

KEYBOARD cKeyboardValue [PLAIN] [CLEAR]

Argument:

cKeyboardValue Any valid character expression.

[PLAIN] Causes the command to ignore key assignments in **<expC>**.

Examples:

```
KEYBOARD "NOT APPLICABLE"
KEYBOARD "{CTRL+HOME}"
KEYBOARD UserName( )
```

KEYBOARD has been around for a while, but FoxPro gave it an enormous boost by making it possible to include specific key equivalents. This arrangement opened the door to producing a live action demo, in which under program control, all the normal user keystrokes can be simulated. Although character expression for **cKeyboardValue** means just that—a character string that can be put into the keyboard buffer—there are actually three major components used with **KEYBOARD**:

- A string of text (characters) in quotes: `KEYBOARD "This is a string."`
- Key equivalents, in quotes and curly braces: `KEYBOARD "{HOME}"`. This might be written like a syntax statement: **KEYBOARD "{ <key label1> }" [+"{<key label2>}" ...]**. All the valid key labels (see the **ON KEY LABEL** list in the *Language Reference* manual) can be used in this fashion. They can also be chained to execute a sequence of keystrokes: `KEYBOARD "{F10}"+"p"+"{DOWNARROW}"+"{ENTER}"`. This example happens to cancel a program using the main menu.
- Functions that return character strings or keyboard equivalents in the string can also be used. With **ON KEY LABEL**, functions are called this way: `DO FuncName`. In contrast, here you must use the normal function format: `KEYBOARD FuncName()`.

CHAPTER WRAP-UP

With the keyboard commands, this chapter has come to the end of a long—and yet incomplete—listing of user interface elements. In Chapter 18, you'll be diving into the area of FoxPro where all the user interface elements are brought to bear on the forms of your application. Your skill in selecting and using the elements introduced here will probably be an important factor in the success of the application.

It's important to admit that much about creating a user interface is intuitive and even artistic. Few application developers have the time or inclination to assiduously study user interface design. It also takes a great deal of time to prepare and polish good user interface routines. Still, there is a temptation to linger over the visual details or to spend hours working on a new interface element.

The temptation, however, is also to forget who it's all for: the user. The user interface has a utilitarian commitment: At worst, it shouldn't get in the user's way, and at best it should make the user's job easier. To accomplish this, working with the user—prototyping, experimenting, and reacting to comment and observation of use—is extremely important in developing a good user interface. You, the developer, may have the brilliant first ideas, and you have control over the look-and-feel issues. But without refinement and modification under the harsh light of user opinion, your user interface runs the risk of rejection.

CHAPTER 18

MASTERING FORMS

The form is too important to FoxPro applications not to master it. The same thing is true of all object-oriented application development systems. Forms *are* the user interface. They are the repository for the majority of your code. They are where you will ultimately spend most of your development time. Consider this a pep talk.

It's possible to build applications using only the Visual FoxPro base class **Form**. You could also use the Form Wizard exclusively. Either way would be a shame, though, because you'd miss most of the design opportunities and user-friendly details. You'd lose most of the power of inheritance and object-oriented programming. It would also be flirting with disaster, because you'd be cobbling together something you don't understand. It would be like a painter working blind or an engineer who didn't understand physics—possible, but not desirable.

The centerpiece of this chapter is the basic data form, the type of form you will build again and again for a typical FoxPro application. Even a basic form presents many options and choices, and this chapter will help you understand the issues involved. This chapter is also designed to bring together the various controls introduced in Chapter 17 and integrate them within the Form. This is probably the most difficult aspect of object-oriented FoxPro programming.

A BASIC FORM FOR DATA ACCESS

The variation in forms is limitless, but in FoxPro, with its emphasis on data management, one type of form stands out. Let's call it a basic data form. It's something you're bound to create for the application framework just by following the rule that users need maintenance access to every table. In addition to the tables most central to the application, you need to provide access to a large number of individual tables. Nothing fancy is required. You need just a basic data form with these specifications:

- Provide access to a primary table.
- Support multiple concurrent users.
- Enter new records.
- Search for records on a number of criteria.
- Display existing records.
- Edit existing records.
- Validate new and edited data as appropriate.
- Navigate through records one at a time.
- Delete (or recall) records.

As basic as this is, it embodies all the issues and techniques you'll need for more-complicated forms, so it's a good place to start.

As illustrated in Figure 18.1, the basic data form represents a constellation of elements working together to accomplish the tasks of the specification.

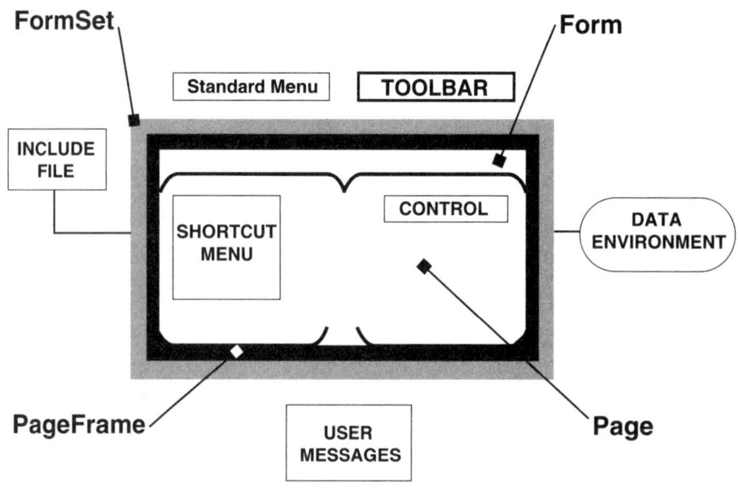

FIGURE 18.1 ELEMENTS OF A BASIC DATA FORM.

You may not need all these elements for every basic data form, but this group is representative. The standard equipment includes the form, an include file, a menu, a Data Environment, and controls. In the example that will be developed for this chapter, we'll add a toolbar, a page frame, and tabbed pages. To give you an idea of where this is going, Figure 18.2 is a screen shot of the Application Users module, one of the utilities on the accompanying disk. This module provides access to the USERS table, a list of people who may use the application and their security assignments.

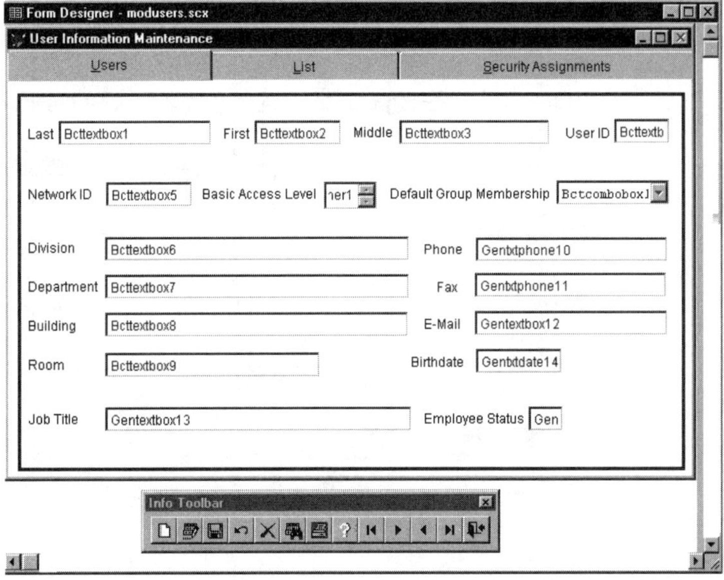

FIGURE 18.2 A BASIC DATA FORM.

THE CLASS HIERARCHY: STARTING A FORM

If you followed some of the examples in earlier chapters, you've already created a form or two that were immediately attached to an application shell and run. This time, we'll focus on the development of a class hierarchy that delivers the elements of a standard data form to the application framework.

The first order of business is to decide whether you want the services of the Data Environments. Unfortunately, it's not a decision you can make for yourself without considerable experience. Some developers consider the DE hard to control and therefore choose to create forms only as classes (which don't support the DE). That's not the position of this book. Data Environments are an important part of FoxPro to Microsoft, and it can be expected that DEs will be enhanced and improved.

Once you make the commitment to using the Data Environment, development of a class hierarchy might result in something like Figure 18.3.

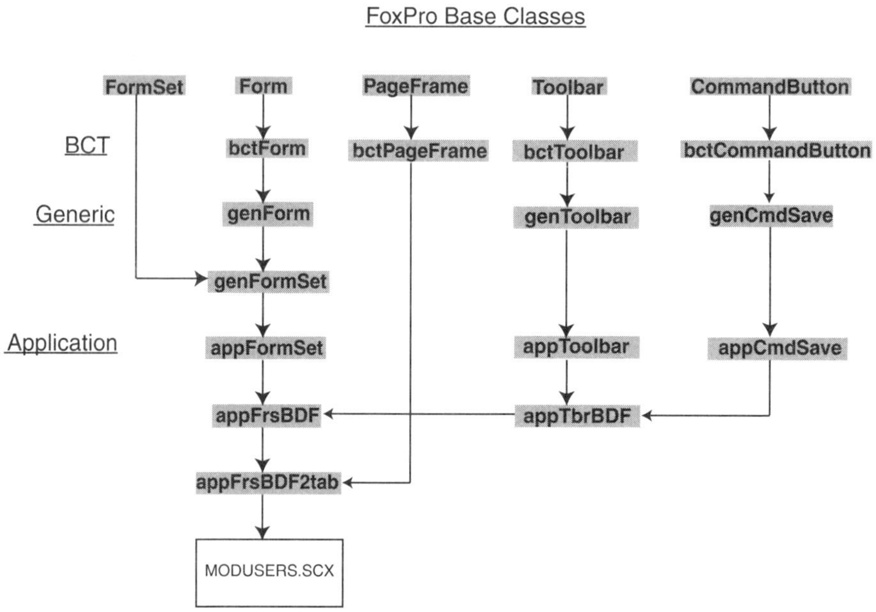

FoxPro Base Classes
FormSet
Form
PageFrame
Toolbar
CommandButton
BCT
bctForm
bctPageFrame
bctToolbar
bctCommandButton
Generic
genForm
genToolbar
genCmdSave
genFormSet
Application
appFormSet
appToolbar
appCmdSave
appFrsBDF
appTbrBDF
appFrsBDF2tab
MODUSERS.SCX

FIGURE 18.3 A FORM CLASS HIERARCHY.

The class hierarchy is arranged in three levels: base class templates (BCT), generic classes (GEN), and application classes (APP). Each level adds something to a class, and the classes become more sophisticated and complex as they go down the hierarchy. Too much code is summarized by this hierarchy to explain it all here, so let's look at an example. The base class template form, **bctForm**, adds only a standard background color, font size, and form size. The generic level form, **genForm**, adds code to the **Activate**, **Deactivate**, **Destroy**, **Init**, and **Keypress** event methods along with a new **RefreshForm** method. These minor enhancements help a form position and display itself. At the application level, major code is added to provide user preferences (window positioning and so on) and a number of properties are created to work with the data and object management.

In the hierarchy of Figure 18.3, the **Form** class is joined by a **Toolbar**, **appTbrBDF**, to become a **FormSet** class, **appFrsBDF**. Then a page frame is added to make the final class, **appFrsBDF2Tab**. By the naming convention, this is an application-level FormSet basic data form with two tabs. This final class is the one entered into the Options dialog box as the template Form (see Chapter 17 for details). When this template is installed, a new form will automatically be derived from the class **appFrsBDF2Tab**. This form looks like Figure 18.2 minus the controls.

NOTE

If you followed the hierarchy just outlined, you need to understand that in a sense, document forms are the end of the line for inheritance. Unless you save a form as a **Form** class, you can't subclass it. That's why in most applications a battery of forms is listed under the **Documents** tab of the Project Manager. They are all SCX forms, and they're ready to be run in a specific application.

As we go along in the next sections of the chapter, more details of the class hierarchy construction will be explained, but there's a lot to cover. It would be worth your time to study the code of this hierarchy on the accompanying disk.

FORM WIZARDS AND BUILDERS

Visual FoxPro has provided a number of supports for the creation of forms. The most obvious ones are the Form Wizard, the One-to-Many Form Wizard, and the Form Builder. As a developer of an application, however, you'll find that some of these supports are a mixed blessing.

The biggest disadvantage of the Form Wizards is the difficulty of linking with your class libraries. By default, everything created in a wizard is built directly from the Wizard classes. This may be a nifty shortcut in some situations, but for application building it leads to a bypass of what should be standard use of your own class hierarchy. In this kind of black box condition, you have a form but you're not sure how it runs.

The Form Builder, on the other hand, provides many of the benefits of the wizards, but it can be called at your discretion to supplement (rather than supersede) your classes. We'll cover the use of the Form Builder shortly.

THE SEQUENCE OF FORM EVENTS

Before we get started with the description of building a basic data form, there's one topic of background information that's vital: the sequence of events that occurs when a form is instantiated (created) and then destroyed. If you don't know about this sequence, it's easy to put code in an event method only to find that it doesn't execute properly (or at all).

Let's say you start one of the forms created from the class hierarchy that is now a form file, USERS.SCX. The command might be `DO FORM USERS.SCX NAME users LINKED` in a menu option of the main menu. This command makes an object of the form with the name USERS. It also starts the instantiation process that goes through each of the events listed next:

```
DATAENVIRONMENT.BeforeOpenTables
FORMSET.Load
FORMSET.FORM.Load
FORMSET.FORM.DATAENVIRONMENT.CURSORS.Init
FORMSET.FORM.DATAENVIRONMENT.Init
FORMSET.FORM.CONTROLS.Init
FORMSET.FORM.Init
FORMSET.Init
FORMSET.Show
FORMSET.Activate
FORMSET.FORM.Activate

FORMSET.FORM.CONTROL1.
```

This sequence presumes the use of a FormSet and a Data Environment, but you can just subtract either element if it's not being used. Remember that if there is no code in an event method, it doesn't fire. If you stare at the list a bit, no doubt you'll see a pattern: a cycling through objects, generally working toward the inside of containers. The big news here is that all controls are initialized *before* the form and form set are initialized. This means that the data to which they are bound must be available or you'll get errors.

Now let's reverse the order and leave the Form by clicking on an **Exit** button:

```
FORMSET.FORM.Click
FORMSET.FORM.CONTROL1.Valid
FORMSET.FORM.CONTROL1.LostFocus
FORMSET.FORM.QueryUnload
FORMSET.FORM.Destroy
```

```
FORMSET.FORM.CONTROLS.Destroy
FORMSET.FORM.Unload
FORMSET.Unload
FORMSET.DATAENVIRONMENT.AfterCloseTables
FORMSET.DATAENVIRONMENT.Destroy
FORMSET.DATAENVIRONMENT.CURSORS.Destroy()
```

As you might expect, on the way out the order is reversed—moving from inner objects to outer containers—with the obvious exception (either way) of the Data Environment.

NOTE

Now is a good time to point out events that FoxPro generates during this process of instantiation and destruction as well as events that are triggered by the user. Events such as **Init** and **Activate** can be triggered only by FoxPro or by your programming. Events such as **Click** and **InteractiveChange** are caused by user actions, in this case a mouse click or a change in value. Incidentally, by convention the events are listed without parentheses: **Click**. Their event methods are listed with parentheses: **Click( )**.

The most obvious importance of this event sequence is that you should not put programming in an event that will fire out of sequence for the code. For example, setting a color property in the `FORMSET.Activate()` event won't be effective, because it's after the `FORMSET.Show()` event, which displays the form.

There are no rules about what should go where; FoxPro doesn't care as long as the code doesn't violate operational requirements. For your own sanity and for those who come after you, though, here are some rules of thumb:

- Put code that is related to the object in the object's events. This principle is fairly obvious, but if the code has something to do with a Form itself, you should use Form events such as **Init** and **GotFocus**. As a common exception, there are times when code is triggered by an object's event but directed at a different object—for example, using the **SetFocus** method.
- Divide the code into three flexible categories: setup, control activity, and cleanup. The Form's **Init** and **Load** events are the most common location for setup code. **GetFocus**, **Valid**, **Click**, and other events most

associated with controls are the locations for code that deals with control activity. **Destroy** and **Unload** in the Form are most commonly used for cleanup code.

- Don't wander around. Keep the same kind of code in the same place in each object for each Form.

NOTE

You can become even more involved with the event sequence by using the Debugger's event tracking capability (see Chapter 13). Although it's used mostly to solve knotty problems with event code, you can also use it to learn how FoxPro moves from event to event.

The Include File

As a good programming practice and part of the application framework, each form should attach one more include files, each with appropriate preprocessor-defined constants. Typically, these files have constants for the **MESSAGEBOX( )** function, standard keys, parameters for important functions, and colors. Examples are available in the accompanying disk (Project Manager, **Other** tab, **Text Files**). Chapter 16 explained all the preprocessor directives in detail. The directives don't show up in the compiled code and take only a few extra seconds in the compiler process. They're well worth your time because of the self-documentation and efficiency they provide for your code.

The include file, which you set in the Form Designer: (**Form**, **Include File**) is the first thing that is processed when the form or form set is turned into compiled code. You can think of it as being at the head of the chain of elements that make up a basic data file.

Multiuser Data Access

It's a reasonable assumption that your application will run on a network and be used by more than one person at a time—a multiuser application. There are database applications for individuals, but they are in the minority. In general, network and multiuser considerations should be built into your forms from the beginning and not added as an afterthought. You should make it a part of the application framework class hierarchy by adding appropriate code (at the generic level) wherever records are added, updated, or deleted.

The principal concern of a multiuser application is the sharing of data. The main purpose of using a database management program as the basis for development is to provide fast, reliable, and controllable access to data by multiple users. For many applications, the control may be most important. This could mean "control" in the sense of security, but it also means the way a data management program protects data integrity and prevents multiple users from stomping on each other's work.

GENERAL MULTIUSER SETUP

There are three pieces in the network configuration of FoxPro: one that is applied generally, another one that is applied to forms, and still another one that is applied (with precision) to specific transactions or data management routines.

The general setup for multiuser applications is to put the following statements in the initialization file or object of your application (see Chapter 8 for a description of the settings):

```
SET EXCLUSIVE OFF
SET LOCK ON
SET MULTILOCKS ON
SET REFRESH TO 5
SET REPROCESS TO 15 SECONDS
```

The exact values of **REFRESH** and **REPROCESS** may need to be adjusted for a particular network.

NOTE

During development and for interactive data management, the multiuser settings can also be made in the **Data** tab of the Options window: **Open Exclusive** for **SET EXCLUSIVE**; **Browse Refresh Interval** and **Table Refresh Interval** for **SET REFRESH**; **Automatic File Locking** for **SET LOCK**; and **Reprocessing** for **SET REPROCESS**.

LOCKING

Locking is the term for permitting only one program to access a table or record. Notice that the word is *program* and not *user*. Many database operations are done by programming and don't require a user. It doesn't matter to FoxPro, because it applies control over the update of tables and records based on the command involved and not on whether it was user-or program-generated.

FILE LOCKING

Before we go into the mechanics of table and record locking, let's consider an initial question: If the object of multiuser applications is to share information, why do tables (in particular) need to be locked? This is not a stupid question, because developers tend to misunderstand the instances and benefits of table locking. For practical purposes, there are three reasons for locking:

- **Because FoxPro requires it.** Certain table operations require an exclusive (locked) use of the table or database file. Most of them (**INDEX**, **INSERT BLANK**, **MODIFY STRUCTURE**, **PACK**, **REINDEX**, and **ZAP**) are fairly obvious, because files must be completely rewritten during the process, and that cannot (or should not) be done while other programs are using them. Other operations require a complete lock of the file (either by exclusive use or by file locking): **APPEND**; **APPEND FROM**; **REPLACE**, or **DELETE**,or **RECALL** with **<scope>** greater than 1; and **UPDATE**.
- **To improve performance.** Because there is less checking and status management, tables opened with **EXCLUSIVE** or **NOUPDATE** (read-only) will process more rapidly. This becomes significant mostly with table operations on larger files (25,000 records or more). Otherwise, table and record locking exacts a small performance penalty.
- **To preserve data values for a period of time.** If you are running a report and must have the most accurate data as of that moment, you lock the relevant tables while the report is running. By doing this, you preserve the stored data values during that period by not allowing other users to make changes or updates. Similarly, if a user doing data entry must complete the entry before anyone else can make changes, you lock that record during the editing.

File locking in these selective situations is useful. Because file locking means that everyone is locked out (except the immediate program), most developers try to schedule operations such as **PACK** and **REINDEX** for times when no one is using the system. At other times, the shortest possible lock is best.

Don't be tempted to confuse data locking with data security. There's a difference between not allowing a user to change a field value at all (security) and temporarily blocking a user from making a change (locking).

RECORD LOCKING

Most decisions to use record locking are based on the notion that each edit of a record is a distinct (one-at-a-time) operation and that all the data in the record must be preserved from additional changes during the time of the edit. Put another way, simultaneous update is not allowed. Is this policy always appropriate?

Consider this record as if it is being simultaneously edited by three people:

RECORD:	LASTNAME	FIRSTNAME	MIDINIT	BIRTHDATE	SSN	SEX
ORIGINAL:	Jones	John	J.	4/14/34	323-23-2443	M
CHANGE 1:				4/15/34		
CHANGE 2:					313-23-2443	
CHANGE 3:		Joan				F

Obviously, changing the sex of the person is worth some consideration. Which of these entries will remain? FoxPro never updates the same record at exactly the same time. Even if two or more users finish editing the same record at exactly the same moment, their entries will be processed to the table sequentially. The problem is that mistakes may be introduced by the sequence of update, and the user will not know that his or her entry has been overwritten.

How important is it for a person working on a record to know that someone else has changed the field or record in the meantime? In our example, there are several significant discrepancies between the entries (first name, birth date, Social Security number, and sex). Which entry is correct? Who is to decide, and how? The programmer might decide that, in the case of this example table, devil take the foremost: The last entry is the best. Or perhaps you believe that the odds of a simultaneous update are so slim, and the relative importance so low, that a few sequencing mistakes are not worth the inconvenience of record locking.

With these issues of file and record locking as background, let's examine the system Visual FoxPro offers to resolve potential conflicts.

DATA BUFFERING

The essence of the Visual FoxPro system is that it takes one or more records from the tables and stores them in a RAM or disk buffer while you work on them. This is a *copy* of the data in the table, and it is compared with the original when the signal is given that editing is complete. By using a copy, FoxPro ensures that the original data isn't accidentally changed, and you have opportunity of canceling the edit.

The buffering system FoxPro uses is conceptually not very complicated:

1. Select one: For buffering a single record, use *record buffering*. For buffering multiple records, use *table buffering*.
2. Select one: *Pessimistic* buffering locks records immediately. *Optimistic* buffering locks records after editing.

That's it—just two items with two options each. The complication, if it is one, is the multiplicity of ways to implement buffering. There are three approaches:

1. Set buffering for all tables involved with a Form or FormSet: **BufferMode** property.
2. Set buffering for each table in a Data Environment: **BufferMode Override** property.
3. Set buffering anywhere (especially outside a form) with **CURSOR SETPROP( )**.

In this chapter we're working with forms, so that aspect will be emphasized. Chapter 19 "Mastering the Database" discusses the programming aspect of buffering and locking with classes. When you're using forms, the path to buffering is simple: Set a form's **BufferMode** to **1** for pessimistic buffering or **2** for optimistic buffering. Visual FoxPro automatically uses table buffering if a grid is associated with any table in the form; otherwise, it uses row buffering. This is usually enough. If you're working with a FormSet that has more than one form (and not just a FormSet with one form and a toolbar), apply the **BufferMode** options there.

If you think that a particular table (such as a cursor in the Data Environment) should have a setting different from the Form or FormSet, use the **BufferMode Override** property with one of the six options:

- 0 = No buffering.
- 1 = (Default) Use the form's **BufferMode** setting.

- 2 = Pessimistic row buffering.
- 3 = Optimistic row buffering.
- 4 = Pessimistic table buffering.
- 5 = Optimistic table buffering.

The pessimistic lock provides maximum protection, because it locks the records for the duration of the edit. That also makes it potentially the most intrusive. It works best when the integrity requirement of a record is high and the simultaneous access requirement is low—for example, access to a hospital patient's records of administered medicines.

Optimistic locking occurs only when a **TABLEUPDATE( )** is issued after the editing is finished. FoxPro locks the records just long enough to compare the values in the buffer with the values in the table. This comparison usually takes only a few microseconds. Then FoxPro automatically updates the table. If the comparison indicates that the table record has been changed, FoxPro generates an error event, which your program must trap and interpret.

NOTE

Because a form's default buffering is none, enabling data buffering is the programmer's responsibility. In a multiuser environment, the no buffering setting has limited use, mostly for tables with static data (little or no update). The real default for most forms' **BufferMode** is **2**, optimistic buffering. This value can be set for all Forms in the base class template or generic level of the class hierarchy. With optimistic buffering as default, when the need arises you can change it to 0 (no buffer) or 1 (pessimistic buffering).

PROCESSING THE BUFFER

In all forms of buffering, you have the option of canceling an edit by using **TABLEREVERT( )**. If you are using optimistic buffering and FoxPro discovers that the data has been changed, it will generate an error that you need to process. Both operations are handled within a form in association with toolbar buttons and menu options, usually with **Save** and **Cancel**. We'll cover the programming involved in Chapter 19.

THE DATA ENVIRONMENT

As you may have noticed, the Data Environment is the first object created as you go into a Form. By definition, a basic data form is based on table information, and the Data Environment becomes a crucial part of the form. This is the point where the database design (Figure 18.4) is used to guide the configuration in the DE (Figure 18.5).

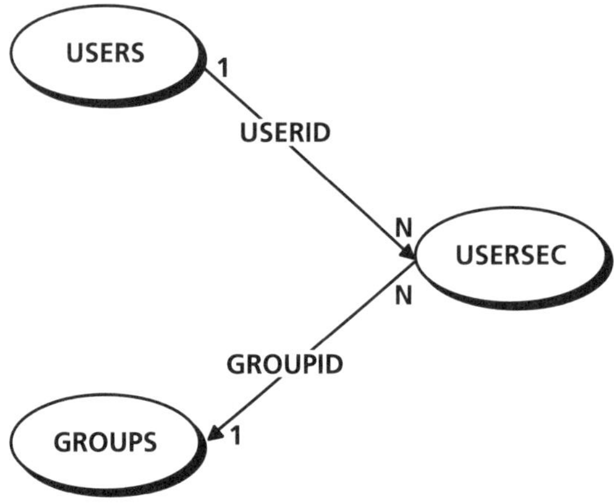

FIGURE 18.4 TABLES FOR THE USER FORM.

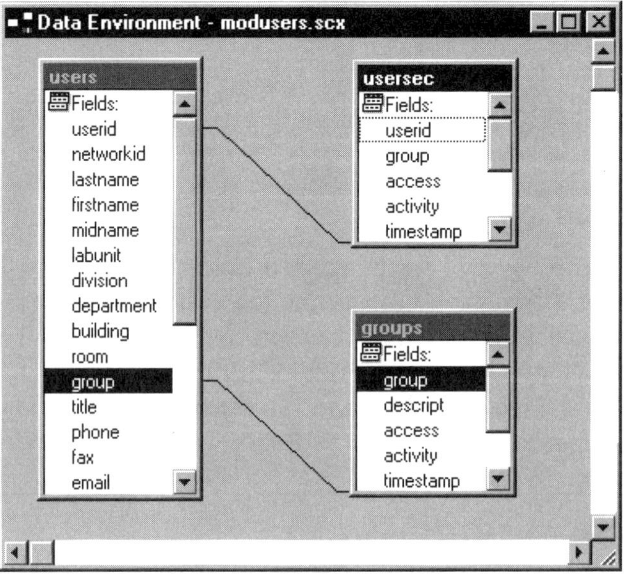

FIGURE 18.5 TABLES IN THE USER FORM DATA ENVIRONMENT.

The example involves three tables: USERS, USERSEC (user security), and GROUPS (groups of users). USERS and USERSEC have a relation based on the USERID. USERSEC and GROUPS share a relation based on GROUP and GROUPID. The user table contains basic information about people who use the application: names, phone numbers, and so forth. It also contains basic security information such as the user's password (encrypted) and access rights. Linked to this table is a detailed listing of the user's specific security rights in the USERSEC table. This user security table is based on assignment of rights to a group (a generic term for almost any functional group of users). The groups are defined in the GROUP table. You can drop these tables from the **Data** tab of the Project Manager and then establish the relations.

The DE itself has two properties that are immediately important to a form: **AutoOpenTables** and **InitialSelectedAlias**. Both properties are set at design time. The first is set to true (`.t.`) if you want FoxPro to automatically set up the Data Environment, and the second specifies which table (alias) will be selected when the form is opened.

In addition to the basic minimum events **Init**, **Destroy**, and **Error**, the DE has two other events: **BeforeOpenTables** and **AfterCloseTables**. These are bookend events, often coded together. The **BeforeOpenTables** does something, and **AfterCloseTables** undoes it. Typically, it would involve setting something in the environment that needs to happen before the Data Environment is created and needs to be removed after the Data Environment is released. An example is shifting in and out of various settings related to international data, such as **SET CURRENCY** and **SET CODEPAGE** (with the **DataSession** property set to **2**, private data session, if the Form will have more than one copy).

OTHER DATA SETUP

Whereas the Data Environment sets the basic pattern of tables and relations, there's often a need to have other channels to data, particularly with SQL queries. For example, many ComboBox controls are used with arrays for selection of small lists of items. If these arrays are populated from table data, as they often are, a SQL **SELECT** statement is coded into the **RowSource** property of the ComboBox or in the **Load** event method of the form. The **UnLoad** event, usually a bookend with **Load**, reverses data settings. In a typical example, you should use **SELECT**s in **Load** to generate active tables or cursors that need to be open throughout the run of the form but closed on exiting.

Building the Basic Data Form

Once the Data Environment has the appropriate tables and relations, you're ready to go to work on the form itself. A basic data form is essentially a maintenance screen, usually without elaborate data entry support or special processing. The example used for this chapter has a few wrinkles: access to security elements such as password and group rights. This feature might call for some extra coding, but most of the form is composed of data-related controls.

Speaking of the controls, which you're about to put into the form, here's a basic design question: On entering the form, is the data visible or not visible? Because the example form deals with application security, it requires some access security itself; the data is relatively private. Consequently, some of the information (password and group rights) is deliberately hidden. However, in general, the person who has access to this form should have already passed one or more security barriers to get to it. Why not show general information? Most basic data forms show information immediately, but this may not be true for other forms.

Here's another question: May the data be modified? This is a maintenance screen, and by definition it is updatable. From time to time you'll build forms that only display data. Given that data in this form can be changed, should the user be allowed to make changes immediately on entry to the form? In this particular form, it's a good idea to make changes deliberate and controlled. That approach has broad implications for building the form. It implies that all the controls are disabled when the user first sees the form and that there is a mechanism to enable the controls.

To accomplish this, as you put each control into the form, you set the default **Enabled** property to `.F.`. This action changes the foreground and background colors of the control, and you may need to adjust them, depending on the color scheme you're using for the form. To update the data, the user must select either **New** or **Edit** (in the form's menu or toolbar). **New** will create a new record, enable the controls, and put the cursor in the first control. **Edit** simply enables all the controls.

All these decisions should be tempered by three requirements: adequate user support and convenience, data security, and data integrity. You want your form to be as informative and flexible as possible; at the same time, you don't want users doing things they shouldn't. The approach taken in the example form is middle of the road: supportive of the user but controlled.

PAGE FRAMES

The tabbed page is a relatively new user interface device that stands out as both practical to use and easy to implement. As an element of a form, Visual FoxPro uses a PageFrame as the primary container class into which you put Pages (themselves a container class for controls). Pages may be tabbed or not, and that gives you some design latitude. However, all pages with a frame must be of the same kind.

In the old days, circa 1993, developers used multiple windows to handle data entry that required more than one screen. It was cumbersome. The page frame changes all that. Now, if you can't fit all the controls you need on one screen, you can add more pages (with or without tabs). Some commercial Windows 95 and NT programs are composed entirely of tabbed forms. Such programs can be visually boring and even confusing to use, but illustrate the usefulness of the approach.

NOTE

The similarity between PageFrame Pages and using multiple forms in a FormSet raises an important question: Which one is preferred? In most cases, the PageFrame is much more preferable, because it is simpler to create, requires little programming machinery to operate, and uses less memory.

ADDING A PAGE FRAME TO A FORM

Adding a page frame to a form is a simple matter of dropping a **PageFrame** class onto the form. This class is usually a "one off" version of the FoxPro base class; an example is the base class template **bctPageFrame** in this book. This version usually has code to size the frame so that it stays with the form window as it changes size. Alternatively, most developers will have several versions of forms and form sets that contain a page frame in their class hierarchy.

Although PageFrames and Pages have the usual extensive complement of events, methods, and properties, only a few are used regularly:

- **Caption property**. Create an appropriate caption for each page. You can use **\<** before a letter to make a hot key. This is important if you want people to be able to reach pages without using a mouse.

NOTE

I always work through the features of a form (toolbars, menus, and tabs) asking myself, How will people use this form if their mouse doesn't work? It happens.

- **PageCount property**. Add more pages by increasing this number. You can't have a page frame with fewer than two pages. New pages are added to the end. You can move them around by changing the **PageOrder** property of a page. However, the page names are not changed, and that could be a problem for routines that work with the order of pages.
- **ActivePage property**. By default, the active page is 1. You might wish to use this property to automatically move the user to a page.
- **Activate event method**. This event fires when the user clicks on a page or the program sets the **ActivePage** property. It's common to use this method to adjust table configuration and control status (enabled or disabled), particularly when the pages have very different content and use different tables.

As you will quickly discover, a form that contains a page frame isn't as easy to edit in the Designer windows as a bare form is. Because of the containership hierarchy, you must first select the form and then use the shortcut menu to select **Edit** before you can get at the controls in the pages of the page frame. It's even worse when you need to edit a grid column inside a page: You must select the grid and do another round with the shortcut menu.

NOTE

A favorite use of tabbed pages is to set aside the first page for editing fields in the "form layout" using controls and labels. The second page is dedicated to a grid layout that presents the same data as a list in row and column fashion. That's how the example basic data file is designed.

Adding Controls

So far, most of the topics in this chapter have dealt with the container framework provided by the form set, form, and page frame. What goes into the framework are controls. In a basic data form, the vast majority of controls will be TextBoxes, with a smattering of other data entry controls. This arrangement makes design easy. In Chapter 17, we explained how to set up a mapping between fields and control classes. Now all you have to do is to drag and drop from fields in the Data Environment or from classes in the Form Controls toolbar.

An important step in adding controls to a form is to configure or check their relationship to the data—how they are bound. Each control is a bit different, and control's behavior can at times be eccentric. The most difficult controls in this respect are ComboBoxes and ListBoxes, which have so many options for how they get their data that it's easy to make a mistake.

The design and layout of a form is a topic in itself—it's a career for some people—but most developers add controls quickly, make sure their data bindings are correct, and then set about moving, shaping, and adding the other esthetic elements (color, font, and so on). Although populating a form with numerous controls is easy, it can be tedious to do the minute details of layout and formatting. Each control has several properties that need to be set, and there's the occasional need for code in event methods. In a form (or page) that has 20 or 30 controls, this becomes a chore. Fortunately, several tools are available to help the process: the Form Builder, multiple selection editing, the Control Builders, the AutoFormat Builder, and the Layout toolbar.

THE FORM BUILDER

In Visual FoxPro, the Quick Form and the Form Builder are one and the same (*Quick Form* is a holdover term from older versions of FoxPro). You can invoke the Form Builder at any time using the **Form Builder** icon in the Form Designer toolbar. Typically, you would call on its services after you've loaded a form class into the Form Designer or Class Designer. You should already have defined the Data Environment and have the needed database and tables open.

As you can see in Figure 18.6, the Form Builder starts with a tab for selecting fields to be placed into the form. This is a typical "picker" dialog box, where you select or deselect the fields. The only complexity may be having too many fields for the size of the form. For that, you can check the **Enlarge form as needed** option on the **Style** tab (Figure 18.7).

The **Style** tab lets you pick from five control styles (standard, chiseled, shadowed, boxed, embossed, and fancy). Which one you choose is a matter of taste and the overall design of your application. When you've selected the fields and style, then **OK**. The Form Builder will churn out a form (based on the one already open) having all the selected fields. The results are not always good composition—you will have usually have quite a bit of adjusting to do—but this approach beats defining and formatting each of the controls individually.

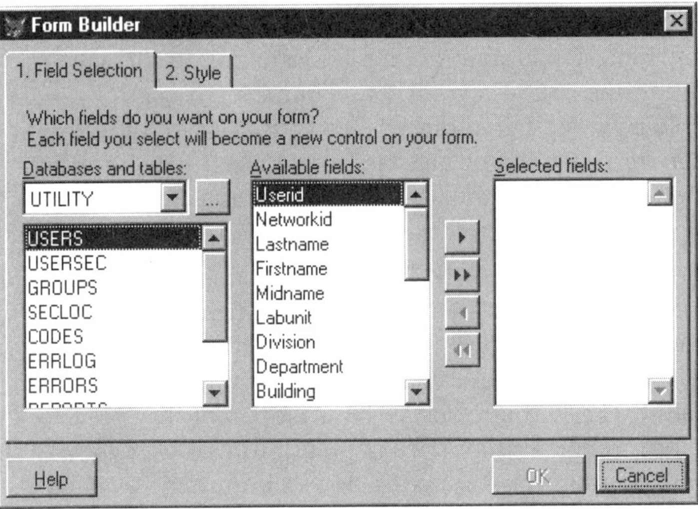

FIGURE 18.6 FORM BUILDER FIELD SELECTION TAB.

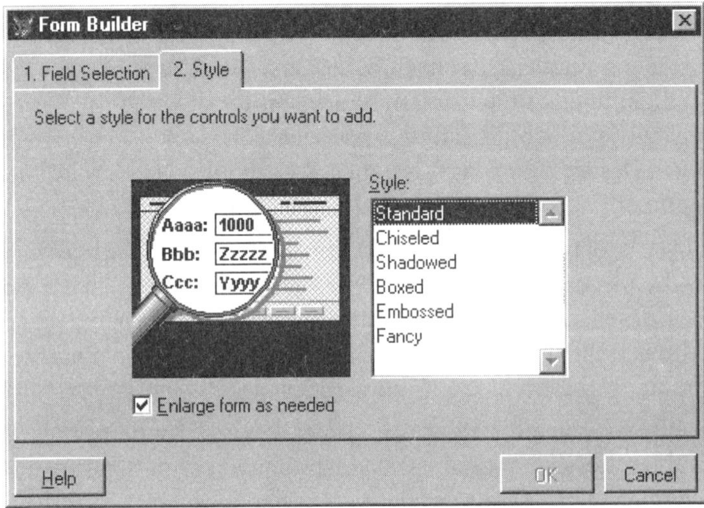

FIGURE 18.7 FORM BUILDER STYLE TAB.

CONTROL BUILDERS

Whereas the Form Builder can help with a gaggle of fields, the Control Builders can help you add individual controls (not necessarily tied to fields). As mentioned in Chapter 17, you can enable the Control Builders with the **Builder Lock** icon on the Controls toolbar. This action will cause the appropriate Builder to appear whenever you choose to enter a control. You can also set this as default behavior in the **Options**, **Forms** tab, but it's more convenient to turn the feature on and off while working in the form. You can also use the Builder retroactively by clicking on the **Builder** icon in the Property window of the control.

NOTE

Except for a few weird behaviors in the Grid and ComboBox Builders, the Builders are great. Put them to good use.

ALIGNMENT

One of the most time-consuming and frustrating elements of form design is the task of getting groups of controls properly shaped and aligned. For the most part, it involves using the Layout toolbar to center, justify, space, and align one or more controls. Draw a marquee (the box with a hand icon) around the target controls and select the desired alignment icon.

For some controls, particularly text boxes and command buttons, the **AutoSize** property is important, because it will configure the control's frame to match the font and size of the content. For example, you would use **AutoSize** to create command buttons that are the same size as their caption (instead of the default all the same size).

NOTE

Use the **Arrow** keys to "nudge" controls for fine tuning of positions on the form. **Alt+Arrow** keys will change the size of the control pixel by pixel.

AUTOFORMAT BUILDER

Occasionally, you will add controls to a form and then decide that they need a different style (or don't fit the prevailing style). Building styles, especially the 3-

D types, is a job for people who have superlative eyesight and enormous amounts of free time. Thankfully, Visual FoxPro has the AutoFormat Builder (Figure 18.8).

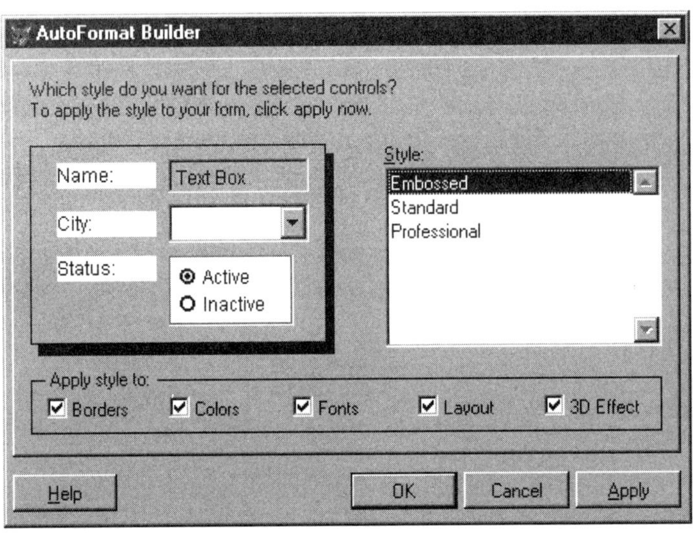

FIGURE 18.8 AUTOFORMAT BUILDER.

To use this Builder, select the controls you wish to change and click on the **AutoFormat** icon in the Form Designer toolbar or the shortcut menu. Then select the style you want and finish with **OK**. The AutoFormat Builder adds the special borders and shading that create effects such as 3-D. For major font changes and other slightly more radical changes in the appearance of the controls, you need to work directly in the Property window.

MULTIPLE SELECTION EDITING

Whereas the AutoFormat Builder changes properties wholesale for a selected group of controls, you can select a group of objects and edit them all property by property in the Property window. This *multiple selection* editing is a new and welcome addition to this version of Visual FoxPro. It works best for one class of control at a time. You can also click the right mouse button on the title bar of the Properties window and select **Non-default Properties Only**, to display only methods and properties that you've changed.

CHANGING DESIGN IN THE PROPERTIES WINDOW

Visual FoxPro provides a large number of design options for controls: coloring, shaping, filling, and assigning fonts, and borders. They are available through the Properties window in the **Layout** tab. The color options can also be set through the Palette toolbar, which provides a simple point-and-click way to color objects in a form. Otherwise, you make individual entries for the properties. Figure 18.9 highlights some of the properties that are often modified, especially for labels and shapes.

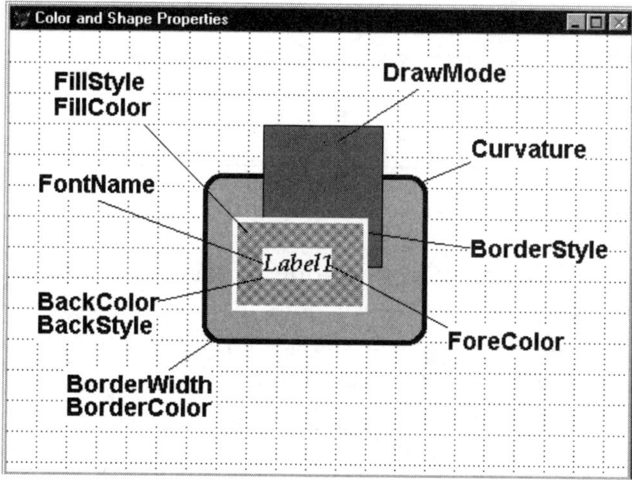

FIGURE 18.9 COLOR AND SHAPE PROPERTIES.

Most of the properties are fairly clear, but a few, particularly those for shapes, are mysterious:

- **DrawMode**. Perhaps the most mysterious and unpredictable property of all. It changes the relationship of the color bits to the foreground and background; depending on what colors are present, the results can vary immensely. Most of the settings are unusable, but a little experimentation can be useful.
- **LineSlant**. The direction of a line shape is controlled by a forward or backward slash key. Figure 18.9 shows lines pointing in many directions; this effect required constant use of the **LineSlant** property.

- **Curvature**. 0 = rectangular corners, 30 = bevelled corners, 99 = circle. Surprisingly, Visual FoxPro does not have a stock curved or circular shape. This is one area of design that cries out for a set of user-defined classes.

NOTE

The design properties of most Visual FoxPro controls are dynamic and can be changed while an application is running. The possibilities are endless for shaping the looks of a form in response to the current status or a user action. For example, you could have a shape that is a square for one selection and turns into a circle for another selection. The coding for that is `shapeobject.curvature=99` (circle) or the reverse: `shapeobject.curvature=0` (rectangle).

TAB ORDER

Once you've placed the controls on the form and have taken care of some of the esthetics, you need to consider the way users move around a form from control to control. This is called the *tab order*: the sequence of controls that receive focus if the user were to continually press the **Tab** key.

There is no standard tab order, because the order should be based on the content of the controls. For example, all address fields should be filled in before the user moves on to employment fields. Tab order is usually left to right, and top to bottom in relatively unbroken sequence, but this order isn't always possible or appropriate.

Tab order in a Form can be set two ways depending on the basic approach you've set in the **Forms** tab of the Option window: **Interactive** or **By List**. The interactive approach starts by selecting **Tab Order** from the Form Designer toolbar or the View menu. Then click the tab box (in the upper-left corner of the control) of the first control to gain focus (a **1** will appear). Thereafter, use **Shift-Click** in the tab box of each control in the order you want them. This technique works best if there are many controls on the form and their tab order is irregular.

The other approach is a Tab List (see Figure 18.10), which should be familiar to you if you have used older versions of FoxPro. Here you change tab order by moving objects up and down the list (grabbing the buttons on the left). This approach works best for changes within a small group of objects.

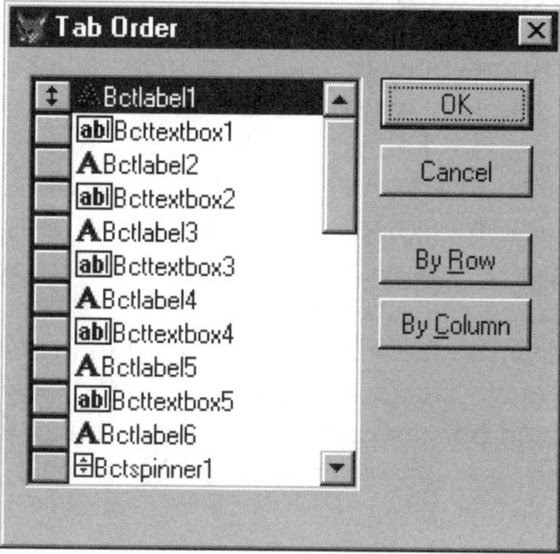

FIGURE 18.10 TAB ORDER DIALOG BOX.

NAVIGATION AND ACTION OPTIONS

Adding controls to a form is done more or less ad hoc for each form. In contrast, the mechanics of manipulating which records the user sees and the actions the user can take should be part of the application framework and class hierarchy. Recall the specifications for a basic data form:

- Navigate through records one at a time.
- Enter new records.
- Search for records on a number of criteria.
- Edit existing records.
- Delete (or recall) records.

These basics of data management entail many issues when you offer them to the users of your application: security, data validation, data retrieval, and performance, to name a few.

Navigation Options

The term *navigation* is something of a holdover from mainframe database terminology. It represents a basic activity of the user: finding the right data. In the case of our USERS form, it means finding user data to edit. Among the ways to select data for editing—such as SQL query, or a FoxPro **SEEK**—for each form you must decide which search methods are appropriate. In most basic data forms, the user can get things started with a search in a list or a **Find** option, supplemented by four standard navigation options that move between records: **Next** (or any word that means to move ahead one record in the table), **Prior** (or any word that means to move back one record in the table), **Top** (move to the first record of the table), and **Bottom** (move to the last record of the table). In Visual FoxPro, these options are almost always available through a combination of menu, toolbar, and command buttons.

Action Options

The *action* options affect one record of a table at a time: add, edit, and delete. Here are some of the basic issues:

- **Prior to action**. Which action options are available to a particular user? The options usually involve security rights and depend on the sensitivity of the data. In some cases, deleting may not be allowed. In other cases, users may have editing rights but can't add or delete data records. Whether certain options are visible or active in your screen depends on the rules you program into the action options. Typically, this means enabling or disabling the action button in a toolbar or menu options.
- **During action**. This is one of the major headaches of event-driven programming: What is allowed while the user is adding or editing? In a tightly controlled form, the user isn't allowed to do anything else during these operations. In a truly event-driven scenario, the user is free to do anything, at any time. Which way a particular form should go depends on the nature of the data. In an accounting program or other kinds of transaction-based entry, the user's options are usually controlled. In a decision support form, where the user's guidance is important, the freedom of the event-driven model is appropriate. In a typical basic data form, a mixture of the two approaches is often used. For example, the user is forced to complete an add but may be allowed to do other things during an edit.

- **Exit from action**. Somehow, sometime, the period of editing or adding a record needs to end. Exit can occur by default, such as when the user leaves the current form or completes a process (such as deletion). It can also occur by intention, such as pressing a **Save** or **Cancel** button. The point for the programmer is that you shouldn't leave any of the three action options in an ongoing state forever. Eventually, the data needs to be dropped or made available and the program execution continues. In some applications, you'll have to guard against the ability of a user to tie up needed information.

In one way or another, all forms that involve data update must deal with these issues. For adding, editing, and deleting a record, you need to make explicit choices about how your forms will behave. Then you need to build that behavior into the application framework through customized toolbars, menus, and command buttons. Following is a description of how the example basic data form works. There are many other themes and variations.

The application framework has a template menu for a basic data form: APPMENU. Among other things, it has options for **New**, **Edit**, **Cancel**, **Save**, and **Delete**. The class hierarchy has a toolbar defined at the application level (**appTbrBDF**) that has icon command buttons for **New**, **Edit**, **Cancel**, **Save**, and **Delete**. This is combined with a form class, **appForm**, to create a FormSet class for a basic data form: **appFrsBDF**.

Each menu option and toolbar button calls a routine that handles the required action. In this case, that call goes to a single method from a class that was created to handle all action and navigation options from either a menu or a toolbar from any form. In other words, the call goes to a generic action manager. The **appActMgr** class was created in the APPPROG.VCX library file (at the application level) and contains several methods to handle the work of updating records and navigating a table. The principal method is called **Action()** and has three arguments: the name of the form, the source of the call (button, toolbar, or menu), and the action requested.

At the initialization of the application, the class is instantiated this way:

```
oActMgr = CREATEOBJECT("APPACTMGR").
```

In each menu option procedure and the **Click()** method of each button, the call looks like this:

```
oActMgr.Action("FORMNAME","CMDBUTTON","EDIT")
```

This generic approach works best when the actions themselves are generic. The routines in the action manager can insert records, enable or disable controls, delete records, search records, move through the table, and enable and disable menu options and toolbar buttons. If the form requires more complex handling of the data or has unusual requirements for controls, then either the action manager must be abandoned, or, hopefully, code can be put into the buttons and menu options to supplement the action manager.

Built into the code of the action manager are the following rules:

- All data entry controls in a form are disabled when data is not being added or edited.
- The user must deliberately signal to call up a new record (**New** button) or to edit a record (**Edit** button).
- When the user is adding or editing, no other search, navigation, or action option is available.
- Adds and edits are ended only with a **Cancel** button—which uses **TABLEREVERT( )** to reverse all changes—or a **Save** button, which uses **TABLEUPDATE( )** to complete the changes.
- The user is allowed to leave the form during adds and edits, and certain menu options, such as **Print**, may be available.

This set of rules works well with a basic data form and its maintenance role. Other kinds of forms would need variations to many of the rules.

NOTE

There's much more to the action manager than can be comfortably described here, so it's worth your while to study the code. I want to stress that this is *a* way of handling these navigation and data update requirements. The point here is to get you thinking about how it is done. You should also look at other approaches, such as the FoxPro TASTRADE project.

Menu and Toolbar

A standard menu is just that—standard. Whether each form has its own menu is another story. It's possible to make a main menu serve double duty for a form, but the necessity of controlling overlapping or unwanted options creates a lot of work. Most developers choose to bring in a different menu for forms. For basic data forms, there are so many similarities between menu options that a generic template menu can work unmodified in most cases.

ADDING A MENU TO A FORM

A menu that has been adapted to a form has dropped almost all the standard Visual FoxPro menu options except the **Edit** bar and submenu, a few options from the **File** submenu, and, at least during development, the **Window** submenu. The example shown in Figure 18.11 is from APPMENU.MPX, an application framework template menu stored in the UTILITY project under the **Other** tab.

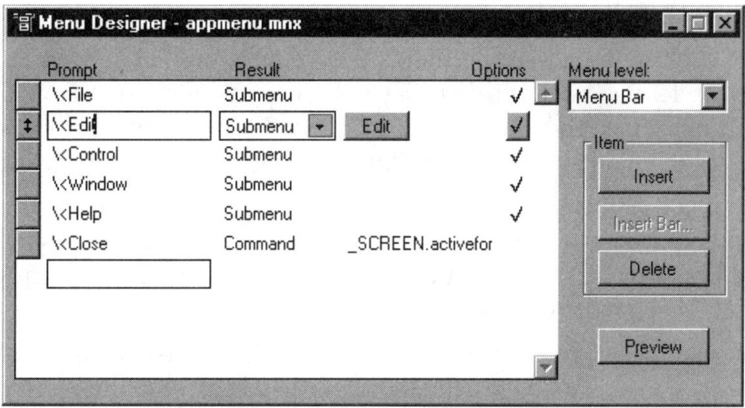

FIGURE 18.11 TEMPLATE MENU FOR A FORM.

To use this template menu in an application, you open the APPFRAME project, open the menu, and save the menu to the MENU directory of your application. Then open the application's project and add the menu to the **Other** tab under **Menus**. It's helpful to keep the APPMENU name so that you can tell at a glance what it is. Once you've loaded it into your application, you can open APPMENU and customize it for a particular form as needed.

Attaching the menu to a form is usually done in the **Load()** method of the form:

```
PUSH MENU _MSYSMENU
DO APPMENU.MPR
```

It is usually removed in the **Unload()** method of the form:

```
POP MENU _MSYSMENU
```

Even if you're working with a form set, put the menu call in the primary form. Consistency helps when you try to locate things.

During the run of the form, except for those menu options handled automatically by FoxPro (primarily the file and edit options), you will need to make choices about which menu options are enabled and when. This is done using the **Skip For** expression. For example, if you don't want the **Add** (a record) option to be available while the user edits a record, then create a property (or variable) `plEdit` and put it in the **Skip For** expression. The variable is set to true (`.t.`) during editing, and this will also disable the menu option. That's how it's handled by the action manager discussed earlier.

Adding a Toolbar

Although toolbars have become standard on almost every Windows program, there is still debate about whether they're appropriate for Visual FoxPro applications. Unlike FoxPro or Word for Windows, many applications have few things that can go on a toolbar. The effort to create one may not be worthwhile.

Even if you accept the need for toolbars, the next question is whether every form should have its own or whether you should try to maintain a single toolbar for the application. As it is with menus, changing and managing one toolbar is generally much more difficult than simply bringing in a new one.

In Visual FoxPro, toolbars are a form (internally that is, not as a class), and that's why you must have a FormSet to be able to add a **Toolbar** class to a Form. This makes sense; after all, the toolbar must be a container, and a form can contain other objects, such as buttons, at the same level as other forms. You can create toolbar classes in the Class Designer or as code. Because they are a visual class, however, it's much easier to create them in a Designer.

Before you start creating a toolbar, it's a good idea to assemble all the needed BMP or ICO files into an appropriate folder and make any desired changes to their appearance with the Icon Editor (provided with the Professional Version of FoxPro) or similar tool. You can do this design work later, but it helps to crystallize your thinking about the use and representation of each button. FoxPro comes with a large number of bitmaps and icons suitable for toolbars. Most of them are located in the \VFP\SAMPLES\GRAPHICS folder.

Before you make the toolbar, you need to make its buttons using the CommandButton control and icons or bitmaps you have assembled. The application framework class hierarchy has two toolbar button types, which are derived from the **bctCommandButton** class. The **genCmdSave** (the end part of the name is the action involved) and all the other generic level buttons carry out actions with simple commands and without needing supporting objects. By contrast, the application-level toolbar buttons, such as **appCmdSave**, use the complete action manager system, which must be instantiated by running the application.

NOTE

One of the easiest ways to distinguish generic-level classes from application-level classes is whether they can be run "as is" or need a lot of supporting machinery (other objects). One of the points of the generic level is that its classes are simple and can be run at any time.

When the button is sized (usually 25x25 pixels), use the **Picture** property to attach the appropriate BMP or ICO file, and define the **ToolTip** property with a description of what the button does. Then add the appropriate action code to the **Click** event of the button. A complete set runs about 12–15 buttons, so it takes some time to put them together. (The beauty of OOP is that once you have constructed this set, you can reuse them forever.)

Then you start a new **Toolbar** class. Keeping in mind that the **Toolbar** class in the Class Designer window can be treated like a Form, you can set whatever properties and methods are appropriate for the toolbar (as distinguished from its buttons), including a toolbar caption and colors. With the toolbar in place, you can begin dragging and dropping the toolbar buttons from the **Classes** tab (see Figure 18.12). If you want groups of buttons to stand out, you can add separators from the Form Controls toolbar.

When you're finished with the toolbar, save it. Then open the Form (or Form Set) that you want to associate with the new toolbar. Shift to the **Class** tab of the Project Manager and expand until you can see the new **Toolbar** class. Drag it onto the Form. If you don't have a FormSet defined, FoxPro will immediately ask to do it for you: otherwise, it can't attach the toolbar.

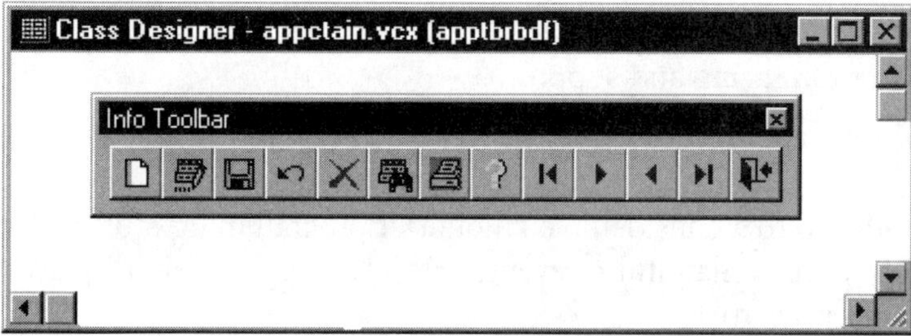

FIGURE 18.12 TOOLBAR AND BUTTONS IN THE CLASS DESIGNER.

If this procedure sounds fairly simple, that's because it is. Adding a toolbar to a form is not a difficult task. However, there are plenty of wrinkles involved in coordinating some toolbars with the actions of an application, and you may want to do different things with the positioning and docking of the toolbar.

MANAGING EVENT METHODS

In object-oriented jargon, it's said that one object sends a *message* to another object. The image this term invokes is slightly misleading from the programmer's point of view, because what actually happens is closer to the standard program *call*. But the point is that one object can use methods, get information from properties, and set properties in another object (as long as they are not protected). With the program executing in one object—say, in the **Click()** method of a toolbar button—it can access information and methods from another object (such as the action manager):

```
oActMgr.Action("MYFORM","NAVIGATE","NEXT")  && access method
IIF(oActMgr.plEdit,SEEK(userid),.F.)         && use property
oActMgr.pcCmdObject = "MYFORM"               && set property
```

In addition to the navigation and action options already described, a typical basic data form may also have coding for the following:

- TextBox or other data control access and validation, as described in Chapter 17.
- General access control, enabling or disabling of groups of controls.
- Changes in layout or design: colors, shapes, and similar properties.
- Action options that invoke processing or other program routines.
- User messaging and support.
- Error trapping and management.

This can add up to a considerable amount of programming, but most of it will be located in only a handful of event methods, supplemented by user-defined methods and properties.

Figure 18.13, combined with Tables 18.1 and 18.2, highlights the most commonly used methods, event methods, and properties. The list does not imply that other methods and properties are not important—far from it—but they're important for specific objects or specific activity and aren't used as often. As they say, your mileage may vary.

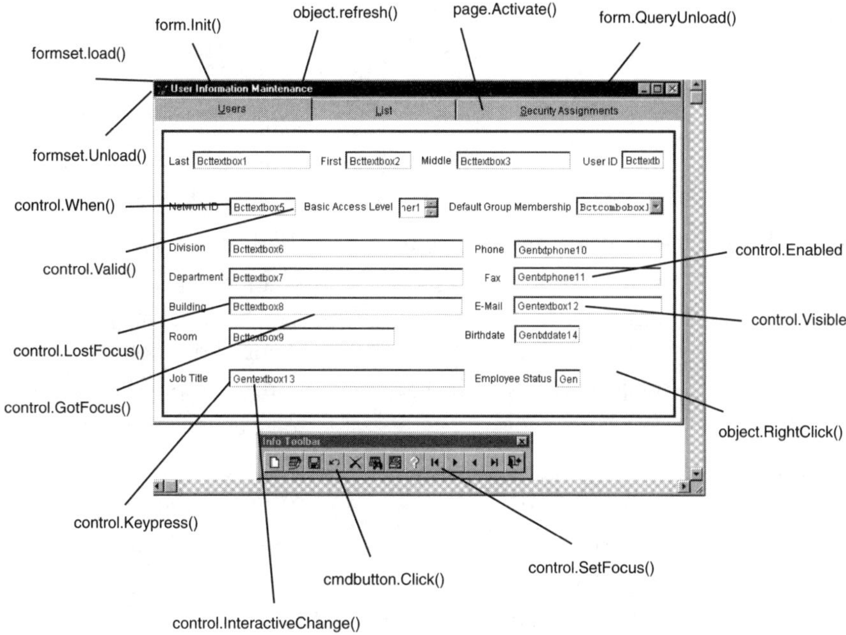

FIGURE 18.13 COMMONLY USED EVENT METHODS.

TABLE 18.1 COMMONLY USED METHODS AND EVENT METHODS

EVENT	DESCRIPTION	USE
Activate	Object is activated.	Test for entry conditions, set properties (Enable).
Click	Mouse click on object.	The main event, especially for action buttons.
GotFocus	Object receives program focus.	Validation of user access, may trigger chain of actions.
Init	At the creation of all objects.	The place for setup code, particularly for a form.
InteractiveChange	User changes a value.	Respond to change while user still in control.

(Continued...)

EVENT	DESCRIPTION	USE
KeyPress	Traps each user keystroke.	Monitor user input in TextBox.
Load	Form data loading.	Use for all data and environment setup outside of DE tables.
LostFocus	Object loses program focus.	Shutdown or change of status in control losing focus.
QueryUnload	Just before releasing a form.	Validate exit from form.
Refresh	Refresh data or screen image for most objects.	Routinely called whenever data or visual image is changed by another routine.
RightClick	Right mouse button clicked.	Initiate shortcut menus from most container objects.
SetFocus	Passes program control to specified object.	Direct user attention to particular controls.
Unload	On releasing form.	Cleanup code for a form.
Valid	Occurs on exiting a data entry control.	Data entry validation.
When	Just before entering a data entry control.	Validate user entry to a control.

TABLE 18.2 ROUTINELY USED PROPERTIES

PROPERTY	DESCRIPTION	USE
AutoSize	A control's box automatically sizes for the content.	Frequently used for TextBox and Command Button controls.
Caption	Set the title or caption.	For all labels, buttons, and objects with a prompt.
Comment	Status bar information.	Routine for user information.
Enabled	Enables and disables access.	Use **SetAll** or do individually.
Visible	Most objects.	Make controls visible only if needed.
Picture	Specify bitmap for control.	For command buttons and other bitmap or icon objects.
ToolTipText	Text for ToolTip.	Routine for user information.

PROPERTIES AND VARIABLES

One of the mental adjustments you need to make when working with forms involves the use of variables. In FoxPro procedural programming, the primary mechanism for storing programmatic data was with **PRIVATE** or **LOCAL** variables and arrays. Within the confines of a form, the programming is done in many event and user-defined methods, where traditional variables of the private or local variety don't survive going in and out of events. You could use global variables, but they are dangerous because they can persist beyond the form and are available all the time and everywhere. The solution is to define properties of the form.

This process sometimes feels different from creating properties for classes, but it's not. You use the **Form**, **New Property** options from the menu and enter one or more properties in the dialog box. After you create the properties, it's a good idea to go directly to the Properties window and enter initial values. The values of the properties are often changed in the **Init()** event method, which fires just before the form becomes visible.

One of the advantages of assigning properties to a form is that they will be automatically released when the form is destroyed. During the run of the form, they are accessible to other objects within and outside the form by use of the form's name for an object reference.

THE FORM INIT EVENT METHOD

The **Init()** method of the form is distinguished by being the only event method that takes user-defined parameters. Suppose you call a form with a command such as this one:

```
DO FORM myform NAME myform LINKED WITH 10, cName, user.last
```

The values after the **WITH** are arguments passed to parameter variables in the **Init()** of the form: `LPARAMETER tnUserCount, tcModuleName, tcUserLastName`. Keep in mind that these parameters do not persist beyond the **Init()**, so if you need them elsewhere in the form, transfer them to properties. Throughout the form remember that properties must be referenced to the form, usually with **THISFORM**. Here's typical code for an **Init()**, which often is used for various kinds of setup:

```
* Set property values from parameters
THISFORM.pnUserCount  = tnUserCount
THISFORM.pcCallModule = tcModuleName
THISFORM.pcUserLast   = tcUserLastName
THISFORM.SetAll("enabled",.F.)
* Instantiate special object for this form
ocstCalc = CREATEOBJECT("CALCTEST")
```

NOTE

Attach methods and expressions that evaluate to a property in the **Init()** method rather than in the Property window. This technique avoids potential evaluation problems during design time. For example, if you reference a UDF that doesn't yet exist or has a bug, the resulting crash could make it impossible for you to edit the form in the Form Designer.

MESSAGING THE USER

During the course of a working session in a form, a user needs at least three kinds of support:

1. **Identification**. Information about what a particular control does or what kind of entry is expected.
2. **Information in response to actions**. This includes warnings, status change information, and procedural dialog boxes.
3. **Help**. Access to the application help system.

The first type of user messaging should be a routine use of ToolTip text and status bar comments with these properties:

- **ShowToolTips**. For forms and toolbars.
- **ToolTipText**. For most controls.
- **CommentText**. For all controls.

The second type is open-ended, but most developers create a battery of standard messages for the **MESSAGEBOX( )** (see Chapter 17) and classes for a variety of standard dialog boxes.

The application help system is a topic in its own right (see Chapter 21). Specifically, in a form you will need to set the **HelpID** property of selected objects if you are using the standard Windows help system provided by FoxPro in the Professional Edition.

LEAVING THE FORM

As a program exits a form, it's usually necessary to have *cleanup* code that undoes, resets, or releases programming elements that were changed going into the form. This cleanup may be as simple as resetting the selected table or as complex as a battery of environmental changes, database changes, and release of variables or objects.

In most cases, there is little or nothing to be done in the individual controls. Most of the setup (**Init**) and cleanup action takes place at the level of the larger containers: Form, FormSet, PageFrame, and sometimes Grid. The usual location for cleanup code is in the **QueryUnload** or **Unload** event of the form. Let's look at some typical code (more samples are in the forms on the accompanying disk) with suggestions on what is appropriate.

The **QueryUnload** event is unique to a form and is designed to provide a way of determining whether the user can leave a form. Here's an example that checks for the exit and uses the **NODEFAULT** command to prevent the DE from unloading:

```
IF NOT THISFORM.BufferClear()
  *Ask user if OK to leave.
  IF NOT MESSAGEBOX(OK_LEAVE,276,"Exiting")
    NODEFAULT                && Do not unload data
    RETURN .F.
  ENDIF
ENDIF
```

Use the form **Unload()** event method for general cleanup related to the form:

```
THISFORM.Visible = .f.      && Quick exit from screen
IF TYPE(oTestBox)<>"U"
   RELEASE oTestBox
ENDIF
SET NEAR (THISFORM.NearSet)
SET EXACT (THISFORM.ExactSet)
```

RUNNING AND TESTING THE FORM

If there are no complications, Visual FoxPro can run a form from the Form Designer using the **Run** icon. This capability is handy and in the class hierarchy might apply to forms created with generic-level classes. However, for a real application that uses application-level forms, certain important external functions, variables, data tables, and so forth are not accessible to a form unless the whole application is running. Under these circumstances, you may need to build the form into an application file before running it.

When the form is running, you can use tools such as the Class Browser to monitor the objects in real time or use Command window statements to monitor and modify properties while the program is running. Here are some typical command expressions you can use:

```
_SCREEN.ActiveForm.BackColor = 200,200,200
_SCREEN.ActiveForm.cmdButton1.enabled = .f.
? _SCREEN.ActiveForm.BaseClass
? _SCREEN.ActiveForm.shpCircle.DrawMode
```

Notice the reference to the FoxPro "screen," **_SCREEN.ActiveForm**, which is necessary to sidestep the actual reference to an object within the running form. You can also use the expressions in the Watch window of the Debugger.

Debugging a running form presents some interesting quirks. Not only must you monitor the line-by-line execution of code, but also you must be aware of the relationships between objects. In standard procedural code, watching the values in variables change is standard debugging practice. You'll still need this approach, but it must be supplemented by examining values in properties and tracking the use of methods from one object to another.

WINDOWS

With the advent of fully object-oriented forms, there is little need for the old FoxPro "window" created with a **DEFINE WINDOW** command. A blank form is a blank window, after all, but with much more capability. However, it's in that regard—form as window—that a number of old functions that once were used to monitor windows are still useful with forms. They've been summarized next so that you'll be aware of their existence and potential use. The syntax details can be found in on-line help.

WEXIST(windowName)

If the named form exists (is defined), it returns `.T.`. Otherwise, it returns `.F.`.

WVISIBLE(windowName)

If the named form is visible, it returns `.T.`. Otherwise, it returns `.F.`.

WLAST([windowName])

Returns the name of the last form active on the screen.

WONTOP([windowName])

Returns the name of the form currently on the top of the screen.

WOUTPUT([windowName])

Returns the name of the form currently the active output form.

WMAXIMUM([windowName])

Returns `.T.` if current or named form is at full screen size; otherwise, it returns `.F.`.

WMINIMUM([windowName])

Returns `.T.` if current or named form is minimized; otherwise, it returns `.F.`.

With 40 options, defining a window is one of the monster commands in FoxPro. You will rarely, if ever, need to create a window instead of a form, so just be aware that there are a number of commands related to window management: **DEFINE WINDOW**, **SHOW WINDOW**, **HIDE WINDOW**, and **MODIFY WINDOW**.

GRIDS

The Visual FoxPro Grid control is so versatile that a book could be written about it. Yet the "queen of controls" (or "king" if you prefer) is not difficult to use, at least for routine tasks.

Like the FoxPro Browse window, the grid is essentially a row and column format—sometimes called a *spreadsheet* format—for displaying data. In a Browse window, the analogy to a spreadsheet is bogus because you have no good way to address an individual row and column junction (a *cell*, in spreadsheet lingo). With a grid, however, the ability to work not only with a cell but also with almost every aspect of the row and column structure has expanded the design potential immensely. You can move focus to cells, insert data in rows, rearrange columns, and perform a thousand other manipulations. This work can become complicated, but it opens the door to creative user interface programming.

As illustrated in Figure 18.14, a complete grid is composed of at least three objects: Grid, Column, and Header. And because controls can also be put in columns, it's clear that the Grid is a sophisticated set of containers. Sometimes this container relationship makes editing a grid cumbersome, particularly if you need to access embedded controls.

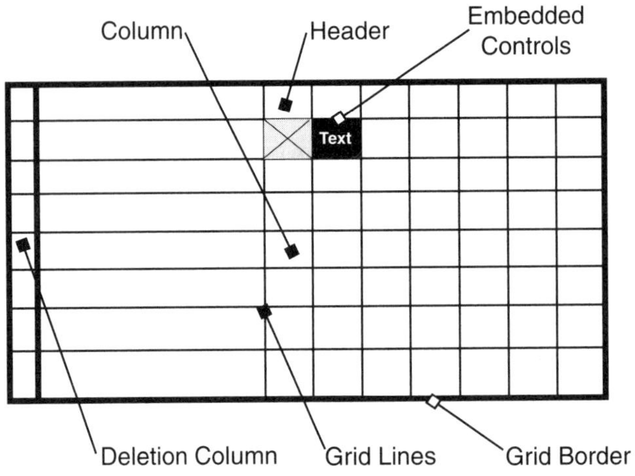

FIGURE 18.14 COMPONENTS OF A GRID.

Grids have other visual properties that are also easily enabled or disabled: grid lines (**GridLines**, **GridLineWidth**, **GridLineColor**), a column for marking deleted records (**DeleteMark**), scroll bars (**ScrollBars**), and a record marker (**RecordMark**). As with the Browse window, you can also set the grid with a partition (**Partition**, **Panel**, **PanelLink**), set the column width (**Width**), and change the fonts for columns, controls, and headers. In short, there's very little about a grid's appearance that you can't change.

ADDING A GRID TO A FORM

There are so many ways to enhance a grid that almost every developer has several variations, all of them classes in the class hierarchy. To install a class as a Grid object in a form, you have several approaches: Drag it from a class in the Project Manager, click the **Grid** button in the Form Controls toolbar, or drag a table from the Data Environment. This last approach works best if you've mapped the Grid object to a generic **Grid** class (such as **genGrid**) and want all or most of the fields of the table in the grid.

THE GRID BUILDER

Arguably, of all the wizards and builders provided by Visual FoxPro, the Grid Builder is the most useful and time-saving. Because many details are involved in setting up a multicolumn Grid—data sources, column content and width, header names, grid style, and so on—you can spend hours tracking down all the elements in the Property window. The Grid Builder does all this in minutes, and, best of all, it retains the inherited code you carefully created in a **Grid** class. To start the Grid Builder, select the grid, click the right mouse button, and from the shortcut menu select **Builder**.

One of the advantages of using the Grid Builder is that changes you make in working with its options are immediately reflected in the grid. This dynamic quality is much easier to accomplish in Visual FoxPro than older versions and is one of the benefits of the object-oriented approach. (By the way, the Grid Builder was created in Visual FoxPro.)

There are four areas covered by the Grid Builder (each one on a tab of a PageFrame Page): **Grid Items**, **Style**, **Layout**, and **Relationship**.

- **Grid Items**. Select the database (if it is not already open), table(s), and fields you want included in the Grid. The order you select them will be the order of the columns.
- **Style**. Choose one of the four default styles (professional, embossed, standard, and ledger), or keep the current style. This **Style** feature alone saves an enormous amount of work.

NOTE

One of the options in the **Style** tab—**<preserve current style>**—is another indication that this builder (unlike most wizards) respects user defined classes. Note too that as you try various styles, they are displayed in the grid of the Grid Builder. In the **Layout** tab, you can use the grid lines to adjust the column widths. All this is possible because the Grid Builder is using an actual FoxPro grid.

- **Layout**. In this tab you can set the caption for the header, the width of a column, and the type of control in the column. Note that using a control in a column is standard practice for Visual FoxPro. This sets the Header.**Caption** and Column.**Width** properties.
- **Relationship**. As is often the case, the Grid can be used for a listing of records in a child table related to a single record of a parent table. This is the familiar customer/orders, suppliers/parts, one-to-many scenario. You can create this relation and establish the data source for the Grid in the **Relationship** tab. It's recommended that you do this before you make the selection of grid items. This sets the **LinkMaster** and **ChildOrder** properties of the Grid.

By the time you click **OK** in the Grid Builder, your Grid is already changed and ready for any necessary tweaking. For this, you must resort to the manual property-by-property approach.

THE GRID'S DATA ENVIRONMENT

The relationship between a Grid and a table (or several tables) is based on the **RecordSource** property and to a certain extent on the **SourceType** property. The **RecordSource** specifies the name of the table used as the source of data. This approach allows only one table to be the source, so if you need to connect with multiple tables for a Grid display, you should use a query or a view cursor to pull together a single table. (You can, however, designate different tables for the columns and controls.) If you use a query, the **SourceType** can be set to **3 = Query .QPR**, and FoxPro will run the query before populating the Grid. The **SourceType** is also used to specify the following: **0 = Table** (or view cursor), **1 = Table Alias** (the default), and **2 = Prompt** (the user is prompted to select a table).

If you want to establish the Grid as part of child-parent relationship (as covered in the Grid Builder), you can use the **RecordSource** property of the Grid to name the child table, the **LinkMaster** property of the Grid for the parent table, and the **ChildOrder** property of the Grid to specify the index (tag) that links the parent and child tables. Finally, use the **RelationalExpr** property to enter the index expression used in the link.

Data for the grid columns is supplied by each column's **ControlSource** property. You can set this property using a normal ALIAS.FIELD format: `users.userid`. The same applies to the embedded controls, which must have the same data source as their column. The relationship between a column and any controls that it contains is set by the **Bound** property.

NOTE

This version of Visual FoxPro is sensitive to errors in grid data. If you specify a data source that doesn't exist or mix data sources for a column and its control, FoxPro is likely to generate an error message or even crash—as in suddenly, without warning and without a message—and return to the operating system.

GRID COLUMNS AND CONTROLS

A column is a container for controls. By default, a column will have only one control assigned to it—typically, a TextBox called TEXT1. You can work with it as a single control, but it functions as if every row of the grid contained that control. The reference to a column's control will be `THISFORM.genGrid.COLUMN1.TEXT1`.

A control in a column has all the same properties, events, and methods as it has in any other container. This means, for example, that all the data entry validation and support described for the TextBox control in Chapter 16 also applies to every TextBox cell in a grid.

When a data type is bound to a column, it also entails a default control—for example, a TextBox control for a character data column. The **ControlSource** for the column, in general, sets the data for the whole column. However, if the **Bound** property is set off, it is possible to set a different data type **ControlSource** for the control. Furthermore, you are not limited to one control per column, although only one can be active at a time.

Why would you want more than one control type for a column? The key to the answer involves the way a Visual FoxPro Grid can alter its manner of presentation to fit the needs of the data, the user, and the programmer. The following three examples (out of thousands of possible examples) show how a Grid can serve all three masters.

MULTIPLE CONTROLS IN A COLUMN

The default control for all grid columns is a TextBox. This control is not ideal for some kinds of data, and FoxPro allows you to substitute another control that is more appropriate. You can also substitute controls based on classes from the hierarchy, so you might replace a standard TextBox with a TextBox enhanced to handle dates. There's more. It's easy to come up with scenarios in which a different control might be used depending on the values in a field. For example, a Spinner control is used for date values less than 10, and a ComboBox for values expressed in increments of 10. Here's how.

First, add the two controls to the column and remove the default TextBox. This is not one of the most intuitive procedures in FoxPro, but it works. Follow these steps:

1. In the Designer window, select the grid column where the controls are to be added.
2. From the Form Controls toolbar, select a control and drop it into the column.
3. Repeat for the second control.

4. Go to the Properties window. In the object selector at the top, find and select the Text1 (the TextBox) that belongs to the column.
5. Activate the Designer window and press the **Del** key.

Incidentally, there's no technical reason for removing the original TextBox control; it's just good form. To manage the activation of controls, put code in the **DynamicCurrentControl** method of the column. This action sets the control to be used depending on the field value: `IIF(overdue<10,"SPINNER1","COMBOBOX1")`.

NOTE

The Column **Sparse** property plays an important role in the display of controls within the column. If **Sparse** is set to true (`.T.`), the control will be displayed only when the user enters the column. When it is set to false (`.F.`), the control will always be displayed in the column. In many cases, such as the preceding spinner example, it is advantageous to hide the control for general viewing.

Changing the Grid's Appearance

Although most layout properties are set at design time or can be changed until the object is created, the grid's dynamic properties can change each time the grid is refreshed (and you can call the **Refresh** method for that purpose). This capability is of enormous value in presenting data to the user, because you can do all sorts of highlighting to guide the user's attention to important information in the Grid.

The key to these properties is that they can take a conditional expression, usually the standard **IIF( )** or logical expression, and apply the property depending on how a field value evaluates in the expression. For example, to change the text to a bold font for all occurrences of "sale" in the field, you would use this code:

```
THIS.appGrid1.Column2.TextBox1.DynamicFontBold = ;
   IIF("sale"$descript, .T., .F.)
```

The dynamic properties are listed in Table 18.3.

Table 18.3 Dynamic Column Properties

Property	**Description**
DynamicAlignment	Alignment of text and controls in the column.
DynamicBackColor	Specify the background color for a column.
DynamicCurrentControl	Specify the control type to be used.

PROPERTY	DESCRIPTION
DynamicFontBold	Make current font bold.
DynamicFontItalic	Make current font italic.
DynamicFontName	Specify the font to be used for column text.
DynamicFontOutline	Make the font outlined.
DynamicFontShadow	Shadow the font.
DynamicFontSize	Change the font size.
DynamicFontStrikeThru	Strike through all characters.
DynamicFontUnderline	Underline all text.
DynamicForeColor	Specify the foreground (text) color for the column.
DynamicInputMask	Change the input mask of a TextBox.

GUIDING USER ACTIVITY IN A GRID

One of the classic problems in the old FoxPro Browse has been to shift the user from one column to another under program control. For example, let's say that the user is about to enter a value in column 4, but to do this the user needs to make an entry in column 2 (of the same record). If column 2 is empty, you want to display an error message and then move the Grid highlight back to column 2. Here are your tools:

- **ActiveRow**. This property returns the number of the currently active row of the Grid. This number is not the same as the record number.
- **ActiveColumn**. This property returns the number of the currently active column of the Grid, counting from left to right.
- **ActivateCell(nRow,nCol)**. This method sets the Grid cursor (highlight) to the specified row and column of the Grid.

As with a spreadsheet, the two properties and the method reference locations in a Grid using row and column coordinates. In the example at hand, you could put the following code in the control of column 4 using the event method **THISFORM.AppGrid1.Column4.TextBox1.GotFocus**:

```
IF NOT THISFORM.APPGRID1.CheckCol2()
  = MESSAGEBOX("Please enter an ID first.",0,"Error")
  nRow = THISFORM.AppGrid1.ActiveRow
```

```
    THISFORM.AppGrid1.ACTIVATECELL(nRow,2)
ENDIF
```

Drag and Drop

Drag and drop has become almost a household word. Because of its widespread use in Windows 95 and NT developers need to put this technique in their toolkit. In Visual FoxPro it's much easier to describe how to use drag and drop than to describe what it should do. You've seen many examples of drag and drop, particularly in dealing with files: Drag the icon of a word processing document to the icon of a word processing program, and the file will run. The essence of the operation, and the FoxPro implementation, is simple when laid out in a diagram (Figure 18.15).

You can execute a drag and drop with one or several objects. The single-object version is more like "drag and move," but it's the same operation. The first object is usually called the *source object*. By default, its **DragMode** property is set to 0, manual operation, which is normally where you'll leave it. The other mode, 1, is automatic, and that means the object can be dragged and dropped at any time. You have no control over whether or not that's appropriate.

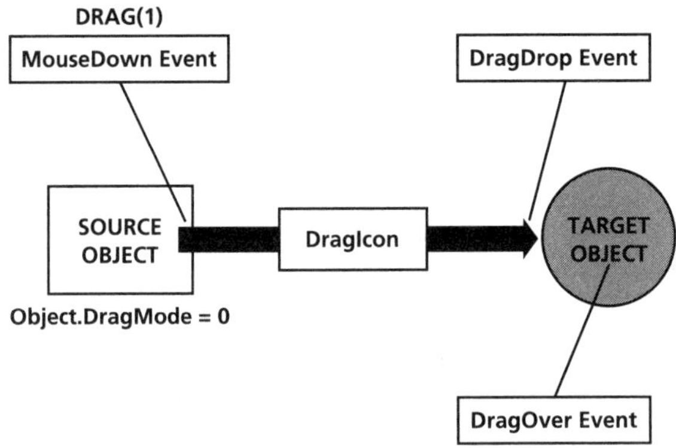

FIGURE 18.15 DRAG AND DROP.

In **DragMode** = 0, the drag-and-drop operation is triggered by putting `THIS.Drag(1)` in the **MouseDown** event method of the source object. When you click and hold with the mouse, **MouseDown** fires and the drag operation is started—that's the meaning of `Drag(1)`. The **DRAG( )** method has three parameters: 0 = no drag, 1 = start drag, and 2 = stop drag. Generally, only the 1 parameter is used, because merely releasing the mouse will drop the object and stop the drag.

NOTE

Don't confuse using the **DRAG( )** method this way with the **Drag** method listed in the object's **Methods** tab of the Property window. If you put code in the latter method, it will override the behavior of the default FoxPro method.

Once the drag is started, you can roam about the screen with the default "ghost shape" icon until you either drop the object on another object or simply move it. If you're working with a single object, all you need to do is to put this code into the **MouseDown** event method of the object:

```
LOCAL nHorizStart, nVertStart
nHorizStart = MCOL()-THIS.Left
nVertStart  = MROW()-THIS.Top

THIS.Drag(1)

THIS.Left = MCOL()-nHorizStart
THIS.Top  = MROW()-nVertStart
```

This code will move the object to the relative position of the mouse when the click is released.

A more interesting use of drag and drop involves at least two objects. The first, the source object, still receives `THIS.Drag(1)` in its **MouseDown** event. The second (target) object has a couple of options (refer again to Figure 18.15). To make the second object sensitive to drag and drop, you put code in either the **DragOver** or **DragDrop** event (or both).

The **DragOver** event is mostly used to inform users that they're "in the neighborhood" of an appropriate drop. In the code window of the **DragOver** event method, you'll see four parameters:

```
PARAMETERS oSource, nXCoord, nYCoord, nState
```

When a drag-enabled object passes over an object with an active **DragOver** method, the `oSource` parameter will contain the name of the source object. You can use this to find out the name, type, and almost anything else concerning the source object:

```
oSource.Name
oSource.Class
```

This information can be used to react to the object and determine whether it's appropriate to drop it, followed by some sort of signal to the user. If a finer reading of the first object's position is needed, the `nState` parameter has three values: 0 = Entering the object's region, 1 = Leaving the object's region, and 2 = Within the region. This might allow you to dynamically monitor the pass so that perhaps only when `nState=2` is reached will the second object react.

The **DragDrop** event method is handled in a similar fashion, except with three parameters:

```
PARAMETERS oSource, nXCoord, nYCoord
```

Again, you might use the `oSource` parameter to determine whether a drop is appropriate and notify the user; or simply process the drop using something like this:

```
DO CASE
CASE oSource.Class = "GRID"
  DO RuKidding()
CASE oSource.Name  = "shpShape1"
  DO TwistnShout
ENDCASE
```

While the mouse is in the drag position, the icon of the original object changes. By default, this is the ghost outline mentioned earlier, but you can change it to any kind of cursor icon you want. Use the **DragIcon** property to specify a CUR (cursor) file of your choosing. (You can't use ordinary BMP files.)

That's all there is to executing drag and drop. It's easy to implement and can be used in whatever ways you can imagine. With this feature, it's fun to set up a test form and have at it.

Chapter Wrap-Up

The user interface of a full-scale application might consist of 10–20 forms or form sets, 15 menus, five toolbars, 30 dialog boxes, one drag and drop enabled form, and 110 messages. Most of these elements contain large numbers of controls, and behind the scenes are the databases and the processing code. This does not describe a big application, but, even so, the numbers tell a tale. Building the user interface of an application is a big job.

As mentioned in Chapters 14 and 15, the class hierarchy is a dynamic product of both formal design and practical experience. Nowhere is this more relevant than in the creation of **Form** and **FormSet** classes and the controls that go into them. You may start by laying out a number of "standard" user interface elements and enhanced basic controls (command button groups with logic for navigating tables, or toolbars with basic action options). You might then incorporate sophisticated controls (Grids with incremental searching, and PageFrames with built-in Grids) and add complete Forms such as a class for a basic data form. As you work to build these elements, you'll need to put them into real applications, and there you will have to struggle between the specific needs of the application and the desire to create generic classes. That's why a class structure, and especially an application architecture, is in a constant state of flux.

CHAPTER 19

MASTERING THE DATABASE

For the last three chapters the topic has been the user interface, admittedly the predominant issue in most applications and the core of the object-oriented approach. But important aspects of the Visual FoxPro database system remain to be covered. For the next two chapters we will look into some of the advanced elements of the database management capability, finally completing the illustration in Figure 19.1.

This chapter explores the relationships between Visual FoxPro database elements and object-oriented programming. In some cases, such as cursors and Data Environments, the database elements are treated as objects. In other cases, such as file and record locking and transaction processing, the data management is almost wholly procedural.

The OOP relationship also covers some of the important extensions to the database, such as Memo and General fields. General fields are the key to the use of OLE objects and thereby a potential enhancement to many applications through connections to other Windows programs.

DATABASE ASPECTS OF OOP

Despite the incomplete alliance between object-oriented programming and the FoxPro data management system, a few points of connection are worth exploring. Most of these points involve working in and around forms and a handful of event methods: **BeforeOpenTables**, **Load**, **AfterCloseTables**, and **Unload**.

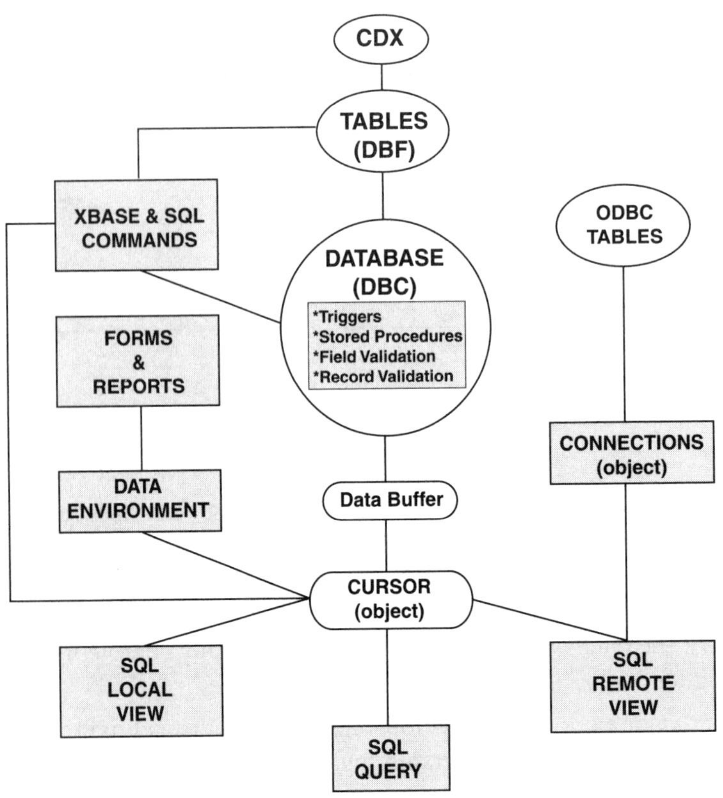

FIGURE 19.1 THE COMPLETE DATA MANAGEMENT SYSTEM.

It's good programming practice for a routine to respect the Data Environment that existed before its being called. This practice applies to forms and it means saving a record of the existing environment on the way into a form and restoring it on the way out. The ideal time to implement this practice is before the tables of the Data Environment have been opened and again after they've been closed: the **BeforeOpenTables** and **AfterCloseTables** event methods.

Because you should do this for every form—and in many other places—it should trigger a little voice in your head that says, "It's generic. Make a class." In the scheme used for this book, such as class belongs in the generic data class category (GENDATA.VCX), because it can be instantiated anywhere in an application and doesn't require extra tables or other application-oriented machinery. As usual, the custom class is presented here in code form:

```
DEFINE CLASS SetReset AS CUSTOM
  *Accessible Properties
  pcSetAlias  = ""
  pcSetOrder  = ""
  pcSetExact  = ""
  pcSetDelete = ""
  pcSetLock   = ""

  *Protected Properties
  PROTECTED pnRecno
  pnRecno = 0

  PROCEDURE Init
    THIS.pcSetAlias  = ALIAS()
    THIS.pcSetOrder  = ORDER()
    THIS.pnRecno     = RECNO()
    THIS.pcSetExact  = SET("EXACT")
    THIS.pcSetDelete = SET("DELETE")
    THIS.pcSetLock   = SET("LOCK")
  ENDPROC
  PROCEDURE Destroy
  LOCAL lcSetAlias,lcSetOrder,lnRecno,lcSetExact,;
        lcSetDel, lcSetLock
    IF NOT EMPTY(THIS.pcSetAlias)
      lcSetAlias = THIS.pcSetAlias
      SELECT (lcSetAlias)
      IF NOT EMPTY(THIS.pcSetOrder)
        lcSetOrder = THIS.pcSetORder
        SET ORDER TO &lcSetOrder
      ENDIF
      IF THIS.pnRecno <> 0
        lnRecno = THIS.pnRecno
        GO lnRecno
      ENDIF
      IF NOT EMPTY(THIS.pcSetExact)
        lcSetExact = THIS.pcSetExact
        SET EXACT &lcSetExact
      ENDIF
      IF NOT EMPTY(THIS.pcSetDelete)
        lcSetDel=THIS.pcSetDelete
```

```
      SET DELETE &lcSetDel
    ENDIF
    IF NOT EMPTY(THIS.pcSetLock)
      lcSetLock = THIS.pcSetLock
      SET LOCK &lcSetLock
    ENDIF
  ENDIF
 ENDPROC
ENDDEFINE
```

If you instantiate this class within an event method, it will come and go within that method. Understanding why is important. When you instantiate a class, you normally assign it to a variable: `oSetReset = CREATEOBJECT("SETRESET")`. This code creates a variable within the method; when the method finishes, the variable is released. When the variable is released, **SetReset** is released and its **Destroy** method resets the environment. Because you want **SetReset** to work for the duration of the form, this approach won't work in a form's methods. Instead, you need to use a user-defined property of the form, such as `poSetReset`.

Classes that have global (application-wide) use are often instantiated in the initialization of the application, and then its members (properties, methods, and events) can be called from other objects within the application. In this case, as an alternative approach, you could create the `oSetReset` object in the initialization file. Then placing a call to `oSetReset.Init()` in the **BeforeTableOpen** method of the form's Data Environment accomplishes the task, as does `oSetReset.Destroy()` in the **AfterTableClose** event of the DE.

NOTE

The **SetReset** class can easily be expanded to include a wide variety of **SET**s and other environmental setup and cleanup tasks. Concerning other database and table-related classes, you might want to take a look at **genDBC**, **genTable**, and **genRecord** in the GENDATA.VCX library.

The Database as Object

A FoxPro database is not an object. In keeping with the approach in other parts of FoxPro, however, you can deal with the database in ways similar to the way you deal with an object, principally with the **DBGETPROP( )** and **DBSETPROP( )** functions.

DBGETPROP() AND DBSETPROP()

In most respects. these functions are identical except that one gets property values and the other sets them. (There are also a few read-only properties that show up only in **DBGETPROP( )**.) As you look through Tables 19.1, 19.2, and 19.3, notice that **DBSETPROP( )** works only for those properties marked RW (read/write). You'll probably notice that these are the same settings and properties you encountered in the Database Designer and Table Designer. Using these functions, you can view their settings from within program code. **DBGETPROP( )** returns a property for the current database or for the fields, named connections, tables, or views in the current database. **DBSETPROP( )** allows you to set some of the same properties.

Command syntax:

DBGETPROP(cName, cType, cProperty)

DBSETPROP(cName, cType, cProperty, ePropertyValue)

Arguments:

cName The name of the database, field, connection, table, or view.

cType The type of item: CONNECTION, DATABASE, FIELD, TABLE, or VIEW.

cProperty The name of the property to return.

ePropertyValue The value to be set for the property.

Examples:

```
IF DBGETPROP("CAPTION","FIELD")<> "RESULTS"
   =DBSETPROP("CAPTION","FIELD","RESULTS")
ENDIF
```

TABLE 19.1 DBGETPROP() AND DBSETPROP() FOR DATABASE PROPERTIES

PROPERTY	CODE	READ/WRITE STATUS	DESCRIPTION
Comment	C	RW	The text of the database comment.
Version	C	RW	The database version number.

TABLE 19.2 DBGETPROP() AND DBSETPROP() FOR FIELD PROPERTIES

PROPERTY	CODE	READ/WRITE STATUS	DESCRIPTION
Caption	C	RW	The field caption.
Comment	C	RW	The text of the field comment.
DefaultValue	C	RO	The default field value.
RuleExpression	C	RO	The field validation rule expression (logical).
RuleText	C	RO	The error message for field validation.

TABLE 19.3 DBGETPROP() AND DBSETPROP() FOR TABLE PROPERTIES

PROPERTY	CODE	READ/WRITE STATUS	DESCRIPTION
Comment	C	RW	The text of the table comment.
DeleteTrigger	C	RO	The DELETE trigger expression.
InsertTrigger	C	RO	The INSERT trigger expression.
Path	C	RO	The table's path.
PrimaryKey	C	RO	The name of the table's primary key (tag).
RuleExpression	C	RO	The record validation expression.
RuleText	C	RO	The error message for the record validation.
UpdateTrigger	C	RO	The UPDATE trigger expression.

Both of these functions are typical of language that's aimed at developers who want to hack the innards of major FoxPro elements, such as like databases, to create their own utilities and supplementary programs. In day-to-day application programming, functions such as **DBGETPROP( )** and **DBSETPROP( )** are used infrequently to provide bits of information for data processing routines.

CURSOR: THE TABLE AS OBJECT

Like the database, a cursor is not truly an object, but it is one of the family—Data Environments, cursors, connections, and relations—that Visual FoxPro treats as a kind of object because its members have properties, events, and methods. To verify this, open any form with a defined DE and select one of the tables. Then open the Properties window and you'll see a number of members defined:

- Events: **Init**, **Destroy**, and **Error** (the minimum set).
- Data properties: **Alias**, **Name**, **Database**, **Read Only**, **BufferMode Override**, **Exclusive**, **NoDataOnLoad**, **CursorSource**, **Filter**, and **Order**. Only the last two may be changed during the run of a program (run time).

A cursor, for all practical purposes, *is* a table. Whether it was created by a SQL View or you used the **CREATE CURSOR** command, a cursor can be used in most situations just as a normal table can be used. However, when you close a cursor, it vanishes along with all its contents. Here's the basic syntax:

Command syntax:

CREATE CURSOR name (fieldname1 [, fieldname2 ...)| FROM ARRAY ArrayName

Arguments:

dbf_name Name of the cursor, as a DBF, although it's not really a file.

fieldname1 The definition of each field requires a minimum of **fieldname** (field name), **type** (field type), and **Precision**. The latter is the same as the width setting and is required for character fields, although you should use it on all fields as a matter of good documentation.

Example:

```
CREATE CURSOR newresult (sampleid C(8), userid C(4),;
   testdate D(8) DEFAULT DATE(), result N(8,3) CHECK ;
   BETWEEN( result, 1200, 1800) ERROR "Check your entry!")
```

Many times during data processing, or even in user interface programming, you may need a scratch table for temporary storage. The property of self-eradication makes the **CREATE CURSOR** command a prime candidate for creating any kind of temporary table.

CURSORGETPROP() AND CURSORSETPROP()

Despite their names, **CURSORGETPROP( )** and **CURSORSETPROP( )** are not for cursors only; they work equally well for "normal" tables. They also work just like their database counterparts, **CURSORGETPROP( )** retrieves values, and **CURSORSETPROP( )** sets values for non–read-only properties.

Command syntax:

CURSORGETPROP(cProperty [, nWorkArea | cTableAlias])

CURSORSETPROP(cProperty [, eExpression] [, cTableAlias | nWorkArea])

Arguments:

cProperty The name of the property.

EExpression For **CURSORSETPROP**, the value to be set.

CTableAlias Specifies the table name (alias).

NWorkArea Specifies the work area, as a number.

Examples:

```
IF CURSORGETPROP("Buffering")=0
   =CURSORSETPROP("Buffering",2)
ENDIF
```

As with **DBSETPROP( )**, only the RW (read/write) properties can be used by **CURSORSETPROP()**. Many of the properties (see Table 19.4) are for managing remote (ODBC) connections, which will be covered in Chapter 20. However, **Buffering** is commonly used in all kinds of programming situations.

TABLE 19.4 CURSORGETPROP() AND CURSORSETPROP() PROPERTIES

PROPERTY	CODE	READ/WRITE STATUS	DESCRIPTION
BatchUpdateCount	N	RW	The number of update statements sent to the back end for buffered tables. 1 is the default. Adjusting this value can greatly increase update performance.
Buffering	N	RW	1 = (Default) Row and table buffering is off. 2 = Pessimistic row buffering is on. 3 = Optimistic row buffering is on. 4 = Pessimistic table buffering is on. 5 = Optimistic table buffering is on.
SET MULTILOCKS must be **ON** for 2–5.			
ConnectHandle	N	RO	The FoxPro connection handle (name).
ConnectName	C	RO	The named (FoxPro) connection used to create the cursor.
Database	C	RO	The name of the database (DBC) for the view.
FetchMemo	L	RW	If true (`.t.`), Memo fields are retrieved with view.

Property	Code	Read/Write Status	Description
FetchSize	N	RW	The number of records retrieved from a remote source. Default = 100; –1 returns all records in result set.
KeyFieldList	C	RW	Comma-delimited list of primary fields for cursor. Required.
MaxRecords	N	RW	Maximum number of records that can be fetched. Default = –1 all records, 0 = no records fetched but view is run.
SendUpdates	L	RW	If true (`.t.`), SQL update query is sent to remote tables.
SourceName	C	RO	The long name of the SQL view or free table.
SourceType	N	RO	1 = Local SQL view 2 = Remote SQL view 3 = Table
SQL	C	RO	The full SQL statement executed to create the cursor.
Tables	C	RW	A comma-delimited list of the remote table names. Required.
UpDatableFieldList	C	RW	Comma-delimited list of remote field names (and local field names) for the cursor.

PROPERTY	CODE	READ/WRITE STATUS	DESCRIPTION
UpdateNameList	C	RW	Comma-delimited list of fields in the view (local and remote).
UpdateType	N	RW	1 = Old data updated with new data. 2 = Record is deleted and new data is inserted as new record.
UseMemoSize	N	RW	Size of column that will trigger the creation of a FoxPro Memo field. Default = 255 characters.
WhereType	N	RW	**WHERE** clause for updating remote tables (constants from FOXPRO.H): 1 or **DB_KEY**. Update remote tables for only the primary fields specified with the **KeyFieldList** property. 2 or **DB_KEYANDUPDATABLE**. Update remote tables for primary fields specifiied with the **KeyFieldList** property and any updatable fields.

(Continued...)

PROPERTY	CODE	READ/WRITE STATUS	DESCRIPTION
WhereType *(cont.)*	N	RW	3 or **DB_KEYANDMODIFIED** (default). Update remote tables for the primary fields specified with the **KeyField List** property and any other fields that are modified. 4 or **DB_KEYANDTIMESTAMP**. Update remote tables for the primary fields specified with the **Key FieldList** property and a comparison of the time stamps.

DATABASE-RELATED EVENTS, METHODS, AND PROPERTIES

Included in the list of things Visual FoxPro treats as objects are the Data Environments. This may seem a little strange, but a DE is really just another form of container. It holds cursors and relations—objects.

QUERYUNLOAD CODE

As mentioned in Chapter 18, **QueryUnload** is the event method in which you should ask users whether they really want to leave the form, because you have the option of using **NODEFAULT** to avoid unloading the data sources and then return to the form. Another aspect of **QueryUnload** may be useful: monitoring how the user is leaving the form. This option is based on using the form **ReleaseType** property, which is set just before **QueryUnload**(Table 19.5).

TABLE 19.5 FORM EXIT OPTIONS

ACTION	RELEASETYPE VALUE	QUERYUNLOAD CALLED
QUIT	2	Yes
CLEAR WINDOWS	1	Yes
RELEASE WINDOWS	1	Yes
Click Close Box	1	Yes
RELEASE THISFORM	0	No

Based on how the user appears to be exiting the form, you might want to intercept with code such as this:

```
*Might be accidental closure of form window
IF THISFORM.ReleaseType = 1
   nReply = MESSAGEBOX("OK to quit?", 292, "Exiting")
   DO CASE nReply = 6
     RELEASE THISFORM
   CASE nReply = 7
     NODEFAULT
   ENDCASE
ENDIF
```

CONSIDERING Z-ORDER

Here's a hypothetical, but common, situation: On your form you have a TextBox that you wish to disable if a certain condition is true—for example, if a payment is later than 30 days and you don't want a NEWORDER field to be used. You've put the following code into the **Refresh** event method of the NEWORDER TextBox so that it will be updated whenever the **REFRESH( )** method is used:

```
=DODEFAULT()
THIS.Enabled = invoice.orderdate > DATE()-30 AND;
  EMPTY(invoice.datepaid)
```

If the ORDERDATE is more than 30 days old and the bill is not yet paid, the expression evaluates to false and the NEWORDER TextBox will be disabled.

Notice the call to the **DODEFAULT( )** method. It's important to underline that putting your code in an event method that has default FoxPro behavior will override that behavior, resulting in unpleasant side effects. Frequently, the solution is to use **DODEFAULT( )**, which searches up the class hierarchy until it finds the default code (even in FoxPro itself) and frees you from trying to figure out where that code is located. But this approach might not work as you expect because of the **ZOrder** property.

The tab order of a form is the sequence of controls that are activated as someone moves through the form with the **Tab** or **Enter** key. **ZOrder** is a similar concept, but it applies to the order in which the controls are refreshed from their data source (presuming they are bound to a table field). By default, the **ZOrder** of a control derives from *when* it was placed on the form. It also relates to the physical placement of controls on a form: whether one control is considered on top of another control. Controls that were added to the form last and are on top are the last ones to be refreshed.

In the example, let's say that ORDERDATE and PAIDDATE were added to the form after the NEWORDER TextBox. This means that they will refresh after NEWORDER, and consequently the expression in NEWORDER will not evaluate with new data. The fix is to send the NEWORDER TextBox to the front of the **ZOrder** so that it will be among the last to refresh (or send ORDERDATE and PAIDDATE to the back). To do this, select the text boxes. From the Layout toolbar, use the **Send to Front** icon, or use the system menu: **Format**, **Send to Front**.

Programming Table and Record Locks

Chapter 18 introduced the subject of file and record locking in a multiuser environment. There, most of the conditions were set and maintained by FoxPro itself within the new data buffering system. This approach covers the majority of requirements for safe and accurate data management in your applications; but "majority" isn't everything when a few altered decimal points or a clutch of trashed records might ruin a report or even a company.

It's the responsibility of the application programmer to handle the various situations that arise in a network setting. This responsibility includes not only various forms of file and record locking but also the resolution of conflicts between users who either have locked or want to lock records or files simultaneously.

WHAT FOXPRO WILL DO

FoxPro, like most other multiuser database management software, has a built-in file and record locking capability for running on a network and multiuser system. However, one locking mechanism is *not* on by default: **SET LOCKS**. This command controls the locking of table operations such as **COUNT** and **REPORT FORM**, in which you may not want to allow update while processing is in progress. When designing your locking strategies, it's important to understand which locking FoxPro will do automatically and what it will or won't do if you SET LOCKS ON. Table 19.6 summarizes what FoxPro does.

TABLE 19.6 FOXPRO FILE AND RECORD LOCKING

COMMAND	WHAT'S LOCKED	SET LOCKS ON
APPEND	Table	
APPEND BLANK	Table header	
APPEND FROM	Table	
APPEND FROM ARRAY	Table header	
APPEND MEMO	Current record	
AVERAGE	Not locked	Table
BROWSE,CHANGE,EDIT	Current records in all related tables	
CALCULATE	Not locked	Table
COPY TO	Not locked	Table
COPY TO ARRAY	Not locked	Table
COUNT	Not locked	Table
DELETEIRECALL	Current record	
DELETEIRECALL NEXT 1	Current record	
DELETEIRECALL RECORD	Record <number>	
DELETEIRECALL SCOPE>1	Table	
DELETE TAG	Table (EXCLUSIVE)	
DISPLAY SCOPE > 1	Not locked	Table
GATHER	Current record	

(Continued...)

COMMAND WHAT'S LOCKED SET LOCKS ON

COMMAND	WHAT'S LOCKED	SET LOCKS ON
INDEX (new)	Table (EXCLUSIVE)	
INDEX (existing)	Not locked	Table
INSERT BLANK	Table (EXCLUSIVE)	
INSERT-SQL	Table header	
JOIN	Not locked	Table
LIST	Not locked	Table
LABEL	Not locked	Table
MODIFY MEMO	Current record	
MODIFY STRUCTURE	Table (EXCLUSIVE)	
PACK	Table (EXCLUSIVE)	
READ EVENT	Data buffering applies	
REINDEX	Table (EXCLUSIVE)	
REPLACE	Current record and records of all aliased fields	
REPLACE NEXT 1	Current record and records of all aliased fields	
REPLACE RECORD <n>	Current record and records of all aliased fields	
REPLACE SCOPE > 1	Table	
REPORT	Not locked	Table
SORT	Not locked	Table
SUM	Not locked	Table
TOTAL	Not locked	Table
UPDATE	Table	
ZAP	Table (EXCLUSIVE)	

NOTE

You can also use this table as a general guide that indicates when locking is necessary, whether locking is automatic or manual.

Looking at Table 19.6, it would be an easy conclusion to say, "Great. Let Fox do it." And perhaps you will, but you should also know the limitations of automatic locking.

- The automatic locks don't always do the locking at the right time and sometimes don't lock at all. This is particularly true in database processing, during updating and maintenance. The automatic locking can't always follow a chain of relations during file processing and put locks on all related records. Occasionally, FoxPro will attempt to do a file lock when it should do only a record lock. Sometimes the sequence of your processing, moving from table to table, will confuse the locking process.
- Automatic locking can make it difficult to trap lock errors properly. Assuming that you have an application error trapping routine, any errors in locking, such as time-outs, too many retries, and unresolved contention, should be trapped, whether from automatic or manual locking. However, with automatic locking it may be difficult to know exactly where the lock failed, and that can make it hard to clean up or respond to the error. If you lock manually, at each manual lock you can create a specific **ON ERROR** response if necessary.
- You have no control over the sequence of locking and unlocking.

Do-It-Yourself Locking

The issues of when to apply locks and for how long spill over into the decisions about automatic versus manual locking. This section aims to show that doing it yourself is easy.

There's one crucial setting for all multiuser locking:

SET REPROCESS TO nAttempts [SECONDS] I TO AUTOMATIC]

This sets the number of times FoxPro will attempt to complete a lock. It can make about three tries per second, depending on hardware, or you can use the optional **SECONDS** clause to have it do one per second (recommended). You can use numbers from –2 to 32,000. Yes, –2 and even –1 or 0. These settings have special meanings: –2 is equivalent to **AUTOMATIC**, and 0 = Forever (an infinite number of retries, the default). If you ever use this setting, you should be prepared to trap for "Attempting to lock" errors, and you should let the user escape if necessary. The –1 setting is much more draconian. The attempts continue indefinitely, no error is generated, and **Esc** can't be used to cancel the attempt. Try this one at home, but not on the users.

Use –2,–1, or 0 only when you know exactly why you're using them. Most of the time, a reasonable number (1, 2, 5, or 10) is better, especially if you're using **SECONDS**. Make the number larger if the locking is an off-hours processing routine; make it smaller when interactive user activity is involved. Remember that functions such as **FLOCK( )** and **LOCK( )** don't kick in and return false (.F.) until **SET REPROCESS** has exhausted its retries.

In a other instances, you will also need to use **SET MULTILOCKS ON**, so it's a good idea to do this with **SET REPROCESS** as a matter of routine.

File Locking

Fortunately, file locking is not required very often during user activity. Standard data entry and grids use record level locks, if any. Locking an entire file in a multiuser environment can be disruptive, and it might be difficult to get a file lock established on a busy network. Most applications avoid operations that require exclusive use of a file or file locks within the interactive user portions. The usual advice is to save the processing and maintenance routines, which usually require file locking, for times when there are no users on the system.

This being the case, it pays to analyze your processing routines to optimize them for speed. This means using **SET EXCLUSIVE ON** or opening files **EXCLUSIVE**, for those files involved with updating, and using the **NOUPDATE** (read-only) clause for lookup files. For example:

```
USE samples  ALIAS sam ORDER sampleid EXCLUSIVE IN 0
USE testcode ALIAS tcd ORDER testid   NOUPDATE  IN 0
```

If this technique isn't possible, you can fall back on the file locking function.

Command syntax: **FLOCK([nWorkArea | cTableAlias])**

Arguments:

nWorkArea Number of the work area to lock.

cTableAlias Alias of the work area to lock.

Examples:

```
=FLOCK("ANALYTES")
```

Returns: `.T.` if the file is locked, and `.F.` if not.

Like all the locking functions, **FLOCK( )** will attempt to set a file lock for the number of retries in **SET REPROCESS TO**. If it fails and returns `.F.`, you'll need to handle that eventuality in the program: Cancel further processing and notify the operator.

Now is a good time to throw in the command that removes locks:

UNLOCK [IN nWorkArea|cTableAlias] | ALL

Although FoxPro will automatically remove record locks when the table pointer is moved and will unlock files when a command is complete, it's a good habit to include an explicit **UNLOCK** with every manual lock. It guarantees the shortest amount of lock time, documents the duration of the lock, and is easy to do:

```
IF FLOCK( )
  DELETE ALL
  UNLOCK
ENDIF
```

A simple method, attached to a generic data class (GENDATA.VCX), can be created to do the file lock, and it can set and reset the **SET REPROCESS TO** value to control how long the program should wait for a successful lock.

In a **FileLock()** method, use this code:

```
FUNCTION FileLock
LPARAMETERS tnSetReproc
IF PARAMETERS() < 1
  tnSetReproc = 5
ENDIF
LOCAL lnOldReproc,lis_ret
lnOldReproc = SET("REPROCESS")
SET REPROCESS TO (tnSetReproc) SECONDS

lis_ret = FLOCK()
```

```
SET REPROCESS TO (lnOldReproc) SECONDS
RETURN lis_ret
*
```

To call it, use `oGenData.FileLock(10)`.

RECORD LOCKING

The mix of automatic and manual locking for records is a bit more problematic than for file locking. There are three principal situations: in a grid, during table operations (**DELETE**, **REPLACE**), and within forms.

Inside a grid it's customary to let FoxPro do the locking, simply because so many records are exposed. If necessary, you can put explicit locking into a grid or **BROWSE** through the **WHEN** event (turn on locking) and **VALID** event (turn off locking). This approach is used mostly to lock related records rather than for the primary table.

For table operations whose scope is a single record—typically, **REPLACE** and **APPEND**—the manual approach involves the record lock command:

Command syntax:

RLOCK(cAlias | [cRecordNumberList,cAlias])

Arguments:

cTableAlias Alias of work area to lock record.

cRecordNumberList A list of record numbers to lock. Requires **SET MULTILOCKS ON**.

Examples:

```
=RLOCK()
=RLOCK("TESTCODE")
SET MULTILOCKS ON
=RLOCK(1,2,5,7,"RESULTS")
```

Returns: `.T.` if the record is locked, `.F.` if the locking fails.

As with the **FLOCK( )** function, it's common to create a simple method to add a bit more capability to the record locking function.

In a **RecLock()** method, use the following code:

```
FUNCTION RecLock
LPARAMETERS tnSetReproc
IF PARAMETERS() < 1
  tnSetReproc = 5
ENDIF

LOCAL lnOldReproc, llret, llerr
llerr = .F.
lnOldReproc = SET("REPROCESS")
SET REPROCESS TO (tnSetReproc) SECONDS

*======================>> TRY THE LOCK
llret = RLOCK()

SET REPROCESS TO (lnOldReproc) SECONDS
RETURN llret
*
```

To call it, use `oGenData.RecLock(2).`

In table operations that involve complex relations, manual locks are frequently used. For the most part, FoxPro will not be able to follow a relational tree and lock all the relevant records. Use of a manual lock and unlock for almost all the commands that require a record lock is the only way to guarantee the shortest possible duration for the lock.

Creating ID Numbers

A good example of manual locking involves the creation of ID numbers. Most applications encounter the need to create IDs—unique numbers or other identification sequences. In fact, the classic advice for relational database systems is to make as many table relations based on a pure ID key as possible.

Creating a sequence of IDs isn't hard, especially if you're using a purely numeric ID. You just increment it by 1 for each new record. But in a multiuser environment, there's a complication: How can you be sure that an ID is absolutely unique while multiple users might be creating IDs at the same time? You need a way to store the current ID, making it available to multiple users. You also need a way to make sure that the ID each user gets is unique. There are several ways to do this. Here's one method:

1. Create a table to hold sequence numbers—for example, SEQUENCE.DBF (Table 19.7).

TABLE 19.7 SEQUENCE.DBF

FIELD	TYPE	SIZE	DESCRIPTION
SEQNAME	C	10	Sequence name (or ID type), primary key.
SEQNUM	N	6	The sequence number or current ID stub.
SYSDATE	D	8	Date incremented or updated.
SYSTIME	C	5	Time incremented or updated.
OPERATOR	C	4	ID of operator.

Whether the SEQNUM field is numeric or character depends on your approach to the IDs. Most experts on relational systems recommend using pure IDs that have no meaning. The classic approach is the familiar sequence of numbers ("000325"), which is padded left with zeros so that the sequences will sort in proper order.

2. Create a user-defined function as a stored procedure in the database file. Use it to access the sequence file and create the ID. The key to this procedure is to lock the sequence number while it is being updated. In practice, this takes only a short time and presents no problem in the usual data entry environment. However, if your data entry is a computer process, which is many times faster, you'll need to check this routine to make sure it doesn't become a bottleneck in your application.

   In stored procedures, use this code:

```
FUNCTION IdMake
LPARAMETERS tcSeqName

LOCAL lcId, lcIdAlias
lcId      = ""
oSR = CREATEOBJECT("SETRESET")  &&preserve file environment
```

```
* Open the sequence file
IF NOT USED("SEQUENCE")
  USE sequence ORDER seqname
ELSE
  SELECT sequence
ENDIF

* Lookup the sequence name
IF SEEK( tcSeqName )
  * Lock and load
  IF oGenData.RecLock(10)
    REPLACE seqnum WITH seqnum + 1
    lcId = PADL(ALLTRIM(STR(seqnum)),"0",8)
    UNLOCK
  ENDIF
ENDIF
RETURN lcId
*
```

Here is how to use it in a field replace:

```
REPLACE field WITH PADL(ALLTRIM(STR(IdMake("field"))),8,"0")
```

Field Locking

Once in a while, and more often in financial/accounting applications, it may be necessary to lock a field and not the whole record—for example, in transaction-intensive applications where several data entry people may be working with the same record at the same time, either because the record is very large (has many fields) or because there aren't many records (or both). FoxPro has no provision for field locking. Fortunately the work-around is simple, although it adds overhead to the table and your program.

For each field you wish to lock, you add a companion logical field. For example:

```
FINRESULT     N   9
RESULTLOCK    L   1
```

In the form, you add the following code to the **When** event of the field TextBox:

```
IF NOT resultlock
  IF oGenData.RecLock(5)
    REPLACE resultlock WITH .T.
    RETURN .T.
  ELSE
    RETURN .F.
  ENDIF
ELSE
  WAIT WINDOW "Field not available for update." NOWAIT
  RETURN .T.
ENDIF
```

This code prevents entry into the field if it is already locked. If it is not locked, this code puts a lock on the field. When the user is finished editing the field, you reverse the lock with a few lines in the **Valid** event method:

```
IF oGenData.RecLock(5)
  REPLACE finresult   WITH nResult;
          resultlock  WITH .F.
  UNLOCK
ENDIF
```

Working with the Data Buffer

Assuming that most applications will run on networks and are multiuser in nature, your database will spend much of its time with the FoxPro data buffering enabled. This means that you will also have to deal with the buffer as an entity. Refer to Figure 19.2 and bear the following in mind:

- Data buffering is most often enabled at the Form level. Set the form's **BufferMode** to 0 (FoxPro 2.x style), 1 (pessimistic locking), or 2 (optimistic locking). FoxPro handles the record vs. table type of locking by automatically making all bound controls record locks and treating grids as table locks.
- You can explicitly enable buffering for *each* table in or out of a Data Environment. In a DE, you use the **BufferModeOverride**; with any table, you use **CURSORSETPROP()**.

- When you turn on data buffering for a table, you are no longer directly accessing the table at any time. If you append records, for example, they go into the buffer and not into the table. Another example: When you edit records in a grid, the records are in the buffer, no matter how many rows are visible in the grid.
- When table buffering is enabled, it does not mean that the whole table is buffered; it means that as you add or edit, each record is stored in the buffer until you issue **TABLEUPDATE( )** or **TABLEREVERT( )**.

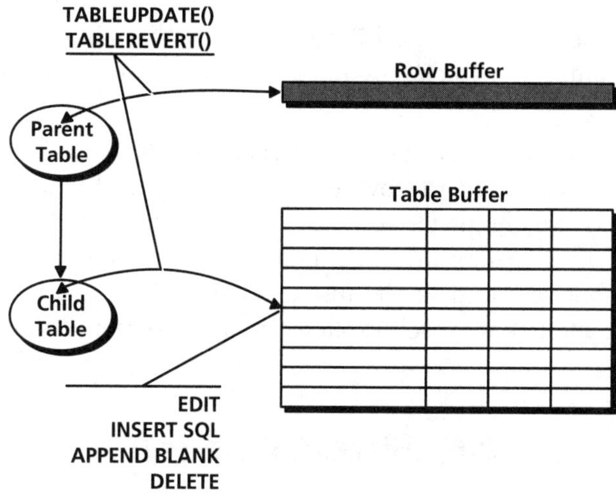

FIGURE 19.2 TABLE AND ROW BUFFERING.

Although the data buffer is not officially an object, it is part and parcel of the cursor management system, a special function of Visual FoxPro. If you want to do something with or know something about the data buffer for a table, you can use the same tools used for a cursor—with some important peculiarities when compared with direct access to tables.

The most interesting difference is what comes back from the **RECNO( )** function after you've added a record to a table buffer: a negative number! Each record added (with either **APPEND BLANK** or **INSERT SQL**) will be one more negative number: –1, –2, –3, and so on. This arrangement is actually helpful, because at a glance or with simple programming you can tell the difference between original records and added records.

This straightforward system for adding records becomes much more circuitous for deletions. You can use **DELETE** in a cursor or buffer in any way you would in a regular table, but what happens after that may vary:

- If a regular record is deleted, use **TABLEREVERT( )** to remove it.
- If an added record is deleted, its record number becomes invalid.
- Using **TABLEREVERT( )** removes all added records, including deletions.
- If you don't remove them, **TABLEUPDATE( )** will write all deleted records to the table.

To navigate in the buffer, the **GOTO** command has been augmented to recognize negative numbers. If you issue `GOTO -3` (and the record exists), **GOTO** won't complain.

Remember that most of the complicated details belong only to table-buffered data; the single record (row) buffering is a piece of cake by comparison and for that reason is the preferred mode. However, table buffering is required for grids or for any situation in which multiple edits must be performed before the whole batch is sent to disk. Because this area of buffering is both complex and important, another approach is offered by FoxPro: transaction processing.

Transaction Processing

In a broad sense, *transaction processing* is any adding or editing of a record (or set of records) from the moment the user (or a program) begins the procedure to the moment when the data is committed to the tables. In everyday terms, a transaction is something like entering the sale of a product or writing up an airline ticket.

Many transactions are simple: an update of a single record in a single table. Extremely complex transactions may involve as many as a dozen tables in a tightly orchestrated sequence of events. Most database management systems provide some means of controlling the transaction process, because it is crucial to ensuring the integrity of the data. At the simple level, this control may be nothing more than locking a single record while the user is editing it. More complex transactions may involve many records in many tables, and the locking and validation must be systematic, sequential, and, most of all, complete.

NOTE

Many of the more complex transaction conflict management routines are used only when optimistic locking is in effect. Under pessimistic locking, the record simply isn't available to other users, so no conflict can occur. But with optimistic locking, it is possible for another user to lock or change the same record, and that situation must be handled.

RESOLVING CONFLICTS

In a multiuser environment in which each user shares the same data resources (your application's tables), there is always the possibility of conflict over usage. Sometimes this conflict is direct: User A wants to edit (and lock) a record, but user B has already locked the record. Other times it may be a conflict over the currency of the data. For example, user A may want to run a report with only the most recent data, but, while the report is running, user B updates half the table.

Fortunately, the most common conflicts are limited to four basic types:

- **Opening a file**. Another user or a program may have opened the database or table in **EXCLUSIVE** or **NOUPDATE** mode. All file opening routines must handle the possibility that the file (table or database) can't be opened.
- **Locking a record (pessimistic).** If another user has already locked a record while your program attempts to lock it before editing, the inability to access the record must be handled.
- **Changes to record (optimistic).** While a user is editing a record, another user makes changes to fields in the record. Because there is no way for the computer to make an intelligent decision about which data is better, the last user to attempt an update should be offered the decision of which data to keep.
- **Locking a record (optimistic).** While a user is editing a record, another user locks the record. This conflict is detected when the first user's program tries to do an update.

The first step in resolving any of these conflicts is to detect them. Some are obvious: If you try to open a file that has been locked, you will immediately get a FoxPro error message. On the other hand, detecting fields that have been changed in a record is not a matter of an error (until you try to use a **TABLEUPDATE**). Before we look at the common conflict resolution routines, you should be introduced to the unique language tools FoxPro provides for the job: **GETFLDSTATE( )**, **GETNEXTMODIFIED( )**, **CURVAL( )**, and **OLDVAL( )**. These functions apply only to buffered records.

The **GETFLDSTATE( )** function detects whether a field has been updated. What's more, it can tell you which of all the fields have been changed.

Command syntax:

GETFLDSTATE(cFieldName | nFieldNumber [, cTableAlias | nWorkArea])

Arguments:

cFieldName The name of the field to return a status.

nFieldNumber The number of a field (as it appears in the Table Designer).

cTableAlias The table name or alias to use.

nWorkArea The work area number to use.

Examples:

=GETFLDSTATE("TESTCODE")

Returns: A number 1–4.

=GETFLDSTATE(-1)

Returns: A string representing the status of every field in the record.

GETFLDSTATE() returns one of the following status codes:

1 = Field has not been edited or deleted.

2 = Field has been edited or deleted.

3 = Field in an appended record has not been edited or deleted.

4 = Field in an appended record has been edited or deleted.

As in one of the examples, using –1 as the record number argument causes **GETFLDSTATE( )** to respond with a character string like this: `1221111112111`. Using the code listed earlier, the first digit represents the deletion mark. Each digit thereafter represents the changed or unchanged status of the fields. You can create several interesting methods to read and translate this character string. For example:

```
FUNCTION RecordChanged
RETURN IIF("2"$GETFLDSTATE(-1),.t., .f.)
```

Whereas **GETFLDSTATE( )** can tell you whether a specific field has been changed, the **GETNEXTMODIFIED( )** function is used to determine whether a record has been changed at all. If it has been changed, the function hunts down each record in a table buffer that has been updated.

Command syntax: **GETNEXTMODIFIED(nRecordNumber [,cTableAliasIn WorkArea])**

Arguments:

nRecordNumber The record number to use for finding the next updated record.

cTableAlias The table name or alias to use.

nWorkArea The work area number to use.

Examples:

```
nRecChange = GETNEXTMODIFIED(0)
DO WHILE nRecChange <> 0
   *Test each modified record.
   ...
   nRecChange = GETNEXTMODIFIED(nRecChange)
ENDDO
```

The `GETNEXTMODIFIED(0)` version is used to find the first changed record in a table buffer. Thereafter, by using the current modified record number as the argument, you can find all the rest of the changed records.

The field values returned by **CURVAL( )** and **OLDVAL( )** can be compared to determine whether another user changed the field values while the fields were being edited. **CURVAL( )** returns the value in the data buffer, and **OLDVAL( )** returns the value in the table. Both functions return different values only when optimistic row or table buffering is enabled.

Command syntax:

CURVAL(cExpression [, cTableAlias | nWorkArea])

OLDVAL(cExpression [, cTableAlias | nWorkArea])

Arguments:

cExpression The name of the field to return a value from.

cTableAlias The table name or alias to use.

nWorkArea The work area number to use.

Examples:

```
cCurField = CURVAL("SAMPLEID")
cOldField = OLDVAL("SAMPLEID")
IF cOldField <> cCurField
  *Notify user
ENDIF
```

Handling the first two conflict types—file opening and locked records—is a matter for the general error trapping system you use in your application (and the topic of Chapter 21). The conflicts arising from optimistic locking are another matter. They often require more-sophisticated techniques to detect and respond to conflicts.

A Transaction Wrapper

In another feature more in common with database server programs, Visual FoxPro has added standard transaction commands:

```
    BEGIN TRANSACTION
    ...do some operation
IF test of operation is NOT ok
    ROLLBACK
ELSE
    END TRANSACTION
ENDIF
```

Between the **BEGIN** and the **END**, you can code any kind of database operation that could benefit from being undone if something goes awry. The important thing about the transaction operation is that Visual FoxPro saves each element of the transaction—essentially each record in a cache (on disk or in RAM)—

until the **END TRANSACTION** command signals that it's OK to write the data to the tables. **ROLLBACK**, on the other hand, deletes the cache and you must start the transaction again from scratch.

NOTE

Transactions are available only for tables contained in a database. Operations with nondatabase elements, such as variables, are not covered, and remote tables are not affected by the transaction commands (they have their own).

The syntax of the transaction commands is clearer than most, although if you nest transactions (set one transaction inside another, up to five levels) you should be scrupulous about issuing a matching **ROLLBACK** or **END TRANSACTION** for every **BEGIN TRANSACTION**.

It's easy to fall into the rut of thinking that the transaction commands are strictly for updating records. In fact, they can be used for any kind of table operation, including packing and indexing.

USING MEMO FIELDS

Bit bucket, text catcher, and miscellaneous data storage locker to the world of FoxPro—that's the Memo field. The General field is a variant of the Memo field and is housed in the same file (FPT). Internally, FoxPro stores into a General field additional information about each entry that is not present in the standard Memo field. That's what makes it possible to use a Memo field for a wide variety of data elements and maintain the links necessary for OLE. Together, the Memo and General fields can now store the following data types:

- Text (ASCII)
- Graphics (bitmaps, BMP format)
- Sound (WAV format)
- Animation (AVI format)
- Any OLE-compliant material

At a glance, you can see that this list opens the door to multimedia. However, this stage in the evolution of the General field presents far more possibilities than finished tools. FoxPro provides ways to display, play, or run some of the data types, but they are limited. There are no data management tools specifically for organizing or using multimedia data. However, there are enough tools to begin the process of turning capabilities into uses in your applications.

Memo fields tend to be taken for granted, probably because they are easy to use. Create a Memo field in your file, bind it to an EditBox in a form, and you're finished.

Memo fields can be used for more than taking notes. For one thing, you can import and export text data for Memo fields. You can scan entire manuals or sales forms into ASCII text files and then store the material in a Memo field. On the output side, in addition to being instantly accessible through the Report Designer, Memo fields can produce text (ASCII) files for word processing. The commands for these operations are simple:

Command syntax:

APPEND MEMO <memo field> FROM <file> [OVERWRITE]

Example:

```
APPEND MEMO notes FROM F:\DOC\COMMENT.TXT
```

Command syntax:

COPY MEMO <memo field> TO <file> [ADDITIVE]

Example:

```
COPY MEMO notes TO F:\DOC\OUTPUT.TXT ADDITIVE
```

For most of the other Memo field operations, the length of the field line is important:

SET MEMOWIDTH TO numberLines

This is a crucial value for many of the memo functions. Be sure that you know the line length each Memo field has been set to (if it is other than the default of 50). Be sure to reset the value when you're finished working in a particular Memo field.

There is an impression that Memo fields are just a big glob of text that can't be searched or manipulated except through the form's editing methods. Not so. This serves to introduce some useful functions provided by FoxPro for manipulating Memo fields (as usual, check the details with on-line help):

MEMLINES(MemoFieldName)

Returns the number of lines in a memo field as measured by the setting of **MEMOWIDTH**.

MLINE(MemoFieldName ,nLineNumber[,nNumberOfCharacters])

Returns the text from the specified line up to the length of the **MEMOWIDTH**.

ATC(cSearchExpression, cExpressionSearched [, nOccurrence])

Returns the position number in the memo field where the search string occurred, or 0 if none is found.

ATCLINE(cSearchExpression, cExpressionSearched)

Returns the line number where the search string occurred, or 0 if none is found.

The following code fragment gets the user's choice of word to find in a Memo field and uses **ATC( )** to find its position. **MODIFY MEMO** has the ability to highlight (select) a piece of text in a Memo field based on its starting position and length. (This function sets the editing selection on start-up and does not require use of the search option in the Edit menu.)

```
*Get search string from user.
lcSearch = GetUserString()
*Set up for memo edit
lnLen   = LEN( cSearch )
lnStart = ATC( cSearch, notes )
MODIFY MEMO notes RANGE lnStart, lnStart + lnLen
```

Most of the time, to change a Memo field you'll need to put the changed text into a variable (as in the preceding sort example) and then use a **REPLACE**. There is no way to use **STUFF( )** in a Memo field on a line-by-line basis. However, other character string manipulation functions will work in a Memo field: **STRTRAN( )**, **SUBSTR( )**, **EMPTY()**, **RAT( )**, and **RATLINE( )**.

There are limitations to the FoxPro Memo field tools: Searching becomes very slow on a record-by-record basis and in large Memo fields. There are, however, a number of third-party utility programs that bring indexing, sorting, searching, and other capabilities to a Memo field if your application requires them.

Extending FoxPro with ActiveX Controls and OLE

The ability to commingle applications—a word processor in one window, a spreadsheet in another, and your FoxPro application in a third—has been a dream for more than 10 years (at least as long as Windows has been around). For one reason or another (lack of hardware horsepower, battles over standards, and so on) the dream has been difficult to realize. Now that we have ActiveX and OLE 2.0, Pentium computers, and Windows 95 and NT, we are finally positioned to use other applications as if they were really part of our FoxPro applications.

Object linking and embedding (OLE), widely pronounced *olé* as in bullfighting, is the means to interprocess communications. This is a fancy way of saying that OLE provides application developers with the ability to link one Windows application to another. In Visual FoxPro, OLE has several faces (Figure 19.3):

- ActiveX an OLE in General fields
- OLE in Forms
- Visual (in-place) editing of OLE objects
- OLE automation
- ActiveX custom controls

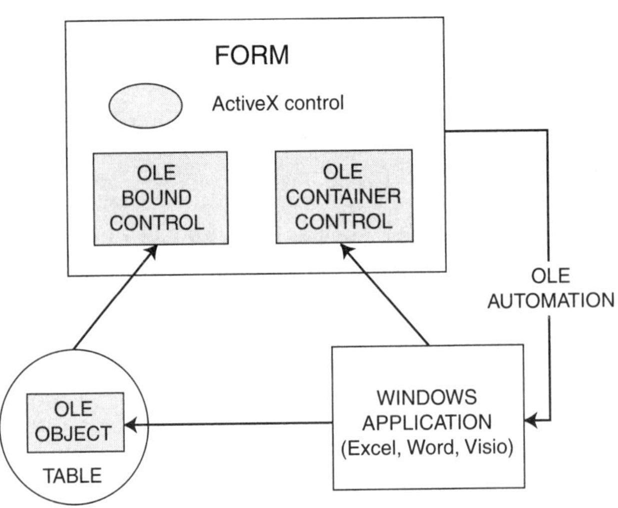

Figure 19.3 Various forms of ActiveX and OLE.

There are a number of combinations, and it can become confusing. After a little background, we'll cover each of the options.

SERVER TO CLIENT

The OLE implementation in FoxPro is both input and output or, to use the jargon of the OLE trade, a *client/server* capability. FoxPro is the client to various Windows applications (MS Word, MS Excel, and so on) that act as OLE *servers*; or those applications use Visual FoxPro as the server to their clients.

You are no doubt familiar with the term *client/server* in its database management context: The server is the database manager software (usually centralized) that receives and processes requests for data (usually in SQL) from client software. The OLE context is different, because it is more of a conversation among equals.

NOTE

Working with any other OLE client/server capabilities shouldn't be undertaken lightly. For one thing, success depends on a favorable environment, which includes available RAM, CPU speed, available disk space, folder (directory) structure, Registry entries, and network settings.

OLE OBJECTS IN TABLES

The first piece of the OLE mosaic is the ability to store OLE objects in FoxPro tables, specifically in the General field. OLE is a conduit for the use of those objects in forms and other programming, and some applications are built around this storage capability—for example, art gallery catalog applications.

NOTE

The art gallery example brings to mind that you shouldn't form the impression that OLE is strictly a visual medium (a way to store pictures). OLE can be used for anything: voice, music, images, movies, graphics, programs, and so on. In a word, multimedia.

OLE AND GENERAL FIELDS

It's useful to think of OLE information in General fields as having three forms: linked, embedded, and static. When you establish an OLE *link*, FoxPro stores the reference to an OLE object (usually but not always a file) in a General field.

That reference contains information about the server, the type of the object, and the location of the object. When you double-click on a General field that contains a link, FoxPro goes to the external file or program it has on reference and displays, runs, or plays the object, depending on the type of the data.

An OLE *embedded* object is stored in the General field along with information about the server and the type of data. In this self-contained unit, which no other application can access, you have the ability to do *visual editing*, also called *editing in place*.

When you insert a *static* object into a General field, you deliberately avoid all links between the client and server and it will not be possible to access the server that created it. Essentially, the General field is not part of OLE, and the links cannot be reestablished.

All three forms have advantages that flow from two attributes: Embedded and static data is proprietary, and linked data is shared. When you embed an OLE object in a General field, it becomes your property, a part of the FoxPro application. At the user's request, it can be changed or updated by running the server program from within FoxPro, but it is not accessible from the server. This implies both security of access and the ability to customize an OLE object for a specific application. The same holds true for a static object except that it can no longer be modified. By contrast, a linked OLE object always has an external existence; it is tied to the server program and usually one of its files. In this form, the OLE object is available to other users and other programs; it's shared.

The decision of whether to link or embed objects or use static objects is made by the application developer on a case-by-case basis. FoxPro, through the General field, makes no attempt to check for OLE type or data consistency. In practice you can mix and match object types as you see fit, even if that means breaking all the rules of relational structure. The disadvantages—a natural result of the complex OLE environment—are the most significant for linking and embedding.

INTERACTIVE OLE

The first way of getting OLE objects into a table—the *interactive* approach—requires that someone (the user or the developer) go through the keystrokes. It has limited use unless this sort of operation is naturally part of the application, as it might be for loading pictures into an art gallery catalog database.

Step 1 is to have a table open that contains the General field you want to use. Then you select a specific record and field (often in a Browse window) and double-click the field, opening a General field window. If the OLE object has not been created, you start with **Insert Object** in the Edit menu; with **Create New** enabled, select the OLE application to use (such as Word or Corel Draw). Create the object—a Word document, a drawing—and, when you return, the new object will be embedded in the General field.

If the object already exists, you have three options, again starting from the Edit menu. In the Insert Object dialog box, select **Create from File** and use the File Open dialog box to select the file you need. Otherwise, with the other OLE application already running, you can cut or copy the object in the Windows clipboard and do one of two things: Use **Paste**, which automatically embeds the OLE object; or use **Paste Special**, which gives you some options.

For using the original object, the **Paste** option is the same as in the menu; the object is embedded in the General field. If you choose the **Picture** of the object, then the **Paste** option will put a static (bitmap) image of the object into the field. If you choose the **Paste Link** option, the object will be a link between the General field and the external file.

Once the object has been placed in the General field, you can play or edit the General field simply by double-clicking on it in the Browse window. If the object was embedded, then you'll have the pleasure of visual editing, which means that the server application will be started and you will be able to edit the OLE object—in a FoxPro window—as you would in the original application.

Visual editing is a slick feature, but you'll need to make some allowances for what it does to your application's menu. With OLE, the server application inserts its menu options into the menu, and that can cause havoc. Here's how to avoid problems when you create a menu for a form that will use visual editing: For each pad in the menu, use the **Options** check box to open the Prompt Options window. Then select **Negotiate** to see the Negotiate dialog box. Use one of the following options. **None**: The pad will not appear when an OLE session is in progress. **Left**, **Middle**, **Right**: The pad will be placed to one of these positions relative to the options of the inserted OLE application.

PROGRAMMATIC OLE

Turning to the programming aspects of OLE, it's not much more difficult than the interactive version. Under program control you can probably make it easier—or at least clearer—for the user to manipulate OLE than do the interactive options offered by FoxPro.

There are only data two commands with specifics for OLE management: **APPEND GENERAL** and **MODIFY GENERAL**. These commands are most important for loading OLE objects into tables and allowing user access to OLE objects under program control.

Command syntax:

APPEND GENERAL GeneralFieldName [FROM FileName | FROM MEMO PictureFieldName] [DATA cExpression] [LINK] [CLASS OLEClassName]

Arguments:

GeneralFieldName The name of the General field.

FROM FileName A complete path and file name, including extension, are necessary to specify the file to be incorporated into the General field. Note that the **MEMO** and **PictureFieldName** options allow importing material from Memo and other General fields.

DATA cExpression A new option for Visual FoxPro, this argument allows transmission of data to the OLE server through this command.

LINK This changes the command from the default embedding to linking of the OLE object.

CLASS OLEClassName Specifies the OLE class to be used.

Examples:

```
APPEND GENERAL notes FROM c:\word\doc\taxes.doc
APPEND GENERAL design FROM d:\corel\draw\horses.cdr LINK
```

This command looks and behaves like the **APPEND MEMO** command with the appropriate additions for OLE-specific information. The OLE class determines the origin of the object and is used to distinguish the OLE application you want to associate with an OLE file object. The extension of the file usually determines which application; DOC indicates a Word for Windows file. However, generic files, such as BMP, might be associated with a number of programs. You would then use the **CLASS** clause to specify which application to use among those named in the Registry or OLE.INI file.

The new **DATA** option can be used to pass data to the OLE server, on the assumption that the server can use the data to create something and return it as an object. Compared with OLE automation, this is a crude approach, but it's sufficient for some uses. For example, you can send raw data to the Microsoft Graph program this way:

```
cGraphData = "  "+CHR(9)+"X-Axis"+CHR(13)+CHR(10)+;
             "Region 1"+CHR(9)+"22000"+ CHR(13)+CHR(10)+;
             "Region 2"+CHR(9)+"45000"+ CHR(13)+CHR(10)+;
             "Region 3"+CHR(9)+"33000"+ CHR(13)+CHR(10)
```

With an open table, a selected record, and a General field named GRAPH, use this code:

```
APPEND GENERAL graph CLASS "MSGraph" DATA cGraphData
```

To look at this graph or at any other OLE object in a General field, you can use the **MODIFY GENERAL** command.

Command syntax:

MODIFY GENERAL GeneralField1 [, GeneralField2 ...]
[NOMODIFY] [NOWAIT] [[WINDOW WindowName1]
[IN [WINDOW] WindowName2 | IN SCREEN]

Arguments:

GeneralField1 [,GeneralField2 ...] Name of the General field to modify.

WindowName1 Name of the user-defined window to use.

WindowName2 Name of the user-defined window to be IN.

Examples:

```
MODIFY GENERAL graph NOMODIFY
```

This command looks and works like **MODIFY MEMO**, **MODIFY FILE**, or even the **BROWSE** command. All these commands are usually handled by defining a window for the **WINDOW** clause and then using a **NOWAIT** to have the window stay open. With the OLE window, which this really is, **MODIFY GENERAL** makes possible an interactive OLE session for the user unless you specify **NOMODIFY**.

Putting the two commands together, the following example method envisions two buttons that ask the user to select a CAD drawing type to put into a General field.

```
DEFINE PROCEDURE LoadCAD
  LPARAMETER tcSample
```

```
DO CASE
...
CASE tcSample = "Design"
  *————————————[ LOAD THE DESIGNS (OLE)
  lcFile = GETFILE("CDR", "Load the Design")
  IF NOT EMPTY( lcFile )
     APPEND BLANK
     APPEND GENERAL design FROM &lcFile LINK
  ENDIF
  * Have a look at it.
  DEFINE WINDOW wgDesign AT 2,0 SIZE 20,60 FLOAT GROW;
    ZOOM CLOSE ;
    TITLE lcFile
  MODIFY GENERAL design NOMODIFY WINDOW wgDesign
  RELEASE WINDOW wgDesign
 CASE...
 ENDCASE
ENDPROC
```

In working with OLE, you'll probably find that distinctions will often be made between OLE objects that are intended for user modification and those that are not. The overhead of interactive objects—both in terms of programming in your application and in the general Windows environment—tends to make programmers conservative with the number of active OLE links, whereas images and sounds that have been loaded into General fields (and usually made static) are simple to maintain and use.

Using OLE Objects in Forms

The source of OLE objects used in forms can be either a table or a server application. If the object is stored in a table, you use an OLEBound control to display it (or, for sound and movie objects, display an icon of it). The contents of this control may change with each record. OLEBound controls are handled like TextBoxes and other more mundane bound controls; you specify the **ControlSource** as the General field.

If the OLE object doesn't need to change, such as a particular spreadsheet that is used each time the form is opened, then you can use an OLE Container control. In this case, the OLE object is stored in the form. (When you embed an OLE object into a form, it, too, is being stored in a General field, except this time in the SCX file of the form instead of a table.) To create a Container control, select its icon from the Controls toolbar and draw its size on the form. When the Insert Object dialog box appears, you can select whether you want to use a file, create a new object, or use an OLE control.

Don't get carried away with OLE objects in forms. The overhead is considerable, and putting a number of them into a form may cause a long wait for the user before the form is fully loaded.

OLE AUTOMATION

Like a few other topics in Visual FoxPro, OLE automation is one of the "gateway" subjects; stepping into it leads to a whole world of possibilities for an application. In this case, you can open the gate into running and controlling other OLE applications. Unlike the other OLE objects, which are largely static links, OLE automation allows you to program in the language of the server application. But there's the rub: To use OLE automation for anything but minor convenience (which isn't necessarily a bad thing), you will need to become familiar with, if not skilled in, another programming language. In most cases this will be Visual Basic for Applications (VBA), the common language of Microsoft Office applications.

I'd love to get into OLE automation, because it's been greatly enhanced in Visual FoxPro 5.0, but it's a huge subject. It needs a book or a few chapters of its own. Not here, unfortunately. If you're interested, start with the meager chapters in the FoxPro manuals and then scan the Internet and your local bookstore for recent information. With the coming of Microsoft Office 97, this is a topic in a state of flux.

OLE CUSTOM CONTROLS

If you are working with a copy of the Visual FoxPro Professional Edition, you will also be able to take advantage of the final OLE feature: ActiveX controls. These are the 32-bit versions of the wildly popular, and important, VBX controls of Visual Basic. VBXs almost single-handedly demonstrated the power of component architecture, the ability to snap together preconstructed components into an application.

Over the past few years, some powerful and creative controls ("controls" in the same sense as the Visual FoxPro control for forms) have been made for Visual Basic, but the format and range of the VBX architecture was limited (and not just because they are creatures of the 16-bit world). To open the architecture, Microsoft promulgated OCX controls, now called ActiveX controls, based on the OLE protocols. Because ActiveX controls are 32-bits and new to the market, there aren't very many examples, and only a few ship with Visual FoxPro. But their availability is expanding rapidly, largely because of the Internet.

Using an ActiveX control is similar to using any other OLE object. You start by selecting the **OLE container** icon and marking the area in the form where you want the control to go. When the Insert Object dialog box appears, check the box marked **Insert Control** and you'll see a list of the ActiveX controls as they exist in the Windows Registry. (Don't be surprised if you see controls from other applications also listed.) As a rule, there will be a few more layers of dialog boxes to go through—depending on the complexity of the ActiveX object—until finally the control shows up in the form.

Once you have the visible control, open a Properties window and you will see exposed for your use all the nonprotected properties and methods of the control, no matter where it was created. Incidentally, you can't create ActiveX controls in Visual FoxPro; this is a job for C++, Visual Basic 5.0, or one of the competitors.

CHAPTER WRAP-UP

Most of the topics in this chapter dealt with extensions or refinements to the Visual FoxPro database system (with a side trip to OLE automation and controls). In building applications, it's important to explore the many ways to integrate data from tables. This chapter emphasizes multiuser table and record locking, in part because most applications will be run on a network and share data resources, and in part because there are many options (or variations).

It would be helpful if you could be given a formula for just how much file and record locking you need for every application. Unfortunately, like many other things in application development, this issue must be decided case by case. There are many factors:

- The number of people using the application, especially the number using it simultaneously.
- The type and performance of the network .
- The concurrency demands of the application: how much data is updated more or less simultaneously.
- The timing and sequencing sensitivity of the data: the issues of whose data is valid.
- The performance requirement, especially for real-time response.
- The security sensitivity of the data, and the amount of protection it requires.

...and others. Certainly almost all applications will use buffered data as the standard, but adjustments to individual tables for row or table buffering depend on the situation. Similarly, decisions to use manual locking depend on specific requirements from some of the factors listed earlier. Transaction processing (**BEGIN TRANSACTION** and **END TRANSACTION**) can be used routinely or applied to special situations that require an extended sequence of updates to complete a transaction.

Virtually all applications use Memo fields, because attaching notes to forms is standard practice. General fields are more specialized and may not be required in every application, but through the use of OLE they present an opportunity to expand your FoxPro application to incorporate documents and direct participation from other Windows applications. Within the limitations of hardware and network transmission, OLE automation is also a powerful tool, especially when you need to call on other programs for specialized support of your application.

CHAPTER 20

ADVANCED SQL AND VIEWS

You've already been introduced to the basics of working with SQL, mostly within the confines of the Query Designer and View Designer. As useful as these tools are, they do not cover all the capabilities of the FoxPro SQL **SELECT** statement. This chapter opens more of the door to the programming of **SELECT** statements and will give you more flexibility to cover situations that can't be handled in the Designers. It should also help to amplify your knowledge of SQL in general.

SQL is also the gateway to the world of client/server database systems and applications. Although there isn't space for a complete treatment of client/server, this chapter will cover some of the approaches involved, particularly the use of Microsoft Open Database Connectivity (ODBC) to connect your application with a variety of database sources and not just in the client/server sense.

This is the realm of the remote view and ODBC connections, the final piece of the Visual FoxPro database picture. It will be useful (or even required) for many applications to tap data in file formats other than FoxPro. Previously, these files had to be converted before FoxPro could use them; with ODBC, you can connect more or less directly to a wide variety of database files. This chapter covers the basics of making that connection and of controlling some of the properties involved.

VIEW AND QUERY PROGRAMMING

At this point, you've hopefully had some experience with the Query Designer and View Designer. Because they put so much under one (similar) roof—

graphing, reporting, cross tabs, and browsing—the Query Designer and View Designer can be used for a wide variety of data retrieval and reporting tasks. However, the Designers are interactive tools and are targeted primarily for individual users, and they are not available for distribution through compiled and linked (EXE) programs. This means that your applications may need other ways to manipulate SQL, especially if you want to give your users some interactive SQL capabilities.

Although you can build powerful queries and especially views with the Designers and you can link them to the Data Environments, you will find that your ability to create SQL statements as command code will become increasingly important for your applications. The more you know about what this direct form of SQL can do, the more ways you will find to use it as the "data generator" for your forms and reports.

Earlier, it was highly recommended that you earn your spurs by using the Query Designer and View Designer to see how they generate SQL code and then do some SQL coding of your own in the Command window. In this chapter, it's time to put some of that knowledge to work in an application and to extend it with some SQL you can't do in the Designers.

You can do a lot of data retrieval with a basic **SQL SELECT**: Name your fields and tables, specify a number of conditions for selection from those tables, and deposit the results in the full array of Visual FoxPro output options. But it's like a warm-up act before the show.

To nail down the specifics of the full command statement, let's go through each element and take a close look at the syntax details, beginning with the **SELECT**. The syntax has been rearranged somewhat from the *Language Reference*, mainly to place the output-related clauses at the end of the statement. This arrangement doesn't cause errors and makes the statement better fit the sequence of execution.

Command syntax:

SELECT [ALL | DISTINCT] [TOP nExpr [PERCENT]]

Examples:

```
SELECT DISTINCT
SELECT TOP 10 PERCENT
```

ALL indicates that all rows of the result should be displayed. Because this is the default, you don't normally need to include it.

DISTINCT allows only unique rows into the result set. This option is frequently used to get an array list for a ComboBox, such as a list of all people in a table in which their names may appear several times.

TOP nExpr [PERCENT], new in Visual FoxPro 5.0, provides a sorely needed way of limiting the number of records returned by a query or view. The **nExpr** means that you can set any number—say, 100—and only that number of records will be returned. This capability is useful for testing. The **PERCENT** option is extremely useful for business reporting when you want not just a list but to show, for example, the top 20 percent of salespeople.

Command syntax:

SELECT [ALL | DISTINCT] [TOP nExpr [PERCENT]]

[Alias.] Select_Item [AS Column_Name] | *

Examples:

```
SELECT tcd.testcode AS "Test", sam.sampleid AS "Sample"
SELECT *
SELECT TRIM(tcd.testcode), sam.sampleid
SELECT COUNT(invoice.invoiceid), customer.lastname
```

The field list, or more precisely the list of select items (fields aren't always involved), may cover as many fields as needed, or you can use the asterisk (*) to mean all fields. When you are working with many fields from several tables, it is much cleaner (and shorter) to use table aliases, the same as **ALIAS** in general FoxPro. The alias must be defined in the **FROM** clause. You can use the **AS** clause to specify an appropriate header for the field (column). In addition to field names, you can also use constant expressions, such as "-" to add a spacing column to the result. Or you can use any of these field functions:

- **AVG(Select_Item)**. Averages a column of numeric data.
- **COUNT(Select_Item)**. Counts the number of selected items in a column.
- **COUNT(*)**. Counts the number of rows in the query output.
- **MIN(Select_Item)**. Determines the smallest value of **Select_Item** in a column.
- **MAX(Select_Item)**. Determines the largest value of **Select_Item** in a column.
- **SUM(Select_Item)**. Totals a column of numeric data.

Command syntax:

SELECT [ALL | DISTINCT] [TOP nExpr [PERCENT]]
[Alias.] Select_Item [AS Column_Name] | *
FROM [FORCE] [DatabaseName!] Table [Local_Alias]

Example:

```
FROM test!testcode tcd, test!sample sam
FROM
```

FORCE tells FoxPro not to mess with the order of tables specified in the **FROM** clause. Otherwise, the query optimizer might rearrange the tables in ways that are not valid for what you want to achieve. Normally, of course, you let the optimizer do its thing.

If there is any ambiguity about the origin of the table, particularly if it is part of a database container file (DBC), you should specify the database. It's good documentation in any case. Depending on how you've structured your application's folders and have specified the default path for FoxPro, you may also need to include full paths for the databases and tables. As mentioned, you define the table **Alias** here in the **FROM** clause.

Command syntax:

SELECT [ALL|DISTINCT] [Alias.] Select_Item [AS Column_Name]
FROM [FORCE] [DatabaseName!]Table [Local_Alias]
[[INNER | LEFT [OUTER] | RIGHT [OUTER] | FULL [OUTER] JOIN
[DatabaseName!] TableName | LocalAlias [ON JoinCondition...]

Example:

```
INNER JOIN invoice ON customerid
LEFT OUTER JOIN testcode ON tcode
```

Every table in the **FROM** clause (except the primary table) must be linked through a join. The sequence of tables linked by a join is important. SQL works best when these joins link primary tables into secondary tables. Joins from secondary tables into tertiary or lower tables can become difficult, problematic, or impossible.

If you don't have indexes on the join fields (or on field expressions), FoxPro will build them on-the-fly, and that may be a problem in a large table. There is no limit (other than your patience) to how many tables may be joined. Too many joins will drastically affect performance and may indicate a need to go to a subquery, which will be explained shortly. The description for **INNER**, **OUTER**, and **FULL** options was given in Chapter 6. The **JoinCondition** is usually nothing more than the field name, typically one that's indexed.

Command syntax:

SELECT [ALL|DISTINCT] [Alias.] Select_Item [AS Column_Name]
 FROM [FORCE] [DatabaseName!]Table [Local_Alias]
 [[INNER | LEFT [OUTER] | RIGHT [OUTER] | FULL [OUTER] JOIN
 [DatabaseName!] TableName | LocalAlias [ON JoinCondition...]
[WHERE JoinCondition [AND JoinCondition...]
[AND|OR FilterCondition [AND|OR FilterCondition ...]]]

Example:

```
WHERE state = "CA" AND tcd.indate > {12/31/94} ;
 OR sam.flag = "A"
```

The duty of the **WHERE** clause is to select records based on conditions. This is where you separate the sheep from goats, so to speak. The **FilterCondition** expressions, which are essentially standard FoxPro logical expressions, usually cover field values but are not limited to fields. You may have statements that have no joins, but it's unusual to have no filter conditions.

Command syntax:

SELECT [ALL|DISTINCT] [Alias.] Select_Item [AS Column_Name]
 FROM [FORCE] [DatabaseName!]Table [Local_Alias]
 [[INNER | LEFT [OUTER] | RIGHT [OUTER] | FULL [OUTER] JOIN
 [DatabaseName!] TableName | LocalAlias [ON JoinCondition...]
 [WHERE JoinCondition [AND JoinCondition...]
 [AND|OR FilterCondition [AND|OR FilterCondition ...]]]
 [GROUP BY GroupColumn [, GroupColumn ...]]
 [HAVING FilterCondition]

Example:

```
GROUP BY tcd.indate ;
   HAVING COUNT(tcd.indate)>50 ;
```

As mentioned Chapter 6, the **GROUP BY**, **HAVING**, and **ORDER BY** clauses can be seen as post–row selection commands, because they operate with sets of data that have usually come through the **WHERE** clauses. Typically, the **GROUP BY** clause creates an invisible cursor, which is ordered so that the specified groupings can be available for the SQL functions listed earlier.

The **HAVING** clause further qualifies a grouping and is similar in effect to the **WHERE** clause but at the group level instead of the record (row) level. In most cases, the expression is meaningful only in conjunction with the field functions, as in the example; otherwise, the expression could just as easily have been applied in the main **WHERE** clause.

Command syntax:

SELECT [ALL|DISTINCT] [Alias.] Select_Item [AS Column_Name]
FROM [FORCE] [DatabaseName!]Table [Local_Alias]
[[INNER | LEFT [OUTER] | RIGHT [OUTER] | FULL [OUTER] JOIN
[DatabaseName!] TableName | LocalAlias [ON JoinCondition...]
[WHERE JoinCondition [AND JoinCondition...]
[AND|OR FilterCondition [AND|OR FilterCondition ...]]]
[GROUP BY GroupColumn [, GroupColumn ...]]
[HAVING FilterCondition]
[ORDER BY Order_Item [ASC | DESC] [, Order_Item [ASC | DESC] ...]]
[[INTO Destination] |
[TO FILE FileName [ADDITIVE] | TO PRINTER [PROMPT] | TO SCREEN]]
[NOCONSOLE]
[PLAIN]
[PREFERENCE PreferenceName]
[NOWAIT]

Example:

```
ORDER BY tcd.indate DESC, sam.sampleid ;
INTO CURSOR temptest
TO PRINTER PROMPT NOCONSOLE PLAIN
TO SCREEN PREFERENCE test1
```

ORDER BY does a sort on the results data set. By default, **Order_Items** contains the fields of your choice in ascending order, but you can specify descending order instead. This clause is relatively independent of the rest of the query and acts as a pre-output process, preparing data for a report or other output format.

Output, in the command syntax, provides many of the same options available from the Query Designer and View Designer. However, in programming, you may put them to different uses, especially with arrays and cursors. The options are summarized in Table 20.1.

TABLE 20.1 SQL SELECT OUTPUT DESTINATIONS AND OPTIONS

OUTPUT CLAUSE	USAGE
INTO ARRAY arrayName	Filling an array with a **SQL SELECT** is a convenient way to load data into List or ComboBox controls. However, it is faster than a simple **SEEK** and **SCAN** only when the results of the query are indeterminate. If you know exactly what to load, a direct lookup is usually quicker than invoking the entire SQL machinery.
INTO CURSOR cursorName	For regular use of **SQL SELECT**, the creation of a results cursor is probably the most efficient approach. Unless they are very large, cursors are left in RAM and are very fast to manipulate. Because most result sets are intended for temporary use, the fact that the cursor self-destructs when closed is a secondary benefit.
INTO DBFITABLE tableName	Because output to a cursor isn't permanent, you can use this clause to create a standard DBF.
TO FILE fileName [ADDITIVE]	This output option sends the results to a standard text file. The additive option makes it possible to load several queries into a single file.

(Continued...)

[PLAIN] TO PRINTER [PROMPT] [NOCONSOLE]	This directs output to a printer. With the **PROMPT** option, the Windows printer setup dialog box will appear. **NOCONSOLE** suppresses output to the screen, and **PLAIN** prevents output of column headings.
TO SCREEN	By default, screen display is sent to a Browse window. This option causes output to be sent to the FoxPro Main window.
(no output clause) PREFERENCE NOWAIT	By default, if you use no output clause, output goes to a Browse window. By adding the two Browse-related clauses (**PREFERENCE** and **NOWAIT**), you can have a Browse window template and have the Browse exit immediately back to program control.

The output options complete the basic **SQL SELECT**, which provides much the same capability as the Query and View Designers. A complete statement that extracts summary data from a laboratory testing process looks like this:

```
SELECT tcd.testcode AS "Test", sam.sampleid AS "Sample", ;
       MAX(tcd.fee) AS "Fee", SUM(tcd.fee) AS "Total" ;
  FROM test!testcode tcd, test!sample sam ;
  INNER JOIN sam ON testcode ;
  WHERE tcd.testtype = "PESTICIDE" ;
    AND tcd.indate > {12/31/94} OR sam.flag = "A" ;
  GROUP BY COUNT(sam.indate) ;
    HAVING COUNT(sam.indate)> 50 ;
  ORDER BY tcd.indate DESC, sam.sampleid ;
  INTO CURSOR temptest
```

Some Uses and Tips

To refresh your memory: The Query Designer produces **SQL SELECT** statements, which are executed to produce the desired output. Query Designer queries can be saved in QPR files, which are nothing more than program files containing a standard **SQL SELECT** statement. These you can program without the aid of the Query Designer.

The View Designer also uses **SELECT** statements but in a different framework. For one thing, it doesn't save them to a text file but instead stores the command statement in a database file. You can accomplish the same thing with programming commands outside the View Designer, bypassing it completely:

CREATE SQL VIEW [ViewName] AS SQLSELECTStatement

The **SQLSELECTStatement** is the same as a query **SELECT** statement. In this case, the view creation command and the query must be executed with an already open database file (a .DBC) that has been opened using **EXCLUSIVE**. Reuse of a **SQL View** is dependent on opening the database. When you call the view—for example, by using it in a Data Environment—it is executed to produce a cursor.

One of the things that drives SQL query users crazy is that the "little" things can mess up the results. That's why there are some query expressions to consider routinely every time you do a query:

```
WHERE NOT DELETED()
```

If **DELETED** is **OFF**, this code will weed out deleted records.

NOTE

Recall that **SET DELETED ON** is like a filter that removes deleted records. If you run your application with the setting **ON** most of the time, you should create an index tag of DELETED with a key of **DELETED( )** for *every* table. The Rushmore optimizer will use this index to optimize removal of deleted records. Without it, the set of result records must be sequentially searched for delete marks, a much slower process.

```
WHERE NOT EMPTY(<field>)
```

In the primary table, this code will exclude records (rows) containing no values.

```
WHERE EXISTS( SELECT * FROM <table> WHERE <condition> )
```

This is a *subquery*, which is often used make sure that at least one item of relevant data exists in a table—for example, that a code definition actually exists.

When constructing your join or filter expressions, don't forget the SQL operators **NOT**, **BETWEEN**, **IN**, and **LIKE**. **LIKE**, in particular, is often overlooked, although it can be one way to find character string matches that are unavailable or difficult to do with traditional FoxPro language. That's because you can use the percent sign (`%`) and underscore (_) wildcards as part of the matching expression: `WHERE lastname LIKE "SM%"`. The `%` acts like the DOS `*` wildcard and matches all characters. `WHERE lastname LIKE "SM_TH"`. The underscore, _, has the same effect as the DOS `?` wildcard and will match any single character.

Some SQL Gotchas

The subtleties of **SQL SELECT** have foiled many a query and have given rise to a cult of SQL freaks who do little but create and solve weird and wonderful **SELECT** puzzles. There are a few **SELECT** statements you can inadvertently create that may balloon a result beyond the capacity of your hard disk.

Avoid any **SELECT** statement that joins two tables with conditions (or lack of conditions) that guarantee that every record in both tables will be included in the result set—for example, `SELECT * FROM invoice, customer`. This produces a *Cartesian join*. If one table has 500 records and the other 900, you will get 500 x 900 (450,000) records in the result set.

Although it was suggested earlier that you use **EMPTY( )** to help eliminate empty records from the query result set, you need to exercise caution with it and with **ISNULL()**. For example:

```
SELECT * FROM matrix, testcode ;
  WHERE testcode.matrixid = EMPTY(matrix.matrixid)
```

In this case, Visual FoxPro will match the empty fields in *both* tables and produce a Cartesian join from them: 1245 empty fields in one table and 2678 empty fields in the other will produce 3,334,110 records in the result set.

NOTE

In general, you need to be wary of **SELECT** statements that could generate very large result sets. This is especially true for remote connections, where a mistake that generates a three million record result could tie up a network for hours. FoxPro does provides you with some tools, such as the **TOP..PERCENT** clause, to limit the number of records returned or how long a query can run. More will be introduced shortly.

Subqueries

Nested queries, or subqueries as they are more properly called in FoxPro, can be useful—and are not supported by the Query Designer and View Designer.

Subqueries have many forms, but they are easiest to use and understand as a tool to pluck information from a table not directly related to the main query tables, with the result to be tested as part of the main query. Here's an example:

```
SELECT customer, invtotal ;
  FROM customer cus, invoice inv ;
  INNER JOIN inv ON cno ;
  WHERE inv.ofcno = IN( SELECT ofcno ;
                      FROM office ;
                      WHERE ofctotal > 500000 );
  INTO CURSOR tmpfile
```

The query: Show all the customers and their invoice totals where the sales office for the invoice is one of those that sell more than $500,000 a year. The information about the sales offices is a subquery that provides a list of qualifying offices for the **IN** function that is used by the main query. Notice this subquery is framed by parentheses, which are required. The general form of the subquery is some variant of the following:

WHERE|AND|OR [FieldName Comparison] [Function] (Subquery)

If there is more than one **WHERE** clause, the **AND|OR** connects the subquery to the **WHERE** clause.

```
WHERE billcode = (SELECT billcode FROM labfees ;
                    WHERE division = "DAIRY")

WHERE totalfee > 1000 ;
  AND billcode = (SELECT billcode FROM labfees ;
                    WHERE division = "DAIRY")
```

The **FieldName** must match the data type required by the comparison operator and must match the return value from the **SELECT** of the subquery. The **Comparison** is any of the operators shown in Table 20.2.

Many subqueries are constructed using only the comparison operators:

```
SELECT * FROM testcode ;
  WHERE labunit = "001" ;
   AND billcode = (SELECT billcode FROM labfees ;
                    WHERE division = "AGRONOMY" )
```

Table 20.2 Comparison Operators

Operator	Description
`=`	Equal
`= =`	Exactly equal
`LIKE`	SQL **LIKE**
`<>, !=, #`	Not equal
`>`	Greater than
`>=`	Greater than or equal to
`<`	Less than
`<=`	Less than or equal to

Using a **Function** is optional, but they often distinguish a subquery. The function is used to contain the nested **SELECT** statement. There are several of these functions, and they provide an important selection capability for SQL queries:

- **FieldName Comparison ANY (Subquery)**. Matches any one result item operator.
- **FieldName Comparison SOME (Subquery)**. Matches more than one result item.
- **FieldName Comparison ALL (Subquery)**. Matches all result items.

```
SELECT tcd.description, tcd.labname ;
  WHERE tcd.matrixid = ANY(SELECT matrixid FROM matrix ;
                           WHERE type = "DAIRY")
```

[NOT] EXISTS (Subquery) is another important variant:

```
SELECT tcd.description, tcd.labname ;
  WHERE EXISTS( SELECT labname FROM codes ;
                WHERE labname = "BIOMED")
```

Whenever a lookup value must exist for the query to succeed, use the **EXISTS** subquery. Under some circumstances, this can be an extremely important part of a query. The function returns true (`.T.`) if the return set contains at least one entry.

The **IN** subquery provides a list to be compared against the values in the **FieldName**: **FieldName [NOT] IN (Subquery)**.

```
SELECT * FROM testcode ;
  WHERE testcode.matrixId IN ;
  (SELECT matrix.matrixId FROM matrix ;
     WHERE matrix.type = "AGRONOMY" )
```

The use of the functions **EXIST**, **IN**, **ANY**, **SOME**, and **ALL** in conjunction with a subquery is common SQL. You should be careful using them in very large tables, because the SQL engine will usually run a row comparison of the main query against the column of results provided by the subquery, and that can be time-consuming.

WARNING

You do not have the same freedom with subqueries as you do with the main **SELECT** query. The following restrictions apply: Unless you use the all-fields wildcard token, *, a subquery can refer only to one field. **UNION** and **ORDER BY** clauses cannot be used in a subquery. Only direct comparisons and **EXIST**, **IN**, **ANY**, **SOME**, and **ALL** can be used to connect a main query to a subquery. Finally, FoxPro does not support subqueries within subqueries (nested subqueries), although you can have more than one subquery at the same level (under the main **WHERE**).

In practice, all subqueries can be reworded to form a **WHERE** expression. However, because there is no difference in performance, most programmers prefer the subquery format for its clarity (self-documentation) when pulling data from a subsidiary table.

SELF JOINS

A *self join* is a variant of the subquery format in which the subquery refers to the same table as the main query. It's used for the same purposes as any subquery: to provide a comparison list or result against which the main query is tested. Here's an example:

```
SELECT cno, lastname, city ;
  FROM customer cus ;
  WHERE cus.salestotal > 1000 AND NOT EXIST ;
     ( SELECT * FROM customer cust ;
         WHERE cust.crtype <> "X" ;
         OR cust.status = "I" )
  INTO ARRAY aCust
```

Notice the explicit declaration of a table alias, which is different from that used for the main query. This makes sense, because you're asking the query to give you the names of customers who have more than $1,000 in purchases while not being in the list of customers who have a bad credit rating or are inactive—all of which comes from the same table.

Adding the UNION

The primary use of the **UNION** clause of **SQL SELECT** was once to simulate an outer join. Now that outer joins have been formally introduced into the statement, we can go back to using **UNION** as the clause that adds one result set to another.

```
SELECT customer.customerId, billing.fee ;
  FROM customer, billing ;
  WHERE customer.customerId = billing.customerId ;
    UNION ;
SELECT customer.customerId, 0, 0 ;
     FROM customer ;
     WHERE customer.customerId NOT IN ;
     (SELECT billing.customerId FROM billing)
```

With complex statements such as this one, it helps to read them from the bottom up. In this case, the second SELECT statement collects all the customers who don't have any billings. Then the first SELECT statement is executed, and that gets all the customers *with* billings. Finally, through the **UNION** clause, the two result sets are merged to create the outer join.

Employing a **UNION** is a bit tricky, but the main strategy for this kind of query is fairly clear: Use subqueries to get chunks of data and then use **UNION** to glue the chunks together. You can use the **ALL** option to prevent the elimination of duplicate rows from the combined results. Also, there are a few restrictions to using **UNION**:

- **UNION** can combine only a main query with a subquery (not two subqueries).
- All **SELECT**s must have the same number of columns specified for output.
- Each column of the result set must have the same data type as the subquery results.

- Only the main query can use **ORDER BY**, which will sort the merged result set.

USES OF SQL SELECT

The output options are the main guide to using **SELECT** inside the programming of your applications. Use arrays for ComboBoxes and other List controls. Use the default Browse options for an interactive screen. Use the DBF or cursor output for further data management and reporting. You should always consider SQL whenever you need to choose a method of extracting data with an unknown result set. The query optimizer will generally do a better job in working with multiple tables than you will. However, if you already know what you are looking for and if it can be readily defined as part of an index, then standard **SEEK** and **SCAN** will probably be quicker.

Because the Query Designer and View Designer aren't available in the EXE form of a FoxPro application, there have been many work-arounds and third-party products to fill the gap. These efforts are aimed primarily at replacing the interactive aspect of the Query and View Designers. In a more modest fashion, you can insert some quasi-interactive SQL into your own applications using either the parameters approach described in Chapter 4 or the following programming approach.

In a form:

```
*Get parameters from user: Last name and city name.
*Call the select method (or procedure).
DO SelectName WITH cLastName, cCityName
```

In a method or procedure:

```
DEFINE PROCEDURE SelectName
LPARAMETER tcLastName, tcCityName
LOCAL lcWhere

IF NOT EMPTY(tcLastName)
  lcWhere = "UPPER(lastname)=UPPER("+tcLastName+")"
ENDIF

IF NOT EMPTY( tcCityName)
```

```
    IF NOT EMPTY( lcWhere )
      lcWhere = lcWhere + " AND UPPER(city)=UPPER("+;
                tcCityName+")"
    ELSE
      lcWhere = "WHERE UPPER(city)=UPPER("+tcCityName+")"
    ENDIF
  ENDIF

  SELECT lastname, firstname, city, state, phone1 ;
    FROM customer ;
    WHERE &cWhere ;
    INTO DBF MailLst

  *Run the report based on the selection
  REPORT FORM MailLst TO PRINT PROMPT

  ENDPROC
  *
```

The query parser must pull apart and preprocess the whole query anyway, so the crucial element, a macro substitution, has no performance impact. This example is bound to a particular table. Using the same macro substitution technique, you can create much more generic SQL statements, which lend themselves to being incorporated in custom wrapper classes.

Programming Views into Reports

Another reason for using command language instead of the Designers is to include **SELECT** statements that can't be created in a Designer (for example, outer joins, self joins, and other nested joins). If you want to include this kind of complex **SELECT** in a Data Environment, here's how:

1. Open a database.
2. Create a view using the command language:

   ```
   CREATE SQL VIEW newtest AS SELECT * FROM testcode ;
    WHERE testcode.matrixId IN ;
    (SELECT matrix.matrixId FROM matrix ;
       WHERE matrix.type = "AGRONOMY" )
   ```

   The view is stored in the database file.

3. In either a report or form, you can now use this view in the Data Environment by selecting **Add** from the DE shortcut menu and picking the view from the list.

THE CLIENT/SERVER ASPECT OF FOXPRO APPLICATIONS

If you work in a corporate environment, where much of the data you need may be located on networks, mainframes, minicomputers, or a multitude of database servers, then the client/server approach to developing FoxPro applications is a must. Fortunately, everything that has been said to this point about FoxPro database management and object-oriented programming still applies, but the client/server approach adds a most important layer to your database design: access to remote data.

Developing client/server applications is a huge subject and can be covered only briefly in a book like this. This section will introduce the topics involved, with a special emphasis on the ODBC capabilities of Visual FoxPro and the ability to include remote data sources in SQL views.

THE CLIENT/SERVER MODEL

The terms *client* and *server* are so well worn that most people in the computer industry can at least attempt a definition. In fact, these terms are so well worn that the jargon has already moved on to a more complex situation—*partitioning*. Here, the discussion is not merely about clients and servers but also about repositories, business rules, and middleware (see Figure 20.1).

The *front end* is the application itself, which is created in an application development environment such as FoxPro. The application (and FoxPro while you're working on the application) is the client. The *back end* is traditionally the database server (products such as Sybase SQL, Oracle, and Microsoft SQL Server). These data management systems specialize in handling large volumes of SQL data requests from client applications.

In the expanded client/server model, which has been forming for the past three or four years, it has been realized that application software must draw information from sources that are both local (database files on the local network) and remote (database servers anywhere). To handle local data—which is often in the form of PC database files such as those from Microsoft Access, Borland dBase or Paradox, and FoxPro—the client software has been given at least a minimal database engine of its own. Management of remote data is the province of the specialist database servers.

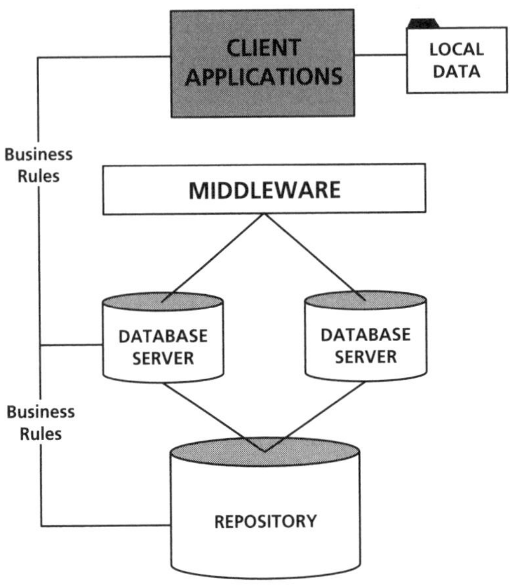

FIGURE 20.1 THE CLIENT/SERVER MODEL.

Accessing server databases directly is a tricky business, however, and it becomes virtually impossible if you try to manage access for servers from different companies. The solution is to use *middleware*: software that manages the interface between a client program and the database servers. The middleware, which for Visual FoxPro is Microsoft ODBC, supports many *drivers*: software routines that handle data requests from clients and translate them into the native language of a particular server.

Although virtually all servers use SQL, they don't all speak it with the same accent. Particular servers have special enhancements, such as triggers and stored procedures. Moreover, they often don't do important SQL functions—namely operations such as an outer join—in the same way. The drivers for a middleware package—which, by the way, don't always come from the same company—are supposed to compensate for the differences between servers and find the best way to translate a client request. This is not always the case, and that is one of the reasons that building extensive client/server applications can become complicated.

Another component of the client/server model is quickly growing in importance: the *repository*, or *data warehouse*, stores the archived data from one or many database servers as well as almost all kinds of information about the data. Repositories are somewhat specialized databases that employ data compression and other archiving techniques to store and retrieve vast quantities of mostly historical data.

Business rules, which you have encountered in several other chapters, are beginning to play a major role in client/server application design. Although business rules are often not formally included as part of the client/server model, it has become understood that they are actually some of the most important data of a working system and that they must be stored and applied with control and efficiency. The issue, however, is *where* the business rules are to be applied. That is part of the concept of partitioning, which is the splitting of responsibility for data and business rules among the various components of a client/server system.

VISUAL FOXPRO AS A CLIENT/SERVER DEVELOPMENT SYSTEM

Traditionally, FoxPro has been seen only as a development environment for local databases, in which data exists on the same local area network as FoxPro. The broader picture of the client/server model was (and still is) considered to be the domain of specialist client/server development systems such as Sybase PowerBuilder and Borland Delphi. The release of Visual FoxPro should change that perception, but it will take a while and will require some marketing support from Microsoft.

Although subject to endless debate, the significant realities appear to be as follows:

- Visual FoxPro has one of the most advanced client (front-end) application development systems available. The addition of a true object-oriented programming capability has made user interface development (among other things) not only easier but also potentially faster.
- Visual FoxPro 5.0 now supports team development and ties directly to Microsoft's version control product, Visual SourceSafe.

- FoxPro has always had one of the best, if not the best, local database engines available. In most one-to-one comparisons, it will run rings around database servers for direct manipulation of smaller sets of data with a moderate number of users.
- Visual FoxPro has added enough server-like capabilities—triggers, stored procedures, and data integrity routines as well as the expandable database container—to compete with servers for data integrity and incorporation of business rules.
- The FoxPro database engine is not designed for very large databases (millions of records being accessed by hundreds or thousands of users). There are limits to its scalability.
- Previous versions of FoxPro, and now Visual FoxPro, support Microsoft ODBC for connections to database servers with as much ease as any product available, if not more. Insofar as the ODBC drivers are good, FoxPro will have good performance in handling data from any ODBC support source. When some local manipulation of the result set is required, it's performance will be better than most.
- Visual FoxPro supports no form of a data repository.
- Visual FoxPro has no formal means for organizing business rules, although their incorporation, even on a quasi-partitioned basis, is relatively easy.
- Visual FoxPro has no formal support for partitioning, but innovative uses of FoxPro have accomplished some very good partitioning schemes.
- Visual FoxPro incorporates no form of upper CASE (design-oriented) tools.

It should be pointed out that no application development system does everything in this list. There are classes of systems. Some systems are intended for large transaction volume and corporate development, and they emphasize repositories, CASE tools, or business rule management. Another group of products aims for medium enterprise and departmental client/server development and often emphasizes partitioning. And then there are the PC database management systems, such as Visual FoxPro and Visual dBase, that can be used for client/server development at least to the departmental level.

Is Visual FoxPro a client/server development system? Emphatically, yes. Is it scalable to all levels of client/server enterprise database management and application development? No.

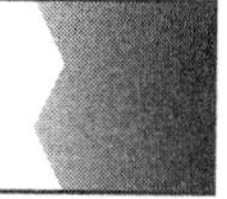

CONNECTING TO ODBC DATABASES

In terms of basic analysis and design, there is little difference between an application for local databases and one that uses remote data. However, when practical issues of performance and reliability come into play there can be major differences. Connecting to remote database servers or even local files from products other than FoxPro can be an adventure, exhibiting all the peculiarities of four different systems: remote data source, ODBC driver, network operating system, and FoxPro. These primary elements of the FoxPro ODBC connection are illustrated in Figure 20.2.

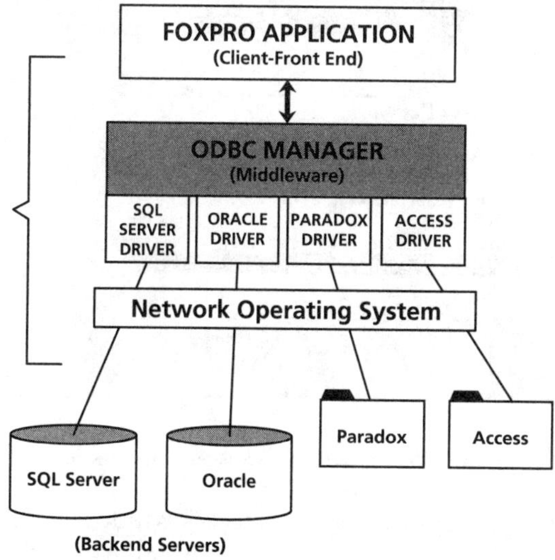

FIGURE 20.2 FOXPRO AND ODBC CONNECTIONS.

Microsoft ODBC has gone through several iterations and has just moved into the 32-bit world of Windows 95 and Windows NT. ODBC joins other major subsystems, including MAPI (messaging application programming interface), TAPI (telephony API), and WinSock (Windows sockets), all of which may become involved in a FoxPro application. Get used to this alphabet soup taxonomy. It's good for you.

All these services have a similar goal: to shield the developer (and the user) from the complexity of working with multiple APIs. ODBC does this by providing translation of SQL statements from any ODBC-compliant application into the native database commands of ODBC-supported file formats and database servers.

The actual translation is carried out by the ODBC drivers. In some cases, such as for dBase, Paradox, and Access file formats, the driver is a database engine, providing processing services to and from the file; such a driver is called a *single tier* driver. In other cases, the ODBC driver merely organizes and passes the SQL data request to a server, which does its own processing. This kind of driver is called a *multiple tier* driver.

The first step in hooking up Visual FoxPro with ODBC is to prepare the ODBC Administrator and select the relevant driver. In Windows 95 or NT, double-click the 32-bit ODBC Administrator. This action brings up the ODBC Data Sources window shown in Figure 20.3. (What you see will vary with the version of Windows.)

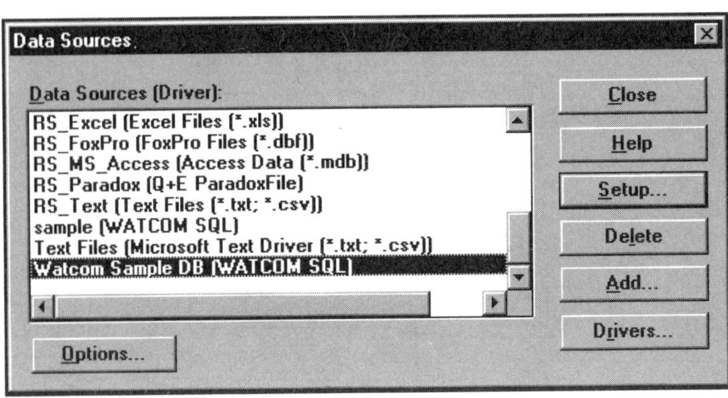

FIGURE 20.3 ODBC DATA SOURCES WINDOW.

More often than not, developers who open this window for the first time have no idea how all those drivers got there. Many programs load their own drivers, or even a set of drivers, during the installation process, with nary a word to the user. It's not unusual to have a driver list of 20 or more.

You can add data sources in this window based on existing drivers. If you need to add a new driver, the **Driver** button gives you access to the Drivers window (Figure 20.4).

Although most drivers are added automatically through setup of a particular application or development product, you can also add (or delete) drivers from this window. Be sure you have the appropriate disk handy, and be prepared to answer questions about where the driver should be placed.

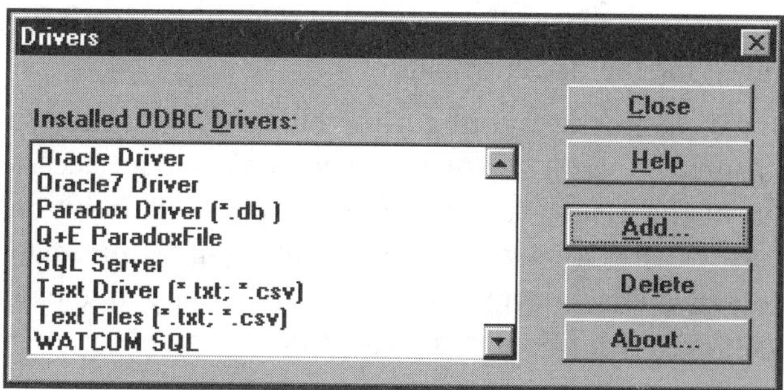

FIGURE 20.4 ODBC DRIVERS WINDOW.

Returning to the Data Sources window, you can create new sources by using the **Add** button, which shows you a version of the Drivers window so that you can select a driver on which to base the source. Next, you'll see the Setup or Configuration dialog box that's appropriate for the driver you've selected (Figure 20.5). The dialog box varies, because the driver for each product is responsible for its own installation and configuration.

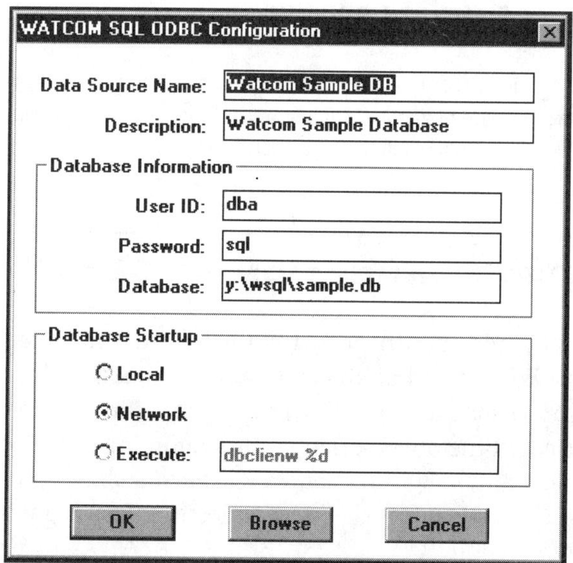

FIGURE 20.5 ODBC DRIVER CONFIGURATION DIALOG BOX.

Sometimes you can guess what information is required, but it's better if you have the documentation for the driver in hand.

In addition to selecting and configuring the driver, you need to set a couple of options for running the ODBC manager, which you can access through the **Options** button of the Data Sources window. The ODBC Options dialog box (Figure 20.6) lets you specify whether ODBC calls will be automatically tracked and recorded in a file. This information can be crucial if you're having problems identifying which calls from FoxPro are functioning or failing.

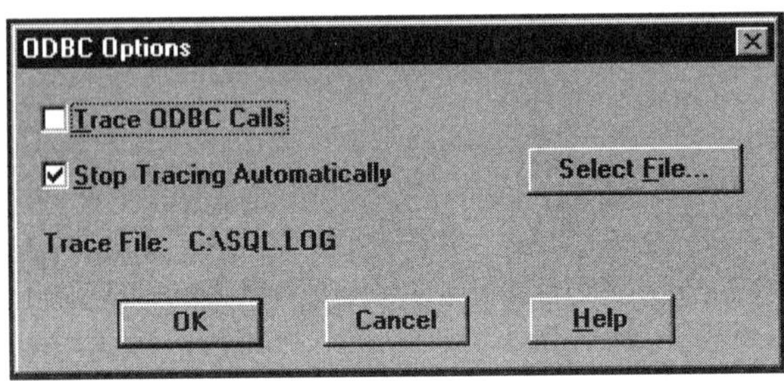

Figure 20.6 ODBC Options dialog box.

NOTE

If you are interested in more detailed information on the ODBC process, the ODBC Software Development Kit (SDK) is available from Microsoft, as are several articles on ODBC in the Microsoft TechNet CD-ROMs.

The FoxPro Connection to ODBC

Once you've configured the driver in the ODBC Administrator, you can turn your attention to FoxPro and establish a named *connection*. In the ODBC context, the word *connection* has special meaning for FoxPro. For one thing, a connection is an object in the object-oriented programming sense. It's also the only way you can attach an ODBC data source to your databases. However, there is more to an ODBC connection than just connecting. It is highly recommended that you do the following:

1. Create explicit *named* connections, which are stored in the database file.
2. Create SQL views that use the remote named connections.
3. Use the Data Environment to integrate the views with forms and reports.

In this way, FoxPro can automatically handle many of the tasks surrounding opening, querying, and closing remote tables. Also, in a SQL view, you are in a much better position to limit the number of records pulled from the remote data source—one of the primary goals of using a server. By using a Data Environment, you can use the object-oriented programming events to help control (even on a manual level) the connection to a remote data source.

NOTE

Connections and views have the equivalent of a base class definition (though not formally). It's called *connection 0* for connections and *cursor 0* for views. These are set with the default values of all properties (as defined in the tables in the following section). You can change the default properties by using **CURSORSETPROP( )** and **SQLSETPROP( )** like this: `CURSORSETPROP("BUFFERING", 5, 0)` and `SQLSETPROP( 0, "BATCHMODE", .f.)`. The 0 represents cursor 0 and connection 0, respectively. These changes remain in effect only during the current session of FoxPro, but during that time all connections or cursors you create will inherit the temporary values.

DESIGNING CONNECTIONS

Establishing a named connection is easy (provided everything works). Open the database to contain the remote connection. It must be opened with **EXCLUSIVE**. Start a new connection from the Project Manager in the **Data** tab: Select **Connections**, click the right mouse button, and select **New**. In the Connection Designer window (Figure 20.7), specify whether the connection uses separate fields for data source, user ID, and password; otherwise, select **Connection string**. Then either fill in the **Data source**, **Userid**, and **Password** fields, or enter the connection string appropriate for the data source.

The **Display ODBC login prompts** options let you specify when the prompts can be displayed: when they are not specified, always, and never.

The **Data processing** options are somewhat dependent on the nature of the data source. Most of the time you will use the default *synchronous* transmission, in which flow is simultaneous. However, some servers also support *asynchronous* transmission, the back-and-forth mode. This option can be desirable under certain network conditions. The **Display warnings** option allows you to shut off display of nontrappable errors generated by the server; you might choose this option if you don't want to alarm users. The **Batch processing** option is usually enabled, as is **Automatic transactions**. In both cases, FoxPro usually does a good job of managing the communications to the server and allowing it to control the transaction processing. There are occasions, however, when you might want to disable these features and use direct control through **SQLSETPROP( )**. This function is analogous to **DBSETPROP( )** for communications with database servers.

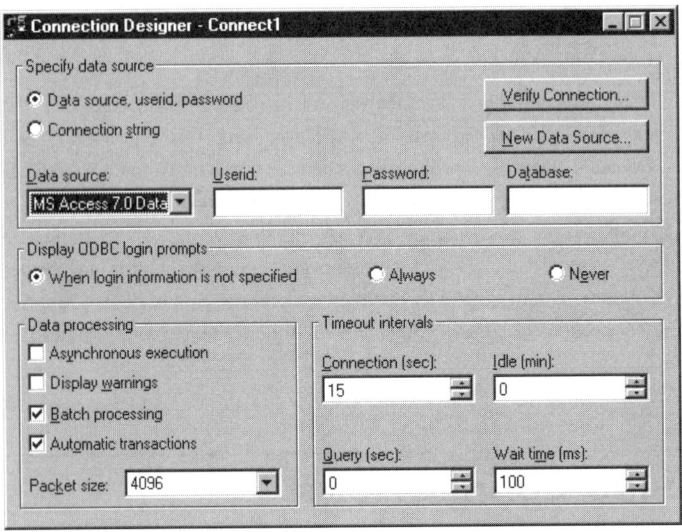

FIGURE 20.7 CONNECTION DESIGNER WINDOW.

The settings in the lower-right portion of the window, **Timeout intervals**, are both intriguing and finicky. Many of them are "tuning" capabilities that differ for every data source on any given network. As a rule, the default settings are satisfactory: 15 seconds for **Connection** time-out (loss of connection), 0 minutes for **Idle** time (how long before an inactive connection is dropped; 0 = indefinitely), 0 seconds for **Query** (how long FoxPro will wait for a query to complete; 0 = indefinitely), and 100 milliseconds for **Wait time** (how long FoxPro waits before checking to see whether a query is finished).

When you're finished setting the values, name the connection. It will be stored in the DBC file.

PROGRAMMING FOR CONNECTIONS

All the options in the Connection Designer can be set through programming. Creating a connection through commands is rare, but occasionally you made need to do one on-the-fly. (See **CREATE CONNECTION** in the *Language Reference* for details.)

Once the connection has been defined, you can address its properties through the CONNECTION type of the **DBGETPROP( )** and **DBSETPROP( )** functions (Table 20.3).

TABLE 20.3 DBGETPROP() AND DBSETPROP() FOR CONNECTIONS

PROPERTY	CODE	READ/WRITE STATUS	DESCRIPTION
Asynchronous	L	RW	`.t.` = Asynchronous connection, `.f.` = synchronous
BatchMode	L	RW	Processing is in batch mode, `.t.` or `.f.`.
Comment	C	RW	The text of the connection comment.
ConnectString	C	RW	The login connection string.
ConnectTimeout	N	RW	The connection time-out interval in seconds. Default = 0 (indefinite).
DataSource	C	RW	The name of the data source as defined in the ODBC.INI file.
DispLogin	N	RW	Numeric value that determines when the ODBC Login dialog box is displayed (from FOXPRO.H): 1 or `DB_PROMPTCOMPLETE`. 2 or `DB_PROMPTALWAYS`. 3 or `DB_PROMPTNEVER`.
DispWarnings	L	RW	Display connection errors that can't be trapped, `.t.` or `.f.`
IdleTimeout	N	RW	The idle time-out interval in seconds. Active connections are deactivated after the specified time interval. Default = 0 (indefinite).
PacketSize	N	RW	The size of the network packet used by the connection. Adjusting this value can improve performance. The default value is 4096 bytes (4K).

Property	Code	Read/Write Status	Description
PassWord	C	RW	The connection password.
QueryTimeout	N	RW	The query time-out interval in seconds. Default = 0 (indefinite).
Transactions	N	RW	Numeric value sets transaction handling (from FOXPRO.H): 1 or **DB_TRANSAUTO** (default). Automatic. 2 or **DB_TRANSMANUAL**. Transaction processing is handled manually through **SQLCOMMIT( )** and **SQLROLLBACK( )**.
UserId	C	RW	The user identification.
WaitTime	N	RW	The amount of time in milliseconds that elapses before Visual FoxPro checks whether the SQL statement has completed executing. Default = 100 milliseconds.

Extending the previous example, you can set any of the connection properties:

```
OPEN DATABASE utility EXCLUSIVE
CREATE CONNECTION excel_temp DATASOURCE excel1_data
=DBSETPROP( "EXCEL_TEMP", "CONNECTION", ;
            "CONNECTTIMEOUT", 30)
=DBSETPROP( "EXCEL_TEMP", "CONNECTION", ;
            "QUERYTIMEOUT", 10)
=DBSETPROP( "EXCEL_TEMP", "CONNECTION", ;
            "IDLETIMEOUT", 120)
```

Using named connections gives you a little more control in defining views and a way of documenting the server and other data sources that your application can handle. For transaction-heavy applications, particularly those running on very busy networks, you may need to define a set of connections that are tailored for specific operating conditions, such as changing all the time-outs for heavy traffic.

SHARING CONNECTIONS

In complex remote data situations, you may find it practical to use one connection for several views. This approach is called *sharing* the connection, and it requires an explicit setting. Follow these steps:

1. From the Project Manager, create a remote view using one or more named connections.
2. With the Project Manager open, select **Tools**, **Options** from the system menu and then select the **Remote Data** tab. In the **Remote View Defaults** area of the tab, check **Share Connection** and then choose **OK**.

   When this option is selected, FoxPro will automatically use a named connection that is already open, or it will open the connection as shared. Sharing connections can reduce the traffic on your network and at the server, but loading a connection "circuit" may decrease performance. This is another of those features that are highly dependent on the data source, network, and the requirements of your application.

NOTE

To improve the performance of a connection, you can test to see whether it's "busy" (carrying a transmission) by using a combination of **CURSORGETPROP()** and the **SQLGETPROP()** function:

```
=SQLGETPROP(CURSORGETPROP("CONNECTHANDLE"), "CONNECTBUSY")
```

This code could be built into a time-out class designed to handle a busy transmission.

REMOTE VIEWS

Remote views are nothing more than regular views that use data sources other than FoxPro databases and tables; put another way, remote views use ODBC. You can also mix local and remote data sources in the same view. The point of the view is simply to deliver a cursor that contains the information needed by a form or report. The source of the data is often of no importance to the user. To you, the developer, it can be of critical importance.

It's worth repeating that views are one of the most powerful features of Visual FoxPro. Unless there is a particular reason for not using them (performance is one reason), you should try to standardize on views as much as possible for multiple table data management.

Incorporation of connections in a remote view is mandatory. Whether you use the Remote View Wizard or simply open a remote view for the View Designer window, FoxPro will ask for the name of the connection (or else you can use the name of the data source) and will immediately test to see whether it can open the connection. If it can't, you won't be allowed to create the view. Most of the time, you will use named connections to create SQL views. As usual, the starting point is in the Project Manager. Follow these steps:

1. In the **Data** tab of the Project Manager, select **Remote Views**, click the right mouse button, and select **New**.
2. You can either use the View Wizard or go directly into the View Designer. The View Wizard can be helpful and will automatically test your ODBC link. As you may recall, the majority of a view is contained in the definition of the filtering **SELECT** statement. Generating that definition is mostly what the Wizard is designed to do.

Once in the View Designer, and assuming you've completed the SQL filter, you can turn your attention to the options in the **Update Criteria** tab (Figure 20.8).

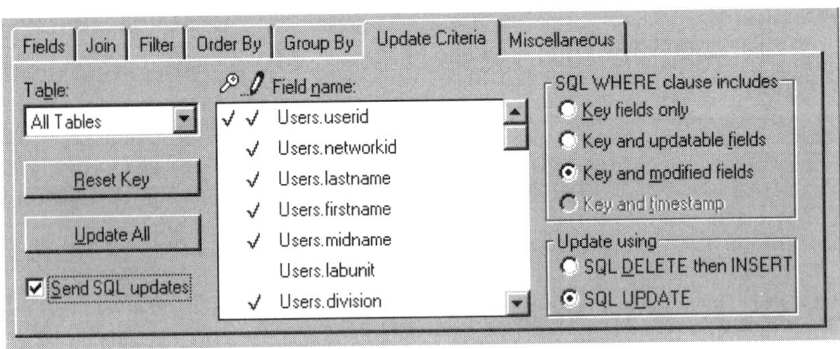

FIGURE 20.8 VIEW DESIGNER, UPDATE CRITERIA TAB.

UPDATING REMOTE VIEWS

Compared with editing of FoxPro tables, the handling of data update in a view—and in remote views in particular—requires more thought and some action. A number of properties affect how view tables are updated, and their settings need to be matched to your data sources. Some of these properties are accessible through the View Designer, and others must be set using **DBSETPROP( )**. We'll cover both approaches.

In the View Designer, **Update Criteria** tab, you can set several of the most important properties, as described in Table 20.4.

TABLE 20.4 UPDATE CRITERIA IN THE VIEW DESIGNER

PROPERTY	DESCRIPTION
Tables	This property provides a list of tables to be included in the remote update. The **Table** combo box defaults to All Tables, but in the spirit of client/server performance—fewer is better—you should include only those tables that contribute significant (updatable) fields. Fields are usually referred to as *columns* in the manuals, in keeping with the SQL jargon. In the View Designer, you can have only All Tables or any one table.
KeyField	As you might expect in a relational system, the linkage between tables is based on key fields (index keys). You must specify a key field for the primary table and for each of the child tables listed in the **Tables** property. In the View Designer, this will be done automatically for each included table (the check mark in the "key" column) based on the Data Environment for the view.
UpdateName	The "name" in this case is the name of the field for each field that you want to be updated. Again, fewer is better. The View Designer defaults to all the fields you selected in the **Fields** tab.
Updatable	Uncheck the "pencil" column for fields you don't need updated. Once again, less is better. You may wish to leave some of the fields for viewing but skip their update.
SendUpdate	The **Send SQL updates** button in the View Designer is the final, vital touch. This option enables or disables updating for the entire view. If you forget to check it, no updates will take place.

(Continued...)

PROPERTY	DESCRIPTION
UpdateType	In the **Update Using** area, you can set how updates should be processed using the **SQL UPDATE** command or executing **SQL DELETE then INSERT**. The latter method is usually faster, but not all data sources support it, especially the non-server source.
WhereType	There are at least three and sometimes four options listed in the **SQL WHERE clause includes** area. The manuals make this more murky than it needs to be; keep the options simple:
Key fields only	Selecting this option will update all selected fields except when a key field has been changed (usually deleted), which will cause the update to fail. This is the least restrictive option.
Key and updatable fields	In this option, the key fields and all updatable fields are compared against the remote data source. If anything has changed in the remote source, the update will fail.
Key and modified fields	For this option, the key fields and the updatable fields that have been modified are compared against the remote data source. If the values at the remote source have changed for these fields, the update will fail. This is the default setting.
Key and timestamp	This option applies only to data sources that support a TIMESTAMP field. In essence, this is a requirement that nothing has changed in the entire record, and that makes it the most restrictive option.

The choice of the updating scheme for a remote view is based on an analysis of the kind of information that flows between server and client, the volume of the traffic, and the security and integrity requirements. In general, as with local networks, you try to minimize the time that data sources are locked or tied up with processing. For remote servers, it may require a considerable amount of testing to find the right combinations.

By default, remote views are buffered and use an optimistic locking scheme (setting 5). This arrangement is sufficient for most uses, but you may also need to go to other locking schemes if the data warrants it.

SETTING VIEW AND CONNECTION OPTIONS INTERACTIVELY

In addition to the View Designer options, you can set a number of view and connection options interactively by going through the menu: **Tools**, **Options**, **Remote Data** tab. These options are summarized in Table 20.5. (See also the tables related to the **SQLSETPROP( )** and **CURSORSETPROP( )** functions for descriptions of the options.)

TABLE 20.5 REMOTE DATA OPTIONS TAB

OPTION	COMMAND EQUIVALENT
Share Connection	CURSORSETPROP("ShareConnection",...)
Fetch Memo on Demand	CURSORSETPROP("FetchMemo",...)
SQL Updates: Criteria	CURSORSETPROP("WhereType",...)
SQL Updates: Method	CURSORSETPROP("UpdateType",...)
Records to Fetch at a Time	CURSORSETPROP("FetchSize",...)
Maximum Records to Fetch	CURSORSETPROP("MaxRecords",...)
Use Memo for Fields	CURSORSETPROP("UseMemoSize",...)
Records to Batch Update	CURSORSETPROP("BatchUpdateCount",...)
Asynchronous Execution	SQLSETPROP("Asynchronous",...)
Display Warnings	SQLSETPROP("DispWarnings",...)
Batch Processing	SQLSETPROP("BatchMode",...)
Automatic Transactions	SQLSETPROP("Transactions",...)
Show Login	SQLSETPROP("DispLogin",...)
Connection Timeout	SQLSETPROP("ConnectTimeOut",...)
Idle Timeout	SQLSETPROP("IdleTimeOut",...)
Query Timeout	SQLSETPROP("QueryTimeOut",...)
Wait Time	SQLSETPROP("WaitTime",...)

The settings for these options are stored in the database file (DBC) along with the views defined while they were in effect. You can use the command equivalents during the run of a program to change the values.

Programming for Remote Views

Much of the configuration for remote views is available through the View Designer and the **Remote Data Options** tab, it's worthwhile asking whether (or when) it might be necessary to use programmatic means to change the settings. The answer, in general, comes in two forms: spot changes and wholesale program control.

There are times when you may need to change one or two connection or view properties as the program is executing. For example, some of the performance tuning properties (such as **UseMemoSize**, **IdleTimeOut**, and **FetchSize**) may need to be adjusted for a particularly large transaction. This adjustment requires nothing more than putting the appropriate **CURSORSETPROP( )**, **DBSETPROP( )**, or **SQLSETPROP( )** function in an event method or processing routine.

Because of the similarity between the three pairs of connection and view property functions, the following descriptions that may help you differentiate them .

- **DBGETPROP** and **DBSETPROP**. These functions read or set properties of the view or connection *definition*, as it is stored in the database file. This is very much like changing a template class definition. The changes are permanent and will apply to every connection or view created with that definition.
- **CURSORGETPROP** and **CURSORSETPROP**. Once the view has been executed and a cursor has been created, you can use these functions to read and modify the *active cursor* properties. The changes apply only to a specific instance of the view and are not permanent.
- **SQLGETPROP** and **SQLSETPROP**. Once a connection definition has become an *active connection*, you can use these functions to read and modify the connection properties. The changes apply only to a specific connection and are not permanent.

Tables 20.6 and 20.7 cover the remaining properties of **DBGETPROP** and **DBSETPROP** as they relate to views.

TABLE 20.5 DBGETPROP() AND DBSETPROP() FOR VIEW PROPERTIES

PROPERTY	CODE	READ/WRITE STATUS	DESCRIPTION
BatchUpdateCount	N	RW	The number of update requests being sent to the server. Default = 1; adjusting may be important for performance.
Comment	C	RW	The text of the view comment.
ConnectName	C	RO	The connection name for the view.
FetchMemo	L	RW	When `.t.`, Memo and General fields are retrieved but only after a direct request to display the data (delayed retrieval). In some cases, this can be a crucial performance setting.
FetchSize	N	RW	The number of records retrieved per time. Default = 100. Setting of –1 retrieves complete result set. This setting can be important for performance adjustments.
MaxRecords	N	RW	Sets the maximum number of records that can be retrieved. Default = –1, all records. 0 = no records but query is run. Use this property to test a data source or when you suspect a gigantic result set may occur. (You will also find the property in **CURSORSETPROP()**.)
ParameterList	C	RW	ParameterName1, DataType1… for the **WHERE** clause.

(Continued…)

PROPERTY	CODE	READ/WRITE STATUS	DESCRIPTION
RuleExpression	C	RW	The record validation expression.
RuleText	C	RW	The error message for record validation.
SendUpdates	L	RW	If true (`.t.`), SQL update query can be sent to update.
ShareConnection	L	RW	When `.t.`, the view can share connection handle.
SourceType	N	RO	1 = Local tables, 2 = Remote tables.
SQL	C	RO	The SQL statement to be executed by the view.
Tables	C	RW	Comma-delimited list of tables in the view.
Updatable	C	RW	Comma-delimited list of fields that may be updated.
UpdateName	C	RW	Comma-delimited list of remote fields to be updated.
UpdateType	N	RW	The update type from FOXPRO.H. 1 or **DB_UPDATE** . The old data is updated with the new data (default). 2 or **DB_DELETEINSERT**. The old data is deleted and the new data is inserted.
UseMemoSize	N	RW	The minimum size (bytes) for a returned Memo field.
WhereType	N	RO	The **WHERE** clause for remote tables (from FOXPRO.H):

PROPERTY	CODE	READ/WRITE STATUS	DESCRIPTION
WhereType *(Cont.)*			1 or **DB_KEY**. Update remote tables for only the primary fields specified with the **KeyFieldList** property. 2 or **DB_KEYANDUPDATABLE**. Update remote tables for the primary fields specified with the **KeyFieldList** property and any updatable fields. 3 or **DB_KEYANDMODIFIED** (default). Update remote tables for the primary fields specified with the **KeyFieldList** property and any other fields that are modified. 4 or **DB_KEYANDTIMESTAMP**. Update remote tables for the primary fields specified with the **KeyFieldList** property and a comparison of the time stamps.

TABLE 20.7 DBGETPROP() AND DBSETPROP() FOR FIELD PROPERTIES FOR VIEWS

PROPERTY	CODE	READ/WRITE STATUS	DESCRIPTION
Caption	C	RW	The field caption.
Comment	C	RW	The text of the field comment.
DataType	C	RO	The data type for a field (in a view).

(Continued...)

Property	Code	Read/Write Status	Description
DefaultValue	C	RW	The default field value.
KeyField	L	RW	A key field is set `.t.`
RuleExpression	C	RW	Field validation rule (as logical expression).
RuleText	C	RW	Error message for field validation.
Updatable	L	RW	True (`.t.`) if field can be updated.
UpdateName	C	RW	The name of the field to update for a remote table.

Passing Through: SQLGETPROP and SQLSETPROP

If you are creating a client/server application and you need to go beyond the capabilities of the View Designer or even of the FoxPro SQL commands, the ultimate channel of approach is the so-called SQL pass-through functions.

For connections, use the following:

- **SQLCONNECT()**. Makes the connection to a SQL data source (usually a server).
- **SQLSTRINGCONNECT()**. Connects to a data source with an ODBC connection string.
- **SQLDISCONNECT()**. Disconnects from an ODBC data source.

For **SELECT** statement execution and control, use these functions:

- **SQLCANCEL()**. Cancels the execution of a query on an asynchronous connection.
- **SQLEXEC()**. Executes a pass-through **SELECT** statement through an active connection.
- **SQLMORESULTS()**. Requests and fills the active cursor with more data from the server.
- **SQLCOMMIT()**. Requests a transaction commitment.
- **SQLROLLBACK()**. Requests a transaction rollback.

For data source and miscellaneous information, these functions are available:

- **SQLCOLUMNS()**. Creates a list of column names and information.
- **SQLTABLES()**. Creates a list of tables in the data source.
- **SQLGETPROP()**. Reads and returns a connection property from an active connection.
- **SQLSETPROP()**. Sets a property for an active connection.

Unlike the ODBC settings, these functions work directly with the data source—in most cases, a SQL database server—and that is why they're called pass-through functions. They open up possibilities for taking advantage of server-specific capabilities and of developing fairly precise control over the timing and processing of data between the FoxPro application and the remote server. They are also risky, temperamental, and difficult to implement; consider their use with care.

The SQL pass-through functions and their relationship to specific database servers are beyond the scope of this book, but you should know about **SQLGETPROP( )** and **SQLSETPROP( )** because they are sometimes used within remote views and ordinary connections.

Command syntax:

SQLGETPROP(nConnectionHandle, cSetting)

SQLSETPROP(nConnectionHandle, cSetting [, eExpression])

Arguments:

nConnectionHandle The number of the connection handle as it is returned by **SQLCONNECT()** or `CURSORGETPROP("CONNECTHANDLE")`.

cSetting The setting (or property, although in the SQL context this is inaccurate).

eExpression The value to be set as any kind of valid FoxPro expression.

Example:

```
IF SQLGETPROP(0, "CONNECTTIMEOUT") = 0
  nOk = SQLSETPROP(0, "CONNECTTIMEOUT", 15)
ENDIF
```

As you can see in Table 20.8, the settings for these functions are almost identical to those for **DBGETPROP( )** and **DBSETPROP( )**:

TABLE 20.8 SQLGETPROP() AND SQLSETPROP()

Setting	Code	Read/Write Status	Description
Asynchronous	L	RW	`.t.` = asynchronous connection, `.f.` = synchronous.
BatchMode	L	RW	Processing is in batch mode, `.t.` or `.f.`.
ConnectBusy	L	RO	Returns `.t.` if the connection is busy, (data is being sent).
ConnectName	C	RW	The name of the connection—not to be confused with the connection handle.
ConnectString	C	RW	The login connection string.
ConnectTimeout	N	RW	The connection time-out interval in seconds. Default = 0 (indefinite).
DataSource	C	RW	The name of the data source as defined in the ODBC.INI file.
DispLogin	N	RW	Numeric value that determines when the ODBC Login dialog box is displayed (from FOXPRO.H): 1 or **DB_PROMPTCOMPLETE**. 2 or **DB_PROMPTALWAYS**. 3 or **DB_PROMPTNEVER**.
DispWarnings	L	RW	Display connection errors that can't be trapped, `.t.` or `.f.`
IdleTimeout	N	RW	The idle time-out interval in seconds. Active connections are deactivated after the specified time interval. Default = 0 (indefinite).
ODBChdbc	N	RO	The internal ODBC connection handle.

SETTING	CODE	READ/WRITE STATUS	DESCRIPTION
ODBChstmt	N	RO	The internal ODBC statement handle.
PacketSize	N	RW	The size of the network packet used by the connection. Adjusting this value can improve performance. The default value is 4096 bytes (4K).
PassWord	C	RW	The connection password.
QueryTimeout	N	RW	The query time-out interval in seconds. Default = 0 (indefinite).
Transactions	N	RW	Numeric value sets transaction handling (from FOXPRO.H): 1 or **DB_TRANSAUTO** (default). Automatic. 2 or **DB_TRANSMANUAL**. Transaction processing is handled manually through **SQLCOMMIT( )** and **SQLROLLBACK( )**.
UserId	C	RW	The user identification.
WaitTime	N	RW	The amount of time in milliseconds that elapses before Visual FoxPro checks whether the SQL statement has completed executing. Default = 100 milliseconds.

A Local and Remote Data Example

As an example of manipulating data sources in the object-oriented programming framework, here's how to design a form that can use both local and remote data.

1. Starting from the Project Manager, open a database.
2. Create a local view.
3. Create a remote view with an identical field structure. The identical structure is key, although it also limits its use.

4. Create the form to use the data.
5. Define a property of the form to signal whether to use local or remote data. For example: `plUseRemote`.
6. Add the local view to the data environment of the form. Because both local and remote views have the same structure, substituting one for the other will be no problem.
7. Because you will need to control the opening of tables to be able to insert your alternative code, set the following properties:

   DataEnvironment.**AutoOpentables** = `.f.`

   Cursor1.**Alias**= "A generic name"

   Controls.**ControlSource**, set to the field names of the Cursor1 alias

   Grids.**RecordSource**, set to the field names of the Cursor1 alias
8. Use the form **Load** event method to set the user-defined property for local or remote data. This property could be set by user decision (with a **MESSAGEBOX** function) or by logic from the program: `THISFORM.plUseRemote = .T..`
9. In the **Init** method of the Data Environment, explicitly call the **OpenTables** method:

```
THIS.OpenTables()
```

10. In the **Init** method for Cursor1, set the **CursorSource** property to the appropriate view using the user-defined property:

```
IF THISFORM.plUseRemote = .T.
  THIS.CursorSource = Name of remote view
ELSE
  THIS.CursorSource = Name of local view
ENDIF
```

Program Control of Remote Connections and Views

Wholesale program control of remote connections and views is a major undertaking. It usually involves a sophisticated combination of the FoxPro settings (set either automatically or manually) and the use of the SQL pass-through commands including **SQLGETPROP()** and **SQLSETPROP()**, which talk directly to

ODBC and thence to the server software. The situation is remindful of the old days of FoxPro table and record locking. The automatic system was quite good—but not good enough—so many developers decided to build their own locking system. In this case, there are plenty of remote data access situations that may require careful and elaborate control of the entire process.

NOTE

If you decide that you need to embark on complete control of remote access, you should assemble the ODBC SDK, all the relevant manuals from the remote data source (presumably server software), and specialist material from the Microsoft Technical Notes, journals, and other books. You will have a steep (and interesting) learning curve ahead of you.

CHAPTER WRAP-UP

If the use of SQL in Visual FoxPro needed any emphasis, this chapter has underlined it. Because of the updatable views, Visual FoxPro SQL is no longer "just" a query language; it's also a means of maintaining data. Your ability to manipulate the **SQL SELECT** statement with facility and imagination could easily be one of the most important skills for developing successful applications. This is not an exaggeration.

Within the context of client/server computing, SQL is the native language—the one you will use when communicating with remote data sources. The process of developing a client/server application is similar to that of a standard FoxPro application except for the work you need to do with remote data. Although this task may also seem familiar (especially the SQL), you may find that in practice there are many complications.

This chapter contains nary a word about an application framework, so let's bring the focus back to that for a moment. All forms of SQL are represented in the database elements of an application framework. Many developers who specialize in data retrieval create their own class library (a VCX) that is filled with classes that support different kinds of query and view building within an application, especially when the user interface requires a substitute for the Query Designer or View Designer.

For those developers who use Visual FoxPro in a client/server role, the best way to handle the myriad tasks involved in setting, tuning, and maintaining connections and their views is to put them into classes. The best of these classes can make the transition from local FoxPro data management to remote server operation almost seamless.

SECTION 7

COMPLETING AN APPLICATION FRAMEWORK

As you have been discovering, there is a lot of application machinery behind most applications. This programming has little or nothing to do with the content (domain) of the application but is dedicated to keeping the program running. Some of is, such as error trapping and multiuser data management is virtually inevitable. Some of it, such as security and file maintenance, is pretty standard. And some of it, such as report and print management and user preference management, is elective but often well appreciated by users.

This section of the book covers these application components along with some of the supporting topics, such as documentation, testing, and application delivery. It also completes the application framework by discussing the framework document and the various larger modules that can be added to almost any application (Section Figure 7.1).

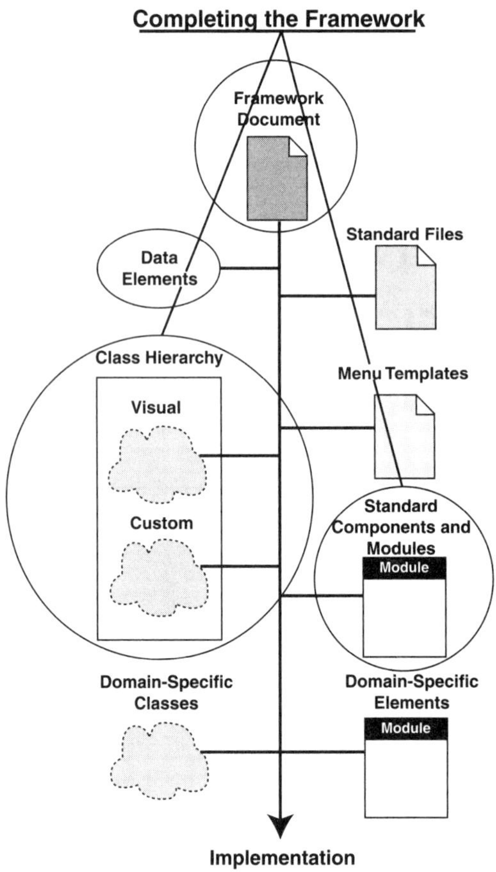

SECTION FIGURE 7.1 COMPLETING THE FRAMEWORK.

As you approach the end of the development cycle, repeat this mantra: Winding up is not winding down. Of course, if your project is on time, on budget, and beloved by the users, you may be ready to relax as delivery approaches. Barring miracles, however, most developers face the last days or weeks of development with an acute sense of the lack of resources (time, money, people, and so forth). This makes the topics of the final three chapters some of the most difficult (in the practical sense).

- Chapter 21, "Testing and Documentation," describes the possible levels of testing for an application and the developer's responsibility to produce adequate documentation.

- Chapter 22, "Standard Components and Modules," includes some of the elements of an application that every developer should eventually have in the application framework. These elements include data maintenance routines, error trapping, backup and archiving, report management, and application security.
- Chapter 23, "Delivering the Application," approaches the final step of the development cycle as being tricky enough not to overlook and simple enough not to overcomplicate—depending on the nature of your application.

It will be stressed here and in the following chapters that the final days of development are usually hectic. That's what makes the business of testing, documentation, utilities, and software delivery easy to talk about and difficult to do. It's also why you should make the effort to plan these elements, or even prepare some of them, long before the crunch days arrive.

CHAPTER 21

TESTING AND DOCUMENTATION

It's important not to think of testing and documentation as necessary evils. Although they're not as creative or satisfying as making new user interface elements, they are important and challenging in their own right. From the user's perspective, testing and documentation ensure that the application will do what you say it will do and that you care enough about the application to help the user understand and operate it. If you underplay these two elements, you risk alienating the user regardless of the brilliance of your programming.

Some parts of testing were discussed in the chapter on debugging, Chapter 13, but, as this chapter will take pains to point out, debugging is not testing. Testing helps to generate bugs, but it should be far more systematic than simply waiting for something to debug. There are several kinds of testing and different stages of testing that occur during the application development cycle.

Documentation is a broad subject, covering not only documentation of the programming and application design but also all aspects of documentation for the user: on-line help, manuals, training materials, and so forth. FoxPro provides tools to help with documentation, but, as you will see, it's an area of development that takes considerable time and discipline, usually at the end of the development cycle when you have the least time and least inclination to be disciplined.

APPLICATION TESTING

You expect that commercial software, such as FoxPro, has had extensive testing. In fact, you demand it. What about your own software? "Well, sure, I'd really like to get it tested, but there isn't much time, and with our budget..." Let's try to be realistic, starting with defining four levels of testing:

1. **Mainstream commercial software.** These programs are distributed to thousands or even millions of people. The software must be heavily tested, not only for reputation's sake but also for practical reasons. If the product isn't close to bulletproof, it will cost a fortune to support and could be dead in the marketplace. Theoretically, the volume of the national (or international) market can subsidize the full-scale effort to test thoroughly.
2. **Vertical market software.** It's a slightly different story for a commercial application with limited distribution. Whether it is a vertical market application such as a dental office package or software developed within a corporation for use at branch offices, there is an implicit and sometimes contractual requirement for custom support. Configuration, setup, and maintenance may all be part of the distribution process and the purchase price. This means that although the software still needs as much testing as possible, it's routinely fudged in lieu of on-site correction. There may or may not be any budget for formal testing, and that tends to put it in the "as can" category.
3. **Custom or workgroup software.** Even further down the testing totem pole are applications customized for one or a few clients. Typically, these programs have little or no budget dedicated to testing. As a result, testing is neither systematic nor extensive. As with vertical market software, there is heavy reliance on the fix-it-as-you-go approach. It's also helped by the fact that the number of users is limited. Just as programmers make lousy testers because they instinctively know how to avoid bugs, a small group of users—especially those who have been involved in the development process—also manage to get themselves into patterns that don't cause problems. This approach doesn't work consistently, but a large percentage of applications survive on this basis.
4. **Personal software.** Some applications are essentially personal. Here, testing is usually synonymous with debugging.

There are a couple of points to emphasize about these categorizations. First, testing is not debugging. Testing produces bugs, but even that doesn't go far enough. Just *using* software produces bugs, especially early in the development cycle. Testing is intentional mayhem; you're trying to produce bugs and, more important, record when and how they occurred. And remember, there are different kinds of bugs: those that crash the application, those that produce an error message but don't cause a crash, and those that are wrong but don't stop the program or even produce an error message. A bad calculation is just as much a bug as a syntax error. Testing must catch them all and may concentrate on finding the things that don't produce an obvious message.

The second point is that real testing is expensive. It's one thing for software theoreticians to wag their fingers and admonish, "Thou shalt test," and it's quite another to come up with the time and money to put software through a complete testing cycle. The more systematic and thorough the testing, the more expensive it becomes. Yet there is no reliable table of cost/benefit ratios to help you determine how much testing is enough. Intuitively, more testing should make a better product, and it probably does. But there are so many exceptions that no one can guarantee that a solid testing regime will provide a solid product. In addition, as is well known, there is no such thing as a bug-free program.

Saying that there are always bugs in software is a cop-out. We all know that testing is necessary, even when it's not sufficient. For most developers, it's a question that's addressed application by application. Although there are patterns for testing and books written on the methodologies, it all boils down to two questions: What does this application need? What can you afford to do?

USER INTERFACE TESTING VS. PROCESS TESTING

It may be useful to consider the need for testing based on how much of your application is user interface and how much is processing. Although both aspects require testing, they don't need the same kind or degree of testing.

The active part of the user interface, composed of menus, buttons, grids, and other controls, needs testing by people who will poke the keyboard in every which way, trample through any data entry, and attempt to try every wrong option in the menus—in short, the average user. There is no way a programmer or a development team can do this because they know too much. In any case, testing is a numbers game; the more people who can test an application, the better. Time, money, and management capability are the limiting factors.

On the other hand, process testing can be done by programmers. Most database applications contain data processes of some kind: updating, transaction processing, calculations, reporting, and so on. The name of the game for this kind of testing is to be systematic. A wide range of test data, simulations, and test reporting can be organized to exercise your application's processing for accuracy and reliability. How much of this you do depends on limiting factors such as time and money. But this kind of testing is more controlled and even predictable.

Of the two kinds of testing, user interface testing is much more expensive and time-consuming. Even if you don't hire professional software testers, the management of a beta test, distribution of the program, support, and response can become very demanding very quickly. If your application has many complex user interface elements, you'll need to plan more extensive testing.

Configuration Testing

From the perspective of commercial software development, the most difficult aspect of testing is the necessity of running an application in a wide variety of computer environments. If you're lucky, you're developing your application to run on a limited number of computers with known specifications. Under these circumstances, you don't need configuration testing. At worst, however, you may be sending your application out into the great unknown, where machines of every age, description, and condition may turn your robust programming into an inert lockup.

If your application will be distributed and you don't know which computers and networks it will run on, you may be forced to do at least a sampling of configuration tests. This can take the form of a public test in which copies are distributed to a number of different people, or you can use the services of a professional testing company. Either way, it is expensive. In some corporate projects, you may have a better idea which computers will be used to run your application, in which case limited configuration tests might be enough.

The Testing Cycle

Throughout the development of an application some form of testing is always going on, even if only by the programmers. In overview, testing is linear, moving from a beginning to an end, but the real work of testing is a cycle (see Figure 21.1).

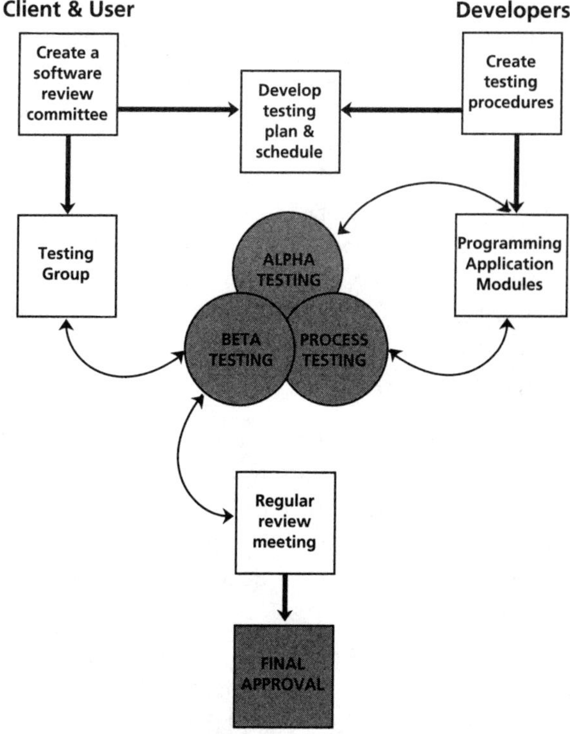

FIGURE 21.1 THE TESTING CYCLE.

As the developers complete segments of the program, they test it (the alpha test) and then send it to users for testing (the beta test); at roughly the same time, performance and stress testing (the process test) are taking place. Each of the testing activities is accompanied by a review (often formal), which produces feedback involving both bug-fixing and program modification. The cycle of programming and testing repeats not only for each module but also several times within a module.

The scale of this cycle varies greatly. For a small project, or when the number of users and developers is small, it may be hard to determine where programming ends and testing begins. But one thing is certain: In the end, the program must run properly to the satisfaction of the users. So some testing is inevitable.

Full-scale professional testing is a complex business. Starting with the adoption of one or more testing methodologies, it includes development of specific *test metrics* (measurement guidelines) and a complete plan and schedule for the testing cycle. Describing such an undertaking is beyond the scope of this book, and probably beyond the budgets of most FoxPro developers. However, at a somewhat less rigorous level, there's still much you can do to test your applications effectively.

NOTE

Unlike much of the programming process, software testing is often intensely interpersonal. Especially if the ultimate users of the software are involved in the testing process (a normal occurrence), the sensitivity to problems with the software can be difficult to manage. This is one of the times when project managers earn their keep.

Planning for Testing

Many developers bridle at the mention of a formal testing schedule. It sounds like something you do for mainframe software, and that's true. It's also true that on small projects or projects that involve only a few people, any kind of formal testing may be unnecessarily expensive. But somewhere between none and too much is a level of testing that fits a full-scale application. To find that level takes thought and planning.

As in Figure 21.1, most testing plans and schedules are a collaborative effort been the developers and the clients. The clients should be working from the specifications developed for the software, and the developers should have decided on their own approach to the technical aspects of testing (debugging information, user reporting, documentation, and version control).

During the planning sessions, which often have the air of contract negotiations, the goals are to develop a mutual understanding of the scope of the project, an approach to testing, and a reasonable schedule. Here are some points that usually apply:

- **Make testing fit the application.** Part of your planning for an application should be to review development procedures and think about how this application should be tested as it develops. A financial or accounting program requires a certain kind of testing, which is different from the testing for a parts list catalog.
- **Stick to the essentials.** Deciding what's important to test is a major task of planning. If you put it on paper (it seldom needs to be more than a 10 page document), you and everyone else involved in the software development should understand what is unique or most

important about an application, and, in that context, which types of testing need to be emphasized. For example, is the database very large? Then performance tests become important. Are there a large number of critical calculations? Then reporting tests and formula checks become a top priority. This kind of evaluation is the key to making the best of limited testing resources. It's the old 80/20 rule: Test the most important things first and hardest. If you don't get to the other 20 percent, it may not be critical.

- **Use documentation as part of the testing process.** Experienced programmers know that certain problems are associated with certain kinds of programming. For example, in database applications, shifting between program modules can cause problems with table pointers, indexes, and relations. This is especially true of event-driven programming. Knowing this, programmers can take extra steps to document areas in the programs where shifts occur from one database configuration to another. The object of this approach is not only to explain what's there but also to speed the process of locating problems during testing.
- **Plan for development test databases.** For most database applications, nothing is more critical to the success of testing than a good test database. This should be no surprise, but creating this database is often easier said than done. So plan for it. If necessary, assign the work and schedule it. Also plan the approach. Depending on the type of application, you may need to create a database from scratch, or perhaps you can make it part of the conversion process.
- **The schedule is never real.** The fictitious quality of software development schedules is legendary. There is almost always a tension between the amount of time it takes to program an application and the time people are willing to pay for it. Even if the budget is large enough to give a project the luxury of complete honesty, it is still difficult to be accurate with schedules because software development is subject to a huge number of variables. In many ways, developing a full-scale application is like mounting a large theatrical production. It's a highly complex and social undertaking, but with an even bigger element of technical uncertainty.
- **Plan for the end run.** The end of a software development period is often the most difficult time. In the early planning stage, it's difficult

to visualize what the delivery is going to be like, but when you get there few people have the time or energy for planning it. Yet this is typically when the most difficult testing takes place—the days of the deep bugs and pressure-filled deadlines. Plan on it, and organize events that help relieve the tension, or at least try to put some breathing room into the schedule.

All this is common sense. But with some planning, it's *organized* common sense.

Error Trapping

Before you launch an organized testing program, it's a good idea to review your methods for handling errors. If you're using the standard FoxPro error trapping and reporting, you need to ask yourself whether it will provide enough information when it's being reported by a user. Programmers become adept at interpreting cryptic error messages when they experience the context themselves; but when that context is someone else's experience, it becomes much more difficult.

As a result, many developers opt for creating an error reporting system. The APPERROR class provided with this book is an example. By doing your own error trapping, you can retrieve far more information and also make it possible for the beta testers (often users) to encounter bugs in a gentler and kinder fashion.

Alpha Testing

By now the terms *alpha testing* and especially *beta testing* are so common that even nonprogrammers are familiar with them. Alpha testing is usually synonymous with in-house (programmer) testing, and beta testing with independent testers, whether professional or otherwise. These two phases are clearest in commercial software. In database application development, it's common for a rudimentary alpha testing to take place, but the emphasis is on putting software in front of the user as soon as possible in a sort of blend of alpha and beta testing. In fact, with the Rapid Application Development (RAD) approach to software development, the blurring of lines between phases of testing is deliberate.

Even so, there is still a process of programmer testing, and it may overlap more or less continuously with beta testing. After all, if the program can't run, there's not much point in a demonstration, much less in turning it over to users for testing. In larger software shops, certain people may be assigned to testing, or, in ideal situations, the work is done by people whose job it is to test software.

Whatever the scale of alpha testing, the basic tasks remain the same:

- Catch all "fatal error" bugs, those that cause the program to crash.
- Do first testing of user interface elements.

In some senses, the work of alpha testing is to "get the worst of it." Machine lock-ups are the one type of error that no one wants to let out of the inner circle. At the same time they write code, programmers generally wander around in the application. In that sense, they are also taking the first crack at testing the user interface. This is rarely, if ever, systematic, but it's often satisfactory for alpha testing.

The final aspect of the alpha phase is configuration testing. This is the most difficult phase for small operations. Access to a wide variety of configurations (computers, peripherals, and so on) may be limited. Access to client or target customer configurations may also be restricted. There is always the possibility of sending your applications to a professional testing lab, but it is very expensive. The truth is, you do the best you can and cross your fingers, hoping that no one is running a vintage 486/66, with 60 MB of hard disk, eight MB of RAM, Windows 95, on a Token Ring network.

PROCESS TESTING

In addition to the first-run alpha testing, most developers become involved in testing the database and data management processing of the application. How much *process testing* needs to be done varies with the type of application, but most database applications should have at least some of it. There are three steps in process testing:

1. Develop a test database.
2. Run processing simulations.
3. Check processing and calculations for accuracy.

Process testing starts with building a good test database. All applications must have such a sample database; otherwise, you couldn't even begin to run the program. But the sample database is not the same as a test database.

If possible, the test database should be appropriately scaled for the application. Those tables that are expected to contain a large number of records should be equally sizable for testing. This is especially true for applications that make heavy use of relations, SQL, and reporting. Performance issues can crop up in unexpected places, so it's important that you are working with tables large enough to truly exercise the application.

Even more important is the loading of data that will test the extremes of an application. Good test data should be deliberately injected with the following:

- Garbage data, such as nonstandard characters (above ASCII 132 and below 20).
- Values that exceed maximum and minimum parameters for calculations and functions.
- Records with severe data integrity problems (such as nulls and improper values).
- Tables with relational problems (missing keys, widow records, and orphan records).

The trouble with introducing this kind of data into tables is that it becomes difficult to distinguish between artificially placed bad data and bad data produced by the program. That's why a controlled use of extreme data means documentation of what the test data is and where it is located. Typically, test suites of data are constructed and run through the application, each one focusing on one of the four main types of problem data.

Whatever pattern you adopt, the test database is used to run simulations of all the table processes in the application: table updating, data processing, reports, and queries—anything that has a programmed sequence not directly tied to interactive user control. At the same time, it's convenient to carefully check calculations and processing in reports, printouts of the database, and other places where results appear.

BETA TESTING

There's an old axiom among businesses that cater to the public: People don't know what they want until you show them what they don't want. Software is no different. No matter how well you think you understand an application, no matter how much interviewing and analysis was done, when you put the application in the user's hands, that's when you find out (maybe) what people want. The "maybe" is there because it takes time for users to become accustomed to all but the simplest of applications. During the first few days, they may reserve their opinion. Then, like a punch to the solar plexus, you'll hear, "This program doesn't work; it's awful." An anguished hour later, you discover what was wrong: two fields that had an incorrect calculation.

Such is the life of beta testing, in which you turn over all or part of application to people who aren't programmers. The testers can range from a spouse to several hundred thousand people. (Microsoft claims it had more than 400,000 people in the Windows 95 beta test.) Only time, money, and management capability are required.

Once again, you are faced with decisions about the scale of the project, the time and resources available, and the target users of the application. If it is a commercial product, you need a fairly large base of beta testers (at least 50 to 100 people) to have a reasonable sample. If it is a corporate project of modest scale or an application being customized for a client, then perhaps 10 to 25 testers might be enough. Smaller projects might get by with only a handful of testers. The more people involved, the more difficult the management and the greater the expense.

The expense of beta testing isn't merely the cost of materials or communications (phone and fax) but also the time it takes to keep the program running. Some one must plan the program, package and ship the beta copies, monitor the testing, and respond to the testers. If you want the maximum benefit from a beta program, you need to go beyond basic bug reporting and learn from the beta testers what they think about the program—get their gut reactions. Soliciting this kind of information takes some skill and even more time. In custom software development, it's a required step. In other kinds of development, it may seem like an elective. It may be, but you're wasting half the potential reward of a beta test.

NOTE

A trend in modern software development is to emphasize the human interaction side of the process. *Usability testing* is an example. This trend is a result of the personal computer becoming the dominant platform. Unfortunately, many programmers and developers still have the notion that they can go off to their space and create great software without the nuisance of dealing with users. The reality is otherwise. The developer who can orchestrate a successful relationship between the development process and the users stands the best chance of creating a successful project. Beta testing is a big part of that relationship.

VERSION AND SOURCE CODE CONTROL

The beta test period is almost inevitably the first encounter with the problem of *version control*. Each time you deliver a portion of your application to beta testing, you've generated a version of the software. In a one-person project, this isn't much of a problem, although you still need to pay attention to what's new and what's not. But in a multiperson development effort, version control is a major issue. Terrible things can happen to code that gets lost between versions.

There are many kinds of version control, and it's usually teamed with source code control. At the most basic level, it involves cataloging components of an application (usually the files), placing them in special folders (subdirectories) for each version, and keeping a record of when these components are updated or incorporated into a version. In some cases, this record is extended to a logging system for developers, who approach the files as part of a library from which they can borrow.

FoxPro has no built-in version control, but Visual FoxPro 5.0 has hooks to commercial version control programs, namely Microsoft's Visual SourceSafe. If you make your way through the menu to **Tools**, **Options**, **Projects**, you'll see an area for Source Control Options (Figure 21.2).

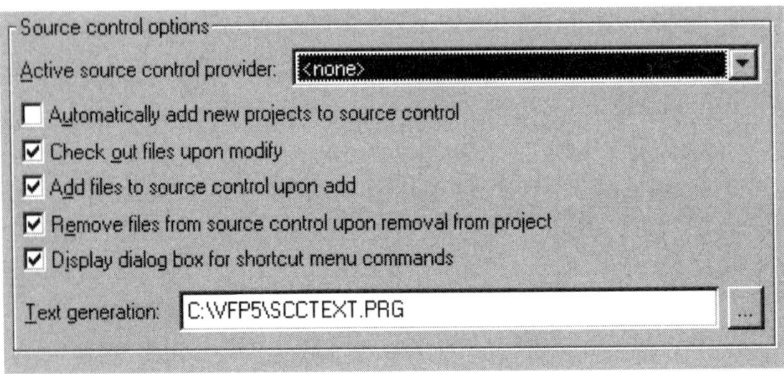

FIGURE 21.2 SOURCE CONTROL OPTIONS.

Version control software enforces file checking out and checking in and maintains before and after comparisons as versions of code. Visual SourceSafe 5.0 has recently been released. In addition to source code file management, it now handles Web site version control.

NOTE

Chapter 29 of the *Developer's Guide* does a good job of explaining how source code and version control work in the context of team programming. If you're considering source code control, that's a good place to start.

For some situations, it's enough to create your own version control system. Good documentation can go a long way. Put version information into the headers of PRG files and by convention in the **Init** method of forms. Various schemes have been devised around the FoxPro Project Manager, and these techniques help with checking out modules of the program. Because the Project Manager is not multiuser-enabled, you can parcel out the application in several Project Manager files. These individualized Project Managers are then assigned or available on a controlled (sign out, sign in) basis. This is usually combined with a folder system that looks something like this:

```
\root\development
      \beta
      \production
```

Programming and alpha testing are done in the development folder, and the beta version resides in the beta folder. When the application is completed, the shipping version goes into the production folder. This system is crude, but it works.

COMING TO CLOSURE

When is an application finished? Being tied to payday, this question is often the most important one faced by a developer. Knowing that software is never completely tested or bug-free, how do you arrive at a point when all parties can say that the beta testing is over and it's time to deliver the product?

Much depends on the kind of software. Different standards exist for commercial shrink-wrap, vertical market, single-client, and personal software. But a rule of thumb applies to almost all situations: Software is deliverable when the users can routinely do the work for which the program was created without errors. The software is said to be *operational*. This doesn't mean that users poking into a seldom-used corner of the program can't press a wrong button and get an error message. It means that all the time in the routine functions of the program, and most of the time in other functions, the program works properly.

Of course, "properly" is a subjective term. You may have created an application that never hits any bugs and runs error-free and yet still have a miserable failure because the performance is terrible. The original specification for the program is usually a guideline in these cases. Hopefully, the testing process has done more than weed out errors but has also given you a chance to achieve a level of performance and usability that satisfies the users.

APPLICATION DOCUMENTATION

Documentation of all kinds tends to fall naturally at the end of the development cycle. Unfortunately, this arrangement often dooms documentation to a dry well for both time and resources. There are two different kinds of documentation—project documentation and user documentation—and that complicates matters. It's difficult and usually not desirable to have the same people produce both kinds of documentation. The project developers (programmers, designers, and analysts) are responsible for project documentation as a matter of routine. User documentation is often more problematic, because frequently the developers don't have the time, skill, or interest to do it. Large software companies get around this by hiring people whose sole job it is to produce user documentation. This practice brings documentation into focus, at least for those people. But for software shops that lack the resources to hire professionals, user documentation can become a major problem.

For most applications, neither kind of documentation comes easy. Software development is notorious for paying lip service to project documentation. That's because it requires disciplined work habits under pressure, a difficult combination. This section deals with the issues in both kinds of documentation within the context of tools and approaches available in FoxPro.

Application Framework Documentation

From the standpoint of reusing code, the application framework document is indispensable. You're just as likely to forget the details of your own methods and properties as those of Visual FoxPro. The best part of an effort to document the framework is that it won't change much and it will be around for all your projects.

Quite a bit has been said about this form of documentation in previous chapters, so let's summarize what, in general and at a minimum, an application framework document contains.

- **Class hierarchy**. This is the lion's share of the application framework documentation. Coverage includes the class categories (VCX libraries), their contents (classes), and the methods and properties of each class. Any language conventions or assumptions about the use of the hierarchy should be spelled out. The emphasis in this part of the document is "how to use," although generalized description is important, too, just as it is with the standard FoxPro documentation.
- **Standard files.** List each of the files: MAIN.PRG, procedures, and include (H). The files should have their own documentation, but

you can describe the purpose of each one and explain how to apply them to an application. Procedure files, if you use them, need the same kind of documentation used for methods in the classes.

- **Menu template**. A listing with a brief description is sufficient except for unusual details or procedures that might be buried in the menu options. Be careful to document any assumptions about the navigation or action options.
- **Data elements**. Documentation for the UTILITY database and its tables, essentially a structure listing and description of business rules (validations) and stored procedures.
- **Standard components and modules**. A complete description of each module, focusing on embedded business rules, design assumptions, and particularly on how to implement each one in an application.
- **Domain-specific elements**. Description of any elements used to handle domain objects such as reports, labels, graphs, and so on.

Covering this much material becomes lengthy, but it doesn't have to be compiled in a week.

NOTE

The APPCLASS.DOC (MS Word 95) file included on the accompanying disk is an example. It, too, is a "living" document that changes over time as new classes are added, old ones reworked, and some discarded.

PROJECT DOCUMENTATION

Project documentation is of, by, and for the people developing an application, but don't forget those who will maintain it. Admonitions to document abound in every discussion (including this one), and all programmers know, in their heart of hearts, that they're right. Yet, at one time or another—if not constantly—every programmer has faced the feeling that, he or she doesn't have time for it. And who's to say what is good documentation? Notes scratched on the back of a napkin? Probably not. Sixteen feet of three-ring binders, like mainframe operating system documentation? Also probably not. No one is asking for more time on documentation than programming, but where does an application developer draw the line?

There is a kind of litmus test: Good documentation allows for rapid comprehension of an application's purpose, design, and programming by someone not familiar with the project but familiar with the context of development. Among other things, this means that if you're a FoxPro developer, you don't need to write documentation so that a C programmer can understand it. It also says that rapid comprehension is really the goal. How fast can someone who's not worked on the project pick up on the work?

At the personal level, whenever you feel the impulse to say, "Why bother?" just remember that you will not be the same programmer six months from now. Your memory will be cluttered with other projects. You will have learned more about programming in FoxPro. Much of your old code will look atrocious, scarcely recognizable. What kind of documentation will it take to jog your memory? Perhaps you can understand specific pieces of code, but what will help you understand how the pieces fit into the whole?

At the group development level, the case for good documentation is even more obvious. Documentation is one of the necessary channels of communication. In the context of an organization that hopes to continue using and maintaining an application, this kind of communication is not optional.

What constitutes project documentation? Some programmers see it as being a printed dump of source code, with maybe a printout of file structures. No, it's more than that. There are at least five *categories* of project documentation: analysis, design (program and data), in-line code, printed code, and code support (cross references). These categories serve to communicate the nature and purpose of the application, the important decisions that were made, and the specific programming choices.

To be complete, the documentation covers the life cycle of the project, including any analysis and design that were done at the inception. It includes major project decisions. In a database application, it usually emphasizes databases: structure, indexes, relations, and so on. Of course, there is the documentation in the code itself. This usually winds up being printed in a mountain of paper and may be bolstered by additional mounds of printed support documentation. And when the application is delivered, maintenance documentation begins.

The scale of a project has a lot to do with the volume and kind of documentation. Small applications scarcely need books of analysis and design. But all FoxPro applications should have adequate data table and in-line code documentation. And because FoxPro gives you a documentation tool, the Documentation Wizard, it's easy to produce the mountains of printed paper.

In the end, the point of documentation is to do it. If you don't, you are taking a calculated risk that whatever time you save now won't be lost 10-fold later.

ANALYSIS AND DESIGN DOCUMENTATION

Even the most cursory preparation for an application involves analysis and design. It's easy to put the primary documents in a binder. It's one small step further to label and index the information. But the most important step is to extract from the chaff the kernels of information that might help other people understand the purpose of the application and the design decisions that went into it.

Perhaps the two most useful types of analysis and design information are diagrams of the application and documentation of the data tables and class structure. Nothing beats a good diagram for a quick presentation of class structure, table relations, and data flow. Unfortunately, not everyone can create diagrams, so a written narrative may be the only substitute. However it's done, the point of this kind of documentation is to provide an overview.

Data table information can be as simple as the **LIST STRUCTURE TO PRINT** or the printout from the Documentation Wizard. Most projects keep a running record of table structure, because it is among the most helpful of all documentation.

IN-LINE CODE DOCUMENTATION

The argument can be made (and is made here) that along with overview documentation (diagrams) and table information, in-line code documentation is the cornerstone of modest but effective project documentation. It's not that programming must read like a novel or that verbosity is its own reward. But as stressed elsewhere in this book, readable, consistently formatted, and intelligently explained code has no peer for communicating how an application was constructed and documenting the crucial programming decisions.

If you're the type of programmer who prefers to work at breakneck speed to get the code out, planning later (maybe) to go back and clean up, FoxPro has help. It was in FoxPro for Windows and not in Visual FoxPro 3.0, and now in Visual FoxPro 5.0 it's back: Beautify (Figure 21.3).

You need to be in a Code or Editing window to get Beautify started. Select **Tools**, **Beautify** from the menu and then configure the options (once done, they remain set):

- **Keywords**. All uppercase, all lowercase, or mixed case. By convention, FoxPro keywords (commands, functions, and so on) are uppercase.

- **Symbols**. Variables, table names, and other symbols are usually in all lowercase. You can also set all uppercase or have the program base the case on the first occurrence of a symbol.

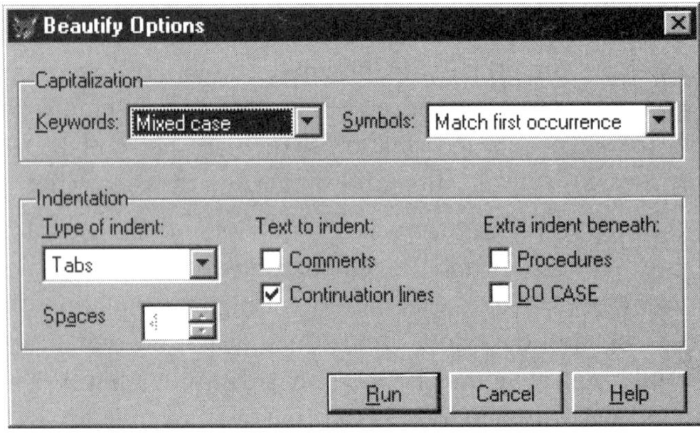

FIGURE 21.3 BEAUTIFY.

- **Indentation**. **Type of indent** is either tabs, spaces, or none. Spaces are preferred, because it's more printer-friendly and editing-friendly, usually set at 3 or 4 for an indent. You can have comments and continued lines indented; the latter is particularly effective. Finally, you can have extra indents beneath procedures and DO CASE structures.

The best thing to do is to haul out one of your methods or program files (one you're least proud of) and let Beautify have at it. Press the **Run** button. In seconds, you'll have something you'd gladly show to Bill Gates.

PRINTED CODE DOCUMENTATION

It seems almost obligatory to print code, because in the eyes of some administrators you haven't done documentation until you've dumped a few hundred pages of code to the printer. Pound for pound and page for page, the utility of this practice is probably one of the most enduring myths in programming. With experience comes the realization that it's much more efficient to go code hunting in the code—on screen, in the file, raw and natural as it should be. However, there's no denying that in this stubbornly paper-bound world, some programmers feel more comfortable scanning a ream of printout. Besides, plunking a massive tome onto the project manager's (or client's) desk lends weight, literally, to your claims of a mighty effort.

These days, there's no excuse for the ugly, endless printer dump of code. FoxPro gives you a useful way to create a lot of printed documentation: the Documenting Wizard.

THE DOCUMENTING WIZARD

If you have the Professional Edition of Visual FoxPro, the Documenting Wizard is one of its added features. You should make at least one run with the Documenting Wizard on a test application and sample all the options. In the long term, however, what you face are decisions about when (or whether) to use Documenting Wizard to make an impression or to be useful project documentation. The difference is mostly a matter of customization.

Before you run the Documenting Wizard, you should know where you want to store its output (which can be voluminous). Typically, you create a specific folder, such as DOCS or DOCUMENT, under the root folder of your project. To start the Documenting Wizard, use **Tools**, **Wizards**, **Documenting**. When the wizard appears (Figure 21.4), just follow the steps as outlined.

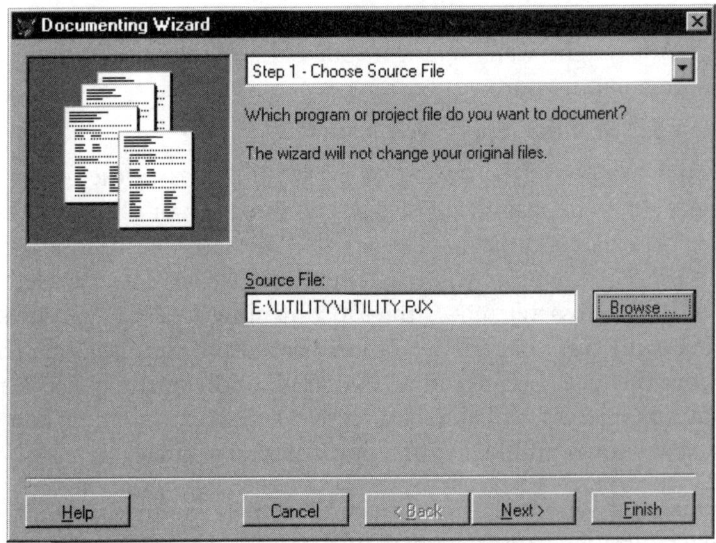

FIGURE 21.4 DOCUMENTING WIZARD, STEP 1.

Step 1. Select the source file. This is usually the Project Manager file for your application.

Step 2a. Choose whether keywords (Visual FoxPro commands and functions) are uppercase, mixed case, lowercase, or no change. By convention in the Xbase language, they are uppercase, but the Wizard default is mixed case. (It must've been written by a C programmer.)

Step 2b. Choose whether symbols (variables and other user-defined names) are uppercase, mixed case, match the first occurrence, or no change. The default is to match the first occurrence, which means it will copy the case from the first example.

Step 3. If you want FoxPro to provide indentation for your code (clegic display), make choices in this step. Otherwise, deselect the defaults. The default is tab indentation, which some people take strong exception to because it doesn't transfer well. Spaces are safer; keep the number low so that you don't force your program lines off the editing windows. The default of 8 is ridiculous. The other three options—comments, control structures, and continued lines—can all be left selected.

Step 4. It usually helps to have the Documenting Wizard add headings to your code unless you're doing it yourself (which you should be). You might want to incorporate the automatically generated information in your own headings.

Step 5. Select the reports you want.

Finish. You have the option of overwriting files in the folder you specified, of depositing all files in one directory, or of having Visual FoxPro create a directory tree for the types of files. The larger the application, the more you may appreciate the tree. If you select the keywords cross reference, the Documenting Wizard will create a table with every occurrence of keywords in the application. Think about this one, because in a large application you may get a huge output table. It's probably best to select this option only when you have a known problem with a particular keyword.

The Documenting Wizard is easy to use. Once it is fed the basic information about your application, it can crank out the requisite ream of paper with little or no effort on your part. This paperwork can be impressive, especially when neatly packaged. However, to cross the line from merely bulk documentation into working documentation is usually a matter of customizing Documenting Wizard. You need to make it truly appropriate to your application, your style of coding, and your needs for debugging and testing.

Customization of the Documenting Wizard has a number of angles:

- Selection of output.
- Customization you can do in your code.
- Modifying the Documenting Wizard keywords file to match your applications.

OUTPUT OPTIONS

There are several Documenting Wizard output selections. They are not equally valuable all the time. Table 21.1 lists the selections and provides a rule of thumb evaluation.

TABLE 21.1 DOCUMENTING WIZARD OUTPUT SELECTIONS

OUTPUT SELECTION	DESCRIPTION
Source Code Listing	How much you allow Documenting Wizard to format your code depends on how much has already been done. Good programmer formatting is often more sophisticated than what Documenting Wizard can produce. But not every programmer has the time or patience. If you're relying heavily on Documenting Wizard to keep code clean, run this selection every time.
Action Diagrams	Action diagrams are one of the most useful things Documenting Wizard can do for you. Not only does it help with checking for control structure errors, but it can also be an invaluable tool for simply reviewing the flow and structure of your application.
Files Listing	Although this listing can be lengthy, it's a standard piece of documentation.
Cross Reference	This option produces a list of the occurrences of all user-defined symbols. If your applications tend to have problems with variables or field definitions, this is a most useful tool. Otherwise, these reports can be huge, chew much RAM, and take time. Use when needed.
Tree Diagram	The tree diagram shows the calling order of programs within your application, but it has some trouble with objects. These text-based tree diagrams can be useful but do not have the clarity of graphical tree diagrams.

DOCUMENTING WIZARD DIRECTIVES

There are a limited number of directives (similar in approach to preprocessor directives) that tell the Documenting Wizard how to perform certain actions. These directives are usually placed in the initialization file of your application or at the beginning of a module or important form.

***# document ACTIONCHARS "abcdef"**

```
*# document ACTIONCHARS " -|+++"
```

The action diagrams use graphic symbols (from above ASCII 132 in the standard PC character set) to create the diagrams. Under certain circumstances, and particularly with different code pages or fonts, these symbols may produce unreadable diagrams. You can substitute other symbols for the standard ones. The preceding example works best as a generic alternative.

***# document XREF cMode**

cMode - ON, OFF, SUSPEND

```
*# document XREF ON
```

Variable cross referencing can be slow and memory-intensive. You can turn the cross reference on and off with this directive or suspend referencing in the current file only.

***# document XREFKEYWORDS cMode**

cMode - ON, OFF, SUSPEND

```
*# document XREFKEYWORDS ON
```

Because the keywords cross reference can produce a huge number of entries in the table, you can use this directive to turn it on only for selected areas of code, perhaps where you suspect problems with keywords.

***# document ARRAYBRACKETS cMode**

cMode - ON, OFF

```
*# document ARRAYBRACKETS OFF
```

By default, FoxPro assumes that brackets are used for arrays (`aState[]`) and that parentheses are used for functions. You can reverse this assumption by turning **ARRAYBRACKETS** off.

***# document EXPANDKEYWORDS cMode**

cMode - ON, OFF, SUSPEND

```
*# document EXPANDKEYWORDS ON
```

Some programmers like to abbreviate FoxPro keywords to four letters (it's legal but unadvisable). This option, when turned on, will expand the four letters into the full command or function name.

***# document ACTIONINDENTLENGTH nSpace**

```
*# document ACTIONINDENTLENGTH 3
```

You can set the depth of indentation in the action diagrams using this directive. The minimum is two spaces; three to five works best.

KEYWORD CONFIGURATION

Over time, developers tend to create their own libraries of classes, functions, and procedures, which are used in many applications. If you have done this or you are unhappy with the default Documenting Wizard selection or handling of keywords, you can configure the Documenting Wizard keyword file: FDKEYWORD.DBF found in the \WIZARDS folder. You can edit this file in the normal manner, such as with a Browse.

There are two fields: TOKEN (for the keyword) and CODE (for the way the keyword should be handled). When you add your own classes and functions, use the same coding as shown in Table 21.2.

TABLE 21.2 KEYWORD CODES

KEYWORD CODE	DESCRIPTION
I	Indent.
U	Undent.
R	Reset indentation to 0, or 1 if in **DEFINE CLASS**.
F	Procedure or function.
D	**WHILE** or **CASE**, or **DO** clause
O	Object.
P	Property.
M	Method.
C	Clause used only as a clause; may not start a statement.

Customizing Documenting Wizard, like most specialized tailoring of the programming environment, takes time. However, once done, 'tis done. From then on, you should get documentation reports, for full documentation and for working documentation, that may actually mean something in the context of your applications.

User Documentation and Support

For most applications, the big question about user documentation is, How much? It would be a rare project indeed that had no user documentation. But the continuum of user documentation is broad:

- **Minimal**. Screen-oriented on-line help. One sheet of installation instructions.
- **Nominal**. Photocopied manual (often with the classic three-ring binder). On-line help system. Basic installation instructions, usually with batch files.
- **Normal**. Printed manual, frequently not typeset. Context-oriented on-line help. Integrated installation software and instructions.
- **Maximal**. Printed manual(s) with illustrations, indexes, and so on. Extensive context-oriented on-line help system. Tutorial material, including computer-based training. Sample and supplementary material such as Quick Guides. Integrated and automated installation software and instructions. Technical documentation for users.

Where your application falls on this continuum depends on many factors: budget, time, complexity of the content, size or scope of the application, target users, life expectancy for use, availability of skilled people for documentation, and more. Depending on the type of application, some elements will be emphasized more than others. For example, an application for professionals in a specific field may require more technical documentation and less tutorial material. If you're targeting the general public, however, you may emphasize the training and tutorial documentation.

As you can see, the line between user documentation and user training is thin, even nonexistent. It's often said that good user documentation is one of the best ways to train. There is, however, a difference of intent between generic documentation, which describes and explains *what is*, and training documentation, which describes *how to*. As user documentation goes from minimal to maximal, it tends to shift from generic to training documentation.

Depending on your perspective, creating documentation for a Windows application draws an inevitable and unfortunate (or fortunate) comparison with commercial software. Microsoft, for one, has set the bar high for quality (and quantity) of documentation in the Windows environment. Can your application compete with this? Should it?

As you consider the level of user documentation to provide, the next three topics (on-line help systems, manuals, and training) might help you put the decision in the context of what FoxPro generates and what you must create yourself.

ON-LINE HELP SYSTEM

Press the **F1** key and up pops the on-line help system. It has become so standard that no application worthy of the name can be without it. On-line help has several advantages in comparison with paper documentation:

- It's always available, unlike paper documentation (which often seems to have legs).
- It can be customized by the developer.
- You can build on-line help as you program.
- Theoretically at least, on-line help should have faster and more convenient lookup.

On-line help is one element of user documentation that should be answered with a definite yes. Then the issue becomes, What kind and how much on-line help? In FoxPro, you have a choice of two on-line help systems.

The DBF help system is a carryover from the DOS versions of FoxPro. It's based on a standard DBF/FPT file. FoxPro provides the necessary machinery to operate this system, including cross-reference links and topic management. With a little work, it can also have open-ended help searches and other amenities.

The other choice is the Windows help system, the standard one used by most commercial Windows applications. When FoxPro calls Windows Help, it's actually executing a separate program (an EXE). This system has a built-in topic search mechanism and also provides bookmarks, annotation, and other amenities to support user references. You can't create Windows Help within FoxPro. It's available as a Help compiler program, a stand-alone product acquired with the Visual FoxPro Professional Edition.

Each system has pros and cons (Table 21.3):

TABLE 21.3 HELP SYSTEM PROS AND CONS

SYSTEM	PROS	CONS
The Windows Help System	It's standard for all Windows applications. It has all Help features built-in. It is a complete Help Development Environment for coordinating help content. You can include graphics and special annotation markings.	It cannot be created inside FoxPro (requires a compiler). It is not user or client modifiable. The mechanics of the system are not programmable at any level. It is a Windows-only system.
The FoxPro / DBF System	It's user-modifiable. It's developer-modifiable with FoxPro. Some of the mechanics of the help system are programmable. This system can be in all FoxPro supported environments.	It's not Windows ***Help*** standard and Microsoft would be glad to see it gone. Enhancements, such as user topic searching, must be programmed.

Under most circumstances, the choice boils down to two major considerations: Windows standard vs. modifiability. The DBF system is more malleable and transportable, even to the point of allowing users to participate in creating help screens, but it is not Windows standard. Most developers will choose the Windows standard help, in part because it will be most familiar to users, and in part because it is heavily supported by third-party products. The documentation provided for Windows Help in the Visual FoxPro *Professional Features Guide* is extensive and won't be repeated here.

Even after you choose your approach and create the first prototype, developing a help system is a lot of work. You need to master and configure the mechanics. You need to create the content, text entry, and screen design. You also need to load and test it within the application. This is not a project to be left until the 11th hour of your first application.

You should be aware that it is illegal to distribute either the Visual FoxPro Windows version help file (FOXHELP.HLP) or the DBF Style help file (FOXHELP.DBF). In effect, if you distribute (not just sell) your application, you must create your own help file.

MANUALS

The creation of professional-quality application manuals is a field unto itself. It's also expensive. Whether or not your application requires this level of user documentation, you should consider using the content of the help file as part of building the manual. The redundancy is helpful, and you will save time by not creating two sources of documentation. On the other hand, people generally expect the printed manuals to be more comprehensive and probably a bit more lavishly illustrated than on-line help.

For most application developers, the most important question about a manual is who's going to pay for it. On-line help can be done by programmers even while they're coding. This approach keeps the cost down. Preparation of a printed manual has a development track of its own. In larger software houses, it is always done by specialists or contract workers. Doing it yourself requires a lot of time, some skill, and access to a laser printer (at the very least) and page layout software.

If your project calls for printed manuals, be sure not to underestimate the time, people, and costs associated with it. It's not unheard of for the cost of commercial manuals to be a significant percentage of the cost of software development.

USER TRAINING AND SUPPORT

The final piece of documentation for an application is the materials and approaches to training and support. As with many other areas of documentation, scale means everything. If your application is intended for commercial sale, you need to put greater emphasis on the training materials and support systems. If it is just a friendly application you're putting together for a work group, then training and support are nothing more than a chat over coffee.

One of the benefits of working on custom database applications is the close contact you'll have with the users. (It's also one of the main drawbacks.) Many developers manage to train the users at the same time the software is being programmed and tested. Although this approach has risks (users tend to become intolerant of buggy software), the rewards are a quicker and less expensive startup time.

CHAPTER WRAP-UP

In some ways, testing and documentation are about the user's relationship to the developer. Whether or not the user is directly involved in the beta testing process, testing software so that it runs reliably is part of a contract with the user. In a slightly different vein, so is user documentation. Very few applications are so intuitive that the user needs no training, manuals, or on-line help.

The problem with documentation and testing is that they are expensive, whether you measure by time or money (or both). In general, applications built with Visual FoxPro are not targeted for the mass market and can't support a payback for testing and documentation that is great enough to justify the cost of a fully professional treatment. This leaves the typical developer of a Visual FoxPro application with some difficult decisions about the depth and sophistication to provide either documentation or testing.

Of the two, testing is where good planning and wise use of resources (such as volunteer help) can cut costs and produce a good product. Because a product that runs reliably is not an option, testing deserves full attention.

This is not to say that the various forms of documentation deserve to be neglected, but it's no secret that it is one of the areas where developers will cut corners. This is not as it should be, but in the absence of clients or employers who understand the importance of documentation—and are willing to pay for it—it is probably an inevitable outcome for many projects. On the other hand, perhaps all that is missing is a sales effort on the part of the developer. Depending on the type of application, you may be able to convince clients that proper programming and user documentation is the way to ensure the long-term justification for the cost of the application. It's the truth, and that should make it easier to sell.

CHAPTER 22

STANDARD COMPONENTS AND MODULES

If you recall the diagram of the application framework shown in Section Figure 7.1, one of the elements was standard components and modules. They've been explained briefly elsewhere, and you probably got the idea that they are important but perhaps elective parts of an application framework.

- Archiving
- Backup and restore
- Data maintenance
- Error recovery
- Report management
- Security
- System codes
- System configuration
- User reference management

They are important, but some of them are elective. If you've ever built one of these components from scratch, you'd certainly want to preserve your effort by putting the code into an application framework for reuse. Other components and modules exist, but they tend to be specialized and you build them as required by a specific application.

This chapter covers all the commonly included components. Many of the descriptions are supplemented by programs (classes or complete modules) on the accompanying disk. With the descriptions here and the programs on disk, I hope to give your applications a jump-start on an area that is too often neglected until the last minute.

NOTE

The best way to access any of the tables, modules (forms), or classes described in this chapter is to use the UTILITY project in the Project Manager. Although it is constructed as a stand-alone program that you can run independently, the elements are easily detached and added to your own applications.

DATA MAINTENANCE

Maintenance may not be a dirty word for developers, but it is usually an afterthought. It's one of those details of an application, even a smallish application, that require time and unwelcome effort at the end of the development cycle. In general, there are three main tasks for data maintenance: index maintenance, file packing, and data integrity checking. With Visual FoxPro, the latter item is no longer quite the bugbear it used to be, provided that you're taking full advantage of the database file and its ability to maintain data integrity triggers and other forms of data validation. This doesn't mean, however, that no data integrity checking remains to be done.

Each of these items requires programming routines, usually quite small but sometimes numerous, that should be run regularly. Tied to these routines is usually a method for reporting results and problems, and that means creating a battery of maintenance reports. These reports are especially important for data checking, because human judgment is almost always required for evaluation.

NOTE

As a rule, the maintenance and utility components of an application are placed under a Maintenance menu option. They are usually protected by a password entry, because you don't want just anyone accessing the internal workings of an application.

INDEXES AND PACKING

Indexing and packing are the two maintenance requirements that are almost always mentioned, probably because a system that makes no provision for them will get into trouble. Although the FoxPro indexes are remarkably robust, no database system is immune to corrupted index files. On a regular basis, and on demand when necessary, an application must make it possible for users (or an application administrator) to rebuild indexes. Similarly, in the Xbase approach in which **DELETE** is being used to remove records, it's necessary to periodically **PACK** the tables. Otherwise, much disk space can be wasted or records will eventually fill the disk. The same is true of memo files, which can become bloated with dead records. For this you use **PACK MEMO**.

There are two approaches to this part of maintenance. One is to code routines for a particular application. They're not difficult, but there may be many of them, at least two for every table in the application. The other approach is to devise a set of generic routines that use information in the database container (DBC) and the tables.

USING GENDBC.PRG

One of the standard steps in both documentation and system protection is to use the GENDBC.PRG file provided with Visual FoxPro. This program will analyze the DBC file and create all the FoxPro commands necessary to re-create the database. This is a great tool. Not only can you keep it on file for a possible emergency in which you need to clone the original design of the database (minus the data, of course), but it is also a useful learning tool for the database commands involved.

GENDBC.PRG is located in the \VFP\TOOLS\GENDBC folder. To run it, open the database to be documented:

```
DO <path>\GENDBC WITH <path><Output file>
```

Then run the program:

```
DO \VFP\TOOLS\GENDBC\GENDBC WITH \DEMO\UTILITY.PRG
```

The file produced by GENDBC will contain the commands. You can run them as is from a utility menu option or modify them to create portions of the database.

DATA INTEGRITY CHECKING

There are many different kinds of data integrity checks for maintenance, some of them specific to an application. We generally recognize four types of integrity checking that should be a regular part of an application's maintenance. All of them are covered by the FoxPro database capabilities: triggers, field and record validation, and index uniqueness. But these tools often need to be supplemented by maintenance routines you create for your applications.

- **Checking key fields for non-unique values and nulls.** As one of the principal rules of a relational system (*entity integrity*), primary keys must be unique and contain no null values. This is a technical way of saying that no two records should be identical. Non-unique keys, in particular, can be the bane of some systems. The Visual FoxPro primary and candidate key enforcement has removed this problem, but you may also wish to check secondary (foreign) keys for similar rules.
- **Checking fields for valid data.** As a rule, each field should contain data of only one data type and of a consistent value for the definition of the field. For example, a ZIP code field should contain only ZIP codes. Not all fields are data-content (*domain-integrity*) sensitive. Large text and memo fields are usually allowed considerable latitude. However, numeric fields are subject to improper values, as are certain kinds of character fields. This varies from table to table, but it's simple to create routines that check fields for appropriate values. Again, good field and record validation in the database and entry forms eliminates some bad data values, but content errors, such as putting a state into a ZIP code, are much harder to detect and often require visual inspection.
- **Checking for widows and orphans in table relations.** Widows are primary keys that have no child records; they have no matching records in related data tables. This condition may or may not be valid, depending on the relationship between tables. Similarly, orphans are child records that no longer point to values in primary keys of the parent table. Guarding against orphans is part of the referential integrity handled by the Visual FoxPro database. You may need to build your own widow checking routine for tables that need it.
- **Table-specific checking for business rule violations.** It often occurs that a sequence of information is expected within a record. For example, if a Social Security number is entered, a birth date should also be entered. These business rules are embedded in the data table and are often handled by record validation. But not all

rules can be checked with simple expressions. You may need to create maintenance routines that employ SQL statements and do results comparison and other forms of checking.

For the most part, maintenance checking routines are simple, much like this example:

```
*Maintenance routine for employee file.
SET LIBRARY TO APPPROG.VCX
oAppErr = CREATEOBJECT("APPERROR")
USE users ALIAS usr ORDER userid
cUserId = userid              && store for comparison
SCAN
  DO CASE
  CASE EMPTY(userid)
    oAppErr.ErrLog("2001","Empty USERID",RECNO())
  CASE cUserId = userid
    oAppErr.ErrLog("2002","Duplicate User ID",RECNO())
  CASE NOT EMPTY(socsecno) AND EMPTY(birthdate)
    oAppErr.ErrLog("2004", "Birthdate Required", RECNO())
  ENDCASE
  cUserId = useridid          && reload for comparison
ENDSCAN
USE
```

The only difficulty may be the requirement for reporting on the results. The sample utilities that come with this book include a table and class (APPERROR.VCX, **ErrLog()** method) that can be used to write maintenance errors to a log. If you're building large applications that run on busy networks, you'll probably need to come up with a method to run your data maintenance routines after hours and then use the reports generated from the error log to fix problems.

BACKUP AND ARCHIVE

On a LAN, it's unusual for an individual application to perform backup. The routine saving of data to tape or optical disk is usually handled by LAN backup software. However, if you're building stand-alone applications or applications used on a small LAN that has no organized backup, you might need to provide the backup routines for the application's data. The basic considerations are simple:

- Applications with small databases can often be backed up to floppy disks. This arrangement has the advantage of being inexpensive and not requiring any special drivers; the FoxPro **COPY TO** routines may be sufficient. However, backup to more than one or two floppy disks becomes a problem, and this technique requires action by a user if more than one disk is needed.
- You need a method for selecting what will be backed up. In some cases, you may back up everything, but a more intelligent routine might select specific files (data and crucial program files) for regular backup.
- If the backup is to be unattended, you will need to create the controlling mechanism (a perfect job for the new Visual FoxPro **Timer** class), a log of action taken, and ways of handling situations that occur during the backup.
- Any backup should be accompanied by a comparison of available storage space with the amount of data involved. This is fairly easy to program. A more difficult task is the ability to recover from a failed backup or at least to warn the user that the backup did not succeed.
- Sooner or later, what is backed up will be restored. You need to provide a way to do this, if only to reverse the copy. Restoration is often trickier than you might think, because a full restoration is not always desirable, and you may need to provide a method for selecting what will be restored.

A number of good backup routines for FoxPro applications are available from bulletin boards or in publications. As with error trapping routines, it's more cost-effective to use these (often free) programs than to construct the whole thing from scratch.

Much of what was just said about backup also applies to archiving, but archiving is usually a function unto itself because it requires long-term data storage and must provide an efficient way of cataloging and recalling the information. Unlike backup, archiving is selective, removing only certain records and leaving others in the table. On the rebound, data coming from archive usually needs the same functionality as regular data, but you don't usually want to mix archive data with current data. All this requires special handling on the part of the developer. If your application calls for archiving, be prepared to spend a considerable amount of time in planning and developing it.

In addition to the considerations mentioned for a backup system, archiving has some of its own:

- You need a method for identifying records to be archived. Such a system may involve flagging (such as an "A" in a STATUS field) or use date fields (such as using a date range for the archive criteria).
- As with backup, you need an archiving routine. Typically, this is a **COPY TO** with the archiving criteria in the **FOR** clause. Although you can archive to standard DBF files, it's common to compress them (if the volume warrants it) using a standard compression program such as PKZIP. The archiving method is often dictated by the volume of information and how often it is recalled from storage. Systems that store huge amounts of data and require frequent retrieval must have more-sophisticated storage techniques and specialized hardware.
- The heart of an archiving system is an archive log (sometimes part of a data dictionary), which tracks the information that was archived, where it went, and when it happened.
- Because archived information is by definition no longer active, you need a deletion or blanking routine to remove archived records from the table.
- Most archiving systems need a specific nomenclature and categorization system for the storage; in other words, you don't just dump the data into one huge folder. Large commercial archiving systems often use *jukeboxes* (multiple optical disk management systems). Although most FoxPro applications won't need that level of storage, you still need a method for storing the tapes, disks, or other storage medium so that you can recall them quickly.
- It's assumed that archived information is destined to be retrieved. You need a retrieval method which is usually tied to the archive log. It often has a fairly sophisticated user interface that allows the user to select the desired data from the archive.
- Once the retrieval selection has been made, you need routines to retrieve the data. This may involve storage manipulation, decompression, and selection of specific records.

- One of the tricky parts of an archive system is to find an appropriate means for displaying the archived data. Normally you would not mix archive data with active data, but users may require many of the same reporting and query capabilities that are available for the live data. There are a number of approaches, one of the best being a way of fooling the normal application into using the retrieved data. What you want to avoid is building a complete (and largely redundant) subsystem for viewing and reporting from archived data.
- In some systems you may need a way to permit user updates (changes) to the archived data. This task can be difficult to do properly, requiring special updating and logging routines.

Many of these elements are not easy to program and must be customized for particular applications. The type of storage device, the volume of archived material, the sensitivity of the data, and the kinds of retrieval required may play important roles in determining the scope of an archiving system. It's almost never a simple module.

Error Trapping and Recovery

If you've been programming for more than a few minutes, you know that FoxPro traps errors and produces error messages. Is this systems sufficient for your applications? Consider these error messages:

"Use of transgressed handle"

"Transgressed node found during compaction"

"Too many relationships"

"Structure nesting too deep"

You can imagine the response of the average user. Obviously, you may want to shield the user from such cryptic messages and, more important, provide remedies for errors, something that FoxPro does not do.

Except for the most Spartan of applications, it's customary for developers to provide an alternative to the FoxPro error trapping facility. FoxPro generates the first response to an error by producing an error event, and then your application uses the **ON ERROR** command or the **Error()** method in all objects to intervene with an error handler. In the error handler, you can inform the user of the error in something more like English. You can also provide ways to fix the error, go around it, or at least make a graceful exit.

Traditionally, if you built your own error handler, the routine would receive error parameters generated by FoxPro and use them to categorize the error, often in a long **DO CASE** structure:

```
PARAMETER nErrNumber, cMsg1, cMsg2, cProgram, nLine

DO CASE
CASE nErrNumber = 3        && File in Use
   ...response code
CASE nErrNumber = 39       && Numeric Overflow
   ...response code
CASE nErrNumber = 1539     && Trigger Failed
   ...response code
CASE...
ENDCASE
```

Visual FoxPro now catalogs 667 error messages, ranging from fatal to inconsequential and covering every aspect of data management, programming, and the user interface. An error handling routine that attempts to respond individually to each error will be very long and complex indeed. Let's look at an alternative approach. (The components are on the accompanying disk.)

Instead of hard-coding errors and error messages into the program, this approach uses a table, ERRORS.DBF. The table can be accessed via the MODFOXR.SCX module (a form) on the accompanying disk. Because the file may be used as a free table, its structure stays within the old 10-character limitation (Table 21.1).

The first two fields are the basic Visual FoxPro error number and description, with the ERRORNUM being the primary key. The CATEGORY field can be used to group similar errors, an aid to maintenance. The TYPE distinguishes between errors solely for programmers that rarely appear for users in a running program, and errors that users are likely to see and need to have explained or handled.

The next four fields are used by the FoxPro **MESSAGEBOX( )** function (see Chapter 17 for details) to inform the user of the error and get a response. The MSGBOXVAL field provides the value that determines the type of message box that is created. For example, using 16 produces a warning message box with a single **OK** button. MSGBOXTTL provides the title (title bar) for the message box window, and MSGBOXMSG is the text of the message you want the user to see. For programmers this might be the raw Visual FoxPro message, but for users you have enough space to explain and clarify. The display routine is written so that a period automatically puts the next line one down in the message box.

TABLE 22.1 ERROR CODES TABLE

FIELD NAME	TYPE	WIDTH	DESCRIPTION
ERRORNUM	N	5	Visual FoxPro error number
DESCRIPT	C	154	Visual FoxPro description of error
CATEGORY	C	10	Category of error, such as FILE,DATA
TYPE	C	1	Type: U = user, P = programmer
MSGBOXVAL	N	3	**MessageBox()** type value
MSGBOXTTL	C	20	**MessageBox()** title
MSGBOXMSG	C	154	**MessageBox()** message
RESPONDVAL	N	2	User **MessageBox()** response value
SEVERITY	C	1	Level of severity (to help response decision)
LOGERROR	L	1	Use **ErrLog()** method to record

The RESPONDVAL field is crucial for handling the error. A number value in this field, in combination with the value from the user's response to the **MESSAGE-BOX( )** options, determines which routine will be used to handle the error; for a record locking error, foe example, it might have a retry method. This error handling is aided by the SEVERITY field, which is used to decide how to respond to an error. The LOGERROR field (true or false) indicates whether the error should be automatically logged (using the **ErrLog()** method).

The programming end of this table is the **appError** class (APPPROG.VCX). Its job is to take over from the Visual FoxPro error event handler, read the table for instructions on what to tell the user, and handle the error. As a class, these methods (and a couple of properties) work together for a variety of error situations while still providing a fairly generic framework. If you find that a particular application needs a more detailed or specialized error handler, you can subclass the **appError** class and add what you need.

Here are some of the features of the class:

- By changing the class's calling parameter with "USERS" or "DEV," you can automatically shift between the developer's error screen and the user's version.
- The **Init** method uses the Visual FoxPro **ON ERROR** command to take over error handling.
- The **Destroy** method resets the error handling back to FoxPro.
- The **ErrorHandler** method has several tasks: It handles any errors that cannot go through the normal display and file opening process—mostly bad file errors. It opens the ERRORS table and reads the error data to the **MESSAGEBOX( )** function. Depending on the user's response and the RESPONDVAL value from the ERRORS table, it handles specific errors. Finally, if the ERRORLOG field is true, the **ErrLog** method is called to record the error.
- The **ErrLog** method dumps the entire memory and environment status into Memo fields of the ERRLOG table, and that gives the programmer complete information about Visual FoxPro at the time the error occurred. The error log table is accessible through the MODERRLG.SCX module (form) on the accompanying disk.

To use the **appError** class, the ERRORS and ERRLOG tables must be available (either in a currently open database or as free tables on the Visual FoxPro path). Instantiate it in the early part of the application (typically the initialization routine):

```
*Instantiate the Error trapping Class
oAppError = CREATEOBJECT("APPERROR","USER")
```

In the old days, before event-driven and object-oriented programming became the dominant trends, this type of error trapping routine was known as *data-driven programming* because it uses data in a table to control much of the action. The advantage of this approach is that tables are much easier to edit and modify than compiled programs are, and the information tables contain is not added to the size of the EXE or APP files. There is some risk that an external table might be corrupted or unavailable, but that's rare.

Using ON SHUTDOWN

One minor piece of trapping (not really error trapping) is the ability of Visual FoxPro to respond to a user quitting the program. If you use the **ON SHUTDOWN** command, you can specify a routine to be run if the user elects to exit the program and a **CANCEL** or **QUIT** command is executed. **ON SHUTDOWN** is like the **QueryUnload** event method for forms. The routine typically asks users whether they really want to quit and responds accordingly. Within any application, you don't generally allow users to exit the program willy-nilly. It usually requires a menu choice or command button, to which you can also attach a user dialog box or perform any necessary processing.

System Codes

Databases, especially relational databases, are peppered with codes that represent data. These codes are the shorthand expressions for identification or abbreviation of information. A typical example is a set of codes for buildings, shown in Table 22.2.

Table 22.2 Example Codes: Buildings

Code	Building Location
SH	J. Smith Hall and Auditorium
BP	Biggs Pool and West Sports Complex
FH	Feldheim Hall and Southwest Annex
HH	Halvorsen Hall and Geographics Library

Instead of loading a database with megabytes of redundant data, in this case the long form of each location, a two-character code is used. The larger an application and the larger its tables, the more likely you are to use codes to save disk space or simplify data entry. Some codes, such as the two-letter abbreviations for states or the postal service ZIP codes, have become so common we rarely think of them in their long form. However, in some applications even these common codes might need translation. That's the problem with codes: They're fine for computers but not always useful for people. You may know, in context, that GA stands for Georgia. But even in context you might not know that UNIT11 is short for Environmental Gas Chromatography Lab.

When you're printing reports or displaying information on the screen, it's often important to include the translation of codes. One of the rules of good interface design is that all codes except the most self evident ones are accompanied by their description. This implies that somewhere you have stored the descriptors for the code.

Some codes are so numerous or important to an application—for example, part numbers for an auto parts application—that they are given their own table with descriptions and other values. However, almost every application has a number of miscellaneous codes with somewhere between three and 100 items. The issue is whether you should create a separate table for each of them, hard-code them into the program, or use another approach. The first way leads to a proliferation of tiny files that become a maintenance problem. The hard-coded technique leads to reprogramming and rebuilding an application if there are changes to the codes (and there will be). The approach many developers prefer is to place all miscellaneous codes into a system codes table.

THE SYSTEM CODES TABLE

By putting all the miscellaneous codes used in your application into one table, you reduce the total number of files and increase the maintainability of the system. As an example, consider the structure of the table shown in Table 22.3 (accessed by the MODCODES.SCX module on the accompanying disk).

TABLE 22.3 A SYSTEM CODES TABLE

FIELD #	FIELD NAME	TYPE	WIDTH	DECIMAL	INDEXED
1	TYPE	Character	10		Primary+
2	CODE	Character	10		+Primary
3	MODULE	Character	8		Secondary
4	DESCRIPT	Character	50		
5	ALPHA	Character	50		

(continued)

Field #	Field Name	Type	Width	Decimal	Indexed
6	NUMERIC	Numeric	10	4	
7	CROSSREF	Character	10		
8	STATUS	Character	1		
9	TIMESTAMP	DateTime	8		
10	OPERATOR	Character	3		

In a table that may have codes of many kinds, it's likely that the code itself will not be unique and therefore can't be used as a primary key. To have precise lookup through a primary key, the codes are paired with a TYPE field. For example, a LIMS application may have units that refer to areas of the lab and units that refer to measurement. The codes might look like Table 22.4.

Table 22.4 Codes for a LIMS Application

Type	Code	Description
LABUNIT	ML	Microbiology Lab
LABUNIT	EDR	Environmental Disaster Research Unit
MUNIT	ml	Milliliters
MUNIT	ppm	Parts per Million

The codes file can also be used as a lookup table for system values and parameters, as in Table 22.5.

Table 22.5 Lookup Table for LIMS

Type	Code	Module	Description	Numeric
SYSTEM	USERMAX	LAB	Maximum number of lab users	12

One of the main benefits of using a system codes table is to make it simple for users or application administrators to make their own changes to application codes. The Codes Maintenance module provided with the accompanying disk (Figure 22.1) presumes that the user will understand the rules for entering codes. The rules could be covered as part of the documentation, or the access form could be extended to provide specific on-line help and entry control for different types of codes.

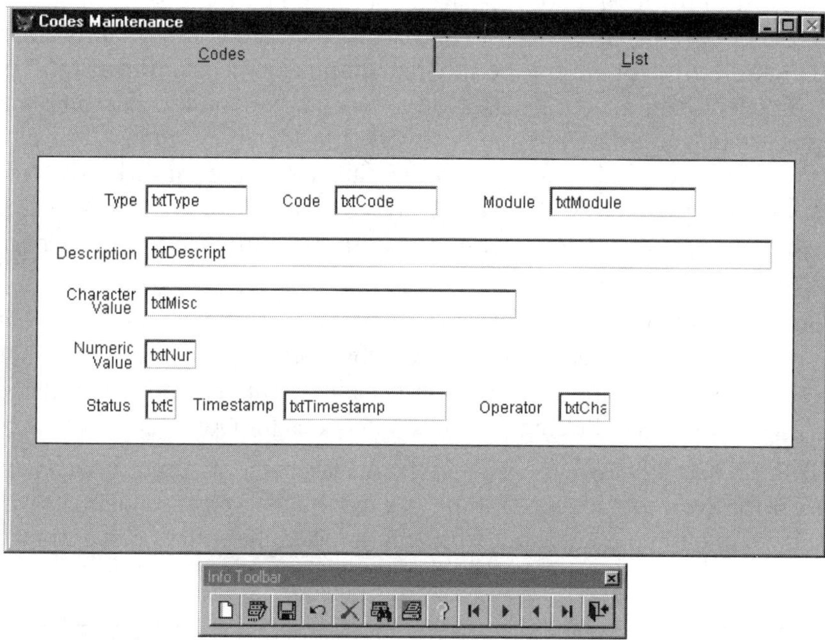

FIGURE 22.1 SYSTEM CODES ACCESS FORM.

Once the codes have been entered, you need to write the routines that use them in your application. These routines come in a number of flavors but usually involve SQL **SELECT**, **SCAN**, or **SEEK**. Sometimes the codes are loaded into arrays for use in list controls, or you can do simple lookups to provide data for a single field value.

REPORTS MANAGEMENT

As with all the application components covered in this chapter, the specifics of an output system are in part a matter of scale. If your application has six reports and two queries, you probably don't need a formal output system. Listing the options on a menu should be sufficient. At the other extreme, if your application hit the road with around 200 reports, label forms, and queries and users are expected to create hundreds more over a couple of years, how can you not have a report management system?

The *system* part of a report management system recognizes that managing a large number of output formats is not easy. There are complications at every turn: multiple types of output, peripheral equipment such as printers and plotters, a frequent requirement for user input dialog boxes, multiuser requirements for concurrency and data integrity, network considerations such as directories and printer queues, and issues of data security and privacy. It's a heady stew, as any seasoned developer will tell you. Only a systematic approach makes it possible for your application to cover all the output requirements without becoming a patchwork mess.

For the most part, FoxPro doesn't do much to help with output management except that it ties neatly into the Windows printing facility. Windows handles the choice of output formats, especially printers, and on a network Windows will also handle some of the connections to network queues.

This still leaves many loose ends in the management of output from an application. Before we introduce one example of a report management system, it's worthwhile to go into more detail about what can be called the structure of output.

The Structure of Output

With interactive FoxPro, output seems direct: Go to the menu, select a report, and run it. It's the same in an application, right? Not quite.

- When you select something for output in the interactive mode, FoxPro assumes that the user knows about file names, directory structures, and the contents of certain FRX files. The user must navigate directories and select the correct report form, label form, or other form, often from dozens if not hundreds of entries.
- Running a report from the menu presumes that the user knows how to make filter expressions and other setup decisions.
- It assumes that no other processing is associated with running an output form.
- It assumes that the user has the rights to run any output form at any time.

Of course, you know what is said about assumptions. None of the conditions in this list is satisfactory for general use in an application. In fact, some of them are impossible in the environment of an application. Your program must be in control of the table setup, network operating conditions, and related processing necessary for output. In short, the interactive mode doesn't fit within the general sequence of output in an application as shown in Figure 22.2.

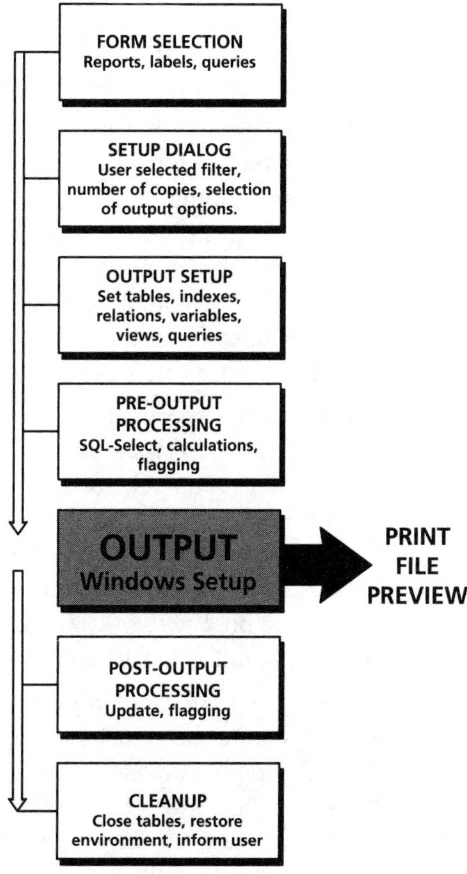

FIGURE 22.2 THE SEQUENCE OF OUTPUT.

It's surprising how many steps can be involved in producing a report or batch of labels. It's also somewhat surprising how many reports require elements from most of this sequence:

- **Form selection**. One way or another the user must choose what is to be output. In FoxPro, this could be one of several *output forms*: a Report Designer report, a Label Designer label, a query from the Query Designer or View Designer, a program file, or a simple output listing. When an application has more than a few dozen output forms (it's easy to break the century mark even with small applications), it's hard for the user to select from among them. At some point, applications need a form selector: a way to narrow down the selections, make their content clear, and remove the necessity for the user to navigate folders to find the desired form. A form selector may also need to apply security restrictions to the selection process.
- **Setup dialog box.** It's a rare output form that doesn't need to have a dialog with the user before running. Standard items to be specified include the number of copies and the destination of the output: print, screen or file. There are also many kinds of conditions that users must (or can) specify, such as date ranges and selection criteria. Some of these items are specific to the report being run, so a large number of output dialog boxes are custom forms.
- **Output setup.** Once the user has specified the output and how to run it, your application begins the setup process. Output setup may include opening tables, indexes, and relations, although the Data Environment is used for most reports. Setup may also include changing some of the environment **SET** values and defining variables that will be used in the output. Before output begins, any necessary conditions for running on a network, especially file locking or selection of output queues, must be taken care of.
- **Preoutput Processing.** Some output, especially reports, may require certain kinds of processing before the actual run. For example, you may need to do a SQL query to prepare one of the tables for a report or do a calculation pass. In other situations, it may be necessary to set certain processing flags or make an integrity check of a table. If needed, this step must be built into your output structure.
- **Output.** You run the report, print the labels, or process the query. You may need to invoke the Windows Report Setup dialog box so that the user can select a printer or other options. Of course, you've been able to handle any output destination (printer, screen, or file) with aplomb,

and you keep the user informed about what's happening.

- **Postoutput Processing.** In a few cases, what was done needs to be undone—for example, if a report is aborted before it finishes—or else an audit trail may be created. This postprocessing usually involves situations in which the output form itself triggers additional data updating, or flagging.
- **Cleanup.** Like any good application routine, the output process cleans up after itself: closing tables, releasing windows and variables, and so forth. At least for printing and file output, the user should be informed that output is complete.

Given the complexity and depth of the output sequence, it's no wonder that developers try to systematize the process. What makes it worth the effort is that once the system has been established, it is used repeatedly. Reporting (and other forms of output) can be repetitive; often, a basic report may have a half dozen near clones. What you need is an approach to organizing the output process that makes short work of such repetitive forms. At the same time, you'd like a report management system that makes the process easier for users without removing all their options.

AN OUTPUT SYSTEM IMPLEMENTATION

The report management system included with on the accompanying disk addresses most of the output sequence and most of the problems encountered with the interactive FoxPro. The software (Figure 22.3) includes an approach for keeping track of all the forms used by an application and provides a mechanism for forms selection by the users. It takes care of some of the basic user output dialog, and it sets the stage for setup, preprocessing, and postprocessing. It's also a good citizen of a network and helps the user keep track of the process. Best of all, it's a form that's based on classes, so you can run inheritance variations to tailor it for your own applications.

Like almost everything in this chapter, the system starts with a table that provides the means to catalog the various output forms: reports, queries, and labels. Access to this table is provided by the MODREP.SCX module (a form) on the disk. Table 22.6 shows the key fields in the table.

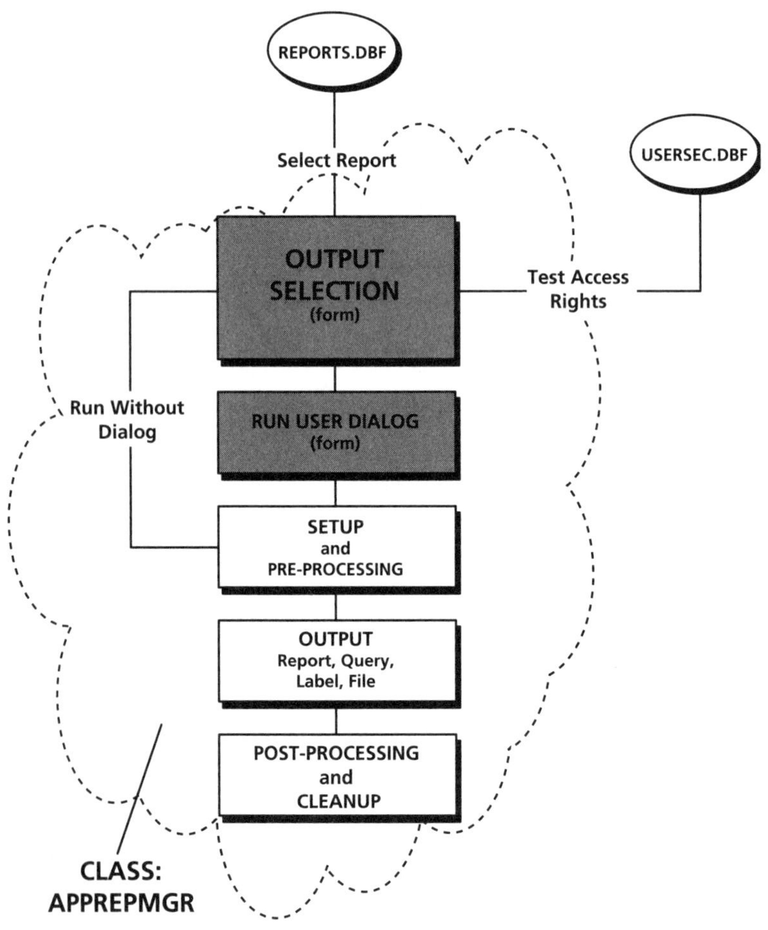

FIGURE 22.3 A REPORT MANAGEMENT SYSTEM.

With these fields you can establish a reasonable description of a form, categorize its type, and provide setup information. The MODULE field is used to filter the forms when the user pulls up a forms selection list. If the module name is passed to the Report Manager as a parameter, only those forms with that name will be available for selection. Similarly, the ACCESS field can be used to place a security requirement on the report. Only those people with an access level equal to or greater than the ACCESS value will even see the form in the selection list.

TABLE 22.6 REPORTS TABLE STRUCTURE

FIELD	TYPE	WIDTH	DESCRIPTION
FORMNAME	C	8	File name or short name for the output form.
DESCRIPT	C	60	Descriptive name of the form, very user-friendly.
TYPE	C	3	The type of form: Report Designer, Label, the Query or View Designer.
MODULE	C	8	The program module associated with this form.
ACCESS	N	1	The security level (access rights) for this form.
PATH	C	70	The path to the output file, if necessary.
RUNFILE	C	70	The path and name of a processing procedure, if any.
DATE_RANGE	L	1	Date ranges used by the report dialog box.
DATE_FIELD	C	10	The name of the field for date matching.
FILTER_EXP	M	4	An output criteria (**FOR**) expression.
SORT_ORDER	M	4	A sort order expression.

NOTE

In many applications, the form is incorporated in the build of the APP or EXE and is not accessible to the user. In this case, a path is not needed for the form, because to find it all FoxPro needs is a name (FORMNAME). However, when the users are allowed to make alterations to the FoxPro report, the report form must be external to the APP or EXE file. Therefore, the form must be on the general FoxPro path, or you can provide an explicit path in the REPORTS table.

When the RUNFILE field is not empty, it is a trigger for a report processing program (often a user dialog box) and provides the explicit location for the program. The FILTER_EXP field contains whatever logical expression is used for the report filter. This expression can be loaded by the developer of the report or, in some cases, is used to store the last criteria entered by a user.

The information entered into the REPORTS table is used by the Report Manager (APPREP.SCX), a form that contains all the elements needed for coordinating the process. The first form (Figure 22.4) is simple: selection of the output form and options to continue or quit.

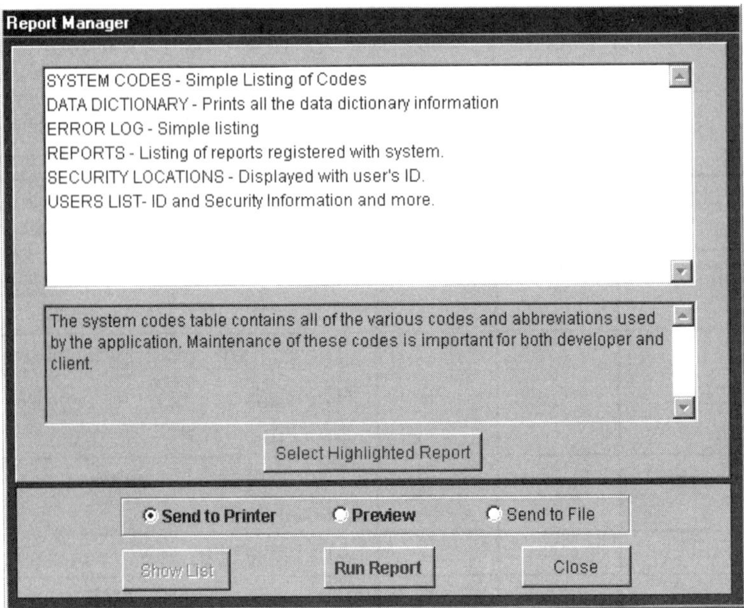

FIGURE 22.4 REPORT MANAGER SCREEN.

The **Select** button is coordinated with a Grid that displays the appropriate forms from the REPORTS table. The forms are prescreened for the current program module by access level. The user selects a form, and information about how to run it is transferred to the properties of the APPREP object.

One of the generic aspects of this Report Manager is that is has built-in seven common types of user dialog boxes that gather information before running a report: beginning and ending date, user-defined filter expression, select sort order, date range and filter expression, date range and sort order, filter expression and sort order, and date range, filter expression, and sort order. These are pages in a PageFrame to which you can add more dialog boxes as needed.

Once the user dialog box is completed, the output form is sent to a handler that is appropriate for the type of output (file, printer, preview, or SQL execu-

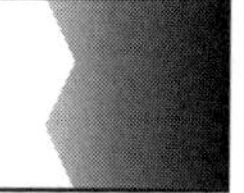

tion). Because this is a Windows system, the Report Manager makes no attempt to control selection of printer or network printer queues; this is usually handled by the user before output. Including the **PROMPT** clause brings up the Windows printer dialog box. At the completion of output, the Report Manager cleans up the environment and returns to the selection form.

SECURITY

Does your application require protection against unauthorized access to private information? Is your data physically secure, on the disk as well as in your program? Is everyone allowed to use your application? These are all security questions.

The requirement for security varies widely. Some applications, including most commercial software, are meant to be used by everyone and therefore have no special provision for security. Other applications have discretionary security, meaning that it can be turned on or off by users to protect certain aspects of their work. Still other applications, such as accounting software, have at least password security and restrictions on access to certain sections of the program. You've probably seen examples of all these types.

SECURITY ISSUES

How much security is enough, and how much is too much? After you've determined that you need security at all, you face the questions of how much security to provide and what it will take to implement it. If you're working on a fairly large application, chances are that somewhere in the project analysis, security came up as an issue—or perhaps it came up as one of its related forms, *data privacy*. Security and data privacy reduce to the same concern: Who has access to what? Security tends to be an issue from an organization's point of view, and data privacy from the individual user's viewpoint, but for the application developer it comes down to two questions: What do I need to protect, and from what?

Protecting data is an obvious need in a database application. You don't want people looking at data they don't have the right to see (for both security and privacy reasons), and you certainly don't want to give people the opportunity to change, tamper with, or trash your application's data.

Protecting the application may boil down to protecting data, but it's an issue at the level of which functions of an application people may use. For example, you may not want every user to have access to all the maintenance routines or the ability to run certain processes.

Protecting the system involves various schemes for making sure that your hardware and software can't be stolen, broken into, or destroyed without having backup and other security measures. For multiuser applications, this aspect of security is largely a matter of the network operating system (such as Novell NetWare or Microsoft Windows NT Server).

The protection "from what" part of security is usually "from people," although you can include protection from natural disasters such as flood and fire. However, the physical aspect of protection is more a part of backup and archiving than it is a part of security. Security in most applications means protection from unwanted access (with or without malicious intent) by people.

To achieve security you put barriers into your application. They come in two flavors: active and passive. PC users are not accustomed to very much active security—security barriers that are visible, such as password entry. Having too many active barriers can turn your application into a kind of data prison, where users feel their every move is being monitored. Perhaps it is, but you don't want the users to feel that way. As a result, much software security is of the passive kind, which occurs in the background and never interrupts the user except in cases of security violation.

Barriers come in many different forms, including password entry, data encryption, and access vetting. They cover all three areas of protection—data, application, and system—and are all related. But when it comes to implementation, there are significant differences.

Security Implementations

Whether you think of security as a system of barriers or of gateways, the point is to think of it as a system. If you determine that your application needs only a single password barrier at startup time, you hardly need to be systematic about that. But if your application requires different kinds of security at different locations in the program, you'll be ahead of the game to treat security implementation as a whole.

NETWORK SECURITY

Any security system you devise for your application needs to work in concert with security measures taken on the network. For example, most networks allow supervisors to assign access rights to folders (subdirectories). The subdirectories that contain your application must allow appropriate access to those who need it.

In this way, the network security is your applications' first level of security. It provides network login and password and network file access rights. Although FoxPro doesn't provide any tools to access network information, you'll find this capability in third-party products. If you need to use the status of various network resources in your application, you may find these tools invaluable.

APPLICATION AND DATA SECURITY

Security inside your application usually has two primary facets: control of access to modules and functions, and control of access to data. To use the common jargon, your application contains various points where it checks the user for *access rights* and then checks for *activity rights*. These checks answer two questions: Can the user gain access to something, and, once in, what can he or she do? This applies across the board to application, data, and system security.

The most intrusive check for access rights is through login and password. This check calls for users to sign in and identify themselves and is often accompanied by password verification. This check is usually applied in three places:

- Application start up login or password entry (or both)
- Module login or password entry (or both)
- For login or password entry (or both)

As the user moves about the application, you can erect login and password barriers wherever required. The emphasis must be on "required." Overloading your application with these active barriers is a quick way to make it unpopular. If people can easily understand why a module or report is protected, they usually won't mind the inconvenience. Still, login and password security should be used sparingly, if at all.

ACCESS AND ACTIVITY RIGHTS

Unlike password and login security, which is active, checking for access and activity rights is passive. It's unnoticed by the user until a security violation occurs and sometimes not even then. For that reason, you can sprinkle these barriers or check points liberally throughout an application. Except for a slight performance penalty, it is an invisible form of security.

What is meant by access rights and activity rights usually varies from application to application. In a broad sense, access rights are enforced by granting the user either general or specific access rights and then checking those rights as the user moves through the application. A simple example is to assign the user an access rights level, often on a scale of 1 to 10. In the application, you have code in strategic spots, such as a menu that is set to allow access only to people with level 7 access rights.

Activity rights are usually defined by what the user is doing at a certain point in an application, typically a data entry form. A user has gained access to a form, but you may want to restrict some users to looking at the data (read only). Others may have rights to change data but not to delete or add. The rights might have a different set of definitions in a processing screen or in choosing reports and queries.

Within an application, access and activity rights can be checked in a wide variety of places:

- Application module rights, usually in system and push-button menus
- Application procedure and function rights
- Data rights: file level
- Data rights: record level
- Data rights: field level

If your application requires security checking all the way down to the field level, you will need a sophisticated system. Implementing the barriers and checkpoints can be complex, not only in the development of the checking routines but also because of the important choices you must make about how to handle security at the level of the individual.

The most fundamental choice in developing a security system is how closely you map an individual to security checkpoints. A related issue is how detailed to make the security at each checkpoint.

If your application has 20 users and is running on a network, and if you have determined that there are 20 places where you need security checking, should you make a table that contains the rights for each user at each security location? And if you have two, three, or four items that are checked at each point, is every user assigned specific clearance for each item? A little math reveals that the application would have to maintain a security matrix (a table of people and security items) with between 800 and 1600 entries. This table would present a significant maintenance problem. Security would need to be important enough to override the difficulty.

In certain government circles, this tight, individualized security is the norm. But in most database application software it would be excessive. This means that you need to devise an approach that's easier to maintain without losing all the individualized aspects of security. One approach is developed in the security system described below.

PHYSICAL SECURITY AND SOFTWARE ENCRYPTION

Most aspects of system security, especially physical control of equipment, are outside the responsibility of your application. This doesn't mean that you can afford to ignore system security. This is especially true of custom software you may be developing, installing, and maintaining on an ongoing basis. If your application is security-sensitive, it may be part of your task to oversee or recommend appropriate security measures for workstations and servers of the network, tape backup equipment, procedures and archiving, and system access through telecommunications.

You may also need to consider using data encryption as part of the protection scheme. This approach has implications beyond your application, because encrypted data is protected even when people are not using your application. In fact, that might be the point. In a way, encryption is a physical alteration of the data for security purposes. The security benefits are obvious, but the penalties and risks should not be overlooked. The process of encrypting and decrypting data usually exacts a performance penalty. More important, encryption always involves some risk to the data.

Data encryption routines are widely available. You can write your own, get routines from bulletin boards, or buy third-party products. All of them can work, but few of them offer a guarantee. Unlike the common data compression products, which only remove redundant data, encryption physically changes the data, bit by byte. For all practical purposes, a damaged and encrypted file can never be restored.

DEVELOPING A SECURITY SYSTEM: A MIDDLE GROUND APPROACH

The software on the accompanying disk contains the **appSecure** class (APPPROG.VCX) for handling application security as a component. Two modules (forms) accompany the system: MODSEC.SCX (security table access) and MODUSERS.SCX (application users' information). Altogether, they make a system that's neither the simplest nor the most rigorous. It has been used in a number of applications in which more than password security was needed, but elaborate user tracking and logging were not required. It's offered here as an example. It's not designed as a "This is the way to do security" approach.

SECURITY LOCATIONS

In the application's initialization routine, you instantiate the security system: `oAppSec = CREATEOBJECT("APPSECURE")`. Anywhere in the application you need to install a security checkpoint, or *gate*, you use the `oAppSec.PassCheck(.T., "MENU09")` method from the APPSECURE object. The method has two parameters: One, a true or false, indicates whether the user should be notified of failing the security check. The other is a SECLOCID, a unique ID assigned to the place where the `PassCheck()` method is used. This is called a *security location* within the application. Because it's a method, `PassCheck()` can be used in an almost unlimited number of places, such as in the **Skip For** snippets of menus or in the **WHEN** clauses of controls (see Figure 22.5).

When triggered, the `PassCheck()` method does a lookup based on the SECLOCID to find the security levels for that location. They are defined in the SECLOC table (the structure is listed in Table 22.7).

TABLE 22.7 SECLOC TABLE STRUCTURE

FIELD	TYPE	WIDTH	DESCRIPTION
SECLOCID	C	5	Unique security location ID, primary key.
MODULE	C	10	The program module associated with the location.
FORM	C	10	The form associated with the location, if any.
DESCRIPT	M	4	The description of the security location.
GROUP	C	10	The required group membership to pass this gate.
ACCESS	N	1	The access level required to pass this gate.
ACTIVITY	N	1	The activity level required to pass this gate.
STATUS	C	1	The status of the location: A = active, I = inactive.

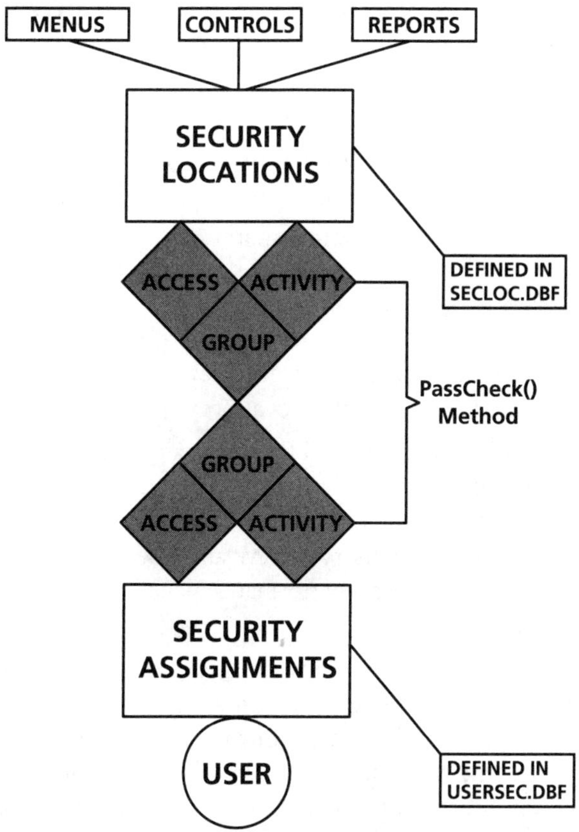

FIGURE 22.5 APPLICATION SECURITY SYSTEM.

For that location you then assign a *group*, such as the Accounting department group. The word *group* is merely suggestive; you could call it a unit, work group, or function area—anything that denotes working groups within an organization. The point of the group assignment is to designate areas of the application that receive specific security: a menu choice for Accounting might be protected by the `PassCheck()` function and require that only people belonging to the Accounting group use that option.

The security levels assigned to each security location are for access and activity rights. The values run from 1 to 5 in ascending order of restriction and have the connotations listed in Table 22.8.

Table 22.8 Access and Activity Rights

Level	Access	Activity
1	Public	Read
2	Departmental	Modify
3	Work Group	Create
4	Management	Move
5	System Supervisor	Delete

Like the group assignment, access and activity labels are suggestive. Any ranking of 1 to 5 would serve. At any security location, the user must meet all the requirements: have clearance for the specific group and have rights greater than or equal to the specified rights for that location.

Normally, the values from the SECLOC table are loaded into an array at the beginning of the application, and the `PassCheck()` method uses **ASCAN()** to find a match for the SECLOCID. If an application has a very large number of gates, however, it may be necessary to conserve RAM and use a direct lookup into the SECLOC table. This technique has a performance penalty, especially for `PassCheck()` placements within menus.

Although the developer must place the `PassCheck()` method in the application, presumably in the most likely spots, this system makes it possible for the user or client to define all, any, or none of the checkpoint gates. Gates may be deactivated by setting the rights fields to zero. The application administrator (or designated user) can define and redefine what group a gate belongs to and the relevant security levels. Some typical settings are shown in Table 22.9.

Table 22.9 Typical Security Settings

SECLOCID	Access	Activity	Group
MM001	2	1	Receivable
MM002	3	4	Payroll
MM003	3	2	Payable

As the security locations are being programmed in the application, it's a good idea to simultaneously enter their IDs and descriptions into the SECLOCID table.

From the control side of security, this approach associates a particular gate with a specific group and requires that a user be a member of that group as well as meet the access and activity levels. This arrangement makes it possible for one user to belong to several groups and to be able to cross work areas within the application while still having more or fewer rights depending on where he or she is working. A typical example is someone in the Payables group who has a high security ranking there (access = 4, activity = 4) and also occasionally works in the Payroll group but has security levels there of only 3 for access and 2 for activity.

A USER'S SECURITY ASSIGNMENTS

The user's part of the security system begins with entering user information into the USERS table. In addition to covering generic information about the user of the application, this table provides information for security, including a default GROUP, ACCESS, and ACTIVITY value and the user's encrypted PASSWORD (see the abbreviated structure in Table 22.10).

TABLE 22.6 USERS TABLE STRUCTURE

FIELD	TYPE	WIDTH	DESCRIPTION
USERID	C	4	Unique ID number for each user (primary key).
NETWORKID	C	8	The user's official network ID.
LASTNAME	C	25	User's last name.
FIRSTNAME	C	15	User's first name.
MIDNAME	C	15	User's middle name or initial.
DIVISION	C	15	The user's division, if any.
DEPARTMENT	C	15	The user's department, if any.
BUILDING	C	20	The building where the user works, if applicable.
ROOM	C	8	The room number where the user works, if applicable.
TITLE	C	50	The user's job title.
PASSWORD	C	8	Encrypted password.
GROUP	C	10	The user's default security group.
ACCESS	N	1	The user's default security access level.
ACTIVITY	N	1	The user's default activity access level.
EMPLOYSTAT	C	1	The user's employment status.

The USERID is the link to another table USERSEC, which contains the user's other security assignments (the structure is shown in Table 22.11)

TABLE 22.11 USERSEC TABLE STRUCTURE

FIELD	TYPE	WIDTH	DESCRIPTION
STAFFID	C	3	Foreign key field from USERS table.
GROUP	C	10	Department, unit or function area as defined in the GROUPS table.
ACCESS	N	1	Access rights, level: 1–5
ACTIVITY	N	1	Activity rights, level: 1–5

For each user listed in the USERS table, you can assign an affiliation with a specific GROUP and the ACCESS and ACTIVITY rights that go with it. For example, let's say that user X works in the Marketing department, where he uses the marketing application with full rights. From time to time, however, user X is called to the Accounting department to fill in for an absent clerk. He needs to have access to some of the accounting application, but only certain parts; in those parts, user X should be able to modify but not add or delete information. The manager of the Accounting department, in great wisdom, has created six function areas within the accounting application: Payroll, General Ledger, Payables, Receivables, Purchase Orders, and Accounting General. The last one is access to the accounting application itself.

In the menu system of the application, where options for the Accounting department are located, the developer has placed the **PassCheck()** function in the **Skip For** snippets of the menu. These code snippets set minimal access rights to each option; for example, the entry into the Accounting submenu has a medium access restriction, GROUP: `ACCOUNTING`, ACCESS: `3`, ACTIVITY: `1`. To get past this barrier, user X would need a corresponding security entry in the USERSEC table (Table 22.12)

The Users form is the place to enter the user's application password (if your program uses any). This password is encrypted using encryption and decryption routines in the class methods. Also among the class methods is `PassWord()`, which can be used to check a user's password in the application.

TABLE 22.12 SECURITY ENTRY IN USERSEC TABLE

FIELD	VALUE
USERID	XXX
GROUP	ACCOUNTING
ACCESS	3
ACTIVITY	2

IMPLEMENTING THE SECURITY SYSTEM

To recap a bit, the steps for using the security system are as follows:

1. Define the checkpoint gates where security should be installed in the application (such as menus and command controls) and assign each one a security location ID. Enter this into the SECLOC table.
2. Install the **PassCheck()**method in the application at each checkpoint gate. Some checkpoints may also require the **PassWord()**method to confirm user identity.
3. The developer or application administrator defines the groups involved in the application and enters them into the GROUPS table.
4. The application administrator defines for each security location the group, access rights, and activity rights.
5. The application administrator defines in the USERS form the names and staff IDs of all the people who will be given access to the application. The network name is important for systems operating on a LAN.
5. The application administrator defines for each user the groups to which the user has access and the access and activity rights that go with the groups. The default access and activity rights are also defined in the USER form, along with a password.

The final part of the security installation is for the developer to initialize the system. This process has two pieces: a routine in the application initialization sequence and a login function.

```
*——————————————————[ Security
#DEFINE SECURITY .T.                && Turn security on/off
oAppSec = CREATEOBJECT("APPSECURE")
```

```
*==================>> LOG IN
oAppSec.Login()
```

The login method, **Login()**, is part of the **appSecure** class and is usually placed in the intialization file. It gets the user's network name either from the user or directly from the network. The login method uses the network or user's name to do a lookup in the USERS table and then into the USERSEC table to load the security values assigned to the user.

As you may have noticed, setting up a security system is quite a bit of work for both the developer and the client. Clients need training in how the system works, and security locations must be set up that tie in with user security clearances. The reward for the effort, however, is a system that can be as stiff or relaxed as needed, for the most part without intruding on the user. It can also be readily adjusted for inevitable changes in personnel and organizational policies.

System Configuration

Most applications of any size, along with all applications that must be shipped somewhere outside the developer's immediate control, need to provide a way to configure their environment. This is sometimes called system configuration or application setup. At a minimum, it involves a table to contain the information and an access module (form) that is triggered when the application is first installed, whenever the program detects the absence of configuration data, or on demand by the user.

User Preference Management

As an example of a purely elective application component, the UTILITY project has a user preference feature. This command tracks various activities of users and saves their work so that the next time they come back to the same place, the previous settings will be restored. This feature is applied in several areas (and more are to be added): window positions, toolbar positions, report parameters, and query parameters.

The classes for user preference are in the APPPROG.VCX library in the **appUserPref** class. As with the FoxPro resource file, which stores the setting made by a user during interactive sessions, you need to have one table per user. The user preference class must contain routines to detect whether the user does not have a preference file and then create one in the correct folder. In this case, it creates the name of the table from the user's application ID (USERID from the USERS table), such as JHMPREF.DBF. Table 22.13 shows the table structure.

TABLE 22.13 USER PREFERENCE TABLE STRUCTURE

FIELD	TYPE	WIDTH	DESCRIPTION
SYSID	C	10	Primary key for lookup.
NAME	C	20	Name of the preference, such as WINDOW or REPORT.
DESCRIPT	C	60	Description of the preference.
C1	C	60	Generic character field 1.
C2	C	60	Generic character field 2.
PATH	C	80	Path for referenced file or table.
N1	N	8	Generic numeric field 1 (1–4 window positions).
N2	N	8	Generic numeric field 2.
N3	N	8	Generic numeric field 3.
N4	N	8	Generic numeric field 4.
MESSAGE	M	4	Error or user dialog box message.
D1	D	8	Generic date field 1.
D2	D	8	Generic date field 2.
DATESTAMP	T	8	Generic DateTime field.

This is another example of a table structure created to hold data that is unspecified when the table is created, and thus it uses generic fields.

NOTE

The user preference table, like the FoxPro resource file, needs periodic maintenance. These tables tend to grow, usually with outdated references, until reaching many megabytes. It's a good idea to review both tables regularly and reduce their size if possible.

The routines for user preference management are a good example of the application machinery that distinguishes the application level of the class hierarchy. The **appUserPref** class must be instantiated when the application begins and before any of the forms or dialog boxes are used, because in the application level all forms have the embedded routines that refer to **appUserPref**.

CHAPTER WRAP-UP

The goal of developing utility, maintenance, and application components and modules is to arrive at the day when you have a complete set: file management, report management, system security, system codes, system configuration, archiving, backup, error trapping, and more. Some of them will produce self-contained objects, and others will be integrated with application-specific objects. In either case, the how-to needs to be fully described in the application framework document.

In any given application, you may use all, some, or none of the standard components and modules (none would certainly be rare), but all of them can be placed into a standard Maintenance submenu and their support files loaded with the application-specific data. The components of user preference, security, and codes management, which are sometimes embedded in the classes at the application level, are more difficult to remove from an application; it would require tracking down all the references and removing them. That's why many developers put these routines into the domain level. This is a matter of what you consider standard for your applications.

CHAPTER 23

DELIVERING THE APPLICATION

The end game of application delivery is a critical time that is made more difficult by the cumulative effects of weeks (or months) of work and the heightened level of attention by the users. Almost without question, you will still be working on elements of the program just before, during, and probably after it is delivered. In many situations, the definition of "delivery" becomes a major issue in its own right. The rule of thumb is that an application is delivered when it is operational for routine work. But there are many variations, and sometimes even the mechanics of delivery become important.

This is especially true when the software is physically delivered to a remote location (away from where it was developed). The choice of how your application is packaged, transported, installed, site-tested, and delivered can become complicated—and important.

APPLICATION DISTRIBUTION

The word *distribution* is used loosely in the context of delivering an application. Running a disk down the hall and handing it to a fellow worker is a form of distribution. So is shrink-wrapped software with a price tag on it. The form of distribution probably isn't one of the make-or-break decisions for your application, but it is something you should give more than a little thought. It's part of the development cycle, and it could take yet more of your time and resources.

In keeping with database jargon, there are two types of distribution: local and remote. *Local* refers to any method that distributes an application while the developer (you) is present or available. In a *remote* distribution, the developer is not available, except perhaps over the phone. There are vast differences between the two. If the developer is present or available, then problems, changes, and fixes can be handled on the spot. If the developer can't be present, then everything must work properly "out of the box," and the developer must rely on the documentation and the client's intelligence to get the application running.

Deciding between local and remote distribution for your application is an important watershed. From that point, decisions on the following topics flow in different directions:

- Method of distribution
- Packaging components
- Installation and configuration
- Data loading and conversion
- Site testing

We'll cover each of the topics in the context of the types of distribution.

Distribution Methods

FoxPro gives you four choices for distributing the application program:

- **Interactive version.** Almost purely a local form of distribution, this method presumes that the site receiving your application has a legal copy of Visual FoxPro for each computer that will run the program. IN some situations (mostly within corporations), co-development or an open-ended modification process might require that the full development material (all forms, menus, and so forth) be available for interactive use. This is a difficult form of distribution to manage and synchronize. Version control can be a significant problem.
- **As an APP file**. Building an APP (application) is a compact way of delivering a program, although it still requires a full copy of Visual FoxPro to run. For local distribution, many developers use the APP file for general installation and bring copies of other development material only when rebuilding on-site is necessary. The availability of an interactive copy of Visual FoxPro for an APP is very helpful during the installation and configuration process. For remote installation, an

APP file is somewhat harder to control because it must rely on each workstation having a properly configured copy of Visual FoxPro.

- **As an EXE file** By far the most efficient (although not necessarily the most convenient) way to distribute an application is to compile it into a self-executing program (an EXE file). This approach requires that you have the Visual FoxPro Professional Edition, which includes the EXE compiler. With this method of distribution, the client sites do not need to purchase copies of FoxPro, and that is often a decisive factor.
- **As an OLE DLL.** This is a more exotic way of delivering an application. It creates a DLL file that can be called by another Windows program as an OLE server.

NOTE

The size of an APP or EXE file will be nearly the same (the APP is 10–15K smaller); although the APP requires a full copy of FoxPro, the EXE must ship with the Visual FoxPro support library file, VFP500.ESL. If you are developing or maintaining an application via remote access software (dial-up programs such as Close-Up or PC Anywhere), you usually install FoxPro or the ESL file locally and then transmit only the APP or EXE file for updating.

Typically, APP files are used for local installation, and EXE files for remote or local distribution.

PACKAGING THE COMPONENTS

Once you've decided on the method of distribution (which might be a mix of methods depending on the phase of the development cycle), you come to a number of decisions and conditions concerning packaging. "Packaging" in this context means the files that are included (or not included) in the build of an APP or EXE, the way the program will be physically distributed (such as disks or tape), and the presentation of documentation related to installing the application.

WHAT YOU CAN'T HAVE IN YOUR DISTRIBUTED APPLICATION

Some mention has been made about elements of Visual FoxPro that are not available for distribution, and now is the time to be explicit. Table 23.1 lists the menus, commands, and file groups that are not legally permitted to be distributed and in most cases are simply unavailable if you build an APP or EXE.

TABLE 23.1 FEATURES AND FILES NOT ALLOWED IN DISTRIBUTED APPLICATIONS

MENU OPTIONS

Database
Form
Menu
Program
Project
Query
Table

COMMANDS

BUILD APP
BUILD EXE
BUILD PROJECT
COMPILE
CREATE FORM
CREATE MENU
CREATE QUERY
CREATE SCREEN
CREATE VIEW
MODIFY CONNECTION
MODIFY DATABASE
MODIFY FORM
MODIFY MENU
MODIFY PROJECT MODIFY QUERY
MODIFY SCREEN
MODIFY STORED PROCEDURE
MODIFY STRUCTURE
MODIFY VIEW
SUSPEND
STEP
SET DEBUG
SET DEVELOPMENT
SET DOHISTORY
SET ECHO
SET STEP

FILES

All Wizard files

All Builder files

TrueType fonts

Microsoft APPS: spell checking, graph

All Microsoft and Visual FoxPro Help files

All Visual FoxPro sample applications files

In summary, you can include almost nothing that is part of the interactive development system: The Project Manager, the Designers (except Report Designer), the Builders, the Wizards, and FoxPro Help cannot be distributed with your program.

Most of these exclusions should cause no problem for 90 percent of the applications you build. However, the exclusion of the View Designer and Query Designer (and their related Wizards) may require some replacement or simulation in certain applications.

USING THE PROJECT MANAGER FOR DISTRIBUTION

As with so much of the development process, one key to distribution is the Project Manager. Only the files listed in the Project Manager and not marked for exclusion will be built into the APP or EXE file. There are important decisions to be made about a few files, because including them in the build means that they are not available for modification. Already mentioned in this respect are report forms (FRX files), which you may wish to allow users to modify. Other files that may need to be accessible (beyond the data files) are memory files (MEM), the CONFIG.FPW file, bitmap files (BMP), and label files (LBX).

Once you've included or excluded the relevant files, you can build the APP or EXE from the Project Manager in the usual fashion, with one exception: For a production build (a completed program), you should turn off the debug information. This will cut the size of your file by nearly 10 percent. Do this in the **Project** option of the system menu under **Project Info.** In the dialog box, clear the **Debug Info.** check box.

NOTE

If you wish to make your application more difficult to copy or reuse, you can encrypt the source code. In the **Project** options of the system menu, select **Project Info.** and check the **Encrypted** box.

Application Files Not Part of a Build

In addition to the EXE or APP file created by the Project Manager, your application may have a number of files that are not included in the build and need to be packaged for distribution. These files may include the following:

- Database, table, index, and memo files.
- CONFIG.FPW.
- VFP500.ESL (for EXE distribution)
- Resource files, typically FOXUSER.DBF/FPT.
- FOXPRO.INT (international characters for sorting).
- FOXFONT or FOXPRINT font files (or other legally transferable font files).
- VFPxxx.DLL, locale (language) specific resource file, where "xxx" is a language code.
- Help files, either FoxPro or Windows type.
- Any FLL, DLL, or other third-party libraries used in the application.
- Report, label, memory, or other FoxPro files explicitly not included in the build.
- ActiveX (OCX) support files, normally found in the Windows SYSTEM folder. The OCX files themselves must be part of the build from the Project Manager.
- ODBC drivers (you can specify their location in the Setup Wizard).

Creating the Distribution Folders

Once you've identified all the necessary files for your application, create a distribution folder structure (directory tree) to organize them. In most cases this structure should be kept as simple as possible, often nothing more than the following:

```
\MyApp    (distribution folder) with EXE file
     \Data
     \Controls (ActiveX)
     \Templates (such as reports not in build)
     \Programs (anything else)
```

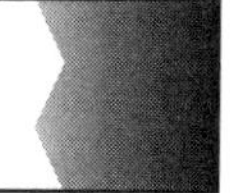

Unless there are a very large number of files in the application folder, there's not much need for additional subfolders. A typical exception might be the need to store a large number of report and label files that are not included in the build.

USING THE SETUP WIZARD

When the distribution folders have been loaded with the application's files, you're ready to prepare the setup for Windows installation. This chore would be extremely difficult if it were not for the Setup Wizard, which handles the tricky business of creating a setup for all flavors of Windows on different disk media. Its inclusion in the Visual FoxPro Professional Edition is alone worth the price of admission.

The Setup Wizard, among other things, analyzes your distribution folders and files, checking to make sure that all necessary components are available. After a lengthy dialog about how you want setup to be created, it compresses and redistributes the files into separate folders, one for each disk used in distribution. For example, this distribution folder structure may be processed to a folder tree holding the disk folders:

```
\MyApp              >       \Disk Images
      \Data                              \Compress
      \Reports                           \Disk144
                                          \Disk1
                                          \Disk2
```

Each disk folder (DISK1 and DISK2) holds enough material for one floppy disk of the size you specify. The folder that holds the disk—DISK144, DISK12, or DISK7—indicates the capacity of the intended distribution disk (in kilobytes). To distribute the application, you copy each disk folder onto a separate disk and label them appropriately.

To start the Setup Wizard, go to **Tools**, **Wizards** in the menu and select the Setup Wizard. The first dialog box (Step 1) asks you to select the source folder of your application, as previously discussed. Be sure you have already loaded these folders with *only* the files you want included with the application. You also need to select the target operating system: **Windows 95** or **Windows NT**. If you need more than one, you will need to repeat the whole preparation process (subdirectories and all) for each version of Windows.

Step 2 (Figure 23.1) is where you specify whether the application is an EXE file and needs the Visual FoxPro 5.0 run-time file (VFP500.ESL), Microsoft

Graph 5.0 run-time, any specific ODBC drivers, and OLE servers. Your selections depend on whether your application uses MS Graph output, ODBC connections, or OLE automation.

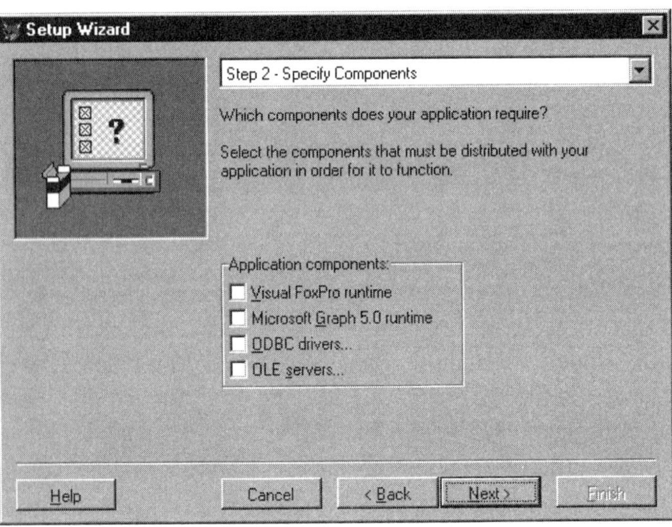

Figure 23.1 Setup Wizard, Step 2, Specify Components.

Step 3 (Figure 23.2) is used to specify where you want the disk images to be put (pick a convenient folder that already exists) and which format(s) you want for disk images. The Setup Wizard can produce all three disk formats in a single pass. The **Netsetup** option is important not only for networks but also if you plan to cut CD-ROM images for distribution.

Step 4 (Figure 23.3) lets you customize the title bar of the setup dialog boxes, add the copyright information, and specify a program to execute immediately following setup. This must be an EXE file, and it can cover any unfinished business of setup, such as loading data, modifying the CONFIG.FPW file, and getting application operating parameters from the user.

Step 5 (Figure 23.4) covers the setup on the user's system, including the default locations of the application folders and files, the name of the Windows program group, and whether the users can modify the directory or group. Normally, the users should have this option, and your application should be able to run in a directory having a different name from the one it was developed in.

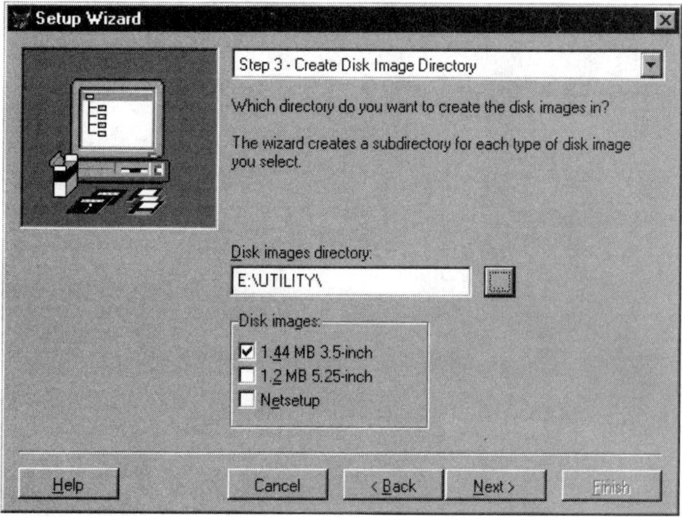

FIGURE 23.2 SETUP WIZARD, STEP 3: CREATE DISK IMAGE DIRECTORY.

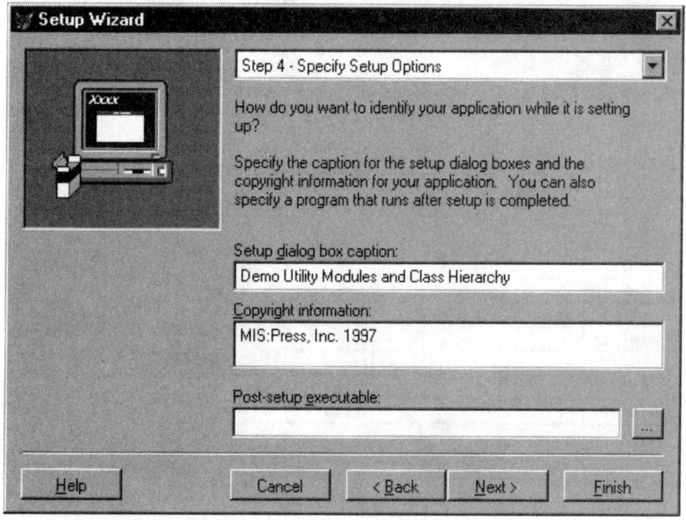

FIGURE 23.3 SETUP WIZARD, STEP 4: SPECIFY SETUP OPTIONS.

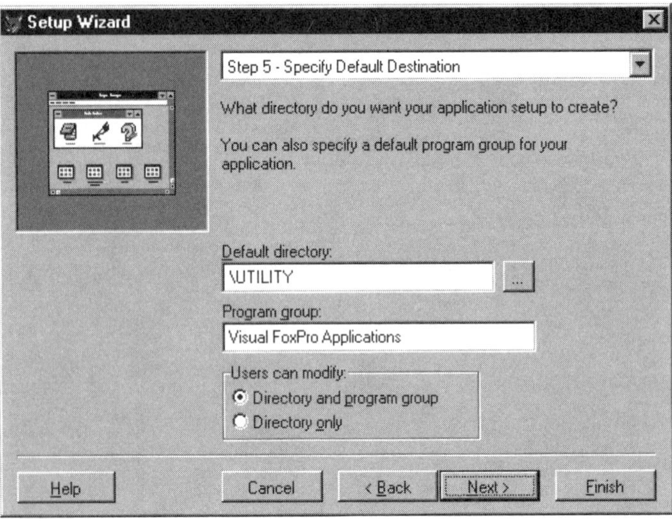

FIGURE 23.4 SETUP WIZARD, STEP 5: SPECIFY DEFAULT DESTINATION.

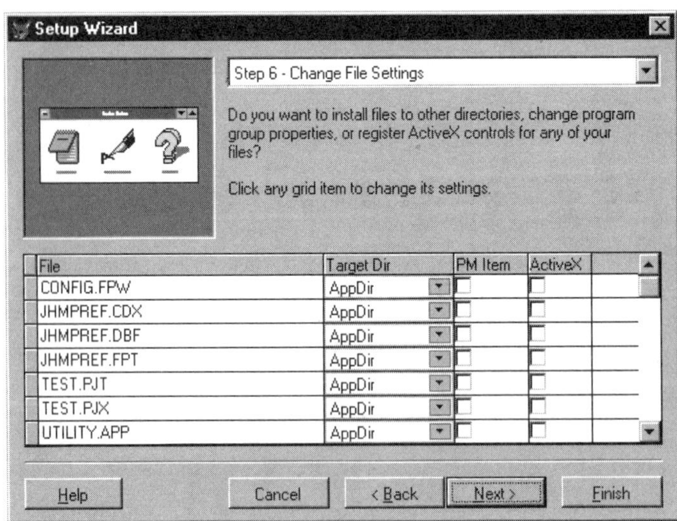

FIGURE 23.5 SETUP WIZARD, STEP 6: CHANGE FILE SETTINGS.

Step 6 (Figure 23.5) is the most laborious. It provides a list of all the files the Setup Wizard found in the source folders and asks you to assign them to destination folders (**Target Dir**), indicate whether they should be included in the program group (for EXE files only), and indicate whether they are ActiveX files. If you select a file for the program group, you will be asked for a caption and a bitmap icon. You should have that information ready, particularly the icon.

The Finish dialog box launches the Setup Wizard into creation of the image disks. This process can take quite a while (depending on hardware); it's not something you want to do more than once a day, at most. The results of the process are well worth the wait—a professional-looking setup routine in the standard Windows mold—and all you had to do was provide some information.

INSTALLATION AND CONFIGURATION

When the time comes for official installation of your application, there are two steps or phases: installation, which is the copying of files to appropriate folders (the computer setup), and the configuration of the application, which includes loading tables and providing operating information. Virtually all database applications, including those created by FoxPro, need special attention not only to get the correct setup but also in loading startup data such as system codes, user names, security assignments, and other information. Which person does this work reflects the original differentiation between local and remote distribution:

1. You (the developer) are there.
2. You are not available, but a surrogate (trained in the application) is there.
3. A computer-literate stranger is available.
4. A computer-literate stranger is the best alternative available.

If the answer is number 3, and especially number 4, you must consider formal ways for your application to be installed.

Part of the job can be handled by the Setup Wizard. For any kind of user installation (and even most of your own), this approach is the easiest and most foolproof. There are several other possible (or necessary) approaches:

- A follow-up program (compiled as an EXE) to the Windows setup (an option in the Setup Wizard). This program can guide the user through a number of data configuration and other application options. It's a good idea but a lot of work.

- An application "parameters" screen, which covers basic operation information such as the name of the client, the location address, phone numbers, and so forth. This was mentioned as one of the possible modules in an application framework.
- Detailed installation and setup instructions.
- Customer telephone (voice or remote access) support.
- A preinstallation training class for the application administrator or key users.

How much setup assistance you provide depends on the complexity of the application, the qualifications of the client or users, the client's computer environment, and whether or not the developer can participate at all. Custom software is almost always accompanied by a developer but may still require a Windows setup, a parameters screen, and user training. Vertical market software usually leans in the direction of a truly remote distribution and must provide enough information and assistance for the user to successfully install the software.

WARNING

If you are planning a remote distribution of your application, do not underestimate the difficulty of creating a successful setup and configuration process. Commercial software developers spend an enormous amount of time and money to develop this kind of software and documentation. You may not have the resources to do it correctly, in which case it's better not to do it at all.

Data Conversion and Loading

For the vast majority of database applications you build with Visual FoxPro, part of the configuration process is to get the databases loaded with startup data. This task might require nothing more than entering appropriate codes, user names, and other system data. Or it might involve entering basic information used in the application's operation, such as mailing lists or parts inventory. Because of preexisting data, it sometimes involves data conversion.

No coverage of application distribution and configuration would be complete without mentioning the possibility of the developer's worst nightmare. There have been data conversion projects that proceeded smoothly, on time, and on budget—but not many.

There are many reasons for this. Because of legitimate timing requirements, data conversion is often done at the last minute. But at this point for the developer, the application is basically finished and the only impediment to getting up and running is the data conversion. For the client, the program is just beginning, and the only impediment is data conversion. One person is ready to be finished with the project, and the other anticipates using it. The data to be loaded is valuable; otherwise, why bother converting it?

With that as the background to a data conversion, it's vexing when the inevitable technical difficulties arise. If you're lucky, you're converting apples to oranges. Otherwise, you might be going from EBCDIC to Xbase. In any case, you are converting between two different systems. If they do not use the same file format, you must first do some kind of file conversion or perhaps several of them—provided that you can find the software tools to make the conversion. Most (but not all) systems can create ASCII text files. Even if you are lucky and both sides are Xbase (DBF) files, there usually are major differences in field names, widths, and types. This discrepancy complicates the move from one type of database structure to another. In all likelihood, your database schema bears no resemblance to the structure used in the old system, so you must split and piece data from various files and put them in various other files.

If you've ever done a major conversion, you know where this is leading. You should estimate the time for conversions based on a factor of 4x. If you think it will take eight hours, it will take 32 hours. Although no two conversion projects are identical, there are patterns. Your success at data conversions may well rest on how well you recognize the patterns and prepare accordingly. The following list covers the basic steps of most conversions. It's impossible to cover all the wrinkles. Most of them require ingenuity, a mastery of FoxPro file manipulation, patience, good record keeping, and luck.

- Identify the *final* file format involved in the source side of the conversion. It may start out as one thing in its native form, but you need to know whether the source software can produce a file format more congenial for the transfer to Xbase. A DBF file is preferred, as are any of the file formats supported by FoxPro. If the format turns out to be some kind of ASCII file, you need to examine it carefully. Parsing it may require complex programming.
- Assuming that the source system can't produce a DBF file, figure out how the source file format gets converted into an Xbase file—not the final FoxPro file, mind you, but *an* Xbase file. It's much easier for you to work with DBF files for final conversion routines. You may need to find a third-party product that can make the transfer

or, if necessary, write your own low level routines (a huge job). The goal is to get all the relevant data into the DBF format without losing its data definition.

- Once the data has arrived in a DBF format (by whatever means), you need to map the field structures to the new database. If the project is big enough, draw a map showing how one field in the source data corresponds to a field in the new data. Indicate what, if any, conversion is necessary: renaming, data type conversion, width, and any other massaging of the data. Many conversions founder when the developer discovers that the source data contains things such as *compacted fields*—fields in which users have jammed two or three fields' worth of data into a single field and, being creative, have used a variety of separators: a comma here, a semicolon there. Untangling strange data constructions is one of the pitfalls in the conversion process.
- Once the mapping has been done, build the necessary conversion routines and test them.
- It's not unusual for a major conversion process to have four, five, or more steps. Many files may be involved in a sequence of processing. At this point, accurate bookkeeping is paramount. Keep records of every step, just as you keep backups of every file.

There are so many possible problems with even small conversions that you never know from one project to another exactly what to expect. That's why the savvy professional developer prefers billable hours for a data conversion. Remember, Murphy's rogue son invented computer data conversion and invoked it with his father's worst imprecation: Conversion? No problem!

SITE TESTING

With custom software or any application that can be distributed locally, you should consider the possibility of conducting site testing before the program is fully operational. Beta testing may accomplish the same thing, but a true site test involves a complete network installation and several users, with a variety of workstation computers. In site testing, the emphasis is on finding all the peculiarities of the client's equipment, especially subtle environmental problems such as power supply, network performance, and oddball computers.

This kind of site testing is almost always conducted with the production version of the software. It's important to (nearly) rule out the software as a source of glitches in the system.

IT AIN'T OVER 'TIL IT'S OVER

Delivery of an application, whether it means shipping it to sales or installing it at a client site, is an important moment, but it's usually not the end of the line for the application developer. Modification and maintenance set in early, sometimes simultaneously with the installation and first use. User support also follows hard on the heels of the delivery, and there's always more documentation to be done. These are aspects of application development that many developers find unpleasant, at best. Others believe that this is where the satisfaction (and a great deal of the profit) can be obtained.

LAST CHAPTER WRAP-UP: PUTTING IT ALL TOGETHER

A big application is a long journey, some of it through familiar territory and some of it through unknown terrain. The more familiar the territory becomes, the more shortcuts you find and the more quickly you can maneuver. That, in a metaphoric nutshell, is what an application development framework is supposed to do for you. You first need to travel that route yourself—build or learn the framework (or both)—before you can begin to reap the benefits. If you recall the diagram used throughout the book, shown in Figure 23.6, you know that each element is a project in itself, with the class hierarchy being by far the biggest.

So what is the minimum needed for a working framework? Allowing for variations dependent on the type, size, and content of the applications you're building, here are some recommendations.

- **Standard files**. MAIN.PRG to get things started and FOXPRO.H for an include file.
- **Menu templates**. APPMAIN.MNX as a template for all application main menus. MODAL.MNX to handle modal dialog boxes. APPMENU.MNX for all forms that have data access.

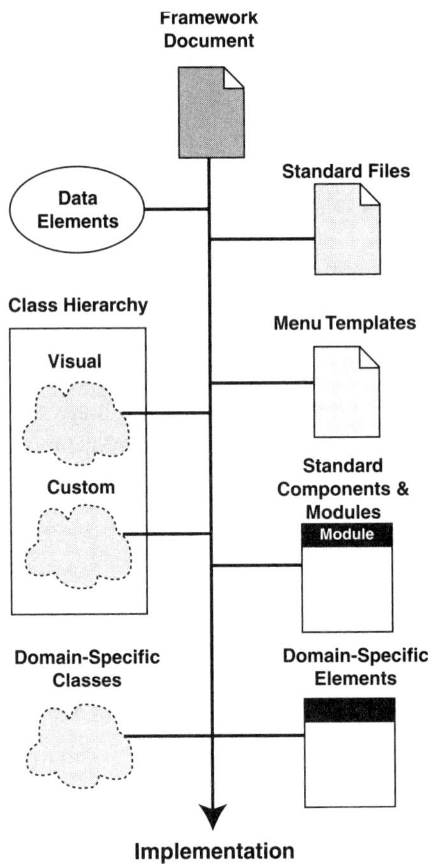

FIGURE 23.6 THE APPLICATION DEVELOPMENT FRAMEWORK.

- **Class hierarchy**. A subclass of every Visual FoxPro base class. Subclasses from that to create standard data forms, dialog boxes, grids, page frames, and toolbars (if you choose to have them). You'll also need custom classes to handle data and environment management. The details, of which there are hundreds, can be gleaned from studying other class hierarchies (such as this book, FoxPro's sample applications such as TASTRADE, and other books and magazine articles.)
- **Standard components and modules**. Data maintenance and error management are necessities. Errors and data maintenance are unavoidable in all applications.

- **Data elements**. A system or configuration table and probably a USERS.DBF are probably necessities, although very small applications get by without either element.
- **Domain elements**. Classes and modules that are aimed at supporting specific applications (their content) can be kept in the framework and reused on similar applications. However, these elements are built as you go along, and not created from a necessity at the start.

You've already seen an example of the shell that's used to organize an application: MAIN.PRG with the **READ EVENTS** command, a menu to access parts of the application, and a **CLEAR EVENTS** to end the application. To this you attach active objects (usually in an initialization routine), include (H) files, and the forms or form sets. It's not a particularly complicated layout, nor does it take very long to get up and running. But, as with so many things, the devil (or the delight) is in the details.

As you may have gathered by now, building a complete application development framework and a correspondingly full-scale application may require many special attitudes, skills, and interests: one person split 10 ways or 10 people working one way. In any case, it's the diversity of tasks that characterizes application development. It isn't all programming, or analysis, or project management, or writing user manuals. It's all those things and much more.

You've been introduced to Visual FoxPro as a tool for developing reusable components and a complete application, and by now you may understand how diverse and sometimes magnificent this tool can be. If you've been working on your own application as you used the book, you have traversed the fields of database management, application analysis and design, object-oriented programming, and software development. If you feel as if it hasn't all sunk in just yet, don't worry—that's normal. Each one of these areas is a *career* in the world of commercial software development.

This book has attempted to stretch your vision of what it takes to create an application, big or small. Sometimes we have covered things in painful detail, but more often it was necessary to leap over topics that should have had entire chapters. No one book can cover all of object-oriented programming, database management, and application development. The more you continue to learn—from other books, magazines, user groups, on-line forums, and, above all, from doing—the more you can fill in the gaps. As you do, you'll continue to see improvement in your programming, and you'll find better ways to put together an application framework. In this business, the process of learning never ends. We wouldn't want it any other way.

INDEX

D

E

Q

R

T